DANIEL YERGIN
and
JOSEPH STANISLAW

THE
COMMANDING
HEIGHTS

*The Battle Between Government
and the Marketplace That Is
Remaking the Modern World*

SIMON & SCHUSTER
Rockefeller Center
1230 Avenue of the Americas
New York, NY 10020

Designed by Irving Perkins Associates, Inc.

Manufactured in the United States of America

1   3   5   7   9   10   8   6   4   2

Library of Congress Cataloging-in-Publication Data
Yergin, Daniel.
The commanding heights : the battle between government and the marketplace
that is remaking the modern world / Daniel Yergin and Joseph Stanislaw.
p.   cm.
Includes bibliographical references and index.
1. Economic policy. 2. Markets. 3. Privatization. 4. Deregulation.
5. Economic history—1945–   6. Competition, International.
I. Stanislaw, Joseph. II. Title.
HD87.Y47   1998
338.9—dc21   97-49089
CIP
ISBN 0-684-82975-4

Photo section created by
Sue Lena Thompson and Bridgett Neely
with Siddhartha Mitter

To Angela, Alexander, and Rebecca Yergin
and
To Augusta, Louis, Katrina, and Henry Stanislaw

CONTENTS

AT THE FRONTIER

Introduction

BOOKS BEGIN in unexpected places. This book began in part on a summer's day on the outskirts of Moscow. The Izmailovo outdoor market sprawls over acres on the southwest edge of the city, almost at the very end of the subway line. Its transformation—from a park for exhibiting painting and crafts into a vast bazaar—was one of the earliest and most visible signs of communism's collapse and the transition to an economy that was no longer state controlled but responded to the demands of the marketplace.

The past and future were simultaneously on sale. Oil paintings of snowy villages and religious icons, many of dubious origin, were commingled with South Korean electronics and cheap videocassettes. Stalls competed to sell old dishes and stained uniforms, czarist mementos, and pins decorated with Lenin's face. There were carpets from Central Asia, swords from the Caucasus, and military souvenirs from both czarist and Red armies. And everywhere were the *matrioshki,* wooden dolls within dolls, but of endless variation—not only the traditional peasant women but also a host of other characters, from Soviet leaders and American presidents to the Harlem Globetrotters. The favored mode of payment for all of this was the dollar—the same dollar whose possession only a few years earlier could have resulted in a stiff prison term.

The market drew all sorts of people, including, on this particular day Sir Brian Fall, the then British ambassador. As a career diplomat in the Foreign Office, Fall had dealt with Soviet and Russian affairs for thirty years, going back to the cold war days of George Smiley. In between, he had held a number of other positions, including senior adviser to three foreign secretaries as well as high commissioner to Canada. This day, however, he was at Izmailovo with his wife and daughter not for diplomatic purposes but, like everybody else, to shop. They were looking for a painting of a rural village scene, an evocation of traditional Mother Russia. But Sir Brian, every now and then, still had to stop to remind himself that the dramatic changes in modern Russia were really happening. Every stall at Izmailovo brought one face-to-face with that change. The market was a metaphor for a society disjointed and confused, but also reenergized, experiencing a transition more wrenching and more rapid than Russians could comprehend, having passed through a revolution they had not anticipated—and were certainly not prepared for.

"How much easier it would have been for the Russians," he said as we wound down one of the aisles, "if the Soviet Union had collapsed in the 1960s or 1970s."

Why?

"Because that was when government intervention loomed large in the West, and national planning and state ownership were the methods of the day. That would have made it much more acceptable for Russia to hold on to its huge state-owned companies and keep pumping money into them, no matter how big the losses. And then the move to a market economy would not have been so severe and traumatic."

His observations brought into sudden and sharp focus how much has changed around the world since the 1970s in thinking about the appropriate relationship between state and marketplace. What was the conventional, indeed the dominating, wisdom of that time is now widely criticized, and in some cases discredited and abandoned. What seemed to be ideas on the fringe, or even beyond the fringe, discussed only around a few seminar tables, have now moved into the center. As a consequence, economies almost everywhere are being reordered, in some cases radically, with immense and far-reaching effects.

All around the globe, socialists are embracing capitalism, governments are selling off companies they had previously nationalized, and countries are seeking to entice back multinational corporations that they had expelled just two decades earlier. Marxism and state control are being jettisoned in favor of entrepreneurship; the number of stock markets is exploding; and mutual fund managers have become celebrities. Today, politicians on the left admit that their governments can no longer afford the expansive welfare state, and American liberals recognize that more government may not hold the solution to every problem. Many people are being forced to reexamine and reassess their root assumptions. These changes are opening up new prospects and new opportunities throughout the world. The shift is also engendering, for many, new anxieties and insecurities. They fear that government will no longer be there to protect them as they become increasingly intertwined in a global economy that seeks to ignore national borders. And they express unease about the price that the market demands of its participants. Shocks and turbulence in international capital markets, such as those that roiled Latin America in 1995 and Southeast Asia in 1997, turn that unease into fundamental questions about the danger and even legitimacy of markets. But all these viewpoints need to be set in context.

Why the Shift?

Why the move to the market? Why, and how, the shift from an era in which the "state"—national governments—sought to seize and exercise control over their economies to an era in which the ideas of competition, openness, privatization, and deregulation have captured world economic thinking? This question, in turn, begets others: Are these changes irreversible? Are they part of a continuing process of development and evolution? What will be the consequences and prospects—political, social, and economic —of this fundamental alteration in the relationship between government and marketplace? These are the basic questions that this book seeks to answer.

Where the frontier between the state and market is to be drawn has never been a matter that could be settled, once and for all, at some grand peace conference. Instead, it has been the subject, over the course of this century, of massive intellectual and political battles as well as constant skirmishes. In its entirety, the struggle constitutes one of the great defining dramas of the twentieth century. Today the clash is so far-reaching and so encompassing that it is remaking our world—and preparing the canvas for the twenty-first century.

This frontier defines not the boundaries of nations but the division of roles within them. What are the realm and responsibility of the state in the economy, and what kind of protection is the state to afford its citizens? What is the preserve of private decision-making, and what are the responsibilities of the individual? This frontier is not neat and well defined. It is constantly shifting and often ambiguous. Yet through most of the century, the state has been ascendant, extending its domain further and further into what had been the territory of the market. Its victories were propelled by revolution and two world wars, by the Great Depression, by the ambitions of politicians and governments. It was also powered by the demands of the public in the industrial democracies for greater security, by the drive for progress and improved living conditions in developing countries—and by the quest for justice and fairness. Behind all this was the conviction that markets went to excesses, that they could readily fail, that there were too many needs and services they could not deliver, that the risks and the human and social costs were too high and the potential for abuse too great. In the aftermath of the traumatic upheavals of the first half of the twentieth century, governments expanded their existing responsibilities and obligations to their populaces and assumed new ones. "Government knowledge"—the collective intelligence of decision makers at the center—was regarded as superior to "market knowledge"—the dispersed intelligence of private decision makers and consumers in the marketplace.

At the extreme, the Soviet Union, the People's Republic of China, and

11

other communist states sought to suppress market intelligence and private property altogether and replace them with central planning and state ownership. Government would be all-knowing. In the many industrial countries of the West and in large parts of the developing world, the model was the "mixed economy," in which governments flexed their knowledge and played a strong dominating role without completely stifling the market mechanism. They would reconstruct, modernize, and propel economic growth; they would deliver equity, opportunity, and a decent way of life. In order to achieve all that, governments in many countries sought to capture and hold the high ground of their economies—the "commanding heights."

The term goes back three quarters of a century. In November 1922, half a decade after leading the Bolsheviks to victory, the already ailing Vladimir Illyich Lenin made his way to the platform of the Fourth Congress of the Communist International in St. Petersburg, then called Petrograd. It was his penultimate public appearance. The year before, amid economic breakdown and out of desperation, Lenin had initiated the New Economic Policy, permitting a resumption of small trade and private agriculture. Now, communist militants were attacking him for compromising with capitalism and selling out the revolution. Responding with his old acerbity and sarcasm, despite his physical enfeeblement, Lenin defended the program. Although the policy allowed markets to function, he declared, the state would control the "commanding heights," the most important elements of the economy. And that, Lenin assured any who doubted him, was what counted. All this was before collectivization, Stalinism, and the total eradication of private markets in the Soviet Union.

The phrase found its way to Britain, via the Fabians and the British Labour Party, in the interwar years; it was then adopted by Jawaharlal Nehru and the Congress Party in India, and spread to many other parts of the world. Whether or not the term was used, the objective was one and the same: to ensure government control of the strategic parts of the national economy, its major enterprises and industries. In the United States, government exerted its control over the commanding heights not through ownership but rather through economic regulation, giving rise to a special American brand of regulatory capitalism.[1]

Overall, the advance of state control seemed to be inexorable. In the immediate post–World War II years, only governments could marshal the resources necessary to rebuild devastated and dislocated nations. The 1960s seemed to prove that they could effectively run, and indeed fine-tune, their economies. By the beginning of the 1970s, the mixed economy was virtually unchallenged and government continued to expand. Even in the United States, the Republican administration of Richard Nixon sought to implement a massive program of detailed wage and price controls.

Yet by the 1990s, it was government that was retreating. Communism had not only failed, it had all but disappeared in what had been the Soviet Union and, at least as an economic system, had been put aside in China. In the West, governments were shedding control and responsibilities. Instead of "market failure," the focus was now on "government failure"—the inherent difficulties that arise when the state becomes too expansive and too ambitious and seeks to be the main player, rather than a referee, in the economy. Paul Volcker, who conquered inflation as chairman of the U.S. Federal Reserve System, explained the reason for the change in simple terms: "Governments had become overweening."

The Greatest Sale

Today, in response to the high costs of control and the disillusionment with its effectiveness, governments are privatizing. It is the greatest sale in the history of the world. Governments are getting out of businesses by disposing of what amounts to trillions of dollars of assets. Everything is going—from steel plants and phone companies and electric utilities to airlines and railroads to hotels, restaurants, and nightclubs. It is happening not only in the former Soviet Union, Eastern Europe, and China but also in Western Europe, Asia, Latin America, and Africa—and in the United States, where federal, state, and city governments are turning many of their traditional activities over to the marketplace. In a parallel process that is more far-reaching and less well understood, they are also overturning the regulatory apparatus that has affected almost every aspect of daily life in America for the last six decades. The objective is to move away from governmental control as a substitute for the market and toward reliance on competition in the marketplace as a more efficient way to protect the public.

This shift does not, by any means, signal the end of government. In many countries, governments continue to spend as large a share of national income each year as the year before. The reason, in the industrial countries, is social spending—transfer payments and entitlements—and almost everywhere, government remains the solution of last resort for a host of societal demands. Yet the scope of government, the range of duties it takes on in the economy, is decidedly receding. The world over, governments have come to plan less, to own less, and to regulate less, allowing instead the frontiers of the market to expand.

The decamping of the state from the commanding heights marks a great divide between the twentieth and twenty-first centuries. It is opening the doors of many formerly closed countries to trade and investment, vastly increasing, in the process, the effective size of the global market. Many new jobs are being created. Still, it is capital and technology that, in this new mobile economy, easily move around the world in search of new opportunities and markets and more favorable business environments. Labor, which does not travel as easily, could be left behind. The result for workers is a double anxiety—about global competition and about the loss of the social safety net.

The word *globalization,* minted not much more than a decade ago, has become the all-too-familiar description for the process of integration and internationalization of economic activities and strategies. Yet the term has already been overtaken by events. A new reality is emerging. This is not a process but a condition—a globality, a world economy in which the traditional and familiar boundaries are being surmounted or made irrelevant. The end of the Soviet Union and communism has redrawn the map of world politics and subdued ideology as a dominating factor in international affairs. The growth of capital markets and the continued lowering of barriers to trade and investment are further tying markets together—and promoting a freer flow of ideas. The advent of emerging markets brings dynamism and opportunity on a massive scale to the international economy. National firms are turning themselves into international operators; and companies, whether long experienced in international business or newcomers, are hastening to generate global strategies. Paralleling and facilitating much of this is a technological revolution of momentous but uncertain consequences. Information technology—through computers—is creating a "woven world" by promoting communication, coordination, integration, and contact at a pace and scale of change that far outrun the ability of any government to manage. The accelerating connections make national borders increasingly porous—and, in terms of some forms of control, increasingly irrelevant.

The Power of Ideas

Underlying all this has been a fundamental shift in ideas. In 1936, in the concluding pages of his famous *General Theory of Employment, Interest and Money,* the eminent British economist John Maynard Keynes wrote that ideas "are more powerful than is commonly understood. Indeed, the world is ruled by little else. Madmen in authority, who hear voices in the air, are distilling their frenzy from some academic scribblers of a few years back. . . . Sooner or later it is ideas, not vested interests, which are dangerous for good or evil."

The dramatic redefinition of state and marketplace over the last two decades demonstrates anew the truth of Keynes' axiom about the overwhelming power of ideas. For concepts and notions that were decidedly outside the mainstream have now moved, with some rapidity, to center stage and are reshaping economies in every corner of the world. Even Keynes himself has been done in by his own dictum. During the bombing of London in World War II, he arranged for a transplanted Austrian economist, Friedrich von Hayek, to be temporarily housed in a college at Cambridge University. It was a generous gesture; after all, Keynes was the leading economist of his time, and Hayek, his rather obscure critic. In the postwar years, Keynes' theories of government management of the economy appeared unassailable. But a half century later, it is Keynes who has been toppled and Hayek, the fierce advocate of free markets, who is preeminent. The Keynesian "new economics" from Harvard may have dominated the Kennedy and Johnson administrations in the 1960s, but it is the University of Chicago's free-market school that is globally influential in the 1990s.[2]

But if economists and other thinkers have the ideas, it is politicians who implement them; and one of the preeminent lessons of this remarkable shift is the importance of leaders and leadership. Keith Joseph, Britain's self-appointed "minister of thought," and his disciple Margaret Thatcher seemed to be embarking on a quixotic project when they set out to overturn Britain's mixed economy. Not only did they prevail, but they influenced the agenda for a good part of the rest of the world. It was a dedicated revolutionary, Deng Xiaoping, who, while genuflecting to Marx, resolutely forced the world's largest country to disengage from communism and integrate itself into the world economy. And in the United States, the victories of Ronald Reagan forced the Democratic Party to redefine itself.

The vocabulary of this march toward the marketplace requires a word of clarification. For Americans, the global battle between the state and market can be puzzling, for it appears to pit "liberalism" against "liberalism." In the United States, *liberalism* means the embrace of an activist, interventionist government, expanding its involvement and responsibility in the economy. In the rest of the world, *liberalism* means almost exactly the opposite —what an American liberal would, in fact, describe as *conservatism*. This kind of liberalism supports a reduced role for the state, the maximization of individual liberty, economic freedom and reliance on the market, and decentralized decision making. It has its intellectual roots in such thinkers as John Locke, Adam Smith, and John Stuart Mill. It emphasizes the importance of property rights and sees government's role as the facilitation and adjudication of civil society. Thus, in this book, when *liberalism* is discussed outside the United States, whether it is in the former Soviet Union or Latin America or elsewhere, it means less government, not more.*

---

* How was the meaning of this word altered so dramatically in the United States? During the First World War, some of the leading Progressive writers began to use the word *liberalism* as a substitute for *progressivism*, which had become tarnished by its association with their fallen hero, Theodore Roosevelt, who had run and lost on a Progressive third-party ticket. Traditional liberals were not happy to see their label transformed. In the 1920s, *The New York Times* criticized "the expropriation of the time-honored word 'liberal' " and argued that "the Radical-Red school of thought . . . hand back the world 'liberal' to its original owners." During the early 1930s, Herbert Hoover and Franklin Roosevelt duked it out as to who was the true liberal. Roosevelt won, adopting the term to ward off accusations of being left-wing. He could declare that liberalism was "plain English for a changed concept of the duty and responsibility of government toward economic life." And since the New Deal, liberalism in the United States has been identified with an expansion of government's role in the economy.

Relinking Past and Future

The reassertion of this traditional liberalism represents a rebirth—indeed, a reconnection—for it had its heyday in the late nineteenth century. Indeed, the world at the dawn of the twenty-first century bears resemblance to the late-nineteenth-century world—a world of expanding economic opportunity and ever-diminishing barriers to travel and trade. Then, as now, new technologies helped foster the change. Two innovations in the nineteenth century decisively broke the bounds of the natural rhythms of winds and tides, that had, from the beginning of civilization, defined commerce. In the early part of the nineteenth century, the steam engine made possible rail and ship transportation of people and goods that was safer, faster, and more expedient than any method known at the time. As early as 1819, the American ship *Savannah* crossed the Atlantic using a steam engine to augment its sails. By the middle of the nineteenth century, steam was beginning to supplant wind power altogether. When the first telegraph cable was laid across the floor of the Atlantic in 1865, after three failed attempts, markets were connected. The spread of these technologies powered a dramatic expansion of world trade. Moreover, they provided outlets for private investment capital. European funds were poured into the construction of railroads in North and South America and in Africa and Asia, and into the mines and plantations they connected to the ports. With British money financing so much of America's railway development, the United States became the champion emerging market of the nineteenth century. In the late nineteenth century and early twentieth century, the world economy experienced an era of peace and growth that, in the aftermath of the carnage of World War I, came to be remembered as a golden age.

Critical Tests

What powered the return toward traditional liberalism around the world? The previous embrace of the state as modernizer turned into disillusionment with state ownership and intervention, owing to the unexpectedly heavy costs and consequences. The financial burden had gone beyond the ability of governments to manage: Debts and deficits had grown too big. Inflation had become chronic and embedded. As the perceived gap between intentions and actual performance grew, confidence turned into cynicism. The implosion of the Soviet system—the great lodestar for central planning—discredited statism of all kinds, while the rise of prospering East Asian economies pointed toward a different balance between state and marketplace and underlined the virtues of participation in the global economy.

Will the apparent triumph of the market endure? Or will government's role expand once again? The response will depend, we believe, on how the answers unfold to several key questions: Will the market economies deliver the goods in terms of economic growth, employment, and higher standards of living, and how will they redefine the welfare state? Will the results be seen as fair, equitable, and just? What will happen to national identity in the new international economy? Will the public be sure that the environment is sufficiently secured? And how will market economies cope with the cost of demographics—the burgeoning of the young in developing countries and the growing proportion of the elderly in the industrial countries? These questions, and the themes they represent, will be integral to the pages that follow.[3]

How does the plot of our narrative proceed? The first three chapters set out how governments took control of the commanding heights in Europe, the United States, and the developing world, achieving what seemed by the 1970s to be an invincible position. Chapter 4 describes the first major counterattack, the Thatcherite revolution in Britain in the 1980s. Chapter 5 explains the forces that led the world in the 1980s and 1990s to change its "mind" about the balance between government and market. Chapters 6 through 8 focus on Asia—the dynamics of the East Asian countries and the forces transforming them after the "miracle," the twenty-year turnaround from communism to capitalism in China, and the efforts to dismantle India's "Permit Raj" and reorient that nation to the world economy. Latin America's wrenching move from *dependencia* to shock therapy is the subject of Chapter 9. Chapter 10 explains how Russia's and Eastern Europe's "ticket to the market" got punched, and the bumpy journey to the world after communism that has followed. Europe's struggle to create a single market and slim down governments—and come to terms with the predicament of the welfare state —is the subject of Chapter 11. Chapter 12 looks at the United States through the framework of the overall process of global change, exploring the impact of fiscal rectitude on expansive government and the contrary directions in economic and social-value regulation. And finally, Chapter 13 looks to the future. What are the essential economic, political, and social issues that are to be confronted in different parts of the world? Will there be a swing back from the market, or are more fundamental and permanent changes in place? Who, after all, will occupy the commanding heights in the next century— government or market?

This, then, is our story, a narrative of the individuals, the ideas, the conflicts, and the turning points that have changed the course of economies and the fate of nations over the last half century. The scope of the story imposes its own discipline. A multitude of volumes could be written on the United States alone, or on any of the other regions and countries; here, instead, we paint them all as parts of a larger canvas—the turbulent battle over the commanding heights, the stakes and the consequences, and the prospects for the next century.

But we begin with a peace conference whose focus was, in fact, on traditional political frontiers. The year was 1945. The place, Berlin.

17

CHAPTER 1

THIRTY GLORIOUS YEARS

Europe's Mixed Economy

THE FINAL MEETING of the Allied leaders took place in July 1945, in what had once been a palace of the kaiser in the Berlin suburb of Potsdam. Their charge was to plan the last act of World War II and to arrange the peace. One of them was the inexperienced new American president, Harry Truman, who had succeeded Franklin Roosevelt not even three months earlier. The second was the Soviet dictator Joseph Stalin—Uncle Joe, as his allies called him, to his great irritation. It would be many years before the full human cost of his brutal dictatorship and gulags would become known. In the meantime, Soviet central planning, with its five-year plans and massive industrialization, had already cast a spell that was to last for decades more. The third was Winston Churchill, grand strategist and implacable leader, whose bulldog determination when England was all alone had embodied and focused the resistance to Axis aggression. He had indeed been "the hero in history"; it would have been hard to envision an Allied victory without Churchill in those darkest hours of 1940–41.

The stakes at Potsdam were very high, and the agenda was filled with tough and acrimonious issues—the timing of Soviet entry into the war with Japan, the mechanism for the German occupation, reparations—and borders, of course. There was also something else. At one point in the conference, having learned of the successful test of the atomic bomb in the New Mexico desert, Truman walked with studied casualness over to Stalin and told him that the United States had a new weapon. It was very powerful, Truman said. Stalin's reply was no less casual. Good, he said; he hoped that the United States would use it. Truman's revelation was no surprise to the Soviet dictator; he already knew about the American bomb from his spies.

After nine days of diplomatic wrangling, there was an intermission, reflecting what must have seemed to the puzzled Stalin a quaint ritual of bourgeois democracy—an election, in this case a snap British general election, meant to replace the coalition that had governed Britain since May 1940. Churchill departed Potsdam on July 25. Although disturbed by a dream in which he had seen himself dead, he was confident that his Conservative Party would win with a big majority and that he would quickly return to continue the wrangle with Stalin. Instead, the British electorate, fearful of a return to the unemployment and deprivation of the 1930s, delivered a landslide victory to the Labour Party. For the man who had led Britain through its terrible wartime crisis, the defeat was a great humiliation. "Scurvy" was the way Churchill described the outcome. A few weeks later, his wife tried to comfort him about the results. "It may well be a blessing in disguise," she said, to which he replied, "At the moment, it seems quite effectively disguised."

Britain was no longer to be led by this extraordinary figure, once called "the greatest adventurer of modern political history"—descendant of the duke of Marlborough, cavalry officer and Boer War hero, swashbuckler and master prose stylist, liberal reformer-turned-defender of Empire. Instead, he was replaced by Clement Attlee, who—moved by the poverty and despair of Britain's slums and inspired by what he called "Christian ethics"—had spent the first fourteen years of his professional life as a social worker in the East End of London.[1]

The contrast with Churchill was enormous. Described by a contemporary as "so subdued and terse," Attlee, as prime minister, prided himself on not reading newspapers, sought to keep his press briefings to ten minutes or under (punctuated by "Nothing in that" and "That idea seems bonkers to me"), and used the fewest words possible at all times. "Would you say you are an agnostic?" he was asked later in life. "I don't know," he replied. "Is there an afterlife?" "Possibly."

And so it was Attlee, not Churchill, who returned to Potsdam. Although Attlee was a professing socialist, there was little change in the composition of the British delegation, and none in its policies. Nor even in the prime minister's manservant—for, learning that Attlee had no valet, Churchill lent him his own. All of this was totally perplexing to Stalin, who thought there must be a trick. After all, as V. M. Molotov, Stalin's foreign minister, suggested to Attlee, surely Churchill could have "fixed" the results of the election. At Potsdam, Attlee was not at all bothered that trade-union leader Ernest Bevin, his new foreign minister, seemed to do all the talking while Attlee sat silent, wreathed in pipe smoke, nodding his head. "You don't keep a dog and bark yourself," he explained, "and Ernie was a very good dog."[2]

With victory in the war close, Attlee and his Labour colleagues—a contentious mix of Oxford intellectuals, trade unionists, and coal miners— had touched a deep chord in the electorate that Churchill could not. And the programs they would launch represented the beginning of an era in which governments—the "state"—sought to scale and control the commanding heights of their national economies. This happened first in the industrial countries, in the name of reconstruction, economic growth, full employment, and justice and equity, and then later also in the developing world—in the name of progress, nation building and anti-imperialism. The Labourites established and legitimized the model of the "mixed economy"—characterized by strong, direct government involvement in the economy—whether through fiscal management or through a state-owned sector that coexisted with the private sector—plus an expansive welfare state. That model lasted for four decades. The efforts of this Labour band marked the beginning of an economic and political tide that flowed around the world until it reached its peak in the 1970s.

Toward the Mixed Economy

Throughout Western Europe, several broad forces shaped the mixed-economy consensus. The first was before everybody's eyes—the appalling destruction, misery, and disruption created by the war. That devastation precipitated a crisis of unprecedented proportions; never had there been a cataclysm like it. The scene, U.S. secretary of war Henry Stimson wrote in his diary, was "worse than anything probably that ever happened in the world." Tens of millions of people were desperately short of food, many of them on the edge of starvation. The crisis could be measured by the human cost—the dead and the injured, the grim survivors, the flood of displaced persons, the shredding of families. It was also evident in the physical destruction—the homes and factories reduced to rubble, agriculture and transportation disrupted. But there was also a devastation that was less obvious to the eye: Machinery was obsolete and worn-out; the labor force in Europe was exhausted, malnourished, and in disarray; technical skills had been dissipated. Extreme weather, culminating in the Siberian winter of 1947, unleashed a grave crisis.

Something had to be done—and fast. The misery was enormous. If relief did not come quickly, it was feared that communism might well capture the entire continent. There was no functioning private sector to which to turn in order to mobilize the investment, capital goods, and skills necessary for reconstruction and recovery; international trade and payments had been disrupted. Governments would have to fill the vacuum and take charge. They would be the organizers and champions of recovery. There was nothing else.

The policies and programs of the mixed economy also emerged in response to the experiences of the immediately preceding decades. First and foremost was the Great Depression of the 1930s and the mass unemployment that was its most striking manifestation. What happened over the subsequent four decades—and where the world economy stands today—cannot be understood without grasping that unemployment was the central structural problem toward which all policies were to be geared. During the 1920s, the market system had not performed anywhere near adequately in many countries, and during the 1930s, it had failed massively. It could not be counted on not to fail again. Governments, therefore, would take on a much-expanded role in order to deliver full employment, extirpate the "slump," regulate and stabilize economic activity, and ensure that the war was not followed by a depression that would make vain all the promises and idealism and sacrifices of the struggle that had just concluded.

At the end of the war, in Europe and throughout much of the world, capitalism was discredited in a way that is not easily imagined today. It seemed infirm, inept, and incapable. It could not be counted upon to deliver economic growth and a decent life. "Nobody in Europe believes in the American way of life—that is, in private enterprise," the British historian A. J. P. Taylor wrote at the time. "Or rather those who believe in it are a defeated party and a party which seems to have no more future than the Jacobites in England after 1688." Capitalism was considered morally objectionable; it appealed to greed instead of idealism, it promoted inequality, it had failed the people, and—to many—it had been responsible for the war.

One other factor was at work as well. The Soviet Union enjoyed an economic prestige and respect in the West that is hard to reconstruct today. Its five-year plans for industrial development, its "command-and-control" economy, its claims of full employment were all seen to constitute a great oasis and antidote to the unemployment and failures of capitalism in the 1930s. The Soviet economic model gained further credit from the USSR's successful resistance against the Nazi war machine. Altogether, these things gave socialism a good name. This respect and admiration came not only from the left in Europe but also from moderates, and even from conservatives. The anguish and brutality of the Stalinist system were not yet very visible, or were not taken very seriously. The limitations and rigidity of central planning—and, ultimately, its fatal flaw, its inability to innovate—were still decades away from being evident. The historian E. H. Carr, although always sympathetic to the Soviet "experiment," was only exaggerating when he wrote in 1947, "Certainly, if 'we are all planners now,' this is largely the result, conscious or unconscious, of the impact of Soviet practice and Soviet achievement." The Soviet model was the rallying point for the left. It challenged and haunted social democrats, centrists, and conservatives; its imprint on thinking across the entire political spectrum could not be denied.[3]

Britain: Making Good on the Promise

For the Labourites in Britain, the specter of unemployment was the starting point, virtually their raison d'être. They wanted to make good, at last, on Prime Minister David Lloyd George's promise at the end of the First World

War of "homes fit for heroes," a promise that had been betrayed in the bitter interwar years. The 1920s, and even more the 1930s, had delivered mass unemployment and hardship, bitter confrontation between labor and management, and preservation of the class system, whereby accent and education (or want of it) denied opportunity and doomed one to staying put. As the Labourites saw it, Britain was a nation whose capitalists had surely failed it; they had underinvested and demonstrated no entrepreneurial drive. Instead, flinty and mean-spirited businessmen had hoarded profits, eschewing new technologies, avoiding innovation, and depriving their workers. These businessmen were hardly the ones to rejuvenate the economy.

The reaction of the Labourites to the 1930s and its unemployment was in fact the culmination of an intellectual movement that had begun during the last decades of the nineteenth century, in response to the poverty and slums spawned by industrialization and to the economic crises and busts of the business cycle. These were the conditions that had led Clement Attlee to stake his career in the East End of London instead of in his father's law chambers. And the response of those who, like Attlee, were appalled by poverty took the form, in varying degrees, of a commitment to reform and social justice, a search for efficiency, a growing belief in the responsibility of government toward its citizens, and an embrace of the British brand of socialism. Much of this was articulated by the Fabians, launched in the late nineteenth century by, among others, Beatrice and Sidney Webb and George Bernard Shaw. This immensely influential society of intellectuals sought to replace the "scramble for private gain" with the achievement of "Collective Welfare"—moving, in Shaw's words, step by step, toward "Collectivism" and "an installment of Socialism." Their method was incrementalism, not revolution.

During the 1930s, the British socialists looked around the world and saw other governments that were "doing things." One model was the optimistic activism, experimentation, and interventionist reforms of Franklin Roosevelt and the New Deal. Others were drawn more to the Soviet Union and what were viewed as the "heroic" accomplishments of communism, socialism, and central planning, which seemed to make the USSR the exception to global stagnation. A segment of the British intelligentsia, led by the Webbs, maintained its romance with Soviet communism for all too long. The Soviet model often impressed the intellectuals more than the trade unionists. Such leaders as Ernest Bevin had become fiercely anticommunist as a result of their battles with the communists for control of the British union movement, and they proved to be among the most resolute opponents to Soviet expansionism after World War II.

War itself had vastly enlarged the economic realm of government. The management of the British economy during World War II provided positive proof of what government could do, and demonstrated the benefits of planning. Indeed, the government took over the economy and ran it far more efficiently, on a much larger scale, than had been the case in the 1930s; the

23

government could squeeze much more production out of the industrial machine than its capitalist owners had done before the war. Moreover, the population rallied together and shared the experience of the "stress of total war," turning the national economy into a common cause rather than an arena of class conflict. Even the royal family had ration books.

All of these historical currents led to a rejection of Adam Smith, laissez-faire, and traditional nineteenth-century liberalism as an economic philosophy. In the immediate postwar years, there was skepticism and outright disbelief in the idea that the individual's pursuit of what Adam Smith defined as self-interest would add up, in the aggregate, to the benefit of "all." No, the sum was injustice and inequality, the few benefiting from the sweat of the many. The concept of profit was itself morally distasteful. As Attlee put the matter, a belief in private profit as motive for economic progress was "a pathetic faith resting on no foundation of experience."

The Labour politicians who took power in the final weeks of World War II were determined to build what they called "the New Jerusalem." To do so, they would apply the lessons of history and transform the role of government. Building on wartime experiences and institutions, they would make government into the protector and partner of the people and take on responsibility for the well-being of its citizens to a far greater extent than had been the case before the war. Moreover, Labour had the blueprint at hand. It was in the Beveridge Report, prepared by a government-appointed commission during World War II under William Beveridge, a sometime civil servant who had been head of the London School of Economics. The report set out social programs to slay the "five giants": Want, Disease, Ignorance, Squalor, and Idleness (i.e., unemployment). The report, published by His Majesty's Stationer's Office, was a phenomenal best-seller. (Two commentaries on the report, both marked SECRET, were even found in Hitler's bunker at war's end.) The report's influence would be global and far-reaching, forever changing the way not only Britain but also the entire industrialized world came to view the obligations of the state vis-à-vis social welfare.

Implementing the recommendations of the Beveridge Report, the Labour government established free medical care under a newly constituted National Health Service, created new systems of pensions, promoted better education and housing, and sought to deliver on the explicit commitment to "full employment." All of this added up to what the Labourites were to call the welfare state—and they were very proud to do so. The term emerged— as used, for instance, by the archbishop of York in 1941—in explicit contrast to what were said to be the "power states" of the Continental dictators. To be sure, it was on the Continent that national insurance for pensions and illness had been pioneered—by German chancellor Otto von Bismarck, as early as the 1880s. In Britain, the reforming Liberal government of 1906 introduced the first state insurance schemes for unemployment and health and old-age pensions. These initial steps of what was at the time called the "ambulance state" were quite modest. By contrast, the comprehensiveness of the Labour Program of 1945 transformed Britain from a would-be ambulance state into the first major welfare state.[4]

Conquering the Commanding Heights

In 1918, the Labour Party had adopted a constitution containing what became the famous Clause IV, which, in language written by Sidney Webb, called for "common ownership of the means of production, distribution, and exchange." But what were these words to mean in practical terms? The answer came during World War II. One evening in 1944, a retired railway worker named Will Cannon, drawn back into the workforce to help in the marshaling yard, happened to drop by a local union meeting in Reading, not far from London. In the course of the meeting he decided to propose a motion calling for "nationalization," which was approved by the local. The motion won national attention, and the Labour Party ended up adopting it in December 1944. Will Cannon's motion would have a powerful global echo.

In July 1945, Labour came into power totally committed to nationalization and determined to conquer the "commanding heights" of the economy, having borrowed the term from Lenin by the mid-1930s. In their quest for control of the commanding heights after World War II, the Labourites nationalized the fragmented coal industry, which provided 90 percent of Britain's energy at the time. They did the same to iron and steel, railroads, utilities, and international telecommunications. There was some precedent for this even in the British system; after all, it was Winston Churchill himself who, as first lord of the Admiralty in 1911, had purchased a controlling government stake in what became British Petroleum in order to ensure oil supply for the Royal Navy. Churchill's rationale had been security, military power, and the Anglo-German naval race.

The premise of nationalization in the 1940s was quite different—that as private businesses, these industries had underinvested, been inefficient, and lacked scale.* As nationalized firms, they would mobilize resources and adapt new technologies, they would be far more efficient, and they would ensure the achievement of the national objectives of economic development and growth, full employment, and justice and equality. They would be the engine of the overall economy, drawing it toward modernization and greater redistribution of income. These nationalizations were carried out quickly by the Labour minister Herbert Morrison, who in the 1930s had honed his expertise by uniting the buses and Underground of London into one authority.

---

* These had also been the themes of the more direct forerunners, the nationalizations of electric power in the 1920s—the Central Electricity Generating Board—and of overseas aviation in 1939—the British Overseas Airways Corporation.

But exactly how was nationalization to be implemented? The British, after some debate, rejected the "Post Office Model"—nationalized enterprises as departments or adjuncts of government ministries. They opted instead for the "public corporation"—the model already used for the BBC —and what later became known around the world as the state-owned corporation. Government would appoint a board, which in turn would govern the corporation. Morrison explained: "These are going to be public corporations, business concerns; they will buy the necessary brains and technical skills and give them their heads." But how were the activities of the public corporations to be coordinated in order to fulfill the Labour agenda? The answer was a resounding appeal to "planning." The word had permeated Labour's 1945 election manifesto; and initially at least, Labour's drive to the commanding heights would rally around the concept of planning as the key to the potential promise of nationalization. And nationalization itself was the new grand strategy that, as Attlee put it, represented "the embodiment of our socialist principle of placing the welfare of the nation before any section."

As it turned out, about 20 percent of the nation's workforce ended up employed in the newly nationalized industries. But these were the industries that for the most part made up the "strategic sectors" on which the nation's economy was built. There were limits, however, as to how far the government could or would go. Policy flexibility was limited at the war's end by the stark fact that Britain was, for all practical purposes, bankrupt. Its balance of payments was in desperate shape as the consequence of the government's having spent an enormous amount of the country's national wealth defeating the Axis, and of having lost so much of its invisible earnings from the forced liquidation of its overseas investments. The severity of Britain's penury became apparent in 1946, when a general economic crisis began. Bankruptcy was now compounded by a calamitous winter and the overall breakdown of international trade and payments. Even the elevators in the Treasury were not working, owing to electricity cuts.[5]

"We Work Things Out Practically"

This crisis, accentuated by the emerging cold war, effectively ended further campaigns to capture any more of the commanding heights. Labour's hands were tied. And thus much of the Labourite rhetoric was never implemented. Despite all the discussions about the grand objective of "planning," not a great deal was actually done, and in due course, it was jettisoned. Ernest Bevin, who had helped direct Britain's wartime command economy, dismissed France's postwar commitment to planning with a wave of his hand: "We don't do things like that in our country; we don't have plans, we work things out practically." The shift was facilitated in 1947, when Attlee transferred the reins of control over the nationalized industries from Herbert

Morrison to Sir Stafford Cripps. Though Cripps was a rather efficient, pragmatic manager, his self-righteousness earned him Churchill's growl that "there, but for the grace of God, goes God." Cripps was also a firm and vocal advocate of a more moderate approach, and his accession to the number-one position represented a clear abandonment of the attempt to centrally plan British industry.

Certainly, the travails continued. Food rationing remained until 1954. Babies were registered at birth as vegetarians so that their parents could get eggs for them; rabbit was the only meat that was not controlled. Even candy remained rationed until 1953. Yet despite hard times, the Attlee government had delivered the goods. The British people had acquired a welfare state, which gave them access to health care and better education and greater peace of mind in the face of the vicissitudes of illness, handicap, bad luck, and old age.

And the number-one giant—the one that, more than anything else, had called the Labourites to battle—was slain. Unemployment in Britain during the 1930s had run at 12 percent; in the late 1940s, it was as low as 1.3 percent. Britain had succeeded in replacing the gold standard, which had been the bedrock of orthodoxy and policy in the 1920s and 1930s, with a "full employment standard." The economy was to be judged not by how many troy ounces there were to the British pound but by the number of jobs it could deliver to a population willing to work.

Members of the Labour Party called themselves socialists. But it was a British brand of socialism that owed much more to the nineteenth-century utopian Robert Owen than to Karl Marx. On the eve of taking power, Attlee defined it thus: "a mixed economy developing toward socialism. . . . The doctrines of abundance, of full employment, and of social security require the transfer to public ownership of certain major economic forces and the planned control in the public interest of many other economic activities." And this "mixed economy," with its welfare state, became the basis of what has variously been called the postwar settlement and the Attlee Consensus. Whatever its name, it would have a profound impact around the world over the next four decades.[6]

France: "The Levers of Command"

In France, the great expansion of the state's role arose out of the disaster of the war. France had experienced neither victory nor defeat but rather collapse and humiliation, collaboration and resistance. Coming out of the war, the nation focused on renewal and the restoration of legitimacy. The old order of the Third Republic could not be reestablished; it had failed. In France at war's end, no less than in Britain, the capitalist system was seen as "rotten." It was held to be backward, narrow-minded, retarded by insufficient investment and a "freezing of the capitalist spirit." The villains were rigid family firms and staid businessmen who, lacking in entrepreneurship, had sought to protect themselves from competition, preserve the family's position, and avoid "creative risk." In fact, the system was already discredited on the eve of World War II. In 1939, the average age of France's industrial machinery was four times that of America and three times that of Britain, while output per working hour in France was one third that in America and one half that in Britain. There had been no improvement in the standard of living since before the Great War; per capita income in 1939 was the same as in 1913. The experience of the Second World War accentuated the critique of capitalism in three ways: France's backward economic organization was a mighty cause of its military and political weakness; the old system was inadequate to meet the overriding needs of reconstruction; and a significant part of French business was deeply tainted by its leaders' collaboration with the Nazis and the puppet Vichy regime.

Across much of the political spectrum, there was consensus on the need to expand government in the face of the apparent weakness of the market system. "The state," General Charles de Gaulle, new head of the provisional government, declared in 1945, "must hold the levers of command." This would be something quite different from what had prevailed before the war. He told the "privileged classes" that they were dismissed because they had "disqualified themselves." There was to be a new France, economically vigorous, built upon an economy divided into three sectors: the private, the controlled, and the nationalized. Nationalization would serve multiple purposes: It would promote investment, modernization, and technological progress; it would solve the problem of monopoly; and it would consolidate and rationalize fragmented industries, some of which were highly fractionated (some 1,730 firms were fully engaged in the production, transmission, and distribution of electricity; another 970 firms were partly engaged in the same enterprise). It would punish the collaborators by taking their firms away from them and turning them over to the "people." Nationalization would also perform one other very critical service: It would enroll the communist-controlled unions in the process of reconstruction rather than leave them outside to wage war on it.

Some precedent for nationalization existed. In the 1920s, for instance, France had created a state oil company, Compagnie Française des Pétroles, to protect and expand French interests and become "the industrial arms of government action." It was the type of firm that would come to be called a "national champion"—a company, either state-owned or closely aligned to the government, that would represent national interests domestically and in international competition—and, as such, would receive preferences from the government. The nationalization of the railroads in 1937 had been a large-scale bailout of that badly bleeding industry. For the most part, however, nationalization and an active state role had not been part of the French tradition. That changed with the Liberation. Through the nationalization acts of 1945 and 1946, the French state decisively asserted its dominion over the commanding heights, taking control of banking, electricity, gas, and coal, among other industries. The state also undertook punitive nationalizations of companies whose owners and managers had consorted with Vichy, including Renault and several important media concerns. By the end of this wave, the French economy had been transformed.

But as quickly as nationalization was implemented, the process was no less quickly halted by 1947. The form of corporate governance adopted in France gave board members from communist-controlled unions inordinate influence over the newly nationalized industries; and the zeal with which they abused this power to pursue their own agenda generated a sharp response. Statutory reforms and a change in political alliances finally wrested control from the communists, but there was little taste left for further nationalization. The communists left the coalition government in May 1947 in the midst of the emerging cold war and, on Moscow's orders, went on the offensive against the state with massive strikes. By 1950, the communist leader who had been minister of industrial production during the nationalization phase was declaring his opposition. Nationalization was "a capitalist weapon," he said, for propping up the capitalist state and resisting the communist tide. Yet when it was all added up, France too had become a mixed economy. The state had acquired a major stake in some of the most critical sectors of the economy, in what was a very decisive break with the prewar tradition.[7]

The Cognac Salesman

The response to the challenge of reconstruction was also to be found in another form of expansion of the state's power over the economy—through *"planification,"* the implementation of a national economic plan that became France's postwar trademark. This process—focusing, prioritizing, and pointing the way—was dubbed indicative planning, to differentiate it from the Soviet system, with its highly directive and rigid central planning. It was very much intended to be a middle way between free markets and socialism.

How appropriate that this plan for a middle way would be developed by a capitalist banker who voted socialist. His name was Jean Monnet, and although he never held high office, he was one of the most influential figures of the entire postwar era. He is best remembered as the "Father of Europe" —the creator and instigator of what is now the European Union. But first he fathered the plan that shook the French economy out of its stalemate and propelled it into the modern age.

Monnet was a citizen of the world who could, when needed, behave like an obstinate French peasant buying or selling a cow. He was driven by drink, so to speak, to his internationalism. Born into a brandy family from Cognac, he left school at sixteen to travel the world selling the liquor—from isolated farms on the prairies of western Canada to villages along the Nile

29

in Egypt. It is said that he ended up, along the way, with a bigger vocabulary in English than in French. On one of his Canadian trips, having traveled from Medicine Hat to Moose Jaw, he found himself in Calgary, looking for a horse and buggy. He asked a stranger for the nearest stable. "Take my horse," the stranger replied. "When you're through just hitch it up here." That, Monnet later said, was his first introduction to the international pooling of resources. During World War I, he played a key role in organizing the Allied supply effort. He also began building up an extraordinary network of friendships on both sides of the Atlantic, which would serve him well in later years. At the Versailles conference, for instance, he met John Foster Dulles (later U.S. secretary of state). Monnet went out of his way to maintain that relationship thereafter, since, he explained, "nothing important is done in the United States without lawyers." In 1919, at age thirty-one, he was appointed deputy secretary-general of the new League of Nations. After two frustrating years, he quit, returned to the family business, fixed its troubled finances, and then gave up cognac altogether in favor of international banking. So extensive and far-flung were Monnet's connections, and so hard did he work them to such productive purpose, that he probably should also be remembered, in today's parlance, as the father of networking.

But it was an urgent matter of the heart that truly demonstrated his unique combination of wits, willpower, persistence, connections, and creativity. In 1929, Monnet fell hopelessly in love with an Italian woman, a painter named Silvia di Bondini. She was not only a devout Catholic but was also already married and had a daughter. Divorce—with child custody —was frustrated at every turn. Even Reno, Nevada, could not meet their needs. It took Monnet five years to find the solution. In 1934, he was traveling aboard the trans-Siberian railway on his way back from a banking mission in China. Monnet disembarked in Moscow. His beloved was there to meet him. Using his connections, Monnet had her made a Soviet citizen in a matter of days and she was immediately divorced. Wasting no time, they married right there in Moscow. Monnet quickly caught a train to Paris, where he deposited his new wife, moved on to New York—and then back to Shanghai to resume his work reorganizing the Chinese railways. He was certainly not a man to stand still. But the marriage lasted forty-five years.

During World War II, Monnet once again operated at the highest levels, serving as supply and reconstruction coordinator for the French government-in-exile as well as economic liaison to the United States. He organized the flow of urgently needed supplies and finance and facilitated overall economic policy among the Allies. He had easy access to Roosevelt's inner circle. (Forever after, de Gaulle suspected him of being an American agent.) He came up with the phrase that the United States should become the "arsenal of democracy," for which Roosevelt's advisers heartily thanked him. They also promptly told him never to use it again so that FDR could reserve the historic phrase for himself.[8]

The Plan: "Modernization or Decadence"?

Monnet, perhaps more clearly than any other Frenchman, grasped the magnitude of the war's destruction and the overwhelming requirements of reconstruction that would confront France afterward. The country was burdened with an industrial engine that had been sputtering for decades even before the war, and France's immediate postwar economic agenda would be dominated both by a huge balance-of-payments crisis and the fundamental need to modernize. The government would have to deal with the first, and the private sector could not be depended upon for the second. Out of these necessities emerged the Monnet Plan.

The more immediate origin of this plan was a conversation Monnet had with de Gaulle in Washington, D.C., in August 1945, a few weeks after the end of the war. "You speak of greatness," Monnet said, "but today the French are small. There will only be greatness when the French are of a stature to warrant it. . . . For this purpose, they must modernize—because at the moment they are not modern. Materially, the country needs to be transformed."

"You are certainly right," replied de Gaulle. Impressed by the vitality and prosperity he saw around him in America, the general turned the problem back to Monnet: "Do you want to try?"

Monnet certainly did. He set up shop at first in Paris in a few rooms in the Bristol Hotel, putting a board across the bathtub to create extra office space, and then moved to a town house that had belonged to Cézanne's art dealer, close to the prime minister's office. There, with minimal staff and maximum behind-the-scenes maneuvering, he drew up the first plan aimed at restoring normal economic life to France.

Essentially, what the Monnet Plan did was prioritize, set investment targets, and allocate investment funds, with the focus on reconstruction, particularly in the basic industries—defined by Monnet as the nationalized electricity, coal, and rail transportation industries, and the nonnationalized steel, cement, and agricultural machinery industries. For Monnet, the importance of the targets lay not in reaching a scientifically optimal level of investment. Rather, establishing an optimistic, forward-looking plan was an end in itself. He wanted action that would generate more action. Initiating momentum would prevent the economy from falling back into its prewar risk-averse ways and again "crystallizing at a low level."

The French also needed a plan as a prospectus for obtaining American aid. The U.S. undersecretary of state for economic affairs, Will Clayton, one of the authors of the Marshall Plan, made this point explicitly, privately exhorting French officials to "be liberals or *dirigistes*. Return to capitalism or head toward socialism. . . . But in either case the government must . . . formulate a precise program proving its desire to give France an economy that will permit it to reach international production costs calculated in man-hours. If it . . . demonstrates to us the seriousness of its program, we shall help your country, for its prosperity is necessary to peace." Thus a feasible plan was essential to secure the aid that eventually flowed into France through the Marshall Plan. Monnet also succeeded in insulating the planning function from the vagaries of French politics. He carried out a brilliant administrative coup by establishing the planning board, the Commissariat Général du Plan, as an independent commission reporting directly to the prime minister.[9]

The formulation of the plan required all of Monnet's formidable skills —as planner, coordinator, financier, and networker. The result was a masterpiece: a plan on which France could hang its hopes, a basis on which the United States could provide aid, and a mechanism by which the French economy could receive the support and restructuring denied it for so many decades by its pessimistic capitalists. Yet the results were somewhat mixed. Some targets were made, others were missed. By 1950, only the coal mines had exceeded the original construction and modernization programs. France also missed its overall investment targets, the growth in its industrial output was well below that of its neighbors, and the aggressive investment program contributed to inflation. But what the plan did do, at a crucial period, was provide the discipline, direction, vision, confidence, and hope for a nation that otherwise might have remained in a deep and dangerous malaise. And it set France on the road to an economic miracle in the 1950s.

Monnet had developed a great love for balance sheets as a boy while poring over the accounts of the family brandy business with his father, and his plan was hailed at the time as "the first attempt in postwar Europe to draw up a balance sheet and overall program for the future." Yet Monnet was not necessarily enamored of central planning. As one future prime minister remarked, "The odd thing is he did not like plans." Monnet did not take a stand one way or the other on nationalization, and he may well have preferred markets, large, open markets to grand plans. But he seized upon the state's monopoly, even if only temporary, over both capital and credit, because he saw no good alternative.

"Modernization or decadence"—that was the choice that Monnet, with his plan, posed for France. In seeking to ensure that the choice was modernization, he expanded the role of government in the national economy and created one of the most credible models for that role, and for planning. And by so doing, Monnet's biographer wrote, "he helped create a relative consensus behind . . . the 'mixed economy' "—and not only for France, but for Europe.[10]

Germany: Lucky Strikes and "Chicken Feed"

Nowhere else in Europe was capitalism so discredited as in the four occupied zones of postwar Germany, owing to the complicity of a good part of big business with Hitler. The Nazis had organized and administered a "warfare state" that had preserved private property but controlled and subordinated it to their own purposes. The SPD—the Social Democrats—was the only party with a record of fighting the Nazis from the first day to the last, and it intended to create a noncapitalist future.

The appalling conditions of postwar life seemed to provide the circumstances for implementing a socialist vision. Germany was a devastated, desperately hungry country. Controls and rationing contributed to a barter economy, with dejected people trooping, by dilapidated trains, to the countryside to exchange whatever household goods they might still possess for a couple of eggs or a bag of potatoes. So pervasive were the black and gray markets that, it was estimated, only half of the country's meager output passed through legal channels. The official currency was almost worthless —one-five-hundredth of its original value. The working currency of the country was not the reichsmark but cartons of Lucky Strike cigarettes, favored by American GIs. Conditions were so deplorable that the Catholic archbishop of Cologne told his faithful it was all right to steal food and coal in order to survive. The mayor of Cologne, Konrad Adenauer, slept in his suit and coat, owing to the lack of heat. His driver managed to do better, sleeping in a bathtub in a hospital bathroom, where at least it was warmer.

Surely in such conditions the new Germany was destined to become a socialist country. The Social Democrats were led by Kurt Schumacher, who had spent ten years in Nazi concentration camps, eight of them in Dachau. Now, in postwar Germany, he and his party were committed to replacing capitalism with nationalization and central planning, much in line with the policies of the British Labour Party. That certainly seemed to be the direction the country would take. Even the center-right Christian Democrats adopted a program in 1947 which declared that "the capitalist economic system" had failed "the national and social interests of the German people" and instead called for public ownership of the commanding heights and a "considerable" degree of central planning "for a long time to come."

Yet within a year Germany was to set off on quite a different economic path. There were a number of reasons. Soviet expansionism was fueling a confrontation between East and West that would lead to the division of Germany and discredit the left wing. Marshall Plan aid was beginning to lay the basis for an integrated European economy. And then there was the matter of the chicken feed.

The food situation in Germany was awful. The average number of daily calories consumed was 1,300, and sometimes as low as 800, just a quarter of the prewar level. "We do not see why you have to read *The New York Times* to know that the Germans are close to starving," General Lucius Clay, the head of the U.S. military occupation, had angrily cabled Washington. "The crisis is now." The German shortfall was part of a global food crisis; European wheat production in 1947 was half of what it had been in 1938. In response, the United States started pouring a great deal of food relief into

Germany. Then, in January 1948, Johannes Semler, the German director of economic administration for Bizonia (as the combined American and British occupation zones were called) made a speech in which he complained that much of the grain that the Americans were sending was not wheat but rather corn, which, he sarcastically pointed out, was what Germans fed to chickens, not to people. The word he used—*Hühnerfutter*—was translated as "chicken feed." That was hardly a gracious way to describe free food aid. The furious General Clay fired Semler. As his replacement, Clay chose a rotund economist named Ludwig Erhard, who had been economic minister of Bavaria for several months after the war. Denied an academic appointment during the Hitler years because of his refusal to join a Nazi organization, he had spent his time quietly doing market research in Nuremberg. Now, suddenly and unexpectedly, he was in a position to lead Germany to an economic future different from what would have been assumed even a year earlier.[11]

The Ordoliberals and the Social Market

Ludwig Erhard belonged to an economic group that called itself the Ordoliberals. Some of its members were centered around the University of Freiburg and thus were sometimes called the Freiburg School. It included such figures as Alfred Müller-Armack, Wilhelm Röpke, Walter Eucken, and Alexander Rüstow. They were committed to free markets, and believed that the disaster of Nazism was the culmination of cartelization and state control over the economy. The Ordoliberals also believed that they had identified the answer to the deeply painful question "of how Nazi totalitarianism could have risen in the country of Kant, Goethe, and Beethoven." The explanation was to be found in the latter part of the nineteenth century, when cartels and monopolies developed unchecked by the state in the new German Reich, leading to greater and greater concentrations of economic and political power and, ultimately, to totalitarianism. Market forces and a competitive economy were the standard for the Ordoliberals. Government's responsibility was to create and maintain a framework that promoted competition and prevented cartels. Competition was the best way to prevent private or public concentrations of power, thus constituting the best guarantee of political liberty, as well as providing a superior economic mechanism.

Yet the Ordoliberals' vision was not simply laissez-faire. The "Ordo" captured their sense of order—"a certain hierarchy or 'natural form' of society"—deliberately meant to be linked to the medieval idea of natural order. They believed in a strong state and a strong social morality. As Wilhelm Röpke explained it: "We want no restriction of the market economy of competition and of the freely floating price mechanism. Nor do we want a mixed economy. . . . We also well know that if we seek a pure free market economy based on competition, it cannot float freely in a social, political,

34

and moral vacuum, but must be maintained and protected by a strong social, political, and moral framework. Justice, the state, traditions and morals, firm standards and values . . . are part of this framework as are the economic, social, and fiscal policies which, outside the market sphere, balance interests, protect the weak, restrain the immoderate, cut down excesses, limit power, set the rules of the game and guard their observance."

Thus, to the Ordoliberals there was nothing inconsistent between their commitment to free markets and their support of a social safety net—a system of subsidies and transfer payments to take care of the weak and disadvantaged. All this added up to what they were to call the "social market economy." The term was invented by Alfred Müller-Armack, one of Ludwig Erhard's senior advisers, and it came to describe the German economic model in the postwar years. In their version, the state might do a great deal. What it was not to do, however, was interfere with the market mechanism by fixing prices or controlling output. Like many other Germans, the Ordo-liberals also saw the root of so much of Germany's misfortune in the hyperin-flation of the post–World War I years that had alienated and virtually wiped out the German middle class, undermining the basis of democracy. Thus they were devoted to a stable currency, a devotion that would later come to be the raison d'être of Germany's central bank, the Bundesbank.[12]

Erhard: "Pay No Attention"

The Ordoliberals' principles guided Erhard. "Our people will be truly fortu-nate," he wrote not long before becoming economics director, "if we can realize an economic order that makes room for free economic activity that is cognizant of its social responsibility instead of the prevailing and univer-sally detested bureaucratic formalism." Now that unfortunate reference to "chicken feed" had put him in the position to act on those principles and put Ordoliberalism into practice.

Events provided support. Soviet obstruction and territorial ambitions led the Western allies to give up on four-power cooperation and instead to shape a western Germany that would be tied to Western Europe. This coin-cided with the recognition that Europe could not recover with a destitute Germany at its heart. The last vestiges of the United States 1944 Morgenthau Plan, which called for the "pastoralization" of Germany, were allowed to fade away. Instead, a revived Germany, its industry rejuvenated, was to be integrated with its neighbors through the Marshall Plan.

The seminal events took place in June 1948. The Americans and British executed a massive overnight currency reform, replacing worthless reichs-marks with new deutsche marks, which created a sound economic founda-tion. Currency reform was essential if the occupation zones were to be fused politically. Not involved in its implementation, Erhard was angry when he found out about it from General Clay only a few hours in advance. He retaliated by jumping the gun and announcing it, as though he had played a key role, on his weekly radio talk show.

Of no less significance was the step toward a liberal economic order that Erhard took a few days later, this time on his own authority. Germany was still gripped by a massive system of allocations and price controls inherited from the Nazis. Now it was Erhard's opportunity to fully turn the tables on Clay. No alterations could be made in the system of price controls without the Allies' approval. But there was no requirement for approval of complete abolition of the system, since no one thought it could possibly be done. That is exactly what Erhard did, simply abolishing most of the price controls overnight, without a word in advance to Clay.

Suddenly, Germany had a functioning economy again. The black and gray markets disappeared; goods reappeared in shop windows. It was Clay's turn to be nonplussed. "Herr Erhard," he said. "My advisers tell me that what you have done is a terrible mistake. What do you say to that?"

"Herr General, pay no attention to them!" Erhard replied. "My own advisers tell me the same thing."

Clay did not disagree. The historians of postwar Germany would describe this meeting as "the 'most fateful' event in the history of postwar Germany"—the beginning of the economic miracle and the launching of the social market economy.

A few days later, on June 23, the Soviets imposed the Berlin blockade in order to stop the currency reform and frustrate efforts to consolidate the three Western occupation zones. They laid siege to Berlin, which, although ninety miles inside the Communist zone, was under four-power occupation. By severing all rail and road transport, they aimed to choke off all supplies to the city until the Western powers caved in on the currency and political unification. The Soviets, however, had not counted on the massive airlift of supplies that the Western allies hurriedly improvised. Had the Russians interfered with that, they would have risked starting World War III. The blockade did further damage to the Soviet position by having quite the opposite effect from what was intended. In April 1949, the North Atlantic Treaty, establishing NATO, was signed, and the blockade only served to speed up the transformation of the three Western occupation zones into a new, unified, Western-oriented democratic state. With the strong support of the Western allies, the Germans promulgated the Basic Law, establishing the Federal Republic (as West Germany was officially known) on May 8, 1949, four years to the day after Nazi Germany's surrender. The Soviets, realizing that they had played their hand badly, called off the blockade.[13]

The Wirtschaftswunder

Thus was created a potential political context for the social market economy. But would the context be there? That depended upon the outcome of the campaign for the Bundestag, the new parliament, and the choice of the first postwar chancellor. And it seemed likely that victory would go to Kurt Schumacher's Social Democrats, with their quite different notions of how the economy should be run. Pitted against Schumacher was Konrad Adenauer, the Catholic liberal who had been mayor of Cologne from 1917 until he was fired in 1933 for refusing to fly Nazi flags over the city hall when Hitler visited Cologne. He spent the Nazi years partly tending his roses, partly in prison, and partly in hiding. He was imprisoned for the final time in 1944, after the German officers' failed assassination attempt against Hitler, initially in a concentration camp and then in a Gestapo prison. "If the advance of the American army had not taken place so surprisingly near us," he wrote a friend in the United States one day after Hitler's suicide, "I probably would have been taken away and killed by the Gestapo." For a time after World War II, he was again mayor of Cologne. No one could doubt his anti-Nazi record; his wife died in 1948 as a consequence of her imprisonment in a Gestapo jail.

The September 1949 election was fought very much, as Adenauer was to say, over the "planned economy" versus the "social market economy." The results were inconclusive, as Schumacher's Social Democrats and Adenauer's Christian Democratic/Christian Socialist parties each received about 30 percent of the vote, with the rest going to a variety of other parties. The choice of chancellor would be decided in the Bundestag. And critical to the outcome would be the votes of the small Free Democratic Party, the one true free-market party in Germany. It threw its support to Adenauer. He was elected by just one vote—his own. "My doctor tells me," the seventy-three-year-old chancellor announced, "that I would be able to carry out this office for at least a year, perhaps for two." As it turned out, he stayed fourteen years. For the entire time, Ludwig Erhard was his economics minister, responsible for building the social market economy. The result was to be the *Wirtschaftswunder*—the German economic miracle.

To be sure, the social market economy looked in many ways like a mixed economy. In 1969, for instance, the federal government owned one fourth or more of the shares of some 650 companies. Public ownership at the federal *Länder* (state) and the local levels was relatively broad in its scope, including transportation systems, telephone, telegraph, postal communications, radio and television networks, and utilities. Partial public ownership extended to coal, iron, steel, shipbuilding, and other manufacturing activities. But there were crucial differences between the German formulation of industrial policy and the French and British models. In France and England, the state took control of the commanding heights so that it could provide prosperity for all. In Germany, the state created—and to a limited extent took control of—a network of organizations around the commanding heights so that the market could work more effectively. The economy operated under the tripartite management of government, business, and labor. The unique nature of this corporatist system was embodied in the supervisory boards, *Betriebsräte,* which consisted of numbers of representatives from all three sectors. This uniquely German formulation, under the aegis of Adenauer and Erhard, propelled Germany from its economic nadir in 1947 to the center of the European economic order in under a decade and firmly established it as the locomotive of European economic growth.[14]

Italy: The National Champion

Postwar Italy did not develop a mixed economy; it inherited one from the Fascist government of Benito Mussolini. In 1933, in the midst of the global slump, the Fascists created IRI—Istituto per la Ricostruzione Industriale—to keep bankrupt companies afloat by extending credit and, in the process, acquiring them. In due course, IRI came to control not only the three largest banks but a significant part of the country's industrial base. "By 1936, the initial phase of the most 'unplanned' nationalization of industry in the Western world" was completed. Thereafter, the Fascists did find a plan—to put IRI to work in an industrial policy meant to strengthen Italy's war-making capabilities. After the war, successively weak governments were unable to assert their authority over IRI, and its various managers ran the component companies to their own liking. IRI was less a tool to capture the future than the continuation of a cozy past. Without centralized control, industrial policy amounted to an amalgamation of the particular strategies of the various parts of IRI.

The decisive break with this IRI past, however, came with a new state-owned enterprise, the oil company ENI—Ente Nazionale Idrocarburi. It was fashioned in the immediate postwar years out of AGIP, a state-owned refining company created as a national champion in the 1920s. That ENI achieved its place as a driver of the Italian economy was the work of one man, Enrico Mattei, the unruly son of a policeman from northern Italy. Mattei, who had dropped out of school at age fourteen, ended up running a chemical company and then emerged as a partisan leader during the war. His managerial and political skills won him the top position at AGIP after the war, and he set about creating a giant new company, dominant in Italy and competitive with the existing large oil companies—what he called the "seven sisters." By the 1950s, ENI was a sprawling conglomerate of some thirty-six companies; their businesses ranged from crude oil and gasoline stations to hotels, toll highways, and soaps.

The president or managing director of every one of the subsidiaries was one and the same man, Enrico Mattei. "For the first time in the economic history of Italy," the American embassy reported in 1954, a government-owned entity in Italy "has found itself in the unique position of being financially solvent, capably led, and responsible to no one other than its leader"—a man, the report added, of "limitless ambition." Mattei was also a man of great magnetism. "Anybody who worked with him would go into the fire for him," one of his aides would later recall, "although you couldn't really explain why."

What could be explained was how potent a symbol the state-owned ENI became. Indeed, it embodied what was so powerful about the postwar state-owned national champion. Enrico Mattei expressed the vision for post-war Italy: antifascism, the resurrection and rebuilding of the nation, and the emergence of the "new man," who had made it himself, without the old-boy network of the IRI crowd or the Fascist past. The company facilitated reconstruction; it promised to deliver natural resources to a resource-poor country. It appealed to national pride. Mattei knew how to capture the imagination of the public. Only a few years after the war, ENI was already building new gasoline stations along Italy's roads and autostradas that were larger, more attractive, and more commodious than those of its international competitors. They even had restaurants.

No private concern in Italy could have done what ENI did, and ENI could not have become what it did, had it not been for the disorganization that characterized the Italian state's precarious hold on the economy's commanding heights. ENI had access to the resources of the state, and it used them to build up what became the eighth-largest oil company in the world. It also generated the human capital and the opportunity for generations of technically trained and commercially adept Italians to become world-class oilmen. ENI not only fueled Italy's economic miracle, it became a major engine of that growth. In symbolic terms, it put fascism into the past and helped shape Italy's postwar future. ENI became a model for what state-owned companies could achieve—and for the very rationale for state ownership. That rationale could be summed up in two words—*growth* and *progress*.[15]

"The Encroachment" of John Maynard Keynes

As the period of reconstruction came to an end and the first signs of prosperity began to appear, management of the mixed economy came to rest on the intellectual foundations of a compelling new economics. It was derived not from socialism but from the work of a reformer of capitalism, John Maynard Keynes, the most influential economist of the twentieth century. Keynes was a product of the late Victorian and Edwardian eras, a period when stability, prosperity, and peace were assumed and when Britain ruled the world economy. Keynes never lost the self-confidence, self-assurance, and indeed the optimism of that time. But his intellectual career, and his profound impact, arose from his efforts to make sense of the disruptions and crises that began with the First World War and continued through the Great Depression.

Descended from a knight who had crossed the English Channel with William the Conqueror, Keynes was the son of a Cambridge University economist. Educated at Eton and Cambridge, he demonstrated from his early years a dazzling, wide-ranging intellect, along with an arrogance and what seemed to some a dismissive elitism. His establishment habits (including the signature homburg normally associated with a City of London stockbroker) and his pride in being a member of what he called the *"educated* bourgeoisie" were combined with chronic social and intellectual rebellion, orneriness, and the lifestyle of a Bloomsbury bohemian and aesthete. His daunting mathematical dexterity was complemented by a considerable literary grace, whether the subject was the subtleties of economic thought or his obsession with the hands of statesmen. He celebrated "vigilant observation" of the real world as one of the requirements of a good economist, and he loved to pore through statistics. His best ideas, he liked to say, came "from messing about with figures and *seeing* what they must mean." Nevertheless, he could not resist endlessly toying with ideas, and he compulsively sought to spin out all-encompassing theories and generalizations from particulars.

As an economic adviser to the British delegation at the Versailles conference in 1919, he became convinced that the Carthaginian peace that the Allies were imposing on Germany would undermine European economic recovery and guarantee new crises. Disgusted, he resigned and retired to the English countryside, where, in a matter of weeks, he brought together his searing criticisms in *The Economic Consequences of the Peace.* That book made him famous. In the 1920s, he focused mostly on monetary issues. He lambasted the decision by Winston Churchill, at the time chancellor of the exchequer, to return Britain to the gold standard with an overvalued pound in a work entitled *The Economic Consequences of Mr. Churchill.*

During those years and into the 1930s, he split his week between King's College in Cambridge, where he did his teaching, and London, where he busied himself speculating in currencies, commodities, and stocks. He was also on the board of a number of investment and insurance companies, and in fact served as the chairman of one. He was a master of markets and their psychology. As bursar of King's College—during the Great Depression— he increased the college's endowment tenfold. He also made himself very wealthy managing his own portfolio, despite periodic reverses. He did not hesitate to take risks. "The academic economist," said a close friend of Keynes, "never really knows what makes a businessman tick, why he wants sometimes to gamble on an investment project and why he sometimes prefers liquidity and cash. Maynard understood because he was a gambler himself and felt the gambling or liquidity instincts of the businessman." As Keynes himself once explained, "Business life is always a bet." [16]

Persistent unemployment in Britain, and then the mass unemployment of the Great Depression, redirected Keynes' intellectual agenda from monetary affairs to unemployment and led to his most influential work, *The General Theory of Employment, Interest and Money,* published in 1936. Here was Keynes as vigilant observer, keen mathematician, self-confident rebel, and grand generalizer. The book constituted a vast assault on the classical economics tradition in which he had been raised. The era that had nurtured classical economics had been destroyed by the First World War, and for Keynes the cataclysms since had demonstrated the tradition's inadequacies. A new synthesis was necessary, and that is what Keynes, working with his "kindergarten" of disciples in Cambridge, sought to create.

In particular, he concluded that classical economics rested on a fundamental error. It assumed, mistakenly, that the balance between supply and demand would ensure full employment. On the contrary, in Keynes' view, the economy was chronically unstable and subject to fluctuations, and supply and demand could well balance out at an equilibrium that did not deliver full employment. The reasons were inadequate investment and oversaving, both rooted in the psychology of uncertainty.

The solution to this conundrum was seemingly simple: Replace the missing private investment with public investment, financed by deliberate deficits. The government would borrow money to spend on such things as public works; and that deficit spending, in turn, would create jobs and increase purchasing power. Striving to balance the government's budget during a slump would make things worse, not better. In order to make his argument, Keynes deployed a range of new tools—standardized national income accounting (which led to the basic concept of gross national product), the concept of aggregate demand, and the multiplier (people receiving government money for public-works jobs will spend money, which will create new jobs). Keynes' analysis laid the basis for the field of macroeconomics, which treats the economy as a whole and focuses on government's use of fiscal policy—spending, deficits, and tax. These tools could be used to manage aggregate demand and thus ensure full employment. As a corollary, the government would cut back its spending during times of recovery and expansion. This last precept, however, was all too often forgotten or overlooked.

Keynes intended government to play a much larger role in the economy. His vision was one of reformed capitalism, managed capitalism—capitalism saved both from socialism and from itself. He talked about a "somewhat comprehensive socialization of investment" and the state's taking "an ever greater responsibility for directly organizing investment." Fiscal policy would enable wise managers to stabilize the economy without resorting to actual controls. The bulk of decision making would remain with the decentralized market rather than with the central planner.

Keynes had worked on *The General Theory* with feverish intensity, convinced that new apocalypses were waiting close in the wings even as the world struggled with the Depression. The alternative to reform was totalitarianism. And it was not only the new vistas of macroeconomics but also the dangers of the time that helped explain the fervor with which others embraced the argument. As one of his students explained, "Finally what Keynes supplied was *hope:* hope that prosperity could be restored and maintained without the support of prison camps, executions, and bestial interrogations."

A new apocalypse came soon enough. With the outbreak of World War II, Keynes moved on to the questions of how to finance the war and then how to develop a postwar currency system. He was one of the fathers of the Bretton Woods accord, which established the World Bank and the International Monetary Fund, and which put in place a system of fixed exchange rates. He also returned to a subject that had obsessed him since the First World War—how to cope with, and limit, Britain's submission to America's financial might. After all, he had come to maturity in an age when Britain ruled the international economy. Now, however distastefully, he struggled to adjust Britain to the new reality of American ascendancy. His last major enterprise was to negotiate a multibillion-dollar U.S. loan for Britain in 1946. It was a very nasty business. The stress literally killed him.

Keynes provided both a specific rationale for government's taking a bigger role in the economy and a more general confidence in the ability of government to intervene and manage effectively. As Keynes' work turned into "Keynesianism" in the post–World War II years, the self-confidence that had animated its author continued to be at its root. Despite Keynes' fascination with uncertainty and his speculative talents in the marketplace, Keynesians deemed "government knowledge" to be superior to that of the marketplace. In the words of Keynes' biographer Robert Skidelsky, the unstated message in its most extreme form was this: "The state is wise and the market is stupid."

In one of the most famous passages of *The General Theory*, Keynes had written, "The power of vested interests is vastly exaggerated compared with the gradual encroachment of ideas." There was nothing gradual, however, in the encroachment of Keynesianism or in its conquest of the commanding heights of economic thinking. Within a few years of his death, it was already taking a dominant place in economic policy making both in Britain and in the United States. How far-reaching its impact, or at least the perception of its impact, was demonstrated by a history of economic thought published in the mid-1960s: "In most Western economies Keynesian theory has laid the intellectual foundations for a managed and welfare-oriented form of capitalism. Indeed, the widespread absorption of the Keynesian message has in large measure been responsible for the generally high levels of employment achieved by most Western industrial countries since the Second World War and for a significant reorientation in attitudes toward the role of the state in economic life." Keynes' self-confidence lived on in his thought.[17]

Trade and National Power

The common acceptance of Keynesianism and the other principles of the mixed economy helped draw the European countries together, despite their many differences, in the three decades after the war. The commonality saw its ultimate expression in what today is known as the European Union.

Jean Monnet first seized upon the potential for securing Europe's future through interdependence. During World War II, he was already envisioning a modern Lotharingia—as the middle of three kingdoms created by Charlemagne's grandsons had been called a thousand years earlier. But Monnet's vision was not a historical dream. It was the response to very practical problems—what to do about Germany and how to prevent another European war. The overarching answer: Integrate a revived, productive Germany into a united Europe. Lotharingia would be the first step. The coal and steel–producing regions at the borders of France and Germany—in Alsace-Lorraine and in the Ruhr—that had been the source of so much conflict would be internationally administered under what was called the Schuman Plan. It was so named for the French foreign minister Robert Schuman, but in fact it was largely the work of Jean Monnet. In the phrase of the time, it "launched" Europe. But the launch was much bolstered by the Marshall Plan, which had insisted that the Europeans draw up a common plan for disbursement of American aid. The Marshall Plan also provided a "code of liberalization" to reduce trade barriers among the European countries in order to facilitate the most efficient use of aid.

The next step came in 1957. Spurred by Monnet's vision and shocked by the dramatic events of autumn 1956—the Suez Crisis, which split the Western alliance, and the Soviet suppression of the Hungarian revolution—the nations of Europe "relaunched Europe" by signing the Treaty of Rome. It established the Common Market, otherwise known as the European Economic Community—an unprecedented joining of diverse economies, built upon three bonds—the mixed-economy consensus, the drive to solve the German question, and the threat from the Soviet Bloc.

Thus, even as the governments of the Western European nations were assuming more responsibility for their national economies, they were also—with the launching of European integration—taking the first steps toward ceding national control by reducing obstacles to trade and investment. In so doing, Europe was part of a larger process of lowering trade barriers and expanding international trade that would serve as the counterpoint to national power.

During World War II, American and British officials had taken the lead in negotiating a comprehensive and unprecedented new system to facilitate and promote international trade. They knew exactly what they wanted to escape from—the fractured interwar trading system, with its quantitative barriers, high tariffs, preferential agreements, blockages, managed trade, and "beggar thy neighbor" policies. Such ferocious protectionism, they were convinced, had contributed mightily to the global slump and the political problems that came with it, and to the ensuing war. Their dream was to recover the open trading system of the late nineteenth century, which had stimulated global growth. They had a foundation on which to build—the reciprocal trade agreements that U.S. secretary of state Cordell Hull, a very traditional nineteenth-century liberal, had championed in the 1930s. But the new system they negotiated during the war, in contrast to Hull's, was to be based upon multilateralism, meaning that many countries would simultaneously accede to reductions in trade barriers. This new system was to be embodied in the International Trade Organization (ITO), which was meant to provide both the framework for multilateral trade negotiations and the mechanisms to design and implement the required rules. It was meant to be the third leg of the postwar international economic tripod, along with the World Bank and the International Monetary Fund.

In 1947, at a conference in Havana, fifty-seven countries concluded negotiations on a treaty establishing the ITO. As it turned out, however, there was little popular or congressional support for the ITO, and much opposition. In 1950, several months after the outbreak of the Korean War, the State Department issued a press release dryly announcing that the plan for the ITO was now in abeyance. Protectionists in Congress thought they had won. "The State Department have written the obituary but I was in charge of the funeral," one senator jubilantly declared. But the protectionists were wrong. President Truman had the executive authority to implement the provisions of a stopgap measure that was part of the ITO negotiations—the General Agreement on Tariffs and Trade (GATT). Administered through periodic meetings, this agreement was the mechanism for negotiating multilateral reductions in trade barriers and for working out rules for world trade.

The GATT did not have the formality or the powers of the ITO. Yet, put into effect in 1948, it became the framework through which the barriers to international trade—whether in goods, services, or finance—were progressively lowered over the next half century. The GATT would become one of the most important propellants of postwar economic growth and would help create a global economy that transcended the borders of individual countries, opening the commanding heights to international competition and eroding the power of the nation-state.[18]

"You Never Had It So Good"

All that, however, was still many years off. At the time, there were more immediate sources of economic recovery. The Korean War, 1950–53, and the military buildup that went with it, provided a major stimulus to growth throughout the industrial world; and thereafter, defense spending continued to be a major driver of growth. There was also continuing anxiety in the West about what were thought to be the economic achievements and high growth rates of the Soviet Union, and as to whether East or West would win the economic race—and who would capture the economic allegiance of what Churchill had dubbed the third world. The Soviet launching of the first

44

satellite, *Sputnik,* in 1957, was not only a dramatic jolt; it also seemed to confirm the vigor of the Soviet-style command economy.

Yet the economic record of the Western European countries in the postwar years was extraordinary. The mixed economy delivered a standard of living and a way of life that could not have been anticipated, or even imagined, at the end of World War II. The 1950s and 1960s became known as the golden age of the welfare state in Britain. "Most of our people have never had it so good," Prime Minister Harold Macmillan replied to a heckler at a political rally on a soccer field in 1957. And "You never had it so good" became his very accurate campaign slogan.

It was true right across Western Europe. For the first time, workers could begin to buy the products of their own labor. In France, the strikes and the threat of a communist takeover receded into memory. This period in France became known as *Les Trente Glorieuses*—"the thirty glorious years." Germany, powered by its social market economy, became the country of the "economic miracle"—*Wirtschaftswunder*—as the country moved toward Ludwig Erhard's goal of "prosperity for all." Both were growing at 5 or 6 percent a year, or even more. By 1955, all the Western European countries had exceeded their prewar levels of production. The scourge of unemployment, which discredited the prewar order throughout the industrial world and which had been the number-one stimulus to action, was banished. In France, average unemployment between 1945 and 1969 was 1.3 percent. In Germany, unemployment dropped to the virtually invisible 0.5 percent in 1970.

This record of success in the industrial countries of Europe vindicated the idea that government must take an active role in overseeing or directing the economy—and in many cases own part of it—in order to provide prosperity for all. On the strength of this unprecedented economic expansion, the mixed economy established itself as the new incumbent system and one whose reach would grow in the ensuing years. The state was either in control of the commanding heights or managing the levers of fiscal policy. Government had created and assumed the responsibilities of the welfare state, and it was dedicated to correcting the "failures" of the market. All this added up to a formula for economic success that consigned the deplorable interwar years and the destruction of World War II to the past. By any comparison, these were, indeed, in economic terms, the glorious years.[19]

CHAPTER 2

THE CURSE OF BIGNESS
America's Regulatory Capitalism

THE EX-TYCOON EXPIRED on a subway platform in Paris in 1938. Hardly any money was found on his person, and newspaper headlines back in the United States said that he had died a pauper. Although disgraced, he was in fact not poor, and his wallet had probably been pinched before the authorities appeared. But it was a better story to say that he had died in poverty. For more than any other American, Samuel Insull and his accession to prominence as a businessman and then his precipitous fall from grace provided the perfect morality tale for the giddiness of the stock market in the 1920s and its collapse in the 1930s. How better to demonstrate the bankruptcy of capitalism than with this fallen figure of Samuel Insull, the equivalent of eight cents in centimes in his pocket. The times, with their sorrow and pain, called out for such morality tales.

What a change from the boom years of the 1920s, when Insull embodied spunk and ambition and ability. Born in 1859, he had gone to work as a boy in London as a telephone switchboard operator and later as a shorthand secretary to the head of Thomas Edison's British operations. In due course, he became Edison's personal secretary, and from that point worked his way up in Edison's organization. When it was broken up, he became head of Chicago Edison and built it into a huge electric power company. He was the king, presiding over a far-flung enterprise that delivered electricity to a substantial part of the United States. Insull was known for his seriousness and his temper (Insult Insull, he was called), but most of all for his drive to create a great empire. He held out a grand vision of the future of electric power: "Every home, every factory, and every transportation line will obtain its energy from one common source, for the simple reason that that will be the cheapest way to produce and distribute it." The mechanism for implementing this vision was to be the kind of enterprise he had constructed—an endlessly complex and bewildering corporate pyramid. Insull's operating companies ran the power plants, dispatched the electricity, and read the meters. His holding companies, whose main assets were stock in other companies, were where the financial engineering was implemented, leaving plenty of room for financial manipulation. Who could make sense of it all? At one point, Insull held sixty-five chairmanships, eighty-five directorships, and eleven presidencies. For a time, "Insullism" was held up as the model for the future. But with the stock market crash and the Great Depression, Insull's empire collapsed, and the stock in his paramount holding company, Insull Utility Investments, plunged from over a hundred dollars a share in 1929 to little more than a dollar in 1932. In its aftermath, people said that Insull himself had never understood his own empire. He could not fail to observe, however, the fury of his investors; and in consequence, he prudently protected himself around the clock with thirty-six personal bodyguards.

As if the rage of his ruined shareholders were not enough, his troubles were compounded by a Cook County indictment for larceny and embezzlement; and Insull hurriedly decamped to Europe. With President-elect Roosevelt promising " 'to get' the Insulls," the U.S. government wanted him back. He moved through France; and Roosevelt asked dictator Benito Mussolini to help in case he turned up in Italy. By then, however, Insull was already in Greece. "Why am I not more popular in the United States?" he asked uncomprehendingly from his exile. "What have I done that every banker and business magnate has not done in the course of business?" The only response from the Greek government was his expulsion from the country, at the request of the United States. With nowhere else to go, Insull became a man without a country, sailing aimlessly around the Mediterranean in a chartered tramp freighter. When the ship docked in Turkey for provisions, he was arrested; and, although lacking an extradition treaty, the Turkish government packed him on a boat back to the United States. He was tried on fraud charges in Cook County. Yet despite the intensity of hatred against him, he won acquittal with surprising ease in 1934. The jury needed just five minutes to reach its verdict. But Insull had had enough of America, and he spent the last four years of his life outside the United States. Once worth hundreds of millions, he had lost much of his wealth; even the ownership of his shirt studs became the subject of a lawsuit. He habitually took the Paris subway in order to save money, although his wife had warned him, presciently as it turned out, that it might be bad for his heart.[1]

Well before his death, Insull had become the nation's symbol for the excesses of capitalism, for the chicanery and greed that had preceded the Great Depression, and, indeed, for all that could go wrong with unfettered markets. His name was invoked by President Roosevelt and the other New Dealers only to excoriate him. So much of the distress was attributed to the machinations of Insull and the other tycoons that Insullism was no longer held up as an expansive vision of the future but rather as one of the major causes of the Depression. In order to clean up the wreckage—and prevent future Insulls from creating future disasters—the New Deal embarked on a far-reaching program of experimentation and expansion of government authority over the economy. State ownership was not out of the question; the Tennessee Valley Authority was a great experiment in public ownership and development economics that electrified the dirt-poor region of the middle South. But for the most part, government would seek to control the key parts of the economy not through ownership but through a distinctly American approach—economic regulation. This thrust contrasted with that in Europe and the developing world. By comparison, the United States was more market-oriented. But government would still hold considerable sway over the market. Indeed, in the American context of the 1930s, the "regulatory idea" became the solution to the problems of the marketplace. This idea would maintain its grip for decades, until new economic disruptions and a growing intellectual critique undermined the consensus.

The Rise of Regulation

Regulation—rule making—has many purposes, of course. They range from health and safety and environmental protection to working conditions, equality, equity, and social policy. National regulation specifically for economic purposes originated in the nineteenth century, beginning during America's development era—with the establishment of the Interstate Commerce Commission (ICC) to regulate railroads, the great new industry of the era. Until then, the national government had been remarkably limited in its activities, as could be measured by the number of its civilian employees. In the early 1870s, the federal government employed a grand total of 51,020 civilians, of whom 36,696 were postal workers. The ICC marked the first major attempt by the government to oversee the national economy. Railways had become not only a critical industry but also a national force, erasing the boundaries of states as they tied the nation together. The ICC was created in order to ensure "just and reasonable" rates and equitable treatment of shippers and communities—and to limit manipulation by the robber barons. With five commissioners appointed to staggered six-year terms, it also became the model for future regulatory commissions. In its early years, its mandate was dramatically whittled back by the courts, only to be expanded again with the rise of progressivism after the turn of the century.

By the late nineteenth century, America was well on its way to being an industrial nation. Its cities were becoming home to millions and millions of new immigrants, along with sprawling factories that spewed dark smoke out of their chimneys. The advent of industrialization and the transformation of living space brought a host of ills, which in turn became the target of a group of investigative journalists known as muckrakers. The term, borrowed from Bunyan's *Pilgrim's Progress,* was first used by President Theodore

Roosevelt, a writer of considerable accomplishment himself. Roosevelt did not mean the phrase as a compliment; he thought the writing of these journalists too negative, their work too focused on "the vile and debasing," and their impact too much a fan for the flames of revolution. Nevertheless, the muckrakers' exposés of the ailments of the new industrial society—dirty food, dirty working conditions, dirty cities, dirty business, dirty money, and dirty politics—set the agenda for turn-of-the-century America, and Roosevelt and other politicians embraced the cause. Regulation was the response to the catalog of abuses.

Much economic regulation focused on one problem—what to do about bigness and monopolies. Combinations to control prices and outputs were, of course, a perennial problem—indeed, one that had much exercised Adam Smith. "People of the same trade seldom meet together," he wrote in one of his most famous passages in *The Wealth of Nations,* published in 1776, "even for merriment and diversion, but the conversation ends in a conspiracy against the public or in some contrivance to raise prices." But those words were written at the very beginning of the Industrial Revolution. Smith could hardly have imagined the scale in America a century later resulting from technology, mergers, takeovers, economic concentration, and the emergence of huge (by the standards of the times) combines. In shorthand, they were known as trusts, often out-and-out monopolies that seemed determined to extinguish the atomistic world of small, family-owned enterprises. Trusts, said the editor of America's leading muckraking magazine in 1899, constituted "the red hot event." They were indeed the dominating national issue of the time.

Something had to be done. But what? Although he earned the sobriquet "trust buster," President Roosevelt was not against bigness per se. Combinations, he said, could be turned back no more easily than the spring floods on the Mississippi. But, he continued, "we can regulate and control them by levees"—that is, by regulation and public scrutiny. He distinguished between "good trusts" and "bad trusts." Only the latter should be destroyed.[2]

The People's Lawyer

Others saw size itself as the enemy and were determined to demolish the trusts. The foremost proponent of that position was "the people's lawyer of the Progressive Era," Louis Brandeis, whose eyes were fixed on one evil—what he called "the curse of bigness." Brandeis was a man of outstanding intellect. Entering Harvard Law School at age eighteen, he quickly amassed a phenomenal record, one of the best in the entire history of the school. He "is supposed to know everything and to have it always in mind," one of his fellow students wrote of him. "The Profs. listen to his opinions with the greatest deference, and it is generally correct. There are traditions of his omniscience floating through the School." Brandeis's subsequent career bore out his promise. He went on to become a formidable advocate, and on nothing was he was so powerful as in his advocacy of the destruction of bigness. He was a masterful attacker in the courtroom and no less masterly as a muckraker. The title of his most famous work—*Other People's Money and How the Bankers Use It*—told all. He was also a trenchant critic of Theodore Roosevelt. The president, he said dismissively, was in favor of "regulated monopoly," while he, in contrast, advocated "regulated competition." As for the public, he feared they "still admire the Captains of the trusts."

The issue of bigness and the trusts was thrashed out in both the political process and the courts. Although differentiating between "good" and "bad" trusts, the Roosevelt administration launched no fewer than forty-five anti-trust suits, many of them long-running. None was more prominent than the prosecution that culminated in the Supreme Court's decision in 1911 to break up John D. Rockefeller's Standard Oil trust.

For his part Louis Brandeis became the chief economic adviser to Woodrow Wilson, who was elected president in 1912. Brandeis thereafter played a major role in designing both the new Federal Reserve System and the new regulatory agency, the Federal Trade Commission, which was intended to police bigness, restrict restraint of trade, and prevent "unfair" trade practices. Yet even Wilson did not fully satisfy the people's lawyer. "In my opinion," Brandeis explained, "the real curse was bigness rather than monopoly. Mr. Wilson (and others politically wise) made the attack on lines of monopoly—because Americans hated monopoly and loved bigness." In 1916, Wilson nominated Brandeis for the Supreme Court, and despite a fierce anti-Semitic campaign, he was confirmed. He served on the court for twenty-three years. He was an outstanding justice and, as it turned out, most committed to judicial restraint.[3]

Normalcy, "Not Nostrums"

And there regulation more or less stood for a number of years. Business seemed, in the worshipful fever of the 1920s, incapable of doing wrong, save for the occasional scandal such as that involving the naval oil reserve at Teapot Dome. Those captains of capitalism who had so exercised Brandeis were now heroes, and the less government did, the better. President Warren Harding opened the decade of the 1920s with a reassuring call for a return to "not heroism, but healing, not nostrums but normalcy." A Republican attorney general denounced the Federal Trade Commission as nothing more than "a publicity bureau to spread socialist propaganda." "Association" and "cooperation" among businesses were encouraged; it was part of rationalization, one of the high values of the day. Even the critics got on board. Lincoln Steffens, among the most famous of muckrakers, declared that "big business in America is producing what the Socialists held up as their goal:

50

food, shelter, clothing for all." * Everything seemed to be working so well. "No Congress of the United States ever assembled," said President Calvin Coolidge in December 1928, "on surveying the state of the Union, has met with a more pleasing prospect than that which appears at the present time."

That prospect did not last long. Ten months later, on Black Thursday, October 24, 1929, the stock market crashed. Thereafter, the entire edifice of debt and credit both in the United States and around the world—banks, stock margin accounts, postwar reparations, loans to commodity-producing countries—came tumbling down. The nascent democracies in Germany and Japan succumbed to dictatorship. With unemployment at almost 25 percent in the United States and the GNP falling by half, it was not all that certain that democratic capitalism in the United States would survive.[4]

The New Deal: "I Never Felt Surer of Anything"

Franklin Roosevelt came to office in March 1933 with a mandate to do something, and to do it fast. Inauguration Day, his wife, Eleanor, observed, was "very, very solemn and a little terrifying." Roosevelt told the frightened country that the only thing it had to fear was fear itself; he immediately set about restoring confidence through words and spirit—and a great fury of vigorous economic improvisation. One line of effort was emergency response—a bank holiday, relief, welfare, and food programs. Another was "cooperation" and national planning. In his second Fireside Chat, in May 1933, Roosevelt called for "a partnership in planning between government and business, with government having the right to prevent, with the assistance of the overwhelming majority of that industry, unfair practices and to enforce this agreement by the authority of government."

While the president was working on the speech, one of his assistants, Raymond Moley, warned him, "You realize, then, that you're taking an enormous step away from the philosophy of equalitarianism and laissez-faire?"

The president was silent for a moment, and then replied with great earnestness, "If that philosophy hadn't proved to be bankrupt, Herbert Hoover would be sitting here right now. I never felt surer of anything in my life than I do of the soundness of this passage."

That thinking was embodied nowhere more clearly than in the National Recovery Administration. The NRA was premised on the belief that the

---

* A few years earlier, in 1919, Steffens had encapsulated the utopian embrace by some Western intellectuals of the new Soviet Union with the immortal phrase "I have seen the future and it works." Actually, Steffens had been playing with the phrase on the train to the Soviet Union before he even laid eyes on the country, trying out variations such as "I have been over into the future and it works."

essential problems were overproduction and too much supply—of virtually everything. In response, the NRA sought to get labor, business, and government to cooperate in a grand partnership—a corporatist combine to reduce output, set prices, and thus push up incomes. Such coordination was essential, it was thought, because America had reached a phase of "economic maturity." The Depression had proved that America could no longer depend on an ever-expanding economy for its well-being. It seemed the country was ready to accept the NRA and its unprecedented intervention—and, in the process, to put aside traditional antitrust considerations. And indeed, the NRA began with an initial burst of enthusiasm, emblazoning its blue-eagle emblem in windows across the nation and filling New York's Fifth Avenue with ticker tape and throngs of well-wishers in a promotional parade in September 1933. But it did not work. America was not so eager to toss aside its deeply rooted suspicion of concentration and cartels, or to put its confidence in the forthrightness of businessmen and government officials to harness these dangerous forces for the public good. In attempting to establish such a system, the NRA violated the tenets of traditional progressivism. The American conscience would not brook such a transgression. In trying to perform his impossible task, the NRA's director, General Hugh Johnson, was reduced from a reformist hellcat to a sobbing alcoholic, and within two years the NRA and its mandate were tossed out by the courts.

Instead, the New Deal pursued another approach—regulation instead of ownership or nationalization, antitrust rather than concentration and rationalization, decentralized control instead of planning. In so doing, the New Deal put in place a system to regulate markets and ensure that they worked better—and, by-the-by, to save capitalism from itself. Despite the wide variety in the purposes of the various regulatory agencies, there were two unifying themes—the failure of markets and the problem of monopoly.

The Securities and Exchange Commission (SEC) was a highly visible and critically important part of this effort. It was meant to make the battered financial markets work better, and to restore confidence in them through increased disclosure requirements and the establishment of a level playing field that did not give insiders an unfair advantage. How better to do it than by putting a financier, Joseph P. Kennedy (father of a future president), in charge? When opponents of Kennedy's nomination pointed out that he had in fact been a master speculator, Roosevelt replied that it was all to the good, because Kennedy knew the tricks of the trade.

The SEC got a great boost when it turned out that Richard Whitney, the distinguished president of the New York Stock Exchange and a leading opponent of the SEC, had himself embezzled $30 million—a truly dizzying number in the 1930s—to cover bad debts. Like Roosevelt, Whitney had attended Groton and Harvard; and when Roosevelt was told of this particular villainy, he was heard to gasp, "Not Dick Whitney!" But, yes, even Dick Whitney. In order to enjoin such behavior in the future, the SEC created a whole series of reporting requirements that were intended to help investors understand in what they were investing. Disclosure and a level playing field were the basic principles. Not only buyers, said Roosevelt, but also sellers should beware. Among other things, they should beware to tell the truth. Echoing Brandeis's book *Other People's Money*, Roosevelt laid out the principle that those "handling or using other people's money are trustees acting for others."[5]

"The Prophet of Regulation"

The guiding hand in the creation of the SEC was James Landis, raised in Tokyo by his American missionary parents and, like Brandeis, a brilliant lawyer. He was tenured at Harvard Law School before age thirty and was its dean before age forty. In between, he joined the New Deal, where he was among the brightest of its young stars. He also became, in the historian Thomas McCraw's phrase, one of the "prophets of regulation"—along with Louis Brandeis, for whom he worked as a Supreme Court clerk. Indeed, Landis looked to be Brandeis's likely heir at the intersection of intellectual work and policy, defining the relationship between state and marketplace for the next generation. He seemed destined for the same sort of grand national career that Brandeis had achieved.

An urgent summons from his mentor Felix Frankfurter, Harvard professor and Roosevelt confidant, took Landis down to Washington on a Friday train in April 1933. Landis expected to stay the weekend, help out, and then head back to Cambridge by Monday. As it turned out, he stayed four years. He was the quintessential New Dealer, working day after day until midnight, often sleeping for a few hours on a cot in his office, drafting legislation almost around the clock through the economic emergency, and rushing back and forth to the White House to confer directly with the president. "You can't drive your mind as though it were a brewery horse," Frankfurter warned him. But he did not give up the pace. Details of daily living eluded him, a sloppiness that would come back to haunt him. His personal life took second place to the national emergency. His wife, invited to bring her husband to a party, responded, "What husband?"

Landis served first as a federal trade commissioner and then as a commissioner on the new Securities and Exchange Commission, which he had done much to create. And in so doing he set out to give all the interested parties a stake in the new system. Among his shrewdest decisions in creating the SEC was to enroll the business community as a partner in the process. For instance, one of the requirements instituted for public companies was the disinterested audit. By instituting this requirement, Landis did much to establish the profession of the independent accountant.

Another of Landis's monuments was the Public Utility Holding Company Act of 1935, which created the structure for the electric power industry in the United States that lasted until the middle 1990s. Electric power was among the issues that most viscerally engaged President Roosevelt personally. Viewing electricity as a great tool for economic development and conservation, he promoted, against enormous opposition, both rural electrification and the Tennessee Valley Authority. The latter was unprecedented —a far-reaching public corporation that built dams, generated huge amounts of power, manufactured fertilizers, controlled floods, restored forests, and replenished the soil—all of it in the cause of economic development. Roosevelt was very proud of it.

But there was also the private side of electric power. Roosevelt regarded holding companies, particularly in electric power, as one of the nation's scourges and a principal cause of the financial collapse. He was intent on banishing "the Insulls" forever. These holding companies, with their "concentrated economic power," constituted a form of private socialism, he said, adding, "I am against private socialism as thoroughly as I am against governmental socialism. The one is equally as dangerous as the other; and destruction of private socialism is utterly essential to avoid governmental socialism."

The result was the Public Utility Holding Company Act. The legislation dismantled much of the holding-company structure and severely restricted what remained, in order to prevent holding companies from "exploiting" operating companies. It also gave the SEC power to promote physical integration of electric utilities to achieve greater engineering efficiencies. The act was bitterly opposed by industry, which enlisted in its cause such legal luminaries as John Foster Dulles, Dean Acheson, and John W. Davis, the 1924 Democratic presidential candidate. It took a full decade of legal challenges before the law was finally accepted.

Landis was not only an activist. He was a theorist, and did more than anybody else to set out the doctrine for economic regulation. As a young law professor he had pioneered the study of the legislative process and the implementation of law. In 1938, having left the SEC, he put down his thinking in what became a classic work on regulation, *The Administrative Process*. Markets themselves, he said, had big problems, problems too large and sprawling for traditional government, which was simply too weak, too incoherent, and too lacking in expertise. "In terms of political theory, the administrative process springs from the inadequacy of a simple tripartite form of government to deal with modern problems." Legislation was the beginning, not the end. There was a need for, in effect, a fourth branch of government—the "administrative branch"—embodied in independent regulatory agencies that would be "quasi-legislative, quasi-executive, quasi-judicial" and that would ensure the implementation of the legislation. And he admonished policy makers not to be cowed by the growth of government activity this task would entail. "A consequence of an expanding interest of government in various phases of the industrial scene must be the creation of more administrative agencies if the demand for expertness is to be met. . . . Efficiency in the processes of governmental regulation is best served by the creation of more rather than less agencies. And it is efficiency that is the desperate need." This branch would be staffed not by politicians or amateurs but by experts who devoted themselves to the issues "52 weeks a year, year after year." How much that sounded like the job description for James Landis himself during the hectic New Deal years.[6]

Landis's words were written in the heyday of regulation, as the New Deal entrenched his strategy through unprecedented extension of administrative regulatory powers. In addition to the preexisting Interstate Commerce Commission and the Federal Trade Commission, both of which were strengthened, the New Deal also bolstered the Federal Power Commission with new responsibilities for electricity and natural gas prices. The Roosevelt administration created not only the Securities and Exchange Commission but also the Federal Communications Commission, the Civil Aeronautics Board, and the National Labor Relations Board. The attack on business took on an added fervor in the late 1930s, when liberals blamed business for a steep recession because of what was its alleged failure to invest (the "capital strike"). Roosevelt denounced "economic royalists" for deliberately fostering the recession in order to undermine the New Deal. Thus, as the 1930s came to a close, the Roosevelt administration had finally completed the blueprint of the New Deal strategy, after its early fits and starts. The cozy partner relationship with business envisioned in the early New Deal had given way to James Landis's more prickly and vigilant vision.

Keynes' American Beachhead

But the true test of the regulatory system was stayed by fresh economic exigencies. The recession in the late 1930s distracted the country from its regulatory fervor. And the government's response reflected the emergence of a new economic strategy—Keynesianism. During the early years of the New Deal, Keynes had written a couple of "public letters" to Roosevelt and, indeed, through the good offices of the ever-busy Felix Frankfurter, had called on the president in the White House in 1934. Roosevelt reported back to Frankfurter that he had had a "grand talk with Keynes and liked him immensely," although comments to others suggested that he had been somewhat irritated by Keynes' patronizing manner. For his part, Keynes said that he had found the talk "fascinating and illuminating." He did, however, complain about Roosevelt's hands—"Rather disappointing. Firm and fairly strong, but not clever or with finesse." There is no evidence that Keynes at this point, although much engaged in writing *The General Theory,* did anything to convert the president—or the New Deal—to his thinking. In fact, Roosevelt was suspicious of deficit spending; in the margin of a book that prefigured Keynes' arguments, he had written, "Too good to be true—you can't get something for nothing."

The General Theory was published in 1936, and Keynes' ideas thereupon crossed the Atlantic with remarkable rapidity. The most powerful beachhead proved to be the Harvard economics department, led by Professor Alvin Hansen and supported by a host of other converts and recruits—from full professors right down to undergraduates. They absorbed, refined, and transmitted the Keynesian message in record time. Their propagatory influence in turn was enormous. The intellectual work was centered in Hansen's Fiscal Policy Seminar, which brought the latest academic research and Washington policy makers together on a regular basis. Keynesianism quickly gained adherents in Washington, in large part because it seemed to provide a way to address basic economic questions "without the dangerously statist features of other, more intrusive methods." In the judgment of Nobel laureate Paul Samuelson, a Harvard graduate student in the late 1930s, "The Hansen influence can be said to have transformed the New Deal of Franklin Roosevelt from its first-term populist melange . . . to a mixed economy pursuing coherent and informed macroeconomic policies." Between 1938 and 1940, Keynesian fiscal policies began to be applied in the United States. And with the arrival of Keynesianism—combined with the focus on recession and the growing specter of international conflict—regulatory innovation passed into the background.[7]

Toward Full Employment

World War II did not help the cause of regulatory intervention. The War Industries Board's management of the economy during the First World War had been considered a great success and was much praised. The leader of the effort, Bernard Baruch, was virtually beatified. World War II would be an altogether different story. The scale of both the economy and this war effort dwarfed the previous world war's. Roosevelt and his wartime administration confronted a much more complex challenge than that which had faced Woodrow Wilson and Bernard Baruch. And the government's record reflected that complexity. The difficulties encountered by the two main coordination agencies during World War II, the Office of Price Administration and the War Production Board, undercut plans for increased government intervention in the economy after the war. The Office of Price Administration, observed historian Alan Brinkley, "may have been the most intrusive bureaucracy ever created in America." Its example was "a jarring reversal of the Second New Deal . . . it reminded much of the public that state power could be used not only to assist but to deny." The War Production Board was the target of similar criticism. Thus the management of the wartime economy stood alongside the National Recovery Administration as a warning to America against highly interventionist policies. "In 1945, the war agencies emerged from four years of effort and achievement with nothing even remotely comparable to the standing and authority the war boards of World War I had enjoyed at the end of 1918. If they served as models at all,

56

they were models of the perils of state management of the economy, not of its promise." Even liberals wanted, in the aftermath of the war, "to find a role for government that would allow it to manage the economy without managing the institutions of the economy." [8]

Moreover, after World War II, capitalism was not in the doghouse in America as it was in Europe. Mobilization by industry had worked; the businessmen attacked as the "economic royalists" by Roosevelt in the late 1930s had rallied to the cause and contributed mightily to the war effort in the 1940s. Now they were heroes, patriotic, get-it-done "dollar-a-year men." And after the war, the American economy, instead of slipping back into a new depression as feared, took off on a great boom.

Yet in the aftermath of the war, all of the major Western nations were engaging in experiments with various flavors of the mixed economy. And despite the negative experience of government intervention during the war and the sharply improved status of capitalists and capitalism, America was no exception. The debate over which direction the American economy would take after 1945 manifested itself in the congressional battle over the Full Employment Act. In its early drafts, the bill contained language that would have guaranteed a "useful and remunerative job" as a *right* to "all Americans able to work and seeking work." The support for such statements came, at least in part, from arguments consciously paralleling the birth of the British welfare state. In 1943 the National Resources Planning Board had published a tract entitled *Security, Work, and Relief Policies.* It was dubbed the American Beveridge Plan owing to the similarity of its content and conclusions to Beveridge's phenomenally influential 1942 report, which had launched the welfare state in Britain. There was, indeed, considerable momentum for America to follow the lead of its allies in constructing a mixed economy.

But ultimately, American political traditions and the unique American war experience limited the expansion of direct government control that would be implied in underwriting employment for all citizens. In the end, the Full Employment Act was transformed into merely the Employment Act and was passed in 1946, loaded down with the very conditional and convoluted promise only that government would "use all practicable means consistent with its needs and obligations and other considerations of national policy . . . to foster and promote . . . conditions under which there will be afforded useful employment, for those able, willing, and seeking to work."

Yet even as America deferred to the forces of the market more than its allies, the regulatory framework of the New Deal remained. Throughout the Truman and Eisenhower years, there was little regulatory conflict. America was in the midst of its own thirty glorious years, and increasing prosperity diluted New Deal–type regulatory zeal. Economic expansion was the spirit of the era, and thoughts of dampening the progress of the market seemed far from the public's mind. Harvard economist John Kenneth Galbraith noted at the time that "everything happens as if Saint Peter, when receiving souls in heaven to send the ones to Paradise and the others to Hell, asked them only one question: 'What have you done on earth to increase the gross national product?' "[9]

Regulation and Reform

Thus, the postwar years were a time of a regulatory equilibrium. The activism and zeal promised by James Landis in 1938 were once again stayed by a changing economic focus. But not everyone was quite so sanguine about the state of regulation. As early as 1946, an investigation concluded that new rules—in the form of the Administrative Procedures Act—were needed to ensure equal treatment and due process. But more troubling was the lack of understanding about exactly how the government would oversee the decentralized and growing hydra of the "administrative branch." In 1949 Truman appointed former president Herbert Hoover to examine the issue. The Hoover Commission recommended that the executive branch be reorganized along functional lines, but it had no idea how to deal with the regulatory agencies.

Dwight Eisenhower was similarly baffled. His team entered office in 1952 as "determined, even jaunty reformers, 'modern' Republicans at last in charge of government which for twenty years has been misused by liberals." But Eisenhower slowly came to realize that he did not even have control over the executive branch. The New Deal had irreversibly extended government obligations with its rhetoric and its creation of a new administrative branch through the process of "delegation" of authority. Regulation during the Eisenhower administration was not particularly vivid or distinguished. It was a stable business, rather clubby in nature.

John Kennedy sought to revivify the regulatory idea. He appointed strong chairmen—such as Newton Minow, at the Federal Communications Commission, who captured national headlines by declaring that television had become a "vast wasteland." But real scrutiny of the regulatory system, which had become entrenched, inefficient, and overloaded with cases that it moved through with none of the vigor envisioned by its New Deal framers, would come from the man who had been so instrumental in creating it— James Landis.

Landis had not fared well after the New Deal. Unlike Brandeis, he had not fulfilled his early brilliant promise. After an unhappy tenure, he resigned as dean of the Harvard Law School, served as head of the Civil Aeronautics Board during the Truman administration until Truman fired him, and then went to work in the private sector for his old boss at the SEC, Joseph Kennedy. He did a variety of odd jobs, including helping with the research for John Kennedy's Pulitzer Prize–winning book, *Profiles in Courage.* When Kennedy was elected president in 1960, he asked Landis to prepare a detailed diagnosis of the regulatory apparatus. And with all his old fire renewed, Landis delivered a devastating critique of the system that had developed unsatisfactorily since his optimistic 1938 work. Whereas in the 1930s he had celebrated the idea of regulation as the means to efficiency, he now denounced the practice for its rigidity and incapacity. The report found that "delay had become the hallmark of federal regulation," and cited as two main causes the absence of an overall regulatory policy and the deterioration of the quality of regulatory personnel. He identified the Federal Power Commission as "the outstanding example" of "the breakdown of the administrative process." It would take thirteen years, he said, to clear up the natural-gas-price cases already pending. And the number of cases likely to be filed over those thirteen years would not be cleared up until 2043—even with a tripling of staff.[10]

Kennedy made Landis a special assistant, with the charge to reform regulation and upgrade the quality of the regulators and their output. Despite his initial impact, Landis never really had a chance to get back into the fray. The reason was personal. It turned out that Landis had failed, for inexplicable reasons, to pay his taxes over several years. He resigned, stood trial, spent thirty days in jail plus a year on probation, and was suspended from the practice of law for a year. His brilliant reputation as the leading thinker about the regulatory idea was spent. A few years later, he was found floating in his swimming pool, dead. His house was seized by the government, to pay off his remaining tax penalties.

While regulation still mattered very much to those who were regulated, it continued to remain well in the background of public concern, partly because things were working. But there was a shift of focus from regulation of the market to regulation of the economy through Keynesian fiscal policies. Keynesianism was about managing the overall economy, not the specific workings of the marketplace. These were years of great economic growth, and tens of millions of Americans migrated from cramped urban life to the green grass of suburban housing. The lawn mower in the garage was as much a symbol of prosperity as the automobile. Keynesianism seemed to be fulfilling its promises of growth and full employment. The good economic performance and long expansion of the Kennedy–Johnson years (until disrupted by the Vietnam War) marked the high point of Keynesianism, offering proof that the economy could be fine-tuned through macroeconomic management and the fiscal tools of taxation and spending. The attitude was summed up by John Kennedy when he received an honorary degree from Yale University. He began by saying that he had obtained the best of all worlds—"a Harvard education and a Yale degree." He concluded, "What is at stake is not some grand warfare of rival ideologies which will sweep the country with passion but the practical management of the modern economy."

These years were the apogee in the United States of the belief in government knowledge. It had taken three decades for Keynes' "scribblings" to move from rooms in King's College, Cambridge, into standard-issue government policy. To underline the point, Keynes made the cover of *Time* magazine in 1965—nineteen years after his death. He was only the second deceased person to be so honored (Sigmund Freud was the first).

The Last Liberal Administration

The most massive effort to actually manage the marketplace came in a subsequent administration, which sought to put in place thoroughgoing government control of wages. What was particularly odd was that this initiative was not the handiwork of left-wing liberals but of the administration of Richard Nixon, a moderately conservative Republican who was a critic of government intervention in the economy. As a young man during World War II, prior to joining the navy, Nixon had worked as a junior attorney in the tire-rationing division of the Office of Price Administration, an experience that left him with a lasting distaste for price controls.

What, then, were the forces that led Nixon to try to impose government management on the most basic elements of the market? Certainly, economic matters were hardly his passion. That was reserved for foreign policy. Even foreign economic policy did not much interest him. There was a memorable time during some moment of international monetary perturbation when he rudely suggested exactly what should be done with the lira. As for domestic economics, he liked to give his radio talks on economics at noon on Saturdays, because he was convinced that the only listeners would be farmers riding their tractors, and they were likely, in any event, to be his supporters.

For one thing, whatever the effects of the Vietnam War on the national consensus in the 1960s, confidence had risen in the ability of government to manage the economy and to reach out to solve big social problems through such programs as the War on Poverty. Nixon shared in these beliefs, at least in part. "Now, I am a Keynesian," he declared in January 1971—leaving his aides to draft replies to the angry letters that flowed into the White House from conservative supporters. He introduced a Keynesian "full employment" budget, which provided for deficit spending to reduce unemployment. A Republican congressman from Illinois told Nixon that he would reluctantly support the president's budget, "but I'm going to have to burn up a lot of old speeches denouncing deficit spending." To this Nixon replied, "I'm in the same boat."

While Nixon may have philosophically opposed intervention in the economy, philosophy took a rear seat to politics. He had lost very narrowly to John Kennedy in 1960—49.7 to 49.5 percent of the popular vote. He sometimes blamed the state of Illinois, whose electoral votes had made all the difference and where the Chicago Democratic machine was known for its effectiveness in getting out all possible voters, dead as well as living. Kennedy won Illinois by just 8,858 votes. But Nixon certainly believed that mismanagement of the economy had also cost him the election. "He attributed his defeat in the 1960 election largely to the recession of that year," wrote economist and Nixon adviser Herbert Stein, "and he attributed the recession, or at least its depth and duration, to economic officials, 'financial types,' who put curbing inflation ahead of cutting unemployment." Looking toward his 1972 reelection campaign, Nixon was not going to let that happen again. And he had to pay attention to economics. Despite the optimism about government's ability to manage the economy, economic conditions had begun to deteriorate. The inflation rate, which had been 1.5 percent at the beginning of the 1960s, had risen to 5 percent. Unemployment was also up from the 3.5 percent level of the late 1960s to 5 percent.

So the central economic issue became how to manage the inflation-unemployment trade-offs in a way that was not politically self-destructive; in other words, how to bring down inflation without slowing the economy and raising unemployment. One approach increasingly seemed to provide the answer—an income policy, whereby the government intervened to set and control wages, whether in hortatory words or legal requirements. Such policies had become common in Western European countries. In the 1970s, the Democratic Congress provided the tools by passing legislation that delegated authority to the president to impose a mandatory policy.

The administration remained overtly dedicated to markets. But there were those in it who believed that the "market" was more an idyll of the past than an accurate description of how the current economy functioned. To them, the economy was like the question that Lenin had expressed—*Kto kvo?*—Who could do what to whom? That is, they saw the economy "as organized by relations of power, status, rivalry and emulation." Government intervention was required to bring some greater balance to the struggles for power between strong corporations and strong unions that would drive the wage-price spiral upward.

A critical push toward an income policy came from Arthur Burns, whom Nixon had appointed to be chairman of the Federal Reserve. Burns was a well-known conservative economist; Nixon paid special attention to Burns because he had warned Nixon in 1960 that the Federal Reserve's tight monetary policy would accentuate the economic downturn and thus threaten Nixon's chances in the race against Kennedy—which is exactly what had happened. Now, a decade later, in May 1970, Burns stood up and declared that he had changed his mind about economic policy. The economy was no longer operating as it used to, owing to the now much more powerful position of corporations and labor unions, which together were driving up both wages and prices. The now-traditional fiscal and monetary policies were seen as inadequate. His solution: a wage-price review board, composed of distinguished citizens, who would pass judgment on major wage and price increases. Their power, in Burns's new lexicon, would be limited to persuasion, friendly and otherwise.

Further reinforcement of the pressures toward control came with the recruitment of former Texas Democratic governor John Connally to fill the critical slot of Treasury secretary. The forceful Connally had no philosophical aversion to controls. Indeed, he did not seem to have strong feelings one way or the other on economic policy. "I can play it round or I can play it flat," he would say. "Just tell me how to play it." What Connally did like was the dramatic gesture, the big play; and grabbing inflation by the neck and shaking it out of the system would be such a move.

A second issue was also now at the fore—the dollar. The price of gold had been fixed at thirty-five dollars an ounce since the Roosevelt administration. But the growing U.S. balance-of-payments deficit meant that foreign governments were accumulating large amounts of dollars—in aggregate volume far exceeding the U.S. government's stock of gold. These governments, or their central banks, could show up at any time at the "gold window" of the U.S. Treasury and insist on trading in their dollars for gold, which would precipitate a run. The issue was not theoretical. In the second week of August 1971, the British ambassador turned up at the Treasury Department to request that $3 billion be converted into gold.[11]

With inflation rising, the clamor to do something was mounting in both political circles and the press. At the end of June 1971, Nixon had told his economic advisers, "We will not have a wage price board. We will have jawboning." But resistance to an income policy weakened with each passing month. The climax came on August 13–15, 1971, when Nixon and fifteen advisers repaired to the presidential mountain retreat at Camp David. Out of this conclave came the New Economic Policy, which would temporarily— for a ninety-day period—freeze wages and prices to check inflation. That would, it was thought, solve the inflation-employment dilemma, for such controls would allow the administration to pursue a more expansive fiscal policy—stimulating employment in time for the 1972 presidential election without stoking inflation. The gold window was to be closed. Arthur Burns argued vociferously against it, warning, "*Pravda* would write that this was a sign of the collapse of capitalism." Burns was overruled. The gold window would be closed. But this would accentuate the need to fight inflation; for shutting the gold window would weaken the dollar against other currencies, thus adding to inflation by driving up the price of imported goods. Going off the gold standard and giving up fixed exchange rates constituted a momentous step in the history of international economics.

Most of the participants at the Camp David meeting were exhilarated by all the great decisions they had made. During their discussions, much attention was given to the presentation of the new policy, particularly to television. President Nixon expressed grave concern that if he gave his speech during prime time on Sunday, he would preempt the tremendously popular television series *Bonanza,* thus potentially alienating those addicted to the adventures of the Cartwright family on the Ponderosa ranch. But his advisers convinced him that the speech had to be given before the markets opened on Monday morning, and that meant prime time. A few of the advisers would recollect that more time was spent discussing the timing of the speech than how the economic program would work. Indeed, there was virtually no discussion of what would happen after the initial ninety-day freeze or how the new system would be terminated.

Nixon's chief of staff, H. R. Haldeman, went in to see the president privately at Camp David the evening before his speech. "The P. was down in his study with the lights off and the fire going in the fireplace, even though it was a hot night out," Haldeman wrote in his diary. "He was in one of his sort of mystic moods." Nixon told Haldeman "that this is where he made all his big cogitations. . . . He said what really matters here is the same thing as did with [Franklin] Roosevelt, we need to raise the spirit of the country, that will be the thrust of the rhetoric of the speech. . . . We've got to change the spirit, and then the economy could take off like hell." As he worked on the speech, Nixon tormented himself, worrying whether the headlines would read NIXON ACTS BOLDLY or NIXON CHANGES MIND. "Having talked until recently about the evils of wage and price controls," Nixon later wrote, "I knew I had opened myself to the charge that I had either betrayed my own principles or concealed my real intentions." But Nixon was nothing if not a practical politician, as he made clear in his masterful explanation of his shift. "Philosophically, however, I was still against wage-price controls, even though I was convinced that the objective reality of the economic situation forced me to impose them."

Nixon's speech—despite the preemption of *Bonanza*—was a great hit. The public felt that the government was coming to its defense against the price gougers. The international speculators had been dealt a deadly blow. During the next evening's newscasts, 90 percent of the coverage was devoted to Nixon's new policy. The coverage was favorable. And the Dow Jones Industrial Average registered a 32.9-point gain—the largest one-day increase up to then.

The Cost of Living Council took up the job of running the controls. After the initial ninety days, the controls were gradually relaxed and the system seemed to be working. But unemployment was not declining, and the administration launched a more expansionary policy. Nixon won reelection in 1972. In the months that followed, inflation began to pick up again in response to a variety of forces—domestic wage-and-price pressures, a synchronized international economic boom, crop failures in the Soviet Union, and increases in the price of oil, even prior to the Arab oil embargo. Nixon, under increasing political pressure from the investigations of the Watergate break-in, reluctantly reimposed a freeze in June 1973. Government officials were now in the business of setting prices and wages. This time, however, it was apparent that the control system was not working. Ranchers stopped shipping their cattle to the market, farmers drowned their chickens, and consumers emptied the shelves of supermarkets. Nixon took some comfort from a side benefit that George Shultz, at the time head of the Office of Management and Budget, identified. "At least," Shultz told the president, "we have now convinced everyone else of the rightness of our original position that wage-price controls are not the answer." Most of the system was finally abolished in April 1974, seventeen months after Nixon's triumphant reelection victory over George McGovern—and four months before Nixon resigned as president.

In retrospect, some would call the Nixon presidency the "last liberal administration." This was not only because of the imposition of economic controls. It also carried out a great expansion of regulation into new areas, launching affirmative action and establishing the Environmental Protection Agency, the Occupational Safety and Health Administration, and the Equal Employment Opportunity Commission. "Probably more new regulation was imposed on the economy during the Nixon Administration than in any other Presidency since the New Deal," Herbert Stein ruefully observed.[12]

Only one segment of the wage-and-price control system was not abolished—price controls over oil and natural gas. Owing in part to the deep and dark suspicions about conspiracy and monopoly in the energy sector, they were maintained for another several years. But Washington's effort to run the energy market was a lasting lesson in the perversities that can ensue when government takes over the marketplace. There were at least thirty-two different prices of natural gas, a rather standard commodity, each of whose molecules is based on one atom of carbon and four atoms of hydrogen. The oil-price-control system established several tiers of oil prices. The prices for domestic production were also held down, in effect forcing domestic producers to subsidize imported oil and providing additional incentives to import oil into the United States. The whole enterprise was an elaborate and confusing system of price controls, entitlements, and allocations. It was estimated that just the standard reporting requirements for what became the Federal Energy Administration involved some two hundred thousand respondents from industry, committing an estimated 5 million man-hours annually.

Malaise and Inflation

Overall, the 1970s were characterized by chronically poor economic performance. The oil embargo, which accompanied the 1973 Yom Kippur War between Arabs and Israelis, delivered a terrific shock to the economy. In 1974, inflation reached the highest level since the end of World War I. Within months, unemployment stood at 9.2 percent, two points higher than at any time in the postwar years. And there was a growing fear that inflation and inflationary expectations were becoming so embedded as to threaten every household, as well as the social order and stability of the nation. As part of their campaign to conquer inflation, members of Gerald Ford's administration took to wearing buttons that said WIN—"Whip Inflation Now." After some ridicule, they were withdrawn. In the 1976 presidential election, Jimmy Carter, running against economic distress and campaigning as an outsider, defeated Ford. Not long after, in an effort to cheer up the nation, Carter's chief inflation fighter renamed inflation "bananas." After protests from banana interests, he switched the code word to "kumquats." That did not do any good either.

At the end of the 1970s, the shah of Iran was toppled from power, setting off a second severe oil shock. The price of oil went from thirteen to thirty-four dollars a barrel, lines at gas stations snarled across the country again, and the nation's ire rose dramatically. So did inflation, rising as high as 13.2 percent. The Carter administration felt itself under siege. "In many respects, this would appear to be the worst of times," the White House chief of staff wrote to Carter. The president retreated to Camp David to meditate on the country's problems. He embraced a new book that identified "narcissism" as the heart of America's difficulties. He also forced five members of his cabinet to quit or resign, and followed up with a speech diagnosing America's crisis of confidence—quickly redubbed "malaise"—as the ailment that was afflicting America's soul. Whatever self-confidence remained was turned into humiliation a few months later, when Iranian students took American officials hostage in Tehran.

There were many reasons for America's affliction in the late 1970s—ranging from Middle East politics and Islamic fundamentalism to the rigidity of labor markets. The two oil crises stunned the global economy with their powerful shocks. The legacy of the Vietnam War included a pervasive national bitterness and a suspicion of and alienation from government. Yet it also came to be seen that a good part of America's ills resulted from the balance between government and marketplace that had been struck over the preceding decades—although it was a balance that had been shifting increasingly toward the side of government. After all, the coexistence of high inflation and high unemployment was new, and that in itself demanded a reassessment. Some wanted to respond with more planning, more controls. But the tide of opinion had turned. "We were at the end of two decades in which government spending, government taxes, government deficits, government regulation and government expansion of the money supply had all increased rapidly," wrote Herbert Stein. "And at the end of those two decades the inflation rate was high, real economic growth was slow and our 'normal' unemployment rate . . . was higher than ever. Nothing was more natural than the conclusion that the problems were caused by all these government increases and would be cured by reversing, or at least stopping, them."

What had been confidence in government knowledge was now turning to cynicism. The Keynesian paradigm was not what it seemed to be. It was not all that easy to manage the economy by wielding the levers of fiscal policy. In fact, it was not clear, with all the lags and uncertainties, that it could be done at all. Indeed, critics argued that the effort to apply Keynesianism was in itself inherently inflationary. Instead of picking up the slack of inadequate private-sector investment as Keynes had proposed in the 1930s, public spending, it now seemed, was crowding it out. Confidence was also ebbing in the ability of government to solve major social problems through big, interventionist programs. However altruistic and idealistic the purposes of these programs, the application of new methods of cost-benefit analysis, combined with everyday observation, led people to question whether the public was getting value for the tax dollars it spent on them. In a low-inflation, growing economy, the public had accepted the tax burden. But with recession and slow growth—and with inflation pushing people into higher brackets—taxes stoked the anger of the public. Conservatives had traditionally argued that high taxes on working people and high transfer payments to nonworkers held back the economy. That had, no less tradition-ally, been dismissed as the "fanciful ideology" of the right. But now this contention could no longer be dismissed; indeed, a new wave of academic research supported the assertion.[13]

All of this was accompanied by the appearance of a fundamental questioning about the system of regulatory capitalism that had emerged out of the New Deal. Although the discussion had been simmering in the intellectual community since the 1950s, it took the economic travails of the 1970s to bring it to the fore. The system seemed to have bogged down. It was too rigid, too slow, too distorting. It could make things worse. It hobbled techno-logical and commercial innovation. Most important, by replacing the deci-sions of the market with its own decisions, it denied markets the salutary effects of competition. It froze relationships, shored up cost levels, and, of critical significance, institutionalized inflation.

Conditions warranted change, and America was ready to go in a new direction. The ideas were there. The specter of market failure had shaped four decades of government economic policies. But the message of the 1970s was that government could fail, too. Perhaps markets were not so dumb after all.

CHAPTER 3

TRYST WITH DESTINY

The Rise of the Third World

MASSES OF PEOPLE filled the streets of New Delhi that evening; it was the beginning of the end of colonialism. With night's fall, torches were lit everywhere, and everywhere the same few chants resounded through the darkness. In the hours before midnight—the time chosen to appease the astrologers—conch shells, traditionally used to invoke the gods in Hindu temples, were sounded. Emotional but controlled in his trademark jacket, Jawaharlal Nehru strode to the podium of India's Constituent Assembly. Only three years earlier, he had been Britain's prisoner—for the ninth time. Now, with midnight about to usher in August 15, 1947, he would assume the role of Britain's successor, the first prime minister of a newly independent India.

"Long years ago," he said, "we made a tryst with destiny"—to win independence for India. "Now the time comes when we shall redeem our pledge." Indeed, Nehru and his allies had made good on their hard-won promise. The world's biggest colony—the centerpiece of the British Empire, the raison d'être for imperial policy, the very symbol of imperialism—was now to be an independent nation, the world's largest democracy. That midnight hour marked the beginning of the end of all of Europe's empires, although much blood would flow before the imperial sun finally set around the world—and much more blood in its aftermath.

But August 15 was not a complete victory for Nehru; the pledge was not redeemed in its entirety. While balkanization into a myriad of states and principalities had been avoided, British India was divided into two countries, the Hindu-dominated India and Muslim Pakistan.* And although hurried British improvisation had averted the feared total "breakdown" into civil war and anarchy, the upheaval that came with Indian independence was enormous. Fifteen million Hindus and Muslims fled as refugees in opposite directions, passing each other across the newly drawn India-Pakistan borders. With their lives disrupted, filled with harrowing fear and resentment, they soon fell prey to savage violence. Trains loaded with refugees were ambushed before they crossed the border. When the doors swung open at the stations, they revealed only corpses inside. In the cities, neighbors who had long lived in peace turned on one another. Altogether, at least a million people are estimated to have been killed in the Hindu-Muslim strife that came with independence.

For the spiritual leader of the struggle for independence, Mahatma Gandhi, who had preached the unity of Hindus and Muslims, the exultation of victory was lost in the pain of a bitter defeat. While Nehru prepared for power, Gandhi spent Independence Day in silent prayer in Calcutta, fasting in the vain hope of halting the communal violence that had engulfed the city.[1]

Nation Building

The British Raj was finished. Now the task for Nehru and his Congress Party was to turn a colony into a nation. They had inherited from Britain the Westminster model and were committed to making India a federal, parliamentary democracy—and keeping it so. But meeting the challenge of "nation building" meant more than creating political institutions. It required the development of a modern economy. In order to do so in a country desperately short of resources and skills, Nehru often said, the state would have to capture and control the commanding heights of the economy. And for the next forty years India would be dominated by Nehru's vision of a modern, planned, industrializing, socialist economy. Advised by talented economists with international experience and reputations, convinced he was drawing on and integrating the best of the Western and Soviet economic models, and buoyed by the electoral dominance of the Congress Party, Nehru found little to stop him from developing one of the world's most thoroughgoing, complex, tangled, and, ultimately, cumbersome systems of national economic planning and administration. Private firms could prosper. But the core of the Indian economy, its commanding heights, was left to an overwhelming array of public enterprises.

---

* At the time of independence in 1947, the total population of the Indian subcontinent was 300 million—95 million of whom were Muslim. Today the subcontinent's population is 935 million in India, 120 million in Pakistan, and 125 million in Bangladesh—a total of 1.18 billion.

This public sector was central to the overall vision of the planned economy, Indian-style. The model would come to have wide appeal. India's economic choices reflected profound faith in rationalism, predictability, quantification—and planning. These choices embodied the dominant economics of the day, which, with the best of intentions, economic thinkers and international agencies were promoting around the world. In one form or another, the prevailing view came down to a single point: The state would have to generate development. There was no other way. The impact of this approach would be far-reaching and lasting, across the entire developing world. The zenith would be reached in the 1970s, when the third world seemed to be on the road to victory in its confrontation with the rich countries. That was before the great disillusion.

Nehru's Discovery

The approach that Nehru articulated grew out of his view of the modern world and his belief in its technology, combined with his confrontation with the realities of Indian society—or, as he put it, his "discovery of India."

The Discovery of India was, in fact, the title he gave to a book he wrote during his twenty months of incarceration in the remote Ahmadnagar fort during World War II. He had started his autobiography during an earlier prison stint but had never finished, because he was released early in December 1941. Not long after, he was again arrested, this time for leading protests against British rule during some of the worst moments of World War II. He generally was not ill-treated during his prison stays. The fact that he had been a student at Harrow, one of England's most prestigious public schools, seems to have won him some special consideration. At Ahmadnagar fort, he spent hours each day digging at the rocky soil in the prison yard, preparing beds for flowers. But he also wrote by hand over a thousand pages of manuscript detailing his expectations for the future—and explaining his "discovery" of India and how it had transformed his life.

Nehru had grown up in a privileged setting in the city of Allahabad, on the banks of the Ganges, in India's northern heartland. His father, Motilal, was among the most prominent barristers in India, successful and increasingly rich. An early leader of India's national economic elite, Motilal Nehru was one of the founders of the Congress Party, which called for independence. Yet he also prided himself on his achievements as a man of the empire. As a boy, young Jawaharlal lived in a house with fifty or more servants, a swimming pool, and the latest European cars. His father, endlessly doting, wanted everything for his only son. Specifically, he wanted him to join the Indian civil service—at the time, the most prestigious appointment an Indian could enjoy in the Empire. He sent the boy to Harrow (where he was nicknamed Joe) and then to Cambridge, to Trinity College, where the young man studied natural sciences with considerable indifference and amused himself in the social life along the Backs, as the banks of the River Cam were called. He then studied to be a barrister in London, spent rather lavishly, toured Europe, and wrote his father about actors and actresses he saw in plays in different cities. He was deeply interested in technology. He followed with fascination the development of aviation. He also had recurring dreams about flying effortlessly in the sky.

In 1912, Nehru returned home to Allahabad, where for eight years he practiced law without much enthusiasm. His lifestyle bordered on the opulent. He worked as a lawyer, went to parties, and read *Punch* on Sundays. But he itched for something more. As a boy he had been stirred by stories of the Indian mutiny of 1857–58. He had also devoured histories about Giuseppe Garibaldi and other nationalists, and dreamed of "greatness." Moreover, he would write, "I was always, like my father, a bit of a gambler, at first with money and then for highest stakes, with the bigger issues of life." By this time, Mahatma Gandhi had begun his long journeys on foot through the country's villages, gathering followers and breathing a new urgency into the Congress Party's independence movement. Emotionally compelled, Nehru grew close to the mahatma, and became engaged in the cause. Even in his own privileged life, he saw that Empire and British rule were a humiliation. The senior officials of the British Raj would come to his father's house and drink his champagne, but they would never invite his father back to their own houses for dinner.

In 1919, the British Army massacred protesters in the city of Amritsar. Enraged, Nehru was raised out of his lethargy and stirred to action. He joined in an independent inquiry that the Congress Party established. But for Nehru, the decisive event came the next year, in 1920. His family had escaped the stifling heat of Allahabad for the elegant Savoy Hotel in the hill station of Mussoorie, leaving him to follow. A delegation of Afghani Muslims was in the same hotel. The British authorities, fearful of Hindu-Muslim collaboration, forbade Nehru to meet them. Rather than be ordered around by the British, he decided to stay at home in Allahabad. At the same time, a group of peasants, protesting against exorbitant taxes and mass evictions, arrived from the hinterland district of Rae Bareli in hopes of finding Gandhi in the city. But he was elsewhere. So instead, they headed for the Nehru family compound. And there they asked Nehru to go in Gandhi's stead, to lead a new inquiry. Nehru, with little else to do, agreed.

What followed would overwhelm him. The peasants built roads overnight so that his car could pass deep into rural India; they rallied together again and again to lift his car when it became stuck in mud. Nehru had never seen anything like the wretched poverty he now encountered. "After all," biographer M. J. Akbar would write, "he was still an Indian sahib in a hat and silk underwear." But under the scorching and blinding sun, Nehru was transformed. "I was filled with shame and sorrow," he later wrote, "shame at my own easygoing and comfortable life and our petty politics of the city, which ignored this vast multitude of semi-naked sons and daughters of India, sorrow at the degradation and overwhelming poverty of India." He had also discovered his political vocation—and the focus for his ambition. To his father, with whom he corresponded candidly, he wrote: "Greatness is being thrust on me." He moved to the fore in the independence movement and emerged as Gandhi's designated heir. Joe, the public-school boy at Harrow, had become Pandit—Teacher—and the leader with Gandhi of the Congress Party.[2]

"Tractors and Big Machinery"

If independence was the central political issue, then fighting poverty was the central economic issue. With independence achieved in August 1947, poverty was *the* problem. Whereas Gandhi and Nehru were united on political objectives, they were divided on economics. For Gandhi, the model was *swadeshi,* self-reliance—simple home production of basic goods, self-sufficiency in the village, and a spinning wheel in every hut. Why should colonial India export cotton to Manchester, only to import it back in the form of expensive clothing? Indians should make their own clothes. Gandhi had little time for socialism and class warfare. After independence, he lectured a group of Communists: "What to me is even more pathetic is that you regard Russia as your spiritual home. Despising Indian culture, you dream of planting the Russian system here." Nehru's view disagreed fundamentally with Gandhi's. He sought a different kind of self-sufficiency—industrialization and the steel mill. His central objective was "to get rid of the appalling poverty of the people." He believed in technology and progress, in machines and industrialization—"I'm all for tractors and big machinery," he said—and he intended to use twentieth-century means to achieve his goal.

Lenin had said that "communism equals Soviet power plus electrification." Nehru offered a variant in his formula for India's development—"heavy engineering and machine-making industry, scientific research institutes, and electric power." He certainly shared in the Attlee consensus. His adoption of the themes and ideas of the Labour Party was evident in his recurrent evocation of the commanding heights, the mixed economy, and the need for planning. But he was also much impressed with the Soviet model, and embraced five-year plans and central planning. While troubled by what communism did to freedom, he wrote during his last term in prison that "the Soviet Revolution had advanced human society by a great leap and had lit a bright flame which could not be smothered and that it laid the foundation for a new civilization toward which the world could advance." Private property, yes, but it was to be subordinate to the state in the building of the Indian economy.

Their sharply differing economic visions put Gandhi and Nehru very much at odds. In 1945, Gandhi accused his appointed heir of being unfaithful to his economic vision of *swadeshi* and an India composed of harmonious villages. "I do not understand why a village should necessarily embody truth and nonviolence," Nehru shot back. "A village, normally speaking, is backward intellectually and culturally and no progress can be made from a backward environment. Narrow-minded people are much more likely to be untruthful and violent." The master's vision, said Nehru, was "completely unreal."

A Hindu extremist murdered Gandhi on January 30, 1948. The country was thrown into shock and pervasive grief. Nehru had lost his spiritual father. But now there was also nothing left to stop his economic program, which he pursued as prime minister until his death in 1964. Under Nehru, India embarked on a socialist course that had already been laid out in the late 1930s in the Congress Party's National Planning Committee—chaired by Nehru. He had then divided the world between two groups of people. There were those "who want to advance the world further and free the people from the chains of imperialism and capitalism. On the other side, there are a handful of people who are deriving benefit from the present state of things." India, he concluded, would take its stand on "independence and socialism"; for, he added, that was what was needed, "in our own poverty-stricken country, where unemployment prevails." [3]

"The Idea of Planning"

A series of measures between 1948 and 1952 established the process of national economic planning, devised the instruments and agencies to carry it out, and designed the first five-year plan. It was to be a mixed economy, heavily weighted toward the state. The Planning Commission was established in 1950 and its preeminence was quickly clear. Chaired by Nehru, it became a quasi-government on its own, the real manager of the economy.

The next several years reaffirmed India's commitment to a government-dominated economy. In 1954, both the Congress Party and the Parliament called for "a socialist pattern of society." But what India actually aimed for was a mixed economy, borrowing from both the European and Soviet systems. As with France, the system was to be tripartite: a state-owned and state-controlled sector composed of the key heavy industries, a state-regulated sector, and a private sector. But the Indian model put much greater emphasis on the role of government. It was to be dominant; it was to provide the "big push," through heavy industrialization, that would deliver development and growth. The state would be the guardian of wisdom and impartiality, with the elite managing the development process in order to ensure that it met the needs of the "nation" and not of "special interests."

To achieve all this, India put in place a more complicated and intricate system of planning than any of the European nations, with detailed tables of economic "inputs" and "outputs," as if the economy were something that could be measured and rationally managed with the precision of a physics experiment. Nehru blessed the entire process. "The idea of planning and a planned society," he said, "is accepted now in varying degrees by everyone."

The hyperrationalist scientism of the Indian "planning-and-control system" reflected the fact that it was shaped by a brilliant scientist who had turned to economics in later life. P. C. Mahalanobis was the outstanding Indian economist of his time, and he influenced an entire generation. Like Nehru, he had gone to Cambridge to study natural sciences; but unlike Nehru, he had done very well indeed, getting a first in physics. He became a statistician and only later an economist. But he retained the scientist's belief in rationality, and thus, in contrast to the indicative planning that Jean Monnet had established in France, he promoted highly quantitative planning, fed by complex mathematical matrices based on "scientific" study of the economy and the linkages among sectors and enterprises. As one of his younger colleagues put it, Mahalanobis subscribed wholeheartedly to the dictum of the British physicist William Kelvin "that qualitative reasoning was nothing other than 'poor quantitative reasoning.' " Mahalanobis sought to apply that precept to the economy of a country of many hundreds of millions of people.

The expansion of the public sector was carried out with great enthusiasm. The state would control some sectors exclusively; in others, existing private enterprise could survive, but the state would take charge of all new undertakings. Economic policy ruled out nationalization of existing companies, with only a few exceptions. Commerce and small-scale activities stayed private, and the large private industrial empires of the Tata and Birla families, and others, remained intact (with the exception of Tata Air, which was nationalized and became Air India). Rather, the state would take charge of all new large ventures. Hosts of new public companies were created—ranging from power utilities to chemical plants to automobile assemblies, even hotel chains—along with state-owned banks.

These various companies would be national champions, the economic embodiment of India's independence. They would demonstrate India's skills and capabilities to the nation and the outside world and they would help tie the new nation together. That last objective was critical to a nation struggling to forge itself out of many provinces, as well as numerous principalities, whose hereditary rulers had dealt directly with the British. And the state companies would be a source of national pride. In their recruitment notices and on their letterheads, the public enterprises proudly announced, after their names, "A GOVERNMENT OF INDIA UNDERTAKING." [4]

The Permit Raj

The impact of the Indian system was felt far beyond its borders. India was the most prominent example of decolonization of the postwar years. Nehru was widely respected, a figure of rectitude, the man who had prevailed against the British Empire without a sword, the leader of the third world bloc. India's many economists were trained in the state of the art; they were committed to their models. They were also worldly and wonderfully articulate. And the Indian economic model seemed to be at the very forefront of development. As a consequence, it proved to be enormously influential.

There was, however, one problem. The Indian economy did not perform as the model had predicted. The creators of the system thought they were putting in place an eminently rational—indeed, the only rational—solution to the conundrum of industrial development for the social good in a country engulfed by poverty. The results proved otherwise. It turned out that the economy of India could not be reduced to the laws of physics. It could not be controlled, at least with any degree of efficiency, by planners at the center; nor could it be satisfactorily "pushed" by a vast collection of state-owned enterprises that were not subject to the discipline and tests of the market. Instead of gaining the perfectly constructed mechanism for the "big push," India developed a thoroughly complex and enormously cumbersome system. It operated through a byzantine maze of quantitative regulations, quotas and tariffs, endless permits, industrial licenses, and a host of other controls—a maze in which incentives and initiative and entrepreneurship either were lost or became hopelessly distorted. All of this made the economy increasingly inefficient; bureaucratic dispensation took over the functions of the market-place. The British Raj, some would eventually say, had given way to the Permit Raj.

The restrictions brought economic stagnation. They frustrated the businessmen who had so ardently supported the Congress Party and independence. They also created a great paradox. India developed an immensely talented world-class pool of scientists and engineers. Yet the emphasis on self-sufficiency and state enterprises meant that India stepped out of the global flow of technology and imposed upon itself a form of technological retardation. In *The Discovery of India,* Nehru had postulated that science and engineering would drive India into economic growth and development. But in the two decades after independence, India was to discover that the system put into place would end up frustrating both economic and technological progress. Its symbol was seen on the streets of India in the "Amby" —the Ambassador—the domestic car modeled on the British Austin of the 1960s, an automotive time warp still being produced in the late 1990s.

The system fell prey to politics, too. As Nehru grew old, the Congress Party's grip on politics began to loosen. Faced with competition, the party turned to patronage and, sometimes, to graft. Public enterprises found themselves caught between the political tugging of constituencies and the bickering of organized interests. As India's democracy grew livelier and more clamorous, the economic structures—imagined by an intellectual elite and based on science and rationality—could no longer be kept above the fray of ordinary, "vulgar" politics.

Yet was there an alternative? None that Nehru and the politicians and

74

technocrats and economists around him could easily see. In the years after independence, the nation's political and economic problems were enormous and the country was terribly poor. There was no capital market to speak of, and not much of a middle class. The past, as Nehru saw it, was mired in mysticism. The future should be based upon rationality. To "develop" meant to harness science and technology. They could not afford to wait a hundred years. Private capitalists were by definition suspect; they would pursue their own private interests. They had no moral or ethical claim. What models, then, were there to choose from? The answer: some combination of the mixed economy of Western Europe and the command-and-control model of the Soviet Union, with its five-year plans and big push into industrialization. So the models were fused and erected upon the partial legacies of Gandhian self-sufficiency and the imperial civil service that Gandhi had fought—and a strong state tradition going back to the Mogul emperors. And at the heart of the whole system was the powerful conviction that necessity required the nation's economic future to be entrusted to the state.

"An Agenda for a Better World": The Development Economists

India hardly existed in a vacuum. On the contrary, that country's experience was to have tremendous impact, both as a focus of effort, the greatest laboratory, and as an example to many other nations. For although India was the largest, it was but the first of the newly independent nations to emerge after World War II. As decolonization cascaded with the disintegration of the European colonial empires, the number of independent countries swelled from fifty-five in 1947 to over 150 by the end of the 1980s (before the breakup of the communist empire). Most were poor; many, desperately poor. Poverty was also endemic in countries whose independence had long pre-dated World War II, as in Latin America.

This specter of poverty was a powerful rallying point. During the war, Franklin Roosevelt had summoned the world to a battle against poverty with the fourth of his four freedoms—the freedom from want. In Britain, the Beveridge Report had simultaneously called for the slaying of the giant of poverty and the creation of the welfare state. Such became the animating spirit for a great effort to bring a better life to what had been called in former days the backward or underdeveloped areas but would soon enough be known as the third world, or, more optimistically, the developing world.

Idealism and altruism were not the only driving forces. The cold war confrontation made development a primary concern for Western governments. The Soviet Union was deploying both its development model and its foreign aid to win countries over to its camp. The competition with communism made the American and other Western governments eager to embrace a noncommunist path to development, one that would lead to stability. And the success of the Marshall Plan and postwar reconstruction—and the experience gained therein—not only reinforced the effort but also provided the confidence to proceed. Indeed, the crusade to overcome poverty and despair in the developing world seemed almost the logical continuation of postwar reconstruction. "After the success of the Marshall Plan," the economist Albert O. Hirschman recalled, "the underdevelopment of Asia, Africa, and Latin America loomed as the major unresolved economic problem on any 'Agenda for a Better World.' "

But how was development to happen? The answer came from a group of economists who enlisted in a crusade. In response to the poverty of newly emerging nations, they fashioned a new branch of the dismal science called development economics and, in so doing, became grand strategists of the crusade. They sought to answer a set of basic questions: What drives economic growth? How can it be accelerated? In a way, these questions had been central to Adam Smith's inquiry in *The Wealth of Nations,* for he had set out to explain "the natural progress of opulence." But in the late 1940s and the 1950s and 1960s, "natural" was unacceptable. For the development economists, the urgent drive was to accelerate—not to wait on what was thought to be a one-hundred-year cycle but rather to see what could be achieved in a decade. They asked how to get something going now. And their work was to prove yet again Keynes' dictum about the impact of "academic scribblers," for their ideas were to be enormously influential in shaping the economic systems of dozens and dozens of countries across two generations of world history. The power of their ideas arose from the fact that they were not only thinkers but also "doers," drawn into the work of design and implementation.

Their beliefs were at least in part an outgrowth of Keynesianism—in the focus on state-driven growth, in terms of the tools of macroeconomic analysis, and in the bedrock of Keynesian self-confidence. The Beveridge welfare agenda also influenced them greatly. But so did India. "Keynes and Beveridge were both proponents of active state intervention," wrote Hans Singer, one of the most prominent of the original development economists. "This preconditioned me to take a direct interest in the problems of development planning, much in vogue in the immediate postwar year, with special focus on India. P. C. Mahalanobis became the prophet (or guru) of the development economists in this respect, and Calcutta became their Mecca."

Idealism, morality, justice, human sympathy, the shock of confronting poverty, the vision of a better world—all of these brought people into the crusade. Their outlook was summed up by Albert Hirschman, one of the most distinguished of the "pioneers of development." As he put it, "These economists had taken up the cultivation of development economics in the wake of World War II not as narrow specialists, but impelled by the vision of a better world. As liberals, most of them presumed that 'all good things go together' and took it for granted that if only a good job could be done in raising the national income of the countries concerned, a number of beneficial effects would follow in the social, political, and cultural realms." The overall objective was to "bring all-around emancipation from backwardness."[5]

Their individual stories help explain their drive to develop an agenda for a better world. Hirschman's life reflected what he called the "calamitous derailments of history." He was born in Berlin, received his Ph.D. at the University of Trieste, served five years in the army during World War II (the French and the American), worked after the war for both the U.S. Federal Reserve and the Marshall Plan, and spent four years as an economic adviser in Colombia. Paul Rosenstein-Rodan was born in Kraków, Poland, and grew up in a world and culture that were to be completely obliterated by the Nazis. During World War II, he helped organize a study group at the Royal Institute of International Affairs in London on the upcoming postwar problems of the underdeveloped countries. His premise was that "if we were to emerge alive, we should not return to the previous status quo but . . . form a better world." As he saw it, the challenge after the war was to move from "the national welfare to the international" welfare state. "Not to do enough about inequality of opportunity and poverty when our world resources are sufficient to improve the situation is the real moral crisis," he wrote.

Jan Tinbergen, who was to win the Nobel Prize in economics, was preoccupied with reconstruction as the director of the Central Planning Bureau in the Netherlands after World War II. Then, in 1951, P. C. Mahalanobis invited him to India. Although Tinbergen had seen want as a result of the war in his own country, "the poverty prevailing in India—as a normal situation—was such a contrast that it redirected my thinking and main activities." Arthur Lewis grew up in St. Lucia, in the British West Indies. He left school at fourteen. A few years later he won a scholarship to the London School of Economics, which launched him on a distinguished career in economics that would lead him, like Tinbergen, to the Nobel Prize. The conquest of poverty was his central preoccupation: Not only should it be conquered, it *could* be conquered. "My mother had brought me up," he recalled, "to believe that anything they can do we can do." Walt Rostow summed up his vocation by citing a few lines from the poet for whom he was named, Walt Whitman: "All peoples of the globe together sail/sail the same voyage/are bound to the same destination."

The development economists looked to history for guidance. Alexander Gerschenkron's masterpiece, *Economic Backwardness in Historical Perspective,* first unveiled in 1951, was enormously influential. Gerschenkron explored how the industrial "latecomers"—Germany, France, Russia— sought to "catch up" with Britain. He showed that there were many paths by which nations industrialized. The latecomers did not get there by Adam Smith's route. Rather, they seemed to move in double or triple time, via much more intense involvement by the state—through the direction of investment and a close alliance among government, finance, and industry. This perspective suggested ways to mobilize capital in the face of inadequate institutions and proved that governments could close the gap and provide the means for speeding up the "progress of opulence." And it struck a deeply responsive chord for the development economists, who were seeking to close the gap for the "late latecomers."

Certain basic assumptions served as the underpinnings for development economics. The third world was abundant in land, labor, and natural-resource potential, but what it desperately lacked was capital. Without capital, markets were disabled or even absent, and the signals they sent were unreliable. The developing countries needed infrastructure—roads, railways, electric power—to provide the foundations for a modern economy, and markets in their then-truncated state were unlikely to mobilize the vast sums of capital such projects required. Governments would have to do it instead, because, unlike private financiers dogged by shareholders in search of near-term paybacks, governments could assume the risks and bear the responsibilities of investments that might take decades to mature.

The development economists were doubtful about the market and its vigor, and for this reason, they were suspicious of the private sector in the developing countries. It seemed desperately small: In the colonies of Africa, it had been kept confined to the traders of basic goods—surely no base for industrialization. Where a larger private sector existed, especially in Latin America, it appeared to consist of a handful of excessively wealthy families, which were content with what was regarded as an "exploitative" social order and were loath to accept change. In short, either the private sector would pursue special interests rather than the "public good" that Nehru had articulated or it would lack the capability, vigor, and "heart" to get the job done. But if they were inherently pessimistic about the private sector, the development economists were optimistic about what governments could do. The result: "the conviction that, in underdeveloped areas, industrialization required a deliberate, intensive, guided effort." There was not to be the "storming" of the Soviet five-year plans. Rather, there was to be a concentration of effort and capital—variously called the "big push" or the "take-off" or the "great spurt" or, less colorfully, "backward and forward linkages"— that would carry the developing country into a new reality.

To be sure, some development economists focused, with more optimism, on the effectiveness and utility of markets, prices, and international trade. Drawing upon his work with rubber farmers in Malaya and traders in West Africa, P. T. Bauer argued that entrepreneurship existed in the third world, too, and that the sum of the efforts of the entrepreneurs would be much more efficacious than government direction. But critics of mainstream development economics like Bauer were considered eccentric and off the mark. As the 1930s had discredited capitalism, so had it discredited market-focused economics. Instead of concentrating on how markets worked, economists emphasized the imperfections and failures of the market. The dominant view in development economics envisioned a much larger

—and central—role for government. The obvious way to correct the imperfections was with a strong state.[6]

"The Bank"

Spurred by decolonization, fueled by the profusion of foreign-aid dollars and the dominant cold war imperative of making allies of the newly independent countries, a vast development enterprise was born. It was made up of governmental donor agencies, private foundations, international development banks, universities, and research institutes, along with ministries of finance, industry, and development. Amid this constellation, one institution was central—the International Bank for Reconstruction and Development, otherwise known as the World Bank. It was the pivot around which policies and funding were put into place, and around which the debate was organized.

The World Bank was created at the Bretton Woods conference in 1944 to coordinate the awesome job of economic reconstruction in what would soon be postwar Europe. But its mandate quickly expanded—exactly as its founders, including Keynes, had intended—to investing in the infrastructure of developing countries. Its first loan to the third world was $16 million to Chile in 1948, for power-plant and agricultural machinery. It made its first loan to Asia (excluding reconstruction loans to Japan) in 1949—to India, for a hydroelectric project. Its first loan to Africa came in 1950—to Ethiopia, for communications equipment. By the early 1950s its focus had fully shifted from "reconstruction" in Europe to "development" in the third world. Its basic mandate was to raise multilateral finance from the capital markets of developed nations and use that money to make long-term loans on concessional (i.e., very favorable) terms to the public sectors of developing countries. Those loans would be secured by repayment guarantees from the developing country. Thus the bank would get capital flowing across borders —old and new. But it had to start from almost nowhere, for "the pattern and flow of international investment were ruptured beyond recognition by the Great Depression and the Second World War."

The World Bank's role was to help ensure that the conditions for market development were in place. Its lending was meant to correct market failure —or what might even be called market absence. That is, it would fund the nonexistent or sorely lacking infrastructure that was required for the development of market economies. Thus, most of its funding went for transportation (ports, roads, railways), communications, and, above all, electric power—often by means of large hydroelectric dams. Such infrastructure, the bank said, was "an essential precondition for sustained economic growth." It was driven to this orientation by, in the words of the bank's historians, "a series of emergency situations." Power shortages were endemic in Asia and Latin America; in Africa, there was little infrastructure at all. It was easier for Brazil to import potatoes into Rio de Janeiro from Holland than to ship them from a hundred miles inland. Deliveries by the Indian railway system were weeks and weeks late. How could private entrepreneurs be expected to make investments and take risks in the face of such obstacles, uncertainty, and disorganization?

The World Bank stepped into this role because the developing countries could not mobilize sufficient domestic savings to get such projects done. Foreign investors could not count on a sufficient rate of return to be attracted to such projects. Moreover, foreign capital was not very welcome during this era of "nation building." Private investment in what were seen as critically important infrastructure projects meant either foreign management and foreign enclaves and the repatriation of profits or further enrichment and power for a few families that were already very rich.

If there was a single model in the mission of the World Bank, it was America's Tennessee Valley Authority, a public enterprise devoted to a great need. The TVA was efficient, with a powerful sense of mission and sufficient scale to be effective, insulated from politics and corruption, a generator and focuser of skills, and capable of the longer view. It had succeeded mightily in the middle South of the United States, and its first leader, David Lilienthal, was the living expression of the dedicated, disinterested, capable public servant who could effectively, and even brilliantly, operate at the intersection of public and private interests. As with the TVA in the United States and the state companies in Europe, so state-owned companies would be the means of development and modernization in the third world.

The image of the TVA fit the charter of the World Bank. The bank could lend only to public agencies, and better than ministries were semi-independent state-owned companies that would mobilize skills and capital to the achievement of important national objectives. Moreover, the bank wanted to encourage scale and efficiency, just as the creation of the TVA had done. And with the passage of time, it became increasingly open to working with state-owned companies in areas other than infrastructure—for instance, industry and finance. The World Bank did create an affiliate, the International Finance Corporation in 1956, to make loans to private-sector companies, but it played a small role for many years.[7]

The Rise of the State-owned Company

Indeed, the most visible embodiment of development economics was the state-owned company. Such corporations would be the specific vehicle for capturing the commanding heights. Since private enterprise assuredly could not raise the capital necessary for development, the government would mobilize and direct resources through the state-owned companies. They would serve as the engines of modernization, the drivers of economic growth, the mobilizers of development, the mechanisms for achieving a better future.

80

They would pursue the public good—the nation's interest—rather than the special interests of particular merchants and industrialists and various clusters of super-rich families. They would be staffed by meritocracy, not by patronage or lineage. They would compensate for market failure and achieve economies of scale. And in these ways and more, they would express sovereignty, dignity, and the birth of national identity in countries that were trying to create themselves as nations. In sum, the state company came to be seen as essential both to development and to nationhood.

The development economists were sanguine about the efficiency of the public enterprises. The "type of ownership," as Jan Tinbergen put it, did not really matter. What did matter for efficiency was "the quality of its management," and that was quite irrespective of ownership. Thus, "efficiency considerations need not be a stumbling block if public enterprise is chosen as a means for furthering a country's development." Rather, public ownership would streamline the process of coordination among ministers, planners, and company managers—all for the greater good.

Indeed, careful coordination would be required if the developing countries were to successfully negotiate the much-desired industrial transition. New industries started off at a disadvantage against established low-cost imports. So governments protected their "infant industries" with trade barriers. Only in this way could they force the process of "import substitution" —gradually replacing imported goods with home production, starting off with textiles and light manufactures and ultimately aiming for heavy machinery and other industrial products. Once the process was securely under way, the trade barriers could come down and the country would reconnect to international commerce. Most developing countries followed this path to some degree. But only a few—particularly in Asia—would prove successful at weaning their "infants" at the right time. In all too many countries, protection and public ownership became commonplace; and rather than facilitating the emergence of the private sector, they would eventually come to constrain and crowd it out. The number of "parastatals," as state companies were sometimes called, grew rapidly, encompassing not only infrastructure but industry, finance, and services. In Argentina, the government even owned the circus.

Public enterprises took a variety of forms. Some were government agencies, branches of existing ministries or government authorities, that carried out a specific task or service. They had neither working capital of their own nor any autonomy. They were directly controlled by the ministry. (This was what the British Labourites had dismissed as the Post Office Model.) Others were public corporations—separate legal entities that existed as companies, with their own capital but overseen by one or more ministries. There were also mixed firms—the government held majority ownership, but a board of directors provided some insulation between management and government. Some of these state enterprises had complete monopolies; others were the national champions, which competed from a favored position

81

with domestic and foreign rivals. Often these companies took on welfare roles—providing workers and their families with company towns, housing, scholarships, and health clinics. They would ensure the development of homegrown "human capital"—a term rediscovered in the 1950s—and perhaps that would turn out to be their most important role of all. But they could also become sources of favoritism and nepotism. Sometimes they were clearly subordinated to the government ministries; in other cases, they became powerful "states within states."[8]

"The Wind of Change"

Development needed customers, and soon there would be many. India's independence inspired nationalist movements and provided a model for decolonization all over the world, launching a tide of independence. In every way, the old colonial order seemed to have lost its force, its historical relevance. Two world wars had thoroughly discredited the European powers' claim to a "civilizing mission." Back at home, colonial rule was losing its advocates, more and more of whom felt that the economic benefits no longer outweighed the growing burden of administering empires. And a new elite was on the rise throughout the colonies, made up of the lucky few who had acceded to Western education and returned with technical credentials as engineers, lawyers, or accountants. This new professional class had also absorbed Western political values, and could ably challenge colonial rule on its own terms. They formed political parties—inspired, in many cases, by the Congress Party of Nehru and Gandhi—and pressed for greater degrees of self-rule. They also became plausible candidates for a peaceful handover of power. In Britain and France—by far the two largest colonial powers—the view grew steadily in the 1950s that decolonization was inevitable. British prime minister Harold Macmillan called it "the wind of change." There would, of course, be exceptions. France would attempt to hold on to two of its colonies, Vietnam and Algeria, by force—an ultimately futile effort that would carry a dire human cost. Portugal would cling to Angola and Mozambique until its own transition from dictatorship to democracy in 1975.

The change was most striking in Africa. France granted independence to almost all its African colonies in a single year, 1960; Britain, more gradually, from 1957 to 1965. Almost everywhere, the process began with an interim self-rule government, the colonial power retaining ultimate control and responsibility for currency, defense, and foreign affairs. As momentum gathered, local groups expanded their scope of responsibility. By the time of the emotional flag-lowering ceremony at government house and the assumption of formal power by the elected local leaders, a peaceful transition had taken place. In the background, economic links usually remained intact.

The new leaders faced formidable challenges. Colonial infrastructure was scant, and what little existed was designed for swift extraction of natural resources, not for bolstering local trade and civic life. Where railways existed, they connected mines to ports; where roads were paved, they served plantations. Villages along these routes grew into trading posts, while historic centers on old commercial routes became backwaters. In the towns, public services were minimal. The typical electricity network in an African country on the eve of independence consisted of erratic diesel turbines that supplied the villas and offices of the colonial administration. Factories and wealthy traders installed their own generators. Water supply and telephones were similarly inadequate. Primary education and public health were rudimentary. With independence, town and country dwellers alike raised their hopes for rapid growth in all of these areas at the same time. And the new leaders, strained by the quick pace of change and the small numbers of qualified technical staff, became the custodians of these aspirations.

"First the Political Kingdom"

In the period of transition, the beacon country from Africa was Ghana, first to achieve independence, in 1957; and the most influential figure was its prime minister, later president, Kwame Nkrumah. When Nkrumah was born in 1910, Ghana was still the Gold Coast, a British colony known for its plantations and for being the world's largest producer of cocoa. Its frontiers were the result of bargains among the colonial powers—Britain, France, and Germany—that did not correspond to the historical boundaries of the kingdoms that preceded colonization, particularly the once-mighty Ashanti Empire. Nkrumah, who came from a modest, traditional family, received his early education at the hands of Catholic missionaries. He went on to train as a teacher and for a few years taught elementary school in towns along the coast. He was popular and charismatic, and earned a decent living. But exposure to politics and to a few influential figures sparked in him a greater interest—to go to America. He applied to universities in the United States, and with money raised from relatives, he set out on a steamer in 1935. He reached New York almost penniless, and took refuge with fellow West Africans in Harlem. He then presented himself at Lincoln University in Pennsylvania and enrolled; a small scholarship and a campus job helped him make ends meet.

In the United States, Nkrumah saw alternatives to the British tradition of government. He also became suffused with an acute consciousness of the politics of race relations. Unlike many new African leaders, who sought to emulate their European instructors, Nkrumah plunged into America's black communities. Founded before the Civil War, Lincoln University was America's oldest black college, and its special atmosphere inspired and comforted Nkrumah. In the summers, he worked at physically demanding jobs—in shipyards and construction and at sea. He studied theology as well as philosophy; he frequented the black churches in New York and Philadelphia and was sometimes asked to preach. He also forged ties with black American intellectuals, for whom Africa was becoming, in this time of political change, an area of extreme interest. Moving to London after World War II, Nkrumah helped organize Pan-African congresses, linking the emergent educated groups of the African colonies with activists, writers, artists, and well-wishers from the industrial countries. It was a time of great intellectual ferment, excitement, and optimism. India's achievement of independence in 1947 stirred dreams of freedom for the other colonies. "If we get self-government," Nkrumah proclaimed, "we'll transform the Gold Coast into a paradise in ten years."

Returning to the Gold Coast in 1949, Nkrumah found that India's independence had set in motion a process of gradual transfer of power in Britain's other colonies. The terms and timing were highly unsettled, and indeed would provoke conflict and violent clashes, but the basic principle of self-government was becoming the consensus. Nkrumah was dissatisfied with the existing nationalist grouping, finding it staid and conservative, overly tied to colonial business interests. With several associates he set up a new party, the Convention People's Party (CPP), in the process demonstrating his supreme organizational abilities. Within two years the CPP had won limited self-rule elections, and Nkrumah became "Leader of Government Business"—a de facto prime minister, responsible for internal government and policy. He set his sights firmly on independence. No amount of autonomy or self-rule, he argued, could match the energy, commitment, and focus of a government and people in a truly independent country. It was a precondition for growth. He summarized his philosophy in a slogan that became famous and influential across Africa: "Seek ye first the political kingdom, and all else shall be added unto you."

To reach this goal, Nkrumah began to work closely with the British administration and reached a compromise with the domestic opposition. The process of transition accelerated—peacefully—and on March 6, 1957, the new flag was hoisted. The country took the name Ghana. It was a deliberate historical misnomer. The old Empire of Ghana had been a glorious African state of the medieval era. But it was not situated in the Gold Coast—instead, it was well inland, in present-day Mali. But the idea of past African glory was paramount; Nkrumah and his associates chose the name that they felt best conveyed it, and nobody complained.

Ghana's route to independence became the model for the rest of the continent. By the mid-1960s, over thirty African countries were independent and many had charismatic leaders, including Jomo Kenyatta in Kenya, Julius Nyerere in Tanzania, and Kenneth Kaunda in Zambia. Their economic views were very much those of the time, in line with the consensus among development economists. Here again, only the state could mobilize the funds and coordinate the activities of economic transformation if it was to be achieved in the leaders' lifetime—let alone during their time in office. Indeed, pessimism about markets was even greater in Africa than elsewhere. After all, the colonization of Africa had come with little regard for local education, health, or infrastructure. It was tainted with racism and contempt. As a result, people were not equipped to participate in markets, or so it seemed. Instead, the new leaders hatched schemes for "African socialism" that could somehow combine modern growth and traditional values. "Capitalism is too complicated a system for a newly independent nation," Nkrumah argued. "Hence the need for a socialistic society." Few disagreed. It was, after all, the received wisdom of the time.[9]

Marketing Boards: The Tools of Control

Ironically, the economic device in which Africa's new leaders invested their trust was itself a colonial invention—the marketing board, a public agency responsible for buying crops from farmers and reselling them for export. Seemingly innocuous and indeed almost boring in name, marketing boards were in fact powerful tools of control for the new governments. They were born of necessity, when the Great Depression drove down world commodity prices and the wartime boom drove them up again. African farmers lived on a shoestring and were highly vulnerable to such volatile swings in world markets. They might overplant in times of high prices and abandon crops when prices fell. Meanwhile, the state would lose both tax revenue and its ability to plan ahead. The marketing boards were set up to correct this situation. They would purchase crops at stable prices. In times of high world prices, they would accumulate a surplus of money; in times of low world prices, they would use that financial surplus to support the local price. This would protect farmers from the tumult of markets, over which they had no control. Because the marketing boards deliberately paid farmers prices other than the world-market prices, they could not function in a competitive market. Hence, they were granted monopolies. Virtually all crops for export had to go through the marketing board. This was the prevailing system at independence in almost every African country. All that varied from country to country was the exact number and range of crops concerned.

For Nkrumah and his peers, retaining the colonial marketing boards seemed the expedient, indeed the sensible, thing to do. The boards would provide the mechanism both to capture the "surplus" generated by agriculture and to raise revenues. The resources levied this way could be combined with investment and foreign aid to jump-start industrial development and the "great transformation" away from rural-based economies toward industrialization. There were some problems, to be sure. When the marketing board imposed prices lower than world prices, how would it stop crops from slipping away into a black market or crossing borders into neighboring countries? Frontiers were artificial and porous, and there was, after all, a considerable history of long-distance African trade. Moreover, if the marketing board did accumulate a cash surplus, who would oversee its sound management and investment?

But amid the enthusiasm for independence and the overriding concern with market failure, these questions seemed of little import. Governments instead threw their energy into enlarging the existing marketing boards and creating new ones for commodities that were hitherto unregulated. They ran their economies through the boards. In Ghana, the Cocoa Marketing Board grew in size, staffing, and power. It was joined in short order by marketing boards for timber and diamonds, and a host of other state organizations aimed not only at exports but also at regulating local trade in foodstuffs, fish, and household goods. This pervasive, confident—or, as some would say, intrusive—involvement of the state in almost every aspect of investment and commerce made Ghana a case of "development economics in action."

The Volta Dam: The High Tide of African Socialism

The same confidence extended as well to the other half of the process—industrialization. Nkrumah very much believed that the "big push" was necessary and could be rapidly achieved. He harnessed his hopes to a dramatic plan for a huge multipurpose undertaking known as the Volta River Project. Ghana had large reserves of bauxite and hence the potential to become a major exporter of aluminum. But this required building a smelter and a very large dam and power plant to feed it. That, in turn, would support a national electricity grid; and the cheap, abundant power would jump-start industrialization all over the country. It was a grand vision that accorded perfectly with development theory. The dam would set in motion the "forward and backward linkages" that the economists sought, and it would give Ghana economic independence. It would also create the world's biggest man-made lake, forcing the resettlement of tens of thousands of people.

When it was all added up, the Volta River Project was the most ambitious and complicated development project of its day, and certainly one of the most prominent. It also gave rise to lengthy and arduous negotiations between the government of Ghana and its would-be partners—the World Bank, the governments of Britain and the United States, and the aluminum firms Kaiser and Reynolds, which agreed to build the smelter. Several years of frustrating discussion culminated in a series of contract documents that one participant described as the world's "most complex since Queen Marie was selling Roumanian bonds."

But the deal was not yet done. As the negotiations dragged on, the stakes grew higher. Nkrumah's views were hardening, reflecting an increasing attraction to "scientific socialism" and a mounting preoccupation with control. Already in 1960, he had made Ghana a republic and proclaimed himself its president. In April 1961, he delivered a "Dawn Broadcast" in which he lashed out at "self-seeking" and "careerism," and which he used to force the resignation of potential rivals. Soon there were political arrests. He also threw out the British officers assigned to train his army.

All this occurred shortly before Queen Elizabeth II was scheduled to make a state visit to Ghana in November 1961 to celebrate the new area of decolonization. But then, after several bombs went off in the capital of Accra, sentiment mounted in Britain's House of Commons that the trip should be canceled, because it was too unsafe. Prime Minister Harold Macmillan feared, however, that cancellation would provoke Nkrumah into leaving the Commonwealth and moving into Moscow's arms. To prevent such a turn, he appealed to President John Kennedy to confirm that the United States would help underwrite the Volta River Project. When, on the eve of the queen's departure, it became apparent that the House of Commons might vote to cancel the trip, Macmillan made clear that he would resign that very evening—even if it meant having to awaken the queen. The vote against the trip did not eventuate, and the queen took off.

As it turned out, the trip was a great success. The local press in Ghana hailed the queen as "the greatest socialist monarch in the world." With the conclusion of the visit and the queen safely back in Britain, Macmillan immediately telephoned Kennedy. "I have risked my Queen," Macmillan said. "You must risk your money!" Gallantly, Kennedy replied he would match the queen's "brave contribution" with his own. The United States signed on to the Volta River Project.

In the same year, Nkrumah visited the Soviet Union and returned much impressed at the pace of industrialization there. He came back with a rigid seven-year plan. "We must try and establish factories in large numbers at great speed," he argued. State-owned companies and public authorities mushroomed in all fields. So did mismanagement and graft. The price was most painfully felt in the countryside as Nkrumah used cocoa revenues, controlled by the official marketing board, to cover the growing losses of public companies. The imposition of unrealistically low cocoa prices on farmers, combined with the bloated organization of the marketing board, devastated the industry. Many farmers switched crops altogether; others found ways to smuggle their cocoa through neighboring countries, where better prices were offered. Ghana lost its mantle as the world's largest cocoa producer. Its currency reserves depleted, it fell back on barter trade and loans from the Soviet Bloc.

Nkrumah became increasingly remote, preferring to focus on grand schemes of African unity than on running the country. He turned the country into a one-party state in 1964, and took to indulging in a sordid cult of personality, dubbing himself Osagyefo, "the Redeemer." It did not take long for resentment to set in. He evaded several assassination attempts. On January 22, 1966, he inaugurated the Volta Dam, proudly pressing the button that released power into the new national grid—unaware that even this project would be only half a success. Ghana's bauxite mines would never be developed; the smelter found it more economic to process bauxite imported from Jamaica. The inauguration would be his last moment of glory. On February 24, as he stopped in Burma on his way to China at the start of a grand tour aimed at solving the Vietnam conflict, army officers intervened at home and took power. "The myth surrounding Kwame Nkrumah has been broken," announced an army colonel on the radio. Nkrumah did not learn of the coup until he arrived in China. Premier Zhou Enlai, unsure of the protocol to follow, went ahead and hosted an eerie state banquet in his honor. Nkrumah ended up taking up exile in Guinea, where another experiment in "African socialism" was in progress. Guinea's president, Sekou Toure, his own rule increasingly repressive and arbitrary, endowed Nkrumah with the title of "co-president." Nkrumah made regular shortwave broadcasts to Ghana, published ideological treatises, and plotted a triumphal return to power until he grew ill and died in 1972, still in exile. The "political kingdom" had crumbled as fast as it had been built. "The Redeemer," who had once inspired a continent, had fallen far from grace.[10]

"Third Worldism"

Ghana was hardly an exception. In the decade of the 1960s, the high hopes of independence gave way through much of the developing world to a continuing saga of coups and political upheavals. In the process, the optimism of the independence era gave way to an intellectual reformulation that saw North and South—industrial and developing countries—as permanent antagonists. The political struggle for independence was transmuted into a continuing struggle against what was variously described as "economic imperialism" and "neo-imperialism"—and, particularly, against the multinational corporation. Indeed, "exploitation" became the fashionable way to view relations between developed and developing nations. Karl Marx had not said much about the developing world, and what he had said was quite ambiguous. He saw capitalism as a necessary improvement on the "Asiatic mode of production." According to Marx, British imperialism definitely served to modernize "backward" lands like India. Nevertheless, most Marxist theorists, dependency theorists, and many plain liberal theorists propounded the argument that developed nations and the dynamics of international trade and investment exploited developing countries. Strong state control was necessary to protect the developing nation against these forces, and the state company would occupy the high ground formerly held by the foreigner.

The problem of national control was most acute for the great many countries that depended for survival on exports of primary products, whether agricultural—like coffee, rubber, or pineapples—or mineral—like copper and bauxite. The choice seemed to be whether foreign multinationals would capture all the "rents" from these products or whether a national firm could step in. If multinationals found it cheaper to export raw materials than to invest in a processing plant, what hope was there that the producer countries would ever turn their plantations to modern agro-industry? And if multinationals brought economic distortion, not growth, then could the humiliating effects of watching expatriate managers drive new cars and enjoy "hardship pay" be justified any longer? Surely a state-owned company, a national champion, could better represent the national aspirations.

The epiphany for the mixed economy and state domination in the developing world was reached in the late 1960s and 1970s, when the Vietnam War generated a liberal guilt about the entire third world. As opinion shifted against the war and the United States, so it did against the economic system identified with the United States. Markets and capitalism seemed to lose legitimacy. The war was partly blamed on them. National liberation movements aimed not only at defeating pro-Western governments but also at overturning the market and replacing it with state ownership in the name of "the people." Socialism and Marxism enjoyed a renaissance. Capitalism lost confidence in itself, and the young rebelled against it. Moral virtue was to be found in the third world and in its solidarity against the first. All this was part of the loose ideology of "third worldism," which enjoyed a vogue in the developed world in these years. But third worldism also came from the third world itself. As more and more countries acceded to independence, they formed alliances, organizations, and a voting bloc in the United Nations. As early as 1955, at the Bandung Summit in Indonesia, Nehru joined Sukarno of Indonesia, Gamel Abdel Nasser of Egypt, and Josip Broz Tito of Yugoslavia in calling for a "nonaligned movement" to bypass the cold war. Despite differences—and Western skepticism—the movement grew, and through the 1960s, third world countries transacted in economic ideas. By the end of the decade, they too felt ready to assert their identity and their true worth on the world stage.

Good-bye, Coca-Cola

In some ways, all this came to a head on October 6, 1973, when Egypt and Syria launched a massive attack on Israel, starting the Yom Kippur War. For a number of days, Israel's very survival was in doubt, until it finally succeeded in turning the tide. But before the war was over, the Arab oil exporters had used the "oil weapon"—an embargo—to punish the United States and other Western nations for their support of Israel. By the time this first oil crisis had run its course, the price of petroleum had increased fourfold.

It was a climactic event. It accelerated the process of nationalization of oil concessions that had begun before 1973. In 1975 and 1976, the great oil concessions of Saudi Arabia, Kuwait, and Venezuela were all nationalized and integrated under the control of newly established state companies that were now expected to dominate the international oil business. The creation of these companies was meant to put an end not only to the concessions themselves but to the humiliation that went with them, and to capture the bulk of the oil earnings for the nations that produced the oil.

But the oil crisis was also considered to be something much more—a radical shift of power in the international political system. As one eminent foreign policy expert put it, the crisis marked the first time since the Japanese had sunk the entire Russian fleet at the Battle of Tsushima in 1905, ending the Russo-Japanese War, that the third world had defeated the first world. It held out the prospect of a no less radical global redistribution of income from developed to developing nations, thus righting the wrongs of alleged exploitation. Plans were bruited for a variety of other commodity cartels, from copper to bauxite, although, eventually, none was to succeed. Nationalization was on the domestic agenda; only the terms were in question. The world's two largest copper-producing countries nationalized the foreign-owned mines on their soil. Kenneth Kaunda's Zambia nationalized peacefully, paying the British mining firms compensation; but Salvador Allende's Chile did it more abruptly and, in so doing, helped precipitate the government's violent downfall. In India, the Janata Party, in power between 1977 and 1980, expelled foreign firms that refused to share their technology with local champions. IBM packed its bags, as did Coca-Cola—penalized for its refusal to reveal its sacred and jealously guarded formula. Around the world, governments were taking over even greater responsibility for the workings of their economies, while multinational companies and foreign investment were derided as evils to be driven away. This was indeed the apogee for government.

As it turned out, many developing countries were among those worst hit by the oil crisis—the markets and prices for their commodities and manufactures declined with the global recession that followed the quadrupling of the oil price. But this reality was submerged by the spirit of third worldism and the apparent solidarity of South against North in what some were to call an international class war over a "New International Economic Order." Developing nations came together as the Group of 77 in the United Nations. Their argument, supported by the Soviet Union, was that, as commodity exporters, they had been exploited by the industrial countries through the low prices paid for their products. Not only, they said, should the developed countries pay higher prices, they should also pay compensatory reparations. In order to mitigate the North-South confrontation, a North-South Dialogue convened in Paris in 1977. It was intended to redistribute income, protect commodity prices, ensure "control," and accelerate the flow of technology. It was also meant to defuse tensions. Despite two years of tractations, there was not much to show for it; at the end, the conferees could not even agree on a communiqué.

The End of an Idea

Yet underneath the rhetoric and expressions of solidarity was the dawning realization of a gnawing, uncomfortable fact. To be sure, the sometimes violent ups and downs of world markets stood to harm the economic programs of developing nations. But the problem, it now appeared, was also internal. In many of the countries of Latin America, Africa, and South Asia, ordinary people were not getting better off. State-led development was falling far short of its promise; corruption and the waste from dubious investments were all too common. And mysteriously, several countries in Asia, which were notoriously poor in natural resources and dependent on imported oil, appeared to have weathered the storm and embarked on an impressive path of growth. All this suggested that commodity prices and world markets were only a part of a problem that, in fact, began at home.

Politics had also degraded in most of the developing countries. On three continents, elected governments had all too often given way to authoritarian ones. Most countries of South America were under military rule by the late 1970s. Notorious autocrats emerged to plunder national resources in increasingly brash and blatant fashion. In the Philippines, Ferdinand Marcos diverted national wealth into private coffers, bankrolling a lavish lifestyle for his family and cronies. Under the guise of economic nationalism, Idi Amin Dada in Uganda expelled and expropriated the Indian traders who were vital to the domestic economy. Mobutu Sese Seko changed the name of the Congo to Zaire and financed extravagant expenses by stealing foreign aid and printing money, making the currency worthless and forcing trade into the parallel economy.

The damage was greatest to ordinary people. Unable to profit from the pervasive reach of the state sector, they suffered from shortages, decaying infrastructure, bureaucratic harassment, petty corruption, and the continual postponement of promised improvements. One of the greatest indictments was the decreasing ability of some agricultural countries to feed themselves. In the late 1970s, it was hard to draw precise links among world markets, state domination of the economy, corruption, poverty, and political decay. But one thing was certain. The hope of the development economists—born out of the cataclysm of World War II and mass poverty in the developing world—that "all good things go together" had come undone, tolling the end of an idea.

Looking back on all the hopes of progress, the eminent economist Sir Arthur Lewis asked himself what fundamental errors development had made. He identified two basic mistakes, each of which had proved very costly. One, he said, was the underestimation of the power of international trade to propel growth. The other, he continued, was being too slow to learn that "market prices are more powerful incentives than ministerial speeches." [11]

CHAPTER 4

THE MAD MONK

Britain's Market Revolution

IT WAS ONE of the shorter emigrations on record. David Young was a businessman, self-made and very successful until the London real estate market collapsed in 1972, virtually wiping him out. By 1975, he had just about dug himself out of the financial rubble. Still, he was increasingly dissatisfied with life in Britain. It was not only that he had to go out of his way to avoid letting people know he was an entrepreneur, although that certainly was a problem. "It was not socially acceptable to work for oneself," he later recalled. "People worked for *big* companies."

What was really driving him to despair was the state of Britain itself. The country appeared to be locked into descent and decay. Indeed, it seemed to be falling apart. Inflation was running at 24 percent. The trade unions had just brought down the Conservative government of Edward Heath. Constant strikes gave unions a stranglehold on the economy and immobilized the nation. Marginal tax rates were high—up to 98 percent—destroying incentives. Britain was well along the road, people feared, to becoming the East Germany of the Western world, a corporatist state, ground down to a gray mediocrity, and one in which any kind of initiative was regarded as pathological behavior, to be stamped out. Young had had enough. He told his wife they were going to leave Britain; they were going to emigrate. Their destination—America.

Young and his wife arrived in Boston at the beginning of a weekend and checked into the Ritz-Carlton, which looks out on Boston's Public Garden. On Sunday morning, they awoke in their hotel room to the sound of sirens. Later, they set off on a walk across Boston Common. Soon there were tears in their eyes—not, however, in sadness for the country and way of life they had left behind. Rather, it was the result of tear gas, loosed by police to break up a riot arising from court-enforced busing of school children. "You must be out of your mind," his wife said to him as they rubbed their eyes with handkerchiefs. "You're crazy if you think I'm going to give up my family for this."

That very night they took a plane back to London. On the return journey, Young said to himself that there ought to be something more he could do than despair and depart. That meant politics. He had been a Labour voter until disappointed by Prime Minister Harold Wilson after 1964. Margaret Thatcher had just been elected Leader of the Conservative Party, and she appeared to have some new ideas about the dismal British economy. But could a woman become prime minister? Like many others, Young was doubtful.

Then, over the next several weeks, he started to read the speeches of a British politician named Keith Joseph. Later, others would call Joseph the "Mad Monk". Joseph would describe himself not much differently—as "a convenient madman." He talked about such things as enterprise, initiative, and the need for entrepreneurship. There was nothing wrong with starting a business, said Joseph; in fact, it was entrepreneurs who created the wealth for society. Joseph's words were completely at odds with the dominant opinion of the day, but they struck a most responsive chord in David Young. He was impressed. At a charity lunch, he went out of his way to introduce himself to Joseph, and to volunteer his services. "But you don't *believe*," responded Joseph. Young took that as a challenge and threw himself into the cause, becoming one of the circle intent on reconstructing economic and political thought in Britain. Joseph was the man at the center. As Young later put it, "Keith Joseph was the architect of the whole thing." [1]

"My Closest Political Friend"

The "whole thing" would eventually extend far beyond Britain's borders. But arguably, Joseph did as much as any other single person around the world to reshape the debate about government and marketplace, to take a variety of ideas and bind them together into a powerful critique of the mixed economy and, in the course of things, help shape them into a political program. That agenda, in turn, was articulated and put into effect by his most important student, Margaret Thatcher. She made the ideas "happen." But it was Joseph who created the package over half a decade, in the second half of the 1970s, at a time when the premises of the mixed economy were hardly questioned and yet the system itself was running into such severe difficulties as to become dysfunctional. Just as the Attlee consensus of the 1940s had become the "text" for governments and politicians for more than three decades following, so what began around the seminar tables in research institutes in the 1970s and took shape in the Thatcher program of the 1980s would do much to set the global agenda for the 1990s. Keith Joseph's name is hardly as well known as Margaret Thatcher's. But she would give him full credit. "I could not have become Leader of the Opposition, or achieved what I did as Prime Minister, without Keith," she said. And, she would add, Joseph was "my closest political friend."

It may well be said in retrospect that the combination of high inflation, slow growth, labor conflict, and social discontent in the 1970s meant that some kind of basic change was imminent. In the mid-1970s, Lord Blake, biographer of Disraeli and historian of the Conservative Party, was so bold as to write, "There are signs of one of those rare and profound changes in the intellectual climate which occur only once or twice in a hundred years. . . . There is a wind of change in Britain and much of the democratic world —and it comes from the right, not the left." It was a daring prediction to make at the time, but Blake turned out to be correct.

Yet the balance among ideas does not just change on its own account. Events, crises, failures—these drive the shift, forcing reconsideration of seemingly unchallengeable assumptions. That is what happened in the 1970s. "A kind of torpid socialism had become the conventional wisdom of Britain," wrote Margaret Thatcher. "The succession of crises—economic, fiscal and industrial—under Labour constantly invited us to think thoughts and propose policies that deviated from both the conventional wisdom . . . and the agreed line." But at such a time there must also be people who are willing and able to press for the reconsideration. And that is what Keith Joseph did.[2]

"The Minister of Thought"

Joseph was the instigator perhaps because he was part politician, part intellectual, part entrepreneur of ideas. Indeed, he had the enthusiast's belief in ideas. He had grown up in considerable comfort. His father, Sir Samuel Joseph, a baronet, headed the family firm, Bovis, one of the biggest construction companies in the country, and also served a term as lord mayor of London. Keith Joseph graduated from Oxford on the eve of World War II. Unlike that of many of his contemporaries, his undergraduate preoccupation was neither studies nor politics but cricket. He came back from the war intent on catching up on the six years he had spent as a soldier. He also came back Sir Keith, owing to the death of his father. Joseph's academic record, despite his interest in cricket, had been good, and he was offered a job teaching law at Oxford, but turned it down. Yet, still attracted to intellectual life, he succeeded in becoming a fellow of All Souls College at Oxford, one of the paragons of British scholarship. But practical life also attracted him. Even while laboring away many nights on his thesis for All Souls—on the subject of tolerance—he was busy laboring during the day, digging holes at building sites for the family firm. He gave up both for politics, beginning with his father's old seat as an alderman in the City of London. Like Clement

Attlee, he was deeply moved by the poverty and distress of the East End and powerfully motivated by compassion and a drive for betterment and social reform, and he threw himself into a wide variety of charities. He was especially devoted to one that assisted middle-aged single women whom the world had passed by because they had stayed home to care for infirm parents. In this particular course, he became a fervent advocate of marriage bureaus.

Elected to Parliament as a Conservative in 1956 at age thirty-eight, Joseph delivered a maiden speech that contained the germ of the ideas that he would be promoting two decades later. The cure for inflation, he argued, was to be found not in controlling demand but rather "by increasing supply." Corporate management, he added, must have its "proper rewards." The 1930s were not necessarily the guide to the future. The "nightmare" of unemployment was a "totally unjustified fear," for "we live in an expanding age." He became a junior minister in Harold Macmillan's government, although he never quite got used to the body blows of parliamentary debate. After his first front-bench speech, Macmillan complimented him on the performance, but added, "If it's any consolation, it will get worse."

Joseph was given to what sometimes seemed to be endless agonizing as well as self-criticism. He was also slightly unworldly. He refused to have a television in his house. Once, dissatisfied with a live television interview that he had just done, he asked to do it over. "I thought you realized, Sir Keith," said the producer, "that this was to be a live interview." "Yes, I know that," said Joseph. "That's why I want to do it again." His odd obsession with ideas was soon evident to his colleagues. Some would eventually conclude that there could be no better post for him than as "Minister of Thought." [3]

The "U-Turn"

Alas, no such job existed in reality; and as it turned out, when Edward Heath became prime minister in 1970, he made Joseph the minister in charge of social services. The Tories had won by a big majority, in response to how poorly the economy had performed under Labour. The mixed economy was severely malfunctioning. The wisdom and knowledge implied in a high degree of government control were proving inadequate to the reality. Inflation was high—7 percent—as were interest rates. Unemployment was also high, and rising; the welfare state and the loss-making nationalized industries were demonstrating a voracious appetite for taxpayer funds; and the costs of the national health system were increasing rapidly, reflecting what appeared to be the "infinity of demand" and the lack of any mechanism for discipline. Labor relations had turned into constant warfare, chronically disrupting society and the economy. The balance of payments was in perpetual crisis; the pound, under constant pressure, and British industry simply could not compete internationally. The entire country chafed under the onerous tax burden that was destroying the incentive to work and driving entrepreneurial people into tax exile. The high tax rates also hit hard those with modest incomes. One of the ministers in the last Labour government had noted that even trade unionists—a group traditionally supportive of tax-and-spend policies—were complaining about having so much of their wages go to taxes. They wanted "more half crowns jingling around in their pockets."

Edward Heath had promised to turn all this around. But it didn't happen that way. Heath was not, by any means, a Tory paternalist. His origins were humble; his father had been a small contractor. Heath called for modernization and competition. But he also believed in the state and in its responsibilities and its interventionist role in the economy. He wanted to manage the system better rather than change it. The Heath government was, in many ways, parallel to the contemporaneous Nixon administration. Both came in as conservative governments intent on reducing state intervention; both ended up expanding it. In Heath's case, it came to be known as his famous "U-turn." Like Nixon, Heath embraced Keynesianism, along with planning and social engineering. Just as Nixon had imposed wage-and-price controls, so Heath sought to impose the most rigid and comprehensive wage-and-dividend-control system that Britain had ever seen. In one extreme example, the minister for trade and consumer affairs even found himself personally telephoning the vicar of Trumpington, near Cambridge, asking him, in accord with the Prices and Incomes Act, not to increase the fee for burials. The public sector swelled under Heath, and his government embarked on a loose monetary policy in a "dash for growth." Unfortunately, that dash ended up doing much more for inflation than for growth. Government's share of ownership of the economy actually increased; the only government-owned enterprises that Heath got around to privatizing were some pubs in the north of England and a travel agency.[4]

Things fell even further apart in 1973 and 1974. The 1973 oil crisis hit Britain very hard and was immediately made worse by a coal miners' strike that turned into a pitched battle. Coal and power supplies were so disrupted that British industry could work only three days a week. Travelers returning from abroad found a nation living in darkness, owing to the power cuts. Families had to dine and find their way to bed by candlelight. Clergymen debated on the BBC's Radio Four whether families should share their warm bathwater to conserve energy. One cabinet minister went on television to advise people on how to shave in the dark. Heath declared a state of emergency. Inflation hit 15 percent. In a desperate effort to win a mandate, Heath called a snap election. He lost. The blunt fact was that the coal miners had brought down a government. No party won an absolute majority, and so a minority Labour government took power, led by former prime minister Harold Wilson.

The "Conversion" of Keith Joseph

In this dismal period, confronted by the crisis, angry at his party and himself, and convinced that Britain was locked into a destructive downward spiral, Keith Joseph experienced what he called his "conversion" to conservatism. "I had thought I was a Conservative," he remarked, "but I now see that I was not one at all." The problem, he concluded, was not that government was not doing well; it was that it was trying to do too much. And the source of the problem was the postwar consensus, with its promotion of the interventionist state. The enemy was "statism." What had to be changed was the political culture of the country, and the way to do it was through intellectual guerrilla warfare.

With the Tories now consigned to opposition, Joseph tried to force a postmortem in the leadership on what had gone wrong with the policies of the Heath government. But from Heath, he got only a stiff back of the hand. "The main conclusion," Heath told his colleagues in the shadow cabinet, "is that our policies were right but that we didn't persist in them long enough." Sir Keith's eyebrows shot up at that statement. Margaret Thatcher, who had been minister of education in the Heath government, showed no expression.

"I was more and more concerned," Joseph later explained. "Put it down to a mixture of impatience with our slow progress and envy of our neighbors. I never focused on America—I thought they were outside our culture and our reach—but our ruddy neighbors. Why should they do so much better, particularly when they had been prostrate and flat on their back after the war?"

To begin with, Joseph turned up on the doorstep of a right-of-center think tank, the Institute of Economic Affairs (IEA), which had become the island of liberal economic thinking in the midst of Britain's Keynesian consensus. Indeed, the Institute—once described as a "confounded nuisance" and originally funded by a farmer who had made a fortune from mass-producing chickens—revived traditional liberalism in Britain. Its head was Ralph Harris, who came from working-class roots in London. He taught economics at St. Andrews University and then wrote editorials for *The Glasgow Herald* until recruited to run the Institute, which was once presented to him as "an anti-Fabian society." Harris was more than receptive. He looked back to the Macmillan government and criticized it for congealing into a "Keynesian-collectivist mold." It was because of those policies, he once explained, that he had chosen the path of "radical reaction" and "started up" the IEA. His partner in building the new institute was Arthur Seldon, also of working-class origins, who had studied liberal economics at the London School of Economics. Seldon shaped the research program. Together, the two ran the IEA until the middle 1980s.

In its early days, the Institute battled against the *dirigiste* indicative planning that, owing to the French, had become so fashionable in the late

1950s. In due course, it aimed its analysis at all the shibboleths of the day—from the unfettered welfare state and union power to Keynesian demand management, nationalized industries, and the growth of the state sector. Altogether, waging the "trench warfare of the footnotes," it delivered a rigorous and thoroughgoing critique of the mixed economy. It even presented a detailed comparison of the American and British phone systems that went so far as to suggest that Britain would be better off with private phone companies instead of having its telephones and service provided by a branch of the post office. One theme underpinned its entire research program: that economists, politicians, and policy makers had promised too much—much more than they could actually control or deliver. As economist Alan Walters put it, the "real thrust of the counter-revolution" was the acknowledgment "that we know little about the forces that determine detailed economic conditions . . . such as prices and employment, exports and imports, output and productivity, savings and investment." Many highly regarded economists published under its mantle, including Colin Clark, who had done the original national income studies for Keynes.

In particular, the IEA provided a platform for two economists, both initially seen as fringe figures during the years when the Institute, in Margaret Thatcher's words, seemed to be "bashing" its head "against a brick wall," but who would go on to have enormous influence. One was Friedrich von Hayek, the most prominent exponent of the free-market "Austrian School" of economics in Britain. An early critic of Keynes, Hayek now renewed his assault, calling for a shift back from Keynesian macroeconomics and the world of the multiplier to microeconomics and the world of the firm, where wealth was actually generated. The other was Milton Friedman of the University of Chicago, whose monetarist theories the IEA propagated in Britain. For the IEA, Hayek's and Friedman's Nobel Prizes—in 1974 and 1976, respectively—would be sweet vindication. This recognition came just at the right time, for the "demand" for such ideas was high and the IEA had delineated the agenda. "Without the IEA," Milton Friedman later said, "I doubt very much whether there would have been a Thatcherite revolution."

Keith Joseph had sporadically worked with the Institute since the 1960s. Now, in 1974, anxious to begin anew, he asked Ralph Harris, the Institute's director, for instruction and help. He wanted books, reading lists, critiques, and articles to educate himself. He absorbed it all.

Next, he established his own institute, the Centre for Policy Studies. Although Joseph saw the Fabian socialists as the originators of Britain's ills, he modeled his strategy on that of the Fabians—to change culture and politics by influencing opinion makers. To differentiate it from the IEA, which was academic in its orientation, Joseph set up the Centre to achieve a very specific political objective. As he later explained, "My aim was to convert the Tory Party." He recruited another MP to be his vice-chairman —the member for Finchley, Margaret Thatcher. Because of their political connections, it was necessary for them to obtain Heath's approval for the new institute. Although suspicious of Joseph, Heath gave it, assuming that it would be good if the two of them actually learned something about both business and the economies of other countries. That should be enough to keep them out of his way. Some have speculated that he had a further reason for assenting: "Heath's intention must have been to give Joseph a chemistry set with which he would hopefully blow himself up." [5]

But what was the Centre to do? At the first board meeting, the directors could identify only one specific thing—Sir Keith should make speeches. Many speeches. Soon enough, however, the Centre developed its program. "Our job was to question the unquestioned," said Alfred Sherman, the Centre's director of studies and Joseph's intellectual partner during this period, "think the unthinkable, blaze new trails." The Centre developed, promoted, and sponsored a flood of ideas through an outpouring of books, pamphlets, seminars, dinners, and luncheons.

Now it was Joseph's turn to hand out reading lists. Among those to whom he provided such lists was his vice-chairman, Margaret Thatcher. And right at the top of the list was Friedrich von Hayek's *The Road to Serfdom*. She had read it as an undergraduate, but now she carefully reread it with a new comprehension. Published in 1944, *The Road to Serfdom* was the seminal work for the liberal critique—in the traditional sense—of the welfare state, the mixed economy, and "collectivism." It was the bible of Joseph and his coterie.

The Centre's aim was, in Joseph's words, to expose the "inherent contradictions" of the mixed economy. The enemy was "thirty years of socialistic fashions" and "statism"—three decades of looking to government to solve problems and run the economy. As Joseph and his partners saw it, this consensus was already turning Britain into the poor man of Europe. Equality for equality's sake meant poverty. What had to be stimulated was risk taking, with its attendant rewards for success and penalties for failure. "Wealth creation" became one of Joseph's favorite phrases, but the goal was wealth creation for society, not for individuals. Permitting individuals to make money and build up assets was, however, the necessary precondition. In Joseph's view, politics had remained too long in thrall to the 1930s and mass unemployment. He had said so in 1956 in his first parliamentary speech. He believed it even more fervently now. The objective should be the generation of wealth, not the subsidizing of employment.

Joseph and his colleagues knew that they were starting out from a minuscule minority position; they fretted and worried about even using the phrase *market economy,* for fear that such an utterance might brand them to the right of Attila the Hun. The world, they decided, was certainly not ready for a term so extreme as *market economy,* although that would become the commonplace term of the 1990s. They did talk about capitalism. But it was "compassionate capitalism." [6]

The Leadership Battle

All that was the intellectual agenda. But reading lists were not enough. There was also a political agenda. Edward Heath would have to go. He was too much a pragmatist, too much a compromiser and middle-of-the-road man. He had once denounced the activities of one company as "the unacceptable face of capitalism," but to many, that phrase had come to denote an ambivalent attitude on his part toward the market system overall. Worse, owing to the current crises, he wanted to move further to the center-left and establish a coalition government of national unity—to be led, of course, by himself. Harold Wilson called a second election in 1974, this time winning an absolute majority. Surely Heath would now depart. But he was stubborn, and showed no sign of giving up the party leadership. Keith Joseph was seen as one of the leading challengers. It was not at all clear, however, that he had the burning ambition to be, as he put it, "out front."

Then, Joseph unexpectedly created a storm of protest with a controversial speech asking whether poor, unmarried single girls really should become mothers in such record numbers. It was likely to be bad for the country. He advocated birth control. Ironically, he had based his argument on the work of left-wing sociologists. But he was accused of being a racist and an advocate of eugenics. The press camped on his doorstep, bombarding him and his family with rude and hostile questions. The attacks shook him deeply. Disregarding the political adage "never apologize," he published a letter in *The Times* that ran more than a column in length, explaining how he had been misinterpreted. It was to no avail. The attacks continued. He agonized over whether to challenge Heath directly.

One afternoon he appeared in the parliamentary office of his unofficial campaign manager for the leadership, Margaret Thatcher. "I am sorry," he said. "I just can't run. Ever since I made that speech, the press has been outside the house. They have been merciless. My wife can't take it," he continued, "and I have decided I just can't stand."

Thatcher was in despair. They couldn't surrender to Heath's "brand of politics." She was ambitious; of that there was no question. But the highest dream she had ever allowed herself was that of being chancellor of the exchequer. Yet she heard herself replying, "Look, Keith, if you're not going to stand, I will."

That night she told her husband of her plan. His initial reaction suggested that he was not exactly persuaded. "You must be out of your mind," he said. "You haven't got a hope." She was not at all sure that he was wrong. But a few days later she went to see Heath. "I must tell you that I have decided to stand for the leadership," she said. His response was cold. He did not try to convince her otherwise. Instead, he turned his back and, with a shrug, said only, "If you must."

She had no doubt that she must, and she did. Heath was clearly expected to be reelected Leader. Thatcher's chances were discounted. One of the confident few was her campaign manager, Airey Neave, who had helped organize the famous escape from the Nazi prison camp at Colditz during World War II. He knew how to organize, and he privately prophesied, "My filly is going to win." And, in an upset, she did, defeating a stunned Heath and becoming Leader of the Opposition.

Thatcher was more steeled than Joseph to critics and the press. She found herself constantly under assault. The attacks came not only from the left, from outside, but also from within her own party, from Heath's men and the High Tory paternalists. The grocer's daughter was accused of promoting the hoarding of canned food and was charged with doing so herself. And then it was even reported that she had been sighted cleaning out a store in north London of large quantities of sugar, which at the time was in short supply. No matter that the reported "store" did not exist and that her family's consumption of sugar was minimal. Moreover, it was most unlikely that a male politician would have been charged with the high crime of secretly shopping for bags of sugar. But Thatcher was not going to give way. "I saw how they destroyed Keith," she told a friend. "Well, they're not going to destroy me."

For his part, Joseph had come very close to grasping the brass ring, but he had no regrets. "You see," he explained, "there's such a thing as instinct, and Mrs. Thatcher has a lot of instinct and flair and I don't, and nobody who knows me would think I had." Joseph was, however, hardly far from power. He was number three in the Opposition hierarchy, in charge of policy and research. He had indeed become the de facto shadow minister of thought, engaged full-time in "the battle of ideas." [7]

"No Time to be Mealy-mouthed"

What both Margaret Thatcher and Keith Joseph sought was conviction politics, not consensus politics. "This is no time to be mealy-mouthed," Joseph declared. And he was the one who would speak up the loudest. Over the next few years, he talked his way from one end of the country to the other, delivering a set of speeches that, in Thatcher's view, "fundamentally affected a political generation's way of thinking." Indeed, much of what later would be called Thatcherism was to be found in those speeches. With them, Joseph had embarked on a grand cause, a campaign to "reverse the trend" of collectivism, as he put it. He set out to challenge the entire consensus upon which the mixed economy rested. His key premise was that the focus should be on the control of inflation through a stable money supply, not full employment through Keynesian demand management. Although the statism that had grown up since World War II was "well-intentioned" and undertaken out of good motives, that did not make it any less wrong or less harmful. The outcome was still a lower standard of living. Incentives had to be restored. "We are over-governed, over-spent, over-taxed, over-borrowed and over-manned," he declared. If the trend was not reversed, he warned, "we shall experience accelerated worsening of job prospects, the growing flight of those with professional skills, talent and ability to other countries, and an increase in the shabbiness and squalor of everyday lives."

The critical intellectual revision was the rejection of the Keynesian commitment to full employment, which was seen as the fundamental error. If that was indeed wrong—and Joseph and his allies thought it was—then there was no longer a salutary "macroeconomic function" to public spending. Such being the case, government spending could and should be reduced, permitting taxes to be cut, and thus providing the real salutary contribution by enhancing the "supply side" of the economy—the side that Joseph had celebrated in his first speech in Parliament in 1956.[8]

· Joseph's campaign included more than 150 speeches at universities and colleges. He spoke to big audiences and small. He was often heckled, sometimes physically attacked, often boycotted. The students tried to ban him from speaking at the London School of Economics. Even when he was speaking, notices were put up saying that the meeting had been canceled, in order to discourage attendance. Yet he enjoyed this part of the campaign more than anything else—at least in retrospect. "It was lovely. Of course it was horrible at the time." These were the audiences that he most wanted to convert—"almost to a girl or boy convinced statists if not socialists." What he talked about was completely foreign to their education—almost, indeed, to their upbringing. One of the students in the audience at an Oxford speech recalled "going to a packed lecture hall to hear Sir Keith Joseph talk about free markets, about monetarism and the perils of corporatism . . . they were the sort of things that a rather respectable parent would warn his son against; the sort of thing that an ambitious tutor would be worried about if his students started flirting with."

Joseph argued that the entire thrust of postwar economic policy had been based upon miscomprehension. "Our post-war boom began under the shadow of the 1930s. We were haunted by the fear of long-term mass unemployment, the grim, hopeless dole queues and towns which died. So we talked ourselves into believing that these gaunt, tight-lipped men in caps and mufflers were round the corner, and tailored our policies to match these imaginary conditions. For imaginary is what they were."

He spoke the unspeakable. He said that people who take responsibility and risk and make money are doing society a favor. "The private sector, the indispensable base on which all else is built, is under attack. . . . Yet we discourage those who make it work. . . . The worker on his own cannot create wealth. We need the wealth-creating, job-creating entrepreneur and the wealth-creating, job-creating manager. We treat them very badly." He invented a term for those who promote economic growth—the "ulcer people," he called them, appropriately enough for someone like himself who had a bad stomach. "They have insecurity and worry. They are meant to take risks. . . . They deserve a chance of reward."

Joseph had no doubt that he shocked his university audiences. "I'm sure they had never heard the moral case for capitalism. . . . What I always said was that it was a jolly imperfect world, and all I was saying was that capitalism was the least bad way yet invented—as Churchill said about democracy." He warned that the incessant, single-minded drive for equality of result would result in a leveling and more general poverty. Again and again, he said something particularly shocking—"What Britain needs is more millionaires and more bankrupts." Greater risks and greater rewards were necessary to achieve a higher standard of living and greater prosperity. He was not, however, he emphasized, saying that the state had no role. "I am not defending a free-for-all. The state must act to make and enforce rules to ensure the security of human life, protection against force and fraud and protection of those values and standards—social, economic, ecological—which represent the accumulated and current aspirations of our community."

At the end of his speeches, Joseph would ask the students which country ran its affairs better than Britain. It was usually the same list—Cuba, China, Yugoslavia. Over time, as the truth was revealed about those countries, the questions were met with silence. At one of the last meetings, after a pause one heckler finally came up with an answer. The Paris Commune of 1871—which had lasted just three months.[9]

"There Are No Trains Today"

Joseph, as the "shadow minister of thought," constantly questioning others and himself, filling his notebooks and then pumping out ideas, became something of a figure of fun. He appeared to be a political Don Quixote, crisscrossing the country to tilt against this windmill and then that. Could he be taken seriously? After all, wasn't he, really, when you came right down to it, beyond the fringe? *The Economist,* at that point very much part of the mixed-economy consensus, could not resist lambasting the Mad Monk. "The trouble Sir Keith takes to leave no confusions undispersed, no misunderstandings of his pronouncements unexplained, has become well known ever since . . . he was lumbered with the roving job of refining, redefining—or re-somethinging—Conservatism. . . . A political sage must be clever as well as holy." Joseph tried to set *The Economist* straight, writing the magazine that his advocacies had arisen "from critical re-examination of local orthodoxies in the light of our own bitter experiences in the early 1970s . . . we are practical people who judge ideas and policies by results."

He carried the same messages into parliamentary debates. A journalist captured him giving a speech: "He crouches—festooned with his own copious notes and with such additional artillery as cuttings from the City pages, pamphlets from various right-wing institutes and study groups, the bulky report of some American midwestern university seminar on Was Keynes a Monetarist? As he speaks, the veins are prominent on the forehead, the brows are coiled, the eyes are half-closed with concentration. The whole head comes to resemble an over-wound-up alarm clock about to go off or burst its springs. . . . He will either be speaking once more about the efficacy of free enterprise, before the glazed or baffled stares of Shadow Cabinet colleagues. Or he will be rebutting some inane intervention about Chile . . . while he is saying that capitalism is crucial to political freedom . . . a necessary, but not a sufficient, condition of freedom. After which the world will go its way with everyone believing what they did before."

Not quite, for Joseph's message was finding more and more resonance. Britain had continued its downward spiral. Was this the best that Keynesian-ism, fine-tuning, and state intervention could deliver? The entire country was on the dole, forced to borrow money from the International Monetary Fund in 1976 in order to protect the pound and stay afloat. As a condition of its loan, the IMF required sizable cuts in public expenditures, setting off a bitter rebellion in the Labour Party. Labour prime minister James Callaghan, who had succeeded Harold Wilson, risked further rebellion by supporting plant closures and labor force reductions at state-owned companies. He also rejected a basic Keynesian full-employment tenet. Deficit spending, he said, would not increase employment. "For too long," he told the annual Labour Party conference, "we postponed facing up to fundamental choices and fundamental changes in our society and our economy . . . we have been living on borrowed time. The cozy world we were told would go on forever, where full employment would be guaranteed at the stroke of the Chancellor's pen . . . that cozy world is gone. . . . We used to think that you could just spend your way out of a recession to increase employment by cutting taxes and boosting Government spending . . . that option no longer exists and . . . insofar as it ever did, it worked by injecting inflation into the economy." If Callaghan's speech sounded more like the Institute of Economic Affairs than the traditional Labour Party, there was good reason. One of the speech's chief authors was Callaghan's son-in-law Peter Jay, economist and journalist, who, among other things, had written several IEA pamphlets.

By the end of 1978, the country was again in crisis, yet another "winter of discontent," as public-sector employees struck. Hospital workers went out, and medical care had to be severely rationed. Garbage was piling up in the streets. Striking grave diggers refused to bury the dead. The truck drivers were on strike, too. Only shop stewards had the right to let trucks bearing "essential supplies" cross picket lines. British Rail put out a terse notice: "There are no trains today." In 1974, the coal miners had brought down the government; now striking unions seemed about to bring the whole nation to a halt. Callaghan contemplated declaring a state of emergency, as Heath had done in 1974. Something was very badly wrong.

On March 28, 1979, a day when even the catering staff at the House of

Commons was on strike, the Labour government fell on a vote of no confidence—losing by just one vote. Callaghan had no choice but to call a general election. He knew well that the bitter circumstances would turn the election into a referendum on the mixed economy. Toward the very end of the campaign, as he drove from Parliament back to 10 Downing Street, one of his aides began explaining how Labour might just squeak through. "I should not be too sure," Callaghan replied quietly. "You know there are times, perhaps once every thirty years, when there is a sea-change in politics . . . I suspect that there is now such a sea-change—and it is for Mrs. Thatcher." [10]

"Now for the Real Battle"

The Conservatives won the general election of 1979, and Margaret Thatcher became prime minister. "We are over the first hurdle," she wrote to one of her confidants. "Now for the real battle." Joseph may well have been the leading promulgator of the ideas, but it was up to Thatcher to implement them. And in so doing she would be the only prime minister of the twentieth century "whose name has become synonymous with a political philosophy."

She was born Margaret Roberts in 1925, and the roots of both her political career and her fundamental ideas went back to her childhood. "At heart, Margaret Thatcher was an extremely bright, lower middle class girl from the Midlands," explained one of her cabinet ministers. "She believed in hard work, achievement, and that everything had to be paid for. If you don't have the money, you don't get it." She was the daughter of a grocery store owner and local political activist in the Midlands town of Grantham. Alfred Roberts had wanted to be a teacher, but owing to the modest finances of his family, he had been forced to leave school at age thirteen to go to work. He saved his pennies and in due course graduated to owning two grocery stores. He was an autodidact, very much self-taught, and one of the very best customers of the local public library. He also was much more interested in local politics than in groceries.

Alfred Roberts was the most important influence on his daughter. "I owe almost everything to my father," she said. Later, she added that she owed him "integrity. He taught me that you first sort out what you believe in. You then apply it. You don't compromise on things that matter." It was he who imparted to her the homilies and examples—about hard work, self-reliance, thrift, duty, and standing by your convictions even when in a minority—that she was proud to cite when prime minister. He told her that it was not enough to be a "starter." You also had to be a "sticker" and "see it through." "Some say I preach merely the homilies of housekeeping or the parables of the parlour," she said in 1982. "But I do not repent. Those parables would have saved many a financier from failure and many a country from crisis." She was also shaped by the family's commitment to Methodism. On Sundays, she was in church two or three times a day. The family's life was simple, even spare. There were few toys, and they lived above the shop. Politics, she would observe, was the best and most exciting part of her father's life, and politics was what Alfred Roberts talked about with his daughter. Along with the homilies, he also imparted to her the lasting passion for politics. The first time she worked in a campaign was when she was ten.

She went up to Oxford University, where she studied chemistry, although without much conviction. Politics was what compelled her. She ended up president of the Oxford University Conservative Association (although she did not debate in the Oxford Union because women were not yet permitted to join). She had settled on politics as her career. In 1945, she went back to Grantham to campaign for the conservative candidate. "The presence of a young woman of the age of 19," reported the *Grantham Journal*, "with such decided convictions, has been no small factor." Her university years were during World War II, and she came to maturity with an unembarrassed, unabashed patriotism that never left her. The war, not the Depression, was her formative experience.

After graduating, she took a job as a research chemist in a plastics factory and then in the research department of the J. Lyons food company, testing cake fillings and ice creams. She had no great interest in being a scientist, but she was determined to support herself away from home. What she really wanted was to be adopted by a parliamentary constituency. She would later acknowledge that she owed the Labour Party one debt. The Labour government raised the salaries of MPs from six hundred pounds a year to a thousand. "From that moment on," she recalled, "it became possible to think in terms of a political career." [11]

She was given a constituency in the southeast of England that traditionally voted a strong Labour majority. She lost. No one had expected otherwise, and she was very pleased to have had her first shot at Parliament. On the night of her adoption for the seat, she happened to meet a businessman named Denis Thatcher, who ran a family paint and chemical company. They were both interested in politics. And, as she put it, "his professional interest in paint and mine in plastics" gave them further topics of conversation, as "unromantic" a foundation as that might have seemed.

They were married in 1951. Having had her fill of chemistry and cake fillings, she studied for the bar and became a lawyer, specializing in patents and tax. She had already achieved some prominence as a young Tory woman. In 1952, she wrote an article for a Sunday newspaper saying that women should not necessarily feel that they had to stay at home. They could pursue careers—including in Parliament, where there were only seventeen female MPs out of 625. And there was no reason not to shoot high, even in Parliament. "Should a woman arise equal to the task, I say let her have an equal chance with the men for the leading Cabinet posts. Why not a woman

Chancellor? Or Foreign Secretary?" In 1959, she was elected to Parliament. She had reached the first rung.

"The natural path to promotion and success at this time," she was to recall, "lay in the center of politics and on the left of the Conservative Party. Above all, the up-and-coming Tory politician had to avoid being 'reactionary.' " Prime Minister Harold Macmillan epitomized it all. He had been greatly affected by the unemployment and despair he had seen in his constituency at Stockton-on-Trent in the 1930s and had advocated Keynesianism and planning almost from the first. Described as a kind of "New Deal Conservative," he had seen it as his duty to embed the Tory Party firmly in the postwar consensus; and he embraced the welfare state, full employment, and planning—all of which he saw as the "middle way" between the old liberalism, on one side, and socialism and totalitarianism, on the other. His family firm, Macmillans, had published Keynes' most important works. Macmillan's book, *The Middle Way,* was regarded in the late 1930s as the clearest political exposition of Keynesianism, and Macmillan was strongly influenced by Keynes and Keynesianism throughout his political career. In his years as prime minister from 1956 to 1963, he worried much more about unemployment than inflation. "Inflation ran at about $2\frac{1}{2}$ percent a year," he later explained, "which is what Keynes always said to me was about right. . . . Nobody would notice."

Margaret Thatcher subscribed to what she called "the prevailing orthodoxy" and moved further up the rungs. In 1961, Macmillan made her a junior minister, and she dutifully followed him as well as his successor, Alec Douglas-Home (who suffered merciless caricature in the press because he had once remarked that he worked out economics problems with matchsticks). Then, as part of Edward Heath's team, she became education minister when he led the Conservative Party to victory in 1970. It was only in 1974 that she and Keith Joseph broke with Heath and the mainstream—amid the economic and social crises, electoral defeat, and the struggle over the leadership. But she had already been much influenced by the Institute of Economic Affairs, with which she had worked since the 1960s.

As Leader of the Opposition from 1974 onward, she left no doubt that she was also one of the Conservative Party's most committed free marketers. In the mid-1970s, not long after becoming Leader, she visited the Conservative Party's research department. One of the staff was partway through his paper advocating that the Tories adopt a middle way between left and right when she brusquely interrupted him. She was not interested in refurbishing Harold Macmillan. Instead, she reached into her briefcase and pulled out a book. It was Hayek's *The Constitution of Liberty.* She held it up for all to see. "This," she said sternly, "is what we believe." She slammed it down on the table and then proceeded to deliver a monologue on the ills of the British economy.

One evening in that same period, she stopped at the Institute of Economic Affairs for a private meeting with Hayek. Following her departure, the entire staff gathered around the elderly economist, who was unusually pensive, to ask his reaction. After a long moment of reflection, all he answered was, "She's so beautiful."

Now, in 1979, just half a decade after the electoral debacle and her rupture with Heath and traditionalist conservatism, she was prime minister. One of the first things she did was elevate Ralph Harris, the director of the Institute of Economic Affairs, to the House of Lords. "It was primarily your foundation work," she wrote him, "which enabled us to rebuild the philosophy upon which our Party succeeded."

On taking over as prime minister, she thought about her father, who had died a decade earlier. "I am sure that he never imagined that I would eventually become Prime Minister. He would have wanted these things for me because politics was so much a part of his life and because I was so much his daughter." [12]

The "Wets" Versus the "Drys"

The ideas—the fodder for battle—were there. Margaret Thatcher knew exactly what she thought. Government was doing too much. "We should not expect the state," she declared not long after taking office, "to appear in the guise of an extravagant good fairy at every christening, a loquacious companion at every stage of life's journey, and the unknown mourner at every funeral." She wanted to replace what she called the "Nanny State" and its cradle-to-grave "coddling" with the much more bracing risks and rewards of the "enterprise culture." She liked Edmund Burke's quote that politics was "philosophy in action." But ideas were one thing. Putting them into place, into action, translating them into policy amid the immense complexities and contentions of modern government and society—all that was something else. And if judged only by its first three years, the Thatcherite revolution might have been deemed a failure. Or, worse, a non-event.

The new Tory government that took power in 1979 discovered that it had inherited an even more dire economic situation from Labour than it had anticipated. The Callaghan government had kept things together with Band-Aids. Interest rates were 16 percent; inflation was programmed to rise to 20 percent; the government deficit was destined to swell. Enormous pay increases were promised to public-sector workers, a sort of postdated check left behind by the Labour government that would guarantee still-higher inflation. The state-owned companies were insatiably draining money out of the Treasury. To make matters more difficult, Keith Joseph's hopes to convert the Tory Party had been only partly fulfilled. At the beginning of her government, Thatcher liked to say, "Give me six strong men and true, and I will get through." She rarely had six. Thatcher was a minority within her own government and did not have control over her cabinet.

The division was, in the argot of the time, between the "wets" and the "drys." The wets were the traditional Tories—partakers in the Keynesian mixed-economy consensus, traditional believers in Disraeli's "one nation," critics of confrontation, legatees of the now-infirm Harold Macmillan and the now-choleric Edward Heath. The drys were those who had absorbed and internalized the messages of Keith Joseph's speeches. They were "one of us," as Thatcher would say—the ones who wanted to make the revolution. But there were more wets than drys in Thatcher's first cabinet.

The 1979 electoral manifesto had also been more cautious than revolutionary. But Thatcher knew what she wanted to go after, right from the beginning. "The two great problems of the British economy," she declaimed, "are the monopoly nationalized industries and the monopoly trade unions." To conquer them, she would have to declare war.

Coming to office in the wake of endless strikes, she was forced to focus on the powerful trade unions. Unless the unions could be curbed and a more level playing field instituted, nothing of substance could be accomplished. The government dug itself in, to varying degrees, on a series of strikes, eager to establish by "demonstration effect" that the union leadership could not do anything it wanted and that the corporatist days of clubby pay settlements over "beer and sandwiches" at 10 Downing Street were finished. It also got critical legislation through Parliament limiting the ability of unions, sometimes battling among themselves for power, to turn every disagreement into a class war.

As secretary of state for industry, Keith Joseph was at the center of the struggles over labor, including what was considered the bellwether steel strike of 1980, the first industrial confrontation of the Thatcher years. The unions finally did get their pay increase, but along with that went a reduction in featherbedding and other restrictive practices, and a commitment to restructuring. Joseph had refused to play by the traditional rules of union-industry-government horse trading. No beer-and-sandwiches deal making for him. "Talking to you," one union leader is reported to have said to him, "is like trying to teach Chinese to a deaf mute." Joseph also bolstered the commitment to make drastic cuts in public spending and thus reduce the ever-yawning requirement for more public borrowing.

Amid everything else, Joseph was not about to forget his vocation to convert. Early in the new government, he presented the senior civil servants in his ministry with a reading list. It amounted to a catalog of the philosophy that was meant to be put in action. A tea-stained copy, obtained by Joseph's biographer, revealed twenty-nine items, including Hayek's *The Road to Serfdom* and two works by Adam Smith—not only *The Wealth of Nations* but also *The Theory of Moral Sentiments*—as well as eight pamphlets by Sir Keith Joseph.[13]

"The Lady's Not for Turning"

At the same time, the government also got busy trying to displace Keynesianism with monetarism. Instead of intervening with fiscal policy, the Tory government believed that its main economic job was to ensure a steady growth in the money supply that would be commensurate with economic growth. This was the most direct assault on consensus thinking. "We're all Keynesians around here," the permanent secretary of the Treasury said privately, and somewhat plaintively, at the time. "But we've done our best to follow the government line." The traditional Keynesian measures of economic management—employment and output targets—were abandoned in government budgetary documents, in favor of targeting the growth in money circulation in the economy. Huge and immensely controversial cuts were made in government spending, certainly reversing the trend of almost four decades. Yet the immediate results were not economic regeneration. Inflation, already deeply entrenched, was made worse by the oil-price shock of 1979 and the programmed public-sector pay hikes. Unemployment also continued to increase. Joseph's vision did not exactly seem to be working out as he had promised; many more bankrupts than millionaires were being created.

Some of the harshest criticism came from within Thatcher's cabinet. One of her ministers denounced the entire intellectual agenda, warning that "economic liberalism à la Professor Hayek, because of its starkness and its failure to create a sense of community, is not a safeguard of political freedom but a threat to it." The public would not be loyal to the state unless the state offered them protection. "Lectures on the ultimate beneficence of competition and on the dangers of interfering with market forces will not satisfy people who are in trouble." Privately, in the cabinet, there were more apocalyptic forecasts still.

Other politicians might well have compromised. Not Thatcher. She was determined. "Oh, yes, I know, we have been recently told by no less than 365 academic economists that such a thing cannot be, that British enterprise is doomed," she said. "Their confidence in the accuracy of their own predictions leaves me breathless. But having myself been brought up over the shop, I sometimes wonder whether they back their forecasts with their money." Her political back may have seemed against the wall, but she almost exulted in the challenge. At a small dinner at Downing Street, she kicked off her shoes and climbed up on a chair to give an unplanned speech. "I am the rebel head of an establishment government," she said proudly.

Still, would she not—as Heath had done—be forced to make a U-turn and reembrace the consensus? Absolutely not. That would be surrender, and that she would not do. The new approach, with its emphasis on market rather than government, might be very controversial, but the old approach had been discredited—it had failed. Yet the clamor for a U-turn, away from the body of ideas that Joseph and she had propounded in the 1970s, grew stronger and stronger. But she would not be budged. At the annual Conservative Party conference in 1980, where many did want a U-turn, Thatcher drew the line. "Turn if you like," she declared. "The lady's not for turning." It would be her most memorable line.

The cure to Britain's ills, she said again and again, would not be painless. But the economic pain continued to mount. And as it did, her popularity declined. What her supporters saw as her resoluteness, commitment to traditional values, and willingness to speak the truth, her critics viewed as elements of a domineering, adversarial, and sometimes gratuitously uncaring personality. It was that set of perceptions that gave the extra enmity to her opponents, both in the nation at large and in her own party. To the former Tory establishment she had become "That Woman"—said with an emphatic bite. When she personally and unceremoniously fired from the cabinet the aristocratic Christopher Soames, Tory grandee and son-in-law of Winston Churchill, he unlimbered himself of a diatribe on the subject of everything that was wrong with her, a denunciation that could be heard through an open window at 10 Downing Street. Included in the catalog of wrongdoing was the fact that he had never before been talked to by a woman in the abusive manner with which she had addressed him. For her part, Thatcher thought that his fury had to do with the fact that he felt he "was being dismissed by his housemaid."

She may well have had her doubts, but she kept them to herself. Despite her certitude, or perhaps because of it, the likelihood of success seemed to be slipping away. The Tories' support in the polls had fallen to 30 percent, and hers, even worse, to 23 percent—she was as unpopular as any prime minister since the start of polling. That was hardly the base on which to make a revolution.[14]

The Falklands War: "The Unexpected Happens"

One of Thatcher's favorite aphorisms was what she called Thatcher's Law—"The Unexpected Happens." Such is what occurred on April 2, 1982. On that day, Argentinian troops invaded the Falkland Islands in the south Atlantic, some two hundred miles off Argentina's coast. Britain had ruled the rugged islands for 149 years; and something less than two thousand Britons lived there. Argentina had long claimed this bare, uninviting piece of real estate; the brutal military junta that ruled Argentina wanted it back and hardly expected significant resistance. But Thatcher decided that Argentinian aggression could not be allowed to stand. Despite very considerable risks, she dispatched an armada to retake the islands. She was very lonely, at that point, in her decisions. "I would not accept it," she later said. "I didn't believe in appeasement, and I would not have our people taken over by dictatorship. Yet had I fed all the factors in a computer—8,000 miles away, winter, problems of supply, their air cover 400 miles away, we had only two aircraft carriers and if one were sunk, three to four weeks after loading soldiers before they could land—the computer would have said don't do it. But we are people of belief."

After several naval battles, a full-scale landing, and three weeks of tough fighting, the Argentinians surrendered. One result was the collapse of the military government in Buenos Aires. The victory also transformed Margaret Thatcher's position at home. "We have ceased to be a nation in retreat," she told her country. "We have instead a newfound confidence— born in the economic battles at home and tested and found true 8,000 miles away." Her confidence in her own conviction and judgment had been immensely bolstered. So had the nation's confidence in her—and in itself. The Falklands War created a new political reality in Britain. Now she could much more successfully put philosophy into action. "I had a very tough time the first three years, a very, very difficult time," she later recalled. "But after the Falklands War, people understood that we were going to do what we said we were going to do."

The Falklands War transformed British politics, and thus helped set the scene for the Thatcher Revolution. Thatcher herself was no longer an unpopular, almost sectarian figure. She had also, by the by, proved that a woman could be prime minister. But the true test would come with the general election of 1983. The Opposition inadvertently did its part to bolster her new position. Moderate leaders split off from a Labour Party unable to extricate itself from the past and established a new Social Democratic Party. The result was to divide the Opposition, a political reality that overrode the high unemployment numbers and the lack of clear public support for the Tory economic strategy.

Despite what seemed to be the Conservatives' strength, Thatcher spent some of her precious personal time before the election in the private apartment at 10 Downing Street, packing things up, just in case she lost and had to move out overnight. The preparation proved unnecessary. She won with a huge landslide—a 144-seat majority—the largest since the Labour victory that ushered in the "New Jerusalem" in the summer of 1945.

Now Margaret Thatcher was in a position to pursue a program that would deserve to be called Thatcherism. It would comprise the many elements already prefigured in Keith Joseph's speeches—a rejection of Keynesianism, a constraining of the welfare state and government spending, a commitment to the reduction of direct government intervention in the economy, a sell-off of government-owned businesses, a concerted drive to reduce absurdly and punitively high tax rates, and a commitment to reduce the government's deficit. The whole package also came with a sharpness of certitude and what seemed to be a repudiation of the compassion of the nanny state; and it was that, perhaps, which seemed to polarize and get in the way of a more dispassionate assessment of Thatcherism.[15]

The Decisive Battle

The two victories—in the Falklands and at the polls—now gave Thatcher the opportunity to fight the next war, to confront head-on the challenge that had to be overcome if the British economy was to be redirected. That was the overwhelming power of the unions, which had become a great force of inertia. The confrontation took the form of a standoff with the National Union of Miners, led by a Marxist militant named Arthur Scargill. The ensuing struggle was dramatic and protracted. It also proved to be the decisive battle.

The coal industry, nationalized in 1947, was losing money at a horrendous rate; the government subsidy had risen to $1.3 billion a year. The industry desperately required rationalization; mines had to be closed and the workforce shrunk if there was to be any hope of revival. Scargill and his militants were unwilling to compromise. Mine pits could not be closed, they said, no matter how large the losses. For them, it was not a battle over modernization but a class war.

Thatcher and her colleagues knew, from personal bitter experience, how a coal strike had precipitated the downfall of the Heath government almost exactly a decade earlier. Out of that event had come the popular assumption that the National Union of Miners could make or break governments. Thus, a confrontation with the miners seemed inevitable and necessary. For Thatcher, too, compromise was not a possibility. In preparation for the campaign, Thatcher's generals made certain that the Central Electricity Generating Board began, quite early, to stockpile coal inventories to see itself through a cutoff of new production. There was to be no repetition of the blackouts and power cuts of 1974.

The strike began in March 1984. It was angry and sometimes violent —thousands were arrested during its course. Not only miners who wanted to continue working but also their families were subject to constant intimidation. The strike became an international cause célèbre. Social democrats in Western Europe collected money on street corners to support the striking workers. The National Union of Miners solicited funds from Libya's Colonel Qaddafi and received money from the "trade unions" of Soviet-controlled Afghanistan and, apparently, from the Soviet Union itself. Despite the intense pressure and the disruption, the National Coal Board and the government held firm. It took a year, but the strike finally petered out, and in stark contrast to 1974, this time the miners' union capitulated. The government had won. The outcome meant a new era in the basic relationship of labor, management, and government—in short, in how Britain fundamentally worked. The decades of labor protectionism—which had cost the British economy heavily in terms of inflexibility, red ink, and lost economic growth —were over.

The Birth of Privatization

The battle with the coal miners was the most visible representation of the turn in economic arrangements. But the most decisive element of Thatcherism, and the one—along with the philosophy itself—that would have the greatest impact around the world was what was to become known as privatization. It represented the sharpest break with the postwar Attlee consensus. Indeed, what has become commonplace in the late 1990s was considered so radical prior to the 1979 election that even Thatcher's most committed supporters dared not raise the idea. The most that could be advocated for state-owned industries was the introduction of "inflexible" financial targets, the exclusion of ministerial meddling, the promotion of efficiency, and the ending of government subsidies. Privatization itself was only a small passing reference in the 1979 election manifesto. Going any farther would mean frightening the voters on the eve of the election.

The first major sallies after the 1979 victory were along the same lines. State-owned companies, some said, should be "commercialized" and made to operate more like private companies. The policy unit at 10 Downing Street investigated "corporatization" of state companies. But others in the government, beginning with Margaret Thatcher and Keith Joseph, thought that was not sufficient. They wanted to go much farther. They thought that getting a state-owned enterprise to "imitate" a private firm was much like trying "to make a mule into a zebra by painting stripes on its back." They had something far more radical and original in mind: They wanted to get the government out of business. To do so, they had to invent a new kind of business, for there were no guidelines in either the developed or the developing world for what they intended.

To complicate matters further, this new "business" needed a name. One obvious candidate was *denationalization*—as in returning to private hands companies that had passed into state ownership through nationalization. But there was a problem. Some companies, like the phone service, had never been nationalized in the first place; they had begun life as adjuncts to government departments. Moreover, *denationalization* had a decidedly negative and unappealing connotation. So instead they reached for another term—*privatization,* although some considered it not much less ugly. Its use in this context went back more than a decade. In the late 1960s, a young conservative politician named David Howell was charged with working out a plan, as he put it, "to unravel Britain's huge state sector and at the same time widen capital ownership in British society." Scouring the United States for ideas, he ran across the word *privatization* in the work of the economic and social theorist Peter Drucker. Howell thought it was an unattractive word; nevertheless, he also thought it described what he had in mind, and he deployed it in a 1969 pamphlet, "A New Style of Government." But then, as Howell put it, the idea lay "dormant," until Joseph and Thatcher picked it up.

The odd thing about the word was that its proponents found it both so ugly and yet so useful. "I don't like it," said Thatcher. "It's free enterprise. But we had to accept it. It was one word." In fact, Thatcher disliked the word so much that for some time she refused to use it at all. But like everyone else, she gave in. "None of us could come up with anything better," wrote Nigel Lawson, who served as both energy minister and chancellor of the exchequer. "And, as this word, or quite literal translations of it, is now used from Siberia to Patagonia, we may as well stick with it."

Thatcher adopted the concept, if not the word, because she saw in it something much more than a means to raise revenue for the Treasury or rein in the unions. It was about changing the balance in society. "I wanted to use privatization to achieve my ambition of a capital-owning democracy. This is a state in which people own houses, shares, and have a stake in society, and in which they have wealth to pass on to future generations." Out of that ambition came her fervor.

The Labour politicians had promoted state-owned enterprise, before and after World War II, as an almost altruistic undertaking. "The public corporation must be no mere capitalist business, the be-all and end-all of which is profits and dividends," Herbert Morrison, the Labour politician who had so much influence on the postwar nationalization program, had said. "Its board and its officers must regard themselves as the high custodians of the public interest." But in practice, argued the Thatcherites, that higher vision could not be attained. Was government going to be any better in figuring out the future than private business? It did not have access to a higher level of knowledge. Indeed the Thatcherites disbelieved in government knowledge. As Lawson put it, governments "enjoy no unique hot line to the future." The record suggested just the opposite—inflexibility in the face of change.

Whatever the vision, state companies had often proved in practice to be highly inefficient, inflexible, poorly performing employment agencies, politically pressured to maintain and expand employment far beyond what was needed. They were also unable to resist the wage pressure from public-sector unions, thus becoming major generators of inflation. Because of their inefficiency, their weakness in the face of union pressure, and their insulation from competition in the marketplace, they piled up huge losses, which they solved by turning to the taxpayers or, as Lawson put it, by "recourse to the bottomless public purse." Every kind of decision ran the risk of becoming a political decision, driven not by the interests of the firm but by the desires of politicians in power, whether it was wage settlements or new investments in plant location, major projects, and equipment. What was missing was exactly what the Labour promoters of national industries had most disliked —the discipline of the market. "What public ownership does," Lawson declared in 1982, "is to eliminate the threat of takeover and ultimately of bankruptcy, and the need, which all private undertakings have from time to time, to raise money from the market." Public ownership British-style also meant that output and products were not adapted to the marketplace and that the needs and desires of the consumer, the buyer, did not count for all that much.

For the Thatcherites, privatization became a cause. It would embody the turning of the tide that Keith Joseph had lectured about up and down the country. Widening ownership and thus giving people a vested interest in private property would change the political culture of the nation. It would decisively limit the role of the state and make at least part of the Thatcher agenda virtually irreversible. It would also make the companies themselves more efficient and deliver more value to consumers. It would eliminate the industries' call on the "bottomless purse" and reduce government's share of the GNP. And, by the way, it would provide for a considerable inflow of money that would, in turn, help finance tax cuts.

With all that said, there was never a sense that privatization had broad popular support. For their part, civil servants did nothing to hinder the process. Their experience with the state-owned companies in the 1970s had been so painful that even those intellectually attracted to the mixed economy had come in practice to despair of its proper functioning. Moreover, they did not have any good alternatives to offer. The traditional ideas were exhausted. "One of the real driving forces for privatization," recalled Thatcher cabinet minister John Wakeham, "was the consensus among bureaucrats that they did not know how to determine anything anymore. Planning, nationalization, and so on—it had all failed. The state-owned industries were running massive deficits. There was willingness to try something new. You found that the response within the bureaucracy to the new conservative government was that 'it could not get any worse than it had already got.' "

Keith Joseph initiated privatization at the Department of Industry, and on the first day of the new government, he appointed David Young to be his special adviser on privatization. "The new government was determined to roll back, to reduce government's spending, and that meant to privatize," said Young. "The big risk was that we had to get companies into a fit state to be privatized. It turned out that it was not the commanding heights of the economy but rather clapped-out coal mines and other industries that were losing lots of money. We intended to sell off those that could be sold, and meanwhile work on the others to reduce losses, to do the necessary closures, to establish management."

In such circumstances, the initial steps toward privatization would be rather modest compared to what came later. Cable & Wireless and British Aerospace were among the first. Also disposed of were gas stations along motorways, hotels belonging to the state-owned railway system, and a company that manufactured radioactive isotopes for medical treatment. As it turned out, the most significant form of privatization in the early years was the sale of "council" (i.e., public) housing units to the people who lived in them.

Sometimes even a small step toward privatization would meet a torrent of opposition from the press, parts of the public, the unions within the state companies—and from the managers of those companies, too, who did not want to see their purview and their realm reduced. It almost did not seem to matter what it was that was being sold off. British Gas's monopoly was far-reaching. The creation of that state-owned company had been the means of creating a modern, integrated gas supply system in the country. Its market was very broad. It even held the exclusive right to sell gas-fired stoves and other appliances through its nine hundred showrooms around the country. In 1981, the government announced that it intended to sell off those stores, because the monopoly reduced competition, led to higher prices, and also discouraged exports. Moreover, the existence of that kind of monopoly was rather ridiculous: What special skill did the government have that it should be the custodian of the nation's gas ranges?

But little did the Tories realize what awaited them. British Gas's unions, egged on by a management that did not want to lose any of its empire, no matter how tangential, joined together with Labour MPs and even some Conservative ones in denouncing the planned move to dispose of the show-rooms. "Few of us realized," wrote Nigel Lawson, "what a storm would be unleashed over what could scarcely be called one of the commanding heights of the economy." The government's opponents, he added, were "remarkably successful in portraying the privatization of this state-owned chain of shops . . . as an ideologically inspired attack on the British way of life. The heart of every community, it appeared, was neither the church nor the pub, but the local gas showroom." In this case, Lawson, caught unprepared by the fury of the attack, negotiated a temporary, face-saving retreat by saying that the sale of the showrooms would be put aside until some new safety legislation could be passed.[16]

But How to Do It?

After the Falklands War, the government had the muscle to begin to privatize what were truly the commanding heights of the economy. But one of the biggest difficulties, Lawson recalled, "was the fact that, to all intents and purposes, it had never been done before . . . there was no departmental dos-sier to dust down." There were many questions to decide. Should shares in the companies be distributed free to all citizens? Emphatically not, said Chancellor Lawson, citing the American revolutionary patriot Tom Paine: "What we obtain too cheap, we esteem too lightly." How to price the shares so that they were not too high (discouraging investors) and not too low (meaning that the government would give up too much value) but still—of critical importance—low enough to ensure that the prices would go up, not down, after the initial offering? How to foster incentives for employees and small investors to buy into the "float"? To facilitate that desire, they created a series of television commercials that urged a fictional modern Everyman named Sid not to miss this chance to become a shareholder.

One of the most urgent challenges, it turned out, was to create meaningful and accurate financial histories for the companies that corresponded to conventional and intelligible accounting standards. "When we first examined the nationalized British Telecom," said Lawson, "we discovered that, in true East European style, the corporation had not the faintest idea which of its activities were profitable and which were not, let alone any finer points of management accounting." Added David Young, "British Telecom was a total mess." One small unit, with five hundred people, had "a clunky accounting system. Everything else was in one great big pot. You didn't know regional costs, or any costs. Once something was bought, you forgot about it."

This pointed to a larger challenge. Companies could not be privatized until they had been "fixed"—loss-making activities reduced, organization restructured, and the basis for profitability established. Otherwise, why would anybody buy stock in the enterprise? British Steel would prove to be an excellent case study. The company lost over $10 billion from the mid-1970s through the mid-1980s. Restructuring was first undertaken to stem the draw on public funds. Only in the 1980s did privatization become a goal. By the time the company was finally sold to the public, its labor force had already been drastically reduced and its productivity dramatically increased, its facilities rationalized. And it was profitable—and internationally competitive.

But there were also special cases with issues that went beyond the "bottom line." How, for instance, when it came to "strategic" assets like oil, to ensure that they did not fall into foreign hands? After all, privatization was following only a few years after the oil crises of the 1970s, which had, in the first place, precipitated the partial nationalization of North Sea oil. On this subject Lawson proved to be very creative. He recalled "the curious voting structures" he had encountered a decade earlier, when working as a stock market columnist for the *Financial Times,* that enabled someone with a "very small slice of equity to exercise quite disproportionate power." As a journalist he had been disapproving. But as a politician he found it a godsend. Thus he came up with the "golden share"—"a special share which would be retained by government after privatization, and which would enable the government to prevent control of the company from falling into unsuitable hands." The term *unsuitable* was a euphemism for *foreign.* However euphemistic, it did the political trick.[17]

A Far Bigger Program

Ultimately, the Thatcher government was able to carry out a privatization program far bigger than anyone would have expected at the start, and one that pushed back the frontiers of the state. In 1982 and 1984, the government's ownership share in North Sea oil and gas was privatized, creating among other things Enterprise Oil, today one of the world's largest independent oil companies. The government disposed of its share in British Petroleum—acquired by Winston Churchill on the eve of the First World War. Ports and airports were privatized. Heathrow and other airports are now owned and operated by a private company, BAA, which also operates airports in the United States.

The first truly massive privatization was the hiving off of the state telephone system into British Telecom. It, more than any other, shifted the balance from production to the "consumer." It would also be the real breakthrough for privatization. Whether the oil and gas reserves of the North Sea were in the hands of the state or private industry did not directly affect people in their daily lives. Telephones did. Relatively few people actually paid attention to the oil and gas privatizations; almost everybody knew that something dramatic was going to happen to the phones. The telephone system, part of the post office until separated by Keith Joseph, embodied many of the worst traits of state-owned companies. Bureaucratic state control repressed innovation. The customer did not count. It took months to get a new telephone. There were only two choices—the design offered or nothing. The only way to get a phone fixed in any reasonable time was to pay a repairman, who freelanced after hours, under the table. The red call boxes were relatively rare, sometimes malodorous, and often out of order.

"When we went into the telephone offices to talk to the staff," David Young recalled, "they talked about office conditions, pensions, and many other things. No one ever mentioned the customers. If British Telecom wanted to move a group out of a run-down office building into a new building, unions extorted compensation—a few hundred pounds for each employee for the 'disturbance' of giving them better working conditions. And when it came to installing new phones, they came along when they were damn well ready."

Other steps were taken prior to privatization. A competitive long-distance service, Mercury, was launched, which stimulated further innovation. On a Tuesday in Thatcher's first term, Keith Joseph stood up in Parliament and announced that in the future, shops would be allowed to sell telephones. Two days later David Young, on the way to work, passed a shop on Lower Brook Street whose windows were filled with hurriedly imported telephones, although such sales were not yet legal. Arriving at the ministry, he rushed into Joseph's office to make an excited announcement, "The market is working."

The actual privatization of British Telecom took place in November 1984. The first tranche, just over 50 percent, was sold to the public for $6 billion. A huge popular market for privatization had been created. Curiously enough, the public's complaints about service rose after the privatization, but with good reason. "In the good old days before privatization, no one complained because there was no point," Young said. "No one was listening." Now there was someone to complain to. British Gas, British Airways, and British Steel followed. Later came British Coal and British Rail. The state-owned water system was privatized in the form of a series of regional water companies. Most massive of all was the breakup of the state-owned electric power monopoly into twelve regional distribution companies,* three generating companies, and one open-access grid company.

The process of privatization encountered many criticisms over a decade and a half. With the larger transactions, there always seemed to be a refrain that the capital markets would not be able to absorb the deal. In practice, that never proved to be a constraint. The pricing of stock was generally criticized, for being either too low or too high. Former prime minister Harold Macmillan, the Tory proponent of the mixed economy and the middle way, weighed in to voice the complaints of many when he declared that the "family silver"—the state companies, all of whose names began with *British*—was being sold off. The obvious reply was that the "family" could not afford to maintain the silver anymore.

Some pointed out that a number of the state-owned companies had become more efficient and raised their productivity prior to privatization. Here the reply was that those improvements were driven by necessity, by the discipline and pressure of impending privatization. After the fact, the growth in compensation—salary and options—of senior managers and board members in the newly privatized companies became a hot staple on front pages, made all the more vivid by the sharp downsizing in employment levels in what had formerly been the woefully overmanned state companies. The recipients of these benefits became immortalized as the "fat cats" and the target of popular rage. Employment in many privatized companies was often slashed by 20 to 40 percent. Beyond question, the quality of service improved and operations became more efficient. But it would be difficult for many of those who lost their jobs—often late in their careers—to find new opportunities. The rationalization that privatization brought about fed for a time a growing tide of unemployment in the new "lean" Britain. Yet the growth in unemployment proved temporary. By the late 1990s unemployment was much lower than on the European continent.

Privatization also introduced the new challenge of regulation. The nationalized industries had operated under the control—often ineffective, to be sure—of the government ministries. Now the provision of basic public

---

* Eleven of them have since been bought, seven by American electric power companies.

services—gas, electricity, water—was being entrusted to private enterprises guided by profitability, not universal service at any cost. To work, this new system required a regulatory body that could ensure competition and protect the consumer. The establishment of such regulation was essential to public acceptance of the new arrangements. Sure that they could improve on the American experience, the Tories sought a solution that would keep regulation as "lite" as possible while still being effective. After all, excessively burdensome or interventionist structures would run counter to the goal of making government smaller. So they appointed for each industry a single individual—known as "The Regulator"—with the mandate to monitor industry practice and set pricing rules with as lean a staff as possible.

But what started out as "regulatory lite" soon grew into much larger regulatory establishments. There had been an underestimation of the regulatory needs posed by the movement from state monopoly to private firms. The risks of private monopolies or "duopolies" forming were great; and on the technical side, the sophisticated pricing mechanisms for industries such as electric power proved complex to run and monitor. For all these reasons, the original conception of "The Regulator" came under fire, and a drift began instead toward full-fledged regulatory agencies, some staffed by hundreds of people.[18]

"A Bit of an Institution"

Margaret Thatcher's third electoral victory, in 1987, confirmed that Thatcherism was not an aberration but a change of direction. "I think I have become a bit of an institution," she said shortly afterward. "People seem to think, 'She isn't so bad is she, this Maggie?' " In the aftermath, she was drawn to add a private project to her manifold of duties—reading the Old Testament from beginning to end and reporting daily to her staff on her progress. "I've been told that the Old Testament is about laws, and the New Testament about mercy," she later said, "but I'm not sure I agree."

But the 1987 victory was also the beginning of the end of an era. The Tory government created a domestic furor by "bashing on" to make a radical change in local taxation in the form of the poll tax. And Thatcher became increasingly nationalistic and angry in her attacks on the moves to strengthen the European Community. She reviled what she saw as a new bureaucratic monster rising up in Brussels that would drain sovereignty away from Westminster. She was particularly enraged about plans to create a single European currency, which, she was convinced, would lead to German hegemony over Europe. Her strident stance did more than anything else to alienate some of those who had been her most important allies in creating the Thatcherite revolution. They were convinced that Britain should be inside Europe helping to shape it, not sitting outside and attacking it. All of this was made worse by the style of Thatcher's leadership. She appeared to have become increasingly confident of her own opinions, increasingly isolated from other points of view. She showed little willingness to brook opposition, and she humiliated even those who had been closest to her. She had become a divisive figure, not only in national politics but within her own party.

There was a brief respite. When Saddam Hussein invaded Kuwait in August 1990, she was attending a conference in Aspen, Colorado, with George Bush and she took the opportunity to ensure that there was to be no acceptance of a fait accompli. "Remember, George," she said to the president, "this is no time to go wobbly." The lessons of the Falklands—and of appeasement—were still much in her mind.

At home, however, her own political position was definitely becoming wobbly. Nigel Lawson, the champion of privatization, resigned as chancellor of the Exchequer in 1989. One of Thatcher's closest allies over the years had been Geoffrey Howe, who had served as chancellor in the first four years of her government and as foreign secretary for the next six. Deciding that he was not sufficiently anti-European, she forced him out as foreign secretary, consoling him with the posts of Leader of the House of Commons and deputy prime minister. After a little more than a year, he had had enough. He could no longer tolerate Thatcher's domineering leadership or what he saw as her crudely nationalistic opposition to the European Community. His resignation speech in November 1990 regretfully but clearly laid out his disagreements. The speech precipitated a contest for the leadership of the Conservative Party. Thatcher was in Paris when she learned that she had come out at the top of the first ballot but without the required majority. That evening, she attended a wonderfully elegant ballet and dinner hosted at Versailles by President François Mitterrand. She demonstrated enormous aplomb. But to another leader who wished her well in the unfolding contest, she replied, "No, it's all over." Warned that she would eventually lose, and anticipating the humiliation that would follow, she withdrew her name from the second ballot. A few days later the new leader of the Conservative Party, John Major, son of a vaudeville entertainer–turned–businessman, succeeded her as prime minister.

The Thatcher era was over. She did not go out amid a great outpouring of sentimentality. Her unpopularity extended right across the political spectrum and into a large segment of her own party. She was seen as self-righteous, rigid, and uncaring. Her strength—her convictions—had also been her downfall. She was, Geoffrey Howe said afterward, "a great prime minister." But, in his view, "her tragedy" was "the recklessness with which she later sought to impose her own increasingly uncompromising views. For Margaret Thatcher in her final years, there was no distinction to be drawn between person, government, party, and nation. . . . The insistence on the undivided sovereignty of her own opinion dressed up as the nation's sovereignty was her own undoing."

Yet her legacy proved powerful and lasting in a way that eludes most politicians. She recast attitudes toward state and market, withdrew government from business, and dimmed the confidence in government knowledge. Thatcherism shifted the emphasis from state responsibility to individual responsibility, and sought to give first priority to initiative, incentives, and wealth generation rather than redistribution and equality. It celebrated entrepreneurship. Privatization became commonplace. Labor unrest no longer continually disrupted the economy. For a number of years Thatcherism seemed anathema almost everywhere. But by the 1990s, it would turn out that Margaret Thatcher had established the new economic agenda around the world.

Numbers give a sense of the economic change in Britain. By 1992, some two thirds of state-owned industries had moved into the private sector. Altogether, 46 major businesses, with 900,000 employees, had been privatized, and the government's take was well over $30 billion. What was once a massive drain on the public purse had turned into a major source of tax revenue. The number of people owning shares tripled to 9 million—20 percent of the adult population—although many of those 9 million owned only a few shares. But the most important consequence of privatization was that, together with labor union reform, it changed the basic institutional relationships that had defined Britain since 1945—and that had brought the country to a standstill by 1979. In that year, 1,274 working days were lost to strikes for every thousand people working. By 1990, that figure was down to 108—less than one tenth. The political and economic culture in Britain had been permanently altered; Keith Joseph's intellectual revolution had, in good measure and despite all the controversies, worked. David Young, the would-be emigrant of 1975, was four years later Keith Joseph's special adviser and then, under Margaret Thatcher, a member of the cabinet. Looking back from today's perspective, he said, "The Thatcher years turned the United Kingdom from being a producer-led into a consumer-led economy, and it was becoming a competitive economy. Conviction drove the process." [19]

"Always with Beliefs"

With the passage of time, the bitterness over Thatcherism has ebbed away. What Joseph and Thatcher started is no longer radical but rather very much the heart of a new consensus in Britain. "New Labour" came into power in 1997 not by attacking Thatcherism but by embracing much of its rhetoric and its policies, although leavened with an emphasis on compassion that was distinctly non-Thatcher.

Ideas and politics were the topic one morning with Baroness Thatcher, as Margaret Thatcher has been known since 1992. "Years ago, ordinary people became Labour to get a better life," she said, poised on a small settee in the second-floor drawing room of the elegant Belgravia row house that is home to the Thatcher Foundation. "Now they understand that freedom and enterprise under law is better than massive government control over industry and people. New Labour has an understanding of what socialism was and how it doesn't work, that somehow you have to create wealth before redistribution. Socialism started with redistribution before wealth.

"Socialism was the flavor of the time for a long time," she continued. "We in this country had an experiment in socialism. The Conservatives, when in power, did nothing to reverse it. I myself never had any sympathy for socialism. For me, it was so simple. The state ought not tell us what to do. My experience reinforced my beliefs. It was becoming obvious to people that the socialist way meant accepting decline." She shook her head. "Can you imagine—people accepting decline?"

And what then are the tasks of government? "First, keep finances sound. Second, ensure a proper foundation of law so that industry, commerce, services, and government can all flourish. Third, defense. Education, the fourth, is the road to opportunity. The fifth is the safety net. Society is more complex and needs to be more sophisticated in how it responds to fundamental questions. How is it to provide an effective safety net without creating or strengthening the dependency culture? How are we to uphold the virtues of civil society? And a certain amount is to be spent on infrastructure and a certain amount on pure research. . . ."

"And," she added, "don't forget Thatcher's Law: The unexpected happens. You had better prepare for it."

For Margaret Thatcher, one of the "unexpecteds" has been the global impact of the program she launched in Britain. "In 1981 a finance minister came to see me," she remembered. "'We're all very interested in what you're doing,' he said, 'because if you succeed, others will follow.' That had never occurred to me." As it turned out, the others—whether acknowledging the impact of Thatcherism or distancing themselves from it—have indeed followed.

At the top of the stairs, she stopped to reflect on the morning's discussion. The Thatcherite revolution itself was unexpected. Who in the mid-1970s would have anticipated the degree of change? "It started with Sir Keith and me, with the Centre for Policy Studies, and Lord Harris, at the Institute for Economic Affairs. Yes, it started with ideas, with beliefs." She paused. "That's it. You must start with beliefs. Yes, always with beliefs." [20]

CHAPTER 5

CRISIS OF CONFIDENCE

The Global Critique

No ONE still quite knows how it happened. In retrospect it seems to have been inevitable, and yet what unfolded on the night of November 9, 1989, was also accidental. What is known is that the border guards along the East German side of the Berlin Wall became wholly confused on that evening. The members of the Central Committee of East Germany's Communist Party were locked in an endless meeting, arguing and maneuvering for power among themselves. And Günter Schabowski, the head of the Communist Party of Berlin, was just about to go on television for a live press conference when party secretary Egon Krenz handed him the draft of a new regulation from the Interior Ministry.

"This could be a hit," Krenz told him.

And indeed it would be. The draft described proposed new bureaucratic procedures for obtaining visas in order to visit the West. It was not central to what Schabowski was talking about in his rambling press conference; he was distracted and was not clear about what he had read, and even less clear as to how he would express it. In any event it was only a draft. Yet in reply to an Italian journalist, he seemed to say that East Germans could go to the West with no restrictions—and at once. Egon Krenz was later to describe those words as "a small mistake"—an understatement, to say the least.

It was now just about seven o'clock in the evening, and much of East Germany was watching the press conference. In response to Schabowski's words, thousands and then tens of thousands and then hundreds of thousands of East Germans headed toward the Wall to test the new policy, whatever it was. Whole families joined the march, many of them in their pajamas. For three hours the throng swelled in front of the Wall, refusing to move and chanting, "Open the gate! Open the gate!" In all the years of communist

125

oppression, the guards had received endlessly detailed instructions about what to do in case people tried to breach the Wall. But now the unthinkable had happened; they had no instructions for this eventuality. There were no directives about how to react in this situation, and so the guards were paralyzed. Were they to shoot, or were they to open the gates? In their confusion, they did the latter. Hundreds of thousands of East Berliners surged through, to be met on the other side by huge crowds of waiting West Berliners, who engulfed them with hugs and doused them with champagne and beer.

It was unbelievable; what West German chancellor Helmut Kohl had only the year before said would not happen in his lifetime had just occurred. The Berlin Wall, for all practical purposes, had fallen. Together, East Berliners and West Berliners danced and sang the night through. Now they were all Berliners. The next day, at an emergency meeting of East Germany's Communist Party, one speaker glumly summed up the new reality: "The party is basically kaput." Soon enough, East Germany was swept away by history. As for the Wall itself, it was demolished, and chunks of it would be sold off as souvenirs of a bygone era. The cold war was over. It had ended with neither a bang nor a whimper but with a party.

The Wall had symbolized the division between East and West, between communism and capitalism. Its fall was a great symbol, too, of the end of the confrontation and the passage into a new era. What also disappeared was an intellectual wall, opening up the frontiers of ideas and knowledge and transforming what had been two different worlds, each with billions of people, into a common landscape—and a common market. As communism was the most extreme form of state economic control, its demise signaled an enormous shift—from state control to market consensus. The apparent success, and thus the prestige, of the communist economic model had been one of the most important drivers of government control. Now, certainly, the failure of Marxism and the communist system constituted one of the most important forces shaping this new era.

It was an era in which conceptual shifts would culminate in a sharp revision in thinking and policy about the organization of economies around the world. Within regions and countries there were many variations. But taken as a whole, this change represented a process through which the issues of national sovereignty were resolved, the residue of classic colonialism and imperialism were relegated to the past, and economics won precedence over politics. Moreover, a common stock of ideas and perspectives would provide the pivot, the hinge, on which the relationship between government and marketplace would swing. And how did it begin? With disillusionment about the mixed economies of the industrial world.[1]

Crisis of Confidence

Experience is a teacher, and what experience taught in the 1970s and into the 1980s was an increasing skepticism about the capabilities of what had become the traditional mixed economy. For some, it would result in an outright rejection of government's abilities. For others, there was unease and the growing sentiment that the economic structures of the postwar era no longer fulfilled the aims their founders had intended. In either case, the change of heart happened over time as, in one form or another, the confidence generated by the thirty glorious years began to dissipate. It was less a revelation than a process of learning about the limits of government's ability to run a modern economy.

For three decades the consensus held that achieving economic growth and improvements in the standard of life and human welfare required some form of central management. The extent of coordination was considered so great that only the state could provide it. This consensus rested upon trust. In order for it to work, the public and business enterprises would have to believe that political leadership—tested and recalibrated by elections, to be sure—could gather the knowledge required to look into the highly uncertain future and apply economic tools to improve a country's prospects and make that future more secure. The governments of the mixed economy did so by using some combination of five sets of tools—regulation, planning, state ownership, industrial policy, and Keynesian fiscal management. These tools could be augmented by a sixth—monetary policy. The actual mix varied considerably among countries, depending upon their traditions and history.

The basic rationale for government's role was the economists' concept of "market failure." Some desired outcomes required a degree of coordination that individual competitors in the marketplace could not muster. As a result of this failure, government would step in and provide that coordination. Time horizons and returns were often important concerns. Business alone could not provide investment; it either would take too long to come to fruition or would generate benefits that went to society at large, rather than the individual firm that had made the investment. Infrastructure was an example of something that took too long to develop, as were expenditures on basic research and development—a case in which the benefits might be quite diffused and thus not capturable by the firm that spent the money.

There was another sense to market failure as well—a failure of acumen, of knowledge. "Government knowledge"—what the government knew and was considered responsible for knowing—was different from "business knowledge." The latter was cultivated in different academies—in schools of law and policy, not business, and certainly not in the "trades." It was thought that the more an economic activity aimed toward the future and affected the broad population, the less sufficient was simple business knowledge to see it through. The instruments of intervention became the tools with which to apply government knowledge. Resources were directed and allocated by the state, by political and bureaucratic decision making, rather than by the elemental forces of supply and demand—forces shaped by the knowledge of those in the marketplace. Valéry Giscard d'Estaing, the former French president, was a star pupil at the École Nationale d'Administration, France's great repository of government knowledge, in the early 1950s. Looking back on his education, he recalled that he was taught about indicative planning and price controls, "but there was no reference, no discussion whatsoever of the market or about the market."

At first, government's assumption of the risks of economic activity seemed logical—and safe. No one could forget the 1930s. Thus government became a sort of national insurance company, guaranteeing growth while protecting the public from the risks of the market. Like vast insurers, governments collected premiums to pay for their outlays via direct and indirect taxes of all sorts. Unlike insurers, they also had at their disposal the prerogative of public authorities—deficit spending, on which they increasingly drew. But as government's role as insurer became entrenched, so too did the expectations of consumers, workers, and businesses. Once established, an interventionist government could only grow larger, not shrink. The expectation that government could and would guarantee growth and expanding benefits became part of the political culture.

Yet who could deny the success of the experiment? From the end of the Second World War until the oil crises of the 1970s, the industrial world enjoyed three decades of prosperity and rising incomes that sparked aspirations and dreams. It was an extraordinary achievement. The children of wartime and postwar rationing became the adolescents of economic recovery and growth and then the parents of the consumer society. Housing improved enormously. Families bought their first and then their second car; they acquired appliances and televisions. They shopped in supermarkets and department stores, they went on vacations and traveled to foreign countries, and they purchased products that had been turned into brand names and status symbols by advertising. And, most of all, they had jobs. Social critics bemoaned consumerism and materialism; they identified the gulf between "private affluence" and "public squalor." But the fundamental fact was that a quality of life had emerged that could not have been dreamed of at the end of World War II. It is no wonder that throughout the noncommunist, industrialized world, voters gave politicians the go-ahead to use that standard set of tools to guarantee a steadily growing economy—and, hence, full employment. In so doing, they deferred to government's superior knowledge of the national economic interest.

The warning flag was inflation. Throughout the 1960s, inflationary tendencies crept upward in the mixed economies, but never to the point of causing serious alarm. However, by the early 1970s, inflationary pressures were becoming more pronounced and visible. The tools governments had used to muddle through—to sustain consumer demand, to match inflation with wage increases—were now inadequate. Keynesian demand management assumed that low unemployment and a low, managed rate of inflation was a sustainable combination. That proved wrong.

The lesson took time to learn, for it challenged all that had been accepted as the received wisdom. The shortage of political will to tackle the problem head-on only gave conditions time to get worse. Inflation was becoming entrenched in many ways: by the growth of government deficits, by the expansion of the welfare state, by the barriers to competition, by the rigidities of the labor market, by the "social charges" added to the labor bill, and by the nature of the bargaining between labor and management over wages and the way they would be passed through the system. A good part of the inflation was a cost of the protection provided by the insurance state against uncertainties, volatilities, and competition. The adoption of wage and price controls became testament to the prevalence of the inflationary dynamics. But controls were no more than a stopgap. They could hold inflation at bay ever so briefly but could not disable its causes.

When the oil crisis of 1973–74 hit, the mixed economy was already straining. What made the dramatic rise in the price of oil truly a "shock" was the extent to which it upset the familiar patterns of costs in the economy. In the slump that followed the oil crisis, inflation and unemployment began to rise together in a deadly and unprecedented spiral. The phenomenon was christened stagflation. And between 1974 and 1980 governments of the left and the right alike learned that attempts to buy one's way out of the crisis by means of deficit spending would be futile and counterproductive. Keynesianism lost its cachet. The economic growth of the preceding decades, formerly much taken for granted, was now sorely missed.

Poor economic performance and the muddling and confusions of government policy engendered a loss of confidence in existing arrangements. Government knowledge was less powerful; governments, less all-knowing. By the end of the troubled 1970s, a new realization had gained ground: More than daily management, it was the entire structure of the economy that had reached its limits. It was imperative to rethink government's role in the marketplace. For the pioneers—the economists, politicians, and technocrats who shepherded the early programs of government withdrawal from the economy in various countries—the task was nothing short of revolutionary. For the first time in decades, governments would seek to reverse direction— to shed assets and to confront at least the idea of giving up some control. The dissatisfactions with the mixed economy were already evident in the industrial world by the end of the 1970s, and they would shortly make their impact felt at the ballot box. In the meantime, while the industrial world was reassessing its arrangements, the developing world was about to encounter its own transforming crisis.

The Debt Crisis and the Lost Decade

Jesús Silva Herzog carried a proud name in Mexican history. In 1937, his father had drawn up the historic bill of complaint against the foreign oil companies that provided the rationale for Mexico to nationalize the oil industry—one of the most important events in modern Mexican history. He himself had followed the path of the new technocrats, in his case getting a graduate degree in economics from Yale. He became his country's minister of finance in April 1982, just as Mexico seemed poised to rise to a new rank in the world. Large new petroleum discoveries were turning the country into a major oil exporter, and the present and projected surge in earnings meant the country would be able to spend liberally on new public investments. President José López Portillo demanded a global leadership role for Mexico. In so doing, he struck a magisterial pose: The economy should not "eat more than it could digest," he declared.

But then, in the summer of 1982, Silva Herzog discovered that it was all a house of cards. Mexico had been on a borrowing spree that nobody would or could stop—certainly not President López Portillo, who had surrounded himself with courtiers and sycophants in order to be told what a wonderful president he was. Some months earlier, a group of officials had screwed up their courage and actually warned the president that trouble was coming. He had rewarded them for their troubles by firing them. But now the truth was clear, at least to Silva Herzog. On August 12, 1982, he concluded that Mexico could not pay the interest on its international debt. The game was just about over. Mexico was about to go bankrupt.

"It was horrible," said Silva Herzog. "We had just committed terrible mistakes on the basis of oil. But there had been this great mood of victory in Mexico. We had been in the largest boom in Mexican history. And for the first time in our history, in those years 1978 through 1982, we were being courted by the most important people in the world. We thought we were rich. We had oil."

Silva Herzog hastened to Washington, where, after very tough negotiations with the U.S. Treasury and the Federal Reserve Board, he worked out the first steps in an emergency rescue package. The American officials had no trouble recognizing the extreme danger. It was not just Mexico, or even the whole of Latin America, that was at risk. So heavy had been the lending to the developing world that most of America's major banks, and indeed the entire global banking system, were in grave peril of collapse.

A few weeks later, at the behest of American authorities, Silva Herzog flew to New York City to meet with the heads of the several hundred U.S. banks that had lent to Mexico in order to tell them how much trouble they were really in. He was accompanied by another senior official, Ángel Gurría. Silva Herzog laid out the bleak picture and described the rescue plans thus far. The banks would have to cooperate by agreeing to allow Mexico to postpone its repayments. The president of the New York Federal Reserve Bank called the postponement a "standstill." American officials did not want to use the word *default,* for fear that it would immediately induce a panic. No one could doubt the gravity of the situation. And this was not just a Mexican problem. They all knew their exposure, and now they clearly understood the interconnections—everyone was standing at the precipice together. It was not a cheerful meeting. So stunned were the assembled bankers that they could hardly muster any questions. Searching for something comforting to say, Jesús Silva Herzog finally told the bankers that over the long term they need not worry about their Mexican debt. After all, he added, pointing to his colleague Ángel Gurría and himself, both Jesús and Ángel would be looking out for them. The reassurance was meager, but it would have to do. The great debt crisis of the 1980s had begun.

Just as stagflation and rigidity had toppled the consensus within the industrial world in the 1970s, so the protracted debt crisis in the 1980s undermined both the confidence placed in the expanding state in the developing world and the adherence to third worldism. The borrowing that began with high ambition and great assurance ended in what has been described as "the most widespread debt problem in history." It had been generated with remarkable rapidity in the second half of the 1970s. In those years, the world's money centers were flush with deposits from the oil producers' windfall. Bankers rapidly recycled these newly dubbed "petrodollars" in the form of loans—many of them to developing countries, both to governments and to government-owned companies. Some worried about the ability of these government and state companies to handle the consequent debt service, but the concern was brushed aside. In fact, with the 1920s and 1930s very much in mind, there was great fear that failure to recycle those funds could trigger a world depression.

At the same time, in the spirit of the day, it seemed to both lenders and borrowers that this was money being loaned to the future. After all, were not global power and influence shifting from developed to developing countries? Wasn't the South redressing the balance against the North, expiating the sins of colonialism and imperialism? Add to it all one other factor: Because of the downturn in the industrial countries, business in the home markets of the banks was poor. Real estate in the United States had just gone bust. Intensified competition among banks led to ever sweeter and more enticing terms for would-be borrowers. In fact, the in thing was to lend to third world countries, and no one wanted to be at the bottom of the league tables. "To a Third World president or finance minister," Federal Reserve chairman Paul Volcker observed afterward, "international banking in the 1970s" was "like receiving a credit card in the mail—with three or four more zeros on the size of the credit line."

In ways that were not very well recognized or accounted for as it was happening, developing-country borrowing exploded. Overall, between 1972 and 1981, the external debts of developing countries increased sixfold, reaching $500 billion by 1981. The infusion of money stimulated, at least for a few years, higher economic growth. By the beginning of the 1980s, the nine largest U.S. banks had committed the equivalent of 250 percent of their capital to loans to developing countries. Those who questioned the rapid buildup of debt were dismissed as grumpy old men. After all, insisted the head of America's largest bank, governments could not go bankrupt.

Right at the top of the borrowing league was Mexico, boosted by its oil boom. By the early 1980s, it owed over $80 billion. Banks fell all over themselves to lend to Mexico. Amidst the feverish lending, one Mexican official was even pronounced, with great admiration, "borrower of the year." After August 1982, however, that was a title no one would want.

How did the borrowing turn into the debt crisis? In retrospect, the formula for bankruptcy was very simple: growing debt, rising interest rates, and falling revenues. The rapid buildup of debt reached its peak at a bad time—just at the moment when, owing to the recession in industrial countries, demand was weakening for the primary products that made up the livelihood of most developing countries. That meant lower prices for their goods, and thus lower income. At the same time, the high interest rates of the early 1980s, aimed at counteracting the inflation in the industrial countries, raised the cost of developing countries' floating debt, increasing the repayment burden. Yes, the borrowed money went into investment, which should have been generating more income. Unfortunately, it also went into things that did not generate much of a return—expensive imports, extravagance, inflation, waste, corruption, and numbered bank accounts. As a result, there was a lot less to show for all the loans in terms of productive assets than might have been anticipated.

During the 1920s, when there was some discussion about debt relief for Germany, President Calvin Coolidge said, "They hired the money, didn't they?" That mistake was not going to be made again. This time around, vast efforts would be expended to help "solve" the debt crisis through rescheduling and repackaging the debt, write-downs and forgiveness, and conversion of existing debt into new kinds of bonds or equity. The alternative was protracted economic misery, with highly uncertain but potentially very serious political consequences. Thus the rest of the 1980s was spent on the cleanup. For parts of the developing world, the 1980s became known as the "lost decade"—a period of either very modest or negative economic growth and, when taking population into account, sharply declining per capita real income. Banks, meanwhile, wrote down their loans, greatly weakening their own balance sheets. All this was the price of ambition and hubris—and imprudence.

The lasting impact of the debt crisis was to fall on the frontier between government and market in the developing world. As part of the rescue packages, the International Monetary Fund became partner to the debt-ridden governments, a sort of international bankruptcy receiver. Imposing tough conditions in its workout deals, the IMF pushed countries to get their fiscal houses in order. That meant removing trade protections that drained resources, devaluing currencies to realistic exchange rates, and restraining wage increases. And, crucially, it meant reducing deficits and fiscal drain. Governments would have to cut spending, stop subsidizing loss-making enterprises, and sell or transfer state-owned assets to the private sector. To help finance this transition and oversee its implementation, the World Bank devised "structural adjustment loans," which it disbursed only when recipients met certain policy conditions. Austerity replaced profligacy.

The debt crisis was the great turning point for the developing world. Far-reaching lessons were drawn from the entire drama. Countries had gotten into these severe straits owing in part to bloated government sectors and inefficient state-owned companies. Nations could not expect the international capital markets to finance a huge, undisciplined government sector. And it was the very expansion of government, justified by the ideas of the times, that had led these nations down the road to what in reality was bankruptcy. Both economic arrangements and the guiding ideas derived from development economics would have to be changed, for they could no longer deliver the economic growth they had promised. Ideas that had been beyond the pale and politically impossible only a few years earlier now moved to the fore, and doors opened to new people who would apply those ideas. Fiscal reality simply would not allow otherwise.[2]

The National Champions

When Franco Bernabè, the somewhat scholarly chief executive of the Italian oil company ENI, came to the United States in 1995, he told a group in Houston, "We have to privatize." Then he added simply, "There is no choice."

What a long arc it had been. ENI, Italy's largest company, would never have come into existence after World War II had it not been state owned. Without state funding and the élan and mission of the national champion, it would never have been able to elbow itself successfully into prominence and technical excellence and grow to become one of the world's ten largest oil companies. Yet what made sense in the 1940s and 1950s no longer held true by the 1990s. Of that Franco Bernabè was sure.

Bernabè's conviction arose from experience—bitter struggles within ENI and the Italian political arena, in which he often found himself on the defensive. Every day, it seemed, he learned and relearned the same lesson— that there was a huge gap between the ideal of the state company and the reality of its predicament. The son of a railway worker and trained as an economist, Bernabè had already played a role in the restructuring of Italy's largest private company, Fiat, by the time he joined ENI in 1983. He had no idea of how bad the conditions inside ENI were. The company was losing money. It was also under constant pressure from Italy's political parties, which regarded it both as a source of funds and as a prize in terms of patronage. The company was not able to function as a coherent business.

From the outset, Bernabè tried to free the company from political influence. But when he began to work on the reorganization of the loss-making chemical business, he found himself subjected to a vicious assault from ministries, parliamentary commissions, ministers, and party officials. That was the turning point for him. "From then on," he said, "I felt a violent hatred for political interference, and I began to think of a way of liberating ENI from the public sector." He quietly started to sketch out a concept for privatization. But then politicians and people in the company who wanted things to stay just the same got wind of his efforts. They unleashed a new war against him; they wanted his head. He was saved in part by the "Clean Hands" investigation into Italy's pervasive corruption that led to the jailing of numerous government officials and businessmen. Among those thrown into prison were twenty senior managers from ENI, including the company's chairman, who committed suicide while in jail. The Clean Hands campaign created a vacuum within ENI. Appointed managing director and CEO in 1992, Bernabè quickly realized that time was running out for the loss-making company. That year, it nearly failed to meet its payroll. Bernabè now set about ferociously restructuring the company, selling off unproductive assets, changing the management, and focusing the company not on meeting the interests of politicians but on creating value for shareholders—although at that time the only shareholder was the state. He also initiated a plan for a privatization. Late in 1995, several months after his visit to the United States, ENI shares were offered, for the first time, on the Milan, New York, and London exchanges.

ENI had been one of the most famous state-owned companies in the world. Although it was uniquely shaped by Italy's political culture, its travails and transformation nevertheless demonstrated in a particularly dramatic form how the position of such enterprises had changed. State companies had come into existence to meet worthy and important ambitions—to secure national objectives, to assert sovereignty and escape foreign domination, to fuel economic growth, to constrain private monopoly, and to ensure that the nation's resources served the interests of the people. They were also to marshal investment and promote technical development. But the difficulties for state companies had already begun to emerge in the 1970s, and indeed, one of the great losers from the crisis of the 1970s was confidence in state-owned companies. The shine of their hallmarks—their corporate cultures, their modes of operation, their pride and sense of mission, their ability to attract skills and mobilize technology—now faded. Coordination had turned into unwieldy control; allocation had turned into distortion; government taxes and revenues had turned into subsidies and obstacles to growth. Political intervention was a chronic ailment. They suffered from inflexibility and inefficiency; they were forced to misallocate resources; and they became an increasing drain on nations' finances. Public enterprises now came to be seen as big contributors to the overall economic crises that nations faced.

The inflexibility of state-owned companies was reflected in the difficulties they faced in innovating. Some were protected from having to innovate because they enjoyed monopolies over domestic markets or exclusive rights to the use of certain basic resources. They did not have to respond to signals from consumers; and entrenched interests within their corporate structures impeded new technologies. In many countries, to be sure, large private companies also fell prey to the failure to keep up with economic and technological change, but competitive economics left them no choice. Many were forced into painful restructurings. State-owned companies, on the other hand, were usually sheltered for all too long. Of course, there were many exceptions. From Norway and France to Latin America and Southeast Asia, one could point to companies that were technological leaders. Yet no less telling was the deplorable condition of public services, equipment, and infrastructure in so many countries. In Argentina, for example, it took over two thousand dollars to get a phone line put in—and several years of waiting. The inflexibility was also obvious in terms of employment. Powerful public-sector unions held an iron grip over labor practices. In many cases, overstaffing and featherbedding were endemic.

Missing were the forces that could have most potently driven the public enterprises to become more efficient, to innovate, to control their investments and expenditures better—competition and the discipline of the capital markets. Whether national champions or outright monopolies, in practice state-owned companies became massive, hierarchical establishments, with a particular culture that seemed endemic to public-enterprise management the world over. Many firms ended up self-regulating: They did what they wanted to do, and some came to resemble "a state within a state." They took pride in their productive, expansionary accomplishments, in the inherent worth of their output, and in their contribution to a nation's development. But their critics said they were also closed off to the rest of the country. They could not control their budgets. And they were not responsive to their customers. Their investment decisions were subject to interference, political criteria, and endless second-guessing rather than to economic realities and opportunities. That would prove to be one of the greatest downsides of the efficient functioning of the state-owned company.

What also became clear was that state ownership creates permanent confusion for enterprises when it comes to their basic purpose. This is what Vijay Kelkar, a distinguished Indian economist and civil servant, observed while serving on the boards of state-owned companies in the 1980s. The experience led him to question one of the fundamental premises of India's development strategy—the ability of governments to run business enterprises. "When the 'people of India' are the shareholders," he said, "it creates multiple and conflicting objectives for the management, which cannot be resolved in any effective way. That makes the companies slow and inefficient and difficult to run. The interests of shareholders and management need to be aligned, and the only objective way to measure performance is through profitability."

There was another consequence of state ownership—what economists euphemistically called "directly unproductive practices"—otherwise known as corruption. The "state within a state" drew in resources—loans, equity, revenues—and attracted fortune seekers. The machinery for nepotism and patronage was in place. Because state companies or governments decided who would get what rights or opportunities under the umbrella of monopoly, those who made such decisions were provided with opportunities for personal enrichment. At times of prosperity, public opinion might be content to accept that kickbacks, contract padding, politically motivated investments, and payoffs to political parties were facts of life. But as growth slowed or transparency increased, the advantages of favored groups became more objectionable and blatant, and were renamed corruption.

The most formidable challenge to state-owned companies was to be found in their bottom line. Although many companies were intended to be self-sustaining, the shelter provided by government ownership gave them greater latitude to spend than what a private firm would have enjoyed. Their spending often exceeded their revenues and they ran ever-larger losses. There was often no discipline. This was the number-one problem. It was inescapable—in developing and developed countries alike. And yet national champions could hardly be shut down. They were frequently not allowed to raise their prices, even if the current prices did not come close to covering costs, for governments feared the inflationary effect—and, no less, angry demonstrations in the streets.

With international lending abruptly foreclosed, the companies could no longer borrow. And so there was only one place left to go for the money—the public coffers. Together, inexorably, companies' losses mounted and government deficits skyrocketed. The financial position of the state itself was now imperiled. Governments acted because they had no choice. They had hit a brick wall. Traditional state-owned companies seemed to have achieved their historic role. But now, they had to be dramatically restructured and reformed, reattuned to the market and financial discipline—in short, "commercialized." Or, more radically, they should cease to exist as state-owned companies and be privatized. Competition and the specter of bankruptcy would work better than monopoly and government funding. The government would relinquish its position on the commanding heights to the capital markets. It would not simply abandon its stake; it would sell the holdings, potentially making a lot of money in the process.

That is what happened with ENI. By late 1997, the Italian government had made $17.6 billion on the sale of its shares in the company; and ENI in turn had generated an annual profit that reached $3 billion in 1996. For Franco Bernabè, the chief architect, the company's transformation arose in part from the need to escape from the struggles and demands of an entangling, corrupt political system. But it was also driven by larger forces. "State companies are finished," he said. "They are basically archaic in a world that has lost many borders and that is becoming global. In fact, state companies are inward-looking and defensive; private companies are outward-looking. In a state-owned company, you are a state official, not an entrepreneur. You're not accountable. Nation-states do not have the tools for competing in a global economy.

"A state company has to do with war, national interest, and self-defense," Bernabè reflected. "And economies were adapted to war until 1990. They were part of closed and antagonist systems. Access to raw materials was considered key to survival. Privatization, on the other hand, is driven by the absence of war, and by the opening of the international system that makes raw materials, money, and technology available to everyone." He added, "The nation-state with all its paraphernalia, including state companies, is a relatively recent invention. The global economy already existed by the fourteenth and fifteenth century. And it's the global economy in which we have to compete." [3]

Red Star Sinking

Call it a model—or an icon. Or call it a spell that was cast upon the twentieth century. For so much of the century was defined by Marxism and the struggle among those who were mesmerized by it and those who rejected it—and those who, through no choice of their own, were caught up in it. Marxism and communism not only constituted a competitive model to market societies but also shaped the terms of the global debate, weighting it toward a powerful role for the state even within capitalist systems. In the aftermath, in communism's ruins, it is hard to understand the enormous prestige the Soviet system garnered around the world first through industrialization and then through the (apparent) very high growth rates of the 1950s and 1960s. That system seemed to have found the solution to the problem of unemployment; it glorified central planning; and it provided a powerful development model, which affected national strategies around the world.

The appeal of Marxism extended beyond the practical questions of how to organize an economy. It also offered a framework for interpreting the ways of the world, an all-embracing theory of everything, from economics, political organization, and relations among nations, to every sort of "structure," whether of the novel, the family, or the sexes. If one could not make it through the impenetrable pages of *Das Kapital,* there was also the romantic appeal of the "young Marx." In its various forms, Marxism attracted intellectuals, provided an outlet for a sense of injustice and outrage and alienation, and delivered a mechanism for political mobilization and control.

And Marxism seemed able to claim so many successes. Was not East

Germany the world's tenth-largest economy on a per capita basis? Did not China's Cultural Revolution show how a decadent society could be both developed and purified? Did not the victory of North Vietnam over the South demonstrate the authority of Marx and the power of Marxism to transform and modernize a backward peasant culture? Even the critics had to concede that there might be something there, at least so long as the curtains—Iron or Bamboo—were firmly in place, impeding the flow of knowledge.

It took decades for those curtains finally to be drawn back. But when they were, reality turned out to be strikingly different from appearances. As an economic system, communism had failed, and spectacularly so. By the 1980s, the sclerotic Soviet economy found its perfect correlative in a series of sclerotic Soviet leaders—the faltering Leonid Brezhnev; the ailing Yuri Andropov, previously head of the KGB; and the doddering Konstantin Chernenko, onetime border guard and Brezhnev crony. By the time Mikhail Gorbachev came to power in 1985, the economy was in deep crisis. Although still a military superpower, the Soviet Union increasingly looked like an underdeveloped country, and a failing one at that. Even before the Soviet Union fell apart in 1991, it had become apparent that communism and Marxism—with their distinctive central planning and pervasive state ownership—had also run into a wall.

The system had worked no better in Eastern Europe, from which the Soviet Union was disengaging. Meanwhile China, although maintaining a rhetorical and political allegiance to Marxism, was rapidly opening the door to the market system—and, in the process, doubling the size of its economy every seven years. The admonition of party leader Deng Xiaoping to the Chinese people was the very un-Marxist "Go out and enrich yourselves." Deng had actually begun the process of reform in the late 1970s, but the dramatic change was not widely recognized until the mid-1980s. By then, China had already taken the crucial step of separating politics from economics in the country's communist system.

In earlier decades in the West, one could have been a fervent anticommunist, appalled by the gulags and the repression, and yet still be influenced by the fact that the Soviet system appeared to be so successful. By the 1980s, that was no longer possible. The result was a vast discrediting of central planning, state intervention, and state ownership. A famous collection of essays by disillusioned former communists published in the 1950s was called, appropriately enough, *The God That Failed*. But now it was the economic model that had failed. "Between the fall of the Berlin Wall in 1989 and the collapse of the Soviet Union in 1991," recalled one of the most senior economic officials in India, "I felt as though I were awakening from a thirty-five-year dream. Everything I had believed about economic systems and had tried to implement was wrong." The spell had been broken.[4]

138

Asian Star Rising

Even as the red star was disappearing, another one was rising, and it accentuated the tilt away from the state-centered economy. It was the "Asian miracle," which began, of course, with Japan. The Japanese, as officials there were fond of repeating, lived in a very small part of a few islands, with hardly any natural resources—in sharp contrast to a resource-rich Soviet Union, which spread across eleven time zones. Yet already by the mid-1980s Japan was becoming recognized as an "economic superpower." It was not alone. Next came the "tigers"—South Korea, Taiwan, Hong Kong, and Singapore. And close behind them came the "new tigers"—Malaysia, Indonesia, Thailand, the Philippines—plus a fifth one, the Guangdong province of China. These became the countries to emulate and from which to learn.

What made Asia a miracle was not just the speed of economic growth. Rather, it was that growth was sustained; that it involved industrial transformation; and, most of all, that ordinary people appeared to share in it, sparking a revolution in lifestyles. But politicians and academics alike hastened to argue that, far from being a miracle, East Asia's success could be explained—and could offer practical lessons for the rest of the world. They set off a vigorous debate over the wellsprings of growth. The arguments came to focus on the role of government intervention—or government restraint. Success was the result of industrial policy, some said—that is, they explained, government had "picked winners" from among domestic companies, nurtured them with subsidies and tariff protection and patronage, and then worked inextricably with these national champions to go out and conquer markets around the world. The results could be measured in growth rates. Others disagreed. They noted that the Asian countries were still much more open to commerce and entrepreneurship than were other parts of the world. Whatever the ambiguities, the Asian nations were, as economist and Nobel Prize winner Gary Becker put it, "by world standards at the time, pretty market-oriented."

The latter view gained ground in the 1990s with the rise of a new formulation that directly challenged the industrial policy thesis. This was the interpretation of the "macro-fundamentalists." The impact of government intervention, they said, was much exaggerated. The decisive factor was that these Asian governments got the economic fundamentals right: low inflation, low government deficits, high savings, education, consistency, institutional and legal frameworks that encouraged enterprise, and—crucially—a willingness to become part of the global system of international trade. In this view, government's direct positive contribution was its promotion of human capital with education and primary health. Picking winners was secondary, and in any event, as an activity it was overrated.

139

New Zealand: "You've Got No Economy"

These lessons had been underscored in the second half of the 1980s and early 1990s by a radical experiment in a remote part of the Pacific Rim—New Zealand. Clothed for decades in a heavy social-democratic coat, New Zealand was an unlikely but important laboratory for economic liberalization. One of the richest countries at the beginning of the century, New Zealand had developed a classic mixed economy in the postwar years that was intended to fulfill the social-democratic dream of "cradle-to-grave security against economic uncertainty." It was highly regulated and highly protected, with a large state-owned sector and a commitment to generate full employment. Wages were controlled; so were prices. As in many other countries, the two television channels were state owned. But unlike other countries, the state also determined who produced television sets and how much they cost. By the 1980s, it was clear that the entire system was malfunctioning. The economy was not competitive; per capita income was falling relative to other economies. Debt as a share of gross domestic product had zoomed up. Unemployment was high. A foreign-exchange crisis in 1984 left no room for maneuver.

The Labour government that came to power after a snap election immediately began a rapid process of liberalization—"breathtaking," some called it—that threw out most of the policy measures associated with left-of-center governments. Over the next several years, the economy was deregulated and state-owned companies underwent a massive program of privatization. Protection of every kind—whether in terms of trade barriers or the job market—was reduced or eliminated. In a direct repudiation of classic egalitarianism, taxes were slashed from the top bracket down. The results were striking. Inflation and unemployment were reduced; growth resumed; debt as a share of GDP went down; and New Zealand became internationally competitive. "Looking back on it, I don't see how we could have avoided it," one prime minister said several years after the reforms began. "You can't have social justice if you've got no economy." Unlike the Asian tigers, New Zealand did not become a household word in the world of economic policy, but its program of change—initiated by an ostensibly left-of-center government—certainly had an important impact on thinking of decision makers in other parts of the world.

New Zealand's reforms ran in parallel to the Thatcher Revolution in Britain. Both reflected a conjunction of an economic crisis with political leadership willing to go against the grain and apply ideas that up until then had mostly had their impact only in theory. But the fundamental framework of economics through which the world was seen was changing. And here was a classic demonstration of the power of ideas.[5]

Friedrich von Hayek and the "Battle of Ideas"

In retrospect, it was the awarding of the 1974 Nobel Prize in economics that first captured, almost by chance, the great intellectual change. The Swedish academy wanted to honor Gunnar Myrdal, distinguished Keynesian, a father of development economics, and a great figure of Swedish socialism. But the grantors, worried about the appearance of choosing so local a favorite, decided that they ought to balance the ticket with a more conservative figure, and they awarded the prize to Myrdal jointly with Friedrich von Hayek. A good part of the economics profession was scandalized by the choice of Hayek; many economists in the United States, if polled, would have hardly even considered him an economist. He was regarded as right-wing, certainly not mainstream, even something of a crank as well as a fossil from an archaic era. As for Gunnar Myrdal, the lore among other Nobel winners is that he was so irritated that he hardly even spoke to Hayek during the ceremonies.

Yet the award documented the beginning of a great shift in the intellectual center of gravity of the economics profession toward a restoration of confidence in markets, indeed a renewed belief in the superiority of markets over other ways of organizing economic activity. Within a decade and a half, the shift would be largely complete. And the eventual victory of this viewpoint was really a tale of two cities—Vienna and Chicago.

Friedrich von Hayek was the figure who tied the two together; he also connected the post–World War I Austrian School of economics to the renewed embrace of markets in the 1980s. A product of the Austro-Hungarian Empire and its collapse, Hayek was shaped by the vibrant, vital culture of Vienna both before World War I and, in its more tortured form, after the war. A second cousin to the philosopher Ludwig Wittgenstein, he came from a family of biologists and government officials, and he was headed toward his father's career, botany. But then World War I fundamentally changed his outlook. As a junior officer in the war, he came face-to-face with the complexities and dangers of nationalistic fervor. "I saw, more or less, the great empire collapse over the nationalist problem," he later said. "I served in a battle in which eleven different languages were spoken. It's bound to draw your attention to the problems of political organization." The war also left him with a compulsion to find an answer to "the burning question" of how to build a "juster society."

To that end, returning to Vienna after the war, Hayek earned doctorates in both economics and law. He went to New York City in 1923 and enrolled in the Ph.D. program at New York University. But he ran out of money and returned to Vienna to continue his work in economics. The war drove him, like many of his young contemporaries, toward an idealistic search for renewal, a quest for a better world—which meant socialism. "We felt that the civilization in which we had grown up had collapsed," he later said.

"This desire to reconstruct society led many of us to the study of economics. Socialism promised to fulfill our hopes for a more rational, more just world." But then, as he began to study economics, he went through a painful and reluctant reassessment, in which he concluded that his idealistic objectives could be better served through a market economy.

His transformation occurred under the influence of Ludwig von Mises, the most prominent member of the Austrian School of economics. In his book *Socialism,* published in 1922, Mises presented a devastating analysis of the central economic failing of socialism. He called it the economic calculation. The problem was that under central planning, there was no economic calculation—no way to make a rational decision to put this resource here or buy that good there, because there was no price system to weigh the alternatives. Central planners could make technical decisions but not economic ones. Over the rest of the century, that criticism would prove to be extraordinarily prescient. *"Socialism* shocked our generation," Hayek later said. Yet, he added, it profoundly altered the outlook of idealists returning from the war. "I know, for I was one of them. . . . *Socialism* told us that we had been looking for improvement in the wrong direction."

Hayek became Mises' student and then, for several years, his research assistant. Owing to the postwar Austrian inflation, he learned firsthand, in his very first job, what inflation could mean. He began at five hundred kronen a month. Nine months later, his salary had swollen to 1 million kronen a month. In 1931, Hayek was invited to become a professor at the London School of Economics (LSE). The invitation was proffered by William Beveridge (who would author the Beveridge Report a decade later) but was at the specific instance of Lionel Robbins, the outstanding British liberal economist. In his inaugural address at LSE, Hayek declared that it was "almost inevitable" that any "warm-hearted person, as soon as he becomes conscious of the existing misery, should become a socialist." But economic study would bring that person to a more conservative point of view. This would happen to people who "have all possible sympathy with the ethical motives" from which radicalism springs and who "would be only too glad if they could believe that socialism or planning can do what they promise to do."

The London School of Economics had been founded by the Fabian socialists in 1895, and since the 1930s it had had a reputation as a leftist institution, dominated by socialists and devoted to propagating left-wing doctrines both in Britain and to the young people who went to study there from around the world. Yet by the 1930s, LSE's economics department, with Robbins, Hayek, and others, became the redoubt of traditional liberalism, battling to uphold the creed as socialism and Keynesianism became the dominant forces of the time. Hayek was at the forefront, not only the most consistent but indeed the most vocal critic of Keynes' work both before and after *The General Theory.* Keynes' approach, Hayek believed, was based on error; it would not solve the slump but would institutionalize inflation.

142

Indeed, in Hayek's view, *The General Theory* was not a general theory of economics at all but rather a dressed-up specific theory to get around a political impasse in Britain. Keynes was no less slashing in his rejoinders. Hayek, he said, had started in one article "with a mistake" and then proceeded to "bedlam." Another Hayek article, he said, was "the wildest farrago of nonsense." In 1933 Keynes wrote his wife about a visit that Hayek had made to Cambridge. Keynes sat next to him at dinner and then lunched with him the following day. "We get on very well in private life. But what rubbish his theory is."[6]

The Road to Serfdom

As World War II progressed, Hayek became increasingly apprehensive about what he saw as the advance of collectivism, central planning, and what would become Keynesian interventionism. In one of his most famous articles, he argued that the problem of knowledge defeats central control of economies: Those at the center can never have enough information to make their decisions. Much better, he argued, was the price system, which, in "its real function" was "a mechanism for communicating information." For Hayek, it was nothing less than "a marvel." He explained, "The marvel is that in a case like that of a scarcity of one raw material, without an order being issued, without more than perhaps a handful of people knowing the cause, tens of thousands of people whose identity could not be ascertained by months of investigation, are made to use the material or its products more sparingly; that is, they move in the right direction."

At the same time Hayek was preparing a full-scale broadside in a much more popular form—*The Road to Serfdom*. That book, which appeared in 1944, might have become a best-seller in Britain were it not for the extreme paper rationing of the war. Nevertheless, at least one copy found its way into the hands of an Oxford undergraduate, Margaret Roberts, not yet Margaret Thatcher. The University of Chicago Press published it in the United States, and Hayek's arguments went on to have much wider fame when *Reader's Digest* published a condensed version. To some degree, Hayek had to make his arguments in code, for it was not acceptable to criticize the Soviet Union, which at the time was a great ally. Even so, after World War II, the four-power-occupation authorities in Germany banned the book there at the behest of the Soviet Union.

Keynes, who read *The Road to Serfdom* while on his way to the Bretton Woods conference, wrote Hayek, more than oddly, that it was "a grand book." He added that he was in "deeply moved agreement" with the whole of it. He then proceeded to lay out his profound disagreement: "According to my ideas you greatly under-estimate the practicability of the middle course. . . . What we want is not no planning, or even less planning, indeed I should say that we almost certainly want more." He concluded by advising

Hayek to take up "the restoration of right moral thinking." For "if only you could turn your crusade in that direction you would not feel quite so much like Don Quixote."

But after the initial splash of *The Road to Serfdom,* Hayek did rather seem a Don Quixote off on a fanciful campaign. In later years, Hayek would ruefully acknowledge that the book was too "popular" for his own academic good and had discredited him within the economics profession. The breakup of his first marriage occurred shortly after, and he married a woman he had first fallen in love with over twenty years earlier. In 1950, Hayek left LSE for an appointment at the University of Chicago. He was professor of social and moral sciences and a member of the prestigious Committee on Social Thought, where his colleagues included some of America's most stellar intellectuals. He was not part of the economics department and did not have much direct impact on students there. He struck people as very much an old-style Central European gentleman—reserved, rather austere. When a young graduate student (much later a Nobel Prize winner) asked him to read a draft essay on economic analysis and political choice, Hayek politely declined. He did not read handwritten manuscripts, he explained.

It was while at Chicago that Hayek wrote what many consider his outstanding work, *The Constitution of Liberty,* published in 1960. In it, he further developed one of his most important themes: Laissez-faire was not enough. Government did have a clear role: to ensure the development and maintenance of the institutions—the laws and rules—that would ensure a competitive economy. And that, whatever emotion might otherwise say, remained the best mechanism for achieving the ideals that had captured him on the battlefield of World War I. Hayek never quite felt at home in Chicago. He kept a car in Paris, and whenever he could, he returned to the Alps with his new wife. Depression began to unsettle him. After a dozen years at the University of Chicago, he took up an appointment at the University of Freiburg, amid the Ordoliberals.

The Alps had already provided the venue from which Hayek would extend his influence. In 1947, he had taken the lead in convening a meeting of a remarkable group of intellectuals, mainly economists, numbering just thirty-six. It was held at a Swiss spa on Mont Pèlerin, and ever after became known as the Mont Pèlerin Society. The first session was such a success that the group reconvened two years later and thereafter on a regular basis, in different locations, with ever-growing numbers. It provided a framework for like-minded thinkers to dissect socialism and collectivism and to debate and argue philosophy and policies. It also provided liberal (in the European sense) economists with the sense of an international community, with a fervor to develop their ideas, and—especially for those coming from countries where liberal economists were few and far between—the means to overcome their isolation and the comfort of knowing that they were not alone.

For Hayek, the meetings of the Mont Pèlerin Society were essential bivouacs in the war of ideas. He believed that the struggle would be a long one; liberal thinking would be on the defensive "for the next ten or twenty years, during which the present collectivist trend is bound to continue." In a paper entitled "The Intellectuals and Socialism," which he circulated after the first meeting of the society, he warned the participants that they should prepare for the protracted struggle, though it was one that they could win. "What to the contemporary observer appears as a battle of conflicting interests decided by the votes of the masses," he said, "has usually been decided long before in a battle of ideas confined to narrow circles."[7]

The Chicago School

Among those attending that first Mont Pèlerin meeting was a young economist from the University of Chicago who was making his first trip to Europe —Milton Friedman. Mont Pèlerin certainly helped Friedman become part of an international network—and at the same time contributed to the dissemination of Friedman's increasingly influential work. Indeed, the fundamental shift in the global attitude toward markets might never have happened, at least in the form it did, had it not been for several decades' worth of highly unfashionable academic "scribbling" by Friedman and his colleagues at the University of Chicago. The Chicago School, as it became known, provided a substantial part of the foundation for the intellectual reformulation, both in the United States and around the world.

Like many great university departments in the United States, Chicago's economics faculty came together in the 1930s and 1940s as an amalgam of distinguished American academics, rising young stars, and eminent Europeans, some of them refugees from fascism. It was a diverse group. The leader was Frank Knight, a free-market economist. But there was also Paul Douglas, a firebrand New Deal liberal, who eventually departed for a career in politics and ended up a U.S. senator. Another member was a Polish refugee, Oskar Lange, who, ironically enough, while at Chicago did much to develop a model for market socialism. Lange was expected to become a major figure in the department but instead left Chicago at the end of World War II to join the new Communist-dominated government in Poland and became its ambassador to the new United Nations.

By the end of the 1950s, people were already talking about a distinctive Chicago School, which, in opposition to the new Keynesianism, emphasized laissez-faire—free markets—and argued against government intervention. What made Chicago special? The economics faculty was committed to famously rigorous and well-defined standards of teaching in the Ph.D. program. People flunked. The department focused on workshops, which brought faculty and students together on a regular basis to thrash out and argue over issues. Members of the department cohered around a particular worldview and set of ideas, which they explored and advanced single-mindedly and which was basic to the training of new Ph.D's. George Shultz, later secretary of the Treasury and secretary of state, noticed the difference as soon as he joined the Chicago faculty after fifteen years at MIT. "It was more a university than anywhere else," he said. "People from all over the university interacted together as colleagues."

"Chicago always had a strong tradition of a belief in the power of markets," said Gary Becker, who went to Chicago as a graduate student in 1951 and won the Nobel Prize in 1992. "Chicago's contribution was to show the power of markets and people's choices, not only in public policy but also in economic science. The department also had very strong leadership. There was a lot of self-confidence that we had the right answers and the rest of the profession was wrong. We saw economic analysis as a powerful way to understand behavior, providing a lot of insight not only into the economy itself, but also how society organized. I think that at most places economics was taught as a game; it was not clear that teachers elsewhere thought economics was a powerful tool. Chicago did."

The Chicago economists believed, in practice, in a very small number of theorems about the way decision makers allocated resources and the ways these allocations led to prices. They trusted in markets and the effectiveness of competition. Left to their own devices, markets produced the best outcomes. Prices were the best allocators of resources. Any intervention to change what markets, left alone, would achieve was likely to be counterproductive. For the Chicago economists, the conclusions for government policy were clear: Wherever possible, private activity should take over from public activity. The less government did, the better. Intervention in the money supply distorted the markets; better instead to have a steady, predictable growth in the money supply. This was the very opposite of the Keynesian idea that government could smooth out economic fluctuations. This aspect of the Chicago approach, and its later variants, became known as monetarism.

Through most of the 1950s, the Chicago School remained obscure and unfashionable, at least as far as the public was concerned. It seemed to contradict the conventional wisdom in almost every respect. But by the end of the decade, all that was changing, partly driven by Milton Friedman, who was not only a powerfully capable economist but also charismatic, optimistic, and unfazed, whether by the spotlight or by the enormous amount of criticism that would be heaped upon him.

While in high school Friedman had fallen in love with mathematics, inspired by a teacher who was so passionate about geometry that he concluded the proof of the Pythagorean theorem by quoting John Keats's "Ode on a Grecian Urn"—"Beauty is truth, truth beauty." Attending Rutgers on a state scholarship, Friedman was eager to find a profession in which he could use mathematics, and he aspired to become an insurance actuary. That ambition was terminated when he failed some of his actuarial courses. But by then he was already interested in economics, again inspired by outstanding teachers, including Arthur Burns, who went on to become chairman of

146

the Federal Reserve Board. Economics was an almost-inevitable career choice for Friedman: "I graduated from college in 1932, when the United States was at the bottom of the deepest depression in its history before or since," he later wrote. "Becoming an economist seemed more relevant to the burning issues of the day than becoming an applied mathematician or an actuary." He enrolled as a graduate student in economics at the University of Chicago and did his doctoral work there, interspersed with research at Columbia.

It was upon becoming a professor at Chicago in 1946 that Friedman truly began to go his own way. He emerged from among the Chicago faculty as an iconoclastic and controversial thinker and leader of what was, by the late 1950s, an all-out assault on virtually every aspect of Keynesian economics. He was a formidable debater. Colleagues joked that people preferred to debate him when he wasn't there. As a teacher, he was demanding and relentless. "Everything you could say, he could say better," recalled one student. His students also developed enormous loyalty to him. There was a great sense of camaraderie. They were part of a small band, fighting for the truth.

According to the Chicago approach, intervention almost always did more harm than good. In a famous early article, "Roofs or Ceilings? The Current Housing Problem," Friedman and his coauthor, George Stigler, rigorously demonstrated that however good its intentions, rent control had the perverse effect of reducing available housing by removing the incentives for landlords and builders to bring new housing to the market. Overall, Friedman would argue, taxation and government spending were appropriate only for the most limited set of "public goods," such as national defense. Everything else was best left alone.[8]

The members of the Chicago School rejected the concept of market failure and the tenets of Keynesianism. They were also much more concerned about the extension of government power than about the dangers of monopoly, the latter having been one of the main motivators of regulation in the United States. They regarded the problem of private monopoly as much overstated, partly because of technological change. "Private unregulated monopoly," wrote Friedman, was the lesser of the evils "when compared to government regulation and ownership."

While Friedman attacked the sacred cows of macroeconomics, his colleagues challenged other aspects of the dominant thought. George Stigler conducted a quiet but no less devastating critique of government intervention through regulation. Gary Becker applied economic analysis to an array of social issues, beginning with discrimination. "I believe that people make rational decisions and that they try to look ahead to the consequences of their decisions," explained Becker. "They are affected by incentives. You can take markets, rationality, and incentives and illuminate issues involving race, education, and the family." Becker's most famous work was a path-breaking analysis of "human capital." Although now more than fashionable as a subject, it was hardly studied at all before Becker took it up. "Human capital," he said, "deals with expenditures on people—for education, training, health—that in a broad sense raise productivity." He agonized, however, about using "Human Capital" as the title. "I was concerned that it would set too many people off. It was unacceptable to many people to link 'human' and 'capital.' Now people are happy to use it." Chicago's 1995 Nobel Prize winner, Robert Lucas, led a new line of research, starting in the 1970s, around the issue of "rational expectations." That work argues that government decisions are not likely to have the anticipated results, owing to the responses of decision makers in the economy. Market knowledge outwits government knowledge.

The Chicago School was derided for being dogmatic, rigid, and reductionist. Friedman was happy to counterattack. He enjoyed the pulpit. He believed his ideas could transform the world—and, arguably, they did. He saw a direct, explicit, and unabashed connection between capitalism and democracy. Free markets produced the best results, and economic freedom rested, in turn, on political liberty. He propounded his ideas not only in a constant flow of journal articles but also in more popular form. His 1962 classic, *Capitalism and Freedom,* was aimed at economists and the general public alike. In 1964, he was economics adviser to the conservative Republican presidential candidate Barry Goldwater. He had become so much a celebrity upon receiving the 1976 Nobel Prize that he found himself, he said, interviewed "on everything from a cure for the common cold to the market value of a letter signed by John F. Kennedy." He conveyed his ideas in a mass-market best-seller, *Free to Choose,* which became a public-television series. In the 1980s, he could recall with some satisfaction that in the 1950s the ideas he and his colleagues were propounding were those of "a small, beleaguered minority regarded as eccentrics by our fellow intellectuals." By the 1980s, those very same ideas were "at least respectable in the intellectual community and very likely almost conventional among the broader public." Still a decade later, in the middle 1990s, MIT economist Paul Krugman would write that Friedman's "long campaign against the ideas of Keynesian economics" had made him into "the world's best-known economist." So much for Keynes.

The Chicago School was hardly alone, and by the early 1980s, "Chicago" itself had become more dispersed. Friedman retired from teaching and, along with others, shifted his base to the Hoover Institution at Stanford, which afforded direct connection to Ronald Reagan and his advisers. But by then it became clear that the Chicago School had carried out a devastatingly successful "neoclassical counterattack" in economics and in its applications. Macroeconomics management did not work, while tinkering with the money supply only increased uncertainty and discouraged investment. And the Chicago School also showed that regulation would inevitably drift away from the ideal of promoting an impersonal public good. Instead, it would be captured by special interests. On top of everything else, government had failed to prove itself as a forecaster. Faith in "big government" fell under the attack.

The work of Chicago—and, more indirectly, Hayek's contribution—proved crucial to a general shift in the center of gravity of economic thinking and to a reevaluation of the appropriate balance of government and marketplace. Fiscal management was no longer seen as an effective tool; fine-tuning was beyond the knowledge and skill of the tuners. Higher inflation did not assure lower unemployment, but it did mean more uncertainty. Smaller government was better; it was all too easy for big government to crowd out private activity. In contradiction to the received wisdom of Keynesianism, reducing deficits, rather than increasing them, could stimulate economic activity. Keynes, it turned out, was not a man for all seasons.

Professors at Chicago felt for many years that other major universities —such as Harvard, Yale, MIT, and Berkeley—did not take Chicago seriously and would not hire its students. Schools like UCLA and the University of Rochester were much more sympathetic. The University of Virginia became a center for free-market thinking, around the figure of James Buchanan. Buchanan and the "public choice" theory applied economic assumptions of self-interested behavior to the actions of politicians, bureaucrats, and voters. A groundswell of Nobel Prizes, beginning with Hayek and Friedman in the mid-1970s, chronicled Chicago's ascendancy. Altogether, since 1974, eight professors from Chicago and another eleven associated at some time with Chicago have won Nobel Prizes in economics. "The shift toward Chicago was clear to me after 1975," said Gary Becker. "It was a result of what was going on in the economics profession and what was going on in the world. They came together."

As Friedman himself saw it, the acceptance of Chicago's ideas resulted first from the stagflation and economic impasse of the 1970s—and then from the fall of the Berlin Wall. "People are not influential in arguing for different courses in the economy," he said. "The role of people is to keep ideas alive until a crisis occurs. It wasn't my talking that caused people to embrace these ideas, just as the rooster doesn't make the sun rise. Collectivism was an impossible way to run an economy. What has brought about the change is reality, fact—and what Marx called the inevitable forces of history."[9]

Grudging Respect

This intellectual migration wrought three changes: in the economics profession, in the minds of those within it, and in national and international economic policies. All three are clear in the career of Jeffrey Sachs. He was "raised" at Harvard as a Keynesian. And in 1976, as a reward for being selected the best undergraduate in economics, he was invited to lunch at the New York Federal Reserve. "I remember," he recalled, "saying the word *monetarist* and almost spitting it out." From the mid-1980s on, he was at the center of economic reform in Latin America and since then in Eastern Europe, the former Soviet Union, Asia, and Africa. His experience in confronting the results of government control of the commanding heights proved profoundly disillusioning; he lost his confidence in the ability of governments to control their economies in a rational way. "The more that I have sat and discussed the economy with government ministers," he said, "the more I have come to believe in the anonymous, competitive processes of the market. And now I am attacked all over the world as a Friedmanite. Considering where I came from, that's amazing for me."

The shift in thinking converged with the experience and learning of the preceding decades. Confidence in market knowledge rather than government knowledge formed the foundations of the global critique. The new viewpoint was powerfully articulated in the 1991 edition of the World Bank's authoritative annual *World Development Report.* The 1991 report signified a sharp break with the conventional wisdom. Instead of intervening, it said, governments should pursue "market friendly" policies—policies that encouraged the private sector. By inference, the bulk of past policies had been "market unfriendly."

The person in charge of the report was Lawrence Summers, then the World Bank's chief economist and currently U.S. deputy Treasury secretary. The nephew of two Nobel Prize winners in economics—Paul Samuelson and Kenneth Arrow—and himself educated at MIT and Harvard, Summers won the Clark Medal for the best economist under the age of forty. "In 1955, it was not unreasonable to focus on the Depression and the impact of World War II," he said. "The autarkic countries of Latin America were doing well, and the Soviet Union seemed to be growing at three and a half times the rate of the United States. Today, the Depression and World War II are much smaller parts of historical experience.

"Three things happened to change people's thinking in recent years," he continued. "First, they have seen how badly the public sector can mess things up. With competition, things seem to go better. Innovation happens. The world is more focused on variety than quantity. Secondly, markets are able to do things that people used to think required government coordination. Markets make it possible to rent videos in every town in America, with no public involvement. There is now a skepticism about the view that you have to have the public sector to get things done. And thirdly, a gradual refinement in economic science has led to an upward revision in elasticities, in how systems respond. There is a greater response to tax rates than people used to think. If you interfere with property rights, business responds by going elsewhere. Maybe it is because economies are more global.

"What's the single most important thing to learn from an economics course today?" Summers asked. "What I tried to leave my students with is the view that the invisible hand is more powerful than the hidden hand.

Things will happen in well-organized efforts without direction, controls, plans. That's the consensus among economists. That's the Hayek legacy.

"As for Milton Friedman," Summers added, "he was the devil figure in my youth. Only with time have I come to have large amounts of grudging respect. And with time, increasingly ungrudging respect." [10]

The Emergence of Emerging Markets

Tom Hansberger was a man with an obsession. It started when he was serving with the U.S. Air Force in North Africa and Europe in the late 1950s. During a mission to Greece and Turkey, he was particularly struck to discover countries that were modernizing with well-run private companies. And no one in the United States seemed to know anything about those companies. That was the beginning of his obsession with global investing, although it was hardly a term that would have been used at the time. Entering the securities business, Hansberger bounced around from Wall Street to Ohio, and ended up running a trust department for a bank in Tampa, Florida. There, at a local meeting of security analysts, he ran into John Templeton. He had seen an article in *Forbes* that described Templeton as the "wise old owl" of investing, and indeed Templeton, working from a small office in the Bahamas, was already on the way to becoming one of the great legends of the business. Templeton was one of those people with the ability to see things long before others. He was also highly disciplined both in his work and his life, and he remained parsimonious on principle even when he became a billionaire. "For John, every investment had its own personality and life," said Hansberger, "and he never allowed emotion to get mixed up in his decision making. Everything was decided on its own merits."

At the time of their meeting, Templeton, who had put up to 60 percent of the funds he was managing into Japan, was just beginning to expand his global investment portfolio. And that was exactly what most interested Hansberger. In 1979, he went to work as chief executive officer of Templeton Investment, which was still a small firm. And the first thing Hansberger did was get himself a passport. Then he bought an extended airline ticket and took off for several months, visiting companies around the world and looking for local specialists. Over the next decade and a half, Templeton and Hansberger would do as much anybody else in the world to open up stock markets in developing countries to American and European investors. It was not all that easy at first. "We would go and see potential investors and talk about investing internationally, but almost no one thought it necessary to do something overseas," said Hansberger. "They would tell us that they didn't need the currency risk, the economic risk, and certainly not the political risk. Sometimes people would laugh at us. Sometimes they would look at us as though we should be committed."

At this same time, the International Finance Corporation (IFC), a World Bank affiliate that focuses on the private sector, was trying to promote the flow of funds into the stock markets of developing countries. Antoine van Agtmael, a Dutch banker, had worked in Thailand in the late 1970s, when that country's stock market went through the exhilaration of its first great boom and then a massive bust. "That left me with three conclusions," van Agtmael recalled. "There was enormous potential in such countries. There was an enormous need for funds for companies that were being completely overlooked by major investors. And there was enormous risk. That argued to me for diversification, investing in a lot of countries." Van Agtmael joined the IFC, working with a small group that sought to promote that kind of investment. "We were fighting," he said, "against the dominant ethos in the World Bank at that time, which regarded these markets as crazy little casinos and which was much more interested in government intervention."

One day, as part of his crusade, van Agtmael went to New York to talk to a group of investors about his pet idea of a "third world investment fund." After he finished speaking, someone from the audience stood up and said, "I think it is an interesting idea, but you can never sell it. No one wants to put money into the *third world investment fund*. You'd better come up with something better." Van Agtmael realized that the criticism was right, and spent the following weekend anxiously wracking his brain. *Underdeveloped markets* was a complete nonstarter. *Third world* wouldn't do. Nor would the World Bank's favorite, *developing nations*. None of those terms would exactly entice Americans to part with their savings—not at the very moment when the debt crisis was shining a huge spotlight on these countries' economic infirmities. "I knew we needed something positive, uplifting, not negative," van Agtmael said. And by the time he came to work on Monday morning, he had the answer: *emerging markets*. That was the magic nomenclature.

But it was a long road from words to reality. In what proved to be a most inauspicious beginning, the IFC helped get the Mexico Fund launched just as Mexico veered toward bankruptcy. It did better supporting the launch of the Korea Fund. Van Agtmael even wrote a book, *Emerging Securities Markets*. Yet by the middle 1980s there was still not much to show for all the effort. The need, if anything, was even more urgent; the debt crisis and the abrupt cessation of lending accentuated the importance of getting money into the cash-starved growth companies of the third world.

Still, with the debt cleanup continuing, few investors were clambering to put their funds to work in what seemed a very risky proposition. Finally in 1986, the IFC, working with the Capital Group, a money management company, succeeded in persuading a group of major institutional investors to come up with a grand total of $50 million for an emerging-markets fund. It was a cautious experiment. The developing countries were going through the wringer, and the opportunities looked to be very limited. Templeton followed suit with the first public mutual fund for emerging markets. "When we launched our emerging market fund in 1986," said Hansberger, "we raised $80 million. Our biggest worry at the time was that we would not be able to invest it, because there were not enough opportunities." Templeton's emerging-market funds now invest over $10 billion.

With the kick start from the IFC, emerging markets began their dramatic growth in the second half of the 1980s. In 1987, the capitalization of emerging stock markets totaled $332 billion, 5 percent of a world stock capitalization of $7.8 trillion. A decade later, in 1996, the capitalization was $2.2 trillion, 11 percent of a total world capitalization of $20.2 trillion. "I always knew that it had to happen," said Hansberger, "but it's come more quickly than I thought." The real propulsion came from the fall of the Berlin Wall. "Billions of people living in communist and third world nations joined the marketplace. That catalyzed the global investing theme. Before that, it had only been regional." By the early 1990s, developing countries were beginning to compete hard for the investment. What had seemed highly risky only a decade ago has become commonplace. Investment experts advise Americans to put 10 or 20 percent of their total savings into emerging markets. Calpers, the mammoth pension fund of California's state workers, currently has over $2.5 billion in those markets.

When Templeton was sold to another fund group, Hansberger decided to start over with his own company. But the circumstances were very different from when he had joined up with John Templeton in 1979. "When I started doing international investing," he said, "there were only seven markets outside the United States in which we could invest. Germany and Japan were the emerging markets at the time, although no one called them that. Now we've invested in forty-seven countries, and we research sixty-two. Altogether there are ninety emerging markets, and the number is continually growing. Technology is helping to speed up the growth. With computers, we can screen twenty thousand companies for investment objectives before lunch. Technology also makes possible the instantaneous transfer of money. You push a button, and in a second you move a billion dollars."

The development of emerging markets was central to economic change around the world. It responded to the specific need in the 1980s to find new sources of money to fuel growth. Governments would not take on new debt, which was not available to them in any event; capital would instead be attracted through local stock markets into private companies in developing countries. In this way, the developing countries could gain access to the savings—as represented in the mutual funds and pension funds—of the industrialized world. And in order to attract capital, countries would have to display stable currencies, encouraging prospects for growth, and a receptive political climate. In practice, of course, the flow of investment also depends on less quantifiable, more psychological factors. And there are those who, remembering the debt crisis, caution that investors often miscalculate risks. With large amounts of money traveling among what are still relatively thin markets, highly sensitive to investor psychology and market trends, there is a constant risk of "corrections" in emerging markets. Yet despite the inevitability of periodic setbacks, sometimes quite drastic, the rise of the emerging markets is entrenched. It has accelerated the shift toward reliance on market knowledge, tied economies together, become a force for change, and created a major counterbalance to traditional government intervention. Across the developing world, government decision makers now have to worry not only about the domestic impact of their decisions but also about the reaction of foreign investors. Officials still can, and often do, intervene as they will; they can impose autarkic policies or put up barriers; they can pursue policies that stimulate inflation or create deficits. But they risk engendering a reaction —a speedy exit from their stock markets—that did not exist before.

Emerging markets are delivering a tremendous jolt to the old system. To understand the impact of the new calculus on governments, the Indian economist Vijay Kelkar suggested borrowing from the psychologist Erich Fromm. Explained Kelkar, "Fromm talks about the balance between 'mother love,' which is unconditional, and 'father love,' which is conditional. What we are seeing is the shift from the unconditional love of the treasury, which takes the form of deficits and endless subsidies for loss-making state enterprises, to the conditional father love, which is the discipline imposed by international capital markets. That father love was not there before."

Financial Integration

The world was already being tied together by continuing increases in cross-border investment by companies and the globalization of their activities. But beginning in the mid-1980s, the development and coalescing of capital markets—financial integration—gave a new meaning to the international economy. The powerful effects of financial integration depended, in turn, upon informational integration. Rapid advances in telecommunications and computing, which linked markets and investors together, provided instant knowledge of performance. As a result, not only national but also global capital markets could vote not every day or every hour but every minute on stock markets—and thus on national economies. A negative vote could mean a very swift outflow of capital.

In ways that could not easily be disentangled, the information and telecommunications revolution was partly responsible for the global critique. State control depends upon a state that is in charge. And one of its most important sources of power is monopoly over information. That was most obvious with the Soviet Union, where oil reserves were a state secret and a factory manager had hardly any opportunity to learn about developments in the rest of the world that might affect his operations unless he took the risk of listening to Radio Liberty or the BBC. In the classic autarkic system, control of information was as important as control over licenses, currency, and investment.

154

But once information began to flow more freely with improved and less expensive phone service, fax machines, and computerization (and, of course, with increased travel), entire economic systems became more transparent. With the speed and reach of new information technology, governments can no longer keep up. As information flies around the world, people can compare and contrast; they can trade knowledge instantaneously; they can act upon it. Investors can make far more informed decisions no matter where they sit. Access to a Reuters terminal or a Bloomberg machine provides a range and depth of information hardly imaginable ten years ago—and without a moment's delay. Inside countries where the walls had been high, people can now learn about alternatives and choices.

The impact of the information and telecommunications revolution is only beginning to be felt. But it is a very different kind of economy when companies establish virtual headquarters and software designers in Silicon Valley and Bangalore, or oil geologists in Siberia and Houston, or auto designers in Detroit and Cologne, function via computer as one team. The effectiveness of state control and the very borders of the nation-state are being eroded. Nations' economic managers become parochial when the market becomes universal. Thus the notion of government knowledge, as decades of planners and regulators had developed it, has come under siege. Government may not know as much as it thought it knew—and may not be able to act effectively on what it does know. The result is increased limits on governments. Political impulses are now subject to economic imperatives as market systems take control of delivering goods, lowering prices, decreasing inflation, and improving universal living standards. But the intellectual victory of the marketplace has also transferred a new set of duties and responsibilities to the market, leading to new questions about just what and how much the market knows and how effectively it will be used—and how badly awry things could go. For global markets also mean global risks. Just as vastly increased travel means that diseases can be transported more quickly, so financial integration means that contagion can pass rapidly among markets.

The dust has yet to clear from this very dramatic reversal of roles in what has become a global economy. Yet there appears to be greater modesty about government knowledge and what government ought to do with the knowledge it does have. For Valéry Giscard d'Estaing, the shift from state control to market control was symbolized by something as simple as bread. As France's junior minister of finance in the late 1960s, he oversaw the implementation of price controls for basic goods. "I had an army of civil servants," he recalled, "whose job was to inspect every bakery in France and make sure the price of a *baguette* followed the guidelines." Thousands of officials fanned out across the cities to bicker and argue with the bakers in every town and village. "This was nonsense," Giscard concluded. "I realized the system could not go on." [11]

CHAPTER 6

BEYOND THE MIRACLE

Asia's Emergence

Is THERE TRULY such a thing as the East Asia economic miracle? Prime Minister Mahathir Mohamad of Malaysia would have an informed view. After all, since the mid-1980s, the country over which he presides had been growing at an annual rate of 6 percent or more. On the day he was to discuss this matter, he welcomed the visitors to his office in Kuala Lumpur a bit stiffly from behind an enormous desk of pristine teak. The prime minister was clothed simply, in traditional Malay dress. He also wore, at chest level, a small, formal tag that read MAHATHIR. All of his aides sported their own tags.

Mahathir was definitely well connected; on a separate table at his side sat four screens, which blinked intermittently. The first served for video conferencing; the second was linked to the Internet; the third displayed a continuous news feed from Reuters; and the fourth provided up-to-the-hour information on developments across Malaysia. To the left, models of airplanes designed and built by Malaysians were displayed on a windowsill.

Outside, downtown Kuala Lumpur—KL, as it is known in Asia—was a boom city, with a forest of gigantic cranes and construction equipment. At street level, youths—Malay, Chinese, and Indian—clad in jeans and T-shirts zoomed on motorbikes through streets jammed with Japanese cars, Mercedeses, and the ubiquitous Proton, Malaysia's national car. The cultural mix was captured by the stark contrast of women in miniskirts and high heels next to women clad head to toe in demure Islamic dress. Twin office towers, astonishingly tall, tapered far up into the sky. Belonging to the state oil company, Petronas, they are the world's tallest office buildings, surpassing the World Trade Center in New York and Chicago's Sears Tower. They are also an extraordinary architectural symbol of an Asian economic growth so sustained and so dramatic that even the World Bank called it a miracle. Embracing Malaysia in its southward sweep through the region, this miracle had transformed what was a plantation economy. "It was only in 1960," Mahathir said, "that we managed to catch up with the per capita income of Haiti"—the poorest nation in the Western Hemisphere. In the late 1990s, Malaysia is an increasingly technologically advanced society that aims to pull even with the industrial West by 2020, if not before. It took just thirty years to turn the former rubber colony into one of the world's largest manufacturers of semiconductors.

When Lee Kuan Yew gave up day-to-day leadership of Singapore, Mahathir emerged as the most articulate, assertive, and outspoken leader of Asian economic growth. He disparaged those who expressed doubts about the sustainability of Asia's economic march, and he forcefully proclaimed the emergence of a "new Asia" that will "look east" and no longer follow the West. But like many others in the region, he did not particularly like the word *miracle*. It seemed to dismiss hard work and sacrifice, and glossed over enormous differences of market size and structure, history, culture, and —what was very important to Mahathir—nationalism. "There is no Asian miracle," he protested. "It is just the realization of an idea, an idea of how to manage an economic system. It is making the right choices, the right mixture of political and economic methods."

In his own wing of the government palace, Mahathir's designated successor, Deputy Prime Minister Anwar Ibrahim, elaborated. "Our success is spectacular in some way," he said. "The increase in openness and the opportunity for income and wealth among all classes are unprecedented in modern history. But we do not like the word miracle. It is too grand—too arrogant. Success in Asia has happened because of the society, health, education, and culture."

Whatever it is called, something very remarkable has unfolded in East Asia—growth at an intensity and rapidity nearly unprecedented in economic history. The "essence of the miracle," as the World Bank put it, was Asia's attainment of the closest thing that economics has to the philosopher's stone —"rapid growth with equity." It is this that has pushed Asia to the forefront, and it is why the rising star of the Asia miracle has replaced the setting star of Marxism and central planning as the model to study—and to seek to emulate. The financial crisis that hit Asia in the second half of 1997 stunned the region and raised fundamental questions about the area's future prospects. Yet what has been accomplished is extraordinary, and the underlying vibrancy and adaptability suggest that the region is entering a period of readjustment, not derailment.

How have these countries achieved what they have? Mahathir offered a phrase to describe the case of Malaysia. He called it "the winning formula." But exactly what was the formula? What was the mixture of government and marketplace? These questions are the subject of vigorous and sometimes acid debate. Some argue that the secret was the guiding hand of the govern-

157

ment—an elite cadre of bureaucrats who endlessly engaged in picking winners and calling the shots. They continually intervened through the management of trade barriers, credit, investment, and competition. They promoted aggressive competition internationally and detailed protectionism at home. Others reply that far more important was the fact that governments were "market-friendly" and thus ensured that the macrofundamentals were right: high savings rates, low inflation, a strong orientation to exports, and high commitment to education—especially education geared to the changing technical skills required by industrialization. Add to all that consistency and persistence, supported by the deep conviction that what was at stake was not distribution but, in the starkest terms, survival in the face of militant communism.

Was it government guidance or was it the market? The unambiguous answer is both. Asia's success has been realized through a balance of government intervention and market forces that, for all their local varieties, remains both distinctive and different. Market and state—business and government —each played its role, against a backdrop of coordination and common purpose, motivated by a drive to work that has been called "a hungry spirit." From its start in Japan, the balance evolved and adapted. Its common elements found separate expressions to fit the perceived needs of countries that ranged from industrial city-states to agricultural giants, from culturally homogeneous societies to those that are ethnically and religiously mixed. There were also some countries that from the beginning were less apt to use government intervention than to go with the market.

Chief among the common threads was a resolute choice to grow the domestic economy by harnessing it to exports—and thus committing to the rigors of international competition. Yet while the countries of the region have "competed out," they have also "protected in"—insulating their domestic economies, to one degree or another, from foreign competition. The entire edifice was built, to varying degrees, on regulation or coercion, in political as well as economic life. Most of the Asian success stories involved, at some point, dictatorship, authoritarianism, or at least regulated politics and a de facto one-party system. Yet at the same time, they built a consensus around the imperative of survival and the visible returns of growth—indeed, what has been called shared growth—which has resulted in growing equality. Most Asian governments did intervene—sometimes quite drastically. But they did so to influence the shape of market outcomes, not to replace or roll back markets. The paradox of Asia, then, was that in many ways it was government knowledge, enforced by political structures, that helped bring about "market-friendly outcomes."

The story of government and market that underlies the Asia miracle could still be summed up in one concept: "Countries, Inc." The analogy of the country as a firm—often employed by the region's leaders—keenly evoked the orientation toward trade, the quest for productivity, and the recourse to regimented organization. But more, these Countries, Inc. have enjoyed a degree of common purpose few firms can match: a nationalistic drive, molded by living memories of colonization, conquest, secession, civil conflict, subversion, or war.

In the late 1990s, as economic development proceeds, a shift is taking place away from the state's "governance" of the market and toward greater reliance on the market as manager and regulator. At the same time, there is growing anxiety, even fear, that the formula for fast economic growth no longer works when these countries reach a certain level of income and openness. And indeed, the currency crisis of 1997 brought that apprehension to the fore.

Local cultures and histories have made each Country, Inc. distinct. But all of the nations shared a reference to a common model: Japan, the first in the region to attain—and, arguably, surpass—the industrial achievements of the West.[1]

Japan: "I'll Go for Income Doubling"

In 1945, Japan was a devastated nation, humiliated by absolute defeat. Its leaders under arrest and discredited, its industry in ruins, a third of its urban housing nothing more than ashes and rubble, the country existed at a bare subsistence level. Its people were demoralized and adrift, their lives torn apart. There was hardly anything to eat. Boys stood by railway lines jumping up and down, begging American soldiers to toss them candy bars from the passing trains.

The confrontation with American power had overwhelmed the Japanese. The vast swarms of B-29's overhead during the war and the total devastation of the two atomic bombs that ended it had driven home the fact of superior American technological prowess. The occupation that followed brought them face-to-face with the American standard of living. They could see with their own eyes what they might dream of attaining. Yet the reality seemed far beyond their grasp. Or was it? "Come, Come, Everybody" was the theme song of Japanese radio's English-conversation program, and the tune, repeated in the streets, became a counterpoint, enticing listeners into the future.

The first several years after the war were excruciatingly hard, dominated by vast dislocations, chronic shortages, and high inflation. By the end of the 1940s, the U.S. occupation—impelled by both the cost burden and the emerging cold war—made what was known as the "reverse course" and began to focus on promoting Japanese economic recovery. As part of that, it imposed the Dodge Plan, which did much to extinguish inflation. The Korean War, beginning in 1950, turned Japan into a supply base for the American forces on the Korean peninsula and stimulated an export boom. The early 1950s were the beginning of recovery. Those years were immortalized in the 1952 best-seller *The General Manager,* whose hero trades in his prewar Datsun for a Ford and then earns enough to buy a Lincoln, which he drives around the outer garden of the Meiji shrine, shouting, "Light as a feather! Light as a feather! It's absolutely like flying above the clouds." No one could possibly think at the time that a Japanese automobile would one day be more desired, and a greater status symbol, than a car from Detroit.

It was only in the mid-1950s that Japan rose from recovery into sustained economic growth, which became the central national objective. In 1960, when Hayato Ikeda was about to move from being minister of international trade and industry to prime minister, he was asked what he would do. "Isn't it all a matter of economic policy?" he replied. "I'll go for income doubling." And that is what Japan was doing. By 1964, on the eve of welcoming the Olympics to Tokyo, Ikeda could proudly declare, "With the 19 postwar years of rapid growth, Japan's national income is approaching the Western European level; we are attempting to do in 20 postwar years what we were unable to do in the 80 years before the war." This could be measured in the standard of living. In the 1960s, consumers were acquiring the "three sacred treasures"—television, washing machine, and refrigerator. In the 1970s they moved on to the "three C's"—car, color television, and air conditioner.[2]

When the energy disruptions of the 1970s hit, the Japanese feared that the game was over. Their growth, based on cheap oil, could not continue, they thought. Yet despite the pessimism at the time, the energy crises proved to be only a temporary setback for Japan. By the early 1980s, its economy was already rebounding strongly, on the basis of rapid technological adjustments—moving from an energy-intensive economy to a "knowledge-intensive economy"—and a new emphasis on efficiency. Japan was now an economic superpower. By the end of the 1980s, the capitalization of the Tokyo Stock Exchange was equal to that of the New York Stock Exchange, and of the world's ten biggest banks, eight were Japanese. The real estate in the area of the Imperial Palace, in central Tokyo, was said to have a higher value than the entire western United States. To stand in the lobby of the Imperial Hotel and watch groups of Western and Japanese businessmen approach each other and bow and exchange business cards was to feel that one was in the agora of the world economy, the very pivot point of global commerce.

Buoyed by a strong yen, Japan went on an enormous shopping spree, buying not only companies but trophies of all sorts—vineyards in France, some of the world's most famous paintings, Rockefeller Center and the Exxon building in New York, and two of the five major film studios in Hollywood. American and European companies and business strategists sought to divine the secret of Japanese commercial success in order to replicate it; and as if indicating the future, the president of Mexico made a point of sending his children to the Japanese school in Mexico City.

There were many elements in Japan's postwar success. It was already a relatively developed country before World War II. The U.S. occupation implemented land reform and broke up the *zaibatsu,* the great industrial/financial combinations. The *zaibatsu* were succeeded by *keiretsu,* groupings of banks and industrial companies, but the links were less tight, and there was room for entrepreneurs like Akio Morita, the cofounder of Sony, to turn their backroom workshops into dynamic global companies. The fundamentals were right: The country had a large and educated workforce, low inflation, and a very high savings rate. American power had demonstrated the centrality of technology, and Japanese companies set out on a forced-pace campaign to obtain and absorb technology from America and Europe. Masaru Ibuka, Morita's partner at Sony, came across the transistor at Westinghouse in 1956 while on a State Department–sponsored tour, and Sony promptly acquired the rights. Firms sought continuing quality improvement as a competitive weapon and invested in ever-greater scale in mass production in order to win market share. All this was sustained on values that included an incredible work ethic, an extraordinarily intense identification with the firm, a shared sense of national identity (and of the country's precarious position), a desire to live better—and the searing memory of the defeat, the harsh postwar years, with the occupation and the humiliation that went with it.

One other factor was absolutely central, and that was Japan's commitment to exporting its way to growth. In the early 1950s, there was a vigorous debate in Japan over what kind of strategy to follow—what was called international tradism versus inward-looking "developmentalism": liberalism versus central planning. International tradism won out, with the result that Japan made a huge bet on the world economy, and one that paid off handsomely. Japan benefited enormously—and very consciously—from the increasingly open international trading system that America took the lead in shaping. Japan was helped by its being ignored as an economic force until the early 1970s. In the United States and Europe, it was regarded not as a competitor but as a source of cheap, low-quality goods. Hardly anyone recalled how effectively it had captured export markets in Asia from the British in the interwar years. And its protectionist policies were also overlooked. As an exporter, Japan moved up the product chain: from textiles and simple manufactures to ships and steel to complex mechanical goods, electronics, and high technology.

The Iron Triangle: "The 1955 System"

All of this was embedded in a market system that was characterized by a particular government-corporate collaboration. It achieved growth and standard of living objectives that, despite the often intense competition among Japanese firms, added up to a system that came to be known as Japan, Inc. It was one in which government bureaucrats often played a dominating role through regulation and something more ineffable but nevertheless potent: "administrative guidance." Some Japanese have recently described this as the 1940s System—a continuation of the system that was established on the eve of World War II, in which bureaucracies and companies worked closely together in order to operate a war economy but in which decisive power lay with the bureaucracies. After World War II, the bureaucracies moved into an even more ascendant position. But it is more relevant to describe it as the 1955 System. That year marked the beginning of the Liberal Democratic Party's ascendancy and the clear establishment of the "iron triangle" of bureaucrats, businessmen, and politicians.

In the Japanese system, this tight coordination between government and business was accepted as the natural order and was reinforced by the precariousness of Japan's position. In the words of one scholar, both bureaucrats and many business leaders "viewed government intervention in industrial affairs as a natural component of economic policy." Regulation of industry was strategic; it was "not considered distinct from the promotion of industry." Firms had to be strong at home in order to compete abroad, and the Japanese government saw no contradiction between promoting overseas competition and strongly regimenting the domestic market.

This system was meant to support producers, not consumers, and consumer prices were high. Such was the cost of ensuring security of supply and the continued health of business. The efforts required to manage this economic system were complex, and depended on a skilled and politically insulated bureaucracy. The whole apparatus of economic management was known as *jukyu chosei*—"supply-and-demand adjustment."

At the center of the *jukyu chosei* was one entity—a single, potent agency that coordinated both external and domestic industrial strategy: the Ministry of International Trade and Industry, which for most of the postwar era represented the command center for the noncommand Japanese economy. It was better known by its initials—MITI. As a former senior Japanese official observed: "There is a word for commanding heights in Japanese, at least up through the 1970s, and that is MITI."

From its headquarters in a gray-brown 1950s office block in the Kasumigaseki section in Tokyo, not far from the walls of the Imperial Palace, MITI coordinated the entire system of industrial policy. It aimed not only to help firms adapt to world export markets but also to help them take the greatest advantage of them. It channeled information and knowledge and facilitated the flow of new technologies. It utilized an array of tools to achieve its objectives: price setting; quotas for imports and market share; licenses; quality standards; industry associations; "old boy" networks; and a nonbinding but clear way of sending a message: administrative guidance. It interpreted changes in world markets to shape the rules of domestic industrial organization, providing continual advice and local interventions through local offices. It tried to ensure that "excessive" domestic competition did not erode the strength that Japanese firms needed in order to compete overseas. It organized mergers and megamergers, coordinated investment to avoid overcapacity, and encouraged the specialization of small and medium-sized companies. It also sought to restrict foreign competitors within Japan through a host of tools and barriers. International trade and domestic industry were thus closely intertwined, and MITI acted as the single coordinator. That was one of Japan's greatest innovations. Only one ministry matched (and some would say exceeded) MITI in prestige and influence, and that was the Ministry of Finance, which wielded control over credit and foreign exchange. But the Ministry of Finance operated in a more rarefied world, and was much less visible.

The people who ran both ministries were the top graduates of the top universities, particularly the law school of Tokyo University. They were called *bureaucrats*—and indeed, with no irony, so described themselves—but the word had none of the pejorative implications found in the United States. It was a Confucian term of respect, connoting responsibility, dedication, and power. And carrying out such far-ranging responsibilities put very heavy demands on Japan's bureaucrats.

MITI's role evolved over time as the Japanese private sector became stronger. The system proved to be, as one former official put it, "a very effective catch-up model." MITI became the focal point of Japanese economic expansion, of Japan, Inc. An entire culture grew up around it. Companies, required to interact with MITI on a near-constant basis, located their headquarters near the ministry, within what was known as the short walk. They served on its advisory councils, which were as much vehicles for receiving advice as giving it. Senior company officials were often careful to show great respect, and bow appropriately, to high-flying MITI officials decades younger than themselves.

MITI worked closely with industrial-sector associations, took their advice, and sought to promote the overall sector. However, some companies became famous for resisting MITI and going their own way. In preparation for international competition in automobiles, MITI tried to narrow down the number of companies to ensure economies of scale. As part of that, it tried to persuade Honda to stick with motorbikes. Ignoring MITI's strong advice, Honda went ahead anyway. The crucial consumer-electrics business developed with little government support. The classic case was VCRs—videocassette recorders. Three Japanese companies succeeded in transforming a fifty-thousand-dollar American invention, which only television stations could afford, into a five-hundred-dollar consumer item. MITI's role was modest at best. Yet whatever the missteps, this system was the nexus of daily life for the Japanese economy, and it was out of this nexus that Japan's extraordinary achievement arose. For the most part, the system performed as intended. It delivered the goods to such a degree that by the end of the 1980s, Japanese preeminence seemed destined to remove the last humiliations of the occupation. The boys who had jumped up and down trying to catch candy bars from the American GIs were now running not only an economic superpower but one that seemed poised to overtake the United States.

Instead, the economy was taken over by a huge and intoxicating speculative boom, which started to burst in 1990. In 1992, Japan went into a deep slump, the most severe economic crisis since the era of high growth had begun. The stock market fell 60 percent, real estate values plunged, and banks loaded up with bad real estate loans teetered on the edge of bankruptcy. The weakness of the financial system proved a persistent drag on recovery. Japan was losing its competitiveness. A glowering pessimism settled over the country. Confidence among consumers and business eroded, coinciding with a splintering of the Liberal Democratic Party and the breakup of the monopoly on power it had exercised for half a century.

These troubles led to turbulent debate as to whether Japan, Inc. was finished. Did the formula for the relationship between government and marketplace need radical revision, with government to be constrained and the economy deregulated? The outcome of this debate, still being fought in the political arena as well as in argument, will determine Japan's economic future.[3]

A "Suicide Act" for Bureaucrats

The battle was embodied in the fate of Masahisa Naitoh, a MITI director general and head of the industrial policy bureau within MITI, who was to become the foremost advocate of deregulation in Japan. Like most of the leadership in the ministry, he was a graduate of the law school of Tokyo University. He entered the ministry in 1961. After participating in negotiations related to Japan's entry into the Organization for Economic Cooperation and Development (OECD) in the early 1960s, he began to harbor doubts about the long-term efficacy of the system. "I thought that planning could not work so well unless all information was directed to a specific center," he said. "But that is very unlikely. So the second best was the market mechanism. From the 1960s onward, the main theme for me was what should be the relation between government and companies. At that time, many in MITI thought only the wisdom of MITI people could guide the economy. But I thought MITI was not almighty. I read American antimonopoly and competition theory. And I always thought how well consumer electronics had done without government support."

As Naitoh rose through MITI, he kept such unconventional thoughts more or less to himself. Instead, he came to be seen as one of MITI's "golden boys." He played a key role in the all-important semiconductor negotiations with the United States, and seemed to have a good chance to go right to the top. By the late 1980s, he was in a prominent enough position to begin arguing the merits of a more deregulated economy. He was opposed on many fronts. "The MITI old boys felt that deregulation would hurt their positions," he said. "The company presidents and politicians also opposed it. Brochures were circulated saying that I advocated the 'destruction' of the current system. But all of this criticism only strengthened my conviction. I thought it should be done."

Naitoh was aligned with the "internationalist" faction within MITI. He was running the powerful Bureau of Industrial Policy and was a very likely candidate to rise to the highest post open to a civil servant, vice-minister. He also became more outspoken. He testified to the Hiraiwa Commission, headed by the chairman of the Keidanren (the powerful Japanese Federation of Employers), on the future of the Japanese economy. He insisted that deregulation was essential to restore waning Japanese competitiveness. He was the only senior official to take that position. "Within the government, what I did was not liked," he recalled. "Others thought government officials should simply implement the laws. I was said to be envisioning a 'suicide act' for bureaucrats."

Then, at the end of 1993, the unheard-of happened. The MITI minister, a politician, intervened in an unprecedented way: he abruptly fired Naitoh, ensuring that he would never be able to occupy the critical post of vice-minister. The firing became a cause célèbre in Japan, the crucible for an unfolding debate. Naitoh left for Washington—to teach and to become, in his words, a "political refugee." His enemies circulated articles in the Japanese press alleging that he was holding secret rendezvous with American CEOs.

But it was too late. By that time, there was a growing movement toward deregulation. The bursting of the "bubble," which had been built on spiraling stock market and property values, hit Japan very hard. Several years of sluggish, or even no, growth upset all expectations about the workings of the 1955 System. The slump showed up the problems with a high-cost, protected, production-geared economy. The financial implications were great. The imperative of cheap money for industry had meant that firms received loans less on the basis of their balance sheets than as a result of a managed system in which administrative guidance and networks played a large part. This system prevented a clear differentiation between stronger and weaker companies. Savings were managed to support the system. High consumer prices provided an incentive to save, not spend. But household savings were channeled into the banks and life insurance schemes, where they earned low returns, whereas their owners should have been able to seek higher returns in more dynamic—or riskier—markets. In an increasingly global financial market, Japan had only a small mutual fund industry. Layers of regulations separated the functions of banks and financial institutions, limiting opportunities for Japanese or foreign firms to offer new financial products. With the population of Japan rapidly aging and increasing numbers of people soon to claim pension benefits, the failure of Japanese savings to achieve better returns took on the character of a demographic time bomb.

Neither the low value of the yen, which helped exporters, nor several waves of government spending on infrastructure projects were sufficient to jump-start the economy. As the recession continued, voices grew louder in favor of a structural change to unharness the economy from its tight regulation and thus to restore its competitive position.

In the first few years of the recession, concerted political action was made more difficult by the instability of several coalition governments. But since 1996, there has been more focus and momentum for regulatory change under the reformed Liberal Democratic Party (LDP) government of Prime Minister Ryutaro Hashimoto. Hashimoto appeared at first an unlikely proponent of structural reform. The head of six ministries at different times during his career, he had, in fact, been forced to resign as minister of finance in 1991, when the ministry's role in a financial scandal became known. For a time considered a spent force, he kept a low profile during the internal turmoil of the LDP and emerged as its leader and prime minister in 1996.

Hashimoto placed deregulation at the center of his political agenda. But it is in fact two forces toward deregulation that are at play in Japan. The first is relatively simple. It concerns certain sectors where the cost differential with competitors has become too extreme, partly because the principles on which the industries were organized are out of date. The imperative of national security, which had long required that all of Japan's oil be refined in Japanese plants rather than more cheaply elsewhere, is now seen to be outdated or transformed. Japan's electric utilities are seeing their traditional monopolies being eroded around the edges by independent power production. Air transport is also to be opened up to more competition. These reforms are significant but hardly universal. In sectors where the cost differential is less extreme, there is far less pressure to change, and the power of established interests, combined with the rigidity of the labor system, remains deeply entrenched.

The more complex force is the one in Japanese finance, which will have a less direct but far more pervasive effect on the way Japan manages its economy. It hinges on what has come to be known as the Big Bang—a series of liberalizations modeled on financial deregulation in London and slated to occur in stages starting in 1998. Beginning with foreign-exchange deregulation and spreading to banking, securities, and insurance, the Big Bang will change the ways that the financial industry does business on the Tokyo market. It seeks to reenergize Tokyo as a financial center, and to re-attract many of the foreign companies that have delisted from the Tokyo stock exchange. It also aims to unravel some of the ties between finance and the criminal underworld that have led to several notorious scandals. But it will have a more pervasive effect in the economy at large, for it will introduce a far greater measure of competition for savings and investment capital. Households will be able to demand higher returns from those who manage their money; and Japanese firms will have to compete among themselves and with overseas markets for investment capital. The financial markets will apply a new discipline to companies, enhancing their competitiveness. The

166

implication will be, among other things, that the market will be allowed to indicate which firms are stronger than others.

The Big Bang is the centerpiece of Hashimoto's agenda, and he has staked much of his political reputation on it. But in fact, it draws on ideas that were nurtured in some quarters of MITI and the Ministry of Finance and which only now have become urgent enough to be advocated in public, owing to Japan's long slump. The two ministries are still the intellectual leaders in the bureaucracy. But the nature of their leadership is changing fast. MITI is no longer the grand architect of industrial policy; nor is the Ministry of Finance, in the run-up to the Big Bang, the sole clearinghouse for the management of Japan's money. Rather, they are increasingly charged with directing the rest of the government toward liberalization. There are even proposals on the table to modify the structure of the government to merge MITI into an economics superministry, which would at the very least have the highly symbolic effect of abolishing one of the most famous acronyms of postwar economic history.

What is clear is that the days in which MITI was synonymous with the commanding heights are already long over. The 1955 System made Japan a formidable competitor. But the future requirements of international competition suggest that Japan, like so many other nations, is likely to move to a market system that is freer and more open than the one that made it an economic superpower.[4]

Korea: Picking Winners

In Rangoon, Burma, on the sunny morning of October 9, 1983, Korean members of the receiving line were taking their places inside the Martyrs Mausoleum. They were awaiting the imminent arrival of South Korea's president, Chun Doo Hwan, who was beginning a five-nation tour in Burma and was due at the mausoleum for a wreath-laying ceremony. The South Korean ambassador, flags flying from his limousine, roared up with a motorcycle escort and hastened into the mausoleum. A Burmese soldier lifted his bugle to his lips. He managed barely two notes before a huge explosion ripped through the mausoleum, blowing its roof off, throwing bodies high into the air, and shaking buildings a mile away. Five South Korean ministers and three vice-ministers were among those killed, including a Stanford-educated economist named Kim Jae-Ik, who had been masterminding the next phase of economic development in his country. But the perpetrators missed their main target, President Chun, who was still a few minutes away. Misled by the motorcade and the Burmese bugler, they had mistaken the South Korean ambassador for Chun and had detonated the remote-controlled bomb too soon.

There could be no doubt about who had organized the bombing: communist North Korea. The objective was to destabilize the southern half of the Korean peninsula. South Korean soldiers immediately went on the highest alert status along the demilitarized border zone that separated the two countries. It was yet another battle in a war that had never really ended. But what had surely changed since the all-out war in the early 1950s was that South Korea was well on its way to becoming an economic powerhouse, shaming totalitarian North Korea. And it was doing so very quickly.

In 1945, when the peninsula was partitioned, South Korea had been left with very little. Most of the existing industry—largely the Japanese-built hydroelectric stations on the Yalu River and the nearby chemical and fertilizer plants—had ended up in North Korea. In 1950, 135,000 North Korean troops invaded the south. Communist China entered the war in support of North Korea, and as the communist troops advanced, it had seemed for a time that South Korea might not survive at all. Seoul, its capital, changed hands four times. The war ended in 1953, with a truce, not a peace treaty— a constant reminder to South Korea of how precarious was its existence and how dangerous was the threat from the north. Kim Il Sung, North Korea's megalomaniacal leader, never wavered in his relentlessly hostile policy. Thus, in the aftermath of the war, South Korea desperately needed to build up its economic strength, especially as both China and North Korea embarked on rapid industrialization, communist-style. But South Korea was in a terrible state, devastated by the war. Seven percent of its population had been killed, including a large proportion of young men, and two thirds of its meager industrial capacity had been destroyed.

This was the inauspicious beginning for the rule of President Syngman Rhee, who dominated the South Korean scene from the end of World War II until 1960. The Korean peninsula had been a colony of Japan since 1895, and the Japanese had jailed Rhee from 1898 until 1904 for nationalist activities. He had then made his way to the United States, where in 1910 he completed a Ph.D. at Princeton University, under Professor Woodrow Wilson. Altogether, he spent forty years outside the country, campaigning for Korean independence. Once in power, he was much more concerned with politics and with managing relations with the United States than with development. Nationalism, not economics, was his forte.

The real push to industrialization came in 1961, following a military coup. General Park Chung Hee emerged as the strongman, running the country from 1962 until 1979. Tough, autocratic, and absolutely committed to economic development, he was the founding CEO of "Korea, Inc.," and he played the part, ruling with an iron fist. He was supported by energetic young military officers, a skilled and increasingly experienced bureaucracy, a broad base of citizens willing to work, and a national commitment to industrial development. The continuing danger from the North drove everything.

Of all the Asian countries, South Korea proved to be the one that most consciously, if ambivalently, adopted the Japanese model. The result was a system that was, in the words of economist Dwight Perkins, "highly interventionist, but with the discipline of having to export." Certainly, there was irony in Korea's focus on Japan. Not only had it been a colony, but the Koreans had a long history of resisting Japanese domination. The Japanese occupation had been brutal and the Koreans were bitter long after independence. They were intent on building up their own nation and their own national identity. As a result of the Japanese occupation, however, many of them had been educated in Japanese-language schools, and they were strongly influenced both by the MITI model and by Japanese culture. Moreover, they could look across the Sea of Japan, where the rise of an economic superpower was all too evident. President Park, who had attended a Japanese military academy and had served two years as an officer in the Manchurian army during World War II, pursued closer Japanese-Korean relations as part of his development strategy.

A MITI variant could serve Korea's urgent interests. The country was very poor; per capita GNP did not reach $100 until 1963. In the first decade of military rule, the government focused on building up exports to compensate for declining U.S. foreign aid. Initially, the export-push system was nondiscriminatory, providing protection and a wide variety of subsidies and support to all comers. But soon the economic planners in the Park government came to a conclusion with far-reaching implications: They were convinced that Korea needed big companies if it was to compete in international markets and withstand foreign imports. To achieve that goal, they promoted a series of national champions called *chaebols*—holding companies that controlled diversified industrial groups. Park and his team selected firms that were already successful in one field (for example, rice milling or real estate or construction), typically run by a strong-willed entrepreneur who was not lacking in self-confidence. These firms were then nurtured with low-interest government loans, tax incentives, and other advantages to enable them to become large, strong, and diversified industrial groups. Thus were born companies whose names are now globally known—Hyundai, Samsung, Lucky Goldstar, and Daewoo.

In 1973, Park's government became even more interventionist, launching what was known as the Heavy and Chemical Industries Initiative—the foundation upon which Korea's global role would be built. It was done mainly for reasons of security. North Korea was a military machine, its objectives could not be doubted, and thus, for South Korea, the issue was basic—escaping extinction. With a Communist victory looming in Vietnam, Park and those around him feared the U.S. security shield would be withdrawn. And South Korea was hardly equipped to go it alone. Its only cannons, of World War II vintage, were not usable; the United States had stopped making the spare parts. It did not have antitank weapons to resist North Korea's T-62 tanks, and its military stores were sufficient for no more than three days of warfare. South Korea's renewed sense of insecurity was greatly stoked by President Jimmy Carter, who in 1976 announced his intention to withdraw U.S. forces from the Korean peninsula. It took some dissuading to get Carter to relent, but he tied the presence of U.S. troops to human rights, further widening the gap with the authoritarian Park regime.

Government officials made the basic investment decisions under the Heavy and Chemical Industries Initiative, and then enforced them through control of credit. The result was a very concentrated economic system, based upon a strong and tight relationship between government and a limited number of large industrial companies. Park himself was the hands-on CEO, selecting companies, monitoring progress, bullying through corporate or bureaucratic impediments, traveling around the country by helicopter to swoop down on the different sites and see them for himself. Park also had his own demanding version of "management by objectives." Each New Year he visited all of his ministers to discuss their goals and how they would be achieved. The following New Year he would return to the ministers and go through the previous year's promises—"sentence by sentence." Those who failed to hit 80 percent of what they had promised were fired. Everybody got the message, and they understood what Park wanted—high, sustained growth.

The government targeted six strategic industries for support—steel, petrochemicals, nonferrous metals, shipbuilding, electronics, and machinery. It pushed the *chaebol*s to pursue aggressively only the most advanced technology, and it pushed for scale. To be efficient, for instance, an automobile manufacturing plant had to produce 300,000 vehicles a year, which was far beyond South Korea's ability to absorb given the fact that at the time, the country had a total of only 165,000 passenger cars. Thus it was imperative to develop an export market as soon as possible and at the same time create a domestic market.

The *chaebol*s had generous access to credit and were insulated from downturns by government support. They were protected from foreign competitors in the Korean market—and from domestic competitors as well. The companies received exclusive licenses for their products, and only one *chaebol* was allowed to sell in the domestic market during the first phase of a new industry. The government forced the *chaebol*s to attain international competitiveness in their fields according to a strict timetable and across a broad range of their products. If they did not, they suffered economic and political penalties. The program was pursued with extraordinary dedication, embodied in a very powerful work ethic. As one manager was to put it, Koreans "overcame poverty with hard work and discipline." In many cases, it went further than that. Government work rules were very tough, workers were highly regimented, and the workweek was close to sixty hours. The *chaebol*s had many advantages, one of which was cross-subsidies within the groups. The heads of the *chaebol*s became enormously rich, which did not prevent them from continuing to work hard and aggressively. But there was no question of who was the boss. They would regularly be called to the presidential palace, the Blue House, where President Park would take them to task for failing to act in the interest of the state. They were to do as they were told.[5]

At the end of the 1970s, the government began to back off from the massively interventionist Heavy and Chemical Industries Initiative program. Part of the reason was the rise of domestic opposition and discontent with the Park regime. A shift to stabilization was seen as a way to placate the population by controlling inflation and spreading the benefits of industrialization more widely. The obvious break came in October 1979, when President Park was assassinated by the head of the Korean CIA. The man who thereafter took power, General Chun Doo Hwan, was even more interested in stability. He was also somewhat hostile to the large *chaebol*s and their considerable influence.

A strong intellectual force in the person of Kim Jae-Ik also drove Korea's change of course. Born in 1938, Kim had attended Seoul National University and then completed a Ph.D. in economics at Stanford University. He first made his influence felt as a member of the powerful Economic Planning Board and then, in 1979, became the architect of stabilization and the promoter of liberalization. His objectives were to get growth under control, reduce government intervention, and create a more level playing field on which small and medium-size firms could flourish.

Kim became President Chun's chief economic adviser, which many found odd—"the dour soldier and the exuberant U.S.-trained economist." But they were unusually close. In the words of a colleague, "he was the man who explained economics to the general." Kim recognized how successful the industrialization strategy had been until then, but he was also convinced that it had to be changed; otherwise the country would come to grief. Many of the *chaebol*s were becoming woefully inefficient and would have been virtually insolvent without continuing government bailouts. The banking system, largely government owned, was accountable to virtually no one. The agricultural system was massively inefficient. Kim's prescription was to pull back the economic frontiers of the state, sell off at least some state-controlled enterprises, free up the financial sector, and reduce import barriers in order to expose inefficient industries to foreign competition. He wanted a bigger role for foreign investment. He recognized that the complexity of the economy had now grown beyond the government's ability to manage it. And to the astonishment of his colleagues, he even made some headway in convincing the generals, who held ultimate power, to trim defense expenditures.

How much farther would Kim, with his self-effacing charm, have gone had he not joined that delegation of senior officials visiting Rangoon in October 1983? The carnage at the Martyrs Mausoleum was a terrible reminder of the dangers South Korea faced. Kim's death was described as "the biggest loss" of the entire event. Although only forty-four at the time of his death, Kim Jae-Ik was to be remembered, in the aftermath, as "legendary."

Building upon Kim's legacy, South Korea thereafter pursued policies aimed at less intrusive indicative planning, an expanded role for the market, and financial and import liberalization. The changes did not come easily. They met considerable opposition both from the powerful bureaucracies and from Korean companies used to being taken care of. In the words of one civil servant, much "hidden regulation" remains in the late 1990s, promulgated by officials who do not want to lose their power.

Korea finds itself no longer a low-wage society. The regimented labor system has shown recurrent strains. The tension began with the massacre of striking workers at Kwangju in 1979, which precipitated the coup that brought down General Park. Periodic labor unrest has continued ever since. Many Korean workers had felt excluded from the benefits of their labor. But in the 1980s, wages went up substantially and job tenure was guaranteed, and after 1987, unions were freed of government repression and control. More recently, however, compounding the trouble, there has been the pressure to make labor markets more flexible, both to enable South Korea to compete with the new tigers and to bring labor laws in line with international practice, as a condition of having joined the OECD. The unions have responded with often-violent strikes and demonstrations.

Worried about prospects for the domestic economy, the *chaebol*s are seeking to maintain competitiveness by investing abroad. The top five *chaebol*s alone are planning to spend $70 billion over a decade on overseas investment. Korea's economy continues to stagger under the weight of non-performing loans used to build up big industries and the persisting need to rationalize and restructure the industries created in the 1970s. Moreover, South Korea does not have the networks of small and medium-sized companies that have been a source of stability for Japan. In addition, Koreans— observing the high price of German reunification—worry about the economic and social costs should North Korea suddenly collapse and the cherished goal of reunification become a reality. Yet with all the ups and downs, South Korea has continued on its enormously impressive growth. And the considered judgment of Asia expert Ezra Vogel stands as a concise view of what was accomplished over three decades: "South Korea was unrivaled, even by Japan, in the speed with which it went from having almost no industrial technology to taking its place among the world's industrialized nations." He adds, "No nation has come so far so quickly, from handicrafts to heavy industry, from poverty to prosperity, from inexperienced leaders to modern planners, managers, and engineers."

Korea is paying a heavy political penalty for its economic success. Massive state intervention created massive opportunities for corruption. Industrial policy Korean-style meant that the state extended enormous largesse to favored companies and there was a price to be paid by those so favored. "If you were not close to the government, you could not survive in the Korean marketplace," one businessman explained. "The Korean businesses that were eager to do business followed the informal rules for the flow of funds in the generation of business"—in other words, kickbacks, bribes, and political payoffs.

In the presidential elections of 1987, a divided opposition had allowed Chun's handpicked successor, Roh Tae-Woo, to take over. But the public became increasingly angry with authoritarianism and repression, as well as resentful of inequality and corruption. The top "managers" of Korea, Inc. —the generals and politicians—had grabbed too much profit for themselves, and the calls for transparency could no longer be shut out. In 1993, newly elected President Kim Young-Sam launched an anticorruption drive that would prove comprehensive in its sweep—and politically popular. As a result, former presidents Chun and Roh were tried and found guilty for their roles in the 1979 coup and the 1980 massacre of pro-democracy demonstrators. At the same time, the heads of eight *chaebol*s were given prison terms for paying bribes to Roh. The "informal" flow of funds to Roh had been very considerable—$650 million, according to the indictment. Ignominiously shackled together, clasping hands, the two former presidents listened to their sentences in August 1996. For Roh, it was twenty-two years in prison; for Chun, a sentence of death. It is said that Roh spent his first nights in jail reading Margaret Thatcher's memoirs, no doubt reflecting on her free-market philosophy and the case against state intervention.

In its way, the outcome was an indictment of the entire system that had propelled Korea to the forefront of the world economy. "What has been normal and necessary in the past as part of a phase of economic development in Korea is now being questioned," observed a key member of a commission charged with reforming Korea's economy. "A more mature economy going into the next stage of development will require the realignment of market, government, and industrialization." The long years of military dictatorship leave a complex and difficult legacy for the nation. Those years turned Korea into an economic powerhouse and raised living standards far beyond what might have been expected. They also ensured that the nation survived in the face of the implacable hostility and threats from the North. Yet many Koreans also opposed the military governments, regarding them as illegitimate regimes that destroyed democracy and ruled in a highly authoritarian manner. How to deal with that past is something with which the nation continues to struggle.[6]

Taiwan: Confucian Capitalism

Sun-Moon Lake, enfolded in the mountains of central Taiwan and often covered with mist, has long been Taiwan's favorite honeymoon resort. It takes its name from its shapes as seen from various nearby hilltops. On one shore is a magnificent temple, dedicated to Confucius and two warrior deities. In 1949, Generalissimo Chiang Kai-shek made his way to Sun-Moon

Lake in search of some respite. He had just fled mainland China to escape capture by Mao Zedong's advancing communist forces. And it was there by the side of the lake that Chiang was handed the telegram telling him the news he had never wanted to hear—of the final collapse of his nationalist forces on the mainland. He turned stone-silent and, for an hour, sat motionless. Then he stood up and set out for a walk in the forest with his son. After a long silence, for want of anything else to do, he suggested that they go fishing. His son paid an old fisherman to take them out in his boat. Lost in depression and hardly paying attention, Chiang cast out a net and, to his surprise, caught a very large fish. The fisherman said it was the largest he had ever seen taken from the waters of Sun-Moon Lake. It was a good omen, he added. Yet that hardly seemed possible. After all, the fall of Taiwan, Chiang's last redoubt, appeared imminent. His old nemesis, Mao Zedong, was on the verge of total victory. And Chiang had nowhere else to go.

The rivalry between Chiang and Mao had defined modern China. The balance between them had seemed very clear in 1949, when Mao's forces won their final victory, taking control of all of mainland China, from the Vietnamese border. Yet a quarter century later, by the time of their deaths, the balance looked quite different. Chiang and Mao both died in the mid-1970s—within a year of each other—at the ages of eighty-seven and eighty-three, respectively. By then Chiang had presided over an extraordinary economic miracle that was catapulting Taiwan into the forefront of industrial nations while Mao had succeeded in creating a series of catastrophes that left mainland China an economic disaster.

Like South Korea, Taiwan was a creation of the cold war, and its postwar history was a "rags-to-riches story," in the words of one of its economic architects. For fifty years, beginning in 1895, it had been a colony of Japan—a "rice bowl"—and then briefly a province again of China after World War II. It became a separately functioning country only in 1949, when Chiang, leader of the Nationalist Party, sought refuge there with upward of 2 million soldiers and civilians. Although outnumbered by the Taiwanese Chinese by three to one, the refugees from the mainland controlled Taiwanese life. The split between them and the native Taiwanese would be of lasting economic, political, and social significance.

For Taiwan, one issue was paramount: survival. As far as the Communists on the mainland were concerned, Taiwan was still a province, its conquest the uncompleted business of the civil war. For their part, Chiang and the nationalists refused to acknowledge that Taiwan was not China, and talked for many years about retaking the mainland. With the passing of the years, however, Chiang's ambition shifted from "a fierce resolve" to "an aspiration, then a myth, then a liturgy." But survival remained the most urgent imperative. At first, it was necessary simply to withstand an onslaught from the mainland. Later, it was to weather Taiwan's isolation as the People's Republic took its place in the international community, snapping most of Taiwan's diplomatic links, including those with the United States. It faced a constant and almost unique struggle for legitimacy in the international system. But Taiwan's precarious position—as Dr. Johnson said of hanging—concentrated the mind, strengthening national unity and focusing resolve on building the economic sinews required for survival.

Things hardly looked promising in the late 1940s and early 1950s. The country had few resources, few entrepreneurs, and no savings, and it had been heavily damaged during the war. Moreover, there was a strong view that the Chinese people were not suited to modern capitalism. They could not operate beyond the family, it was said; nor would they save. They were too suspicious; they were not innovative. No less an authority than the great sociologist Max Weber, in his study on the rise of capitalism, had declared that Confucianism was incompatible with capitalism. In 1949 some attributed the nationalists' defeat to their being mired in a traditional Confucian system. This view sounds quaint today; after all, the Asian miracle is now sometimes called "Confucian capitalism."

Yet Taiwan did have a few strong foundations. A legacy of its fifty years of Japanese colonization was the heavy emphasis on education; by 1949, half of the population was literate. Also, the totality of defeat on the mainland turned into a strength, for the nationalists went through a deep and painful soul-searching about what had brought them to disaster. They identified a number of causes—hyperinflation, corruption, inequality, lack of agrarian reform, arbitrary government power, failure to embrace modern science and technology. These became the lessons they methodically sought to apply on a much smaller stage. Early on, the Nationalist government carried out a land reform that created a strong agricultural base and promoted equality. It inculcated a powerful anticorruption ethos in its new bureaucracies. Almost from the beginning, there was also the conviction that government's prime role was to create an environment in which entrepreneurs could flourish, and then it would withdraw incrementally. Planning would guide Taiwan toward a market system. The objective, in the words of one of the senior planners, was to manage "a process of the gradual depoliticization of the economic system."

"Gradual" would prove a fair description. Through most of the 1950s, Taiwan concentrated on the familiar import-substitution strategy, with a heavy investment in infrastructure and a focus on labor-intensive production, backed up by protective tariffs and tax incentives. It also embraced state-owned enterprise. It did so in part because it had to do something with the state companies the Japanese had left behind. It also saw such companies as essential for aggregating the scarce skills and resources that were available. And it was influenced by the very evident rise of state-owned enterprise in Europe.

U.S. foreign aid was very important in this period, enabling Taiwan to invest in equipment while still paying for its imports. But by the late 1950s, Taiwan could see that American aid would end (as it did in 1965) and thus there was an urgent need to be able to earn foreign exchange. At the time its

175

number-one export was sugar, which would hardly do. Thus it made a decisive shift into a new phase—toward export of manufactured goods into the world market. This meant not only an opening up but also, although less obviously, the beginning of relaxation of domestic controls. The government supported these new would-be industries through low-cost loans, lower tariffs on imports that went into making exports, and aggressive scouring for technology. It also encouraged direct foreign investment, in order to facilitate the transfer of skills and technology and upgrading of quality. The results were spectacular: Exports rose from $123 million in 1963 to $3 billion in 1972. A new phase began in 1980, with an emphasis on technology and research and development; and from there on, the trend toward liberalization became more explicit.

The government was consistently concerned with promoting the emergence of an entrepreneurial class. Sometimes it had to do the "emerging" itself, hunting down businessmen to whom it could entrust specific tasks. For instance, it needed to find a private businessman to take over a government polyvinyl chloride plant originally financed by the U.S. aid program. After much looking, it finally identified a Taiwanese candidate, Y. C. Wang, who was working as a lumber salesman in Japan. Persuaded to come back, he built his Formosa Plastics into the world's largest manufacturer of PVC—and ended up one of the two or three richest men in Taiwan. But in striking contrast to Korea, Taiwan's overall development rested much more upon small and medium-sized businesses, frequently family owned and often operating in networks.[7]

The Supertechnocrats

One of the smartest things Chiang did was leave economic policy making to what became known as the supertechnocrats—very able officials, many of them scientists and engineers, who operated without a great deal of political interference. They were able to call upon Chinese living abroad, including a number of prominent economists in the United States, and eventually on generations of Taiwanese who had gone abroad for their education—and turned what had been feared as a "brain drain" into a "brain bank." Chinese studying or working overseas became a tremendous resource, among other things providing an exceedingly effective network for technology transfer.

From the early 1950s until the mid-1980s, just five men had preponderant say over economic policy making. They combined old and new. They played, observed one scholar, "a role much like that of good traditional Confucian advisors, but both their style and the content of their work were new in Chinese history. They were part of the world scientific and development communities, and they believed in growth and progress." Indeed, for forty years, two of these men, moving among a number of key positions, dominated the entire process.

The first was K. Y. Yin, who orchestrated the move into the export phase and who became known as the "father of Taiwan's industrial development." Trained as an electrical engineer, he had worked all over China before World War II. During the war, he had been a member of the Chinese government's purchasing mission in the United States. And from 1949 through the early 1960s, he was Taiwan's chief planner. He thought like an engineer. "An engineer is a scientist who is knowledgeable about economics," he said. He became a voracious reader of economic texts. He could argue over the details and the finer points in Adam Smith—yes, government did have the role of providing for defense—and offer emendations on Keynes. In planning Taiwan's future, he embraced both Walt Rostow's concept of the economic takeoff and Arthur Lewis's emphasis on export-led growth. He was also a believer in moving the system toward the market. After his death in 1963, people said that his towering monument was the simple phrase "Made in Taiwan," inscribed on quality goods that could be sold in advanced industrial countries.

His place was taken by his deputy, K. T. Li, who held sway until the end of the 1980s and who became known as "the father of the nation's economic miracle drive." Graduating with a degree in physics from one of China's most prestigious universities, Li won a scholarship in the early 1930s and went first to Scotland and then to study nuclear physics at Cambridge. After Japan invaded China, he returned home to join the war effort, working in the military industries. He, too, thought in technical terms. "Economic modernization," he explained, is a "huge engineering system that requires extremely careful and elaborate planning." But as time passed, he was also intent on progressively withdrawing the state from the market—replacing "the arbitrary political power of the government" with "the automatic adjustment mechanism of the market."

Li was obsessed with creating conditions in which entrepreneurship could flourish and business could develop beyond the immediate family unit. This meant that the government had to focus on getting infrastructure in place, developing a rational institutional and legal framework—and looking at things from the entrepreneur's point of view. "Since there is not a textbook on how to improve the climate of business," Li said, "I put myself in the shoes of investors and then rely on scientific method to provide the answers."

The technocrats studied the Japanese experience repeatedly and with great care. Yin took a deep personal interest in the Meiji Restoration, which, beginning in 1868, initiated Japan's modernization, and he sought to sort out its lessons. Li's first job after World War II, before his flight to Taiwan, was to investigate the industry that the Japanese had built in northeast China, which made him a lifelong student of how the Japanese did things. In Taiwan, both men adapted aspects of Japan's bureaucratic structure—MITI-style, yet without the sense of permanence that characterized the Japanese system. They also came to the conclusion that Taiwan, like Japan, would need to export to survive, which meant continually improving quality while remaining price-competitive. That, in turn, required the constant and efficient absorption of technology. It also meant protecting the domestic market sufficiently to safeguard infant industries from more advanced foreign competitors. In short, they adopted the Japanese approach—"competing out and protecting in." But the protection would be allowed to phase out, as Taiwanese firms were deliberately subjected to the rigors and tests of international competition in their home market.

The supertechnocrats bludgeoned domestic companies to get their products up to world standards and down to world prices, and encouraged foreign investment to promote new export capabilities when they felt domestic firms were not up to the task. But Yin and Li ran into powerful opposition in promoting what Li called the "openness orientation." They were both accused of colluding with individual businessmen. Many wanted protection to continue. Li responded: "For those with the mentality of the 1950s— glorification of public enterprise and resentment of the intrusion of private [former imperialist] Japanese capital—the events of the 1980s have been traumatic. All these policy innovations amounted to the abandonment of some highly treasured vested ideas, which were vaguely associated with nationalism"—but which could not stand up to the realities of the world market.

In the late 1990s Taiwan faces the same squeeze as the others of the first generation of high-growth—but no longer low-wage—Asian countries. They are pressed on one side by the low-wage, newly industrializing countries (including mainland China) and on the other by high-technology products from the established industrial countries. Taiwan has tried to respond by augmenting its high-technology capabilities. Also, Taiwanese entrepreneurs have, in the quest for low wages, stepped up their foreign investment, including a great deal on the mainland. A second challenge is the continuing transition away from authoritarianism to a more democratic rule, which has gone hand in hand with economic development and the broadening of the middle class. The Kuomintang long kept a tight grip on power, appointing rather than electing the president. Chiang Ching-kuo, Chiang Kai-shek's son, held that post for ten years. Then, in 1988, the party appointed Lee Teng-hui, a former agricultural economist who had graduated from Cornell University. Although a member of the Nationalist Party, he was also a native Taiwanese, not a mainlander. In 1996, he was renewed in his post, this time in free, contested elections that went on despite Chinese naval maneuvers in the Formosa Strait.

The biggest and by far the most complex challenge is indeed Taiwan's relation to the People's Republic. Economics is drawing them together. Taiwanese firms have invested tens of billions of dollars on the mainland over the last decade, making it by far the biggest foreign investor. But fifty years after Mao's victory on the mainland, politics keeps them apart. The People's Republic still regards Taiwan as an errant province to be regathered. In Taiwan's schools, children learn in detail about the geography of China, memorize its dynasties, and study maps that show Taiwan as a province of

China. But there is no taste to be absorbed by the People's Republic. In the aftermath of the return of Hong Kong in 1997, Taiwan's status has moved front and center. How Hong Kong fares in its new situation—and how well its distinct status is respected—will be scrutinized closely in Taiwan. No near-term resolution of their differences is evident. Time, however, could provide the answer. As per capita income rises in China, and as its brand of socialism comes to look more and more like capitalism, then the gulf between the two could begin to look less significant.

As rags-to-riches stories go, Taiwan's is spectacular. Its per capita income rose from $100 in 1949 to almost $14,000 today. For several years, its central bank held the largest foreign reserves of any country in the world. Today it produces 30 percent of the world's notebook computers and half of the world's computer keyboards, monitors, scanners, and motherboards. Yet the progress was never smooth.

At the beginning of Taiwan's independence, government played an overwhelming role in the economy. There was hardly an alternative. Time has seen a progressive withdrawal of the frontier of government, along with a continuing emphasis on the macrofundamental agenda: The supertechnocrats put policies in place to encourage very high savings. With inflation and the defeat on the mainland entwined as a permanent nightmare in their minds, they relentlessly fought inflation with budget discipline and monetary restraint. They put sustained emphasis on education and on the development of technology and skills. They paid attention to equity and income distribution. They sought deep engagement with the world economy. And they were willing to surrender that most addictive of all of government's allures—the exercise of power.

"Countries with a Chinese cultural tradition are often perceived as having entrenched, powerful bureaucracies and central governments," K. T. Li was to observe. "This not only is historically true but is still true for Taiwan. Nevertheless, what we as policy makers did in Taiwan was to help various parts of the economy first to stand and then to walk. And then we let go."[8]

Singapore: The State as Venture Capitalist

When Dr. Goh Keng Swee, nearly eighty and frail, entered the restaurant of the venerable Raffles Hotel, everybody turned to look at him. After all, he was a father figure. If Lee Kuan Yew was the patriarch of modern Singapore, then Dr. Goh was next in line, its economic architect, the man who designed the system that delivered Singapore's economic miracle—7 to 9 percent growth rates almost every year for three decades. But, Dr. Goh would insist, the source of that miracle is greatly misunderstood. "The lecturers in the universities are all wrong," he said. "The critical factor was our decision to emphasize science and math courses in the schools, and the mothers' insis-

179

tence that their children take science and math. It was the mothers that were really responsible."

It was, of course, fitting to see Dr. Goh at Raffles. After all, it was Sir Thomas Stamford Raffles who in 1819 arrived at the island and, finding only a small Malay community, began to build it into a British colony as well as an entrepôt for the region. In the 1930s, the young Goh was picked out, as was the custom with the promising young native Singaporeans, to attend the elite school named for Stamford Raffles in order to be trained to enter the local government. He was then sent to England, where he earned a Ph.D. at the London School of Economics. It was only after he returned to Singapore and joined the civil service that he teamed up with Lee Kuan Yew.

Also educated at the school named for Raffles before going off to Cambridge University, Lee had come home from England determined to throw himself into the anticolonial movement. Before the struggle was over, Lee would not only overcome the British but would also best the Communists in a bitter battle for control over the nationalist movement. His dream was of a single country comprising both Malaysia and Singapore, but in 1965, after just two years of such a union, the experiment fell apart. Lee wept in public. He was left the leader of a much diminished nation, the city-state of Singapore, with fewer than 3 million people. Somehow he would have to make a nation out of what was there—a poor and poorly educated population, 75 percent of whom were Chinese, with most of the rest Malay and Indian, with no sense of national identity. Gangs, crime, and communists all made life in Singapore a permanent crisis, and its prospects were quite problematic.

If Singapore was to find a future, there were only two obvious resources —the people and the leadership. In Lee Kuan Yew, Singapore had a man with an unusual combination of talents—he was a charismatic leader, a skilled and shrewd politician, a superb technocrat with a broad view, and a visionary. "To build a country, you need passion," he once said. "If you just do your sums—pluses, minuses, credit, debit—you are a washout." He had passion, and he evinced little doubt about his own judgment or authority. He also had, as he would note later in life, a formidable talent for persuasion.

In Dr. Goh, the country had a pragmatic economist. "If we were economic pioneers," Goh said, "it was due to simple economic necessity. The key to success is not a matter of planning but rather the ability to adapt to changing situations." The country's one and only foray into five-year plans was in the 1960s. But, said Goh, it was "cooked up during a long weekend" as a sop to keep the World Bank happy. Yet whether there was a plan or not, the system that Lee and Goh created provided the state with a strong, guiding role in the economy. The results have been given many different names: "the administrative state," "the state as venture capitalist," and, occasionally, "capitalism with socialistic characteristics."

All this was a response to the situation at hand. In its early years, Singapore was a country besieged. It had no great confidence that it could make it, or even survive. As there was so little to work with, Lee, Goh, and their colleagues were not very confident in the capabilities of local entrepreneurs. They were also much influenced by the postwar British Labour Party and the postwar trend toward state ownership. Indeed, they began their public careers as committed socialists, but they ended up professing their faith in the market, albeit with a strong government say. For the most part, they developed the system on their own. If there was one major external influence, it was a Dutch economist named Albert Winsemius, originally an expert in the economics of ice cream. Winsemius was their guide to the international economy, helping them decide which industries to encourage and providing pep talks during times of uncertainty and despair. Yes, they could do it; they could create a viable economy out of what was essentially a port backed up by small farms.

Goh and Lee established the Economic Development Board to guide the creation of a modern economy. They put in place state-owned companies, which they went out of their way to staff with the best they could find. They forced civil servants to think like businessmen, tying their promotions to the profitability of the state-owned enterprises they ran. They financed social services—health care and housing—but were always careful not to make them so complete as to deprive Singaporeans of their sense of personal and family responsibility. As one of the current government ministers put it, a less-than-total welfare system "helps Singaporean people see the future more clearly." And they built upon the Chinese propensity to save by promoting a very high savings rate. In fact, they implemented it through the Central Provident Fund, which at its height took 50 percent of all wages. The money was used to finance infrastructure, industry, and housing. The most famous example of the infrastructure development was the transformation—masterminded by Goh—of a wide expanse of swamp called Jurong into a vast industrial park. Many regarded the project as ridiculous and likely to fail, and it became known as Goh's Folly. Today, however, it is synonymous with Singapore's economic success.

They also made an enormous commitment to education—but they charged, at least at the university level, something for it. Nothing in Singapore should be free. In 1968, the country produced no engineers; now it aims to turn out twenty thousand a year. Throughout the process of modernization, the government was a very active facilitator. It was the agenda keeper, the long-range planner, a strategic player in its own right, and the manager of resources. A small elite of bureaucrats, selected meritocratically, ran the whole system. The sense of immediate vulnerability, the small size of the country, the unfolding success, and Lee's considerable talents as a mobilizer and implementer—all created a national consensus, a common purpose, and effective coordination that made Singapore look like a very cohesive company. After all, even the secretary-general of the trades union council was a member of the cabinet.

Yet state domination was only part of the story. For over the same period of time, Singapore made a crucial commitment to international commerce—in an era when import substitution and protection were the order of the day. Lee and Goh were all too conscious of Singapore's diminutive size; it was, in their view, simply too small to go it alone. They would seek to anchor it firmly in the world economy. "There was no choice except to produce for export," said Goh. "Our domestic market was too small, and the skills of local enterprise at the time were too low."

First, Singapore would create an environment conducive to economic growth—low inflation, stable and predictable "rules of the game" for business and foreigners to operate by, a high savings rate, an anticorruption ethos, and a climate friendly to business. As one economist put it, "In Singapore, companies are good." Second, it made the very unfashionable decision to court multinational corporations, for these firms would move in with a crucial dowry—technology, skills, capital, and access to markets. The firms were vetted carefully for what they brought and what industries they represented. Singapore was looking for stable companies with strong technologies and a willingness to invest with a long-term perspective. It wanted high-visibility projects that would contribute to building, as one minister put it, the Singapore "brand name"—embodying quality, reliability, and a comfort level for foreign investors higher than available elsewhere. One of the very first companies to be so enticed was Texas Instruments, which arrived in 1968 to begin manufacturing transistors. In those years, Singapore benefited greatly from the upheavals of Mao's Cultural Revolution, which lured multinationals away from Hong Kong and Taiwan and instead toward Singapore, which had the great virtue of being farther from China. The government went out of its way to facilitate the activities of foreign companies with everything from infrastructure investment to aligning its educational programs to their needs.

In the late 1990s, Singapore worries about losing out to the newer low-cost production areas, and it has sought to protect itself by moving up the value chain to higher technologies and by carving out an "external economy," new spheres of economic activity—as, for instance, in the "second Singapore" it is overseeing in China. It began this redefinition in the 1970s, but the urgency has grown. "When Singapore was a colony," recalled Dr. Goh, "everything in every store were items that said 'Made in Britain.' Now the dominant insignia is 'Made in China.' "[9]

Malaysia: The Sons of the Soil

Three of the first four "tigers"—Taiwan, Singapore, and Hong Kong—were all Chinese communities. In the "tigers" that came next—Indonesia, Malaysia, and Thailand—the ethnic Chinese have been engines of the local economies. In the case of Malaysia, however, the entire thrust of development has been aimed specifically at solving its "Chinese problem"—dominance of economic activity by the local Chinese, with their long commercial tradition and markets, although the Malays, rural and poor, made up the majority of the population. "Malaysia's subsequent success," observed a close student of its economy, "results in large part from its effort to solve its racial problems." And it was so successful that the country in two decades was transformed from an exporter of rubber and palm oil to one of the world's largest manufacturer of computer chips. With just 19 million people, it is the thirteenth-largest trading nation in the world; it trades more than Russia (with a population of 147 million) and twice as much as India (with a population of 935 million). It also has the thirteenth-largest stock market in the world, and 83 percent of its exports are manufactures. "Not bad," in the words of Prime Minister Mahathir, for a country that was considered "a primary candidate for the dustbin of history."

The turning point was the 1969 anti-Chinese riots—sparked by a strong Chinese showing in elections. Malays—three quarters of whom lived in poverty—saw the little political power they had slipping away to the Chinese. Democracy was suspended, and a "New Economic Policy" was launched, intended to promote rapid growth but also, crucially, to bring about redistribution. It was a massive program of affirmative action, quotas, and favoritism that was meant to lift the majority *bumiputras*—the sons of the soil, that is, indigenous Malays—out of poverty and into schools and universities and then into the middle class. There was no end to the ingenuity of the program. All business enterprises were to have at least 30 percent Malay participation. The government offered *bumiputras* lower mortgage rates than non-*bumiputras*. And on and on.

Yet at the same time, the government sought to ease the social frictions and build broad support for the New Economic Policy. To be sustained, redistribution required wealth creation first and foremost, and the entire population began to benefit—including, very considerably, the Chinese. The program involved a high degree of state ownership, much regulation, and a large bureaucracy. It also entailed a massive investment in education. In 1957, when Malaysia became independent, it did not have a single Malay-language school. "The purpose of Malay education," a noted British colonial educator had declared, "is to make them better farmers and fisherman." As if in reply, Prime Minister Mahathir, himself the son of a teacher, would later proudly point out, "The sons of rice farmers and fishermen own and run billion-dollar companies successfully." Foreign investment was encouraged. The country was launched on a high growth curve—7.8 percent per year in the 1970s. Per capita income rose from $390 in 1970 to $1,900 in 1982. The country also developed national unity. There was enough economic growth to go around.

But by the early 1980s, the New Economic Policy floundered. The government had expanded public enterprise and made a very large investment in heavy industry, which was not working. Losses and inefficiency were mounting. The deficit of public enterprises grew markedly as a share of the GNP. Economic growth faltered. At that point, Prime Minister Mahathir and his finance minister, Daim Zainuddin, engineered a sharp shift to the market.

In instituting these changes, Mahathir was moved less by economic philosophy than by what had always been his motivating force—nationalism. His father was the first Malay head of an English school in British-controlled Malaya. As a teenager during World War II, Mahathir was a pushcart vendor, but he went out of his way to avoid selling fruit to the occupying Japanese. At the war's end, he joined the anti-British colonial movement even before going off to study at the King Edward VII College of Medicine in Singapore. By age twenty-one, he was already a member of the anticolonial United Malay National Organization (UMNO), which in 1997 was still the ruling party. In 1969 he wrote a book, *The Malay Dilemma*. Its criticism of the lack of governmental response to the economic weakness of the Malays vis-à-vis the Chinese got him kicked out of the UMNO, and it was banned. Three years after the anti-Chinese riots, and after the kind of remedies he had proposed in his book were being implemented, he was invited back into the party. He held a succession of positions until becoming prime minister in 1981. It was only then that the ban on *The Malay Dilemma* was lifted.

As prime minister, Mahathir took steps to make it clear that there was now going to be a new emphasis on efficiency and modernization. To symbolize the change, he required that all government employees, including members of Parliament, punch in on a time clock. He also set out to apply relevant parts of the Japanese model to the Malaysian economy. At one point, he spent several weeks traveling incognito in Japan seeking to uncover "its spirit and roots." Books about Japan were often best-sellers in Malaysia, and Mahathir made a point to read them, underlining key passages and insisting that his aides study them as well.

The nationalist struggle continues to define how Mahathir looks at the world. Despite Malaysia's increasing integration with the world economy, he frequently rose up in anger and indignation at what he saw to be any instance of condescension, judgment, or unsolicited advice from Western sources. Mahathir restricted domestic criticism, and viewed criticism from outside the country as expressions of colonialism. To a German environmentalist campaigning against logging, he wrote, "Stop being arrogant and thinking that it is the white man's burden to decide the fate of the peoples of the world." He has banned a number of Western publications and reporters, and attacks what he calls the "so-called Western controlled free press." His Malay nationalism is now becoming an Asian nationalism. "Asia cannot be stopped," he said. To those who questioned the sustainability of high growth, he sarcastically replied, "This belief in our infinite ability to fail and in our limited ability to succeed is touching."

But in the early 1980s, when he directed the turn in the Malaysian economy, it was because of the crisis that had hit the economy and because of his judgment that it was now strong enough to relax state control and—

striking for such a nationalist—to open up further to foreign investment. The country needed the growth and rising national income if it were to solve the Malay economic dilemma. "By the early 1980s, Malaysia had developed the managerial skills and expertise to go forward, including an entrepreneurial class," said Mahathir. "That did not exist in the 1960s and 1970s. Thus, in those years, you had to have stronger state control. Once these were in place, however, you could pull back and leave it to the private sector and the markets to perform." It helped that Thatcherism was in the air. "In a sense, we took advantage of Thatcher and what she was doing to promote our own work," Mahathir said. "Thatcher became a reinforcing catalyst. The real concern was the drain and limitations of government resources. The projects were too expensive for the government to finance. The money used for these projects could be better used for what government would be doing, which is education, health, and removing poverty."

Between 1984 and 1986, a Mahathir-appointed national commission developed the rationale for privatization. "We said it was not the business of government to be in business," explained Mahathir. "The private sector would be the primary engine of growth." The actual privatization has not been laissez-faire, however. The government has continued to hold large, even controlling, stakes in many firms. Asset sales were often far from transparent. The beneficiaries, critics said, were prominent Malay business-men with connections to the ruling party. The government replied that all it was doing was picking "winners"—people who would make a success of the partly privatized companies. And it included among the beneficiaries the broader Malay population, which acquired stakes in the firms through state-sponsored pension and trust funds. These funds mobilized a form of popular capitalism, giving ordinary people a stake alongside the insiders.

Mahathir codified the shift in government strategies in a new program, the National Development Policy and Vision 2020, which aimed at 7 percent annual growth, meaning that the GNP would double every ten years. In this enterprise, the private sector would operate in close "partnership" with the government. "Our idea of Malaysia is Malaysia, Inc., very much along the lines of Japan," said Mahathir. "We have adopted this very explicitly in order to develop the social consensus that the market is the way for Malaysia to go. We want strong cooperation between government, companies, and the community. After all, government depends upon the profitability of compa-nies as much as companies themselves do. If companies don't make money, the government doesn't make money. If companies make money, the govern-ment is guaranteed thirty percent of those profits in the form of taxes. It's simple, but profound."

Just as Malaysia came charging after the first generation of "tigers," it will also face competitive challenges from the next generation. And like others in the region, it will have to temper its ambitious plans for infrastruc-ture development. Yet in the meantime, the country has racked up an extraor-dinary record—not least, keeping ethnic tensions at bay by spreading the benefits of growth. "The political climate was ripe," explained Deputy Prime Minister Anwar. "Indians, Chinese, and Malays are now more tolerant of each other than in the 1960s. Efforts to accommodate each other are part of the system. And leadership can influence the values in the culture, and alter the path of development. Put all these things together in a box and shake it up." Anwar vigorously moved his hands up and down for a moment. Then he smiled. "The result is success." [10]

The New Role

Many of the same basic interactions between government and market have played out in the other countries of the region, although refracted through their histories and cultures and the defining nature of their anticolonial struggles. In Indonesia, there was a long clash between two groups of technocrats—the "engineers," who wanted to undertake big high-visibility projects, and the "economists," who wanted to reduce government control and intervention. Unlike Taiwan, Indonesia was unable to resolve that clash until the late 1980s, when the country made a major turn toward the international market and deregulation. It was certainly influenced by the opening up of other countries in the region. Its major objective was to free itself from excessive dependence on oil and gas exports. "Bureaucrats must take on a new role," said Ali Wardhana, one of the leading Indonesian economists, at the time. "Instead of intervening to control private economic agents, bureaucrats need to avoid intervention and facilitate private activity."

The program has generally worked. Indonesia is now a high-growth country that has successfully moved toward being a significant diversified exporter and away from a heavy reliance on oil and natural gas exports. With 203 million people spread over seventeen thousand islands, however, it does not have the same kind of focus that the smaller Asian countries enjoy. It faces major questions about regional development, the link between education and economic advancement, the prominent role of the Chinese entrepreneurs, equity and income distribution, and corruption. Its political system has become a new target for international human rights activists. Hanging over all of this is the question of what will follow the departure of General Suharto, who took power in the face of an imminent Communist coup in 1965 and has maintained control through an essentially one-party system ever since.

Thailand's growth since the mid-1980s was propelled by foreign investment, led by the Japanese. The country went through some tough political battles, centered on a struggle for power between various military and civilian groups. But Thailand is unique among the countries in the region in that it has had a king, Bhumibol Adjulyadej, who has ruled for half a century and provided continuing stability and legitimacy—and moral conscience— through the various crises. Thailand is a classic case in which the infrastructure—roads, and pollution control, for example—has not kept pace with the rapid rise in the GNP.

Since the early 1990s, the government has sought to reduce its role in the economy through large-scale privatization. "The policy of privatization was carried out for two reasons, necessity and prudence," said former prime minister Anand Panyarachun. "State companies needed the injection of more state funds if they were to survive and grow. The state could not afford to do that even if companies were profitable. The public was demanding leaner government, getting rid of the fat, and did not want to see state-owned companies to be continued as state employment agencies without any productivity effect or long-term potential." Anand spoke of another force behind the move toward privatization: "The timing of the end of the communist system was also a major factor in propelling the global trend toward the free market. All fears of capitalism's failures and my belief in the dominance of the state were cast aside with the collapse of the communist state and, with it, of government control."

The country for which communism remains the central fact is Vietnam. With a population bigger than Taiwan's, Korea's, Malaysia's, and Singapore's combined, it is poised to enter the league of the fast growers. It has a well-educated population and, in many ways, the attributes to spur growth. Yet its transition is likely to be more difficult than that of the other countries in the region, for the system's legitimacy and ideology are rooted in the Vietnam War and a hostility to capitalism and the West. To embrace the market would be to call into question the fundaments of the regime, which is hardly something that the current leadership wants to do. Thus, for the time being, Vietnam is suspended between state domination and private initiative. There is a market system, but the private sector has not been freed up, nor has reform of state enterprises begun in earnest.

Perhaps the surest sign that East Asian growth is a comprehensive, regional phenomenon comes from the Philippines. For many decades, the country operated far beneath its economic potential. Social inequalities were extreme. The government was a dictatorship of the landed elite, with the notorious and profligate Ferdinand Marcos at the helm. Unlike other authoritarian leaders in the region, Marcos rarely channeled his ill-gotten wealth back into the local economy. Instead, he and his cronies stashed it in Swiss banks and spent it overseas. The thousands of pairs of shoes belonging to his wife, Imelda, came to symbolize the corruption of the system.

Marcos fell in 1986, overthrown by the popular front led by Corazon Aquino. Her husband, Benigno, an outspoken opponent of Marcos, had been assassinated three years earlier by Marcos gunmen when he landed at Manila's airport. The Philippines remained a suspect destination for trade and investment, its chronic corruption and disorder contrasting with fast growth elsewhere in the region. Yet the peaceful political evolution under Mrs. Aquino and her successor, Fidel Ramos, set the stage for the Philippines to claim its connection to the rest of Southeast Asia. Aquino and Ramos brought economic policy into line with their regional partners. Thanks to freed currency markets and the lowering of trade barriers, the black market has become less pervasive. Manila, the capital, is still known for high crime, pollution, and poverty. Yet with sustained growth rates of 4 percent or higher since 1994, and having made progress toward ending its chronic electricity shortages, the country has become a newly attractive emerging market—a full-fledged "tiger"—and is narrowing the gap with its neighbors.[11]

Asia, Inc.?

All across Southeast Asia, the economic model is changing as governments, to one degree or another, pull back from an interventionist role in the economy. The reasons for this are not the same as those to be found in other parts of the world—disillusionment, a sense of failure, harsh economic realities. Despite periodic setbacks, change in Asia is in large measure a consequence of success. The growing middle class wants more participation and a bigger say. Its members want the economic system to affect their daily lives positively; they want their growth and income levels to translate into an improving quality of life. The growing complexity of economies makes government management more difficult. The requirements of competition —innovation, speed, flexibility, and adaptability—can all be impeded by bureaucratic intervention.

A growing fear of "hollowing out"—losing their industrial strength— is gripping many of these nations as they worry that their domestic export industries will lose competitiveness, owing to rising wages and to the coun- tries moving up behind them. Indeed, one finds a pervasive anxiety through- out the region that the same set of attributes that propelled their growth— low wages, a skilled and disciplined workforce—could work against them as other nations capture them in turn. That fear spurs the competition for investment, adding to the pressures to reduce government regulation in order to lower costs and increase flexibility. Consumers—and investors—are eager to look outside for better values.

Ironically, Countries, Inc. is being undermined by the growth of Asia, Inc., the new integrated regional economy, which will be a central fact of the twenty-first century. This economy began to take shape in the middle 1980s, as Japanese investment in Asia mounted, seeking lower costs. The flow accelerated after Japan's huge shopping spree in the United States and Europe came to grief. It has made Asia into an export platform—as well as a market—for Japanese companies. "Japanese investment was a catalyst for change," said Anand Panyarachun, Thailand's former prime minister. "Thailand decided to establish competitive terms to attract Japanese invest- ment in our country rather than see it go to Malaysia, Indonesia, or elsewhere in Southeast Asia. It was a decisive policy to seek that investment yen and to create a more open economy for foreign investment. It represented a conscious move on Thailand's part to try to help establish a regional market and to be part of it."

Japan's capital exports did much to tie the Asian economies together, but Korea, Taiwan, and Hong Kong have also become big investors throughout the region, seeking, like the Japanese, lower costs. Trade within the region has grown quickly as these countries become important markets for each other. Companies and entrepreneurs have been increasing their own cross-border stakes, while the rise of locally based multinationals is also tying the region together. Meanwhile, rapid economic growth has turned tens of millions of people into consumers. The growing demands for choice and quality of life are shifting the economic rationale of societies from a producer logic to a consumer logic. Many of the Countries, Inc. have relatively small populations, so the regional Asian economy gives them access to a larger market, of which they are part, which helps them get to scale.

Something else provides unique sinews for the regional economy—the connections among the *hua ch'ia* ("the Chinese across the bridge"), the ethnic Chinese who live, trade, invest, and collaborate across the region. They have proved to be a major force, tying economies together as well as lessening government control. An estimated 25 million Chinese live in Southeast Asia. They make up 32 percent of the population in Malaysia, 15 percent in Thailand, 4 percent in Indonesia, and 1 percent in the Philippines. The ethnic Chinese have an inordinately large entrepreneurial and commercial role; they boast twelve families worth $5 billion or more and are estimated to control at least $2 trillion. They are famous for doing their deals without contracts, lawyers, bankers, and consultants—even when values run into the billions of dollars. Kinship-based rules of the game assume the role that contract law performs elsewhere, facilitating trade, investment, and the movement of capital. Their collective GNP—a somewhat metaphorical concept—has been estimated at $450 billion, which would make them, as a separate country, the world's ninth-largest economy.

While the regional development is testament to the success of Countries, Inc., it also reduces the ability of nations to continue to run themselves as Countries, Inc. It becomes more difficult to deploy government knowledge and to exert the guiding hand, for the span of economic activity—investment, alliances, trade, market development—extends beyond the borders of national sovereignty, and thus beyond the ability of governments to manage and intervene as they did in earlier and, by comparison, simpler times. The result is a new mixture, featuring greater privatization and deregulation, fewer rules, less control, and reduced protection. At the same time, governments are facing pressure to take on the new role of coordinator of economic relations among the nations of the region. The current framework for cooperation is ASEAN, the Association of Southeast Asian Nations, which grew up during the 1970s and 1980s as a political bulwark against communism in China and, more so, in Vietnam. Its vocation is no longer exclusively political. Indeed, ironically, Vietnam is a recent admittee.

Regional integration brings risk. It will take even more complex coordination to keep the dynamic economies of Asia, Inc., in harmony as they integrate. Explosive growth and the removal of barriers to trade and investment have brought new regional dangers—overheating and overlending, dependence on external capital flows, artificially propped up financial systems, overvalued currencies, and speculation. This was all too evident in the second half of 1997, when a severe currency crisis swept over Southeast Asia. It began in Thailand, brought on by the bursting of a real estate bubble, a weak banking sector, high foreign debt, and a fixed currency that encouraged expansive borrowing and lending. It quickly led to attacks on the Malaysian ringgit, the Indonesian rupiah, and the Philippine peso—and dramatic collapse in regional stock markets. Underlying the crisis was the deeper apprehension that the competitive strengths of these nations were eroding in the face of rising wages and a new intensified competition, and that they might end up caught in a sort of no-man's-land of "middle technology." The financial crisis generated many recriminations. By far the most vocal came from Mahathir Mohamad. The prime minister of Malaysia blamed international speculators for "villainous acts of sabotage" and "the height of international criminality." Despite the acerbity of his comments, Mahathir did capture the shock that many in the region felt on discovering not only their exposure but their vulnerability to the volatile and sometimes drastic movements of money in an integrated global financial system. As they saw it, the currency attacks wiped out 20 or 30 percent of the national wealth that had been laboriously built over several decades.

But the institutional side of the international financial system also came to their rescue. Asian governments mounted a regional intervention—a $17.2 billion bailout led by Japan, in which the other countries of the region, including China, participated—to stabilize the Thai baht and contain a "domino" crisis of a modern type. The International Monetary Fund had to be called in to help restore financial equilibrium. A $23 billion bailout of Indonesia followed. In order to improve their balance of payments and financial credibility, many governments quickly announced cutbacks in expensive and visible investment projects. At the same time, the devaluation of currencies renewed their competitive position in world markets. And at least as some saw it, the crisis also cooled off overheated economies. "Lawyers, accountants, and engineers were resigning their positions to go into the stock market," observed a Malay businessman. "We may be better off in the long run with 6 rather than 8 percent growth. It's more manageable."

The countries in the region have gone through a series of currency and capital-markets crises in the past. Ironically, the impact of the latest is a sign of how far they have come, for none before had either the visibility or the regional and international repercussions. Some see in the 1997 crisis similarities to the bursting of the Japanese "bubble." They fear that weak financial sectors, overbuilt real estate, and industrial overcapacity will mean that difficult economic times lie beyond the miracle. Yet one of the hallmarks of these countries over the years has been their flexibility and adaptability, and necessity now provides the opportunity for them to once again restructure their economies and return to sustained growth.

Throughout Asia, one encounters a recurrent phrase—the countries of the region, it is said, need to find a "new modality." It is a frustratingly elusive and abstract term, but it reflects a conviction that a new balance has to be struck between government and marketplace that takes into account not only national needs but also the imperatives of the new regional economic context. These countries have proved to be expert competitors, but new competitive pressures are driving a change. In particular, it is highly likely that the future of Countries, Inc. will be dramatically affected by the coming competition from the two giants that bestride the region: China and India.[12]

CHAPTER 7

THE COLOR OF THE CAT

China's Transformation

WHEN THE FRENCH LINER docked in Marseilles in December 1920, most of the group of Chinese students on board stood about dazed, confused, not knowing what to do. One, however, was immediately busy, organizing their luggage, arranging their disembarkation. The young man, just sixteen, was Deng Xiaoping, and he was already demonstrating the take-charge organizational skills that would make him the dominating figure in China sixty years later. In the last two decades of the twentieth century, he would set his country on a course to create a capitalist economy within a communist political system and turn it into a major force in the global economy. This was remarkable in that he was seventy-four when he finally became the paramount leader and launched China on its era of reform. No less remarkable was the extraordinary resilience he displayed in the face of the enormous setbacks, challenges, deprivations, and falls from favor that preceded his final rise to power.

Deng was the son of a prosperous landowner-turned-local-government-official in the populous inland province of Sichuan. As a boy, he started in a traditional Confucian school, but then, amid the tumult and fragmentation that followed the Chinese Revolution of 1911, switched into a school equipped with both a more modern curriculum and links to France. That is how he came to be sent to France for further study. His education there proved to be spotty, and he held a number of jobs, working in a Renault plant and steel and rubber factories, and also doing time as a kitchen hand and as a fireman on a locomotive. He developed two lasting passions in France—one was for croissants; the other was for communism. The two were not totally unconnected: It was Ho Chi Minh, later the leader of North Vietnam, who would tell him where in Paris to get the best croissants.

Prime Minister Winston Churchill confidently returned from the Potsdam conference for the 1945 British election. Afterward, his wife called Churchill's stinging defeat "a blessing in disguise." He responded that it was "quite effectively disguised."

Clement Attlee, a former social worker in London's East End, touched a chord among voters that Churchill could not. With Attlee as prime minister, the post–World War II Labour government captured the commanding heights of the economy and established the welfare state.

3

At the end of World War II, German girls worked together to rebuild their homes. The nations of Western Europe collaborated on reconstruction aided by America's Marshall Plan. Its emblem (right) appeared on all goods sent to Europe, from flour to tractors.

FOR EUROPEAN RECOVERY
SUPPLIED BY THE
UNITED STATES OF AMERICA

4

German finance minister Ludwig Erhard (center) created the social market economy, making Germany the economic motor of Europe. With France's Charles de Gaulle (left) and German chancellor Konrad Adenauer (right).

5

New Year's Day, 1947. British coal mines, formerly privately owned, were national-ized "on behalf of the people." Government ownership was key to economic growth and social justice.

Onetime cognac sales-man Jean Monnet became the "Father of Europe." He also created the economic plan that propelled France into the modern age.

In 1934 the fallen tycoon Samuel Insull was returned to Chicago to stand trial after fleeing the country. The collapse of his electric-power empire during the Depression galvanized New Deal regulation.

James Landis worked feverishly around the clock during the New Deal to design securities and electric-power regulations. Brilliant lawyer and "prophet of regulation," Landis was warned to stop working his mind "like a brewery horse."

President Franklin D. Roosevelt initiated the Tennessee Valley Authority, embodying the New Deal commitment to public works and public power for economic development. Below: TVA's Wheeler Dam under construction in 1936.

10

11

So great was his influence that economist John Maynard Keynes made the cover of *Time* magazine in 1965, nineteen years after his death.

JOHN
MAYNARD
KEYNES

12

"Now, I am a Keynesian," said Republican president Richard Nixon in 1971. With Treasury secretary John Connally shortly before announcing wage and price controls.

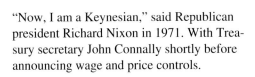

13

Mahatma Gandhi and Jawaharlal Nehru, the two great figures of Indian independence, in 1946. United in political objectives, they differed strongly on economics.
Gandhi advocated village self-reliance and a "spinning wheel in every hut." Nehru
was "all for tractors and big machinery"—and massive governmental control.

Electric power
comes to rural India
in 1962.

Queen Elizabeth II, visiting Ghana in 1961, was hailed as "the greatest socialist monarch in the world." President Kwame Nkrumah (left), calling himself the Redeemer, achieved political independence for Ghana but ruined the country's economy.

"Sing-Song." Conservative parliamentary candidate Margaret Roberts—later Prime Minister Margaret Thatcher—accompanied voters on the piano in a sing-along after a brief political debate in a pub.

"Minister of Thought" Keith Joseph, intellectual architect of the Thatcher Revolution. "I could not have . . . achieved what I did as prime minister without Keith," said Thatcher.

18

During Britain's "winter of discontent" in 1978–1979, garbage piled up in the streets of London, owing to a "dust-men's" strike. Leicester Square in the West End became an official rubbish dump.

19

21

20

Striking hospital workers (left) took a tea break as labor unrest paralyzed Britain and set the stage for the 1979 victory by Margaret Thatcher (above)—and the Thatcher Revolution in Britain and around the world.

22

Deng Xiaoping, age sixteen, as a student in Paris, where he embraced communism—and opened a bean-curd shop.

23

Deng Xiaoping (right), with Mao Zedong (left) in 1962, in the aftermath of the disastrous Great Leap Forward. After Mao's death, Deng would overturn his policies and transform China.

24

The Iron and Steel Complex in Anshan, China, employs more than a quarter of a million people. Its managers are responsible for their workers' housing, children's schooling, and even grandmothers' care. The 15th Party Congress in 1997 slated such enterprises for radical reforms.

Economic reform in China began with agriculture. A smiling farmer in Sichuan brought his geese to market in 1986, knowing that he would keep the profits.

25

26

A Chinese official examined the newly issued stock certificates of a Beijing department store in 1987, as private ownership began.

27

Deng Xiaoping overseeing construction in Shenzhen. As paramount leader, he sponsored such Special Economic Zones, which drove China's remarkable growth.

General Park Chung Hee, iron-handed dictator and "the founding CEO of Korea, Inc.," pushed the industrialization that made Korea an economic powerhouse. He was killed in a 1979 coup.

28

29

Students and workers protesting in 1989 in Seoul, demanding the arrest of President Roh Tae Woo and Chun Doo Hwan. In 1996, the two (left) stood convicted of massive corruption.

30

As the union between Singapore and Malaysia acrimoniously broke down in 1965, Lee Kuan Yew took to the airwaves. Over the next quarter century, he led Singapore's awesome economic development.

31

32

Lee Teng-hui, the first democratically elected president of Taiwan, leader of the Nationalist Party—and a native Taiwanese.

33

Japanese farmers protest against rice imports and U.S. pressure to reduce trade barriers. By the late 1990s, Japan's long economic slump had increased the pressure to deregulate.

Anti-Chinese riots in Malaysia in 1969 resulted in the launching of new policies to promote rapid growth and redistribute wealth toward native Malays.

Prime Minister Mohamad Mahathir, sporting his habitual name tag, has emerged as the most assertive spokesman for Southeast Asia's dynamic economic growth.

The tallest buildings in the world— the Petronas towers in Malaysia's capital, Kuala Lumpur—symbolize Asia's increasing stature in the world economy.

A 1967 campaign poster for Indira Gandhi, who dominated India's politics for almost two decades.

In 1991 P. V. Narasimha Rao (left) became India's prime minister. Although his cabinet was attacked as "old wine in old bottles," he broke with the Nehru-Gandhi legacy and initiated sweeping economic reforms.

In the 1970s, international companies were driven out of India. In the 1990s, Coca-Cola, along with other firms, was happy to return to a market of nearly 1 billion people.

40

Dictator Juan Perón and his charismatic wife, Eva, in 1952. Mixing populism and nationalism, Perón cut Argentina's links to the world economy— accelerating the decline of what had been one of the world's richest nations.

41

With Argentina on the edge of economic collapse in 1989, President Carlos Menem (right) appointed Domingo Cavallo (left) finance minister. "The broommaker's son" swept aside decades of state control with one of Latin America's most radical reform programs.

Hyperinflation hit Bolivia in the 1980s. A worker in Bolivia's central bank counted bills at a time when people had to carry huge amounts of currency even to make small purchases.

42

43

The authors of "shock therapy"—Bolivia's Gonzalo Sanchez de Lozada (left) and economist Jeffrey Sachs (right)—"created a market economy overnight."

In 1994, Fernando Henrique Cardoso, now Brazil's president, introduced the real, the new currency that helped stanch Brazil's chronic inflation.

44

Alberto Fujimori, running as an outsider and campaigning on a tractor, defeated novelist Mario Vargas Llosa in the bitter 1990 Peruvian presidential election. Dramatic economic reforms—"Fujishock"—followed.

Solidarity in Poland in the early 1980s initiated the unraveling of communist power in Eastern Europe.

46

47

Lech Walesa (second from right) at a memorial for slain workers at Gdańsk shipyard. In 1991 he was elected president of Poland.

As confused East German guards looked on, the Berlin Wall came down on November 11, 1989—signaling the end of the cold war and the demise of centrally planned economies.

The currencies of East and West Germany were unified on a one-to-one basis in June 1990—at a very great cost.

48

49

50

Television coverage of the critical 1996 Russian presidential election. Boris Yeltsin (left) came from far behind to defeat Communist candidate Gennady Zyuganov (right), reaffirming Russia's commitment to reform.

Finance minister Yegor Gaidar inherited a collapsing Russian economy in 1991—it was, he said, like going into the cockpit of a jet, and discovering "that there was no one at the controls."

51

52

Russian prime minister Viktor Chernomyrdin (center) went to work to stabilize the Russian economy. Inflation has been cut dramatically and 90 percent of industrial production is now privatized.

Friedrich von Hayek, critic of Keynes, proved Keynes' axiom that "ideas are more powerful than is commonly understood." Nobel Prize for economics in 1974.

53

After visiting Margaret Thatcher, economist Milton Friedman leaves 10 Downing Street, carrying his own book. Nobel Prize for economics in 1976.

54

55

The University of Chicago economists celebrated free markets. What began, in Milton Friedman's words, as "a small, beleaguered minority, regarded as eccentrics," turned into a vastly influential movement.

5

George Stigler, critic of government regu- lation. Nobel Prize for economics in 1982.

Gary Becker developed the concept of "human capital." Nobel Prize for economics in 1992.

56

French president Valéry Giscard D'Estaing and German chancellor Helmut Schmidt at the 1978 Brussels summit where they launched the European Monetary System, a major step toward European economic unity.

Altiero Spinelli, whose dream began in Mussolini's prison during World War II, "relaunched" the drive for European unity in the mid-1980s.

President François Mitterrand after his 1981 election victory, holding the symbol of the Socialist Party. Two years later France would be forced to embark on the "Great U-Turn" toward market reform.

President Ronald Reagan with Federal Reserve chairman Paul Volcker, who set out to "slay the inflationary dragon."

In 1993 Bill Clinton introduced his ill-fated health plan to Congress. The Republicans' Contract with America in 1994, announced on the steps of the Capitol, promised a drastic rollback of government. The clash between the Clinton administration and the Republican Congress shut down the federal government in the winter of 1995.

The White House Visitor Center is closed due to government shutdown.

All White House tours are cancelled.

European Commission president Jacques Delors campaigned for approval of the Maastricht Treaty, designed to unite Europe, in the 1992 French referendum. It barely won.

65

German chancellor Helmut Kohl addressing the European Parliment in Strasbourg in 1996. After reuniting the two Germanys, he set his sights on a federal Europe.

66

67

"Chancellor, here is my last shirt" — German miners protest in 1997 against deteriorating economic conditions.

68

New Labour Tony Blair promised that his party would not be the one that "bungs up" taxes, while New Democrat Bill Clinton declared that the era of "big government" was over.

The spread of communism among the handful of Chinese students in Europe was inspired by the May 4 Movement in Beijing, which had erupted in Tiananmen Square on May 4, 1919, to protest the humiliation of foreign domination of China in the aftermath of the Versailles treaty. Communism became a powerful vehicle for Chinese nationalism. For Deng it became a vocation. One of his chief sponsors and mentors was Zhou Enlai, who had imbibed Marxism while a student in Japan, before moving to France and becoming a leader of the tiny Chinese communist movement in Europe. Years later Deng was to call Zhou "my elder brother," and Zhou, as a good older brother, would shield Deng from the worst excesses of the Cultural Revolution of the 1960s. During their French student days, Zhou put Deng in charge of producing the communist newsletter, which led to his being jokingly granted a Ph.D. in mimeographing. In February 1926, the French raided the house where Deng lived, but they were too late. He had left for Moscow the day before.

In Moscow, Deng studied at the University of the Toilers of the East and Sun Yat-sen University. These were the days when China's nationalists and communists were collaborators and not yet enemies. Their shared objective was China's modernization and renewal. The Comintern, Stalin's international apparatus, was teaching the nationalists how to construct a revolutionary party, and members of the Chinese Communist Party were also active nationalists. Wealthy nationalists were financing the training of young revolutionaries in Moscow who would restore China's dignity. Among Deng's fellow students was Chiang Ching-kuo, son of the Nationalist Party leader Chiang Kai-shek. Much later, in the 1980s, the younger Chiang would succeed his father as president of Taiwan.

Deng returned to China a convinced communist, prepared to dedicate his life to the revolution. His organizational skills quickly carried him forward. By the age of twenty-three he was chief secretary of the Central Committee of the Communist Party and then became an organizer in the countryside. China was in violent disarray. Warlords were battling for control of various regions, and the nationalists' alliance with the communists broke down as they competed for power. The Communist Party itself was riven by deep factional splits that spilled over into bloodshed. Deng, following Zhou, allied himself with the faction led by Mao Zedong. At one point, Mao's enemies within the communist movement imprisoned and interrogated Deng, probably tortured him, and repeatedly tried to force him to recant political "crimes."

Deng was part of the Long March of 1934–35, the six-thousand-mile trek that Mao led to escape the nationalists. Over its harrowing course, the communists were decimated. The march began with ninety thousand communist soldiers and ended with a paltry five thousand. Yet that experience was to provide the myths and cohesion that, within a decade and a half, would help to carry the communists to victory and rule over all of China.

The Japanese invasion of China in 1937 created the circumstances for the renewal of communist power vis-à-vis the nationalists. That war also turned Deng into a soldier. Once again his organizational talents brought him to the fore, first against the Japanese and then against the nationalists after 1945. He became one of the most prominent military leaders; indeed, he played a key role in the Huai-Hai campaign, which broke the back of the nationalists in 1949. This battle, which destroyed a nationalist army of five hundred thousand, is considered one of the most important land battles of the twentieth century. Deng's wartime role enhanced his credibility as a leader and established a network of relationships and connections that would bolster his political position and—at crucial times—protect him.

During his wartime administration of the Taihang region, in northwest China, Deng also laid out a set of pragmatic economic precepts that would prefigure his policies of the 1980s and the 1990s. Economic incentives were appropriate. "Some comrades say this is too much, but I don't agree," he told senior cadres during the war. "If they've acquired it through their own labor and not corruption it's entirely appropriate. Those who are lazy and unenthusiastic should suffer." Economic change should come gradually; people should feel the benefits directly. And—of critical importance—socialism depends upon proper organization and economic strength, and must be built upon "capitalist production." In other words, capitalism was not the total enemy of socialism. But where Deng did not waver was in seeing the party as the necessary instrument of modernization.[1]

Catching Mice

After the victory over the nationalists in 1949 and the establishment of the People's Republic of China, Deng emerged as one of the most senior leaders of the Communist Party. He became secretary-general and number four in the hierarchy. When Mao led a delegation to Moscow in 1957, he pointed Deng out to Nikita Khrushchev, the Soviet leader, and said, "See that little man there? He's highly intelligent and has a great future ahead of him."

Deng, for his part, remained deeply loyal to Mao, though he stood aside when Mao launched the Great Leap Forward. It was supposed to channel the enthusiasm of the "masses" so that China could do in fifteen years what the capitalist nations had taken 150 years to accomplish—and to secure complete control over the countryside. Farmers throughout the country were herded into regimented communes, and backyard pig iron furnaces became the symbols of the Great Leap. As it turned out, however, it proved to be a great leap into disaster. Undertaken without any regard for fundamental economics, it did nothing to advance China's economy. On the contrary, tens of millions of people died of starvation as agricultural and industrial production and internal trade—all totally disrupted—plummeted.

Deng was one of the chief figures who had to pick up the pieces. Gradual investment was to replace mass mobilization; education and expertise were again to be respected. It was at this time that Deng, not known for his aphorisms, made his most famous statement: "It doesn't matter whether a cat is black or white so long as it catches mice." Although he himself would later say he was not sure exactly what he had meant, it was very clearly an affirmation of pragmatism in economic policy in the aftermath of the fanaticism of the Great Leap. It was also a phrase that would find resonance around the world.

This pragmatism was held against him in the mid-1960s, when Mao launched the Cultural Revolution. Mao was deeply dissatisfied with the lack of ideological zeal in the country, and apparently very angry that he was no longer receiving the veneration due him as the paramount leader. Mao complained that Deng and his colleagues "had treated me like I was their dead parent at a funeral." In revenge, Mao mobilized young people in a savage assault on the established order. The number-one target of the Cultural Revolution was the party. This was heresy to Deng. For him, the united Communist Party was the foundation of China's regeneration. The chaos of the Cultural Revolution threatened everything he had devoted his life to since the early 1920s. Once offered a copy of Mao's Little Red Book, the bible of the Cultural Revolution, Deng unceremoniously turned it away. For his part, Deng was attacked as a "capitalist roader" and subjected to intense abuse; he spent two years in solitary confinement. He and his wife were both put to work in a tractor repair plant. His son was paralyzed as a result of a physical assault by Red Guards. What saved Deng from even worse was the network he had established through the army and his personal camaraderie with his "elder brother," Zhou Enlai.

In the early 1970s, after the Cultural Revolution had run its course, he came back into the leadership. During his time in confinement, he had spent many hours pacing the courtyard, asking himself how modernization had failed and how it could be restored. Now he could put his hard-earned conclusions to work as he helped direct the economic recovery. He returned to the principles he had favored before—education and economic incentives rather than ideology and exhortation. But criticism mounted against Deng for bowing to capitalism, and once again, with Mao against him, he was stripped of power. The death of Zhou made Deng's position very precarious, and he was forced to sign yet another self-criticism. He was portrayed as everything evil—from a counterrevolutionary to a "poisonous weed" who was trying to undermine the glorious revolution. But again his old comrades from the army shielded him.

The death of Mao in 1976 liberated Deng. The "Gang of Four" (including Mao's wife), who had masterminded the Cultural Revolution, were arrested; and Deng returned to the center of power. He immediately became engaged in the bitter struggles that followed Mao's death. Hua Guofeng was Mao's designated successor. "With you in charge, I'm at ease," Mao had told Hua. Deng, however, challenged Hua, who was known as the "chief whateverist." ("Whatever decisions Chairman Mao made, we resolutely support," said Hua. "Whatever instructions Chairman Mao made, we will stead-fastly abide by.") If he was to have his moment, Deng realized, this was it. He carried out the battle against Hua with every resource available to him. By the end of 1978, Hua was out, and Deng emerged as China's paramount leader. Yet again he was in the position of picking up the pieces. Out of them he would lay the foundations for China's real great leap forward.

In subsequent history, December 1978 has come to rank with 1911—the Chinese Revolution—and 1949—the communist victory—as one of the great turning points in twentieth-century Chinese history. The Third Plenum of the 11th Congress of the Chinese Communist Party assembled that month, and although a series of major decisions was made in the months before and after, the plenum encapsulated the fundamental decision: to reorient China toward the market.

There was no grand plan, but rather certain practical steps. In their entirety, they reflected a break with Maoism. The shift bore Deng's imprima-tur. Whatever worked economically was more or less all right with him—as long as the party remained in control. Results were what counted. Deng wanted to create a wealthy and powerful China, not a utopian or messianic paradise. He was a nationalist, and communism and the party were the mechanisms by which to reach that objective. And behind it all was a straightforward decision. "I have two choices," said Deng. "I can distribute poverty or I can distribute wealth." He had seen enough of the former un-der Mao.[2]

The Reform Begins

The initial reform effort centered on agriculture. Mao's collectivized agricul-tural system had produced dismal results. Output in many regions was no greater than it had been at the time of the communist victory three decades earlier, and in some cases it was actually less. Despite the investment and the use of new techniques, productivity was no higher under collectivization than it had been under China's old medieval system.

But it took a local crisis to begin replacing the old system. China's entire economic reform began with rainfall—or, more correctly, lack of it. Anhui province suffered a severe drought in 1978—the kind that was said to happen no more than once in a century. The ground was so dry that neither tractors nor plows could break it. Starvation became endemic. Dysentery, encephalitis, hepatitis, and other diseases swept through the region, and as hundreds of thousands of people fled from their homes, the militia mobilized to try to prevent them from flooding into Shanghai. A film of the suffering was shot. Shown to members of the Politburo, it made them "cry out, cover their faces with their hands, and weep." The only way to break through the parched land was through the hardest personal labor. But the peasants would not do it unless they could benefit. They appealed for the return of the "old ways." By this they meant what came to be called the household responsibility system, earlier versions of which had been tried at various times during the history of the People's Republic—and which allowed a family to keep some of the benefits of its labor. The peasants got their wish and the system was implemented. Desperation drove the decision. Even so, the first peasants to sign on insisted upon swearing a common oath to take care of each other's children should they "come to grief" by being arrested for participating in the new program.

Their fears were more than understandable given what had happened during the Cultural Revolution. But the outcome this time was different. The experiment proved successful and was widely approved. The responsibility system was thereafter adopted throughout the country, and material incentives replaced the Maoist strictures. The commune system and collectivization were undone; each family was responsible for the land it tilled. Peasants had to deliver a certain amount of their production to the state; above that, they could keep the output, consume it, or sell it. With that, free enterprise was launched.

The results were stunning. Over sixteen years, output increased more than 50 percent, something that had completely eluded the Maoist system. The introduction of markets in agricultural products instantaneously generated an entire trading apparatus; farmers involved themselves in transportation, house building, repairs, private food markets, and hiring workers. In short, these changes created a whirlwind of entrepreneurship. In 1978, just 8 percent of agricultural output was sold in open markets; by 1990, the share was 80 percent. Between 1978 and 1984, real income in farm households rose 60 percent.

The rapid improvement in agriculture was the beginning of China's economic reforms. The success in the countryside created a pro-reform constituency not only among farmers but also among city dwellers, who could find more food and more variety in the marketplace; it thus provided momentum for the next steps. Gradual decontrol of prices also began at this time. Although what Deng wanted was results, not lessons, there was herein a very important conclusion. As the economist Dwight Perkins put it, "The political lesson for future reformers from China's experience is obvious but often forgotten—try to begin the reform process with a clear winner."[3]

"Bird in a Cage"

Agriculture proved easier to reform than industry and the urban economy. Farming was essentially a local matter. Improvisation—"crossing the river by feeling the stones"—could be tolerated. Not so with the industrial sector. Industry was interconnected: It was controlled from the center, the scale was large, and it generated much of the government's revenues. It was key to the state's financial solvency. Thus, any change in the system could throw the entire country into economic disarray. Moreover, the focus of Marxist economics was industrial production; in both the Soviet Union and China, the agricultural sector was exploited to support heavy industrialization.

Still, the highly inefficient industrial sector was in desperate need of reform, and as a result, a major and acrimonious debate unfolded over the relationship of state and marketplace. The irrationalities of the system were candidly discussed. For instance, it was argued that the way the state collected revenues from enterprises ended up "whipping the fast ox"—that is, punishing firms that were more efficient. The higher the firm's profits, the greater the proportion of profits that went to the government. There was much discussion about increasing the autonomy of enterprises and moving to some system of market socialism. Yugoslavia's self-governing firms were seen as a model. But the state was still to be dominant. The "plan" would rule. The Wuxi conference in 1979 brought economists and party cadres together to discuss these issues. Two economists summed up the prevailing attitude in saying that China "cannot allow Adam Smith's 'invisible hand' to control our economic development." For "if individual consumers in the market make decisions based on their own economic interests, this will not necessarily accord with the general interest of society." Planning had to be made more effective, but that was not the same as giving over to the "blindness" and "anarchy" of capitalism.[4]

While some movement was made toward granting firms more independence, reform in the industrial sector was stifled for several years by conservatives—conservatives of a sort, that is. They were led by Chen Yun, a party elder like Deng. Chen had joined the party in 1925, at age twenty. He had organized both peasants and workers in Shanghai, and had spent some time in Moscow as part of the Chinese delegation to the Comintern. In contrast to Deng, Chen's forte was economics, not politics. He had held senior planning positions since the late 1940s, and although at times he had been one of the few in the leadership who dared to disagree with Mao's economic nostrums, he came to be seen as the party's leading expert on economics. He was disparaging about both the Stalinist economic model and Mao's efforts to replace economics with the enthusiasm of the masses. Like Deng, he was purged during the Cultural Revolution. Rehabilitated before Deng, he was among those who urged that Deng be returned to the leadership. The experience of the Cultural Revolution confirmed Chen's conviction in favor of steadiness and his opposition to "rashness." He was a technocrat and a socialist and a fervent believer in planning. He was vigorous in his criticism of "the petroleum group," the economic managers who simply wanted to pour more and more resources into heavy industry—the classic socialist ailment of "production for the sake of production." But he had no desire to introduce a full-blown market system, nor was he keen to attract foreign investment. He warned that "foreign capitalists are still capitalists," out to make a profit; and he despaired that "some of our cadres are still very naive about this." He worried about foreign "pollution" of Chinese socialism and feared the effects of the shortages, inflation, and dislocations that would come, he was convinced, with a shift to a more market-oriented economy and the resulting "rashness" of high growth.

Chen Yun was unhappy with central planning to date, but he did not believe a country as large and poor as China, with limited resources, could jettison planning. He wanted to improve it—make it more scientific and more balanced. He was interested less in reform than in "readjustment." In his words, the "whole country [was] a chessboard." Chen and the other planners at the center would be in charge of moving the pieces rationally and methodically. In short, the planned economy was "primary" and it should remain primary. While a market economy providing less essential elements had a role to play, that role was very definitely "secondary" and supplementary. Yes, the market was useful, but it was also dangerous.

Chen summed up his attitude to visitors who came to his house at the end of 1982. The relationship between improving the economy and economic planning was like that between a bird and its cage. "You mustn't hold the bird in your hands too tightly or it would be strangled," he said. "You have to turn it loose, but only within the confines of a cage. Otherwise it would fly away."

This became known as the birdcage thesis, and Chen and his allies were intent on keeping the bird in its cage. The "readjusters" largely carried the day in the early 1980s, bolstered in their efforts by other factors that prompted caution. First was the sudden emergence of Solidarity in Poland in 1980, which raised alarm among Chinese leaders. If they did not exert care, said Chen, and "did not pay attention to the two issues of propaganda and economics, then events like that in Poland could happen in China, too." Second, the leadership was caught up in debate and uncertainty over how to deal with the legacy of Mao. There was also a limit to how much change the system could withstand. Deng went along with the more conservative readjusters because of the threat to the party, whose "stability and unity"— and unchallenged dominance—were at the heart of his politics. Such a party was essential to the central goal of modernization. "Without such a party," said Deng, "our country would split up and accomplish nothing."

But by the mid-1980s, the "go-slow" argument was losing its credibility. The economy was growing much faster than anticipated without the severe problems that Chen Yun had forecast. Agriculture was achieving considerable success. As surprising as the improvement in agriculture was the great stimulus it had given to the emergence of rural industry and commerce. Reform now had both a constituency and a track record. Moreover, the Chinese were no longer looking at Yugoslavia, which was experiencing economic difficulties, or at Poland, where Solidarity had been outlawed, but rather at Hungary, which was experimenting more actively with market mechanisms. They read the works of the Hungarian economist János Kornai, who at this time was also beginning to have much influence on young Russian reformers.

The most dramatic lesson, however, came from closer to home. The Chinese were also waking up to the fact that Japan had become an economic superpower. Visiting Japan and seeing its dynamism firsthand shocked the Chinese communists. No less a figure than the head of the propaganda department of the Chinese Communist Party noted truly astonishing things in his report: One out of every two households in Japan owned an automobile; over 95 percent of households possessed television sets, refrigerators, and washing machines. He was also overwhelmed by how people were dressed—by the variety of clothing and its cleanliness. "One Sunday we went out to a busy street. Of all the women we saw, no two wore the same style of clothes." He added something even more astonishing: "The female workers accompanying us also changed clothes every day." [5]

"Socialism with Chinese Characteristics"

The mid-1980s was the turning point for the Chinese economy, the time when it indeed entered into high-speed growth. The leadership under Deng embraced economic reform and liberalism even while striving to maintain political control. "Some of our comrades are most worried about whether we will become capitalist," Deng declared. "They are afraid of seeing capitalism suddenly looming up after having worked all their lives for socialism and communism, and they cannot stand such a sight." Deng sought to reassure them. He described what was happening as the "building of socialism with Chinese characteristics." That became the title of a book he published at the end of 1984.

No doubt, he had Chen Yun more than anybody else in mind in his criticism. They were the two elders, veterans who had joined the party at almost its very beginning. They had both risen to senior positions, only to be purged and humiliated during the Cultural Revolution. They had come back together as allies, intent on redressing the deep wounds of Maoism. But increasingly they had become rivals. Chen believed that Deng took too much credit for himself and that he, Chen, was being denied due credit for helping shape the original reform package. Their struggle would describe the terrain of reform. Their disagreements began over such matters as whether peasant farmers could hire extra laborers. To Deng, it was simply a pragmatic matter, and he supported it. To Chen, it represented a return to capitalism in the countryside, and he was opposed. Deng carried the day, although the term "hired labor," with its Marxist connotation of exploitation, could not be used. Instead, it became "asked-to-help labor." By the end, their battle was over nothing less than what kind of future China could attain.

But what did the "building of socialism with Chinese characteristics" mean? From 1984 onward, debate about the future of the Chinese economy began to move beyond Marxist categories to a discussion of how to create a market economy. It was a decisive turn. The market, some factions now began to argue, would do a better job of allocating resources than planning had done. Increasingly, economic data competed with Marxist catechisms in the fashioning of arguments.

The result was a continuous, complex, and acrimonious debate, pitting not only devotees of central planning and the socialist tradition against reformers but also reformers against other reformers. As the debate accelerated, some who were reformers in the late 1970s became, by the mid-1980s, the conservatives. If Deng was the paramount leader of reform, then Chen was the paramount critic. The issues were enormously complicated: How was the huge economy to be transformed? How could an economy that was partly command and partly market, with two different price systems, move forward? Did reform and high growth inevitably mean overheating and high inflation? At the heart, of course, was the question of the proper relationship of state and market.

For the conservatives, the danger was not only dislocations and inflation but also chaos and loss of political control—which Deng feared. The conservatives wanted to reassert centralization, stabilization, and mandatory planning. The reformers wanted to reduce the control of the center and party secretaries and instead make enterprises responsive to market signals. The reformers got partway there with the introduction of the "contract responsibility system," which, echoing the "household responsibility system," allowed state enterprises to keep earnings above a certain target. By December 1987, 80 percent of China's large and medium-size firms had adopted such a system.

But it was not enough. These state firms remained inefficient. They were losing out in the growing competition from new companies established by local villages and towns. The two-track system of prices stimulated inflation and encouraged corruption. One prominent economist, Wu Jinglian, cited Ludwig Erhard (and the 1948 German currency reform) and Milton Friedman in calling for a massive price reform. But Wu still subscribed to the widely held belief that large and medium-size enterprise was the "backbone" of the economy and insisted that the government must play the central guiding role in the economy. If China were to introduce "a type of economic mechanism reminiscent of Manchester capitalism of the nineteenth century," he said, the result would be "historical retrogression." [6]

Another prominent economist, Li Yining, challenged the entire premise of state control. He had begun as a follower of Oskar Lange, the Polish economist who had advocated market socialism with a system of state ownership. But during the years of the Cultural Revolution, Li thought back on the debates between Hayek and Lange and concluded that he had come out on the wrong side and that Hayek had been more correct than Lange. The Soviet economic model could not work. The most important—and the most required—reform was the creation of property rights. Only ownership could introduce responsibility into decision making and channel motivation. How far the debate had moved—from Marx and Stalin and Mao to Friedman and Hayek.

Reform and Retrenchment

As for Deng, his interest was in results—China's wealth and power. He wanted to make up the wasted years. Party general secretary Hu Yaobang, a strong reformer, had Deng's support until Deng—pressured by Chen, who regarded Hu as too liberal—purged him. The mantle of reform was then taken up by Zhao Ziyang, who was premier and then became general secretary. In order to sell reform as something other than the repudiation of socialism and the embrace of capitalism, Zhao emphasized the imperatives of the "new technological revolution." He read Alvin Toffler's *The Third Wave,* which was about the impact of information technology, and vigorously urged other people to read it as well, in order to understand what China was missing.

Zhao had been propelled into the leadership by the success of his reform program in Sichuan, Deng's home province. In turn, Zhao also became the chief proponent of the "great international cycle of development." The idea was to quickly build up new industries geared to export, particularly in the coastal areas. This approach meant adopting the Asian export-led growth strategy that the Chinese could see working all around them. It offered the solution to multiple problems. These new industries would earn hard currency, and they would absorb surplus labor coming out of the agricultural regions in the country's interior. "China should seize the current opportunity," said Zhao, "take part in international competition, and push the coastal areas into the international market." [7]

At the center of the strategy would be the Special Economic Zones (SEZs). They, more than anything else, engendered China's engagement with the world economy. The original SEZs were created in 1980. Three were established in Guangdong province, including Shenzhen, across from Hong Kong, and in Fujian province, across from Taiwan. Their whole orientation was outward; they were export-processing zones, and they were the magnet by which to draw in foreign investment. Beijing gave local authorities in the SEZs unprecedented autonomy in trade and investment decisions. The concept was expanded to a number of cities in the mid-1980s. From then on, the coastal cities drove the Chinese economy forward.

For all the success of the SEZs, accelerating inflation fueled a conservative backlash that by the end of 1988 had forced Zhao and his allies to go on the defensive. The conservatives attacked the opening to the outside world. "We must not think that the moon in foreign countries is fuller than in China," declared one conservative. Another warned that there were "some people who wanted to go toward bourgeois democracy, as if the moon in bourgeois democratic society were brighter than our sun." There was even a

"Mao Zedong craze," which combined attacks on reformers and the current leadership with nostalgia for the old order.

The specter of capitalist-style crime and corruption—along with materialism and the appearance of inequalities—also drove the reaction. "Honest people can barely make a living," said one economist, "whereas opportunists and the corrupt live in abundance and are envied by others. Nothing corrupts the moral climate in society more than this." Other substantial economic issues emboldened the conservatives. The big state enterprises were losing out. Adaptation was enormously difficult, and their losses were mounting, which meant that the government's revenues were falling precipitously.

Deng remained reform's number-one cheerleader. He backed plans for a massive new price reform. "We are not afraid of stormy weather but will pass all the hurdles braving the wind and the waves," he said. But all that changed in August 1988. Anticipation of a price reform ignited a run on banks and a panic buying of goods. Deeply shaken, the government—Deng included—abruptly changed course. Now the focus was on economic stabilization and retrenchment, not new reforms.[8]

Tiananmen Square

But there were unexpected political consequences. The economic difficulties, the conservative turn, and the thwarting of democratic aspirations strengthened a "democracy movement" among students. Thousands of them, mourning the death of the purged reformer Hu Yaobang, occupied Beijing's Tiananmen Square in April 1989. To conservatives, it was an act of rebellion, the consequence of ten years of too much reform and too little control. To those like Deng, it challenged the sacred precept: the supremacy of the party, which was the bulwark against disorder and chaos. It also reminded Deng too much of the Cultural Revolution and its militant students. He was the core leader, and the core of modern China was in danger. Survival and order took precedence over reform. The risks were evident, for communism was collapsing in Eastern Europe. "Concessions in Poland led to further concessions," an angry Deng declared. "The more they conceded, the more chaos." And chaos was the enemy. Tiananmen Square was a frontal challenge—not only because of its visibility and physical location but also because of its key location in modern Chinese history. It was there, forty years earlier, in 1949, that Mao had proclaimed victory and the establishment of the People's Republic of China. And thirty years before that, on May 4, 1919, it had been the scene of the nationalist student demonstrations that had helped give birth to the Communist Party. At the beginning of June 1989, the order was given to the military to clear the square. About a thousand people are thought to have been killed in the ensuing struggle.

Retrenchment and controls were stepped up. The collapse of communism in Eastern Europe, Mikhail Gorbachev's talk of multiparty democracy in the Soviet Union, the attempted coup against him, the rise of Yeltsin—all this reinforced the Chinese conservatives' drive to rein in reform and reassert control. Economic growth slowed and dissent was stifled. Deng was still the paramount leader, but reform was in retreat, and so was his influence. His old rival Chen Yun was in ascendancy again, and Chen's denunciations of the market and his embrace of central planning were trumpeted. He declared that the "proper ratio" of planned economy to market economy was eight to two. "Chen Yun Thought" was now celebrated in a way all too reminiscent of the adoration given to Mao Zedong Thought. Chen spoke nostalgically of how Mao had "talked to me three times about studying philosophy" and recommended reading the works of Marx, Engels, Lenin, Stalin, and, of course, Mao. And Chen attacked Deng directly, charging that his policies were responsible for the trends that had culminated both in the overheated economy and in the events in Tiananmen Square. Chen and his allies singled out the Special Economic Zones along the coast for some of their most violent criticism, charging that they were capitalist in character and conduits for forces that would destroy communism in China.[9]

The Nanxun: *Deng's Last Campaign*

But Deng would not give up. Everything he had tried to accomplish over the last fourteen years now seemed at risk. Three times before in his career as a communist, he had been pushed onto the defensive, disgraced, forced to recant. It would not happen again. He would respond in kind, confronting his enemies on the very terrain they had denounced. In January 1992, even as the conservatives appeared to be consolidating their position, the eighty-eight-year-old paramount leader set out in his private railway car on yet another campaign. He headed south. It was called his *nanxun,* or "southern journey," and it lasted a month. It would be his last campaign.

His enemies had attacked the Special Economic Zones, which he had sponsored. He would defend them by going there himself. The most important destination was the Pearl River delta in Guangdong province and, in particular, the Shenzhen SEZ, which borders Hong Kong. He gave speeches, met local officials and businesspeople, posed for photos, even shoveled dirt at a construction site. What he saw was enormously changed from what he had viewed in 1984, when Shenzhen was still very much a rough, unfinished city in the making. Now it was a modern high-rise urban area. Deng said he would never have believed that such changes were possible. "Having seen it, my confidence has increased." Yes, he said, many problems had resulted from the much-criticized growth period, 1984–89. But the results had been stunning. It had been a "flying leap"—the real great leap forward. Shenzhen was no longer an experiment; now it was the model for the future.

The man who would not distinguish between black cats and white cats similarly dismissed the catechistic distinctions between capitalism and communism. "Market economies need not be surnamed capitalism," Deng said. "Socialism has markets, too. Plans and markets are simply economic stepping stones . . . to universal prosperity and riches." He had one other very important message: It was not the reformers but Chen Yun and his allies who could be the destroyers of socialism. In what would prove to be his most widely quoted remark from the *nanxun,* Deng urged his fellow party members to "watch out for the Right, but mainly defend against the Left." Commenting on his elderly opponents' opposition to change, he said that old age made people stubborn, and if such people could not show more flexibility and openness in their thinking, then they really ought to "go to sleep." Replying to Chen's recent reading list of communist classics, Deng offered the stunning revelation during his *nanxun* that he had never bothered to read Marx's *Das Kapital.* He had had neither the time nor the patience.

The response to the trip demonstrated how severe the struggle was. In the first month, in fact, there was no response—no newspaper reports, no film, no commentary. Silence. Deng's opponents were strong enough to make it seem a nonevent. But then word filtered from Shenzhen through Hong Kong and back to the mainland. After a month's delay, the nonevent turned into a decisive event. The *nanxun* became the subject of extensive press coverage and much discussion. With the economy still gripped by recession, Deng's message found wide resonance; indeed, it changed national policy. It was Deng's final victory. Support for Chen's position began to fall away. Replying to Chen's calls for severe restrictions on the SEZs, one vice-premier sarcastically advocated the introduction of "special Leftist zones," to which the hard-line Marxists could be sent. "Let us carve out a piece of land where policies favored by the Leftists will be practiced," he said. "For example, no foreign investment will be allowed there, and all foreigners will be kept out. Inhabitants of the zone can neither go abroad nor send their children overseas. There will be total state planning. Essential supplies will be rationed and citizens of the zone will have to queue up for food and other consumer products." He urged the leftist critics to sign up for their places without delay.

Deng's campaign culminated in the 14th Party Congress in the autumn of 1992, which affirmed a new commitment to reform. It hailed Deng's "brilliant thesis"—that China should shift from a "socialist planned commodity economy" to a "socialist market economy." Reform was back on track. It was Deng's final victory. At age eighty-eight, he had reaffirmed, once again, his position as the paramount leader.[10]

The Two Economies

With his trip, Deng wanted to convey a specific message about China's future. Guangdong, he said, was the head, the engine, of China's reforms. And the province, he added, should accelerate its reforms so that it could overtake the four tigers—Korea, Taiwan, Singapore, and Hong Kong—within twenty years. He was, in fact, pointing to the basic reality of China's future economic development. China's overall record would be remarkable. Between 1978 and 1995, the economy grew at an average annual rate of 9.3 percent. During that period, it also moved an enormous distance from being a Soviet-style command economy toward being governed by market forces.

But that growth record concealed a deep divide between state and market. On one side of the divide were the state-owned enterprises, middle-size and large. They were also complex social systems, providing a full range of social and welfare benefits to their workers. The large state companies numbered about ten thousand; their labor forces ranged from five thousand to, in some cases, five hundred thousand. A few made headlines by managing to free themselves from these obligations or carry them out in less onerous ways. But the bulk of the large companies were wasteful and highly inefficient; they produced goods that were not matched to demand; they drained financial resources out of the national budget instead of putting them in. They did not pay their debts. Yet because of their political clout and their social role, they were not easily reformed. By some estimates, three quarters of them lost money. They lacked financial discipline and were not responsive to market signals. Their senior managements, in the words of one Chinese steel executive, were "too tired to take care of their businesses. They spend their time managing their employees' housing, the children's schooling; they take care of their workers' grandmothers." A good part of China's recurrent inflation was attributed to their ability to extract credits from the state on unsound financial criteria.

On the other side of the divide was the new economy, the source of growth and dynamism. Not all of it was private. "Collective" enterprises, owned by villages and localities and the army but run by entrepreneurs, emerged to become one of the main drivers of economic growth. They represented alliances of entrepreneurs, local officials, the military, and enterprise managers, and absorbed the labor let loose by the increased productivity of agriculture and the tightening constraints on traditional state companies. They received little in the way of subsidies, they competed with firms from other provinces, and they responded to market rules. These firms, not the large state industrial enterprises, have proved to be the real backbone of China's economic growth. They also created constituencies with strong local roots for openness and reform.

Foreign investment plays a significant role in China. From 1990 through 1995, it grew tenfold, from $3.7 billion a year to $38 billion. This growth is all the more striking in that it has taken place in a foreign-investment system that has not been wholly inviting. Indeed, it is not firmly fixed at all. The Cultural Revolution abolished lawyers and most commercial laws, and there does not yet exist the kind of contractual, legal framework—or the clear-cut decision making—that most foreign investors seek. Yet despite the insecurity, the inflow of foreign investment continues to grow. "The lure of a billion-plus customers can offset many worries," said Dwight Perkins.

The greater part of foreign investment has derived from ethnic Chinese, and a good deal of that has been oriented not to the domestic market but to exports. Indeed, the investment insecurity has favored investment by the overseas Chinese. They tend toward smaller investments with quicker payback periods. They do not have to worry about twenty-year contracts. The fluidity and lack of well-defined legal systems also puts a premium on what is to the advantage of the overseas Chinese—*guanxi.* These are the informal connections that tie overseas Chinese to friends and relatives on the mainland and that operate not only at the high levels but right down to the local neighborhood. Western and Japanese businessmen may well find themselves received in the highest precincts of the Chinese establishment, but they cannot begin to match the overseas Chinese in terms of the *guanxi,* which get the job done. Nowhere has this been clearer than in the case of Guangdong province.[11]

"A New Tiger"

As Deng emphasized on his *nanxun,* nothing could compare to the frenetic growth on the southern coast in Guangdong province, and in particular the Pearl River delta. Guangdong and neighboring Fujian were selected as the provinces to house the first SEZs not because they were already well developed. On the contrary, they were backwaters with little industrial development. Mao had shortchanged them, instead concentrating resources on building up the internal economy far away from the coast, which he feared would be vulnerable to military attack. The two provinces were chosen because they were distant from key cities like Beijing and Shanghai and thus, it was thought, "contamination" from the outside world could be limited. They were also, of course, on the coast, which would facilitate exports.

By looking outward again, Guangdong was reconnecting to its past. Merchants from Guangdong had dominated Southeast Asian maritime commerce until this trade was banned in the sixteenth century by the Ming dynasty. When the ban was lifted in 1685, it was too late. Although trade revived again, the Europeans dominated it and Guangdong never regained its historic prominence. But two factors were to prove decisive for the rebirth of Guangdong in the 1990s. The first was *guanxi,* which served Guangdong particularly well. Eighty percent of the 30 million overseas ethnic Chinese trace their origins to Guangdong, and they would invest billions in the province. The second was the strategic location of Shenzhen, which was adjacent to Hong Kong. That proximity would prove essential to the dramatic takeoff of the region.

The Pearl River delta, which makes up about a quarter of the total area of Guangdong and includes both Shenzhen and Guangzhou, has been described as the "crown jewel of the Chinese economy," a new tiger, and the "Fifth Dragon." Between 1978 and 1993, Guangdong's economy grew at 13.9 percent, well above the national average. The delta's growth rate was still higher—17.3 percent. Forty percent of all China's exports come from Guangdong. And 70 percent of Guangdong's exports, in turn, come from the Pearl River delta. The population of the delta is only 23 million, about the same as Taiwan and Malaysia. This means that, excluding Hong Kong, a region that holds only 1.4 percent of China's total population is responsible for generating about 30 percent of the entire country's exports.

This kind of sustained high-speed growth exceeded anything registered by any of the "Asian miracle" economies. And it was reflected in the changing landscape. Agricultural land was transformed into what seemed an endless boomtown construction site and then into modern high-rise cities. When Électricité de France, the French utility giant, built its $3 billion nuclear power plant in 1993 to help meet the burgeoning electricity demand, the site was a desolate waterfront, Daya Bay. Once a road was built to the plant, miles of what had been empty land turned into a vast series of new factories. Shenzhen itself, once a border post of some thirty thousand, grew to 3 million in less than twenty years. But a border still separated Shenzhen from Hong Kong, one of the original tigers.

"One Country, Two Systems"

Hong Kong was born of the Opium Wars, which set British traders against the Chinese Empire in the mid–nineteenth century. The island part of the territory was ceded to Britain in 1842, and by 1898 the territory had taken the frontiers that it was to have up until 1997. The revolution of 1912 that overthrew the Qing dynasty gave way to turbulent decades in which southern China was the terrain of battles among nationalists, communists, and warlords of varying allegiance. Hong Kong offered a secure trading outlet as well as a safe haven for assets of businessmen and industrialists. The communist takeover of 1949 cemented Hong Kong's role, as many of the traders and industrialists of China's economic capital, Shanghai, scrambled to move to the British colony. From this upheaval Hong Kong acquired a business community with advanced education, entrepreneurial skills, and connections to the mainland that would come, in time, to be very useful indeed.

Beyond these human resources, Hong Kong had little more than its strategic location, and particularly its deepwater harbor. In the same manner as Singapore, it came to live off trade. Until the communist takeover, it was a major conduit for China's imports and exports. After 1949, it turned toward exports farther afield; and the investment of displaced Chinese, combined with the availability of cheap labor, fostered a mushrooming of local assembly plants, textile workshops, and factories for light manufactures. These prospered thanks not only to the enterprising spirit of their founders but also to the unusually market-oriented business environment that the British administration let thrive. Politics in Hong Kong was of the clubby colonial sort: Opposition was permitted only in small amounts, the legislative council was for many decades appointed rather than elected, and the top administrators were British, sent over from the Colonial Office in London. But if political life was heavily regulated, economic life was decidedly freewheeling. The currency was pegged to the U.S. dollar, and capital was allowed to flow as it pleased. There were no trade or exchange restrictions, and there was no central bank. Labor legislation was light; taxes were very low. All of this contrasted with the other Asian tigers, in particular with the other entrepôt economy, Singapore. In Hong Kong, it seemed, the particular advantages of location and the accident of history that had brought enterprise and investment after 1949 acted as a substitute for government regimentation of economic life. The most powerful government figure was the finance secretary; and that post was occupied by a succession of administrators with explicit laissez-faire beliefs. The classical liberal system in the colony contrasted sharply—and ironically—with the mixed-economy system that prevailed back home in the United Kingdom.

In the 1960s Hong Kong began to switch from the production of apparel and light manufactures to consumer electric and electronic goods. The economy was geared entirely toward exports on the basis of plentiful investment and cheap labor. Hong Kong–made products became ubiquitous on the American and European markets, threatening to displace traditional textile and manufacturing sectors in those countries. But Hong Kong's apotheosis in the global economy would come only in the 1980s. It was intimately linked to Deng Xiaoping's program of reforms on the mainland, which reopened the door to travel, trade, and investment across the border. By establishing the first Special Economic Zones near Hong Kong, Deng invited investment into the Chinese hinterland's vast pool of labor and resources. Hong Kong capital wasted no time in exploiting the opportunity. Manufacturers began to shift the most labor-intensive parts of their production onto the mainland. The fast growth of the SEZs lent even more texture to the increasingly dense urban fabric, turning the Pearl River delta into a real megalopolis, with Hong Kong and Guangzhou as its twin poles.

But the most dramatic change, and the one for which Hong Kong was to become best known, was its transformation into one of the world's preeminent financial centers. That change came about, in part, with the explosion of international investment finance in the 1980s. It was helped greatly by the climate of unbridled laissez-faire capitalism and the well-established presence of major trading houses, known as the *hongs*, many of them a century old, and large local fortunes seeking profitable investment outlets. But the changes in China contributed, here again, mightily. The relaxed restrictions of the SEZs meant that firms there were often free to raise capital on the stock exchange. Although China began to develop its own stock exchanges in the 1990s—at Shanghai and Shenzhen—the Hong Kong exchange was the foremost, logical place to list a company. In addition, as China's fast growth began to attract foreign capital in large quantities, Hong Kong became the center of investment expertise which helped channel that money onto the mainland. All this added to the colony's underlying role as semiclandestine conduit for money from the "renegade province"—and economic success story—that was Taiwan, as well as its formal and informal role as financial center for the overseas Chinese.

China itself began to take an interest, and indeed a financial stake, in Hong Kong's future well in advance of the political handover. By the late 1980s, China's state firms had invested heavily in Hong Kong's frenetic real estate market, and were beginning to take stakes in a number of its productive industries. The state-owned Bank of China built one of Hong Kong's most distinctive and dramatic harborfront skyscrapers. By the time of the handover, Chinese firms had interests in many of Hong Kong's important industrial conglomerates and in the private monopoly utilities that delivered much of the territory's public services. As jitters over the handover rose and then subsided in the early 1990s, the frantic rush of Hong Kongers to transfer capital away from the territory to such alternative homes as the United States, Canada, or Caribbean tax havens gave way instead to a stock exchange rush on the so-called red chips—Chinese state firms registered in Hong Kong but with tight financial and political connections to the mainland.[12]

On June 30, 1997, in accord with the 1984 agreement between China and Britain, Hong Kong was returned, culminating in a sober midnight ceremony in which, under a monsoon rain, the Union Jack went down and the Chinese flag went up. From the promenade of the new convention center that juts into the harbor, the display of fireworks across the water was extraordinary. It was a momentous event. It also posed momentous questions about future political developments and the nature of life in Hong Kong, and its relationship to both China and the rest of the world. Already before the handover, Hong Kong's wealth—in per capita terms, more than 20 percent higher than Britain's—contrasted uncomfortably with standards of living on the mainland. After the takeover, and despite the fast growth and increasing integration of the delta region, that contrast was made starker still by the difference in economic ideology, outlook, and regulations. Hong Kong property values, taken for granted there, certainly would strike the rest of the world as remarkable—$800 million for a plot of land on which to build twelve condominiums. And the values on the Hong Kong stock exchange rested, in part, on such prices.

China is bound by the terms of its agreement with Britain to preserve Hong Kong's economic system for at least fifty years after the handover. To make sense of this contract, and indeed to help abide by it, Deng Xiaoping left his successors with a guiding concept: "one country, two systems."

There was nothing wrong, he felt, with the coexistence of two economic systems so long as they could be made to function well together. It was a logical extension of his pragmatic thinking on the subject of cats and mice. It also vividly displayed, in a country where ideological pronouncements continued to carry considerable weight, how far he had taken the ideology of the Communist Party.

The China Bean Curd Shop

Deng's trip to the Pearl River in 1992 had preserved the course of reform—and, so doing, secured the conditions for the "one country, two systems" experiment. Thereafter, in the run-up to the Hong Kong handover, Deng remained uncontested paramount leader, though he held no formal title. His health was failing rapidly. Yet he had prevailed. He had shifted the course of the Chinese Revolution away from ideology toward the more pragmatic objectives of wealth and power. He had led another long march—this time from communism and central planning toward a market economy. At the Central Party School in Beijing, familiar courses on Marxism, Leninism, and the history of the Communist Party of the Soviet Union have given way to courses on marketing, accounting, and international business.

The march is not over. Progress is uneven; the country has moved through periods of boom, bust, and retrenchment. Yet the results have been extraordinary. In 1997, on a purchasing-power basis, China's gross national product is second only to that of the United States, and it is the only country in the world with a reasonable chance, at least as seen from the current perspective, of overtaking the American economy in size.

At the same time, the warnings of Chen Yun and other conservative critics have, at least to some degree, been borne out. Corruption is a major issue. Tens of millions of underemployed and unemployed people float between the countryside and the cities. Inflation periodically sweeps through the economy. Crime has become much more common. The new stock markets have engendered more than their share of panics, and in some cases riots. The central government and the provinces are in continuing confrontation. Meanwhile, human rights issues remain a source of tension between China and the United States.

Overriding everything is the balance between economic and political change. The one political verity for Deng was the Communist Party. Flexibility was possible on everything save the monopoly role of the party. He was dedicated to the party; without it, chaos threatened. There was no obvious mechanism for a political transition. And yet can party control survive in a society that has nurtured a thriving market and opened to the world? Hard tests await the political system of China as the nation continues its march to the market. Yet certainly, what is remarkable is how far China has already moved to become a market economy integrated into the world economy. It is the world's number-one manufacturer of shoes, sweaters, toys, and sporting goods. None of this was inherent in Mao Zedong Thought. To accommodate such change, a society must massively adjust its myths. And that is what China has done, beginning with the paramount leader.

Deng Xiaoping died early in 1997, at age ninety-three, half a year before the return of Hong Kong and the practical application of his theory of "one country, two systems." In his funeral oration, Chinese president Jiang Zemin traced Deng's career—the victories and the seemingly fatal setbacks from which he managed to recover. What Jiang called Deng's "three rises and three falls" encapsulated most of China's twentieth-century history. Yet Deng ultimately prevailed and launched China on its course of reform. As Jiang put it, Deng "broke with conventions." When he came to power, China was desperately poor: 60 percent of China's people lived on less than a dollar a day. Reform launched China on high growth. Between 1978 and 1995, China's foreign trade increased from $36 billion to $300 billion. Per capita income doubled between 1978 and 1987 and doubled again between 1987 and 1996—a rate almost unheard of in modern history. It took Britain sixty years to double its per capita income; the United States, fifty years. In instituting reforms with such effect, Deng did something that no one else in history has ever accomplished—he lifted upward of 200 million people out of poverty in just two decades.

Half a year after Deng's death, in September 1997, the 15th Party Congress assembled in Beijing to reaffirm China's march to the market. In 1978, the 11th Party Congress, under Deng's tutelage, had taken on the question of agriculture. Two decades later, the 15th, in Deng's shadow, took up the other half of the question—the state-owned sector. Its financial plight had become of overwhelming urgency. Although some of the companies were well managed and profitable, the overall sector was inefficient, loss-making, and inflexible. Nonperforming loans to these enterprises accounted for as much as 40 percent of the total loans by the state banks. But solutions were much tougher than in agriculture, in terms of both ideology and practice. To the older generation of leadership, the very word *privatization* was unacceptable, while the concept of the "iron rice bowl"—guaranteed work and sustenance for urban workers—was a basic principle. Moreover, decisive change would not only upset deeply entrenched interests but also threaten social tumult; for reform held out the specter of millions or tens of millions of unemployed workers. Shifting assets out of the state's hand also opened the door to corruption. Yet the system could not continue; the piling up of debt by the state sector posed a grave risk to the country's overall financial stability.

The party congress declared that most of these enterprises—as many as a hundred thousand—would be divorced from the state and operated on the principle of what is sometimes called *ming ying*—"people-owned companies." This is an ambiguous phrase that certainly could include ownership by shareholders. As China's president Jiang Zemin put it—with a very

212

conscious lack of precision—in his report to the congress, "Public owner-ship can and should take multiple forms in its realization." The tools for reform would include merger, bankruptcy, and, as Jiang put it, "downsizing." How long would this process take? Some said ten years. Zhu Rongji, a leading reformer promoted to the top of the hierarchy at the congress, said that the aim was to get the main work done within three years. "The role of government and enterprise," he said, had to be "urgently . . . separated." Though less noticed, the congress also endorsed the expansion of direct elections from village level up to the larger townships.

At his death, the party confirmed a new status on Deng Xiaoping. "We must hold high the great banner of Deng Xiaoping," declared President Jiang. From now, "Deng Xiaoping Theory" would be "the guiding ideol-ogy"—joining Marxism-Leninism and Mao Zedong Thought as the party's "guide to action." How could Mao's thought and Deng's theory be made compatible? Through pragmatism. And in lifting the banner of Deng Xiao-ping high, the communist leadership was enshrining his sacred principle of pragmatism.

By then Deng had already been cast in many roles—revolutionary, soldier, communist, statesman, reformer, patriarch. But in the 1990s, a new one was added—businessman. A Shanghai newspaper reported the generally unknown fact that while the young Deng was in Paris becoming a communist in the early 1920s, he had also opened a restaurant called the China Bean Curd Shop. He did this at the behest of none other than his "elder brother," Zhou Enlai, who had initiated him into the revolutionary underground. Here, too, Deng's organizational skills came into play. The bean curd was good, the restaurant was a success, and Deng expanded both his menu and his seating space. The moral was evident—one could be a good communist and a fervent nationalist, seeking to assure a unified China the wealth and power it deserved, and at the same time be a good businessman, providing some-thing of quality that people would actually want to buy. That melding, more or less, is just what Deng sought to accomplish during his two decades as China's paramount leader.[13]

CHAPTER 8

AFTER THE PERMIT RAJ

India's Awakening

MANMOHAN SINGH was due for lunch at friends' in New Delhi on June 21, 1991. That very morning, however, his wife called up the hosts to say that they would have to cancel. "Sudden work" had come up for her husband. Shortly after eight that morning, Singh had received an unexpected phone call from the new prime minister, P. V. Narasimha Rao. So instead of going to lunch, Singh found himself being sworn in as finance minister amidst one of India's worst economic crises. Yet it looked to many as though Singh would soon be free for lunch again, for it was thought that Rao's government was weak and would not last long. Instead, it stayed the full five years of its term, and in the process fundamentally redirected India's economy away from its state-directed course. The result could well make India one of the most dynamic forces in the world economy of the twenty-first century.[1]

In changing course, Prime Minister Rao would break decisively with the ideas that had governed India since independence and that, indeed, had dominated the Congress Party since the 1930s. Rao had none of the drama or flair of his most famous predecessors. He might well have been expected to be more caretaker than revolutionary, the tail end of a dynasty rather than the man who would overturn the ideas that had knitted it together.

During all those years, India certainly did seem to be governed by a dynasty. The father, Pandit Nehru, had led the nation into independence in 1947 and served as prime minister up to his death in 1963. His daughter, Indira Gandhi, was prime minister for fifteen of the seventeen years between 1967 and 1984, when she was assassinated. In turn her son Rajiv was prime minister from 1984 to 1989. In 1991, he was assassinated while campaigning for a political comeback.

Yet through all of its travails, India remained a democratic country. And

India's continued commitment to democracy stands as one of the great achievements of the second half of the twentieth century. Its free elections, independent judiciary, free press, and free speech were in marked contrast to political realities in much of the rest of the developing world, which succumbed for long periods to dictatorship, ethnic wars, and political fission. The accomplishment was all the more remarkable given the size of the country—which comprises almost 20 percent of the world's total population —and its complex multiethnicity. The system was often tested by religious and ethnic strife, corruption, and political ambition, but it had shown remarkable resilience.

When it came to economics, however, the story was quite different. Enthralled by idealism and ideologies, India initially embraced a program that held back development that could have alleviated its massive poverty. And in the process it marginalized itself in a rapidly growing world economy. The great idealist cause was the spirit that had motivated Mahatma Gandhi and captured Jawaharlal Nehru on his car trip into the mud of Rae Bareli in 1920—the conquest of poverty. The problem was not the ideals but rather the means. Their ideas shaped by Fabian socialism and communist central planning, the leaders of the Congress Party distrusted the market. They thought competition was bad, and they had what has been described as "contempt for the price mechanism." Instead, they believed that central planning, strong state control, and government knowledge would do a better job of allocating investment and determining output than would many millions of individual decision makers. Bureaucratic diktats were better than the give-and-take of prices in the marketplace.

There was a great deal of economic analysis—highly persuasive, technically expert, sometimes beautifully argued—to support this approach. As an outstanding Indian economist wryly commented, "It is not entirely wrong to agree with the cynical view that India's misfortune was to have brilliant economists: an affliction that the Far Eastern super-performers were spared." But behind all that was a great sense of urgency. Both natural and economic resources were very scarce in the country. They had to be directed; otherwise, as a government official once explained, they might be frittered away producing nonessentials like lipstick. The problems facing the country were too immediate, the human suffering too massive, to take that risk. The government would concentrate its resources in the spirit of Soviet central planning, focusing on heavy industry. And, in what turned out to be a crucial mistake of emphasis, the focus was on investment itself rather than on the productivity of the investment and the quality and value of what was produced.[2]

The consequence of all this was an economic system that had three self-defeating characteristics. The first was the "Permit Raj"—a complex, irrational, almost incomprehensible system of controls and licenses that held sway over every step in production, investment, and foreign trade. The control system had begun as an emergency improvisation during World War II, but after independence it became far more, with much greater ambitions. What was meant to be the embodiment of the all-knowing allocator and balancer of the economic national interest turned into an endlessly arbitrary bureaucracy. Everything needed approval and a stamp. If a businessman wanted to shift from making plastic shovels to plastic pails, he had to get approval. A company had to get approval before it could increase output. Indeed, any company worth over $20 million had to submit all major decisions, including the membership of its board of directors, for government assent. Even trivial decisions required stamps. All of this meant hanging around interminably in government offices and seeking to curry the favor of a myriad of officials. But if you had the licence and the stamp, there was a consolation—protection against competition from those who did not have the necessary approvals. The result was a host of interests that did not encourage economic growth—"the politicians who profit from the corruption, the bureaucrats who enjoy the power, the businesses and the workers who like the sheltered markets and squatters' rights."

The second characteristic was a strong bias toward state ownership, reflecting what has been described as the Fabians' "measured and slow-paced ascent up the Marxist mountain." The public sector rose from 8 percent of GDP in 1960 to 26 percent by 1991. The central government owned about 240 enterprises, excluding traditional state industries like railways and utilities. Their importance can be seen in their scale. By the end of the 1980s, 70 percent of the jobs in the large "organized" sector of the economy were in state-owned companies. Moreover, it was estimated that half of the 240 firms were in fact terminally bankrupt. Rather than letting "sick" companies fail, the government took them over and ran them. Workers assumed that salaries were the guaranteed "rewards" for being employed while overtime was their pay. Even when their enterprises were closed down, they still expected to be paid the overtime. State-owned companies generally operated in totally sheltered markets, with no discipline from competition. The result was a state-owned sector that had no incentive to be efficient, that did not respond to customers, and that racked up ever-growing losses.[3]

The Hindustan Fertilizer Corporation made for a truly brilliant example. In 1991, at the time of the economic crisis, its twelve hundred employees were clocking in every day, as they had since the plant had officially opened a dozen years earlier. The only problem was that the plant had yet to produce any fertilizer for sale. It had been built between 1971 and 1979, using considerable public funds, with machinery from Germany, Czechoslovakia, Poland, and a half-dozen other countries. The equipment had looked like a great bargain to the civil servants who made the basic decisions, because it could be financed with export credits. Alas, the machinery did not fit together and the plant could not operate. Everyone just pretended that it was operating.[4]

The third self-defeating characteristic was a rejection of international commerce. What has been described as "export pessimism" settled over decision makers. India adopted the inward-looking drive for self-sufficiency that had been so fashionable in the developing world in the 1950s and 1960s. By rejecting foreign trade and foreign investment, it excluded itself from the world economy. India developed a very large cadre of highly talented scientists and engineers, but, as in the Soviet Union, there were major obstacles to deploying new technologies in the marketplace. The hostility toward foreign investment, the severe limits on international trade, and the constraints on competition all closed down the avenues by which innovation moves into nations. India fell behind technologically. Often, technology was frozen at the level at which it had been in the 1950s or 1960s.

The Dynasty

Indira Gandhi did little to adjust the lines of economic policy that her father had established.* Indeed, she had learned power from an early age. Her mother had died when she was eighteen, and as a result it was Indira who became Nehru's confidante, hostess, and travel companion on official visits. As prime minister, she would prove crafty and masterful—and also short-sighted. Charismatic but haughty, she earned considerable personal prestige from India's military successes against Pakistan and from her country's successful explosion of a nuclear device in 1974. At home, however, she centralized political power around herself, straining the limits of India's democracy. She eroded the powers of the states in favor of the federal (or "central") government. And she marginalized dissidents in the Congress Party, causing many to defect and form rival parties. In 1975, the courts accused her of minor voting irregularities in her home district. Enraged, she declared a nationwide state of emergency, suspended civil liberties, and imposed censorship—India's only experiment with authoritarian rule. But the public outcry was too great, and in 1977 she was forced to relent and call general elections, in which she was trounced. But the ragtag coalition that replaced her lost its bearings almost from the start. Its economic policies proved incoherent, and it was during this time that many international com-

---

* Indira Gandhi, Nehru's only daughter, was briefly married to Feroze Gandhi—no relation to the mahatma.

panies, fearing nationalization, decided to leave India. The coalition foundered on its endless squabbles. By 1980, her reputation tarnished but her charisma intact, "Mrs. G." swept back into power.

But politics had changed. No longer invincible and infallible, the Congress Party was losing ground in the states—to regional interests. Mrs. Gandhi's stubborn, uncompromising response only exacerbated tensions, fueling separatism in some areas, notably among the Sikh community in the northern state of Punjab. In June 1984, she ordered the army to storm the Golden Temple, the holiest of Sikh shrines, where extremists had taken refuge. It was her fatal mistake. The following October, her bodyguards, who were Sikhs, took revenge; they opened fire on her while she strolled in the prime ministerial garden, killing her.

It had been very clear that Mrs. Gandhi expected Sanjay, her younger son and closest adviser, to succeed her—despite damage to his reputation during the emergency years, when he was found to have promoted a program that rounded up villagers and forced them to undergo medical sterilizations in exchange for transistor radios. But Sanjay was accidentally killed in 1980 while flying a light plane. Mrs. Gandhi had then turned to her older son, Rajiv. He stepped first into Sanjay's place, and then, after his mother's death, into hers, becoming leader of the Congress Party. Then, riding on a great wave of sympathy, he became prime minister. Rajiv was the quiet son, unassuming, married to an Italian, and much more passionate about flying than about politics. He had been a pilot for Indian Airlines, the domestic carrier. In the course of the normal in-flight pleasantries, he would simply announce himself over the PA system as Captain Rajiv.

By the time he became prime minister, mounting losses by state-owned enterprises turned into steadily increasing government deficits. As public debt soared, the government tried to catch up by borrowing, both domestically and internationally. Rajiv Gandhi pledged to reform the Permit Raj. He and his relatively young advisers, known as the "computer kids," talked about the importance of innovation and freer markets. Gandhi also had an intuitive feel that India needed to change. Why? After all, he was the grandson of Fabianism. The reason, it has been suggested, was that he was "the first prime minister to have done honest work outside politics. He thus had seen for himself, and through his friends, the system that he sensibly deplored and would seek to change."

But there was no broad consensus to support reform. The various proposed measures were scorned and attacked as "against the common man." And after his initial burst of enthusiasm, Gandhi himself seemed to lose conviction, especially as his government became immersed in a weapons-purchase scandal involving a Swedish arms maker. The drive to reform dissipated and Gandhi was turned out by the voters in 1989. But there were two consequences of his government that would directly affect reform—one positive, one very negative. The first was the surfacing and discussion of a set of reform ideas, however mild. The second, and more important, was the turn—in the face of soaring deficits—toward borrowing, which was what ultimately led to the crisis. As the end of the 1980s approached, the government's deficit was mounting and it was harder and harder to service the debt. Meanwhile, because of the growing debt burden, it had to cut investment, which meant reducing spending on infrastructure, which, in turn, further choked back growth.[5]

Gandhi's successors, riven by political conflicts over religion and caste, were unable to keep their grip on power. Rajiv launched a comeback campaign. But in May 1991, he too was assassinated—at a village campaign stop, by a Tamil suicide bomber seeking revenge for Indian intervention in the Sri Lankan civil war.

Some in the Congress Party once again looked instinctively to the Nehru-Gandhi dynasty. But both Rajiv and Sanjay were now dead, Rajiv's children were too young, and his Italian wife, Sonia, although now an Indian citizen, promptly ruled herself out of the race. Thus the elderly P. V. Narasimha Rao was elected president of a shocked Congress Party.

The Crisis

Rao looked to be at best a caretaker. For many years he had been a faithful servant of the dynasty. A Congress Party functionary and a sometime speechwriter, he had held a host of senior positions—from foreign minister to home secretary. He had always done what he was supposed to do. Even at a time when several of his children were living in America, he would deliver the ritualistic attacks on the United States that Mrs. Gandhi demanded of him. Yet he was not only a shrewd politician but also a man of considerable personal accomplishments. He knew a dozen languages and was also a translator and a poet. He came from a small Brahmin subcaste from the state of Andhra Pradesh. The members of the caste were known both for their talent for survival and for their intellectual achievements, and many of them lived in the United States.

At the time of Rajiv's assassination, Rao was seventy and had been preparing for retirement. As he had lived his entire political career in the shadow of the dynasty, he was going with certain mixed feelings, perhaps because he had not received the recognition that he felt he deserved. If he had bitterness, it was toward Mrs. Gandhi, who had abused and belittled him, as was her habit with many around her. Rajiv, by contrast, had treated him with respect and civility. Later, the walls of Rao's private quarters would be adorned with informal photographs of Rajiv but with none of Rajiv's mother.

Owing to Rajiv's assassination, Rao postponed his planned retirement. Although he had never been elected to a national office, he was chosen to lead the Congress Party in the elections—not because he was a bold and charismatic leader, which he certainly was not, but because he was a conciliator, a balancer, a compromise candidate, who did not seem likely to challenge the other party barons. When, as the newly designated prime minister, he unveiled his cabinet, it was dismissed as "old wine in old bottles." His government, it was said, would not last long. That seemed a reasonable expectation, since it was a minority government. As events turned out, however, it stayed the full five years. In the first hundred days of his term Rao would launch a full-scale attack on the state-controlled economy—the first assault in what would prove to be a protracted war.[6]

Circumstances drove it. Rao and his colleagues did not have the luxury of debating or dallying, for India was in severe economic straits. On August 2, 1990, Saddam Hussein had invaded Kuwait. The sharp increase in the price of oil hit India's already fragile balance of payments very hard. In addition, Indian workers in the Persian Gulf states stopped sending their earnings home, further weakening the balance of payments. On the edge of a financial crisis, India was virtually bankrupt.

Although the country's turmoil was triggered by the Gulf crisis, it was fundamentally homegrown. Entangled in the Permit Raj, India was prevented from reaching anything close to its potential.

"No Head for Figures"

Over a matter of weeks in the summer of 1991, a small group responded to the crisis by changing India's direction. Indeed, the most important decisions that Prime Minister Rao made were in the ministerial portfolios. Not all, in fact, were old wine. Along with all the familiar figures, he deliberately selected some men who would break with the past. One of the key decision makers was Rao himself, the old Congress Party hand and the wily politician. He had no intention of trying to be a Margaret Thatcher—or, for that matter, a Lee Kuan Yew. He saw himself very much as a social democrat. "I do not believe in trickle-down economics," he emphatically declared. As a politician, he would not be rushed; he would think things through deliberately, carefully, and, to the frustration of some, exhaustively. He also recognized how the Congress Party had weakened and fragmented over the years. Once, he compared the party to "a railway platform where all sorts of people come and go as they like." And although he had looked weak and tired when he took over—he had already had open-heart surgery in Houston—he turned out to be more vigorous, and much more in command, than had been expected. It was the consequence, one of his aides wryly remarked, of his absorbing the most important vitamin of all—vitamin P, as in *power.*

The second figure was the finance minister, Manmohan Singh. A Sikh, Singh had been born into a poor family in a drought-prone village in the Punjab region that is now part of Pakistan. Talent and scholarships had carried him far. In the tradition of India's brilliant economists, he had earned his undergraduate economics degree at Cambridge and then his Ph.D. at

Oxford. Subsequently, he had made a considerable career in India as an economic bureaucrat; he held a senior post on the all-important planning commission. Although no one doubted his economic acuity—after all, he had won the Adam Smith Prize at Cambridge—he was modest and understated; when he wanted to avoid a question, he would somewhat implausibly murmur, "I have no head for figures."[7]

The third key figure was P. Chidambaram, the commerce minister, a member of a leading industrial family from Madras, with an MBA from Harvard. Singh would deal with macroeconomics, while Chidambaram would battle down in the nitty-gritty of trade policy, the Kafkaesque world of licenses and permits. Reserved and rather austere in style, he knew exactly what he intended to do, which was to deconstruct the Permit Raj. His reaction was more visceral than Singh's, the response to fifteen years spent practicing administrative law and grappling with the system on a daily basis: "It became clear to me that both the public sector and the private sector were being mollycoddled by a protectionist environment. The poor quality of goods and services was so apparent. I saw how intrusive, oppressive, and inefficient government had become, stifling entrepreneurial spirit, killing every idea, and not delivering anything in turn."

Each of these men, confronting the impending economic wreck, recognized that four decades of policy making had steered the country badly wrong. They were, however, in a minority. Within the dominant Congress Party, there was still no broad support for change. But there was a clear set of ideas that served as a critique of the old policies and guided the new. And when he and the other reformers examined the workings of the economy, they saw it had not delivered growth. Productivity was low, government spending was uncontrolled, and high-minded planning had degenerated into mindless control. All these ailments could be traced back to overwhelming government intervention. "The left had been dominated by the idea of market failure," said the economist and civil servant Vijay Kelkar. "Yet government failure had over time become very well documented. We could see all the data that was piling up. We responded to experience."[8]

Waking Up

Data were also coming from outside the country. The collapse of Soviet communism had a decisive impact on India's redirection. Central planning, with its appearance of rationality, had long ago captured the imagination of intellectuals and officials. Even before independence Nehru had written that "communists and socialists point with confidence to the way of socialism" because "they have science and logic on their side." Indians wanted to emulate the Soviet economic system (even as Russians craved, when they went to India, the opportunity to go shopping). "We tried to implant a Soviet economic model on a Western parliamentary system on an Indian social system," said Jairam Ramesh, one of India's new technocrats. "It was a heady cocktail." It also created a massive hangover. The failure of the Soviet economic model destroyed conviction in the ability of government to manage the economy. The ignominious end of the USSR meant not only the extinction of India's leading trading partner; it also undermined confidence in the system of central planning. India, the elite came to realize, had hitched its future to the wrong star.

To make matters worse, Indians awoke at the same time to what was happening in East and Southeast Asia. For decades they had ignored the emerging "Asian economic miracles," first Japan and then the tigers, all of which were much smaller than India and many of which were allied with the United States. "We tended to dismiss those countries as lackeys of the United States, running dogs of American imperialism," said one economist, "and closed our ideas to their performance, to how amazing it was what they had done in one generation."

By the end of the 1980s, the reality could no longer be denied. These countries, on a consistent basis, were growing much more rapidly than India, which, it was said apologetically, seemed consigned to a lower "Hindu rate of growth." The annual differences in growth rates had now added up to a huge gap, a fact that was vividly demonstrated for Manmohan Singh when he made a trip to the Far East. Singh had reasonable socialist credentials, which had made him acceptable to the Congress Party as finance minister in 1991. (He had previously served as the secretary of the South Commission, very much a repository for believers in third world state intervention. Indeed, the chairman of the South Commission was Julius Nyerere, whose commitment to altruistic socialism had been ruinous for the economy of Tanzania, the country he had led to independence.) But in 1987, Singh made his trip to East Asia. He was stunned. The comparisons were astounding. South Korea and India had been at the same economic level in 1960. Now South Korea's per capita income was ten times that of India, and it was applying for membership to the OECD.

Singh struggled to understand what had made the difference. Certainly, all the accouterments of the Permit Raj—the controls and licenses—had held back the economy. But two things really struck Singh. In East Asia, the governments engaged in what he called "promotional activities" supporting business, whereas in India the emphasis was on regulation. But perhaps the most striking difference of all was the degree to which the East Asian countries had oriented themselves toward international trade and captured its benefits, while India had insisted upon turning inward. The numbers spoke for themselves. In 1990, the OECD countries imported just $9 billion of manufactures from India—and $41 billion from South Korea, whose population was one twentieth the size of India's. East Asia was not the only international influence. "What happened under Mrs. Thatcher was an eye-opener, a revelation," said Chidambaram. "After all, we had gotten our Fabian socialism from Britain."

One more factor reinforced the conviction that India was on the wrong track. Many Indians had emigrated, moving to North America and Western Europe in the 1960s and 1970s. The first wave may have started off poor, but they worked very hard, and by the late 1980s, they—and their children —had established themselves as successful businesspeople and professionals in their adopted countries. Indians owned 46 percent of the budget-motel rooms in the United States. They were responsible for much of retail trade in Britain. They had also built large industrial and commercial firms overseas. Known as NRIs—nonresident Indians—they were now coming back to visit their families and rediscover their roots. Their impact was considerable, and raised an endlessly fascinating sociological question: Why are Indians such a success outside India? It couldn't be the drinking water. It had to be the economic systems under which the NRIs flourished. Their achievements outside the country became another indictment of the Permit Raj within.[9]

"A Functionless Capitalism"

Rao was sworn in as prime minister on June 21, 1991. The next day, his new finance minister, Manmohan Singh, briefed him on the state of the economy, going through all the numbers. The central government's deficit was 8 percent of the GDP, while its internal public debt amounted to 55 percent. Interest payments on just the domestic debt consumed another 4 percent, while interest payments on foreign debt amounted to 23 percent. At the conclusion of this dismal recitation, Rao said, "I realized the position was bad but I did not realize that it was this bad." The nation had just a few hundred million dollars' foreign-exchange reserves left, enough to pay for imports for only two weeks. The nonresident Indians, panicking, were pulling out their deposits. There was even desperate discussion about selling off the Indian embassies in Tokyo and Beijing to raise quick money. Rao and Singh knew they would have to go to the International Monetary Fund for loans; but as it turned out, the IMF's conditions would reinforce rather than define the ensuing agenda for reform. Indeed, the Rao government ended up going far beyond the terms the IMF would have required.

The crisis gave Singh and Chidambaram the opportunity to force a change that would cure the fundamental ailments of the economy—too much regulation and control and not enough competition. India suffered, Singh would say, from what he called a "functionless capitalism"; that is, "people can make a lot of money without any concern for technical progress, quality, and cost reduction." As much as anything else, the change would mean a change in ideas. "India needs to think afresh on many fronts," Singh said just after his appointment. "The old methods of thinking have not taken us anywhere." He added, "You must not underestimate the force of ideas."

Singh and Chidambaram realized that they had an audience of one.

223

They would have to convince the cautious prime minister to push as much reform as possible as quickly as possible. Rao would admit that his knowledge of economics was less than encyclopedic, and his view of the world had been shaped within the confining walls of the Congress Party, which had for so long heralded the preeminence of the public sector. Chidambaram understood what he was up against. "For 20 or 30 years," he told the prime minister, "you were raised on a diet of controls and regulations which you thought was the right thing. To suddenly say that we want to decontrol and delicense can be quite traumatic."

"Yes," replied Rao, "for some of us it is difficult because it is not an easy thing to make a break with what we thought was the right course."

Rao had continuing moments of doubt as reforms got under way. After Singh made a controversial decision not to reduce the price of kerosene, a fuel of critical importance to farmers, Rao put his head in his hands and moaned, "What am I to do with these technocrats?" But finally Rao made the break with the past. His government, he said in a nationwide radio broadcast, was committed "to removing the cobwebs that come in the way of rapid industrialization." [10]

The decisions for reform were made by a small circle of officials working, it seemed, almost around the clock. In presenting the emergency budget in late July 1991 in a speech to Parliament, Singh could not help but note that his wife was very unhappy with his long hours. "The House will agree," he said, "that it is not good for the health of our economy if the finance minister of the country has strained relations with his own finance minister at home." He took that occasion to propose lower taxes on kitchen utensils.

Singh's budget speech was an extraordinary document, not only as a definition of new policies, but also as a penetrating and incisive diagnosis of what had gone wrong. Its overall message was that India was in dire straits and that its only hope was massive reform. The country was "at the edge of a precipice," Singh told Parliament. "There is no time to lose. . . . The room to maneuver, to live on borrowed money or time, does not exist anymore." Again and again in the speech, he showed how performance had fallen very far short of ideal and expectation. India had the third-largest number of scientists and engineers in the world, but that was hardly reflected in the country's technology. He came back to what had hit him in 1987 in East Asia—it was imperative that India become "an internationally competitive economy." He invoked the dynastic pantheon—Nehru and Indira and Rajiv Gandhi—to bless the efforts. But there was no question that he was using the crisis to try to break with the past.

Both bureaucrats and Congress Party members kept sniping away at the reformers, warning them that they were going too far too fast, that they were denying the heritage, the beliefs, that were at the heart of the party. "We're in the business of making changes," Singh told one group of officials. "Anyone who has reservations should speak up." When he was criticized for spurning Nehru's legacy, Singh invoked Mahatma Gandhi's vision of *swadeshi*—self-reliance—and shot back, "No, no, it follows from self-reliance. Self-reliance means trade and not aid."

In a matter of weeks, the Rao government did succeed in changing course: It devalued the rupee. It cut subsidies for domestic products and for exports. It reduced tariffs and trade barriers, eliminated licenses for 80 percent of industry, and did away with the requirement that larger firms get advance approval to expand or diversify. It even dared to reopen the door to foreign investment. And it began a process of disinvestment—that is, selling off some of the government shares in companies.

With such rapid-fire reforms pressing so hard against four decades of government policy, a firestorm of strong opposition might have been expected. But the circumstances of the crisis and the clarity of the reformers somewhat mitigated the opposition. The crisis gave them a freer hand than they had any reason to anticipate, and the worst they got were protests over reductions in subsidies for fertilizers. In the meantime, they started a process that would gather momentum and prove surprisingly durable.[11]

"A Vastly Different Role"

"The economic reforms since mid-1991 have," in the words of two Indian scholars, "signaled a vastly different role for the government in the Indian economy." But there have been many upsets and controversies since. In 1996, the Congress Party lost the elections and was eventually replaced by a minority coalition government led by H. D. Deve Gowda, the former chief minister of the state of Karnataka. The Congress Party supported the coalition. But barely a year later, in May 1997, Congress temporarily withdrew its support; the ensuing political crisis resulted in the appointment of a new prime minister, the veteran diplomat Inder Kumar Gujral. His government faced the challenge of maintaining cohesion. Yet throughout the political tumult, India stayed on the course of reform, reinforced both by the vast shift in thinking in the country and also, specifically, by the fact that both Deve Gowda's and Gujral's finance minister was none other than P. Chidambaram, who as commerce minister had been one of Rao's two key reformers.

When all the changes are added up, they have been quite considerable. The licensing and approvals of the Permit Raj were mostly eliminated. Foreign trade was opened up. So was foreign investment, including what has been described as "the revolutionary step" of allowing foreign and domestic private investment into such infrastructure areas as electric power, ports, and telecommunications. That kind of investment would seem to have challenged the very essence of the commanding heights, at least as it was under the old system. But now there was an urgent necessity to ensure, for instance, that there would be adequate electricity to support economic growth and to avoid the brownouts and blackouts that had become habitual. Moreover, it was now recognized that the investment required for infrastructure would be so large that at least part of it had to be met with funds originating outside the country—otherwise, what was needed would not be built in time, and the costs would be measured in lower growth rates.[12]

Foreign direct investment did, to be sure, ignite some visible controversies. A Kentucky Fried Chicken restaurant in Karnataka was besieged by opponents, who included a religious faction that attacked it on dietary grounds. Of larger importance was the effort by the Hindu nationalists who ruled the state of Maharashtra (which includes Bombay) to overturn a contract signed with an international consortium led by Enron, the U.S. natural gas and electric power company, to build a $2 billion power plant. Through more than twenty-five court challenges, India's independent judiciary and legal system upheld the contract, and after some renegotiation, the project progressed. "The experience demonstrated that India has a good legal system that upholds binding contracts," said Kenneth Lay, Enron's CEO. "We believe that India will continue to grow at a significant rate, and that it will become a more liberalized economy, and we're planning to be in India for the long term." With that said, it was still hard to find a potential foreign investor in the electric power sector that could not recite the prolonged frustrations caused by what has remained a highly complex and somewhat mysterious approval process, involving multiple federal and state agencies and frequent legal wrangles. Overall, while growing, foreign investment in India is still small given the size of its economy—$5.6 billion in 1996, in contrast to the $42 billion that went into China in the same year.

The two areas that have proved the most difficult to reform in India are public finances and state-owned enterprises. Government has avoided the word *privatization* and instead has adopted a program of "disinvestment," generally intending to sell off partial ownership but retain majority control. And it has had an understandably very difficult time in figuring out what to do with highly inefficient, loss-making state-owned enterprises, which employ many people.

Although the bulk of industry remained state owned or state controlled in 1997, there is a considerable private sector in India, most notably the powerful private conglomerates built up since colonial days by legendary entrepreneurs and their heirs. These houses—such as the Tatas and the Birlas—had retained their assets because Nehru wanted to set up new state-owned firms, not nationalize existing private industry. The Permit Raj protected India's industrialists from outside competition, but they soon came to resent and oppose it, because it stifled their energies. As restrictions were lifted, they began to dust themselves off. Their formidable scope—the Tata group ranks among India's leaders in iron and steel, electrical equipment, heavy machinery, tea plantations, and even publishing—meant that it was unlikely they would be swept away by competition and new investment.

Around the old conglomerates, a new private sector is also on the rise, particularly in technology and services—markets that Nehru's planners of the 1950s could not have anticipated. And all of these private firms, old and new, trade and make contracts daily with the state-owned enterprises. Although inefficient and overstaffed, the public sector possesses some firms that function reasonably well—and some that have performed remarkably. Embedded as they are in a complex industrial economy, increasingly subject to domestic and international competitors, Indian public enterprises cannot be cordoned off from reform.

Change from Below

There have been many signs of change. The nonresident Indians are going back to invest and trade, and so are many multinational companies. The southern city of Bangalore has become a second Silicon Valley, a world center for information-technology development. "You can buy programming services in Bangalore, India, for half the cost you can buy it in the United States," said Larry Ellison, chairman and CEO of Oracle, the information-technology giant. "We have a big research center in Bangalore and the quality is fantastic. The reason we're there and expanding is not because we're saving so much money; it's because the quality of the work is so good." Meanwhile, Indian politicians and officials talk more and more about the importance of the government spending its money on such needs as health and education, rather than on subsidizing losses for government-owned businesses. They talk about economic growth as the precondition for healing poverty. While the number of the country's poor is measured in the many hundreds of millions, the Indian middle class is often estimated at up to 300 million—bigger than in the entire population of the United States and the same as Western Europe's. That is a huge number, both as a consumer market and as a source of economic activity. However, as Western consumer-goods companies have discovered, the Indian middle class does not have anything approaching the income or purchasing power of the European or American middle class.

For the first time in memory, change is coming from below—from the state capitals, and no longer just from "the center," New Delhi. The loosening of the central government's controls is accentuating a shift of economic power to the states. At the same time, the regional parties that emerged to resist Indira Gandhi's centralizing tendencies have matured and assumed power in many states. They are concerned with getting the best deal out of reform for their constituencies, which are strictly local. At first, regional leaders relied on charisma and corruption—several of them were former stars in popular movies, and one became known as Madam Ten Per Cent, for the extent of graft she encouraged. Prodded by voters, they have become increasingly canny and aware of what it takes to attract investment. The state of Orissa, long considered a desperate backwater, is today the site of a radical liberalization and restructuring of the electric power system. In West

Bengal, the Communist Party of India (Marxist), in power since 1977, openly invites foreign private investment. The technology-inclined chief minister of Andhra Pradesh was negotiating in 1997 the first-ever direct World Bank loan to an Indian state for comprehensive economic reform. Perhaps the surest sign of vitality from below is the new role of regional parties in federal politics. The coalition partners who took control in 1996 were largely based in the regions. The rise of power brokers steeped in regional politics and guided by a concern for regional development reflects a powerful change in Indian government toward giving more voice to state-level experiments and results. The benefits move one step closer to the people.

One of the oddest things about India since independence has been the economic disconnection between rigid government controls and the powerful commercial traditions of the people. "The springs of entrepreneurialism run very deep in India," observed Vijay Kelkar. "That's not the problem. Bad policies are the problem." But those policies are being changed. As the constraints are eliminated and India integrates with the world economy, the outlines of a high-growth country are beginning to emerge. It is not expected to be a dragon or a tiger. Instead, some Indians suggest the appropriate zoological analogy is the elephant—slow to rise and get up to speed, but, once in motion, fast and steady, moving through thicket after thicket.

"Our mission is very simple," said Chidambaram. "Sustain seven per-cent growth, allow eight percent growth, and abolish poverty as we know it by the year 2020. Markets must work. That does not mean that the state will wither away. Rather, it will have to act decisively in favor of the poor in such areas as education and health and use its power to intervene where there is a palpable importance. But the state must keep away from producing goods and services. On a scale of one to ten, in terms of changing the role of the state, we started close to zero. I'd say we're now at two or three. But we will get there in time. The biggest risk is that we get too enamored of the wonders of the market and do not pay enough attention to the basic human needs of the poor. If we do not solve their needs, there will be a reaction."

The complexity of politics in the world's largest democracy could well slow things down. As the regions become more empowered, the risk of conflict and stalemates increases. Religious sectarianism has been on the rise. And the social structure, built around the caste system, is creating conflict over access to opportunity. Yet the changes to date suggest that India will become much more important to the world economy in the future—as a market and, increasingly, as a competitor. "The transition is here in thought," said Chidambaram. "People accept it. The difficult part is always to deal with the lobbies and the established interests that are blocking the process of change. This is the time when we should not lose nerve or direction." He paused. "The last mile of reform is indeed the most difficult."

During the 1991 crisis that began the reforms, Manmohan Singh quoted Victor Hugo: "No power on earth can stop an idea whose time has come."

He went on to say, "The emergence of India as a major economic power in the world happens to be one such idea." During the dismal days of 1991, that might have sounded like a rhetorical flourish or even a dream. At the end of the 1990s, it is a realistic prospect.[13]

CHAPTER 9

PLAYING BY THE RULES

The New Game in Latin America

GONZALO SÁNCHEZ DE LOZADA—known by the nickname Goni and president of Bolivia from 1993 to 1997—was always fascinated by the American bank robbers Butch Cassidy and the Sundance Kid. It had to do with his having been born Bolivian but then growing up in the United States—a consequence of his father's exile after a military coup. In Bolivia, coups were commonplace—189 took place in the 172 years after independence. At every New Year during their exile in the United States, Goni's family would make a toast: "Next year, may things change and we will go home." That year never seemed to arrive. But finally, after Goni had completed a degree in philosophy at the University of Chicago, the political situation did change sufficiently and in 1952 he went home.

It was not easy. Even the physical adjustment was difficult. La Paz, the capital, is eleven thousand feet high in the Andes, and walking just a block or two up one of its steep cobbled streets leaves one badly winded. Goni tried to get himself started as a filmmaker, which proved to be a whimsical pursuit in such a small economy. To make a living, he took up aerial photography for oil exploration companies looking for promising terrain and then went into the business of delivering supplies to exploration camps in the jungle.

But the dramatic story of Butch Cassidy and the Sundance Kid maintained its hold on his imagination. The famous desperadoes had escaped to Bolivia one step ahead of the law, and there, still pursued, they perished. "America's Old West," Goni liked to say, "died in the mountains of Bolivia." He researched their story and wrote a film script, which MGM optioned for a few thousand dollars; but it never got made. When the version starring Robert Redford and Paul Newman came out much later, based on somebody else's script, he considered suing for plagiarism, but a lawyer persuaded him that the costs of fighting the case would be prohibitive. Disappointed, Goni gave up scriptwriting—it had been a sideline anyway—and instead went on to become a founder of a successful mining enterprise, as well as a campaigner for democracy. He also married Miss Bolivia of 1959.

Shock Therapy: Decree 21060

Years later, in the mid-1980s, Goni came to write another script—one called "shock therapy." It was not a movie but a program for a rapid and massive —indeed almost overnight—economic shift from a government-dominated economy to a market economy. Although the script has now been played out around the world, it began in Latin America, and Goni deserves credit as the original author. Moreover, he wrote it in record time, with a deadline imposed not by a studio but by looming disaster.

In the mid-1980s, Bolivia was in terrible crisis, its economy gripped by hyperinflation and in total disarray. At the time, Goni was a senator, and then he became minister of planning in a new government that came to power in 1985. Bolivia had a classic Latin American economic system: In the name of development, nationalism, and anti-Americanism, preceding governments had taken direct ownership of much of the economy. What the state did not own, it heavily regulated. But whatever the ambitions, government was not up to the task. The governmental machinery was incompetent and inefficient, blatantly open to corruption and favoritism. The spigots of spending were wide open. Workers were courted with large salary hikes and then lost their money through inflation, which was endemic. Almost no taxes were collected. Only 3 percent of government revenues came from taxes: The rest were from the central bank. The country groaned under its burden of international debt. Both poverty and inequality were increasing. With the added blow of the debt crisis, which had begun in 1982, hyperinflation had reached the rate of 24,000 percent, and there was fear that it could soon multiply to 1 million percent. Very little time was left to act.

Yet there was little agreement on what to do. Large-scale change in the basic organization of the economy was, for most people, unthinkable. Goni thought otherwise. "The hyperinflation was frightening," he explained. "A lot that seemed unimaginable became imaginable with hyperinflation and the debt crisis. No amount of intellectual persuasion could have gotten governments and people to take the steps they did without them. But what really influenced me was my experience as a businessman. I had been inside the system, and I saw that it didn't work. The private sector tried to profit from the public sector's workings, and the public sector was undermining the private sector. That experience, plus the long struggle for democracy, convinced me that the old system just couldn't work anymore."

But what were the alternatives? Goni saw himself as "left of center."

231

He explained, "I always recognized that I live in a poor country and that you have to figure out how to address poverty." Still, he found something of an intellectual role model in Germany's Ludwig Erhard. Goni was a regular reader of *The Economist* and from its pages followed what was happening elsewhere in the world, including Mrs. Thatcher's Britain and the Asian economic miracles. Two things had a particular impact on him. "The first," he said, "was New Zealand, where, in order that the country could grow, a labor government had to dismantle the command-and-control economy that had been created many years earlier by a conservative government. The second was China. Mao had always been portrayed as the cutting edge. But I was impressed when Deng came to power and initiated changes. I was particularly impressed by his statement that he didn't care what kind of cat it was so long as the cat caught mice."

Goni took to quoting Deng on the subject of cats. And these examples reinforced his conviction that the only way to restore Bolivia's economic health was by eliminating statism—by taking dramatic steps. The first draft of his shock-therapy script was Decree 21060, in August 1985. It eliminated price controls, instituted drastic budget reductions, slashed tariffs to introduce competitive pricing into the economy, and began a radical restructuring of the public sector and a reduction in its spending. Goni and his colleagues took a huge risk in doing all this backed by only $1.5 million in the central bank—almost nothing. The reason they dared to take the risk was that the information system was so poor; he said, "We didn't know that was all we had."

Over the next several months of 1985, Goni and his team put the rest of the plan for shock therapy in place. They needed advice, but this was not the sort of help the World Bank was providing at that time. Some months earlier, however, in Cambridge, Massachusetts, Harvard economics professor Jeffrey Sachs had received a notice about a seminar on Bolivia. He was deeply interested in the bizarre phenomenon of hyperinflation, and Bolivia's was the first case in forty years. He wandered into the meeting and was mesmerized. Since he was also the only member of the economics faculty who had bothered to show up, he was drawn into the discussion and, like a good professor, ended up at the blackboard. After a while, from the back of the room, came a variant of a proverbial question: "If you're so smart, why don't you come to Bolivia?" He went.

At a cocktail party in La Paz, Sachs met Goni, who realized that the professor was just the man he was looking for. Sachs provided a good deal of the analytical work and expert guidance they needed. The objective was clear—to end inflation very quickly. Bolivia had 450 different taxes, most of which were never collected. Sachs helped Goni and his team reduce the number to 7 easily collectible taxes. He provided input about how to manage the central bank and what kind of financial controls were necessary. And he helped give them the confidence to stand by their convictions.

What unfolded in Bolivia between 1985 and 1987 brought stability to the country. The inflation rate was reduced from 24,000 percent to 9 percent. Government spending was reduced, subsidies were cut, prices and trade were liberalized, taxes were collected and the tax system reformed, and an emergency social safety net program was put in place. In 1987, Bolivia was able to implement the first debt-reduction program under IMF auspices. Altogether, the Bolivians had done something that was unthinkable in Latin America. "We created a market economy overnight," said Goni. "The issue was shock versus gradualism. But there was no gradualist solution; the system had broken down. There was only a brief time to act. Things that seemed impossible to do became possible."

Goni was not only taking on Bolivia's crisis but also helping initiate a radical turn away from what had been the traditional Latin American approach to state and marketplace. For decades, these governments had thoroughly dominated their national economies. Despite the obvious differences among countries, common features tied the region together: Militarism, Marxism, anti-Marxism, populism, and anti-Americanism were all intertwined in various ways. Some military dictators strutted around in quasi-fascist uniforms; others mouthed the slogans of socialism. Whatever the garb, the state controlled economic life through direct ownership, clientelism, and patronage; government was deemed the central engine of economic growth.

In the late 1990s, that model is being broken. No single system has emerged to take its place, but the general direction is clear—toward freeing markets, reducing and redefining the role of the state and removing it from production through privatization, taming inflation by constraining government spending, lowering trade barriers, and shifting traditional activities out of the state's hands. For the most part, this process has gone hand in hand with a remarkable rebirth of democracy in a region where military dictatorship too often seemed the norm in the past.[1]

Dependencia *Rules*

The traditional statist approach in Latin America was greatly influenced by what was known as *dependencia,* or dependency theory. It rationalized state dominance—high import barriers, a closed economy, and a general demotion of the market. And from the end of the 1940s right up to the 1980s, *dependencia* ruled. Its origins were in the late 1920s and 1930s and the Great Depression, when the collapse of commodity prices devastated the export-oriented economies of Latin America. Meanwhile, in line with the tenor of those times, "national security" became a justification for governments to take over "strategic sectors" of the economy to meet the needs of the nation, not those of international investors. This led, notably, to the founding of state oil companies in a number of countries. After World War II, the shift toward a much greater reliance on the state was propelled by the

233

emergence in the West of both the welfare state and Keynesian interventionism and by the prestige of Marxism and the Soviet Union. One other thing motivated both Latin American economists and their governments: anti-Americanism—fear of the colossus to the north, and antipathy to what were seen as exploitative American corporations operating in the Latin arena.

The *dependencia* theorists rejected the benefits of world trade. By the end of the 1940s, the essential elements of their thinking were already articulated and promoted by the United Nations Economic Commission on Latin America (ECLA)—and most notably by an Argentinean economist named Raúl Prebisch, who headed the commission from 1948 until 1962. He began his career, in his words, as "a firm believer in neoclassical theories." But "the first great crisis of capitalism—the Great Depression—prompted in me serious doubts regarding those beliefs." Prebisch and those who joined him at ECLA propounded an international version of the inevitability of class warfare. They argued that the world economy was divided into the industrial "center"—the United States and Western Europe—and the commodity-producing "periphery." The terms of trade would always work against the periphery, meaning that the center would consistently exploit the periphery. The rich would get richer and the poor would get poorer. International trade, in this formulation, was not a method to raise standards of living but rather a form of exploitation and robbery, committed by the industrial nations and their multinational corporations. The victims were the peoples of the developing world. This belief became the received wisdom in universities across Latin America.

So instead, the periphery would go its own way. Rather than exporting commodities and importing finished goods, these countries would move as rapidly as possible toward what was called "import-substituting" industrialization (ISI). This would be achieved by breaking the links to world trade through high tariffs and other forms of protectionism. The infant-industry logic became the all-industry logic. Currencies were overvalued, which cheapened equipment imports needed for industrialization; all other imports were tightly rationed through permits and licenses. Overvalued currencies also discouraged agricultural and other commodity exports by raising their prices and thus making them uncompetitive. Domestic prices were controlled and manipulated, and subsidies were widespread. Many industries and activities were nationalized. A jungle of controls and regulations grew throughout the economy. The way to make money was by making one's way through the administrative and bureaucratic maze rather than by developing and serving markets. Overall, what guided the economy were bureaucratic and political decisions, not signals and feedback from the market.

Until the 1970s, the approach seemed to work. Real per capita income nearly doubled between 1950 and 1970. Over the same period, the role of the state continued to expand, as did state-owned enterprise. Tariffs and other trade barriers were raised. The biggest criticism at the time was that governments were not doing enough and that they should move closer to the centrally planned model of the Soviet Union and Eastern Europe. The deep weaknesses of this system were mostly hidden—until the beginning of the 1980s.[2]

The Lost Decade

The debt crisis hit Latin America very hard. The buildup in borrowing had been enormous. Between 1975 and 1982, Latin America's long-term debt almost quadrupled, from $45.2 billion to $176.4 billion. Adding in short-term loans and IMF credits, the total debt burden in 1982 was $333 billion. Yet no one was paying much attention to that ominous increase until August 1982, when Mexico teetered on default. What ensued was a double bank-ruptcy—financial and intellectual. The ideas and concepts that had shaped Latin American economic systems had failed; they could no longer be funded. *Dependencia* had caused them to go broke. The years that followed, in which Latin America struggled to reshape its economies, became known as the "lost decade." And with good reason. For at its end, in 1990, per capita income was lower than it had been at the beginning of the decade.

Over those years, the full costs of the old system came to be reckoned. The industrial enterprises—both private and state owned—that it had fos-tered were inefficient, owing to protectionism, lack of competition, and isolation from technological innovation. For the most part, they put little emphasis on quality and scale of service. Agriculture was seriously dam-aged. Budget deficits swelled. With inflation pervasive and deeply en-trenched, family savings were devastated. As a result, people could not retire. Inflation rose to astounding levels, driven by the deficits and loose monetary policy. The domestic economies were denied the benefits of international trade, and there was no improvement in fundamental social inequality.[3]

The New Consensus: "We Asked Too Much"

In the first few years of the debt crisis, the urgent need was to pull the countries back from bankruptcy and stabilize their economies. Their balance of payments had to be restored, much of which was accomplished under the aegis of austerity and the "conditionality" of the International Monetary Fund. The IMF took the lead in implementing emergency programs of loans, credits, and debt reschedulings if the countries, in turn, would take steps to shrink their burden of debt, reduce their deficits, temper inflation, and make their exchange rates more realistic.

But in the late 1980s and into the 1990s, something more fundamental began to unfold throughout Latin America—a drastic reordering of the basic principles regarding the role of the state in the economy. The emphasis shifted from government to the market as the basic allocator of resources in the economy. One of the leading analysts of the new thinking described it as nothing less than a move toward "developing and using the market, rather than denouncing, repressing, and distorting markets." The retreat of government meant large-scale privatization and, in general, fewer controls. It also meant lowering the barriers to both trade and foreign investment, in order to replace the lending that had dried up with the debt crisis. Governments focused on reducing deficits and inflation, and reforming their tax systems. To the degree possible, public expenditures would be driven more by economic returns than by political exigencies. Exchange rates would be competitive and more predictable. Property rights were to be strengthened. And throughout the economy, competition, rather than monopoly and control, was to be encouraged.

Perhaps only those who had grown up in the old system could fully grasp the extent of the change. For many years, Enrique Iglesias was associated with ECLA, working closely with Raúl Prebisch. He is now the head of the Inter-American Development Bank. "I would never have imagined this much change," he said. "For forty years following the Great Depression and the Second World War, we looked to government to take on the task of reviving our economies. We asked the state to deliver the goods. We asked too much of government, for too long. We had to make a choice. Now we have taken a sharp turn back to the market economy. I could not have imagined this forty years ago."

Altogether, this new stock of ideas would shape the economies of Latin America in the 1990s. And like any such group of ideas, it acquired a moniker—in this case, the Washington Consensus. It is a term that its promulgator, the economist John Williamson, has regretted ever since. In the interest of promoting "policy reform in Latin America," he observed, "it is difficult to think of a less diplomatic label." It refueled all the old emotions and revived the specter of Yankee domination. As one critic of the Washington Consensus put it with good old-fashioned gusto, the term "was coming clean about who made policy in the late twentieth century—not governments, but Washington. 'Washington' . . . embraced not only the IMF and the World Bank but also their less than shadowy master—the U.S. government—and behind it, its shadowy masters, the American economics profession and Western business interests."

Good stuff for a conspiracy theory or a film. But such a diatribe missed the whole irony. The Washington Consensus was developed in Latin America, by Latin Americans, in response to what was happening both within and outside the region. Government failure was what now loomed before people's eyes, not market failure. The old system could no longer deliver economic growth. People struggled to live with hyperinflation and woefully inadequate basic services.

External factors also loomed large. As in many other parts of the world, the collapse of communism undermined Latin America's faith in socialism and central planning. Castro's Cuba no longer looked like the vanguard of

236

revolution, or indeed the vanguard of anything, but rather like an archaic relic that had managed to stay afloat only on a sea of Soviet subsidies. Even as the failures of the Soviet model became completely apparent, Latin American economists began to focus on the economic success of Asia. It was really a process of discovery, for they had mostly ignored the region until then. The Asian economies were less regulated and much less inflationary, and their exchange rates were competitive and less volatile. Unlike the Latins, the Asians had rebounded quickly from their debt crisis. And in striking contrast to the strictures of *dependencia*, the Asians had manifestly anchored themselves in the world economy. By the late 1980s ECLA, formerly at the forefront of *dependencia*, began, in what was nothing less than a complete turnaround in thought, to talk about the necessity of "outward oriented" economies and a shift away from government control.[4]

The Technopols

The process of reconceptualization was made possible by the emergence of a group of market-oriented economists throughout the region. Many of them had gone north to earn their Ph.D.'s at institutions such as Harvard, MIT, Yale, Stanford, and Chicago. Their senior teachers had been shaped, to a large degree, by the market failure of the Great Depression. But the economic problem of the day for them, and for the younger faculty members, was government failure. In the mid-1970s, for instance, Pedro Aspe, Mexico's future finance minister, was doing his Ph.D. at MIT, where the future finance minister of Chile, Alejandro Foxley, was a visiting professor, while Domingo Cavallo, the future finance minister of Argentina, was writing his Ph.D. thesis at Harvard. They talked together and jogged together, and became friends of people like Lawrence Summers, now U.S. deputy Treasury secretary, and Jeffrey Sachs, both of whom were doing Ph.D.'s at Harvard at the time. They met MIT faculty members Rudiger Dornbusch and Stanley Fischer, now deputy managing director at the International Monetary Fund; and Harvard professors Benjamin Friedman, an expert on fiscal policy, and Martin Feldstein, who showed how high taxes function as disincentives.

When these Latin American economists went home, many of them not only took teaching jobs but also established research institutes of their own, went into government, and generally set about trying to implement the new consensus. They became known as the "technopols," in contrast to the "technocrats" of earlier years. They were not only making the machine of government work better; they also, if they were to be successful, had to be good politicians. After all, they were seeking to make massive changes in the workings of their economies, and with so many institutions and interests having so much at stake, that was a manifestly political task.

"To do a good technical job in managing the economy, you have to be a politician," said Foxley. "If you do not have the capacity to articulate your vision, to persuade antagonists, to bring people around on some unpopular measure, then you are going to be a total failure." He added, "Economists must not only know their economic models but also understand politics, interests, conflicts, passions." Foxley could speak with some authority on this subject. A highly trained economist, he was also one of the foremost critics of the Pinochet government during the years of dictatorship, and then he proved to be a very effective finance minister in the first democratic Chilean government that followed.[5]

Chile: The Ambiguous Role Model

Chile became a laboratory for an approach that was wholly at odds with the Latin American experience since World War II. But it was regarded with great ambiguity—and, indeed, suspicion and outright rejection—because its implementation was so entwined with repression and dictatorship. Yet over time, it became a role model for the rest of the region.

In 1970, the socialist government of Salvador Allende came to power and embarked on a program of massive nationalization and expropriation, along with price controls, that seemed aimed at creating an Eastern European–style economy in Chile. The result was economic chaos. The Allende government was toppled in a coup led by General Augusto Pinochet, who in turn established a repressive dictatorship. Obsessed with the fear of communism and internal enemies of all sorts, Pinochet enforced a harsh reign, suppressing trade unionists, journalists, students, and others deemed subversive.

Pinochet and his military colleagues knew little about economics. Beyond "national security" and repression of the left, they had hardly any program at all. But they had to do something. A program diametrically opposed to Allende's existed in a document called *El Ladrillo—The Brick* —a massive manuscript originally prepared by the economics faculty of the Catholic University of Chile for the Christian Democratic presidential candidate in 1970. It advocated a strong free-market approach. Its chief author later said *The Brick* had been composed as "something for our nerves, a kind of therapy. . . . We didn't see that it had any future."

But *The Brick*'s program was what the Pinochet government adopted. And along with it came "the Chicago Boys"—market-oriented economists, many of whom had been educated at the University of Chicago under an exchange program with the Catholic University. The intellectual mentors of this group were two Chicago professors—Milton Friedman and, even more so, Arnold Harberger. The Chicago Boys set about to turn the program in *The Brick* into reality. But the task was hardly easy even for a regime that had centralized power in its hands. One economics minister said that he spent 90 percent of his time "trying to explain to the generals and the country what a free market was. This was a totally new experiment, and there was huge resistance." Tired and irritated by one long economics tutorial, Pinochet cut off the discussion by sternly reminding the economists that he was the one who held Chile's "pot by the handle." One of the leading Chicago Boys replied that if the economy continued to suffer, Pinochet would be left "holding just the handle." The general was furious. No one was supposed to talk to him like that. Nevertheless, the lectures continued.[6]

The Chicago Boys rapidly instituted a host of fundamental reforms. They freed prices, liberalized trade, and deregulated the financial sector. They privatized massively, reducing the number of state-owned companies from five hundred in 1973 to just twenty-five by 1980. They wanted to do everything as fast as they could. Their aim was to dismantle the "developmental state" that had run the Chilean economy since the end of the 1920s and mediated among the various strong interest groups. It was ironic that they used the power of a military dictatorship to try to impose what would be, in economic terms, a minimalist state.

The reforms produced results, and even though the Pinochet regime continued to be an international pariah, it won grudging respect. In 1982, however, the country went into a severe economic tailspin, owing to the overall debt crisis, errors in currency management, and inadequate supervision of the financial sector, which was shaken by scandals and failures. The entire program of the Chicago Boys appeared to be discredited. The military government was disoriented, and its efforts to adjust were not very successful. It had to take over so many banks that the period became known jokingly as the "Chicago road to socialism." A second generation of reformers took charge in 1985. They were less pure-bred than the original Chicago Boys—indeed, fewer came from Chicago and more from Harvard—and less austere in their policies. They succeeded in correcting many of the mistakes. And over the next several years Chile became the outstanding Latin American example of market reform. Growth rates were high, inflation was low, and exports grew and became more diversified. Quality Chilean wines found their place on the shelves of the world market.

Finally, at the end of the 1980s, the military, defeated in a plebiscite, stepped aside. What was most decisive about the presidential campaign of 1989—beyond the advent of democracy—was that all three candidates, including two who were outright opponents of the dictatorship, endorsed the reforms. The economics minister in the new government was Alejandro Foxley, who had created a think tank at the Catholic University that had become one of the leading sources of criticism of the military government, though garbed in the language of economics. In the early 1980s, he had still argued for the state to play a large interventionist role, including, among other things, "picking winners." "Truthfully," he later said, "I had less confidence in the free market and more confidence in the state." A decade later, as economics minister, he was intent on addressing the neglected social problems of poverty and inequality. But his fundamental objectives were to strengthen the consensus in favor of a market economy, make the new

239

system work better, and consolidate and continue reform. He found that he had to defend the market reforms against newly victorious democrats, who wanted to dismantle any and all handiwork of the dictatorship. Simultaneously, in response to the Chicago Boys' efforts to deconstruct the interventionist state, he sought to build what he called "the competent state." His goal, he explained, was to combine a "progressive social policy with an austere, some would say conservative, fiscal policy."

That course has continued under the government of Eduardo Frei. "To understand Chile, you need a broad view," observed Energy Minister Alejandro Jadresic. "It is not easy. Many people were against the original reforms because they came from an illegitimate military government. How to preserve the reforms that were rational, and go further with more reforms? That was one of the reasons why people like me got involved in politics. We were afraid that the reforms would be undone. The democratic governments have made important modifications to the reforms. There is now a strong equity consideration, stressing social needs, housing, the health system, education, the environment. But let the market system create the wealth. Let markets develop."

The 1989 presidential election in Chile proved decisive. Despite the bitter strife and deep pain of the previous two decades, notwithstanding the passions and costs, few wanted to roll the market back. That—along with the economic achievement itself—sent a powerful message to the rest of the region, particularly at a time when it needed a role model. No longer could the market economy be dismissed as an artifact of dictatorship. Chile was where the new liberalism was nurtured and from whence it spread to the rest of Latin America—most immediately, across the Andes to Argentina.[7]

The Paradox of Argentina

Argentina had long been an economic paradox. How did a country that was one of the world's richest in the first decades of the twentieth century end up in such economic disorder? A good part of the answer rested with Juan Perón. He is now best remembered, of course, as the husband of Evita, but in the years after World War II he was the embodiment of populism with an almost fascist tinge. Building on the prewar popularity of fascist ideas, Perón turned Argentina into a corporatist country, with powerful organized interest groups—big business, labor unions, military, farmers—that negotiated with the state and with each other for position and resources. He incited nationalist passions, stoked pretensions of grandeur, and pursued stridently anti-American policies. He nationalized large parts of the economy and put up trade barriers to defend them. He cut Argentina's links to the world economy —which had been one of its great sources of wealth—embedded inflation in the society, and destroyed the foundations of sound economic growth. He was also wildly popular—until Evita's death in 1952. Thereafter, however, the economy became so chaotic that he prudently went into exile.

The years that followed were characterized by a revolving door of elected presidents and military juntas. Perón returned from exile to become president again in 1973. He died shortly thereafter, leaving as president his new wife, Isabel, who was not really prepared for the job, having previously been a nightclub dancer in Panama. The country descended into further chaos. A new military junta took power, and it waged a vicious "dirty war" against the left and others, many thousands of whom were "disappeared" à la Chile—some simply thrown out of airplanes over the Atlantic. The military showed no competence in running the economy, which was mired in persistent inflation and a deep recession. In 1982, in a desperate gamble to restore its authority and popularity, the military attacked the British-owned Falkland Islands (known to the Argentines as the Malvinas). It was the same war that gave Margaret Thatcher the political clout to undertake large-scale privatization in Britain. The defeat of the Argentine military dictators undermined their authority. In the one thing at which they were supposed to be expert—warfare—they had proved quite incompetent. In 1983 they surrendered office to a democratically elected president, Raúl Alfonsín.

Alfonsín had campaigned on the slogan DEMOCRACY OR ANTIDEMOCRACY. Argentina had had an abundance of both. Between 1930 and his election in 1983, the country had gone through twenty-four presidents and twenty-six successful military coups and several hundred unsuccessful ones. Alfonsín's great contribution was the restoration of democracy and civic institutions. But with the beginning of the debt crisis, his improvised efforts to stabilize the economy failed. The country remained in a deep economic crisis, and his administration was in disarray. One of his economics ministers, who had ridden on the shoulders of the crowd in the first year of Alfonsín's government, was by the end of his term spit upon by his own neighbors when he dared to venture outside his home.

Alfonsín was succeeded by a flamboyant, almost improbable, white-suited provincial governor, Carlos Menem. Once described as "a psychoanalyst's nightmare," Menem was also pragmatic, quick to adjust to circumstances, and hardly wedded to any set of ideas. Indeed, his policies were initially described as "a mismatch of misunderstood notions, some from Mussolini, some from Maynard Keynes." He ran as a Peronist—he was described as "Perón with sideburns"—with a platform of populism, handouts, and spending. He derided his opponent, who advocated privatization and a freeing up of the economy. Once elected, Menem promptly adopted his opponent's ideas and launched one of the most radical, speedy, and all-encompassing market reform programs in Latin America.

There was really no choice. Argentina had run into a wall. Hyperinflation had reached 20,000 percent, the economy was contracting, and food riots were taking place in the streets. The debt burden stood at $58 billion when Menem took office, and there was no obvious way to pay it off. It was no longer possible to play the old Peronist game of inflationary wage hikes. "We have already seen that movie," Menem once explained. Meanwhile, next door, Chile demonstrated that there was an alternative. Yet even within Argentina an alternative could be found. In the late 1970s, a candy manufacturer and a building contractor had gotten together and endowed the Instituto de Estudios Económicos sobre la Realidad Argentina y Latinoamericana (IEERAL), an economic research institute in the inland city of Córdoba. Its members were sick of corporatism, with its wheeling and dealing among major interest groups. Smaller entrepreneurial businesses, they believed, were the poor relations, simultaneously ignored and smothered by the system. Researchers at this institute studied market reforms in the rest of the world and then, in their own work, related them to Argentina's experience. By the time Menem came to power, they had articulated and indeed legitimized a host of ideas for reforming the economy. Menem, who had the political momentum, was ready to accept any suggestions if he thought they would help solve Argentina's problems. But he lacked one thing—ideas of his own. He needed someone with ideas. And he found such a person at the institute in Córdoba.[8]

The Broom-maker's Son

The head of the institute, and the one who shaped its agenda, was the economist Domingo Cavallo, who would prove to be one of the most influential figures in recasting the relationship of state and marketplace in Latin America. He was born in 1946, the same year that Juan Perón took power. If he had one nemesis in his career, it was Perón, for many of his intellectual and political efforts were aimed at refuting and rejecting Peronism. Cavallo grew up in the interior province of Córdoba, which he would later say had inured him to Peronism. "It is in the provinces, away from Buenos Aires, where one most easily noticed the pernicious effects of an overexpanded and arbitrary economic system." His own origins were very modest; his father owned a small broom-making shop that was connected to the family house.

Cavallo did his undergraduate studies in Córdoba and then worked in the state government, where he found himself increasingly dissatisfied with what he had learned in university. "At the time, there was a lot of emphasis on market failure and the role of planning," he recalled. "I didn't have the feeling of the market economy." He began to educate himself. He was much influenced by *The Principles of Economics* by Raymond Barre, a French economics professor and later prime minister of France. Barre focused explicitly on "the rules of the game"—how an economy is organized, who the players are, how they behave. The rules of the game would turn into a lasting preoccupation—and an oft-repeated phrase—for Cavallo. He also plunged into nineteenth-century Argentinian thought on the constitutional basis for a market economy. "I could not relate those ideas to what I was taught in university," said Cavallo. "I decided to go to the United States to understand the market economy better."

Cavallo ended up doing his Ph.D. at Harvard in the 1970s. He focused on Argentina's persistent inflation and monetarism, out of which came the ideas that would shape his subsequent policies. Argentina's inflation had been created by the fiscal irresponsibility of political leaders, who would spend and intervene no matter what the cost—motivated in part by grandiose illusions. Cavallo believed that the way to check inflation was to rein in the politicians, not the money supply. He was contemptuous of the *dependencia* theorists. Argentina's long decline, he argued, was the result not of external forces—the terms of trade—but of the internal political culture. Instead of complaining about international trade, Argentina ought to have been expanding and diversifying it.

Returning to Córdoba, Cavallo organized IEERAL; the presidency of this new research institute gave him the platform from which to propound his ideas and develop a cohort of like-minded researchers. His objective was to understand why the Argentinean economy had gone so badly wrong. "Argentina had been the most successful emerging economy in the world in the trade system that Britain created in the second half of the nineteenth century," he said. "What happened?" The attempt to identify the rules of the game became the perennial starting point for any research project at IEERAL.

In the mid-1980s, Cavallo published a book entitled *Economy in Crisis*. He wrote it in four weeks, although it was based on a decade of thought and analysis. The book was a best-seller and made him a national figure in Argentina. His diagnosis of Argentina's ailment became famous; the nation's essential problem, he announced, was the coexistence of "a socialism without plans and a capitalism without markets." He got himself elected to Congress. Despite their differences, he and Carlos Menem became good friends. Menem recognized that Cavallo could be very useful to him.

Cavallo was the logical choice for finance minister when Menem won, but his appointment was strenuously opposed by powerful business interests, which wanted to preserve their position and feared competition and deregulation. And so instead, Menem made Cavallo foreign minister. After all, he did speak English very well. Meanwhile, the economy continued to sink further into crisis. Having gone through three economics ministers in his first nineteen months in office, Menem finally turned to the obvious choice, Domingo Cavallo, and handed the economy over to him.

Cavallo was often blunt, abrasive, argumentative, and tactless. Sometimes he could not resist calling in to radio talk shows to set the speakers and listeners straight. But he also demonstrated a remarkable skill at the required politics—identifying goals, communicating, folding groups in, creating and shaping a broad consensus in favor of reform, and building up relationships with the international institutions and financial community whose confidence would be essential. Of course, he was aided by a sense of desperation. No one could doubt that the country was in a severe crisis. The cost of failure was evident—hyperinflation.

Determined to implement shock therapy, Cavallo moved quickly on several broad fronts. First, he rapidly reduced trade barriers and introduced reforms to encourage competition and a new export orientation. Second, he pegged the peso, the Argentinian currency, to the dollar. According to the Convertibility Law, the central bank was obliged to convert the austral into dollars at a fixed rate. This step decisively removed a classic form of sovereignty; no longer could politicians and the central bank feed inflation by manipulating the exchange rate and wantonly expanding domestic credit. The mandatory convertibility was of overwhelming importance in bringing down inflation. As Cavallo explained, "We needed to change the minds of Argentinians. That became very important in contributing to discipline. Before that, politicians and participants in the economy did not have any idea of a budget constraint." [9]

Privatization

The third element was privatization. The government owned an enormous portfolio of companies, ranging from the traditional utilities to the state oil company and a circus. Most of them, burdened with antique organizations and onerous labor regulations, racked up huge losses year after year, draining vast sums out of the national treasury. As such, they were one of the main sources of inflation. Privatization was intended to achieve several objectives. It would stanch such losses and get business off the public dole. It would help reduce Argentina's debt burden. It would also reduce the size of the state, decentralize decision making, and take government out of an economic role that was inappropriate. It would provide a way to improve the quality of woefully poor services in such areas as telephones and transportation. And finally, there was no hope in the long term of taming inflation without privatization.

Argentina would in fact carry out one of the most far-reaching and radical privatization programs of any country in Latin America. Cavallo and his colleagues learned as they went along. "The first privatizations brought us a lot of money but none of the benefits of competition," said Cavallo. "The most important thing we learned from the initial experiences was the need to maximize efficiency and benefits to consumers. We needed to improve the quality and quantity of services and to lower costs. All this would increase the productivity and competitiveness of the entire economy." Thus, Cavallo came to focus on deregulation as the necessary precedent to privatization.

The biggest privatization was that of YPF, the national oil company and the very embodiment of the Peronist state-owned enterprise. Menem and Cavallo selected José Estenssoro, an urbane executive with three decades of experience in the international oil service industry, to run the privatization.

Estenssoro presented two alternatives: Either dismantle the company and sell off the parts, or "rightsize" the company to its strategic core. The latter approach was chosen. As a first stage, noncore assets were shed, among them supermarkets, movie theaters, clubs, airplanes, and even churches. The second stage was restructuring—introducing an entirely new management organization and a host of new systems to support that structure. The central issue was employment. It was reduced by almost 90 percent, from 52,500 employees to 5,800. The extent of the reduction was evidence of how inefficient the company was. Unless it addressed employment, it could never cease being a loss maker. "The reduction in the labor force was the most painful decision," said Estenssoro, "but it took place without strikes, social unrest, or work stoppages." Indeed, it was handled with extreme care—with a mixture of early-retirement packages that included a year of retraining followed by generous severance packages, along with the transfer of employees with assets that were sold off.

The restructuring turned YPF into a firm that looked like a modern company, not a sprawling branch of government administration. Only then was it ready for privatization. The result was a stock offering in 1993—at $3 billion, the largest initial public offering up to that time in the history of the New York Stock Exchange. A lumbering, inefficient, inward-looking company dependent on protection had been transformed into a dynamic international competitor, operating throughout Latin America and, later, in the United States and Asia.

The retreat of the state from direct ownership did not mean that it was out of business. Rather, it held a new role—to which Cavallo and his colleagues had to devote considerable effort—and one that very much fit in with his preoccupation with the "rules of the game." It was the creation of regulatory rules and bodies to ensure that the now-privatized monopolies did not take advantage of their position. That effort would become controversial. Moreover, relations between Menem and Cavallo deteriorated badly after Menem's reelection in 1995, and in 1996 Cavallo resigned. It did not take long for him to become a very outspoken critic of Menem's administration; he made dramatic charges of corruption, judicial manipulation, and mafia control. Yet their bitter differences have not disrupted Cavallo's basic judgment: "Menem was the man for the circumstances. No one else could have implemented so many changes so fast. He was the man for the job."

Menem and Cavallo came to office in a country where, in the words of José Estenssoro, it was very difficult "to think about the future," and they succeeded in rescuing Argentina from its past. For decades, Argentina had been an inward-looking country, which fit its strongly nationalistic temper. Thus, opening up to the world was a dramatic turnaround. "Those years were very stressful," said Cavallo. "We went into battle every week, every day. But I was helped a lot by the young people I would meet in the street or in the stores, who would wish me well in creating a new Argentina. We did accomplish much more than we expected." Argentina had been decimated by inflation. It could not collect its taxes, it could not approve its budget, people with money desperately finagled to get it out of the country, and services were in a downward spiral. The credibility of the new democracy was at stake. The country was trapped by a dangerous and suffocating past. But in the short period of half a decade, it regained a future.[10]

Peru: The Agronomist and the Book Writer

During the "lost decade" of the 1980s, Peru experienced one of the most stunning descents into economic darkness of all the countries in the Western Hemisphere. From 1968 to 1980, it had been ruled by a left-wing military dictatorship. Influenced by Fidel Castro, proclaiming its commitment to social reform, and wrapping itself in nationalism, the regime took over much of the economy, strangled private enterprise, nationalized domestic and foreign businesses, and set the country back enormously. One simple example: By the end of the 1960s, Peru had built up a substantial fishing business, which provided many jobs; its fleet, in fact, was larger than Japan's. The military government nationalized the business and in due course it simply collapsed. Yet despite its nonperformance, the fishing business still continued to draw huge state subsidies. The beached rotting hulls of the fishing boats told all.

The first postmilitary government in the early 1980s did not change much in the way the economic system operated. The second made things worse. It was the leftist government led by a young politician named Alan García. A charismatic and captivating orator, he was drawn to the balcony overlooking the square—but even more by the power that came with the balcony. García and his cronies used their positions to hand out favors and, in the process, to enormously enrich themselves. Their economic policy was a recipe for economic collapse. They slapped on price controls, severed Peru from the international financial community, promoted generous wage increases, cut taxes, and opened the floodgates for government spending. Toward the end of his presidency, García went out of his way to establish diplomatic relations with North Korea, a source of funds and weapons. Meanwhile, Peru was in deep economic crisis: Real wages of the army and government employees had declined by two-thirds, the economy contracted 25 percent between 1988 and 1990, and by early 1990 inflation had reached 3,000 percent. The country was broke.

It was also in the grip of an intense political crisis, instigated by a civil war led by Sendero Luminoso, the Shining Path. Although often described as Maoist, the ideology of the Shining Path was almost impenetrable, but the way in which it sought to impose itself was all too clear—through violence, savagery, wanton bloodshed, and havoc. Led by Abimael Guzmán, a philosophy professor in the Andean city of Ayacucho, it had spread its control through sheer terror over much of the highlands and was waging war on the capital, Lima, through murder, bombings, kidnappings, and blackouts. By some estimates, half of the country was under its sway.

Yet in the 1980s, the country was afforded another path. Indeed, *El Otro Sendero—The Other Path*—was the title of a book that put forth a liberal alternative for Peru. The appearance of the book, written by the economist Hernando de Soto, reflected the percolation of reformist ideas among some intellectuals and businesspeople. Indeed, both Friedrich von Hayek and Milton Friedman were among those participating in the symposia in Lima that had laid the basis for the book. The researchers associated with *El Otro Sendero* concluded that there were over five hundred thousand laws and executive orders that applied to economic activity. They conducted an unusual experiment to discover how difficult it was to start a small business in such a highly regimented and complex system. They set up a small workshop in Lima with two sewing machines and then tried to register it as a business. "To register the workshop," they reported, "took 289 days and required the full-time labor of the group of four assigned to the task, as well as $1,231. . . . At the time, that was the equivalent of 32 monthly minimum wages. This means that the process of legally registering a small industry is much too expensive for any person of modest means." The system discouraged economic initiative or forced would-be entrepreneurs into illegality and the black market—what became known as the "informal economy."

But interest in the other path was restricted to little more than a small circle. That all changed at midday, July 28, 1987, when García delivered a speech announcing that he would nationalize all banks and financial institutions. The writer Mario Vargas Llosa, vacationing with his family at an isolated beach in the very north of Peru, heard the speech over an ancient portable radio. He was infuriated. The results would be more corruption, more poverty, more dictatorship. "Once again in its history, Peru has taken yet another step backward toward barbarism," he said bitterly to his wife. He said much the same in an article entitled "Toward a Totalitarian Peru." A manifesto followed, and then a demonstration that, instead of attracting a few thousand professionals, drew at least a hundred thousand—and caused Alan García, watching it on television, to smash the screen in rage. Mario Vargas Llosa became the leader of the Libertad movement, which intended to roll back the state.

Vargas Llosa was Peru's most distinguished man of letters. A very adept literary critic, he had written his dissertation at Madrid University on the Colombian novelist Gabriel García Márquez. But it was his own novels—beginning with *The Time of the Heroes* and continuing with the likes of *Aunt Julia and the Scriptwriter* and *The War at the End of the World*—that had made him an international literary figure, equally at home in London, Madrid, and Paris as in Lima. In the way of so many Latin American intellectuals, he had flirted continually with politics since his student days, but he had gone through a much more thoroughgoing transformation than most. He had begun as a student communist and had staunchly defended the Cuban revolution. But when he dared to criticize Castro for imprisoning writers, a hail of invective from Castro and his intellectual defenders around the world fell upon Vargas Llosa. Increasingly, he came to see that communism meant repression and, at the same time, failed to deliver on its vaunted promises. He became a social democrat.[11]

Still unsatisfied, Vargas Llosa turned to the study of economics, and ended up settling on liberal economics as the best bet for both delivering economic growth and protecting freedom. Leftist intellectuals heaped calumny on him, and he returned it in kind. He denounced "cut-rate intellectuals," who went with the fashions and were profoundly ignorant of economics. "You cannot be a modern man and a Marxist," he declared. He mused endlessly on why intellectuals were so fascinated with state control and Marxism. Part of it was patronage, part of it was fashion, and part "their lack of economic knowledge." He reserved some of his greatest contempt for Latin American intellectuals who made a career, in his view, of denouncing the "imperialist" United States while at the same time finding much succor from professorships at its universities and grants from its foundations. Perhaps nothing so much brought home the distance he had traveled as when he encountered his old friend Gabriel García Márquez one evening at a theater in Mexico City. García Márquez had never abandoned Fidel Castro, and he was strongly critical of Vargas Llosa's repudiation of the left. They got into an argument, and Vargas Llosa ended up knocking García Márquez out, which is something that one hardly ever gets to do to the subject of one's doctoral dissertation.

Now, in the aftermath of Alan García's nationalization announcement, Vargas Llosa emerged as the leader of a political movement, Libertad, which became the vehicle that brought into Peruvian politics the reform ideas that had spread elsewhere on the continent. The more learned members argued about whether they should adopt the "market economy" or the "social market economy" and debated which path Ludwig Erhard would have endorsed. More immediately, Libertad's leaders methodically developed over three years a "white book" of ideas and plans for radically reforming Peru's economy. The reshaping of political discourse was almost unimaginable. "I see it but I don't believe it," Felipe Thorndike, a prominent engineer, said to Vargas Llosa. "You talk about private property and popular capitalism, and instead of lynching you they applaud you. What's happening in Peru?"

By 1990, Vargas Llosa was the front-running candidate for president. But he had to conduct his campaign under enormous pressure. There were simple things—like the daily phone calls threatening to kill his family. There were physical attacks. In addition to the risk of assassination by García's supporters, there was also the constant threat of the Shining Path, particularly in the Andes, where his campaign workers were gunned down. During all the months of campaigning, Vargas Llosa struggled to keep in touch with his intellectual interests. Every morning during the campaign, when he was in Lima, he withdrew to his study to read and reflect on Karl Popper and the open society. At night, for solace, he read the Spanish poet Góngora.

Vargas Llosa took a highly publicized trip to Asia in order to demonstrate the other path—what he described as "economic freedom, the market, and internationalization." Leftists, he noted, depicted Taiwan as "a semicolonial factory" of the United States. In the middle 1950s, Peru's economy had been superior to Taiwan's; both countries had per capita incomes under $1,000. Yet by the time of his visit, per capita income in Peru had slipped by half, while Taiwan's had risen to $7,530. He also visited Margaret Thatcher, who told him that he should press on. But there would be a cost. "If you continue," she said to him, "you will have to endure a great deal of loneliness." [12]

All this assumed that Vargas Llosa would win. What was not factored in was Alberto Fujimori, an agricultural engineer and university rector. It was very hard, at least at first, to take Fujimori seriously as a candidate; he was even harder to take seriously than a novelist candidate. He had no political following and belonged to no party. Insofar as he was known at all, it was as host of a television talk show that dealt with farming and socioeconomic issues. He was also an outsider, a member of Peru's small Japanese community, his family having immigrated to Peru in the mid-1930s. He identified with those excluded from Peruvian society—the poor and the Indians. And he was filled with anger at what he saw as the collapse, despair, and looting of his country.

Initially, he was hardly noticed, left vying for last place with the prophet Ezequiel of the Israelite Church of the New Covenant. Even his family told him that he was crazy to run. But Fujimori was determined. It is said that he sold his tractor and pickup truck to help finance his one-man campaign. He put together a coalition of evangelists and the dispossessed, who campaigned door to door for him in the shantytowns. He built support by criticizing Vargas Llosa's talk of shock therapy, privatization, and the slashing of government employment. He did not get into specifics; his slogan was "Honesty, technology, and work." Television viewers were treated to footage of him driving tractors over the Andean highlands.

Fujimori was attacked because he was Japanese, because his mother did not speak Spanish, and because none of his relatives was buried on Peruvian soil. He counterattacked with pictures of his son taking communion, and by observing that if Peru was going to emulate the Asian countries, then he was better prepared to implement it than was someone of European descent. Fujimori portrayed Vargas Llosa as the candidate of the small Peruvian elite—white, well off, privileged, and separated from the mass of the poor and the reality of society. Physiognomy became an issue—Vargas Llosa's striking European looks, evoking the Spanish conquest four centuries earlier, in contrast to Fujimori, whose facial features were closer to those of the Andean Indians.

In the initial round of the elections, Vargas Llosa and Fujimori came out first and second, respectively. After much soul-searching, Vargas Llosa offered to step aside if Fujimori would adopt his reform program. The offer was spurned. In the second round, Fujimori won handily, and the next day Vargas Llosa flew off to Paris, bitter and sick of politics, eager to return to his writing. But what he left behind was the detailed script for reform.

Fujishock

Within two weeks of taking office, Fujimori, who had run as a populist and had called for gradual reform, unleashed a program of shock therapy so much more far-reaching than anything Vargas Llosa had proposed that it became known as Fujishock. Public spending was slashed and the currency effectively devalued, the beginning of a very rapid and thoroughgoing reform program. Fujimori also demonstrated a style of governing that put little emphasis on coalition creation and institution building. He took his own counsel and kept decisions to himself.

Yet Fujimori was determined to do two things simultaneously—combat terrorism and implement the kind of reforms that had been laid out in Libertad's white book. "It was a very difficult problem to fight violence and at the same time to make economic reforms," he said one day in the baroque presidential palace in Lima. Sitting very straight at the head of a long table, he talked quietly, often gazing down at the table, sometimes looking sideways at his visitors, occasionally with a little smile at the corner of his lips. "It was very risky to do both of them at the same time, because any economic reform would bring some instability in the short term. But we ran the risk. It was the turning point for success in our economic program.

"My mind worked as an engineer's even on the Shining Path," he continued. "People, even the archbishop of Lima, were talking about fighting poverty before violence. That was a fallacy. We had to fight violence, and then poverty." He stretched out his arm. "I had a conversation in this room with some of the leaders of the business community. They had no hope. But I saw things completely differently. I was convinced that the strategy we established would be a success. I was not lonely. I was sure. In that sense, I have the Oriental patience. I wait for the result. I was very firm. Even stubborn."

The campaign against the Shining Path was reorganized and intensified; Fujimori involved himself directly. Now, instead of fighting on the periphery, they would go after the heart of the movement. It took two years. The police came to focus on a house in Lima. They observed that it was turning out garbage on a daily basis considerably in excess of what might have been expected to be generated by the two people living there. In September 1992, they mounted a raid, and in the ensuing attack, they found that it was indeed a safe house where Shining Path members were living secretly. Among them was the number-one quarry—Abimael Guzmán, the leader. Captured and paraded on television, Guzmán was no longer the fearsome philosopher-guerrilla; he implored his colleagues to lay down their arms.

The winding down of violence provided the context in which Fujimori could carry out the next phases of Fujishock. Labor and financial markets were deregulated, tariffs were reduced and simplified, privatization was initiated, and the tax base was broadened, while taxes themselves were reduced. Peru was reopened to foreign investment and, in complete reversal of Alan García's policies, reintegrated into the international financial community. Peru started to experience substantial economic growth, and in contrast to the fast-growing Asian countries, it began to be talked of not as a tiger but as a puma. "I tried to make a very fast pace," Fujimori explained. "My economic experts did not understand how far we wanted to go to the market economy. I wanted a real authentic market economy." Indeed, he jettisoned his original advisers and ended up with a cabinet composed entirely of people who had originally not supported him.

"The situation here was such a mess, with many kinds of controls that were against the poor consumer and favoring big political power," he said. "The role of the state is in fields like education, health, security, and the judiciary," he said. "I had this thinking, these ideas, because I was a full-time engineer and because I was independent. I make my own evaluation. That is critical for me. The way I think is not the way a politician thinks. My way of thinking is logical and objective. I see a problem as an engineer. Once an engineer sees a problem, he wants to find a solution, even if it is a limited solution."

The reforms were accompanied by many traumas. In April 1992, Fujimori dissolved the Congress, suspended the constitution, and dismissed much of the judiciary. Critics called it a coup and charged that Fujimori was making himself into a strongman. Yet in a survey about the performance of forty-four Latin American presidents, he received the highest score for making appointments on the basis of merit rather than patronage. His wife unleashed a furious public feud with him, which culminated in her joining a dozen other candidates, including former U.N. secretary-general Javier Pérez de Cuéllar, in running against him for president. Nevertheless, Fujimori won a second term on the first ballot, with over 60 percent of the vote.

In December 1996, guerrillas belonging to the small Castroite Tupac Amarú revolutionary group, disguised as waiters, seized the residence of the Japanese ambassador during the huge annual party celebrating the Japanese emperor's birthday. The initial lot of six hundred hostages (including Fujimori's mother) was reduced to seventy-one (including both Fujimori's brother and his foreign minister). Negotiations got nowhere. The Tupac Amarú guerrillas insisted on the release of all their imprisoned brethren. They would not compromise. Nor would Fujimori. Release of the prisoners would undermine everything that had been done to restore order and security. On day 125 of the hostage taking, Peruvian soldiers carried out an expertly executed rescue. Only one hostage died—apparently, of a heart attack. Immediately after the raid, Fujimori's popularity soared, but then fell again owing to discontent with what was seen as his authoritarian style of rule and a wave of political scandals. In the meantime the economy continues to grow.

Fujimori still summons the rage that initially prompted him to run. "I was angry both about the economy and the security," he said. "Most of the first society, the people who enjoyed the results of the economy, did not even know what was happening in the shantytowns. They were afraid of those shantytowns coming down to invade the rest of Lima." He recalled an incident that had fueled the anger that had led him on what had seemed an overwhelmingly quixotic presidential bid. "One day in 1988 I couldn't fly from Huancayo to Lima because of bad service. Aero Peru passengers would have to wait twelve hours in the terminal. Finally, I drove a car. I had to go very slowly because of rocks on the road, and because of the risks and dangers of the Shining Path, who would stop cars. It took me fourteen hours." He smiled. "Now you can do it in five." [13]

Mexico: The Diffusion of Power

It always seemed that Mexico was different. Since the revolution of 1910, it had managed to avoid most of the political upheavals that the other Latin American countries had experienced—the populism, the military crackdowns, and the worst of the repression and violence. This relative peace came largely thanks to Mexico's unique political system, which set it apart from the rest of the region for most of the century. The consolidation of power that followed the revolution put government firmly into the hands of a single, dominant political party. Even its unusual name—the Institutional Revolutionary Party, or PRI—signaled the ambiguity of its mission, identity, and purpose. But its successive leaders managed to devise and apply the political tools that would grant Mexico relative political order and stability.

Mexico's presidents had a firm grip and did not tolerate dissension beyond a point. PRI was not the sole legal party, but it guaranteed its role by buying off potential opponents, coopting faction leaders, and, when all else failed, controlling the outcome of elections. It took care to preserve, at base, a broad measure of bedrock popular support to give legitimacy to the process. A single trade union confederation, for example, mediated among workers, private business leaders, and the government. Its leaders, who were well rewarded for their efforts, helped take the rough edge out of industrial relations. Meanwhile, factions formed and re-formed within PRI, negotiating among themselves and dividing up positions of influence. PRI devised "rules of the game" to ensure something close to fairness within the confines of its one-party logic. The national constitution stipulated that the country's president could serve only one six-year term. And nobody could become president who had held a cabinet-level post within the previous six months. To conform with these requirements, PRI developed an unwritten but unshakable practice known as the *dedazo*—the pointing of the finger—by which the outgoing president would designate his successor, to be rubber-stamped by less-than-transparent national elections.

Not all was manipulation, payoff, and sleight of hand. *Priista* presidents also took measures to give the people a sense of welfare, improved living standards, and control over their country's economic destiny. Most notable was the nationalization of the oil industry in 1938 by Lazaro Cardenas, by most accounts the most popular and revered Mexican president of the century. And in the post–World War II era, Mexico's record of economic growth and social order stood in contrast to the hyperinflation, the recessions, and especially the civil strife and military dictatorships spreading in the rest of Latin America.

All this came under severe threat by the beginning of the 1980s. Despite its advantages and political stability, Mexico too had operated on the economic logic of import substitution, and it too felt the strain of that system. The collapse of commodity markets and the accumulation of debt and dwindling foreign reserves hit hard. And the time-honored ways in which PRI retained its grip did not help. After all, the bargain with organized labor came at the cost of a vast patronage system; and the bargain with the wealthy private industrialists of northern Mexico was based on protecting their markets from competition. The now-familiar array of massive state enterprises bred heavy expenses, and the Mexican president of the late 1970s, José López Portillo, made matters worse with his notoriously profligate spending habits.

Such was the situation when the debt crisis hit in August 1982. The bailout came with a heavy cost. Mexico's credit was shot, and it had to rebuild its reputation step by step within very tight constraints and during a deep economic slump. It was imperative that deficit spending and the public debt be reined in. And since much of the trouble was structural, inherent to PRI's way of running the country, that too would have to be questioned. The political implications were daunting, and an influential faction formed within the old guard of PRI—they would later be called the "dinosaurs"—to ward off such dangers. Against them was a small set of reformers scalded by the shock of the debt crisis. Over time, they would come to transform the political landscape and turn the Mexican economy inside out, from import substituter to participant in continental free trade. But the transition was to be far from simple, and punctuated by several dramatic pauses and reversals.

It would take several shepherds as well. First among them was Miguel de la Madrid, who became president, according to schedule and the rule of the *dedazo,* in December 1982, amid all the financial torment. Although he had once been López Portillo's budget minister, he sought very rapidly to distance himself from his predecessor. He had ample opportunity to prove himself, as he had to assume responsibility for very tricky debt renegotiations. In these, he succeeded in conveying to the bankers the sense that something had changed. He also did the unheard-of politically: Within his first year in office, he allowed the opposition to win a series of local elections. This, however, was felt to be too much, and in the next set of local elections PRI returned to its old ways.

De la Madrid set to work with the help of two key ministers. His finance minister was Jesús Silva Herzog, the scion of a political family, whose father had played a central role in the oil nationalization of 1938. The planning and budget minister was Carlos Salinas, a young, slight economist who had studied at Harvard's Kennedy School of Government. Of the two, Silva Herzog was certainly the more cautious and Salinas the more adventurous. But both knew something had to change. "It was not easy to find another country with as high a deficit as ours," Silva Herzog recalled. "We needed to bring it down and to get rid of debt service." Their job, as Salinas explained it, was "the taming of the budget dinosaur." They clamped down on spending with ferocity, moving the budget from a deficit of 7.3 percent of GDP to a surplus of 4.2 percent. They devoted every possible resource to repaying the debt. And most of all, they began to unravel the tangled web of public enterprises. "At the end of 1982, there were over eleven hundred public companies," said Silva Herzog. "Some were top priority, like electricity or the railroads. But we also owned hotels, restaurants, a bicycle factory, and a blue jeans factory. We even owned a nightclub in Mexico City. It was probably the only nightclub in the world losing money."

To take on this complex was nothing short of revolutionary. If they had the courage to take tough measures, they were not, however, helped by luck. A devastating earthquake in Mexico City in 1985 caused damage estimated at 2 percent of GDP, and was followed soon after by a fall in the price of oil, which generated more than half of Mexico's total export revenues. These obstacles, combined with the difficulties of keeping internal opposition at bay, meant that by 1988, when de la Madrid stepped down, inflation remained very high (upward of 100 percent per year), and the real incomes of ordinary people had plummeted. The budget deficit had crept up again. And the early emphasis on privatization had its pitfalls, too. "Overnight billionaires" had sprung up. "Most people were convinced there were many cases of corruption," said Silva Herzog. "It was a question of moral credibility." At the same time, Mexico had joined GATT, the General Agreement on Tariffs and Trade, which meant removing the protections on a number of privileged sectors. All this portended the unknown and threatened the confidence of working people.

Perhaps for this reason, the election to succeed President de la Madrid in 1988 looked to be more contested than most. A powerful alternate candidate had sprung up to rival PRI. He was Cuauhtémoc Cardenas, who attacked the PRI's economic policies from the left. His name said it all. He was the son of the legendary President Lazaro Cardenas; his first name was that of an Aztec emperor. A gifted orator, he toured the country as the candidate of the Party of the Democratic Revolution (PRD), lambasting corruption and raising hopes that there was an alternative. It was up to de la Madrid to designate the PRI candidate. Silva Herzog was the leading contender, but de la Madrid instead picked Salinas. This seemed an unlikely choice: Salinas was young and unpopular with the public, seen as technocratic and close to foreigners. When the results of the July 1988 election were announced after a week of suspicious silence, Salinas had 50.4 percent of the votes—winning by the lowest margin in Mexico's modern history, so low as to lead to charges that Cardenas had been robbed of victory.

Whatever the merits of his election, Salinas surprised Mexicans by soon winning them over. In a lightning strike with a military squadron, he defeated the dictatorial boss of the oil workers' union, gaining respect as a tough leader, not just a technocrat. He moved privatization forward, selling off majority stakes in major industries such as telecommunications. He sold off the banks, which López Portillo had nationalized in 1982 as a parting shot. The receipts went to pay off the debt. He also balanced the budget, and in this way helped bring inflation down to wholly respectable levels, considerably increasing the real value of wages. The motor of this economic drive was his finance minister, Pedro Aspe, who led a team of experts once called "the most economically literate group that has ever governed any country anywhere." A member of the original crop of technopols, Aspe studied first at the Technical University in Mexico, a privately funded institution set up to rival the public National University. He went on to MIT, where he earned his doctorate in 1978. Returning to Mexico, he joined a *camarilla*, a group of civil servants loyal to a central figure, which was a prerequisite for advancement. Usually *camarillas* served patronage functions. The difference with Aspe's was that its central figure was Salinas and that its membership was exclusively comprised of brash young economists, all of them appalled at Mexico's recent economic history. In time, Aspe would form his own group of loyalists, and once he became finance minister, he was able to disseminate them among the various ministries, greatly facilitating coordination. He also showed his political skills by designing a "social pact" on wages and prices that helped drive down inflation.

By mid-1993, the Salinas government seemed to have achieved the impossible—turned Mexico around—for good, it appeared. Public finances were fundamentally sound for the first time in decades, and a real political opening seemed to be under way, with the center-right National Action Party (PAN) in power in some states in the industrial heartland of the north. In a major achievement, Salinas negotiated the North American Free Trade Agreement with the United States. The acceptance of free trade represented a turning inside out of Mexico's once desperately inward-looking economy. It also carried profound psychological weight, setting Mexico, at least in the minds of some, on an equal footing with its northern neighbor.

Yet extraordinary events were to call the entire process into question. On New Year's Day 1994, masked rebels took over the town center of San Cristóbal de las Casas in the impoverished southern state of Chiapas, which was remote, heavily populated by Indians, and had little to show for the reform process. There they "declared war" on the Mexican state. It was a dramatic reminder of the distance to be traveled and the range of interests to be considered in reform. It was also a reversion to the debilitating peasant wars that had festered in previous decades all over Central America. Although localized, the Chiapas conflict was to flare up and down, and to be placated by uneasy compromises over land rights and improved infrastructure and services. Then, in March 1994, in Tijuana in Baja California, former budget minister Luis Donaldo Colosio, Salinas's designated successor, was assassinated as he addressed an electoral rally. It was Mexico's most shocking political murder in sixty years. Although a suspect was identified and rapidly tried, most Mexicans felt there was more, much more, to the story. In due course the investigation would become enmeshed with other inquiries in a complex weaving of political and financial scandals that appeared to involve Salinas allies and relatives and corruption and drugs. (Later, Salinas would prudently remove himself to Ireland, with which Mexico had no extradition pact.)

To replace the murdered Colosio, Salinas selected yet another unlikely dark horse, Ernesto Zedillo Ponce de León, who assumed office after an apparently clear election victory, although he became known in the process as the accidental president. He was born to a modest family in Mexico City but grew up primarily in Mexicali, on the United States border, a rough town at the crossroads of industry, immigration, and shady dealings. A gifted student, he studied economics and went on to become another of Mexico's new generation of technocrats, in the process earning the reputation of being dull and gloomy. He wrote his Ph.D. thesis at Yale in 1981, presciently arguing that Mexico's debt predicament should be blamed on the government and not on the banks that had provided the loans. That earned him a job, after the debt crisis began, at the central bank, whose head shared his views. It also set out an economic stance that he pursued unwaveringly, if quietly, in various technocratic positions under de la Madrid and Salinas.

Yet the first economic decision of the new Zedillo presidency was to prove costly. The peso had been overvalued for some time, but Salinas refused to adjust it for reasons of politics and prestige. Zedillo's finance minister announced a devaluation. Unfortunately, it turned out that he had miscalculated the effect on the unexpecting financial markets. Mexico's stock exchange took a dramatic dip, which set off a domino reaction around Latin America. Dubbed the "tequila effect," it was another unfortunate sully to Mexico's financial reputation. It was less grave, however, than the debt crisis, and over time was reinterpreted in investment circles as a correction or caution rather than grounds for a full stop. It helped as well that the United States mounted a $20 billion bailout in short order.

Zedillo's most notable achievements have come in the political realm. His determination to push forward the investigations of Colosio's death, despite the possible political entanglements, has earned him some respect as a champion, in at least relative terms, of the norms of justice. Most strikingly, he has allowed the political arena to open up substantially. He entrusted elections to an independent commission, effectively distancing the operations from the PRI old guard. In the midterm elections of 1997, the results —remarkably—confirmed the opinion polls. PRI lost its absolute majority in the National Assembly, as well as in several states. Cuauhtémoc Cardenas became mayor of Mexico City, a newly created elective post and, by virtue of the city's size—it has 20 million inhabitants—the country's de facto second-most-powerful position. For the first time in modern history, Mexico has coalition politics beyond PRI rather than factional accommodations and horse trading within it. The implications for the economy in the near term are uncertain. Yet despite the rocky progression of reform since the trauma of 1982, the economy has been transformed in no small measure. The record of public finance and macroeconomic management is still shaky. But the structure has changed, as privatization and accession to the international trading system have moved economic power toward export-oriented industries and more and more to the private sector and the stock exchange.

There are gigantic social aspirations to be fulfilled. "We have serious problems of income distribution," cautioned Silva Herzog. "The rich got richer and the poor have become poorer." The new patterns of industry are uneven, which makes some jobs more stable and lucrative than others. "Our export sector is as competitive as any in the world," he said. "But our nonexport sector is very backward." Mexico's challenge is to harness political change and economic management to meet these aspirations, while avoiding the mistakes of the past. For Pedro Aspe, who drove the reforms under Salinas, the openness of the political system is the key to the future. "It all started with de la Madrid," he said. "He knew that when he opened up the economy it would foment political change." Despite numerous accidents, that process is still in motion in 1997. "When we open up, it has a tremendous force," Aspe continued. "No party, no government, no bureaucrats can stop that. People are doing deals—with the U.S., with Canada. No one can stop it." [14]

Brazil: Dependentista *Turned Inflation Slayer*

In Brazil, reform has been hampered by the very character of the country— its size, its diversity, the depths of its problems, its demographics, the federal structure and the multiplicity of interests, and the entrenchment of corruption. Democracy returned to the country in 1985 after twenty-one years of military rule, but Brazil inherited considerable economic problems. At the time the debt crisis broke, Brazil owed $87 billion, making it the world's largest debtor. A culture of inflation engulfed the nation. Inflation hit 1,500 percent by 1990. Indexation became a way of life. The price of virtually everything was linked to one of the many indices that were published in the newspapers. Prices changed every day; even bank accounts were indexed. The poor suffered the most. And corruption threatened to undermine the legitimacy of the new democracy; the first directly elected democratic president resigned in 1992 to avoid impeachment on corruption charges.

Yet despite all this, Brazil moved toward an open market economy, although more slowly than most of its neighbors. More than anybody else, the architect was the current president, Fernando Henrique Cardoso. There was more than a little irony in this, for Cardoso described himself as belonging to the "radical tradition" of Latin American thought and, indeed, was one of the premier architects of the *dependencia* theory and its critique of capitalism and the "center." He was an intellectual hero of the Latin American left and one of the most trenchant critics of capitalism and "imperialism." His personal transformation was more thoroughgoing than that of his country and dramatized how far the weight of ideas shifted.

Cardoso, strongly influenced by Marxism while a student at the University of São Paulo, was forced to go into exile after the 1964 military coup. He ended up in Chile, working under Raúl Prebisch, the father of *dependencia*. A sociologist, Cardoso ran a research institute affiliated with ECLA and coauthored a classic text on *dependencia*. He taught at other universities, including the radical Nanterre campus of the University of Paris, where the student uprisings of 1968 began. Cardoso returned to Brazil in 1969. He was promptly stripped of his university professorship by the dictatorship, but nevertheless managed to establish a research institute that turned out criticism of the military regime and its policies. He gravitated toward politics and, after the return of democracy, emerged as a leader of a new social-democratic party and won election as a senator. In 1992, he became foreign minister and then, the following year, finance minister.

It was as finance minister that Cardoso took the key steps to stabilizing the Brazilian economy. He slashed government expenditures and improved tax collection. He also reduced the transfer payments from the federal government to the state and local governments. And with inflation running at 7,000 percent, he acted decisively. The mechanism was his Real Plan, which, like that in Argentina, tied the currency to the dollar. It worked. Within a month, inflation plummeted to less than 10 percent. The plan brought respite to the main victims of inflation: the poor and the working class. It laid the basis for record foreign investment and spurred a rapid growth in trade. Cardoso became the hero of stabilization. On campaign tours, he found himself mobbed like a soccer star. In 1994, he was elected president.

His first few years as president did not go smoothly. There were banking crises and a botched devaluation. In any event, reform was not easy in a country in which the constitution, adopted as late as 1988, explicitly mandated government ownership of part of industry and in which the Congress is dominated less by parties than by interest groups. Nevertheless privatizations, some of them large, continued in Brazil, many of them at the state level. By late 1997, equity sales in such key sectors as steel, electricity, and telecommunications had raised $29 billion. Reforms of the civil service, the tax system, social security, and education have been slower.

Cardoso may have acted like one of the new breed of Latin American neoliberals, but he did not talk that way. His language was still that of a social democrat, with the focus on poverty and equity. But now he had a "regulated free market" and Western Europe's mixed economy as his model. The tenets of *dependencia* were overtaken by changes in the world economy, technological advance, and competition. The overweening, inefficient, intrusive state was a cause of economic problems, not a solution to them.

"In the whole world," Cardoso said, "the force of change-oriented utopia, of a socialist hue, has lost attraction." The traditional left has been left behind. Today, he asked, "what is the left? The left has lost its bearings. If the left identifies with what in history has materialized as the left, it is finished. Especially here in Latin America, the thinking of the left had been based too much on the idea that development was fundamental, that the state was the central agency for such development, and that collective instruments of action had precedence over individual ones. . . . It has to be more rational." But he also rejected the view that "the smaller the state, the better. . . . For a correct solution to the problems of social welfare, it is not enough to make idle references to Chile and bless it on the altar of privatization. . . : One cannot make the private sector the universal salvation, because it is not. The market does not solve the problem of misery. The problem of poverty has to be solved along the lines of coordinated actions by the state."

Yet this father of *dependencia,* formerly one of the leading intellectuals on the Latin American left, now finds that his main political opponents are on the very ramparts of the left that he abandoned. He has no doubt that the left helped restore "the rule of law" in Brazil. But even without the socialist goal, "the notion of a strong state as the main instrument of development is still alive," Cardoso said. "Reforms are needed." [15]

Rediscovering the State

The character and responsibilities of the state are at the top of the agenda in Latin America. With the economic rules converging across the continent and the ghosts of *dependencia,* import substitution, and military dictatorship laid to rest, policy makers are starting to consider the challenges ahead. Their countries remain plagued by deficiencies in infrastructure, human welfare, and the standard of education. In all of these areas they fare far worse than do the Asian tigers. In Latin America, the rates of economic inequality, the gap between rich and poor, are among the world's highest—and have been, by some measures, for centuries.

After decades of state ownership of the core industrial sectors that for so long made up the commanding heights, the change has been great but incomplete. By privatizing airlines, telephone systems, and electric utilities, governments have stopped the financial hemorrhage and relieved the state of a considerable burden that carried high political stakes. The subsequent record of these privatized companies has, however, been uneven, and in some countries it is quite mixed. As privatization spreads across the continent, it also takes on different forms. In all of this, governments face a new challenge: regulating the new private firms that provide politically sensitive services, in some cases on a monopoly basis. Having repudiated the old state-owned firms, governments now sometimes lack the skills, the staff, the information, and the experience to ensure that private owners and contractors maintain high standards of service and are not allowed to collude to keep prices high or service inadequate.

The "technicity" of the technopols—a blend of education and credentials, professionalism and motivation, and a measure of luck and opportunity —does not spread deep in bureaucracies. These have been stripped of much of their means, and civil servants are underpaid and often demoralized. Provincial administrations and the agencies responsible for decentralized services such as primary health care and education do not enjoy the clout and efficiency of the central Finance Ministry. Tax collection is anemic. Local authorities are subject to corruption and cooption.

"The discovery of the market," said Moises Naim, a Venezuelan economist and former minister, "will soon force Latin American countries to rediscover the state," for the market cannot work with a malfunctioning state. Just how to refocus government toward alleviating poverty and regulating private enterprise, at a time when the state itself is discredited, is the special challenge of Latin America's reforming economies. The pioneers among them have gone further than anyone else in opening their "strategic" sectors to the outside world. They now routinely experiment with the most sophisticated technical tools of the market economy. But at the same time, there is no guarantee that electricity and other crucial infrastructure services, not to mention improved health care and education, will be delivered to the large numbers of people who are excluded. Failure to improve conditions will only redouble Latin America's already gaping contrast between rich and poor, and set the continent on a drastically different course from its rivals in Asia. It will also stir political jitters and memories of less democratic times.[16]

Bolivia, the country where shock therapy was born more than a decade ago, has recently provided an innovative approach to consolidating popular commitment to the move to the market. During his term as president of Bolivia from 1993 to 1997, Gonzalo Sánchez de Lozada and his reform team observed the ways that other countries privatized and decided that Bolivia should have a somewhat different approach, its own variation on the common theme. They would sell off the chief public enterprises, including those in energy and telecommunications, but in a particular way. Goni had in mind what happened high up in the Andes, where the Indians divided the harvest between those who owned the fields and those who worked them. He borrowed that approach for his program. For each sale of a state company, the government would select by a bidding process a strategic partner—typically, a consortium of foreign firms experienced at the job. The partner would own 50 percent of equity and wield exclusive management control.

Where Bolivia innovated was with the remaining 50 percent, which it handed over to national pension funds—whose management it soon privatized as well. At the end of each year, the pension funds, using the revenue of the privatized firms, are to pay out a dividend to every Bolivian above the age of sixty-five. The dividend has started off small—$250 per elderly Bolivian. But because it is more than 10 percent of annual per capita income, the amount is quite significant. Goni refused to call the plan *privatization*. In his mind, the word was too heavily loaded with ambiguity and negative political connotations. Instead, he found a word that had eluded Margaret Thatcher and so many other privatizers around the world. He called it *capitalization*—a term which tried to say that market opening and tangible welfare improvement can go hand in hand. The use of the pension funds accomplishes two fundamental objectives. The first is the application of the Asian principle of shared growth—giving the population a stake in the enterprise and direct benefits of its performance. The second is legitimacy, for a good part of the enterprise remains in the hands of the "people."

The current Latin American experience demonstrates that implementation of the new rules of the game is the beginning, not the end. With the market restored, attention returns to the rediscovery of the state. It is no longer to be the controlling, suffocating state, nor the state as business manager, but the competent state that can play an appropriate role of fair regulator—and address the heavy legacy of human needs. That script is still to be written.

CHAPTER 10

TICKET TO THE MARKET
The Journey After Communism

THERE ARE STILL those in America for whom the image is embedded in memory—either from the era itself or from some piece of film. The handsome young man stumping across the country, his hand slicing through the air, his Boston twang—and his ringing declaration: "We must get this country moving again."

Less well remembered than John Kennedy's refrain during the 1960 presidential campaign is *why* he said the country had to get moving again. Just three years before, in 1957, the Soviets had lofted the first *Sputnik* into orbit, shocking American self-confidence. And then, in 1959, Soviet leader Nikita Khrushchev had thrown down the gauntlet at a luncheon in Los Angeles, growling: "We will bury you." Soviet ideology and power appeared to be militantly on the march.

All of this was made possible by apparently high Soviet growth rates, much higher than American rates. If the United States did not get moving again, then capitalism and the West were going to fail in the race for world leadership and lose the allegiance of nations to communism and the Soviet Union. Kennedy argued that the future could belong to the West, but the confidence he expressed was not at all deeply entrenched.

Just three decades later, by the beginning of the 1990s, the race was over. The outcome was decisive. Communism, with its extreme state control, was defunct, bankrupt; the Soviet Union was fragmented; and Russia, its main successor state, was moving to turn itself into some kind of market society. The red star, which had captured the imagination and support of so many people, had dropped from the sky. All of this would have seemed quite improbable to John Kennedy in 1960.

The collapse of communism and the end of the Soviet empire constitute the defining events of the end of the twentieth century, just as the revolutions in Russia, along with World War I, defined its beginning. Nowhere else has the recasting of the relationship between state and market been so extreme as in the former communist world, for the upheaval has set off a turbulent struggle to establish market systems in the very countries where markets had for so long been banished. The communist system claimed to be the vanguard of the future, but it buckled under the pressure of its inner decay. The machinery of central planning and state ownership failed to foster innovation and distribute the benefits of economic growth—and then it failed to deliver any growth at all.

The pervasive economic failure of communism brought about the political revolution that, beginning in 1989, swept across Eastern Europe and the Soviet Union. When the collapse came, it happened so quickly that there was no time for considered adjustment. The successor states to the Soviet empire had no recipe for replacing the communist economic machine with capitalism, and in their first years of existence, they wrestled with travails that had never been anticipated and that were indeed almost beyond imagination. Many of the people in those countries felt as though they had been transported to the other side of the moon. The old apparatus of central planning and control disappeared, and all the rules that had governed economic organization and daily life were gone, with nothing at hand to replace them. Instead, people confronted hyperinflation, massive insecurity, a fierce battle for control of state assets, and what seemed to be pervasive chaos. The construction of market systems out of the rubble of communism is still very much unfinished. Yet for all the human pain of what is somewhat abstractly called "transition" and for all the unevenness of the process, most of the old Soviet empire has been brought into a market economy faster than was anticipated. That transformation—and the struggle of ideas that shaped it—is as compelling as the collapse of the communist states themselves and the demise, around the world, of their ideology.

Poland's Crisis: The Beginning of the End

The end of communism did not begin at the center, in the Soviet Union, but on the frontier, along the coast of the Baltic Sea. The huge Lenin Shipyards in the Baltic port of Gdańsk were meant to be one of the showpieces of the Polish communist state. In fact, discontent was rife among its workers. On a December day in 1979, many of them gathered in front of the green-gray gates for a memorial—to mark the massacre of protesting workers on the same spot by police and soldiers some nine years earlier. A stocky electrician with a droopy mustache worked his way to the front of the group. "I appeal to you to organize yourself in independent groups for your own self-defense," implored Lech Wałęsa, who had been fired by the shipyard for political activism. And, he said, if the government would not build a memorial to the slain workers, then all those there should return in a year, each bearing a stone, and they themselves would build the monument, stone by stone.[1]

What they built instead was the beginning of a movement, Solidarity, that would do the almost inconceivable in a communist country: challenge the government. The following August, workers in the same shipyard, some of them clambering down from half-completed ships, went on strike. Soon, thousands of workers were occupying the shipyard and representatives from other striking enterprises joined them. After almost three weeks, the government capitulated to their demands, including the right to form independent unions and to strike. Never had a communist government gone so far as to grant liberties to its citizens. Solidarity had won, at least temporarily.

The Polish opposition was made possible in part by something not available in any other communist country—the powerful support, both open and covert, of the Catholic Church. And yet the full weight of that support would not have been brought to bear were it not for an event in Vatican City two years earlier—the unexpected death of the newly anointed pope, John Paul I. He was succeeded by a Polish cardinal, Karol Wojtyła, the archbishop of Kraków, who took the name John Paul II in honor of his predecessor. In July 1979, John Paul II made a triumphant tour across Poland; one group he spoke to numbered two million. The visit of the Polish pope kindled a new sense of faith, confidence, and national unity; it also inspired the opposition. Educated in an underground seminary during World II, John Paul II had consistently stood against Communist Party power. During his years as cardinal, he helped nurture—at great risk—what became the democratic movement. Now as pope, he created a sanctuary for dissidence and mobilized the Roman Catholic Church as a powerful opponent of communism. During the August 1980 strike in the Lenin Shipyards, a portrait of the pope decorated the gates behind which the workers rallied. His presence seemed to give them strength. The powers in the communist world recognized what a dangerous antagonist they faced in the Polish pope.

Solidarity had emerged as a protest against deteriorating conditions— sinking standards of living and growing shortages. Indeed, the "shortage economy" would become the alternative name for the centrally planned communist economies. Since the late 1960s, the Polish economy had suffered from economic decline and an absolute inability to reform within a communist framework. Hungary had tried to implement reform by experimenting with a more flexible "market socialism," otherwise known as "goulash socialism." It introduced elements of a market system into the centrally planned economy. But, except for the private agriculture that survived in Poland, the Polish Communist Party leadership would have none of it. They stuck to orthodoxy.

Yet labor unrest meant that the leadership had to do something. Rather than try major reform, however, the Polish government in the early 1970s turned to the West, on the assumption that it could borrow its way out of its troubles. It contracted enormous loans, thinking it could use that money to keep food prices down, import Western technology, and thus improve its economic performance without tampering with the system. That turned out to be the fatal assumption. Easy finance led the country into a situation from which it would not be able to extract itself. By borrowing from the West, it took on huge loans that it could neither service nor repay. By the end of the 1970s, Poland's debt burden had reached $25 billion.

The Poles largely wasted the borrowed funds. Instead of bouncing back, the economy was doubly burdened by its structural problems and by the repayment obligations, which it could not meet. Poland soon faced a massive balance-of-payments crisis. It had turned into an enormous food importer, and yet it was now severely constrained in its ability to pay for food imports. Shortages were everywhere. In these stringent circumstances, following the occupation of the Lenin Shipyards, Solidarity grew. In a matter of months, its membership approached 10 million.

Moscow was progressively more alarmed by this unprecedented threat to communist power, and Soviet pressure on the Polish government became enormous. Some maintained that the Soviets were behind the May 1981 assassination attempt on Pope John Paul II in St. Peter's Square. Finally, in December 1981, after a year and a half of strikes and agitation, the government counterattacked. Tanks moved into the center of Warsaw, roadblocks sectioned off the country, and telephone lines were cut. The government declared martial law. Solidarity was banned; its leaders, arrested. Yet all that did nothing to improve Poland's prospects. Over the 1980s, the economic situation deteriorated further. Solidarity struggled to survive underground, and Wałęsa was under house arrest. Finally, in 1989, in a desperate effort to bolster the still-sinking economy, the Communists convened a national "roundtable," which included both Solidarity and Catholic Church leaders, to discuss the Poland's bleak future and initiate a more open dialogue.

The Phone Call

At this point, the Soviet Union, preoccupied with its own problems, was beginning to disengage from Eastern Europe. It started withdrawing its troops. Experts close to the Kremlin had begun to argue that the costs of empire in Eastern Europe outweighed the benefits, and they were heard. In Poland, in the aftermath of the 1989 roundtable, Solidarity was relegalized. The next step was free elections. The results were cataclysmic for communism. In the newly reconstituted Upper House, Solidarity won ninety-nine out of a hundred seats. In the Lower House, thirty-five Communist Party candidates were running unopposed. Still, in order to be elected, they had to gain over 50 percent of the vote. Polish voters—many of them bringing their children to the polling booths to witness their acts of defiance—carefully crossed out the names of the Communist candidates. All but two of the thirty-five Communists were defeated.

As so often in the past, the Polish regime turned to Moscow for directions. But this time the answer was different. Mikhail Gorbachev talked by phone with the head of the Polish Communist Party. Gorbachev's message was stunning. The Soviet Union, he said, would accept the outcome of a free election—in this case, a government with a Communist minority and a non-Communist prime minister. That phone call ended the cold war.

Solidarity hardly felt itself prepared to take power. It was a broad political coalition, a protest movement, not a party. With Solidarity holding only one third of the Lower House, its leaders worried about whether they should—or even could—take power. Their new economic adviser was Jeffrey Sachs, the Harvard professor whose role in Latin America had already earned him international recognition. One Solidarity leader told Sachs that the movement did not have enough votes in the Parliament to do anything and that Poland was an economic basket case. It certainly looked like a basket case, Sachs replied, but looks could be deceiving. Poland shared a border with Germany, it was in the center of Europe—and the Poles were not lacking in economic skills. In short, the results could surprise everyone. That was what Sachs had learned in Latin America. After hours of impassioned discussion, he finally offered a simple message: Do it; take power. The Solidarity leader sighed a very long sigh. "I'm very unhappy with this conversation," he said, "because I think you're right."

The Solidarity leaders asked Sachs and his colleague David Lipton to prepare the outline for an economic program for rapid and comprehensive change. "And, please," they were told, "start the outline with the words 'With this program, Poland will jump to the market economy.' We want to move quickly; that is the only way that this will make sense." Sachs said that he and Lipton would go back to the United States and write a plan. No, they were told, there was no time for that. It was needed the next morning. The two Americans stayed up all night, wrote a plan, and then went to Gdańsk the next day to meet with Solidarity members to explain it.[2]

"My Ludwig Erhard"

Tadeusz Mazowiecki became Poland's first nonCommunist prime minister in August 1989. He did not know exactly what sort of economic program he wanted, but he knew he wanted rapid action—and that he wanted someone who could implement the kind of program Sachs and Lipton had drafted. He was looking, he said, "for my Ludwig Erhard."

Mazowiecki found his Erhard in a Polish economist named Leszek Balcerowicz, who was the author of the economic program that would end up carrying not only Poland but also much of Eastern Europe, and even the Soviet Union, into the market economy. This was the year that communism collapsed, dominolike, throughout Eastern Europe. As the joke went, Poland took ten years to throw off communism; Hungary, ten months; Czechoslovakia, ten days; and Romania, just ten hours, which culminated in the execution of its dictator, Nicolae Ceauşescu. Through all of this upheaval, Poland led the way in terms of economic reform, and that was the work of Balcerowicz.

Balcerowicz had been preparing for this moment for two decades. He had spent two years studying business at St. John's University in New York City. Subsequently, he had investigated the dynamics of Korean and Taiwanese growth. At one point he went to West Germany to study Ludwig Erhard's reforms of 1948, which turned out to be a brilliant decision; when he was picked to be Mazowiecki's "Ludwig Erhard," he actually knew what Erhard had done. He had also assiduously examined what had worked and not worked in the various Latin American stabilization programs.

In Warsaw, from 1978 onward, he had directed what became known as "the Balcerowicz group," a long-running study group that was devoted to analyzing the "problems" of socialism and the question of how to reform the Polish economy. It focused on such basic questions as property rights, the proper role of the state in the economy, inflation, and what was increasingly becoming the true hallmark of socialism—shortages. All of this convinced Balcerowicz that "gradualism" was doomed to failure. Unless enough changes were combined and applied rapidly, the necessary "critical mass" would not be reached. Unlike many economists, he also dabbled in social psychology. He was particularly impressed by the theory of cognitive dissonance. As Balcerowicz summed up its significance for economic reform: "People are more likely to change their attitudes and their behavior if they are faced with radical changes in their environment, which they consider irreversible, than if those changes are only gradual."[3]

Market Revolution

Balcerowicz became finance minister and deputy prime minister in the new Solidarity government on the condition that the only transition he would implement would be a very rapid and massive one. It became known by the term already popularized from Latin America—*shock therapy*. But Balcerowicz preferred the term *market revolution*. Whatever the name, he knew the policy would be very risky and would meet much opposition. But of one thing he was sure: Gradualism would certainly not succeed. Over the next few months, Balcerowicz and his team worked feverishly to devise a plan and write all the laws that would be necessary. They did so amid an ever-worsening economic situation. Inflation was now running at an annual rate of 17,000 percent, making Poland the fourteenth case of hyperinflation in history. By this time, the country was in default on a debt of $41 billion, and many enterprise managers were engaged in what was euphemistically called "spontaneous privatization"—stealing as quickly as they could the assets of the enterprises they managed.

January 1, 1990, was the day of the "big bang," the promulgation of Balcerowicz's shock therapy, the critical salvo in the market revolution. And it was a shock—a decisive break with the communist past. Most prices were freed. The currency, the zloty, was devalued and made convertible. Controls were imposed to forestall an explosion in wage increases. The government deficit was to be reduced from 7 to 1 percent of the GDP. Taxes were reformed and a restrictive monetary policy put in place.

Balcerowicz and his colleagues waited nervously to see what would happen. They knew prices would go up, but they estimated a 45 percent rise. Instead, prices jumped 78 percent in a matter of days. Reserves of grain, meat, and other foods were low and the shortages continued. They held their breath. Food riots, demonstrations in the street—these could undermine the entire reform program and send Poland spinning back to authoritarianism. But by the end of January, something began to happen. First in a trickle, then in growing numbers, farmers started to drive into the cities from the countryside, bypassing the state distribution system and selling their produce from cars and trucks or on the sidewalk. Industrial wares showed up in the same way. Instead of demonstrators and rioters, Poland had acquired merchants overnight. As shortages disappeared and supplies increased, prices started to come down. Balcerowicz's aides tried to reassure their tense boss by telling him to focus on eggs. Yes, eggs would be the critical indicator of success or failure. By the end of the month, it was confirmed: The price of eggs had leveled off, and in some parts of the country, it had actually declined. Balcerowicz heaved a great sigh of relief. The eggs constituted a great victory. Markets were working.[4]

Yet shock therapy was a shock, and criticism and opposition rose very quickly. Gradualism, many argued, was the better way to go. Underlying the debate was a fundamental difference of mind—between those who looked, even after communism, to the state to be the arbiter and those who had confidence in the dynamics of markets. The press was filled with articles about the decline in the standard of living and the GDP. But the assertions failed to take into account the fact that official GDP numbers did not capture what was happening in the new, still "informal," market. There were constant calls for propping up and reviving the huge state industrial concerns. To Balcerowicz, this would be throwing good money after bad, for so many of the firms no longer had a purpose, a market, or a future, and were extremely inefficient and wasteful. In too many cases, they existed in their current dimensions only because Stalinist economic dogma had ordained that they should exist.

"Stop Looking to the Top"

Balcerowicz had to fight off attacks from many quarters. To an angry convention of Solidarity members in Gdańsk, he declared, "We have to break away from old habits and attitudes. In particular, we have to stop looking to 'the top,' to the state, because it is a relic of the old way of thinking." Again and again he had to remind Wałęsa, who was elected president in December 1990, that economic failure would mean disgrace.

Meeting John Paul II at the Vatican, Balcerowicz was forced to answer the pope's stern question as to whether it was possible to create a "just market economy in Poland." He endured all sorts of abuse; he even had to deal personally with angry individuals who managed to get into the Ministry of Finance, demanding to see him. He was thankful that his government security officers also happened to have degrees in counseling.

The privatization of the large state concerns proceeded slowly. To begin with, while Balcerowicz regarded privatization as "the key part of the institutional restructuring," he saw no point in trying to privatize before stabilization and the creation of what might be called a market society. Otherwise, privatization would become meaningless in the "chaos of hyperinflation." Subsequently, when a Polish system was devised for privatizing large firms, it proved to be cumbersome and ponderous.

If that part of the reform program was disappointing, other parts greatly exceeded expectations. Nothing so dramatized the birth of the new economy —or made it possible—as the explosion of small business. Between the end of 1989 and mid-1992, over seven hundred thousand new companies were registered. In mid-1997 the number was over 2 million. The "shortage economy" disappeared as a consumer-oriented system emerged. Real wages rose sevenfold between the end of 1989 and June 1992. By 1992, the new private sector was generating over half of the entire GDP. The predicted mass unemployment did not occur because the new private firms created 2 million new jobs within two years. Poland was importing more, but now it could be paid for. Its imports and hard currency exports doubled between 1989 and 1993, and many of the exports were items such as consumer appliances—something that no one had predicted. Geography—Poland's being close to Germany and the rest of Europe—and freedom to trade turned out to be much more valuable assets than had been anticipated. The most extraordinary outcome of all was Poland's overall performance—economic growth averaging 6 percent a year since 1994. People started to talk about Poland not as a basket case but as Europe's "new tiger."

By that time, Solidarity had lost much of its luster, owing both to acrimonious infighting and the social discontent that came with shock therapy. Still, when the former Communist Alexsander Kwasniewski defeated Wałęsa for president of Poland in 1995, Kwasniewski made clear that he had no intention of diverting Poland from its economic course. Wałęsa departed from office embittered by his defeat in a free election. Yet he also owed himself a great measure of satisfaction. His courage and conviction had been decisive. And so much had been achieved in so little time. In the 1997 parliamentary election, Solidarity emerged the leader of a coalition government. The new finance minister was Leszek Balcerowicz, who had written the script for Poland's market revolution.[5]

The Two Václavs

Czechoslovakia was considered one of the greatest achievements of Wilsonian national determination to emerge from the mapmaking at the Versailles conference after World War I. It fused two linguistically similar but culturally different Slavic populations of the Austro-Hungarian Empire—the Czechs and the Slovaks—into a new state. Despite the high hopes, its history proved mostly unhappy. Dismembered at Munich in 1938 and then brutally occupied by the Nazis during World War II, it managed only three years of independence before falling under communist control in 1948. In 1968, Soviet tanks crushed the effort led by Alexander Dubček to create a "socialism with a human face." Finally, in 1989, four decades after the communists seized control, dissidents succeeded in implementing a relatively smooth transition to democracy. It was carried out under the tutelage of the writer Václav Havel—imprisoned under communism—who provided the moral authority and vision for what became known as the Velvet Revolution.

As it turned out, however, the Czechs and Slovaks had no great desire to maintain the marriage made at Versailles. After experimenting with an unpopular "dual household," they followed the Velvet Revolution in 1992 with the amiable separation of a Velvet Divorce. Slovakia, with its preponderance of inefficient military-oriented state enterprises, would prove slow to change. But the Czech Republic, the geographically more western and economically more advanced part of the former nation, turned swiftly to the market under the aegis of the two Václavs—President Havel and Prime Minister Klaus. If Havel was the embodiment of principle and democratic values, Klaus was the man responsible for what happened economically. He led the reforms that rapidly turned the Czech Republic into an economic success story. He also found himself sometimes criticized by Havel for not giving enough consideration to the social costs of shock therapy.

Václav Klaus was, to turn around an old phrase, gamekeeper turned poacher. As an economist in one of the hardest of hard-line communist regimes, he had been entrusted by his bosses with the critical responsibility to "know the enemy"—to read, analyze, and master such dangerous advocates of market liberalism as Hayek and Friedman. The problem was that the more he studied their work, the more persuasive and convincing he found them. Amid the war of ideas, he underwent a battlefield conversion. "I am proud," he once said, "of having been . . . accused of being a Friedmanite and a Chicagoan, even in the dark days of communism." He even wrote an essay entitled "The University of Chicago and I." Liberal ideas governed his policies when he launched the Czech version of shock therapy in January 1991, exactly one year after Poland's. As far as Klaus was concerned, there was no alternative. The debate between shock therapy and gradualism was irrelevant and unrealistic when it came to the realities of transition. "Such a choice doesn't exist, because governments don't have as much control as they think over the speed," he explained. "What we do know is that the more they put brakes on the transformation, the more costly and painful it will be." [6]

The Czech program followed along the lines of Poland's: immediate freeing of most prices, currency convertibility and devaluation (combined, in this case, with import surcharges to provide some protection), and tight monetary policies. The effects were much the same as in Poland—a great burst of inflation to begin with, and then a quick settling down, followed by strong economic growth. There was, however, one outstanding difference between the two countries. The Czech Republic went for quick and massive privatization, on the premise that it was better to get property into private hands than wait for restructuring or a fully developed legal and institutional framework. As early as 1990, some property was returned to the people from whom it had been confiscated when the Communists came to power in the late 1940s. The government experimented with a variety of privatization measures. The best known was a voucher system. Books of vouchers were sold to all citizens over the age of eighteen who wanted them. These vouchers, in turn, could be used either for direct purchase of shares in companies or for indirect purchases through voucher funds.

To be sure, the Czech Republic went into its "market revolution" with certain decided strengths. Its experience under communism notwithstanding, it was a country with a strong mercantile tradition and a historic orientation to the West. Some argue that on the eve of World War II it was more technologically advanced than Germany. It had relatively little trouble returning to the market.

The Soviet Command Economy

In the Soviet system, there was no obvious battle between government and market for a very simple reason—because there was, at least officially, no market. In the 1920s the communists had tried to run a mixed economy, permitting private ownership in agriculture and small business so long as the state held the commanding heights (Lenin's dictum). It did not work. Shortages spread, as did recriminations between the followers of Trotsky and those of Stalin and Bukharin. As Stalin rose to power, he clamped down on both economic and political life. He nationalized production, and by the end of the 1920s, with the initiation of the first five-year plan, the "command economy" was born.

In the command economy, supply and demand were irrelevant; they were exiled. Resources were allocated by bureaucratic decision rather than by the tens of millions of individual choices that add up to supply and demand. What mattered were the preferences and goals of the political leaders, which were implemented through the mechanisms of central planning. At the center was a series of government agencies that made the whole system work. Their names all began with *gos,* which is an abbreviation of the Russian word for government. Gosplan determined the plan, while Gosten set prices and Gossnab allocated supplies. Labor and wage policies belonged to Gostrud. With the coordination of the Communist Party, the ministries in Moscow were responsible for all the critical decisions—what a firm would produce, where its supplies would come from, what those supplies would cost, who the customers would be, and what the price to the customers would be. They also decided the number of people who would work in the enterprise, what they would be paid, and what kind of investments would be made. In practice, the process of planning also involved a lot of negotiations with enterprise managers and local party and government officials.

The economic tests of profitability and efficiency were not part of the Soviet system. What really mattered was "fulfilling the plan"—or at least being seen as fulfilling the plan. Oil drillers were not judged on whether they found oil at some economically sensible price; they were judged by how many feet they drilled. From the 1930s into the 1970s, this system enjoyed immense prestige around the world, for it was seen to be delivering the goods in terms of rapid industrialization and high growth rates. The draconian concentration of resources did deliver high growth as it moved the Soviet Union from agriculture to industrialization—most spectacularly in the military-industrial complex, whose expansion and technical prowess had so alarmed John F. Kennedy's generation. But that concentration spelled neglect for agriculture, services, and consumer goods. It also imposed extreme rigidity on the system, breeding inefficiency of all sorts. The system became even more complicated and irrational. The key to its apparent success in the 1950s and 1960s also proved, over the long term, to be the source of its downfall.

Certain markets did exist on the fringes of the system, in the shadows, but they had a crucial role in lubricating the entire system and actually enabling it to work. A tiny proportion of arable agricultural land was available for private farming plots. However reluctantly, the state officially sanctioned these private plots—and a good thing, too. Although postage stamp–size by comparison to the state and collective farms, they proved essential, producing over 25 percent of the meat and up to 50 percent of the potatoes. No such official sanction existed for the black market. Its operators were denounced as "social parasites," and were sometimes imprisoned. Yet it, too, was essential to urban life. There were no chickens in the stores. But if you wanted a chicken for dinner, you could buy it on the black market if you knew "the man on the corner"—and many people did.

The command economy, as developed under Stalin and operated by his successors, did have a purpose. It was not, despite all the rhetoric, about the well-being and standard of living of the people; rather, it existed to promote rapid industrialization with which to feed the military-industrial complex. An enormous part of the country's GNP was concentrated in that sector, and

272

the overall economy was subordinated to its needs. While Soviet satellites circled the earth and the country's nuclear submarines prowled the seas, the system delivered a standard of living much lower than most people understood—in the 1980s, a level as low as one tenth the West's.

Already by the early 1970s, a fatal weakness was becoming clear in the system: It could not, for the most part, innovate. There was no reward, no reason to do anything new. In fact, there was a strong predisposition to avoid change of any kind, for change caused enormous bureaucratic headaches. The best thing was to keep doing what had been done before. In more advanced economies, innovation was essential to the promotion of economic growth. But in the Soviet system innovation was characterized mainly by its absence. And that applied to everything—whether it was small changes to make processes work better or the introduction of new products. The only exception was in parts of the military sector. Rigidity also applied to the overall distribution of investment. Year after year, vast amounts of money went into irrigation projects—twenty times as much as went into communications. "For twenty years there was no visible improvement in the harvest as a result of this huge irrigation project," said the Russian economist Yegor Gaidar, "but it was completely out of the question to reduce, even by a small amount, this investment because this was how it had been done a year ago, two years ago, five years ago, and ten years ago."

The growth rate plummeted. The system had been able to promote growth by brute force, but now its rigidity was preventing growth. Western technology was being imported, but as in Poland, it could not be applied very effectively. A good part of it simply rusted away. The system that had driven economic growth was now in the process of destroying itself. Yet just then, like the deus ex machina in a Greek tragedy, a savior appeared—but as it turned out, it was only on temporary assignment. It took the form of the vast oil resources in west Siberia, which were discovered and initially developed in the late 1960s. This oil became much more valuable in 1973–74, when the first oil crisis led to a quadrupling of petroleum prices. The Soviet Union, as one of the world's major petroleum exporters, benefited mightily. The enormous increase in hard currency earnings, from oil and then gas exports, provided the critical financial resources to keep the failing system going without forcing reforms or diversion of resources from the military-industrial complex. "It created the ability not to think about the crisis for a decade and a half," said Yegor Gaidar.[7]

The Marriage of the Hedgehog and the Snake

The succession of geriatric Soviet leaders in the early 1980s—Leonid Brezhnev, Yuri Andropov, and Konstantin Chernenko—was a fitting symbol for an economic system in advanced decline. It was only in 1985, when a younger, dynamic leader—Mikhail Gorbachev—assumed power that the leadership was willing to think about the crisis. Gorbachev came in intent on promoting reform. He was a child, as he described himself, of Nikita Khrushchev's 1956 secret speech to the 20th Party Congress denouncing Stalin and Stalinism, and he wanted to implement what Alexander Dubček had attempted almost two decades earlier in Czechoslovakia: socialism with a human face. Gorbachev initiated *perestroika*—restructuring—and what became known as *glasnost*—openness. That latter included an openness about the Stalinist past, and the subsequent revelations helped undermine the legitimacy and credibility of the system. Gorbachev wanted to reform socialism, to make it work, although he and those around him had no clear idea about how to merge central planning with the market economy or multiparty democracy with the Communist Party. His nemesis, Boris Yeltsin, would later describe Gorbachev's error as wanting "to combine things that cannot be combined—to marry a hedgehog and a grass snake."

The severe economic crisis became much more acute just after Gorbachev took over. Oil prices collapsed in 1986, severing a major part of the hard-currency lifeline at a time when the costly military-technical competition with the United States had intensified. Recognizing the crisis, Gorbachev took important steps that helped create a foundation for a market economy. He gave much more independence to directors of factories and other enterprises, who had previously been straitjacketed by the plan. And he gave some sanction to private firms, particularly with a 1988 law that legalized any company with three or more owners, counting it as a "cooperative." That was a door through which many people passed, and it was on the basis of this law that many types of enterprises—from manufacturers of weight-lifting equipment to restaurants to banks—were first built. "Cooperatives" proved to be a fig leaf for what were, in reality, private businesses.

Overall, however, Gorbachev's efforts to reform the old economic system failed. He dismantled the machinery of central planning, including the dominating position of the Communist Party, which had coordinated the complex system. But he did not replace it with anything. There was nothing left to keep the parts working together. He launched a vigorous anti-alcohol campaign to try to stem the endemic alcoholism that crippled the society. But the tax on alcohol and other liquors was one of the state's major sources of revenue, and the campaign ended up depriving the state of a great deal of money without contributing notably to national sobriety. The reduction in imports of consumer goods reduced work incentives, while the increased imports of equipment were either poorly used or not put to work at all. Inflation and shortages were much evident; there were now shortages even of simple things like detergent and spoons. The shelves in the shops became more and more empty; the lines outside them grew longer and longer. On warm days in the summer, there was no ice cream.

Meanwhile, the industrial sector of the economy continued to be enormously irrational, inefficient, wasteful, and polluting—to an extent that was almost incomprehensible. It took the Soviet paper industry seven times more timber to make a ton of paper than it took the Finnish industry. The price system was truly lunatic. The Swedish economist Anders Aslund catalogued some of the most stunning examples: Because of price controls, a ton of oil —worth about $150 on the world market—was worth about as much in rubles as the free-market price of exactly one pack of Marlboro cigarettes. The regulated cost of an airfare from Vladivostok to Moscow—a distance of four thousand miles, over six time zones—was seven dollars. But it cost ten dollars to take a taxi from Moscow's airport to a hotel near Red Square.[8]

Market Making

There was one central question now: how to move from a system in which there was no market to a market system. There were no recipes, no cookbooks for this transition, only the lessons and experience still being accumulated—very much on the run—in countries like Poland and the Czech Republic. But there were differences. Poland had 40 million people; the Czech Republic, 10 million. The Soviet Union, almost 300 million people strong, was a nuclear superpower. No one had ever faced the scale and the urgency of the Soviet situation.

Such was the legacy of Marxism and Stalinism that right up to the beginning of the 1990s, not one of the fundamental conditions for a market system existed in the Soviet Union or its immediate successor, the Russian Federation. There was no price mechanism to convey information about supply and demand. Nor were there any of the rules of the game—neither norms nor laws—to guide behavior in the marketplace. And there certainly was no system of contracts or private property rights. All this had to be built from scratch—and almost overnight. At the time, it seemed an almost impossible job—and there was no laboratory in which to practice.

To whom to turn? The Gorbachev-era economists were trapped in a no-man's-land between the dismal inheritance of a command economy on the one side and some kind of market economy on the other. Younger economists, however, were prepared to think more radically, in particular those grouped around the Institute for System Analysis and the Central Mathematical Economics Institute, both in Moscow, and a smaller, more informal network in Leningrad (now St. Petersburg). They had traveled to the West; they had been able to gain access to Western economic literature held in the *spetskhran,* the classified area in libraries that required special permission. They knew foreign languages well enough to read the Western writers. They had also become very cynical about their own system.

The turning point for one of them, Andrey Konoplyanik, came with his dissertation. He had been a very good and energetic Young Pioneer and Young Communist. In the late 1970s, he wrote a doctoral dissertation on the economics of North Sea oil. His adviser insisted that he begin the thesis with a learned quote and disquisition of Marx and Engel's views that would be relevant to North Sea oil. Alas, Marx and Engels had died many, many decades before the discovery of North Sea oil. Nevertheless, realizing that necessity was necessity, Konoplyanik found a quote. That was not enough. His adviser, reading the final draft of his dissertation, told him that he had made a very major mistake—an unacceptable mistake. He had failed to quote the then-glorious leader Leonid Brezhnev. But, insisted Konoplyanik, Brezhnev most assuredly had never said anything of value and relevance to North Sea oil. Instead of arguing, the adviser whipped out his pen and wrote into the draft dissertation a citation from the brilliant theoretical work of Leonid Brezhnev, meant to serve as the intellectual underpinning of the entire thesis. Thereafter, Konoplyanik could never take Marxism-Leninism seriously. He became part of a cohort of what might be called establishment dissenters.

Among the most prominent of this new generation of economists was Yegor Gaidar, who would do as much as anybody to move Russia toward a market economy. But he was also very much part of the past, in a peculiar way. "It's our family's fate to be so completely intertwined in the tragedy of Russia in the twentieth century," he said one afternoon, sitting in the long, wood-paneled study of his apartment on the edge of Moscow. Gaidar belonged to one of the first families of the October Revolution, and thus it was a special irony that he would help bring down the very system that his grandfather had helped create—and in which his grandfather held a mythic place. "My grandfather Arkady Gaidar was one of the biggest heroes of communism of the socialist era," he said. "He was one of the most famous people in our history."

Arkady Gaidar joined the revolution at the age of fourteen. By the time he was seventeen, he was commander of a Red regiment in the civil war. In time, he was held up as a role model and much celebrated for his courage and bravery. In the interwar years, he achieved even more fame as one of the nation's most beloved writers of children's books. He was a paragon of communist ideology. He died in 1941, fifteen years before Yegor Gaidar was born. But Yegor grew up under his grandfather's influence and shadow. "I worked hard to win gold medals at school just so I would not have to hear that I was not living up to my grandfather Arkady Gaidar."

With such a pedigree, Yegor Gaidar started out to be a very good communist himself. His father was a journalist, and the family was living in Havana during the first years of Castro's revolution. "It was still a very happy revolution, and it was a splendid thing for a boy," he said. "Che Guevara would come to our house, and I saw our country defending all good people in the world against American imperialism." His first doubts came with the Soviet Union's invasion of Czechoslovakia in 1968. "I had a lot of Czech friends, and I talked with them, and the official explanation of what had happened was impossible to believe." His father was something of a liberal, at least within communist terms, and around the family's kitchen table, the young Gaidar listened to his father and his father's friends talk about the Hungarian reforms, about goulash socialism, and about what Khrushchev had revealed about Stalin's crimes in his 1956 secret speech.

But perhaps the key turning point for Gaidar came when his family moved to Belgrade, then the capital of united Yugoslavia. The Communist leader, Marshal Tito, presided over a somewhat more open society in terms of debate and contacts with the West. Gaidar was particularly interested in the discussions about market socialism, which was then being applied in various forms in both Yugoslavia and Hungary. Returning to Moscow, he became part of a group of students and young professors who, at least in the late 1970s and early 1980s, thought that market socialism was the answer, that the Soviet Union could become more open, like the Hungarian system —an economy that mixed state control and ownership with private decision making and some private property. Yet even that was considered very radical. In 1986, a Soviet economist of the older generation asked a Western visitor to leave his office and walk down the street so that he could tell him a secret without the risk of being overhead by bugs. The secret? That the Soviet Union was much bigger than Hungary, that the Hungarian economic model could not be applied to the Soviet Union, and that it was offensive even to consider making the comparison.

By this time, however, the younger generation of economists was coming to an even more startling conclusion—that even market socialism could not work. Such a system could not deal with the meat-and-potatoes issues of wages, unemployment, and capital movements. Nor did it permit the creation of private property.

On all these questions, they were tremendously influenced by one author, János Kornai, a Hungarian economist who taught part-time in Budapest and part-time at Harvard. The one living economist who could claim to have influenced the minds of a whole generation living under communism was Kornai. He meticulously dissected the centrally planned system and demonstrated its irrationality and self-destructiveness. He also demonstrated the inadequacies of its would-be variant, market socialism. "He was the most influential on all of us in the 1980s," said Gaidar. "He focused on the practical mechanisms of socialism. His analysis of the economy of shortage, in the early 1980s, had a great impact on all of us. He was addressing our problems. We knew all his books."

Which among the Western writers were also influential? "Of course, Hayek," Gaidar replied. "He gave a very clear and impressive picture of the world, as impressive as Marx in his way." [9]

An Orderly Transition?

These young economists began to think about something more daring than market socialism: a transition, an orderly transition, to a market economy. But was an orderly transition possible? That will never be known because

e very late 1980s, the system was in such distress that there was no way
plement one. The economy was headed toward chaos and hyperinfla-

Between the end of 1989 and the summer of 1991, some fifteen major
economic programs were introduced, and most of them adopted, without any
positive effect. The most famous and influential was the radical program
developed by Grigori Yavlinsky and other economists. It did what no other
plan did at that time: Instead of reforming the Soviet economic system, it
advocated the system's transformation, at forced pace, into a market economy. It was the intellectual bridge between communism and capitalism in
the Soviet Union. And it was much influenced by what was already unfolding
in Poland.

Of all the countries in Eastern Europe, it was Poland—and the changes
there—that would matter the most for what transpired in the Soviet Union.
Poland was of special significance in the Soviet sphere. It was the largest of
the Eastern European countries, and also the most strategically important.
Stalin broke with his allies at the end of World War II over his bid to gain
control of Poland and incorporate it into his empire. Poland preoccupied
Soviet military planners thereafter; it was the potential invasion route. That
was why Gorbachev's phone call in August 1990—accepting a non-
Communist government—was so significant. And that was why economic
reforms in Poland were to have so great an impact on shaping what came
soon after in the Soviet Union. Grigori Yavlinsky was the man who transported the message and, so to speak, translated it into Russian.

Yavlinsky had given up on the centrally planned economy years earlier.
In his view, it was senseless and could not be fixed. In order to avoid
spending inordinate time reading Marx and Lenin, he had become a labor
economist. But when he did a critical report on conditions in coal mines, the
KGB began to interrogate and pressure him. He was threatened with expulsion from the Communist Party—a rather hollow threat as he was not, in
fact, a member. He then found himself hospitalized by force and subjected
to many treatments for an ailment he did not have. The treatments and
persecution stopped only when Gorbachev came to power. Yavlinsky was
then back in business as an economist. He ended up doing economic research for the Council of Ministers and was dispatched to Poland in 1990,
just in time to see the Balcerowicz reforms go into effect. "It was so amazing. I will never forget seeing how prices were moving down. It's very rare
for an economist to see prices come alive." He wrote a very positive report—
so positive that the appalled Soviet ambassador refused to send it. Yavlinsky
managed to slip it into the hands of one of Gorbachev's senior advisers, who
in turn sent it to Gorbachev, who distributed it to the Central Committee.

Back in Moscow, Yavlinsky told senior government officials that they
were wasting their time tinkering with the economy. It was time, he said, to
"stop lying." Instead, he began to develop a plan to radically transform it
into a market system. He was also much influenced by a month-by-month

analysis he had conducted of what had happened to the Japanese economy between 1945 and 1951. The Japanese experience, he concluded, was very relevant. "Japan, too, had experienced a catastrophe. If Japan could do it, why couldn't we? Japan's economy, of course, had benefited from the Korean War. That was a very painful thought for us. I kept thinking what could we do. I came to the conclusion that we could replace the Korean War in our recovery with natural resources."

Yavlinsky and his team laid out a plan for the Soviet Union to move to a market economy in four hundred days, subsequently amended to five hundred days. It was written under a joint mandate from Gorbachev, president of the Soviet Union, and Boris Yeltsin, president of the Russian Federation, which, at the time, had very little power. (During this period, Yavlinsky said to Yeltsin, somewhat undiplomatically, "You are president of a country that does not yet exist. You have no banks, no currency, no tools to do anything, nothing except an independent laundry." A bad feeling would persist.) Yavlinsky's plan eventually took shape as a report entitled, aptly enough, "Transition to the Market." It advocated speed—rapid reform of every part of the economy. The report was a landmark; it did not genuflect to Marxism. It rejected socialism and embraced the market, including swift price liberalization and privatization. But there was also enormous opposition to such ideas. They were not implemented, because no senior politicians wanted them. Gorbachev flirted and danced with them before finally veering away from reform and turning back to the right, to the old Communists, in order to hold on to his position. It would do him no good.

The crisis was worsening. Gorbachev considered privatization. At the same time, ethnic nationalism was being reborn within the borders of the Soviet Union, and Gorbachev initiated something else that was anathema to the traditional Communist hierarchy: He began negotiating a treaty with the fifteen restive Soviet republics on creating a voluntary union—with him as president. The crisis reached a climax in August 1991, when hard-line Communists mounted a coup. They put Gorbachev under house arrest in the Crimea. Despite their initial success, they met determined resistance— immortalized in the photograph of Boris Yeltsin astride a tank. Some of the plotters sank into an alcoholic stupor. The coup fizzled after a few days. Gorbachev returned to power for what proved to be four humiliating months, during which his power ebbed away and he found himself presiding over the dissolution of the Soviet Union. During this period, the Polish reformer Leszek Balcerowicz met Gorbachev in Moscow. "The Soviet Union is interested in discovering the Polish path to economic reform," Gorbachev told him. But it was much too late for the Soviet Union—or Gorbachev—to discover anything. As 1991 ended, the Soviet Union disintegrated. The fifteen Soviet republics had become fifteen independent nations, of which Russia was by far the largest and most important. Gorbachev handed over power—and the nuclear codes—to Boris Yeltsin, president of the Russian Federation, and became part of history.

Over the preceding few months, Yeltsin had been preparing for Russia's sovereignty and his assumption of authority. Shortly after the August coup, he had invited five competing groups of economists to come up with an economic strategy, and they set to work, in government dachas around Moscow, developing their competing programs. The various plans ranged from support for the military-industrial complex to a reform of central planning. Yegor Gaidar was the leader of the group calling for radical reform. He and his team were convinced that shock therapy was the only way to go.

Gaidar's theories coincided with Yeltsin's instincts. Having decided to move toward reform, the Russian president did not want to draw things out; he wanted to move forward as quickly as possible. "If our minds were made up, we had to get going!" he later said. Yet he was still wavering about whether to place his bets on—and risk his future on—the young Gaidar. But then he was reminded that Gaidar came from a special family—that of the revolutionary Arkady Gaidar, who happened to be one of Yeltsin's great heroes. That pushed him over. He chose Gaidar and his team.[10]

Revolution—Or Radical Reform

"As late as the summer of 1990," said Gaidar, "I still believed we could make an orderly, state-organized transition. But by the fall of 1990, it was evident that a blowup lay ahead; the system was falling apart and we were living through open inflation. A revolution was coming, like the Bolshevik or the French Revolution. In that kind of setting, no orderly reform would be possible, only crisis management. All of this was very well known to those of us who knew about revolutions." Gaidar paused for a moment, then added, "The only thing I could not foresee was that I would be in charge of managing that crisis."

In November 1991, Gaidar was made deputy prime minister and minister for finance and the economy. Even before taking office, he had done one very important thing: He drafted Yeltsin's October 1991 speech laying out the basic case for swift and massive economic reform. "The period of small steps is over," said Yeltsin. "A big reformist breakthrough is necessary." He summoned up the failed August coup: "We have defended political freedom. Now we have to give economic [freedom], to remove all the barriers to the freedom of enterprises and entrepreneurship, to give the people possibilities to work and receive as much as they earn, after having thrown off bureaucratic pressures."

However confident the words, the reality was very tough. "The vast majority of people in the world do not understand the dangers of November 1991," said Gaidar. "A nuclear superpower was in anarchy. The army was not reporting to anyone. No one knew what was happening. I can't overemphasize the dangers." Economically, it was chaotic too, with fifteen central banks in fifteen independent republics. "Everything was in a terrible, unbelievable mess," said Gaidar. "We had no money, no gold, and no grain to last through the next harvest, and there was no way to generate a solution. It was like traveling in a jet and you go into the cockpit and you discover that there's no one at the controls." Public finances were falling apart. The government deficit was 20 percent or more of the GDP. The old economy was plunging into a deep depression, with the output plummeting as the orders for tanks and other military equipment disappeared. Inflation was soaring, shrinking pensions day by day. Coal supplies were disrupted, and there was a good chance that Moscow and St. Petersburg would have no heat in the winter.[11]

Everything—As Rapidly as You Can

"Clearly, all our theoretical ideas about the proper sequencing of reform measures were nonsense," said Gaidar. "It was a time when you do everything you can do, and as rapidly as you can. There was no time for reflection." Gaidar and his colleagues knew what they had to do: prepare for price liberalization (i.e., freeing prices from controls), begin opening up the economy, and get ready for convertibility of the ruble and for privatization. The Yeltsin government moved quickly—more quickly than it wanted—to free prices and reduce the huge distortions that were doing so much to contribute to the crisis.

The most immediate problem was grain: The cities were running out of bread. And Gaidar and his colleagues well knew how important grain shortages had been in Russian history—helping to provoke the revolution in 1917 and leading in the late 1920s to the creation of the Stalinist economy. "I wasn't sure we would make it through the spring of 1992," said Gaidar. He feared food shortages, riots, and hyperinflation. There were no longer state procurement agencies—the legatees of Stalin's agents, who had requisitioned grain from the peasants in the early 1930s. As in Poland, all the government could do was count on the incentive of newly freed prices to solve the problem, and wait. In June 1992 the first harvest began to reach the cities.

Other controversial reforms were initiated and partly implemented. Many prices were decontrolled, and Russia started down the hard road of restoring public finances and reducing inflation. Foreign trade was liberalized and economic activity was freed. Military procurement was cut by 70 percent. Subsidies to enterprises were slashed, and attempts were made to reduce the cheap credits that enabled factories to continue to do what they had always done.

But opposition to the reformers intensified, delaying implementation, sometimes very nearly derailing the entire process. The enterprise managers and industrial bureaucrats had an enormous amount to fear from the test of the market. The military saw its resources disappear. The elderly held the reformers responsible for the high inflation that was devouring their pensions, not understanding that it was the cheap-credits policy of the central bank (whose head was opposed to reform) that was fueling inflation. Local politicians saw the enterprises that supported whole towns collapse. The social safety net was much frayed; the enterprises had provided their workers with the bulk of their social services—housing, child care, medical care, recreation. Perhaps the firms no longer had their military-industrial role, but if they shrank or collapsed, who would provide these services? Those who lived on state salaries—whether they were teachers or doctors or researchers in the institutes—saw the value of their wages decrease to the equivalent of less than fifty dollars a month.

And there was a fundamental difference in ideas. For managers, workers, and pensioners in the older generation, the "market" was a source of great stress, indeed some alien creature that had invaded their lives, attacking the body of society, disrupting all they knew, and devaluing their experience, throwing into question the very rationales that had governed their lives and justified their sufferings. This was also true of the older economists, even those who had been liberals under Brezhnev and Gorbachev. In short, they took the market to mean anarchy. They thought that either there should be a return to central planning or at least the state should still play the dominant role, controlling prices and wages. The market could not be trusted. It did not accord with Russia's unique situation. Fundamentally, what seemed to be unfolding before their eyes was immoral; it ran against their deepest instincts. Money made in the market was automatically suspect. *Speculation* was the all-purpose term of opprobrium and insult. Anything that smacked of trade was considered mafia. They had been accustomed, as part of the natural order, to the black Zil and Chaika limousines of the old regime roaring down the specially reserved central lanes on Moscow boulevards with their curtains drawn. That, they could accept. But they were repulsed by the growing number of Mercedeses filled with arrogant and tough-looking young men, holding cellular phones, and heavily made-up young women.

What has been described as a "ruthless populism" built up against the radical reformers, who showed no deference to the old system, to the apparatus that had resisted Hitler and put the first *Sputnik* into space. Yeltsin's vice-president—and later opponent—Aleksandr Rutskoi attacked Gaidar and his team as "small boys in pink shorts and yellow boots." In an effort to stabilize the political situation, Yeltsin made Viktor Chernomyrdin prime minister in December 1992. He had been the most successful industrialist in the country as the head of Gazprom, the state gas monopoly, which has since become the largest energy company in the world. He was widely respected and had enormous authority among the industrial managers. No one would dare say that he was a small boy in shorts. He also had the great virtue of not coming directly from the military-industrial complex.[12]

The actual reform process moved ahead, but in an uncertain way—

sometimes slowed down, sometimes reversed. But it continued to move. Yeltsin himself had no deep economic views, and he was under constant pressure to back away from reforms. But reform and necessity had their own inescapable logic. Whenever he heeded the advice of those who said to slow down or go into reverse, the results were disastrous. Inflation would rise dramatically or the ruble would collapse in value, and such developments would push Yeltsin back onto the path of reform.

By September 1993, Yeltsin and the parliament were deadlocked over reform. Social discontent was very high. Yeltsin dissolved parliament, but parliament refused to be dissolved. Its members occupied the "White House," the parliamentary building; Yeltsin replied by throwing troops around it—in effect, a siege. When armed supporters of the deputies tried to seize the mayor's office and the television tower, Yeltsin dispatched tanks through the streets of Moscow and ordered the use of cannons, setting the White House on fire and forcing the total surrender of the occupants. This was the same Yeltsin who twenty-six months earlier had stood on a tank in defiance.

In December, Yeltsin's opponents, capitalizing on the social distress, scored big gains in parliamentary elections. One month later, in January 1994, a shaken Yeltsin accepted Gaidar's resignation from the post of deputy prime minister. Viktor Chernomyrdin now took direct responsibility for the economy. In order to placate the opposition, the government retreated from financial austerity and opened the flood gates of credit again. The result was an astonishing collapse in the value of the ruble. Chernomyrdin had no choice but to resume the reform path. He had become converted to sound money and low inflation.

By then Russia was already a country of two economies: the old state-controlled Soviet military-industrial system—dedicated to mindless production, and despondent and demoralized and spiraling downward in decline—and a raw, ambitious new market-based society, responsive to consumers' needs and desires. The lead role in the latter was being taken, to a considerable degree, by younger people, the postcommunist generation.

The Essential Element: Creating Private Property

Yet there could hardly be a market system without private property. Yeltsin laid out the principle in his reform speech of October 1991: "For impermissibly long, we have discussed whether private property is necessary. In the meantime, the party-state elite has actively been engaged in their own personal privatization. The scale, the enterprise, and the hypocrisy are staggering. The privatization of Russia has gone on, but wildly, spontaneously, and often on a criminal basis. Today we have to seize the initiative, and we are intent on doing so."

Yeltsin entrusted the implementation of privatization to a group of young economists, who formed the nucleus of the State Committee on the Management of State Property, which became known by its Russian initials as the GKI. Its head was an economist named Anatolii Chubais, who had graduated from the Leningrad Institute of Engineering Economics in 1977 and subsequently taught there. Although he had been a member of the Communist Party committee at his institute, he also became the leader of a semi-underground local group of young economists who studied and debated reform. He was appointed chief economist for the city of Leningrad, which was returning to its old name of St. Petersburg under a reformist mayor, who wanted to attract Western capital and make the city a market showcase. As part of his responsibility, Chubais oversaw the privatization of shops and small businesses. Then he was tapped to go to Moscow as a senior member of Gaidar's team. He was to demonstrate considerable talents not only for economic analysis and policy making but also for bureaucratic infighting and sheer politics, and would eventually become Boris Yeltsin's campaign manager in 1996 and the presidential chief of staff. But it was in implementing privatization, against odds that could only be called insurmountable, that he was to truly hone his skills.

For Gaidar, Chubais, and those around them, privatization had one central objective. Chubais described it as the creation of "a broad stratum of private owners." Or, as he said, to make reform and the end of communism "irreversible." In short, they set out to create a large property-owning population that would have a stake in the market economy and that therefore could counterbalance the managers, bureaucrats, party apparatchiks, angry nationalists, soldiers, and nostalgics. This objective shaped the entire process and provided the reformers with the tenacity required to overcome the opposition and the obstacles.[13]

That was the goal. But how to attain it? The privatization process was, in the words of some of Chubais's chief advisers, guided and made possible "by the power of some key economic ideas." The first was a conviction that Russians belonged, like the rest of the world, to the species *homo economicus* —economic man—and would respond to economic incentives. In the early 1990s, the dominant view was quite different, whether it emanated from Russian politicians or older Russian economists, or traditional Western Sovietologists. Russia had been ruled by Bolsheviks for three quarters of a century, and the results had been catastrophic for people in the market economy. The soil left behind, it was said—and no doubt rightly—was not exactly the fertile sort from which entrepreneurs could be expected to spring easily. Nationalistic opponents of privatization claimed that Russia was different, a special case, that Russians were not like other people. Critics said that Russians were lazy, given to alcoholism, and that their attitude toward work was summed up by an epigram under communism: "They pretend to pay us, and we pretend to work." But to Chubais, all this had less to do with DNA than with the system of economic organization. If the incentives and

institutions were there, he believed, people would act accordingly. He si
did not buy the "Russians are different" thesis.

The second idea was that Russia's central economic ailment was [
cal control and domination and that the cure was to take economic activity
out of the hands of bureaucrats and ministries to the greatest degree possible.
That would also reduce corruption by decreasing the necessity to ask bureaucrats for permission to do things. All this led to a commitment to mass
privatization. Russia did not have time for careful Western-style privatization
—on a case-by-case basis, after careful evaluation and restructuring. If it
took its time, by the twenty-second century it would still be privatizing, the
bureaucrats would still be in control, the economy would still be stagnating
—and there would be plenty of potential for attempted U-turns back to
communism.

The third idea was one that grew out of a view of property. Legally
recognized property was not immutable; rather, it amounted to a collection
of rights. Government by itself did not really own the assets that were to be
privatized; they belonged, in varying measures, not only to the state but also
to the managers, employees, and local authorities. Each of them had certain
rights, and the managers, employees, and local authorities constituted the
"stakeholders." Thus, concluded the Chubais team, if privatization was to
succeed, all the stakeholders had to get a piece of the action, to be part of
the deal. The stronger the coalition, the better the chances of success against
the entrenched bureaucracies. That meant that one more group of stakeholders was essential—a group that did not yet exist as stakeholders: the general
public.

Yet circumstances seemed most unpromising. The parliament tried to
block privatization; the ministries attempted to reassert their control; and
enterprise managers stole whatever assets they could get their hands on.
Amid all of this, Chubais's GKI set out to design its program. The first
step was to "corporatize" state-owned companies, rechartering them as
joint-stock companies, with the state initially holding all the shares. The
directors came from the government—but from the GKI, not from the traditional ministries. That created another bottleneck. Private property can exist
only within a framework of contracts and laws, and the GKI ran up against
a problem that would astonish people in a country like the United States—
an acute shortage of lawyers.[14]

A Ticket to the Free Economy

The reformers concluded that the Polish model of privatization, with its
case-by-case sales and mutual funds, had not worked very well. But the
Czech model, which handed out vouchers on a mass basis, was more promising. And it had the potential to reduce corruption insofar as it elimi-

nated back room-negotiated deals and made privatization as transparent as possible.

The Russian government issued vouchers, worth ten thousand rubles each, to every Russian citizen, children included. They could be picked up at local offices of the state bank for a nominal transaction fee. Eventually some 144 million out of 147 million Russians received their vouchers. They looked like currency and were like currency—up to a point. They could be exchanged for shares in companies through the mechanism of auctions. For Yeltsin, the vouchers became the symbol of privatization. "We need millions of owners rather than a handful of millionaires," he declared. "The privatization voucher is a ticket for each of us to a free economy."

Vouchers became the first liquid security in modern Russia. People could hold on to them and acquire shares in specific companies (or the company in which they worked), exchange them for shares in mutual funds, or sell them. Markets grew up for the buying and selling of vouchers, which could even be bought in local bazaars. In west Siberia, women sold vouchers from stalls, "just like carrots or cabbages." The price fluctuated between four dollars and twenty dollars. The designers of the program had struggled over the critical question—what share of a company the current managers and employees could obtain and how much the public and outside investors could acquire.

The first major privatization was the Bolshevik Biscuit Factory, in 1992. (The workers won control in that transaction and then ended up selling a controlling interest to France's Danone, parent of American Dannon Yogurt.) Thereafter, the program moved ahead despite constant attack by the parliament and by the ministries and politicians who sought to stop the process or gain control over it. The opponents appealed to nationalism, national security, and the unique Russian character. The minister of publishing said that all publishing houses should remain in government hands because "publishing is our ideology." The transportation minister argued that all trucks must belong to the state because they would be needed for mobilization in war. But the coalition strategy worked and the momentum was maintained. Some nine hundred thousand workers a month moved from the state sector to the private sector via voucher privatization. Vouchers were popular; indeed, the song "Wow Wow Voucher" reached number five on the Moscow hit parade.

The voucher privatization program ran for less than two years. It began in October 1992 and was over by July 1994. During that time, the greater part of Russian industry was privatized. A property-owning stratum had, indeed, been created. There were many stories of workers bilked out of their vouchers—and of managers manipulating the shares. Still, as a result of the program, some 40 million people were shareholders, either directly in companies or as members of mutual funds. Both insiders—the managers and workers—and outsiders—the public—had a stake in these private firms. Privatization in itself did not, by any means, answer the problem of restructuring. Rather, it was a precondition. But it did provide the incentive for companies to do better, to improve their products, to find markets and adapt to them, and to manage costs.[15]

The privatization of the medium- and larger-size firms was only part of the process. The state also owned housing, which for most people meant apartments. Yet in many cases, those who lived in the apartments had quasi ownership. Apartments were passed down as inheritances, from generation to generation. The occupants could buy their units at very low cost, and by October 1994, some 10.5 million apartments were in private hands.

Shops and small enterprises were left to their localities. Here the program began with the auctioning off of a few shops in the city of Nizhni Novgorod. Under the watchful eye of television viewers across the country, a group of sturdy women went from total despondency at the thought that they were about to "lose" the bakery in which they had worked for so many years to uncontrollable glee at learning that they had just won the bidding for the store. It became quickly evident that the quality of service in stores that had been auctioned was higher than the service in the stores that had merely been given away to the members of the "collective" who had worked there.

There were important limitations on the privatization effort. "Strategic" and certain defense companies from the military-industrial complex were spared the privatization process on the grounds that their important national mission could not be risked. The reformers realized that opposition would be much stronger for these politically sensitive and well-connected companies than for others, and the better part of valor was to get done what they could get done rather than risk losing the entire battle. In a later stage of privatization, banks were able to acquire a substantial number of shares still in government hands by loaning money to the revenue-starved government. Some observers saw this as an ill-concealed method to strengthen the hands of insiders, with whom the banks were closely allied, or for banking groups to acquire shares on the cheap. Others argued that such strong outside shareholders would promote restructuring.

There was one very large exception to Chubais's voucher privatization. Yuri Luzhkov, the popular mayor of Moscow and a principal ally of Yeltsin, managed to get much of the state assets in Moscow excluded from the national program. Instead, the city sold them or leased them out on its own terms—to the great benefit of its coffers. Under Luzhkov, who was reelected mayor with 90 percent of the vote in 1996, Moscow is undergoing a vast refurbishment, replacing the shabbiness of Soviet days with color and frenetic construction. All this—combined with the speed with which Moscow has raced ahead of the provinces—has led to a reformulation of Stalin's 1930s dictum about "socialism in one country." Moscow has become "capitalism in one city"—or, as one Russian politician put it, switching communist theoreticians, "Moscow and the rest of the country are like Deng Xiaoping's theory—one country, two systems."

Since becoming mayor in 1992, Luzhkov has emerged not only as the city's boss but also as one of the country's most important politicians. While maintaining close relations with Yeltsin, he has become an outspoken critic of the reformers in the Yeltsin administration—dismissing them as the "youth squad"—and castigated their reform and privatization policies as something that "could only occur to theoreticians far removed from everyday life." He delights in describing the "heartburn" he causes them. Luzhkov favors intervention, state capitalism, and a strong hand. "The Russian being has always counted on the government," he explained. "To break that tradition would mean to force upon the people not reform but betrayal." Luzhkov makes his presence felt in everything from decisions about the construction of the new underground shopping mall near the Kremlin to the promotion of Russkoye Bistro, a fast-food chain he set up to compete head-on against McDonald's. Luzhkov may well aim to be Yeltsin's successor as president. On foreign affairs, he strikes a more aggressively nationalistic posture than Yeltsin. Recognizing the importance of the media, Luzhkov has had Moscow establish its own national television network. The city controls the offices and services of the national newspapers, and their coverage of the mayor is more cautious than that of other politicians. And, with the city holding hefty financial resources, Luzhkov is building alliances with cities in other regions. Luzhkov leaves no doubt as to who calls the shots in Moscow. Given the results evident in the city, his brand of reform certainly gets a very receptive reaction from those who have been whipsawed by the turbulence and disorder of Russia's modern revolution.

When everything is added up, what is the overall judgment on Russian privatization so far? The answer, not surprisingly, is hardly simple. The program is impressive, all the more so because of the almost impossible challenges it faced, and yet there is an enormous amount still to be done. The scale is awesome. By 1996, some 18,000 industrial enterprises had been privatized—including more than three quarters of all large and midsize industrial firms and something close to 90 percent of industrial production, bringing the proportion of industrial workers employed in the private sector to 80 percent. Over four fifths of small shops and retail stores are also now privatized, including 900,000 new ventures established by Russian entrepreneurs. And 70 percent of GDP is generated in the private sector.

But privatization is no longer at the top of the hit parade. It has lost its popularity for many reasons—not the least of which are the job cuts that go with restructuring. It is also associated in the popular mind with other afflictions—high inflation, the disappearance of the social safety net, and widespread social distress, especially for the elderly. The blunt fact is that corruption and inside dealing were features of the privatization process—which, combined with suspicion of the whole process, soured the public. Some people, by cornering assets and assiduously aggregating coupons, have gotten very rich. Many others see privatization as theft of the labors of the "Soviet people"—whether they believe the perpetrators are the nomenklatura (the old Communist bureaucrats and managers) or the mafia and shady speculators or the banks and financial institutions of the new Russia. Criticism ranges across the spectrum, from the old communists to the new democrats. "Privatization is not working because they are not creating private property," said Grigori Yavlinsky. "They are creating cartelization."

According to the National Russian Survey, a comprehensive joint Russian-U.S. project, privatization was never as good as the high hopes for it—or anywhere near as bad as the current criticism. Something on the order of three-quarters of the privatized Russian firms are thought to be in need of radical restructuring, and a good part of those in turn are actually bankrupt. Many of the managers simply do not have the capacity, experience, competence, or desire to restructure. It takes outside ownership to force change.

Much of that could come through the new financial-industrial groups that have emerged as potent political and economic forces. Great fortunes have been made out of the transition years—by accumulating privatization vouchers, taking advantage of subsidized credits, and selling at world prices commodities acquired at low domestic prices. But will the growing impact of banks and other financial institutions promote modernization, or will it simply mean a new concentration of economic and political power in what critics call cartels and "financial oligarchies"? The ultimate consequences of privatization will be known only when that question is answered.

Certainly, there is a lot more to do on privatization. In the meantime, a substantial amount of ownership has been depoliticized. Yet despite the newly created fortunes, Russia remains a country of "capitalism without capital." The success of restructuring will require the development of financial markets, which can efficiently provide the capital that industry needs—and at the same time support the development of skills and competencies that a market economy requires. That, in turn, goes back to the basic question: the rules of the game.[16]

"The Massive Retreat of Government"

While privatization has advanced the objective of the depoliticization of Russian economic life, government—at the federal, provincial, and local levels—continues to exert heavy political control over the economy through arbitrary taxes, regulations, and direct intervention. But now, against government power, stands the countervailing force of private property. And private property has become the basis for economic activity and market institutions. Indeed, along with the freeing of prices, privatization has set in motion forces that will carry Russia forward into the world of market economies and that will be very hard to retard, whatever the political events ahead. Privatization stalled after 1994. From 1995 onward, the government's biggest economic achievement was on the macroeconomic front. In the face of great skepticism, it did an outstanding job in bringing down inflation and stabilizing the ruble. It also began reining in the state budget. The leader in all this was a convert to economic orthodoxy, Viktor Chernomyrdin. These efforts laid the basis for economic recovery. But in other ways, reform faltered during this period. The government wasted huge amounts of money in subsidies and cheap credit to industry. The disastrous war in Chechnya claimed tens of thousands of lives and wasted billions of dollars.

The presidential election of 1996 demonstrated the difficulties ahead. Yeltsin managed an extraordinary political resurrection. He went from popular approval of just 5 percent to victory several months later—over a number of candidates in the first round, including an outspoken Grigori Yavlinsky and then, in the runoff, over Gennadi Zyganov, the Communist candidate. Yeltsin's campaign was well funded by the new rich, who feared that they would lose a great deal were the Communists to win. In the hurly-burly of the runoff, Yeltsin's advisers forgot to mention that he had suffered a heart attack on the eve of the election. Nevertheless, his victory reaffirmed the nation's reform course—and the fact that a steady 60 percent of voters has supported reform in a series of elections and referendums since 1993. At the same time, the tepidness of many Yeltsin voters ("the lesser of two evils") and the strong showing by the Communists demonstrated the estrangement and outright hostility of many Russians to the emergence of the market system.

And for good reason. Even as the new economy grows, the old one continues its decline. The nation suffers severe environmental problems—a lasting inheritance from communism—for which it has few funds for remediation. Russia's infant mortality rate is three times that of the European Union countries. Life expectancy for Russian males has fallen to fifty-seven years, compared to seventy-two for males in the United States and sixty-seven in China. Pensioners go for months without receiving their pensions; workers, even longer without receiving their wages. The predictability and physical security (for the average citizen) of the communist era are gone; the low-level but universal social safety net is in tatters. Nonpayment of bills is endemic in the economy—beginning with the government, which cannot collect taxes.

The pervasive problems of corruption and crime threaten the legitimacy of the new system and undercut the consensus necessary to its effective functioning. The extent of corruption is not surprising. Hundreds of billions of dollars of state property were up for grabs; the scramble to get a share was bound to be frenetic and rough. Corruption has been further promoted by the lack of clarity and uncertain speed of reform, both of which have provided plenty of opportunity for favors and private deals. Foreign investors are not on secure grounds; Russian partners can still abscond with a joint venture, and courts hardly provide a recourse. Organized crime—the Russian mafia—has managed to extend its tentacles deep into the new economy. Protection rackets are endemic, and the rich, well-armed criminals are more than a match for a demoralized and underpaid (and sometimes unpaid) police force.

The 1996 election was followed by eight months of lassitude. The main item on the agenda after Yeltsin's victory was his open-heart surgery. His recovery was marred by double pneumonia,which left both his allies and his opponents focused, to an unusual degree, on his physical fragility. The Duma (parliament) continued to be dominated by antireform forces, both Communists and nationalists. The political system had become what has been described by Russian analyst Lilia Shevtsova as a "hybrid regime," made up of "seemingly incompatible principles of democracy, authoritarianism, populism, oligarchy, nepotism, and even anarchy." The most striking development since Yeltsin's reelection has been the growing political power of the new business elite concentrated in the seven big banks, which dominate the media and are gaining control of significant parts of industry. Just a few years ago, the heads of these banks were poorly paid engineers, scientists, and academics. Now they are billionaires, and known as the oligarchy. "They are oligarchs," said one prominent politician, "because they have money, power, and the media." And they unabashedly wield their power in the continuing struggle over ownership of state assets.

It was only after Yeltsin's recovery early in 1997 that the commitment to reform renewed. The first sign that "Boris the czar" had bounced back was another housecleaning by Yeltsin and the appointment in March 1997 of Anatoly Chubais as first deputy prime minister. A memo for Chubais warned him of the risks of not coming to grips with the urgent problems of the budget, taxation, pensions, and corruption. Taxation was particularly difficult, as the rates were ridiculously high and confusing and the actual collections ridiculously low. Overall, the authors of the memo declared, the government was facing an "extreme lack of trust," and failure to make progress on these issues would "destroy the credibility of the entire reform effort." The memo also urged him to isolate the "odiousniks"—the antireform "odious ones"—in the government.

Shortly thereafter, Yeltsin appointed another first deputy prime minister —Boris Nemtsov, a physicist-turned-politician. As the popular governor of the province of Nizhni Novgorod, Nemtsov had pushed the pace of reform faster there than in any other region. He proudly styled himself a "provincial" who had come to Moscow. When Yeltsin was courting him, Nemtsov asked him, "Boris Nikolaevich, how do you want to go down in history. As a good and great tsar . . . or do you want the contrary?" Yeltsin replied, "I do not want to live in a bandit state." On the basis of that, Nemtsov took the post of first deputy prime minister. He saw a good part of his job, as he put it, in implementing "understandable, clear rules, which are identical for everyone." For, he explained, "the period of initial accumulation of capital —which always, even in America, was accompanied by banditry, corruption, lobbyism, and so forth . . . that period is ending in Russia."

Yeltsin's new team is seeking to reinvigorate reform—from continued budgetary and tax reform to regulation and control of monopolies to the construction of a new safety net. The government also has to find a way to solve the politically explosive problem of getting workers and the elderly their unpaid wages and pensions. At the same time, Yeltsin and his team have sought to distance the government from the oligarchy—the bankers— and rein them in. "The state will not put up with any attempt at pressure from the representatives of business and banks," Yeltsin firmly told the Russian parliament in the autumn of 1997. And he declared that the retreat of government was over: "From the policy of nonintervention, we are going resolutely going over to a policy of preemptive regulation of economic processes. . . . In itself, the market is not a cure-all. In any civilized state, the market mechanism and state regulation work in harmony." The fundamental mandate has now changed. It is no longer to dismantle the Soviet system but rather to create a modern government. "The Russians are building a new state," said Thane Gustafson, an expert on Russia's new capitalism, "not a Soviet state that is owner and direct manager, but rather a regulatory state that is the referee over the playing field."

This means getting the rules in place so that people can make decisions with greater confidence and predictability. On banking and securities regulation, considerable progress has been made on both rules and operations. In 1993, there was no real stock market in Moscow. In 1996 and through most of 1997—spurred by Yeltsin's political and physical recovery—the Russian stock market was the best-performing emerging market in the world. Increasing investment is flowing in from the West, and the officially reported volumes have risen from $5 million a day in 1996 to upward of $100 million a day in 1997 (until the turmoil). By one estimate, at least three hundred companies could qualify for Western equity investment.

The biggest failure—and biggest threat to reform—continues to be the legal process, particularly as it relates to property rights, which are still the fundament of a market system. The legal system functions poorly; courts are underfinanced and beholden to local political forces. "The major impediment to private investment is that ownership is still not clear and the legal system does not protect property rights," observed Sergei Vasiliev, one of Yeltsin's chief economic advisers. This is a particular threat to new businesses, whether small or not. Several hundred thousand new firms have appeared. These entrepreneurs are particularly vulnerable to corruption and uncertain taxes, the unwanted "management hand" of local and state politicians, protection rackets, and the demoralizing threats—or worse—of violence. As Vasiliev noted, "Violence is much more dangerous to the market than corruption. You can fight corruption by deregulation, but you cannot fight violence by deregulation." Yet those new companies bring innovation and dynamism, new people and new ways of thinking, and they will have a major role—bigger than many anticipate—in shaping the new economy and creating the jobs it requires. They are the innovators that must be nurtured. As Thane Gustafson observed, "The most serious shortcoming for the future of a prosperous Russia is the slowness with which small business is developing."

With all that said, the speed of change in Russia has nevertheless been enormous. The "transition" is past. "Russia is a market economy," as Yegor Gaidar put it, "a young, immature market economy, but still a market economy." Its prospects could turn out to be better than is conventionally expected. Perhaps the analogy—for all of the differences—of Japan's economic miracle is relevant. Indeed, the basis may already be in the process of being laid for a Russian economic miracle—a *chudo*—by the beginning of the next decade. The country possesses a highly educated population with considerable skills. For the first time in seven decades, its great scientific and technical capabilities are linked to the marketplace—something heretofore impossible. A postcommunist generation has already emerged, eager to partake in the building of a modern industrial country. An enormous pent-up demand for goods and services, built up over decades, waits to be satisfied. The nation, now open to international trade and commerce, is tied into the global community by the enabling technologies of computers, Internet, telephone, and fax. Indeed, the impact of being plugged into the world economy after three quarters of a century of isolation could prove enormous. And the country possesses a huge abundance of natural resources. What it still needs are the rules of the game.[17]

The Vodka Maker

Continuities wind through history. More than a century ago, in Tolstoy's masterpiece *Anna Karenina,* the painter Golenishchev complained about "the new Russians." They were commercial people, he told Anna and Count Vronsky, garish, devoid of culture, and focused on wealth. That is almost exactly the same critique that some members of the Russian intelligentsia make today when they talk about the modern "new Russians." And yet it is the new Russians who will create this postcommunist economy.

One of the most famous faces in Russia today belongs not to a politician or a media star but to a thirty-three-year-old engineer-turned-entrepreneur, whose photograph adorns what is now one of the best-selling vodkas in Russia. The visage belongs to Vladimir Dovgan. Husky, with black hair and a thick black mustache, he has the focus and willpower, along with the conviction and persuasive skills, that often animate entrepreneurs, whatever their country. A vivid example of Russia's new entrepreneurs, he operates out of a modern office building on the bank of the Moskva River. As a reminder of the risks of the new Russia, security at the building is tight. Outside, one runs through a cluster of guards, then passes through two sets of thick security doors, only to be met inside by more guards, who carefully scrutinize visitors.

Dovgan's experience underlines the role—despite the focus on restructuring existing enterprises—of new business as a source of growth and innovation. For him personally, it is really a case of reconnecting a cord that had appeared to be irreparably severed by bolshevism decades earlier. He grew up in a small village in the taiga of the Far East. His father, orphaned at the age of eleven when the rest of his family was killed by communists, wandered eastward until he ended up in Siberia. His mother's father had been an entrepreneur.

There were few prospects in the taiga, and in order to get Dovgan a decent education, his parents decided to move back to European Russia. Moscow was impossible—they did not have a permit to live in the city, and in any event the waiting time for apartments was twenty years. Instead, they went to Togliatti, on the Volga River, six hundred miles south of Moscow, where a giant joint-venture auto factory was being built with Fiat. The plant was slated to produce hundreds of thousands of cars a year, and workers were needed. There, the family could get an apartment, and their son, an education. After studying at an engineering institute, Dovgan went to work on an auto assembly line. A talented athlete, he wrote a small book on karate in the late 1980s. It sold six hundred thousand copies. That provided the capital which, along with his restless energy, led him, after Gorbachev had legalized cooperatives, to start a small machine-making venture for the food business. However, as the Russian economy plummeted in the early 1990s, the business ran into trouble. He started a franchise pizza company that flopped because the franchisees did not pay attention to quality.

But then one night he had a dream—literally—about vodka. "I saw a bottle of vodka with the label DOVGAN VODKA on it," he said. Tens of thousands of people were dying every year from impure vodka, and, reflecting on his dream, he thought that he could develop the business in a new way. He switched his team from machine building to learning everything they could about vodka making. Within a few weeks they were producing their own vodka; and it was not all that long before they were the market leader, producing dozens of different types of vodka. Dovgan has kept a relentless focus on things that had never mattered in the Soviet economy—consistent quality and quickly developed but carefully conceived design work that is integrated into marketing (which did not exist in the Soviet Union). Each bottle comes with an exquisite label that includes the portrait of none other than Vladimir Dovgan, in a tuxedo. His message is that he stands behind his product. On the other side of the label is another picture, of a prerevolutionary Russian—his grandfather. Billboards for his products are all over Moscow. Dovgan is now producing dozens of other food products—from sardines to macaroni—all emblazoned with the same two photographs. Every bottle of vodka, each can of food, comes with a Dovgan lottery number. Every week the numbers are drawn on a Dovgan television show; the lucky winners get a car or a trip to Paris. The viewership is immense.

Dovgan is always trying to move on. "I erase information I don't need," he said. "A part of me is always in the future." He has established a management school for his employees, which they attend on weekends.

"These are people who should not know limits. We need to create a launching pad for new businesses. If somebody has a good idea, we are in the business within a year." He has also introduced other things that are new: brainstorming sessions and highly intense, concentrated meetings that are known, translated from the Russian, as the "Japanese sweat-squeezing working system." Altogether, over the last few years Dovgan has established about thirty companies, which range from foods and beverages to chemical distribution to construction to printing and publishing. Rather than buying up food factories, he contracts for their services—teaching, for example, an old-style Soviet sardine company how, despite its antiquated equipment, to interface with the new marketplace. "Last week," he said, "I was in the Astrakhan region. Several years ago, if we had discussed the idea of bringing the plants there back to life, we would have been looked at like a crazy person. But now they come to us and ask for help to restart the plants.

"It may seem that in Russia, as in a traffic jam, there are no rules. But people are beginning to understand that they need rules. For example, taxi terminals died out in Togliatti. They went bankrupt. But when I went back recently, I found that the whole city is full of taxis with great service, mobile phones, and low prices. I believe that I saw a real miracle. Not a big miracle, but a miracle." Those are the kinds of miracles that Russia awaits.[18]

CHAPTER 11

THE PREDICAMENT

Europe's Search for a New Social Contract

IN 1941, on the island of Ventotene, off the coast of Italy near Naples, Altiero Spinelli and two fellow prisoners set about to write a manifesto for a new Europe, a united Europe. Were it not for the desperation of the time, it would have seemed a quixotic undertaking. Hitler had conquered Western Europe, his troops were rolling across the Soviet Union, and panic had gripped the Soviet leadership and population alike. The United States had not yet entered the war, and Britain was virtually the last point of resistance to total fascist control of Europe. Yes, Europe seemed about to be united— but by Hitler's Reich, not by democratic self-determination. In such circumstances, Spinelli's manifesto, composed in prison, seemed less like a vision than a hallucination, a dying man's feverish dream of a better world.

By this time, however, Spinelli was a hardened survivor. He was in the fourteenth year of his incarceration. He had joined the nascent Italian Communist Party in 1924 to fight the dictator Benito Mussolini and his Fascists, who had just seized power. In 1927, at the age of twenty, Spinelli was sentenced to prison for organizing opposition. Had he said the right words to the court, he might have been spared jail, but he refused. In 1937, repulsed by what he had managed to learn in prison about Stalin, he renounced communism and instead became a democratic socialist.

Not long after, he was transferred to Ventotene, where the emperor Nero had been exiled almost two thousand years before and where the Fascists kept many of their political prisoners. There he began to read smuggled books, pamphlets, and articles—many by British thinkers who argued that Europe should follow the model of the American Revolution and create a federal union. Spinelli was also much impressed by what he read of the Federalist Papers and by the thinking of the American founding fathers.

Here, in these "Anglo-Saxon" tracts, he found the solution to the cataclysm that had engulfed the world. And in collaboration with two other prisoners, Eugenio Colorni and Ernesto Rossi, he set out the solution in what became known as the Ventotene Manifesto. It argued that nation-states were inherently self-destructive, for they bred nationalism, which became virulent, leading to dictatorship, economic crisis, and war. The only way to avoid such catastrophes was through the creation of a federal Europe, in which individual countries would become more like the American states. The economic component of this plan was a socialist version of the mixed economy. The manifesto was smuggled off Ventotene by Colorni's wife, who even managed to get published the first issue of an underground newspaper, *European Unity.* But it is hard to believe that anybody paid much attention at the time. There were more immediate things to worry about, such as survival.

Two years later, in 1943, the tide of war turned. The Soviets had held on the eastern front and were beginning to push the Nazis back. The Allies had landed on Italy's coast, and Mussolini had fallen. Released, Spinelli returned to the Italian mainland with the manifesto in his pocket, a few ideas in his head, and a handful of people who would look to him for leadership. His former fellow prisoner and coauthor Eugenio Colorni died from a beating that fascist thugs gave him on a street in Rome. Spinelli later married Colorni's widow, who had smuggled his work out of Ventotene. He also made his way to Switzerland, where he established contact with a few like-minded Europeans and launched what became the movement for European unity. The Ventotene Manifesto would be their rallying cry. Yet in the last months of the war, and then in the immediate postwar years, there was not much interest in European unity. The immense problems of reconstruction and the emerging cold war dominated thinking. But Spinelli's decade and a half as a political prisoner had engrained two things deeply into him —determination and patience. And in 1947, with the Marshall Plan, the first foundations of European unity began to be laid.

Four decades later, by the 1980s, the European Economic Community was a reality. Europe had achieved a level of income and prosperity inconceivable at the end of World War II, and despite the cold war, the peace had held on the Continent. Still, nation-states continued to control their own economies. Jean Monnet, the "Father of Europe," was dead, and Altiero Spinelli was now the grand old man of Europe. He was also becoming increasingly disappointed and disillusioned. For all that had been achieved, the European project had been stagnating for years; it was not much more than a glorified customs union. What kept coming to his mind was *The Old Man and the Sea,* by Ernest Hemingway. "You must all know the short story by Hemingway," he told the European Parliament in 1983, "about an old fisherman who, after catching the biggest fish of his life, tries to get it back to shore. But bit by bit the sharks eat it, so that when the old man returns to shore, all that remains is a skeleton." That, he feared, would be the fate of federal Europe. He was ready for one last campaign. Already in his late seventies, he took the lead in launching the battle for a treaty for European union. His campaign was the catalyst for a new stage in European integration, much closer to the dream he had had on Ventotene—the dream of a federal Europe.[1]

The Double Retreat

At the end of the twentieth century in Europe, where the mixed economy and the modern welfare state were born, the economic role of the state is in fact being significantly reduced—from two directions. On one side, the nation-state's capacity to manage its economy is being sharply restricted by the broadening of the powers of what has now become the European Union, the implementation of the "single market," and preparations for a common currency.* On the other side, the state is retreating by means of privatization, deregulation, and reduced intervention. The realm of competition is expanding. At the same time, there are increased pressures to rein in and reduce the expansive welfare state. As Europe unites, companies and workers are becoming part of a system that flattens—and indeed transcends—borders. Instead of looking to a national regulator, firms must reorient themselves to compete against other firms that can muster Continent-wide resources. Failure to do so can mean outright failure, since the traditional safety net of the national bailout no longer exists.

While the players in national economies are hastily preparing themselves for far more intense competition, the full impact awaits the introduction of the euro, the currency of a united Europe, at the end of the 1990s. Paper money—with its images of monarchs, presidents, prime ministers, finance ministers, generals, and heroes—embodies national identity. Control of currency is one of the essences of sovereignty. Handing over that control to supranational institutions truly represents a diminution of national sovereignty.

Movement in this direction started in the mid-1980s, with the campaign by Spinelli and others to revive the European project. But it was preceded by a dramatic reconceptualization of the role of the state in the marketplace and the wholesale emergence of a new kind of socialist—socialists without socialism. And nowhere on the Continent did this occur more vividly than in France, for it is the country of Colbertism (named for Louis XIV's domineering finance minister) and *dirigisme* (as the French call their traditional

---

* The European Economic Community or "Common Market," founded in 1957, became in 1987 the European Community, which in turn in 1992 became the European Union, its current nomenclature.

298

system of centralization and state economic control). The changes in France set the stage for the changes in Europe.

France: "The Break with Capitalism"

Paris is a city on whose streets national politics, at critical moments, are acted out. And May 10, 1981, was such a time. That evening, the city exploded with old-fashioned fervor and joyous street parties. All this was to celebrate the election of François Mitterrand as the first Socialist president under the Fifth Republic. It was a very close race, but Mitterrand had done it. A few days after the election, he visited the Pantheon in the Latin Quarter to pay respects to the dead; he paused an especially long time by the mausoleum of Jean Jaurès, the great French socialist leader of the turn of the century and patron saint of the noncommunist left ever since. Mitterrand was clearly laying claim to being his heir, and with very good justification. He was coming to office committed to creating a socialist France, declaring war against the "wall of money," and delivering the decisive and long-promised "break with capitalism."

Mitterrand and his Socialist comrades in the new government were determined that the government would, in the name of the people, build upon and expand France's traditional *dirigisme* and exert much greater direction over the economy through both nationalization and other kinds of control. That was what all those celebrating supporters expected, and that was what Mitterrand delivered—for a time. The French Socialists began with the boldest drive in recent decades to implement "more state" in the industrial world—all the more striking as it took place contemporaneously with Margaret Thatcher and Ronald Reagan's efforts to move in the opposite direction. Mitterrand's program was an amalgam of Keynesian economic management, nationalization, and state control. But ideology would not be able to resist cold economic realities.

Mitterrand was a master survivor in French politics. The man who would be France's president until 1995 was already a cabinet minister at age thirty in the 1946 Ramadier government, at the end of World War II. In the days of the Fourth Republic, he was on the center-left, a Radical. Like Charles de Gaulle, he knew the importance of playacting and self-creation, and over the years he cast himself as a thinker and man of letters —though not without reason, considering his literary gifts. He also seemed the perennial challenger—losing the presidency first to de Gaulle in 1965 and then, by the slimmest of margins, to Valéry Giscard d'Estaing in 1974. In 1981, he went back for a return bout against Giscard. And that time he won.

The 1981 victory was the result of a decade of work by Mitterrand and his allies to recompose—indeed, dramatically transform—the left in France.

In the ten years from 1971 to 1981, they built an organizationally strong Socialist Party to replace the weak and compromised remnants of the left from the Fourth Republic. In addition, they forged a unity pact with the Communist Party that portended class warfare and much greater state control of the economy, including extensive nationalization.

Indeed, the Socialists could not advance without the Communists. Even at the end of the 1970s, the French Communist Party was a potent political force, frequently winning 20 percent of the vote in elections. Still characterized by a sectarian Stalinist gloom, the dour French party had eschewed the internal reforms and debates that had moderated the Italian and Spanish Communist parties into what became known as Eurocommunism. In the new government, Mitterrand gave the Communists just four ministerial places—out of a total of forty-four. All were secondary posts. At the same time, he took care to signal the rest of the world not to worry. On the very day that the Communists entered the government as ministers, he made a point of receiving as his guest of honor Vice-President George Bush.

Mitterrand and his associates were determined to assert government sway over the economy. They launched a broad set of measures intended to stimulate the economy out of its sluggishness. In the classic Keynesian tradition, the government would spend on a vast scale in order to jump-start the economy. At the same time, the state increased its control and coordination of the major industries to ensure that they acted in the "right way." It nationalized banks (96 percent of deposits) and many large industrial companies, including thirteen of the twenty largest industrial corporations, and took controlling shares in many other companies. It vastly increased social spending, cut an hour from the workweek with no loss of pay, increased paid vacations from four to five weeks, and hired another hundred thousand government workers. This program of public spending and nationalization, along with increased taxes on high incomes, became known as *la relance*—or "the relaunching."

But *la relance* immediately set off widespread panic in the capital markets, leading to continuing assaults on the value of the French currency. Instead of stimulating growth, *la relance* bred inflation, stimulated capital flight, and drained money out of the treasury. Unemployment increased dramatically. The newly nationalized industries were losing enormous amounts of money, contributing mightily to the swelling budget deficit. France was heading for bankruptcy, and the Socialists, for disaster. Mitterrand and his colleagues had to be saved from themselves.[2]

M. Delors and the Second Left

That task fell to Jacques Delors, who was once described as the "most successful European Socialist of his generation." The son of a messenger at the Bank of France, Delors certainly grew up with better working-class credentials than the graduates of the elitist *grandes écoles*. When the Germans marched into Paris in 1940, young Delors and his mother fled by train, truck, and foot, finally finding refuge with his grandparents in the countryside. The conditions of the war and its aftermath denied Delors the opportunity to go to university. Instead, he found a low-level job at the Bank of France, took courses at night, and proceeded to rise by dint of intellect and hard work. He was an autodidact; he never stopped studying. One of his early mentors, the politician Pierre Mendès-France, once said of him that "Delors is a good workhorse—his asset is to be self-taught and therefore concrete." He was obsessed with American jazz and film and even established his own film club.

He also became a socialist, although not a Marxist. He once described himself as "the only man on the French left" who had "never been fascinated by communism and Marxism." Instead, he was drawn to the Catholic left, and in particular to the philosophy of Emmanuel Mounier, who died in 1950 at age forty-five. Mounier propounded what became known as personalism, which advocated solidarity, community, and an internal spiritual renewal as well as a political renewal. It set itself as much against the individualism of liberal capitalism as against Marxism and totalitarianism. Over the years, Delors would read and reread Mounier, whose ideas would provide the underpinnings of his politics and his commitment to the European model for the social welfare state.

While still working at the Bank of France, Delors became active in the Catholic trade union, and soon emerged as head of the union's research department. His gift for offering simple, understandable explanations of complex matters helped thrust him forward. Many years later Mitterrand, commenting on Delors's clarity, asked, "How do you manage it?"

"If I'm clear, it's because I have had little education," Delors replied. "As I'm not clever, before understanding something I have to make a huge effort."[3]

In the early 1960s, Delors went to work for the Commissariat Général du Plan, which had been founded by Jean Monnet after World War II to guide France's reconstruction. His work caught the eye of senior officials, including Charles de Gaulle, and Delors began to advance up through the bureaucracy. At the same time, he was active in politics, in the "Second Left," which rejected Marxist dogmas of the traditional so-called Jacobin left and was critical of statism and bureaucracy. At the end of the 1960s, Delors became economic adviser to a reformist Gaullist prime minister, which engendered great suspicions among other Socialists. He had, they thought, gone over to the other side. Nevertheless, as the Socialists reorganized themselves in the 1970s, François Mitterrand, who cared much more about politics than economics, recognized that he needed help, and he brought Delors in from political purgatory to be head of the international economics department of the Socialist Party. With the Socialist victory in 1981, Delors became Mitterrand's finance minister.

"Cash-Flow Incinerators"

Delors was not swept up in the same euphoria that engulfed his Socialist colleagues. After all, he was the only one among them with practical experience in government. Immediately upon taking office, he tried to calm the panic in the capital markets over the Socialist program. He sought, unsuccessfully, to minimize the nationalization campaign. But his room for maneuvering was slim. His Socialist credentials were problematic in the eyes of many; although he was the finance minister, he was only sixteenth in the order of protocol, and the budget function was hived off and handed to a young Mitterrand protégé, Laurent Fabius, who was enthusiastically promoting the Socialist agenda. Delors was not able to prevent Fabius from driving vast increases in social spending. He had to sign off on those expenditures, as well as on the billions of francs in compensation to the expropriated shareholders of the now-nationalized companies. He then had to find still billions more to cover the companies' losses. The nationalized companies proved to be, in the words of one businessman, "cash-flow incinerators," and the government's losses continued to mount. The overall economic situation deteriorated rapidly, and throughout 1981 and 1982, the franc was under constant pressure.

Now began a battle to alter radically the course of the Mitterrand government. It was led by Delors. "On board this locomotive, I was the one demanding that we put less coal in the engine," he once explained. He eventually found an ally in prime minister Pierre Mauroy, who had come to see that the spending frenzy was not bringing the promised results. He and Delors conspired to impose discipline and austerity and to combat the leftist "Jacobins" who dominated the government. They would sometimes win Mitterrand's assent by day, but by night, influential "evening visitors"— nicknamed after the title of a famous French film—would slip into the Élysée Palace to see Mitterrand and lobby otherwise. The evening visitors urged protectionism and told Mitterrand that France should delink its currency from the other European currencies, particularly the deutsche mark. Mitterrand, who believed that political will could overcome economic problems, would backtrack and endorse the positions of the evening visitors.

The struggles were played out in the cabinet as well. "There is no option but growth," one of Delors's opponents declared in a cabinet meeting. "We have to mobilize savings, launch major borrowing campaigns."

"All you talk about is borrowing," Delors retorted. "And when we come under International Monetary Fund receivership, you'll blame me. There is no money left. We cannot borrow!"

"We have to reduce consumption, cut back on purchasing power," added Delors's ally, Prime Minister Pierre Mauroy.

Silent up to this point, Mitterrand abruptly interjected, "I did not appoint you here in order to pursue Mrs. Thatcher's policies." [4]

Yet political will could do only so much in the face of economic reality. The balance of payments was in awful shape, and getting worse. The speculative assault against the franc was relentless. France even had to resort, however humiliatingly, to an emergency loan from Saudi Arabia to try to stem the speculation against the franc.

The Great U-Turn

March 1983 proved to be the critical moment for France, and in a certain sense for Europe. The Socialists did terribly in local elections. Tensions worsened. How to break out of the inflationary cycle? How to protect the franc? What was, after all, to be done? It was at this dismal moment that Delors, with Mauroy, engineered what became known as the Great U-Turn.

The critical issue was money. In 1978, Valéry Giscard d'Estaing and German chancellor Helmut Schmidt had negotiated the European Monetary System (EMS), which tied the franc and several other currencies to the deutsche mark, allowing them to fluctuate only within agreed limits. Now the franc was persistently straining the lower bounds of the system, and some—including the "evening visitors"—argued it should simply be taken out. Delors, however, was convinced that a breakdown of the EMS would be devastating for European unity. He persuaded a skeptical Mitterrand that exiting the EMS would reduce the franc's value by 20 percent, resulting in an enormous increase in interest rates, which would further hurt the economy and weaken the balance of payments. Then, in a weekend of talks in Brussels, Delors blustered and threatened the Germans into agreeing to a compromise: A revaluation of the mark would accompany the devaluation of the franc, and France would stay in the system. Mitterrand rewarded Delors by making him head of a superministry of economics, finance, and budget, moving him from sixteenth to second in the order of protocol.

Delors's success brought an end to the devaluations. From here on, France would keep its currency closely linked to the D-mark. Because the D-mark was strong, the franc would be strong too. Thus was born the policy idea and powerful symbol of the so-called *franc fort,* or "strong franc." And the requirement of a strong franc meant that growth could not come from artificially high exports, protectionism, or uncontrolled public spending. Instead, it could come only from increased productivity. By recommitting to the EMS, the Socialists were shifting their focus from the demand side to the supply side. France was also now lodged much more firmly in the market and institutions of the European Economic Community. It could no longer think in the traditional national perspective.

The stabilization of the franc through the EMS was the beginning of the Great U-Turn. The reestablishment of the EMS meant that the original Socialist program was out the window. Inconsistent with the currency imperative, it could not be pursued. International financial markets had gained a

303

major veto over national economic policy. Recommitment to European monetary cooperation also meant that the economy had to be modernized and made more efficient. Holding back productivity were a number of profoundly archaic, antiquated structures in the French economy, including many that were strangling banking and the stock market. In fifteen frenetic months, Delors began the great task of modernization that his successors would carry on. Delors also took a very hard line against the traditional policy of bailing out troubled companies. In 1984, the steel and engineering group Creusot-Loire, once a crown jewel of French industry, stood on the verge of bankruptcy, felled by international economic change and the rise of new competitors. Arguing that twenty-five thousand jobs were at stake, management demanded a state rescue package. Delors said no. "This was our third time helping Creusot-Loire," he said. "I opposed the plan because once again, it would have meant privatizing the gains and socializing the losses. That's why I refused their blackmail over bankruptcy and the loss of jobs." [5]

Socialists "Efface the State"

After the Great U-Turn, the Socialists maintained their new course of market reform. They controlled spending and continued to modernize the financial sector so that nationalized companies could turn to capital markets and not just the government for funding. This, combined with the sell-off of subsidiaries belonging to state-owned companies, constituted the first steps in what was a sort of "backdoor" privatization. Instead of the "break with capitalism," their rhetoric was now peppered with words like *modernization, industrial dynamics, efficiency,* and *competitive technology.* The change was evident even in Mitterrand's language. "The state," he declared, "must know how to efface itself."

Yet from 1983 onward, Delors's position as French finance minister deteriorated. It didn't help at all that he had been proved right or that his personal popularity had remained relatively strong compared to the other Socialists'. Mitterrand was a crafty, cunning politician. He liked intrigue and maneuvering, and he was not at all comfortable with Delors, who was a Catholic socialist and a devotee of personalism and had a huge appetite for work. Indeed, at one point Mitterrand complained, "Delors smells of the sacristy." He feared being outshone by Delors. Explaining to Delors why he had not made him prime minister in 1983, Mitterrand—recalling a tenth-century dynasty—said, "You would have been the grand vizier, and I would have been the *roi fainéant* [the "lazy king"]."

When Mauroy resigned as prime minister in July 1984, Mitterrand told Delors once again that he would not become prime minister. To make matters worse, Mitterrand then proceeded to appoint Delors's nemesis, the thirty-nine-year-old Laurent Fabius, as the next prime minister. But there was one position in which Delors was most interested. The presidency of the European Commission, the executive and administrative arm of the European Economic Community, was opening up. Delors had become convinced that the real playing field was not bounded by national borders. It was Europe.

The selection of the Commission's new president depended very much on the two countries that formed the inner core of the European Economic Community, France and Germany. The Germans did not have a candidate. Chancellor Helmut Kohl, impressed by what he had seen of Delors, conveyed to Mitterrand that if there was going to be a French president, it would be Delors and no one else. And such an appointment would serve one clear purpose for Mitterrand—it would get Delors out of town. On July 18, 1984, the governments of the EEC chose Delors to be the next president of the Commission. As he departed the ornate front hall of the Ministry of Finance for the last time, to the applause of the staff, Delors left Mitterrand a very important bequest: He had set France on a drive for economic modernization and increased reliance on markets that would carry on without him. In the words of one of his rivals in the Socialist Party, Delors "played a fundamental role in reinserting a vision of the market economy in French social democracy." His policies had helped finalize the divorce between the Socialists and the Communists. Mitterrand did not need them anymore. In 1984, the Communist Party exited the government with a blast that it was "no longer part of the presidential majority." That did the party no good. It was reduced from being a force to being on the fringe.[6]

Stagnation and Euro-pessimism

Delors arrived in Brussels to take up his position in a European Community that had been largely stagnant for almost two decades. The Community's origins went back to the Marshall Plan, when the United States provided billions of dollars of aid to Europe, in the face of its imminent economic collapse, to promote reconstruction after World War II. As a condition for loaning its money, the U.S. government had insisted that the Europeans cooperate on economic reconstruction, look at problems in a European context, and draw up common plans. It also provided the impetus for launching the unification movement. As Altiero Spinelli put it, "The discussions about the Marshall Plan reopened the idea of European unification." In turn, the Marshall Plan helped lay the foundations for the predecessor organization to the EEC: the European Coal and Steel Community, which exercised common management of those resources between France and Germany. Jean Monnet was the man who envisioned this community; and he—along with French foreign minister Robert Schuman and German chancellor Konrad Adenauer—hammered it into existence.

Then in 1957, six European countries—Germany, France, Italy, Belgium, the Netherlands, and Luxembourg—signed the Treaty of Rome, which brought the European Economic Community into existence, neatly enveloping the Coal and Steel Community in the process. This was the first "relaunching of Europe." Indeed, the various institutions of the Coal and Steel Community became the core institutions of the new EEC. But what type of community was it to be? Here ensued a bitter battle that went right to the heart of the matter. Charles de Gaulle advocated a Europe of nations, cooperating but retaining their sovereignty. He wanted the European Commission, the executive arm of the Community, to be subordinate to the national governments, not to have authority over them. Majority votes were insufficient; there had to be absolute unanimity. Otherwise, a nation's sovereignty might be impaired—in particular, France's sovereignty.

Monnet and Spinelli wanted something much more: a federal Europe. The nation-state, which had been born in Europe, would be subordinated to a supranational state, which would have the final say. The venerable countries of Europe would become less like sovereign nations and more like the individual states of the United States. Such a transformation would not happen all at once but would be accomplished by building institutions that had specific authorities. Reality would be changed, though gradually. But de Gaulle wielded his veto, said *"Non,"* and won. As a result, from the late 1960s onward, movement toward a federal Europe stalled. Although the Community gained new members—Britain, Denmark, and Ireland joined in 1973—the energy and economic crises only added to the stagnation. The principal new evolution was the establishment of the European Monetary System—which not every member joined—in the late 1970s. Aside from that, the EEC continued to be stalemated by battles over its authority, its budgets, and—since it did not tax directly—how much its member governments would contribute. In one memorable moment, British prime minister Margaret Thatcher, angry over the huge amounts the Community spent to subsidize uneconomic but politically critical farmers, declared, "I want my money back." Europe, it seemed, was destined to decline, afflicted by "Euro-sclerosis," unable to engage the United States as an equal, and threatened by competition from Japan and other Asian countries. Jean Monnet's optimism, however hardheaded it had been, had given way to rampant and pervasive Euro-pessimism, which was the hallmark of the 1970s and the early 1980s.[7]

The Single Market: Relaunching Europe

It was under these circumstances that Delors moved to Brussels to become president of the European Commission. During his tenure, just one portrait decorated his office wall—that of cognac-salesman-turned-statesman and expert networker Jean Monnet. The imperatives that drove Monnet—to put an end to European civil war, to solve the German problem in the context of Europe—had also shaped Delors. His father had been grievously wounded at the Battle of Verdun in the First World War and had never buried his antipathy to the Germans. When Delors fled with his mother to the countryside during the Nazi occupation of Paris, he made a best friend who carried messages for the Resistance. The friend was captured by the Nazis and died at Auschwitz. That was the past that Delors wanted to be sure would never return.

In due course, Delors would become the incarnation of the "new" Europe—the Europe of the single market. He would be celebrated as a visionary engineer, who tirelessly found solutions to seemingly intractable problems and who was leading Europe toward a unified, truly open market. He would also be criticized for hubris and arrogance, for pomposity, and for progressively confusing himself with Europe as a whole. He would be attacked as the French bureaucrat par excellence, who needlessly applied the French propensity for *dirigisme,* regulations, rigidity, and paperwork to an entire continent, which needed more economic freedom, not more control.

Delors was determined to preside over a new relaunching of Europe. To do so, he needed a big idea, one that would have far-reaching impact. Otherwise, what was the point of doing the job? He had spent the previous autumn canvassing Europe for such an idea, and he had found it in the concept of the "single market." Along with that, he would also promote a single currency. Together, they would add up to his contribution. And if successfully implemented, they would make a federal Europe almost inevitable and create an integrated Continental economy.

Delors wasted no time. On January 14, 1985, just two weeks after taking over as president of the Commission, he went before the European Parliament to call for the removal of all "internal frontiers" to a single market by the end of 1992. The 1957 Treaty of Rome had eliminated traditional customs duties. Now Delors was determined to go much further, to do away with every kind of barrier that stood in the way of a single open internal market. By June, the Commission had come up with 297 proposals to flatten the barriers. Physical barriers at frontiers were to go. No longer would there be customs between members. Technical barriers were also to go. Each country would accept standards on goods or services imposed by another country. This was the key principle of "mutual recognition," which was also applied to banking, stockbroking, mutual funds, and insurance. If a firm was authorized to ply any of these trades in one country, then it could do so in all the others. Governments could no longer play favorites with their national champions; the playing field was meant to be level. Further circumscribing the prerogatives of the nation-state, governments would have to permit any European firm to bid on major contracts rather than reserve them for favored national companies.

Delors enjoyed the support of the Community's three newest members —Greece, Spain, and Portugal, which formally joined on January 1, 1986. For all three, full membership marked a historic watershed in their modernization—they went from being Europe's poor cousins, ruled by dictatorships and long the source of agricultural products and cheap migrant labor, to becoming democracies and full-fledged participants in economic integration. In addition, all three were ruled at this time by "new" socialists much influenced by the French experience—most compellingly symbolized in the figure of Spain's young and charismatic prime minister, Felipe González.

The mechanisms needed to create the internal market were embodied in the Single European Act, which was approved by all twelve members of the European Community on July 1, 1987. By the end of 1992, all barriers to the internal market were to be eliminated. To facilitate implementation of the act, the principle of unanimity—so sacred to de Gaulle—was overturned for many purposes. Majority votes among the governments would be enough to ensure approval of new initiatives. This would be a very key change. The twelve members also committed themselves to develop a common European foreign policy.

Yet the Single European Act did not command anywhere near the attention that might have been expected. It was treated as another of those European stories and received only glancing attention, even from readers of serious newspapers. Altiero Spinelli lived just long enough to see it take shape. But even after spending almost a lifetime of struggle for European unity, he did not bother to hide his disappointment at this outcome of the "relaunching" campaign he had helped initiate in the 1980s. Shortly before his death in 1986, he dismissed the plan as insignificant—nothing more than a "ridiculous mouse." It would take time to realize how much the Single European Act would shift power away from national capitals to Brussels and toward the Community and, in particular, to the Commission, which had the exclusive right to initiate laws.

To turn the act into reality required an enormous amount of lawmaking, on the European scale. In the first half of 1988 alone, the European Community made more decisions than it had in the ten years between 1974 and 1984. All sorts of goods and services were to be "Europeanized" and to have common rules about content, safety, and labeling. Sometimes the obstacles were too great, as in the case of beer. Some countries sold nonalcoholic beer that contained no alcohol. Others sold nonalcoholic beer that had up to 1 percent of alcohol. Germany, meanwhile, had a "purity law" for beer that dated back several centuries, which the beer of other countries did not meet. If beer was to be a freely traded good, then convergence was required. In this case, the rule makers had to compromise. The most they could do was oblige each country to honor other member countries' standards about what constituted beer.

No less bitter has been the battle between candy makers and the European Union over how to create a single market in chocolate. British and Irish confectioners, who liberally mix milk in with their chocolate, may be ordered to relabel their candy bars as "milk chocolate with a high milk content" or "household milk chocolate." There has been no sweet talk in the response of British candy makers, who insist that the issue goes to the heart of national character. "The British have always preferred more milk in their chocolate," insisted one expert, "just as we like milk in our tea." The bad taste left by this struggle makes clear that harmonization is not a smooth process.[8]

Flying in the Face of History?

The march toward the single market ignited an acrimonious debate. The single market was more than acceptable to the likes of Margaret Thatcher as long as it was viewed as nothing more than a sort of super-duper free-trade zone; and she, along with the other European leaders, put her signature to the document in 1987. But what the critics now increasingly saw was the transfer of sovereignty from national capitals, the homes of elected parliaments, to Brussels and the large, self-referential bureaucracy of the European Commission, implacable in its efforts to assert its authority and insulated from both national governments and direct democratic controls. It did not help when Delors was dubbed the Czar of Brussels.

Indeed, for Thatcher, the expansion of the Commission's power threatened to undo what she had enunciated as her goal for Britain. "The European Union is flying in the face of history," she later said. "It will not work. It will not work." In her eyes, a unified Europe meant vesting too much power in a bureaucratic *dirigiste* commission in Brussels that sought to get its tentacles into all sorts of activities where it did not belong. It also ran counter to the Thatcher revolution. She declared at the time, "We have not successfully rolled back the frontiers of the state in Britain only to see them reimposed at a European level with a European superstate exercising a new dominance from Brussels." And as far as she was concerned, Delors was the epitome of the "new breed of unaccountable politicians" running the Community—building, as she put it, "their Tower of Babel on the uneven foundations of ancient nations, different languages, and diverse economies."[9]

But Thatcher was shortly to fall from power, and the implementation of the Single Market Program—involving about three hundred separate pieces of legislation and regulation—was virtually completed by the end of 1992, on its appointed timetable. The competitive landscape was transformed. Each country was open. The Single European Act had removed the sway of governments over large parts of the commanding heights. One area, however, remained a bastion of sovereignty: money.

Buba Knows Best?

With the single market, Europe was ready for more unity. In fact, in 1988, Delors had already headed a committee that was charged with figuring out how to create a single currency. That was clearly a logical requirement for an integrated market. The mood was upbeat, and a united Europe appeared to be on the way.

Then came the *annus mirabilis* of 1989, and another unification got in the way of Europe's. This one, however, in contrast to the European time-tables, was unplanned and unexpected. In 1988, Helmut Kohl had prophesied that German unification would not occur in his lifetime. In January 1989, Erich Honecker, the Communist apparatchik who ran East Germany, stretched the horizon even farther, predicting that the Berlin Wall would last fifty or even a hundred years. But by then, events that would dramatically and unexpectedly negate all such predictions were already in motion. That year would bring the collapse of the Communist governments of Poland, Hungary, Czechoslovakia, East Germany, Bulgaria, and Romania—and the fall of the Berlin Wall.[10]

The era of the cold war was over, inevitably upsetting fundamental calculations. One of the main impetuses for European integration had been to offset communist power in the East. But now, instead of the specter of Warsaw Pact tanks heading west, the Western Europeans feared a flood of economic refugees. Rather than uniting to resist communism, Western Europeans had to devise common economic policies to meet the challenge from the east. To make matters even more pressing, these former communist countries would soon be banging at the Community's door, seeking association and membership. But how could they join in the single market? They did not yet even have market systems. All of this provided new urgency to develop a common foreign policy.

A second fundamental calculation concerned the role of Germany—the ever-present German question. The collapse of communism drastically rewrote that question. The basic postwar formula went back to Jean Monnet and the European Coal and Steel Community: Germany would best flourish, in both its own interests and those of its neighbors, when integrated into a democratic Europe. Germany's might would be balanced off against France's and, after its entry, against Britain's. But the collapse of communism put within reach what had been the rhetorical holy grail of postwar German policies—reunification. This would make Germany the preponderant power in Europe, thus creating an enormous challenge for the entire continent.

Germany itself faced a huge challenge. The East German economy had once been trumpeted as the tenth-largest industrial economy in the world, on a per capita basis. If anybody could make communism work, so it was said, it was the Germans. But the collapse of East Germany revealed its rusted innards. It turned out that the East German economy was a ramshackle, broken-down, highly inefficient, wasteful system, kept afloat by aid and credits from West Germany. How to integrate the two economies? How to help the "Ossies"—the East Germans—achieve their great objective and bring them up to the standard of living of the "Wessies"? The answer, in one way or another, would come down to money. Ludwig Erhard's currency reform of 1948 had created the foundations for the German economic miracle and four decades of growth. How the relationship between the West German and East German currencies was handled would be central to future economic development.

The man who was in charge of Germany's money, Karl-Otto Pöhl, the president of the Bundesbank, was convinced that the right answer was to move with great caution. The Bundesbank was truly the keeper of Europe's economic orthodoxy. Because it was Germany's central bank and because of its constitution, the Buba—as the Bundesbank is known to currency traders —was the dominant central bank in Europe. Its power was rivaled only by that of the U.S. Federal Reserve. The Buba determined interest rates not just for Germany but for all of Europe, because the other central banks had to calibrate their interest rates in relation to Germany's, to maintain stability in exchange rates. The Bundesbank had been established with considerable autonomy, to protect it from short-term political interference. Its constitutional obligation was expressed in the 1957 act that had established it: to fight inflation. Because its power was so great, the Buba, ensconced in its black, modernistic castle on the outskirts of Frankfurt, was often criticized as a "state within a state"—overly obsessed with inflation, at the expense of employment and social peace. Its reply was that inflation was the great destabilizer, the plague; if not checked, it would ultimately destroy the productive economy, shredding both jobs and social peace in the process.

The Bundesbank's orthodoxy was deeply rooted in the German past. Two historic memories—both about inflation—were fundamental. The first was the hyperinflation of the early 1920s, memorialized by photographs of wheelbarrows filled with almost-worthless paper currency. It had wiped out the savings and stability of the middle class and helped set the stage for the collapse of the Weimar Republic and the rise of Hitler. The second was that of the massive post–World War II inflation that Ludwig Erhard had eliminated overnight with the 1948 currency reform, creating the conditions for the German economic miracle. The moral was straightforward: Inflation destroys the foundations of society.

Despite his orthodoxy, Pöhl came to the Bundesbank by an unusual route. He was fifteen in 1945, waiting to be drafted for the last wave of cannon fodder, when World War II ended, and like so many after the war, he was adrift in a nation of ruins. His memory of the years leading up to Erhard's currency reform was basic. "Our problems were very immediate," he said. "We didn't have anything to eat." At the age of eighteen, he went to work for a socialist newspaper, and even if his intellectual allegiances would shift, he never lost his emotional allegiance to the socialists. "I admired those people," he recalled. "They came back from the concentration camps, from emigration. They were the only people who had stood up against the Nazis, except for the communists, and because of what we knew was happening in eastern Germany, no one wanted to be a communist. I was eighteen years old when I joined the Social Democrats in 1948. They did a lot for me. They helped me go to university. I have a certain moral obligation."

At university Pöhl concentrated on economics, studying under Karl Schiller, an outstanding economist. (Later, upon becoming Germany's first socialist finance minister in the postwar era, Schiller announced that his ambition was to merge Keynesianism with the economic philosophy of Ordoliberalism, which had shaped Germany's social market economy in the years of reconstruction.) Pöhl came into the government in the early 1970s as an adviser to Helmut Schmidt, then the finance minister. In 1974, Schmidt, who came from the right wing of the Social Democratic Party, replaced Willy Brandt as chancellor. In 1977, Schmidt appointed Pöhl to the Bundesbank board, and by 1980 he was the bank's president.

In 1982, a coalition led by the Christian Democrats took power in Germany and Helmut Kohl, the party's leader, became the new chancellor. Over the next decade and a half, he was to become Europe's dominant politician—known as the "big man of Europe" not only because of his considerable size but also because of Germany's economic preponderance. The son of a tax official from the Rhineland, Kohl grew up with a gargantuan appetite for politics. He joined the Christian Democrats in 1946, at age sixteen. No one could doubt his consuming ambition, though it was not at all clear that he would achieve the chancellorship. In 1979, as opposition to him mounted in his party, he went through what he was to call his "valley of humiliation." But he was not to be outmaneuvered, and four years later he was chancellor. He so identified with the Federal Republic's first chancellor, Konrad Adenauer, also a Catholic from the Rhineland, that he would describe himself as "Adenauer's grandson." Thinking him dull and plodding, Kohl's opponents continually underestimated him, which turned out to be a great advantage for him, as his rivals discovered as they fell by the wayside. He also had a tremendous sense of the political moment. But the reunification of West and East Germany appeared a distant objective, and thus, as a practical politician, it did not much engage him—until the events of 1989, which culminated in the fall of the Berlin Wall.

Suddenly, the central question was not *when* reunification would take place but the much more practical and immediate *how*. That pushed the matter of exchange rates right to the front. Karl-Otto Pöhl recognized that the exchange rate between East and West Germany would be crucial to future economic development. Some were talking about exchanging one East German mark for one West German deutsche mark. This, Pöhl thought, would be ludicrous. The Bundesbank estimated that it must be about four to one—that is, four East German marks were more or less equivalent to one deutsche mark. The productivity of East German workers was, at best, only 40 percent of West Germany's. A one-to-one exchange rate, and the imposition of the West German social and labor system, would make East Germany totally uncompetitive. Its industry would be bankrupt. The result would be to turn East Germany into a giant welfare-dependent entity. The right approach, according to Pöhl, was suggested by Poland's experience. Wages there were much lower than in Germany, reflecting the lower productivity. And that was good, not bad, because it made Polish goods competitive on world markets —which meant jobs, more investment and modernization, and expanding opportunity.

Pöhl recognized all this. He was not even sure that rapid political unification was a good idea. To his mind, it was overrated—and somewhat unhistoric—as a national ideal. Perhaps it would be better, he thought, to allow East Germany to remain a separate democratic German state for a time. Let it sort out its economic, social, and political problems—including the legacy of the Stasi, the secret police, which had turned East Germany into an extraordinary informer state. East Germany and West Germany could then be reintegrated within the larger framework of the European Community.

"The D-mark Comes"

The politicians were thinking otherwise. The wave of emotion—the exultation after forty years of division—was overwhelming. At the same time, Chancellor Helmut Kohl was increasingly fearful of another kind of wave— a tidal wave of East German workers flooding into West Germany, seeking streets paved with gold. Pöhl argued, "After a certain time, when people realized that they couldn't make a living, they would have gone back." But Kohl could see the numbers swelling already, and East Germans were now demonstrating in the streets—not against the Communist government but in favor of the deutsche mark. "If the deutsche mark comes, we stay here," they chanted. "If it doesn't come, we'll go to the deutsche mark." The refrain alarmed Kohl, who was convinced that East Germany was about to implode. He could envision half a million refugees moving west in 1990, creating vast social tumult. No one could assure him that anything short of currency unification could hold back the flood. There was another factor as well. Kohl thought that monetary union would complete the job of reunification, just as the currency reform of 1948–49 had led to the fusing of the three Western occupation zones to create West Germany. Kohl would certainly earn himself a unique place in history by doing something great and carrying out this national mission. If successful, he would indeed be a chancellor on the level of an Adenauer—even a Bismarck.

On the evening of February 5, 1990, on his way to meet the head of the East German central bank, Pöhl stopped in Bonn to see Theo Waigel, the finance minister. Pöhl reviewed the arguments against hasty action on the currencies. Waigel suggested, in an oblique way, that things might work out differently and that the Bundesbank might very soon have to take over monetary responsibility for East Germany. He did so by quoting a popular line from the German-dubbed version of the television series *Mission: Impossible:* "Cobra, take over control." Pöhl, he was saying, should stay tuned. But Pöhl missed the cue. After all, Waigel liked to make jokes.

Pöhl immediately went on to Berlin to meet with his East German counterpart. In East Berlin, on February 6, 1990, he publicly declared that monetary union was absolutely not on. It was a fantasy. But a few hours earlier on the same day, in Bonn, a small group met with Kohl in his office, including Waigel and economics minister Graf Otto von Lambsdorff. There they decided to expand the deutsche mark into East Germany. This momentously important decision was made, as decisions so often are, in an improvised manner. Under the intense pressure of events, none of the decision makers anticipated the enormous economic toll ahead. The decision was announced in Bonn that same afternoon, before Pöhl could be informed.

For the most part, the immediate reaction was euphoric. Kohl and his colleagues had convinced themselves that currency unification was exactly what the doctor had ordered and that East Germany would soon be on an economic fast track. They simply could not conceive what the consequences would be. By this point, Pöhl was perhaps the only senior official who was willing to speak aloud the fear that the decision would be an economic disaster for East Germany, that it would kill off its industries and would prove immensely costly for Germany as a whole. At a cabinet meeting shortly afterward, Pöhl made his position clear. "The Bundesbank had not been consulted," he said. "But it was a political decision." He was very mindful of the criticism of the Bundesbank's power. The bank was not a second government. It was an agency in charge of monetary policy, and it would do its job as part of the government. "We can manage the currency," he finally said, although hardly with enthusiasm.[11]

Currency unification did, however, serve an overarching national objective, as Kohl had hoped. It drove political reunification. In October 1990, less than a year after the fall of the Wall and three months after currency unification, Germany was reunited as one country. Germany became the major power in Europe, and the Bundesbank would become even more dominant across the Continent. But unification also turned out to be far more difficult and painful—and costly—for West Germany than almost anyone had anticipated.

Not long after, Pöhl, exhausted and frustrated, resigned. The economic consequences of unification were as he had foreseen. The East German economy disintegrated. "We know how to carry out heart transplants, kidney transplants, liver transplants," explained a prominent West German economist at the time. "But here, we are changing all the organs at once." East German wages rose toward the level of West Germany's. Much of East German industry went bankrupt; it could not compete. The German government had to subsidize the east—to the tune, between 1990 and 1997, of about $700 billion, a good part of which went to pay unemployment and other social benefits. West German companies did benefit, because they got to replace the decrepit infrastructure and because the East Germans went on a buying spree. But soon the extraordinary exultation of 1991, on both sides of the former Wall, gave way to pervasive bitterness.[12]

From 1990 onward, the Bundesbank sought to forestall the inflationary risks of monetary unification by holding to tight interest rates. This had consequences far beyond Germany. As a result of the stringent monetary policy, economic growth throughout Western Europe stalled and unemployment rose to levels never seen in the postwar years. What happened in Germany would have a decisive impact on the course of European unity.

The Coin of the Realm

In December 1991, the European summit leaders met in the Dutch market town of Maastricht to conclude a treaty on the single currency and on establishing common foreign, security, and internal policies. Not all the economic consequences of the collapse of communism and German unification were yet clear, but enough was evident to affect the proceedings. The leaders recognized that they were in a new world. The decisions they approved at Maastricht would define the course of European unity well into the twenty-first century. Politically, they agreed to much tighter cooperation on foreign and security policies. But their most important decision was to create a common currency—the euro—and a European central bank to manage it. According to the plan, the euro will come into existence as the official currency in January 1999. Governments, central banks, and corporations will conduct their business and write their accounts and invoices in the euro. The familiar national coins and bills will continue to be used in everyday life but, owing to the fixed link, only as an "expression" of the euro. Thus, invoices and bank accounts will be denominated in the euro, while individuals will walk into shops and pay for their croissants and sausages with the familiar physical bills and coins they know. The actual changeover in circulating currency is slated to occur between January and July 2002. At that point, the euro will come into physical existence in the form of coins and bills in people's pockets, and the national currencies will be withdrawn from circulation.

With the euro comes the European Central Bank (ECB) to manage it. Currently in nascent form as the European Monetary Institute, the ECB is modeled on the Bundesbank. This is not exactly surprising, given both the Bundesbank's predominant role in Europe and the fact that it was Karl-Otto Pöhl who chaired the committee that drafted the ECB's statutes. In fact, its explicit constitutional commitment to fight inflation is even stronger than that of the Bundesbank. If it comes into existence as designed, the ECB will drastically reduce the monetary power of national governments, for fundamental decisions about interest rates and currency will be conceived and implemented at the supranational level of the bank, marking something altogether new—in Pöhl's words, "the denationalization of money."

Yet it is not absolutely clear that all this will happen, at least on the timetable planned. A common currency requires economic convergence, and this means that economies must march to the same drummer when it comes to such factors as debt, deficits, and inflation. To achieve that, the Maastricht treaty contains a series of extremely tough "benchmark criteria," which must be met if a country is going to climb aboard the euro wagon. The key criteria include: inflation at no more than 1.5 percentage points above the average rate of the three countries with the lowest rates; a national budget deficit that is less than 3 percent of GDP; a national debt below 60 percent of GDP (or headed there); and a national currency that cannot have been devalued within the previous two years. It is expected that some countries will be able—and willing—to meet these requirements; others will not. The result will be a two-tier Europe, at least for some years.

While the criteria have been attacked as unrealistic and arbitrary, the treaty does have some flexibility in how these criteria are interpreted and applied. In the run-up to the euro, it is Germany that has insisted on a very literal and inflexible interpretation. Some see reflected in the toughness of the Maastricht criteria Germans' fears that their "hard" deutsche mark will be replaced by a softer European currency, too vulnerable to the inflationary temptations of politicians. For its part, Germany pushed hard for a pact to punish any country that strayed from these criteria after opting into the euro. The European summit in Amsterdam formally adopted, in June 1997, such a "Stability and Growth Pact." Penalties could reach as much as one half of 1 percent of gross domestic product, which could become a very big number. Imagine, for instance, the spectacle of a European Central Bank in Frankfurt fining France some $8 billion—no doubt at the very time when unemployed French workers are demonstrating in the streets. Indeed, Yves-Thibault de Silguy, the European commissioner responsible for currency matters, has described the Stability and Growth Pact as a "monetary nuclear weapon"—too powerful to use.[13]

Certainly, if high unemployment and low growth persist against the backdrop of the tough Maastricht criteria, public resistance to a common currency will grow. There is already growing hostility toward a united Europe, for many people see it as linked to stagnation, not renewed growth and prosperity. They also see the lifting of restrictions as benefiting capital much faster than it benefits labor. In response to these anxieties, manifested in the 1997 French elections, the Amsterdam summit established the fight against unemployment as a high priority. Politics and the demands of electorates are forcing such a reassessment, for if the euro is derailed, then "United Europe" will be put into question.

In a considerable irony, while Germans worry that they will lose control over their economic fate through the "socialization" of the deutsche mark

—that is, its absorption into the euro—some in the other countries fear that the euro and the ECB will mean that the Bundesbank and its rules will prevail over all of Europe. That is not the way that everybody sees it, however. In the French view, for instance, the Bundesbank is Europe's de facto central bank right now, and neither France nor any other nation gets to have a vote. They see themselves gaining more power through their membership in the European System of Central Banks, which will have authority over the new European Central Bank. If it does not mean the socialization of the mark, the creation of a European Central Bank will at least mean the dilution of the Bundesbank. One way or the other, however, Frankfurt—whether as the Buba's home or as the future home of the putative European Central Bank—will be calling the shots on Europe's money.

Privatization

The need to reduce deficits, in accordance with Maastricht, is helping to accelerate the process of privatization in Europe. What is unfolding represents a wholesale retreat from the classic commanding heights of the mixed economies. The numbers are very large. Since 1985, over $100 billion in assets have been sold off in Europe. Venerable national champions in industry—from Volkswagen, Lufthansa, and Renault to the oil companies Elf-Aquitaine of France and ENI of Italy—have been subject to reorganizations followed by partial or complete sales. The sale of stakes in government-owned telecommunications providers has begun, its pace set by the $13 billion public offering of 26 percent of Deutsche Telekom—Europe's largest privatization on record. Before the year 2000, another $300 billion in government assets could be sold off. Finance ministers are attracted to privatization for several reasons. It brings in big money, which helps reduce deficits (although the sales revenues themselves do not count against the Maastricht deficit criteria). It cuts the outflow of subsidies and creates the potential for greater tax revenues. And it also shifts unfunded-pension responsibilities away from the state, which is of increasing importance as demographics tilt toward the elderly. But those are not the only reasons.

A fundamental change in outlook is also taking place. In many, but not all, cases, the mystique of the state-owned company has dissipated. Once it was seen as the modernizer, the champion, the engine of progress, the means for technological advance, the embodiment of national purpose. And for many years state companies did play such a role. But state ownership has increasingly come to be seen as a liability, actual or potential, which promotes inefficiency, limits a firm's flexibility and ability to cope with increased international competition, and hinders technological innovation. Because it is state owned, it ends up making decisions that respond to political pressures, and politicians find it mighty hard to resist the temptation to intervene. "There is a mystery about state-owned companies," mused former French president Valéry Giscard d'Estaing. "They are managed by good people—the best names of the elite. And yet they are unable to operate efficiently. Instead, they resist change, they are above events. It is mysterious."

The dynamics of the single market force change as well. The European Commission is agnostic on the issue of public or private ownership of firms, but it insists on the lifting of obstacles to competition and market entry. This doctrine explicitly challenges public monopolies; and sectors once considered natural monopolies, such as electric power, are now being eroded by competition on their fringes. When there is no longer a protected "national market," state ownership can become a definite hindrance. And public monopolies might find themselves excluded from opportunities further afield. "If our companies are to be ready for the future, they must be exposed to competition and the real growth markets," said Alberto Clô, Italy's former minister of industry. "And people from those markets should compete in Italy. ENEL—Italy's main electric company—is one of the largest public utilities in the world, but it operates in a country where electricity use grows at only 1 percent a year. The future of power is Asia, Central Europe, and Latin America. ENEL must be able to compete in those markets. To do so, we need to open the Italian market to foreign investment."

Another factor is driving privatization as well—technology. "When I started in the Labor Party in 1973, I spent a week learning about Marxism, how changes in the forces of production change the structure of society," recalled Jens Stoltenberg, recently finance minister of Norway. "The force was technology. It was only a question of time, we were taught, before technology would create socialism. Today technology is creating change, but it's not creating socialism. It's encouraging capitalism. It's creating more competition. We had only one television channel until the end of the 1980s. It was forbidden to establish another. In the 1985 election, this was a big issue. Our party was against it; we said it was bad for Norway's population, it was too commercial. But then came satellite dishes, and the policies became ridiculous. We had to give in—to change—because of technology."

For all the convergence among countries that this "wave of privatization" implies, there are key differences in the ways each country goes about it. In France, most big sales have involved the transfer of a controlling packet of shares to so-called *noyaux durs*—"hard cores" of strategic investors whom government trusted to anchor the firm for the long term. In Italy, privatization has meant unbundling the central holding company Istituto per la Ricostruzione Industriale (IRI). In the process, it has brought to light many of the tangled legal and financial dealings of Italian business and government. And in Germany, although local governments sometimes oppose privatizations that would lead to plant closures and job losses in their region, the drive to privatize at the federal level is strong, and it benefits from the country's unique experience of having privatized industry and trade in the former East Germany. Over just five years, a special office called the

Treuhandanstalt sold off 13,700 East German firms for a total of approximately $25 billion. In its final act, after it had completely cleared its shelf of its inventory, it privatized itself.

Privatization is leading to a major new growth industry in Europe: regulation. When governments owned companies, there was no need for independent regulation. The ministry set the prices for such services as telephone, water, natural gas, and electricity. But the newly privatized companies are now in charge, and they set prices and the terms of operation. Government's role has, therefore, changed. Its job is to protect consumers by ensuring competitive prices, safety, and standards of quality. To do this requires designing new institutions to regulate prices and practices. Having gotten the early start in privatization, Britain was first to set up a regulatory system, which it is still adjusting and which is also proving to be much bigger than originally anticipated. Autonomous regulatory boards of various kinds have sprung up all across Europe.

Privatization still involves tough negotiations with unions, as well as complicated compromises among European Union members about the rules of future competition in each industry. Yet what was once almost unthinkable has become a standard and accepted tool of government in Europe. What looms ahead is a far more complex and difficult battle—one that goes to the very heart of the European social contract: the future of the welfare state.[14]

The Costs of the Welfare State

In addition to industrial restructuring, Maastricht forces a reining in of social spending, which has soared over the years to reach an average of 42 percent of GDP in Western Europe. Europe's first convergence after World War II— long before Maastricht—was on the mixed economy combined with the welfare state. The mixed economy, it was felt, would deliver full employment and growth. A significant part of that growth would, in turn, be redistributed through social spending that would ensure security and social peace. The welfare state has also proved to be one of Europe's leading growth industries —at least until recently.

The signal that Europe's social systems have gone wrong is unemployment. In the mid-1990s, it has replaced inflation as the headline, the alarm bell, and the dominant issue in elections. Old jobs are being eliminated by plant closings, downsizing, restructuring—and competition from outside national borders. Governments are much less prone to subsidize loss-making firms in order to preserve employment. During the 1970s, unemployment in France rose from 262,000 to over 1 million. In 1982, the French Socialists feared crossing the threshold of 2 million unemployed. In 1997, the number is over 3 million. Among school dropouts the rate of unemployment is 29 percent. On average in industrial Western Europe, unemployment hovers between 10 and 15 percent. In southern Europe it is worse. Full employment was to be one of the main guarantees of the mixed economy. But increasing numbers of people are, in effect, employed only by the government agencies that disburse unemployment benefits.

Rising unemployment signals a broader challenge—to the entire edifice of welfare, entitlements, social spending, and protections in the labor market. It is the crisis of a system of pensions and compensations that has been overtaken by demographics and can no longer pay for itself. "When Europe's welfare systems were originally set up, they were very good and fair," recalled Valéry Giscard d'Estaing. "But the current life span now greatly exceeds the anticipated life expectancy of the original schemes." The demographics are only going to get more difficult. By the year 2030, the proportion of people over sixty-four to those between fifteen and sixty-four will be 40 percent in France and Britain, and nearly 50 percent in Germany.

Among the Continental countries, the Netherlands has done more than its neighbors to come to grips with the problems of the welfare state. In the 1980s, the Netherlands found itself suffering from poor economic performance. The "Dutch disease," as it was dubbed, had its origin in Holland's particular circumstances—the rapid growth of natural-gas production and the great wealth that came with it. In the words of former prime minister Ruud Lubbers, "The welfare state had 'overmatured,' through a combination of political blindnesss and the easy temptation of rapidly increasing national income due to natural-gas reserves." Ever-growing benefits were handed out with ease. Unemployment assistance was so close to wage levels as to decrease the incentive to work. Soon almost one third of the workforce was on unemployment, disability, or other social benefits.

Forced to confront the illness, the government discarded the orthodox Keynesian prescription and began to redirect the economy—reducing the budget deficit, cutting taxes, promoting "wage moderation," and making it easier to hire and fire and to employ part-time workers. Unemployment benefits were reduced. Since these reforms, the Netherlands has bounded back with lower unemployment than its neighbors and is discussed as a model for a moderate redesign of the welfare state. Critics, however, argue that the real unemployment rate is much higher than the official numbers. And certainly, no one would say that the welfare state in the Netherlands remains anything but generous.

"Fango *in the Morning*"

The contrast in attitudes between the United States and Europe is striking. In America, the term *welfare* is almost a dirty word. By comparison, the welfare state is seen by Europeans as one of the Continent's greatest achievements, an essential element of a civilized society and the foundation of social consensus. When it is criticized, it is for its excesses, not for its concept. Governments of both the right and the left are committed to it. The Germans, for instance, recollect that it was the Iron Chancellor, Bismarck—hardly a socialist—who created the first modern pension system, beginning in the 1880s. In the words of a prominent Spanish industrialist, "In Europe, the welfare state is highly respected. According to the European social contract, the government guarantees the safety net, and it is quite a high safety net." The modern welfare state is part of national identity, and when Europeans speak of "solidarity," they mean not only the overcoming of class and ideological battles but also the sum of the welfare state.

But the welfare system has also been overtaken by its own generosity. In Germany, the typical paid vacation time is six weeks. Unemployment benefits are a high proportion of wages, and pensions are unrelated to work. "It is an amazing situation in Germany today," observed one businessman. "Ours is a society in which a person who worked for thirty years of productive life and then retires gets paid the same pension as someone who for thirty years was unemployed—someone who did not work his entire life. Something has gotten out of hand." The generosity extends to the range of treatments and services that the system will cover. Many Germans, in the grand tradition of Goethe's poetry, like to go to spas to take a "cure," and they are encouraged to do so by their doctors. The social welfare system pays. One much-favored therapy is the mud pack, otherwise known as the *fango,* which has given rise to a little epithet for the joys of such taxpayer-paid cures: "*Fango* in the morning and tango in the evening."

Mushrooming expenses to meet the commitments of an overextended social welfare system drive up "social charges"—the amount of money that taxpayers and employers must contribute to keep the system running. For employers, those charges have reached levels so high that they discourage the hiring of new workers. Reams of labor legislation, meant to help protect workers, now bog down the system, forcing employers to carry the costs of a problem that lies beyond their grasp—and discouraging them from creating new jobs. At the same time, the level of unemployment benefits is so high that it can create a disincentive to work. The rigidities also include the legal and institutional power of unions to impede change and innovation. It took the management of a major German company three years to get its unions to permit the introduction of voice mail. These costs and regulations fall particularly hard on start-up and entrepreneurial businesses. Yet such businesses have proved to be among the most important engines of job creation in the United States. The overall results can be measured in employment figures. Between 1993 and 1997 net employment in the United States grew by 8 percent, while in Europe it remained flat.

Yet today, in the minds of many Europeans, the realization has grown that the social model is in need of significant repair. There is a sense that the welfare state has expanded too far and must be rolled back and reshaped, in terms of both its benefits and regulation. "What we are confronting in

321

Western Europe is the end of the welfare state in its classical form," observed Karl-Otto Pöhl. "It cannot be reversed completely. You can't undo developments of the last hundred years. But there has to be a restructuring."

The challenge is to conceive and carry out structural changes in the social sector and to reorganize the welfare state so that its services are carried out at lower cost and with greater efficiency—and to do so with popular consent. And all this without losing sight of the basic values of solidarity. That is the issue facing Europe's politicians, both left and right of center, as they try to adapt to what Peter Sutherland, the former European commissioner and first head of the World Trade Organization, called "the new consensus of low inflation and sound public finance." This adaptation is particularly hard for social democrats. Having given up the case for massive state control, their main missions today are the protection, reform, and revitalization of the welfare state. And employment will remain the acid test. "It was the failure of the social-democratic parties in the 1970s that they couldn't deliver job security," said Norway's Jens Stoltenberg. "If these market-oriented policies don't provide jobs either, then people will look for something else." [15]

"A Predicament"

"I do believe that there is enough vitality in Europe," observed Helmut Schmidt, who was chancellor of West Germany for eight years, from 1974 to 1982. Before that, he was defense minister and finance minister. He brings an unusual authority and historical sense to the current dilemmas. A British prisoner of war when World War II ended, he threw himself into socialist politics after the war and rose up through the Hamburg city government. He was on the right wing of the Social Democratic Party, a man of the West, and a partisan of NATO. He is considered by many to have been the most able statesman of his time, with an unusual grasp of both politics and economics. One quality he famously lacked was patience for those whose understanding, he thought, did not keep pace.

He was reflecting on Europe's condition in his office at *Die Zeit,* the prestigious German weekly of which he is the publisher. The day in Hamburg outside was very cold, but the light coming in through the window was bright and knife sharp. Occasionally during the conversation, he took out a plastic box and inhaled snuff with deep breaths. "Yes," he said, "the European nations are capable of getting out of the present-day structural difficulties. But the public does not always understand that there is a problem, a predicament. Once the European public does understand, there will be the need to reduce the burden of social services, reduce taxation, find new ways to produce new goods in order to be competitive in the global economy. In the 1970s, I had every confidence that liberalization in the European Community would work. I did not see the great changes taking place in China in

1978 and after, and the enormous success it would have. I did not really believe in the success of Japan or the tigers. Now the Asians have become the lead players. Europe has lost great points of advantage.

"A critical factor in the decline of Europe is the overexploitation of the welfare state," he continued. "The welfare state is such a good idea, but it has been driven to extremes by Sweden, by France, by Germany, by all the European countries. As the nations' societies are getting older and older, the age of death gets higher. The necessity to provide pension cover for much longer times will create financial situations that will continue to deteriorate. This leads to too-high taxation, too-big budgetary deficits in every European state. For far too long, everyone believed that they were safe financially. Now we know that they are not." He paused. "At least, some of us know."

Indeed, as Schmidt sees matters, Europe's current difficulties are the consequences of Europe's success in putting the past behind it. "One of the reasons for the slowing of growth in Europe," he said, "is the fact that in Britain, France, Italy, or Germany, or wherever in Europe, the generations who are now in power—in politics, business, unions, the bureaucracies— are people who hardly suffered from Hitler, from World War II, and the occupation. Their predecessors were driven by the will to rebuild society, so that the catastrophes of the preceding hundred years would not be repeated. The current leaders grew up in different circumstances, in which their parents were better off every three or five years. They have taken improving standards of living for granted. It is an intellectual feeling, a social feeling, a political feeling. There is no motivation to drive to build and rebuild. Now the market is moving faster than political leaders can keep up with. The political leadership in Europe is lagging behind the thinking in the marketplace. Politicians still deal with misplaced economic perceptions; they have hung on to the past they know." [16]

But that past is gone. Reforming the welfare state, and redefining responsibilities between governments and citizens, now emerges as one of Europe's central missions. Rather than retreating from the welfare state, Europe will seek to renew its social contract by redefining "solidarity," adding a concept of personal responsibility to what has been the overriding principle of rights and entitlements—that is, citizens would bear some share of the costs of social services and would take greater responsibility for funding their retirement. The debate will confront old and new ideas of the "public interest." Inevitably, it will also question the future of work—its length, its flexibility, its rules—and the balance among generations.

All this is provoking a good deal of consternation and anxiety. The high standard of living and high degree of security stand as great achievements of Europe's mixed economies. Yet Europeans no longer feel that they "never had it so good." The overextended welfare system undermines the ability to create the wealth required to pay for it. The current system reflects the deep-seated obligation of the state to its citizens. Adding now to the anxiety is the sense that the state itself will erode as Europe implements the federal vision that Altiero Spinelli dreamed about on Ventotene during those hopeless days of World War II. The existing arrangements will certainly be transformed by competitive pressures from both a single European market and the integration of global economies, and by still-unclear new rules of governance. The payoff will be the renewal that can undergird solidarity in Europe's twenty-first century.

CHAPTER 12

THE DELAYED REVOLUTION

America's New Balance

THE LAST SUPERPOWER on earth shut its doors on December 16, 1995. The United States government was running out of money. Owing to a deadlock between the Democratic administration of Bill Clinton and the Republican-controlled Congress led by Newt Gingrich and Bob Dole, funds were not available to pay the government's bills.

Several hundred thousand federal workers were sent home. Hundreds of thousands more received partial paychecks or no paychecks at all. The Defense Department was funded and thus kept working, but many other government agencies were not. Because it was essential to safety, the Weather Bureau was running, but there was no way to pay its employees. In some agencies, only "essential" workers came to the office. Since there was very little that they could do in the absence of their colleagues, however, they were advised to bring crossword puzzles. Even the Senate cafeteria closed. With workers not coming to work, Washington's streets were as empty as on a major holiday. The Washington Monument was closed. So was the memorial to Abraham Lincoln. Most of the museums were shuttered as well. A unique exhibit of twenty-one of the thirty-five known paintings of the Dutch master Vermeer was kept open only after private funds were scrounged up to pay the security guards.

All across the country, the federal government was shut, including some 397 national parks. In Florida, the entrance to the Everglades National Park was blocked by barricades and emblazoned with a sign that said CLOSED DUE TO BUDGET IMPASSE. Angry tourists were hardly mollified when they were turned away with a letter from the park's superintendent explaining the nation's budget problems. "They are playing 1996 politics with people's lives," said a tourist who had driven from Pennsylvania to Florida, only to be denied admittance to the Everglades park. People could not get their mortgages approved because the Federal Housing Administration was operating with a skeleton staff. Nor could they obtain passports. Would-be visitors to the United States could not get visas, because American embassies around the world were closed. In Clinton's home state, Arkansas, the Office of Disability Determination, which depended on federal funding, closed with eighty-five hundred applications pending. A seaside lodge in Washington State that had won four kisses in the book *Best Places to Kiss in the Northwest* had to close summarily because it was in a national park, breaking the hearts of honeymooners.

The shutdown created confusion, befuddlement, and anger. Federal workers, unsure whether or not they would be paid, put off mortgage payments and dentist bills and also worried about the stability of their jobs. All in all, it was a very odd spectacle for the country that had just won the cold war.[1]

Bill Clinton had gone to Washington in 1993 with an ambiguous amalgam of "New Democratic" politics. This emphasized restraint by government in contrast to the more traditional liberalism that critics had taken to calling "tax-and-spend." The president put all his prestige on the line in 1993 to push through a deficit-reduction program in the face of very tough opposition. The administration had also launched an ambitious plan for the federal government to assume responsibility for the largest sector of the economy—medical care—and to create a national health care system, but that program had foundered on its very complexity.

The Republicans came back with a vengeance in 1994, winning control of both the House and the Senate. Their manifesto was the "Contract with America," a list of undertakings aimed to assuage the anxieties of middle America, in particular about crime, "family values," and the national budget deficit, along with the promise to cut back on regulation and intervention. Altogether, the Contract with America pledged to shrink the American government. And at its heart was a commitment to contain government spending and balance the budget. Not only would the Republicans propose deep cuts in the annual budget; they would seek to pass a constitutional amendment to require, henceforth, a balanced budget—in other words, they would outlaw the deficit. Yet, just as the Democrats were divided between traditional liberals and deficit hawks, so the Republicans were at odds among themselves over which was more important, tax cuts or deficit reduction. But the Republicans intended to use the budget to force a makeover of the United States government. Now, with the shutdown, the two sides were engaged in a tense and deadly political struggle. Every step of the way, they consulted the modern version of the oracle—not chicken innards or Delphi but opinion polls, with their daily swings.

Certainly, the battle was part of the run-up to the 1996 presidential election, but it was also a struggle over the role of government—whether to expand it, keep it as it was, or indeed contract it. Though Clinton himself often seemed more conservative than many of his political advisers, no accord could be reached. The Republicans' goal was to enact a budget that would end the federal deficits within seven years. Specifically, they proposed curbing the growth in Medicare (health care for the elderly), various welfare programs, and Medicaid (health care for the poor)—as well as sending welfare and Medicaid back to the states to administer. They also wanted big tax cuts. Clinton vetoed their budget, and the Republicans in turn refused to pass the continuing resolution that would have provided the temporary funding to keep the government going. This had happened first in November 1995, leading to a six-day shutdown, and then again in December. The shutdown continued through Christmas and then New Year's Day. Each side blamed the other.

Earlier in the year, Gingrich appeared to have become America's de facto prime minister, while Clinton looked like a lame duck. But now Clinton was gaining in the polls and Gingrich was dropping fast. His "negatives" were rising steeply. To their surprise, the House Republicans discovered that they were losing the public; they had underestimated the depth of national sympathy for federal workers. Still, they thought they had the leverage to force Clinton to give in by driving the federal government to the edge of default. They assumed that the catastrophic specter of default would force the administration to capitulate. Here, however, they had made a major miscalculation. For months, they had been telegraphing their intention; and that had given Treasury secretary Robert Rubin, an expert poker player from his days on Wall Street, plenty of time to get prepared. Treasury had the authority from 1990 legislation to borrow from various government employee retirement trust funds, and by the time of the December shutdown, it was more than ready. It turned to the trust funds, thus pushing any potential default off for months. When they realized how Rubin had outmaneuvered them, some of the Republicans were so furious that they talked of impeaching him.

The Republicans made one other critical error. Between Christmas and New Year's, Clinton, going against some of his advisers, accepted one of the proffered Republican proposals. But the House Republicans, whom Gingrich was having trouble holding together, rejected Clinton's acceptance. "The Republicans wouldn't take yes for an answer," one of Clinton's senior advisers later said. "History turns on small things. If the Republicans had accepted the president's offer, it would have been a great victory for Gingrich, the Republicans would have been able to say that they had achieved what they set out to achieve with their Contract with America in less than a year, the federal government would have shrunk more, and Clinton might have lost the 1996 election. But they didn't."

Finally, early in the new year, a compromise of sorts was reached. The budget cuts were reduced, as were the tax cuts. Still, the administration accepted in principle, more or less, a budget that—as scored by the Congressional Budget Office—would end deficits in seven years. And that was the

Republicans' most important objective. At the end of the first week of January 1996, an extraordinary blizzard blanketed Washington. Hardly any vehicles could venture out, and senior officials on both sides could not even meet to continue their negotiations. But, snow notwithstanding, the shutdown was over.

In retrospect, the shutdown and the budget debacle were counted as a Democratic victory. Yet they were also a turning point for both the country and the Democratic Party. That became clear when, addressing the nation a few weeks later in his State of the Union address, Clinton said, "The era of big government is over." In fact, he said it twice in that speech. As in so many other countries, America's economic policies were now affected not only by public opinion but also by the judgment that the financial markets, including the trillions of dollars in pension assets, made on the probity of those policies. And the market's view could not have been clearer: large deficits were unacceptable. The mainstream of American politics had changed course. And in the process, Bill Clinton had emerged as a legatee of a transformation that had begun, in fact, two decades earlier.[2]

The redefinition of the relationship between state and marketplace has been less dramatic in the United States than elsewhere because, while government did expand after World War II as in other countries, it did not do so through state ownership. If the great expansion of government activity in the United States was based originally upon the notion of market failure, then the redefinition of the relationship of state and marketplace reflected a shift in attitudes—toward less confidence in the ability of governments to correct market failures and more confidence in the ability of markets to sort things out themselves. Yet how much of this shift represented mainly a change in language and beliefs? And how much did it reflect a real redrawing of the frontier between government and the marketplace?

The United States was always thought to be the true homeland of capitalism in the Manichaean contest between communism and capitalism. It was considered the land of entrepreneurship, innovation, risk taking, opportunity, and the "creative destruction" of the market. Yet government was hardly absent. Whereas intervention in other countries often took the form of state ownership, its characteristic form in the United States was regulation. And the United States also developed a large and growing welfare state and system of entitlements. As a result, the battle in the United States was —and still is—being played out in the arenas of regulation, taxation and spending, the welfare state, and (although less visibly) privatization. Regulation itself is going in two directions. One direction is toward less economic intervention in markets. The other is toward more intervention to uphold social values. Overall, however, the nation has waged battles over fiscal discipline that parallel those in most countries on the eve of the twenty-first century. The struggle began two decades ago.

The Outsider

When Ronald Reagan won the Republican presidential nomination in 1980, he seemed so much on the political fringe that during the convention, there were intense semisecret negotiations about making former president Gerald Ford his vice-presidential running mate. But Ford was not to be a normal vice president. He was to have far-reaching responsibilities as a kind of copresident with responsibility for foreign affairs and the budget. He would also be "super executive of the office of the President." As proof of the seriousness of the initiative, none other than the master negotiator himself, Henry Kissinger—along with the master of money Alan Greenspan—represented Ford, and by extension the Republican establishment, in the discussions.

After a few days, however, the entire plan foundered, not only on its inherent implausibility and apparent constitutional infringement. There were also those jokes: Ford would be president before nine, after five, and on weekends. And Reagan was not exactly won over by the fact that during the campaign against Jimmy Carter, he would be known as Governor Reagan while Ford would be Mr. President.[3]

Yet the very fact that this bizarre idea was considered underlined how unreliable and inexperienced Reagan was deemed to be despite his having been governor of California, the nation's most populous state (at the time there were 20 million inhabitants) for eight years, compared to Jimmy Carter's four years as governor of Georgia (which had a population of 4.5 million). But Reagan was regarded as outside the mainstream of American politics, a genial figure from the far right. He was an ideologue using a vocabulary made obsolete by Franklin Roosevelt's New Deal. He talked about rolling back government and cutting programs; he promoted free enterprise and celebrated the magic of the market. That was understandable if one was a spokesman for General Electric, or even the successor to the "Old Prospector" as the host of the television series *Death Valley Days*—as Reagan had been in his final years as an actor—before going into politics. But surely that was not the kind of rhetoric that was expected of a president of the United States.

Reagan liked to say that he did not mind being underestimated. It gave him an advantage. As it turned out, Ronald Reagan and his presidency did change the language of American politics, and he helped to set in motion a struggle to redefine the relationship of state and marketplace.

"Mugged by Reality"

Ideas created the context for Reaganism. In this, the Chicago School loomed very large. The skepticism generated by the economic difficulties of the

1970s helped to enlarge further the growing influence of the Chicago economists, who argued that government was the problem, not the solution. But
the Chicago School was hardly alone in this. Harvard's Martin Feldstein,
who served for a time as the head of Reagan's Council of Economic Advisers, and others did major work assessing the costs, in terms of lost investment and initiative, imposed by high tax rates. The public-choice theories
emanating from the University of Virginia provided an influential explanation for government's problems—that special interests turned government
activities to their own benefit. There also emerged a group of writers and
economists who quickly became known as "supply-siders." This group fervently believed that inflation was society's principal enemy, that the best way
to fight inflation was by controlling the money supply, and that the international currency system should be based upon fixed rates, ideally gold. But
the most famous concept associated with supply-side was the notion that the
revenues lost through tax cuts would be more than made up by the additional
tax revenues flowing in as a result of higher growth rates.

If various groups of economists dislodged assumptions about the way
America was working, a second set of ideas would provide a parallel political,
social, and even cultural critique that bolstered the redefinition: neoconservatism. This movement emerged in the United States in the late 1960s and early
1970s. Its cadres, numbering only a few dozen at first, were disillusioned
liberals—in the words of one of the leaders of the movement, Irving Kristol,
"liberals mugged by reality." Many had migrated from far on the left—from
youthful Marxism of one kind or another. Kristol himself observed that he did
not mind being tagged as an ex-Trotskyite fifty years after the fact because
he had first met his wife at a meeting of young Trotskyites in Brooklyn.

Neoconservatism had been energized into existence in response to the
"countercultural" explosion and the youth rebellion of the late 1960s, the
New Left and student assaults on universities, and the celebration of mili-
tancy and radicalism. The enemies of the neoconservatives were not only
socialism, Marxism, communism, and statism. Another enemy was the dominant American liberal ethos, which they believed had so permeated politics,
the media, and universities as to be almost unchallengeable. The neoconservatives became convinced that liberalism spawned laxity, decay, and moral
decline and that, ultimately, it would mean the degeneration of the United
States. They criticized ambitious government programs for failing to deliver
what they promised, for creating cultures of dependency, and for making
things worse instead of better. They based many of their most potent arguments on the law of unintended consequences. Public housing, for example,
created slums instead of eliminating them and, in the process, bulldozed
what had been affordable housing for lower-income working people. The
"neocons," as they came to be known, were also reacting against "third
worldism," which portrayed the United States as the source of the ills afflicting developing nations, the exploiter of the third world and purveyor of
oppression, and the blighter of human aspiration—in contrast to the benig-

330

nity of socialism and the Soviet Union. Tying it all together in the minds of the neocons was what they saw as the liberal predilection for guilt and self-flagellation, and the liberal culture of apology and quest for absolution, all of which led to disastrous policies at home and surrender abroad.

The neocons were intellectuals, and they, as much as the Hayeks and Friedmans, believed that their battle was about ideas. They were engaged in an ideological struggle against a set of dominant ideas that had held the commanding heights in American thinking for several decades. "The truth is that ideas are all important," Kristol wrote in the mid-1970s. "The massive and seemingly solid institutions of any society—the economic institutions, the political institutions, the religious institutions—are always at the mercy of the ideas in the heads of the people who populate these institutions. The leverage of ideas is so immense." Thus, the neocons carried out their campaign not in precincts but in print, developing and shaping their ideas in journals like *The Public Interest* and *Commentary,* and, of crucial importance, on the editorial pages of *The Wall Street Journal,* the only mainstream media outlet that carried their beliefs. The group included, at least some of the time, some of America's best-known intellectuals—Nathan Glazer, James Q. Wilson, Norman Podhoretz, Jeane Kirkpatrick, Michael Novak, Ben Wattenberg, Peter Berger, and perhaps the political-intellectual Daniel Patrick Moynihan (Daniel Bell, although sometimes tagged a neocon, distanced himself from the movement). Though not easy to pin down, the influence of neoconservatism was considerable. It redefined the boundaries of political debate. It provided a new set of ideas for conservatives. "The weakness of liberal social policy was becoming evident," recalled Kristol. "We gave conservatives a way of critiquing social and economic policies. Part of the impact arose from the peculiarity that we were a group of social scientists, not literary intellectuals, who came up with studies that Congress could understand and that the media could not dismiss merely as the work of New York intellectuals."

The neocons thought of themselves, at least at the time, as Democrats. Many of them were children of the New Deal. The Republican Party was for people who belonged to country clubs, not for people who had gone to City College. Indeed, as a young man Irving Kristol had written an article on discrimination in country clubs that had been informed by his underlying puzzle about why anyone would want to belong to a country club in the first place. But the nomination of George McGovern as the Democratic presidential candidate in 1972 convinced most of the neocons that they no longer had a home in the party, because it had been captured by the liberal left, which, in their view, was naive about communism and Soviet power and soft on defense.* "Though none of us was a Republican and few of us even

---

* Some years later, McGovern, long defeated and for a time an innkeeper, would blame the failure of his business on excessive government regulation.

knew any Republicans," Kristol recalled, "our political landscape was in the process of being transformed."

The neoconservatives called for a shrinking of government. With increasing vigor, they also offered an optimistic and confident affirmation of capitalism and the marketplace. Norman Podhoretz, the editor of *Commentary,* once suggested to Kristol that, since the word *capitalism* was somewhat "besmirched," he should instead write about *free enterprise* or *free markets.* Kristol would not budge. In his view, "the fight to rehabilitate the reputation of the system would be incomplete unless its name was rescued from discredit as well." As he later added, "That's the word. Use it."

"We had no economist in the original group around *The Public Interest,"* said Kristol. "I was not then a great admirer of Chicago. I was still a liberal, a skeptical liberal. What happened was that around 1980, the free-market school of thought and the neoconservative school of thought fused. Maybe Reagan did it." [4]

The irony was that the market system, as it was then, looked increasingly impaired. But under the influence of conservative economics and the neoconservative social critique, a profound change began to take place in views about the role of the American government. The process would take a long time. It really began with a crisis that preceded the Reagan administration: the inflationary turmoil of the late 1970s. As it had in the other industrial countries, that crisis signaled the weakness of the prevailing economic system and brought about its eventual transformation.

The Central Banker

The White House swearing-in ceremony on August 6, 1979, was unusually sober. Inflation was rising to levels never seen before in modern America, frighteningly high levels. It seemed to have become embedded in the very fibers of the country. Confidence was ebbing. Three weeks before, President Jimmy Carter had proclaimed a national "crisis of confidence" and had fired members of his cabinet. The move was meant to show resolve and steady the nation, but instead it further rattled the country. Carter appointed a new Treasury secretary, businessman William Miller, which in turn meant that the president had to fill Miller's former position—the chairmanship of the Federal Reserve Board. It would be a critical choice, for the Fed, which by statute operates as the nation's independent central bank, had a decisive role in the war on inflation. But whom to appoint? Carter was told that Paul Volcker, a longtime monetary expert and at the time president of the New York Federal Reserve, had the necessary capabilities and reputation to provide financial backbone. In fact Carter had never heard of Volcker, but he was desperate to restore some modicum of confidence and authority to the management of the economy. That was how Volcker ended up in the East Room of the White House. Considering the subsequent impact that his policies would have on the economy and their contribution to the outcome of the 1980 presidential election, Carter may later have wished that he had never heard of Volcker at all.

But on that August day Volcker knew exactly what his task was, even if he did not know exactly how to achieve it. "We are face-to-face with economic difficulties really unique in our experience," he said, suitably glum-faced at the swearing-in. "And we have lost that euphoria that we had fifteen years ago, that we knew all the answers to managing the economy." His mission was, he put it later, "to slay the inflationary dragon." If he failed, the consequences could either be a Latin American–style permanent inflation or another Great Depression. The political consequences could be even worse and would threaten the very foundations of American democracy. He was absolutely convinced of one other thing: Gradualism and half measures would not work.

At a White House tea party after the swearing-in, Volcker confided to a reporter, "I'm boring. It's the job of all central bankers to be as boring as possible." That was an exceedingly harsh self-appraisal for the man who would wage war on inflation and, against very high odds, win—and, in the process, set the United States on a new economic course.

Volcker was cut out for the part. At six-foot-seven, with a cigar often jammed into the corner of his mouth, he had been an unmistakable figure on the international financial circuit for years. It was said that he was the only man who could talk down to you and over your head at the same time. If somewhat shy, he was also self-confident and commanding, with considerable technical and political skills, a strong intuitive feel for markets, and a widely recognized integrity. In most of his career he was a public servant, and he lived a life of probity. His family remained in New York City, to which he returned on weekends, while during the week he lived in a small Washington apartment cluttered with old newspapers and fishing flies. Once a week, he packed up his laundry in a suitcase and took it to get washed at his daughter's house in northern Virginia. His personal style was enigmatic. Well schooled over the years in the tools of central banking, including the importance of surprise and secrecy, Volcker had perfected a talent for obfuscation and the central banker's mumble, which mixed profundities and banalities and non sequiturs in such a way as to be deliberately indecipherable.

Volcker had learned early to worry about inflation. At Princeton, some of his economics professors were from the Austrian School, which had spawned Hayek. For them, post–World War I inflation—with its devastating consequences—was the defining event. Although Volcker assimilated the Keynesian tools for analysis, he was always skeptical of the ability to manage something so complex as the economy. "The Kennedy and early Johnson administrations were absolutely the high point of hubris of economists," he said. "They thought they had the answers, that they knew how to pull the levers. I had a visceral reaction against it. I always thought it was too cocksure." Volcker was also shaped by his experience in the Federal Reserve. "I was a central banker," he said. "I was always worrying about inflation, even in the 1950s, when it was considered very threatening at two and a half percent." As undersecretary of the Treasury in the Nixon administration, he played a key role in the shift from the Bretton Woods world of fixed exchange rates to floating rates.[5]

As chairman of the Fed, Volcker was determined to extinguish the inflationary expectations that gripped the United States—what had become, as he called it, the national "bet on inflation." His weapon was a modified monetarism. Instead of explicitly setting interest rates (the price of money), the Fed would control the actual supply (or quantity) of money by managing bank reserves. It was a blunt weapon. But Volcker saw no choice. The effects were dramatic. As the Fed restricted the money supply, interest rates shot up, to 20 percent and above. The economy slowed and then contracted, falling into the deepest recession since the Great Depression. Unemployment rose to as high as 10 percent, houses went unsold, companies struggled with liquidity problems, cars sat on dealers' lots. The slump was—along with the Iran hostage crisis—a major factor in Ronald Reagan's defeat of Jimmy Carter in 1980. After Reagan's election, the Fed, and Volcker in particular, continued to be a prime target for angry politicians, who feared the political backlash. Yet Reagan himself never quite attacked Volcker. "People in the White House and Treasury put pressure on Reagan, but they could never get Reagan to criticize me," Volcker said. "Slight musings, yes. But Reagan had this visceral feeling that fighting inflation was a good thing." On the subject of conquering inflation, Reagan would say to his secretary of state, George Shultz, "If not us, who? If not now, when?"

Meanwhile, public anger against Volcker and the Fed mounted. Farmers surrounded the Federal Reserve building to protest the high interest rates. Auto dealers sent in coffins with car keys to symbolize the vehicles that went unsold because of high interest rates. Volcker himself would read heartbreaking letters that people wrote to him—about how they had saved for years to buy a house for their parents, but now, because of the high rates, could not. He was deeply upset by these letters, but he still saw no choice.* If inflation were not stamped out, there would be a much greater collapse. And he was convinced that, at last, he had support for tackling inflation head-on. "There was a sense that you wouldn't have won a majority of voters but you would have won a lot of votes," he said. "People were scared. Something had to be done. But none of us quite understood how tough it would be. Some things we never expected. Interest rates of twenty percent!

---

* Volcker was, however, personally stung when German chancellor Helmut Schmidt, who had bolstered the courage of Volcker and other American officials to take up the battle against inflation, later bitterly criticized what he derided as "the highest real interest rates since the birth of Christ."

Who ever expected twenty percent interest rates? But you get caught up in the process, and you can't let go. You don't want to let go. Letting up, giving up—that was not in my psychology."

It took three years. By the summer of 1982, the conquest of inflation was in sight. In fact, inflation that year would fall below 4 percent. Volcker's singular achievement was to conquer inflation at a time when defeatism was rampant. He set the United States on a new economic course. The risks of not succeeding were often on his mind. So was history. Once confronted with the accusation that he was behaving like a German central banker, he replied, "I don't take that as criticism. That's a compliment. I'm in pretty good company there." [6]

Beyond Tax-and-Spend

Thanks to Volcker's efforts, monetary restraint was obtained quite early in the course of the Reagan administration. And Reagan's unwaverng stance in the air traffic controllers' strike of 1981 helped change the tone of labor relations, indirectly contributing to the muting of inflationary psychology. But there was still fiscal policy to be dealt with—the ways that government raised its revenues and the ways that it chose to spend them. The rise of welfare demands, entitlements, and obligations toward the middle class, the poor, and especially the elderly made spending politically necessary as a source of votes. The problem, of course, was how to finance the outlays.

Ronald Reagan's advisers came to office with the intention of cutting both taxes and spending. But they soon found out that it was easier to achieve the first of these objectives than the second. The reason was simple: politics. It was popular to cut taxes. And taxes did come down substantially. The top marginal rate was reduced from 70 percent to 28 percent, the tax base was broadened, and many deductions and loopholes were eliminated. But it was unpopular to cut spending, and the Democratic Congress bridled at the extent of the cuts that the president proposed. Reagan did not take on middle-class entitlements. He also spared the Defense Department from the ax, and indeed initiated, over the course of his two terms, major increases in defense expenditures, including the "Star Wars" space defense program.

Some in the Reagan camp were optimistic, despite the failure to cut total government spending. They were the advocates of what traditional Republican economist Herbert Stein—echoing the music of the day—called "punk" supply-side economics, which made sweeping assertions that reductions in tax revenues resulting from tax cuts would be more than made up for by higher tax revenues generated by economic growth. It did not turn out that way. Because spending did not come down with taxes—and indeed defense spending went up sharply—and because the tax cuts did not feed back into the economy to the extent hoped, both the federal debt and the annual deficit ballooned; and in 1981–82, the economy was in a deep recession. In September 1982, in its first effort to repair the damage, the Reagan administration followed the "largest tax cut in history" with the "largest tax increase in history." But there was no catching up. By the end of Reagan's first term, the supply-side logic was discredited in the eyes of many, and the inability to bring taxes and spending down together stood in marked contrast to Volcker's victory over inflation. David Stockman, Reagan's first director of the Office of Management and Budget, left the administration dejected, disillusioned with supply-side economics, and chastened by the realities of the political process. Failure to achieve fiscal-policy change, he argued, was a clear vindication of the "triumph of politics"—of entitlements over austerity, and of the enduring pork-barrel tradition of American legislation over any cold economic logic. "I joined the Reagan Revolution as a radical ideologue," he wrote. "I learned the traumatic lesson that no such revolution is possible."

The triumph of politics and what Stockman called the "fiscal error" that went with it spawned a new monster, which would come to occupy center stage in policy debate: the deficit and the federal debt. Between the beginning and the end of the Reagan presidency, the annual deficit almost tripled. So did the gross national debt—from $995 billion to $2.9 trillion. Or, as Reagan and Bush administration official Richard Darman put it, "In the Reagan years, more federal debt was added than in the entire prior history of the United States."

There simply was no quick cure to the scale of spending. In the minds of some, however, there was another logic to tax cuts: Reduce taxes and government revenue, and eventually the pain and scale of deficits—and the threat of national bankruptcy—would force a retrenchment of government spending. That thought was not restricted to fervent supply-siders, and ultimately it would end up true. But not for some years, and certainly not during the Reagan years.

When George Bush took office in 1989, the annual deficit stood at $152 billion. Taxes could not be raised substantially for devastatingly powerful political reasons—as Bush found out when his retreat from his solemn "read my lips" campaign promise of "no new taxes" became his most damaging political liability. There was no choice but to contain spending. And luckily, international events afforded a good opportunity to start tackling the problem. The fall of the Berlin Wall and the crumbling of the Soviet empire made possible a tapering-off in defense spending. Still, this was not enough. Owing to the recession of the early 1990s, tax revenues fell, and in 1992, as Bush was ending his term, the deficit peaked at $290 billion.

By that time, out-and-out fiscal conservatives, proud to call themselves such, had gained ground in both major parties. The ideas that underpinned the "Reagan revolution" had acquired much wider resonance. "Tax and spend"—after all, the two basic functions of any fiscal policy—became a pejorative term, an epithet to avoid. On the Democratic side, a group calling themselves New Democrats criticized the traditional Democratic approach, and came to influence more and more of the party's agenda.

One of their best-known figures was the governor of Arkansas, Bill Clinton, who springboarded to the presidency. The division between Democrats ran right through his administration. Treasury Secretary Lloyd Bentsen and Robert Rubin, head of the the newly established National Economic Council, were convinced that the best way to promote economic growth was by reducing the deficit. That would bring down long-term interest rates. It would do so directly; it would also do so by engendering confidence in the bond market that the deficit really was being tackled, which would reduce the inflation premium in interest rates. And lower rates would be the best stimulus to investment-led growth, much better than the traditional Keynesian spending stimulus. In fact, any gains from a stimulus package would be more than offset by the higher interest rates with which the market would respond. In this, they were much in accord with Alan Greenspan, who had succeeded Volcker as chairman of the Federal Reserve Board in 1987, and who had watched the swelling deficits with increasing dismay. Greenspan was convinced that the continuing growth of deficits not only would mean higher taxes and slower growth but could well end in catastrophe. The traditional liberals among Clinton's officials and advisers were appalled. Clinton had not fought the election, they argued, to promote "Republican economics." The Democrats were betraying their traditional constituencies in order to pamper the rich. They wanted stimulus programs, increased government spending, and higher taxes, especially on the upper income. But Clinton had already made his choice. "During the transition," recalled Rubin, now Treasury secretary, "the president expressed his unequivocal commitment to making the deficit his priority." The deficit was enemy number one. That meant that spending would have to be restrained.

The president went all out in 1993 for a deficit reduction program that involved both spending cuts and some tax increases. The political battle was, as one participant put it, "murderous." The program just squeaked through Congress; Vice-President Al Gore had to break a tie in the Senate. "I said at the time that we would only get lower rates if the market believed in the deficit reduction," Rubin later said. "How long would it take for that to happen? The markets believed in our deficit reduction program, more quickly than I had thought they might." Passage of the program in August 1993 indeed proved to be the turning point. The bond market became persuaded that the deficit would be reduced. Long-term rates started down, and the economy moved into a state of reasonable economic growth and low inflation.

Yet this reorientation did not happen in a political vacuum. It was given high visibility by the 1992 third-party presidential bid of Ross Perot. The drive for spending cuts gained immensely in popularity in the early 1990s, culminating in the Contract with America, the Republicans' capture of both houses of Congress, and the ascendancy of Newt Gingrich. The confrontation between Clinton's Democratic administration and the brash Republican crusaders of the 104th Congress and the resulting government shutdown shifted the center in American economic policy. The Republicans used the specter of a prolonged battle over a balanced budget amendment to galvanize debate on current spending. They challenged virtually every area of traditionally "untouchable" government expenditure. They even proposed shutting down or merging entire executive departments, eliminating cabinet positions in the process. All this made the budget the chief focus of relations between the White House and the Congress. Overruling his more liberal advisers, Clinton adopted the principle of the proposed changes, including the balanced budget. But he stopped short of going as far as the Republicans advocated. That maneuver—which became known as triangulation—deprived them of much of their agenda.

The battle over the budget shifted the center of American economic policy, even of American politics. The ease—in relative terms—with which budget deals have been made since then shows how much this center has grown.

While the economic expansion actually began in the Bush administration, subsequent deficit reduction was central to its continuation—an acknowledgment, among other things, that the United States, no less than an emerging-market nation, is judged every day by the capital markets. As Rubin explained, "The threshold issue had to be the deficit and how quickly you can gain credibility with the markets, since ultimately it's interest rates that drive the economy."

The speed with which the deficit has come down—from almost 5 percent of GDP in 1992 to less than 1 percent in 1997—has surprised almost everybody. During the 1993 budget battle, both the administration and the Congressional Budget Office predicted that the 1997 deficit would be over $200 billion. It came in at only a tenth of that, $22.6 billion, the lowest level since the early 1970s. How did this dramatic turnaround come about? Partly through reductions in spending (primarily from defense), partly through higher taxes, and certainly through the flow of additional tax revenues generated by a strong economy. Whatever the reasons, the result is, as economist Benjamin Friedman put it, "a great achievement, and there is plenty of credit to go around." The next stage may well be a battle over what to do with an anticipated surplus—whether to pass it on to the public through tax cuts, or use it to chip away at the $5.7 trillion national debt, or spend it. All that assumes, of course, that there is no recession along the way that would reduce tax revenues and require increased transfer payments. In the meantime, at least one downside to the falling deficit has been detected. "The deficit is disappearing so fast," mused one senator, "that we may not be able to take complete credit for the decline."

In 1990, when the United States hosted the G-7 economic summit in Houston, its economy was hobbled by deficits, recession, and a pervasive loss of confidence. Americans anguished about competitiveness, jobs, and

338

innovation; they worried about the rise of Japan to preeminence in the world economy, and obsessively tried to discover the secrets of its success. America's "decline" was the theme of the day, and *declinism* was, in fact, the term coined to describe the school of thought that focused on America's apparent fall from economic grace. By the time of the 1997 summit in Denver, everything had turned around. The United States was the best-performing of the major economies. It had created 12 million jobs, compared to a net loss of 1 million for Europe and Japan combined, had brought unemployment under 5 percent, had cut its inflation rate in half, and had dramatically reduced the budget deficit. It was in the seventh year of an expansion, compared to almost seven years of slump in Japan. American business had gone through a wrenching process of remaking itself, and "Silicon Valley" (which included not only the actual geographic entity but stretched from Seattle to Houston to Boston's Route 128) was driving change in the world economy. All that added up to a reconfirmation of America's market system, and generated a recovery in self-confidence.

"It's unbelievable what has happened since 1990," observed Deputy Treasury Secretary Lawrence Summers. "It's almost a new world in economic terms since then. In 1990, an economy was defined very much by its automobile industry. Today, it's defined by its service industries, its software industries, and its 'content' industries. The change in the United States has been driven first and foremost by the restructuring of American industry itself. One of the country's comparative strengths has proven to be that, unlike in most other countries, bankers in America will give money to guys without ties."[7]

A Delayed Revolution

It had taken more than a decade and a half from Ronald Reagan's election to dilute the Keynesian imprint on government policy: to steady monetary policy, and to significantly restrain spending and taxation in ways that both parties could discuss and compromise on. The substance of the Reagan revolution was realized well after Reagan's passing from the political scene and well after the logic of supply-side economics had been discredited. It was not, therefore, the revolution the Reaganites had had in mind. But it was no less a revolution in its long-term effects, for it saw the government painfully but genuinely reducing its scope of intervention in the economy.

That applied to regulation as well. Ever since the New Deal, America had placed much of its confidence, in terms of overseeing the economy and avoiding abuses, in its web of regulatory agencies, combined with the powerful judicial antitrust tradition. From the mid-1930s until the mid-1970s the system did not change much. The regulators and the courts played their appointed roles. They came to resemble each other in procedure and style. But from 1975 onward, regulation began to change—drastically. In many areas, America experienced so-called deregulation—meaning the withdrawal of many regulatory restrictions over economic activity, although often with the requirement that new ones be devised as well. Yet in some other areas—particularly health, safety, the environment, employee and consumer rights, and affirmative action—there has been a great deal of new regulation. In some cases, the balance is ambiguous or still shifting. All in all, however, regulation remains a central means for government in the United States to effect major changes in the way the market, and individuals, behave.

From Capture to Competition

Economic regulation emerged with the establishment of the Interstate Commerce Commission in 1887. Over the next several decades, the rationales for such regulation were progressively elaborated. They included the promotion of economic development, equity and fairness, the requisite counterbalance to monopolies, and the provision of economically affordable universal services. From the New Deal onward, market imperfections and failures became a dominating rationale. And in the postwar years, government presence came to be felt in almost every economic enterprise.

Though the Reagan administration arrived with a promise to roll back economic regulation, the process had actually begun in the Ford and Carter administrations, in the middle and late 1970s. By then there was already a well-articulated critique of economic regulation, the result of the attention that economists and other social scientists had been devoting to the subject for a decade and a half. The Chicago School had been at the forefront, owing to the critique of American-style regulation by George Stigler. Stigler had spent much of the 1960s plowing through mountains of data on electric power regulation, stock exchange rules, and antitrust cases. "My findings were often surprising," he said. "The regulation of electric utilities did not help residential users; the regulation of stock issues did not help the widows and orphans who bought these issues."

From these findings came Stigler's famous theory of "regulatory capture." He concluded that the regulated firm always knew more about its own activities than the regulator could find out, and could use this information advantage to shift regulation in its favor. Entrenched regulation had come to serve the firms it was once meant to restrain. Later, students of Stigler would extend this theory to explore how special-interest groups and lobbies could take over the process. Because it challenged the notion that regulation could serve and protect an abstract, impartial public interest, Stigler's theory of regulatory capture was a head-on challenge to James Landis's ideal of disinterested regulation. On the contrary, Stigler argued, it was all too "interested."

The Chicago School also minimized the risks of monopoly and market power that had been central to almost a century of American political think-

340

ing and that had animated, among others, Theodore Roosevelt and Louis Brandeis. Instead, the Chicago School emphasized the negative costs of government control. By the mid-1970s, such arguments found a welcoming audience. The unhappy experience of inflation and wage and price controls, the rapid growth of regulation in the Johnson and Nixon administrations, persistent inflation, and then, after the 1973 oil price hike, the deep recession, all led to wholesale questioning of the entire regulatory structure. It was too rigid, too slow, too distorting, and ever more cumbersome. It hobbled technical and commercial innovation. The need to do something about inflation made deregulation particularly urgent. It was said that regulation not only fixed but drove up prices; deregulation would encourage competition and thus lower prices. And regulatory bodies were having to run harder and harder to keep up with the multiplying economic issues that resulted from technological change. Meanwhile, the growth of international trade and global competition made traditional antitrust less relevant.

With the passage of time, competition increasingly came to be seen as preferable to regulation. The very concept of natural monopoly—the economic name for a situation where multiple suppliers would lead to higher, not lower, costs—was questioned. If people who were now prevented from doing so really wanted to get into a business, and could feasibly do so even if only on a small scale, then the market would not, in fact, be a natural monopoly. Instead, it would be "contestable"—that is, subject to competition. And perhaps competition could better serve the objectives that regulation was supposed to achieve. The results would be lower costs to consumers.

Stigler and the Chicago economists were certainly not alone in their criticism. In 1969, for instance, the politically centrist Brookings Institution initiated a critique of the regulatory system that eventually ran to multiple volumes. That work had wide influence. The critique continued to mount. Some economists and political scientists built a theory of regulation based on the idea that participants in the process were rational actors, pursuing particular interests, and treated the political and regulatory systems as variants on markets in which outcomes were "bought" and "sold." Others examined organizational flaws in the system and the inability of regulation to keep up with technological change. If market failure had been the goad to regulation, then "regulatory failure" became a focus for critique. Regulation would fail to do its job because of poor design or because regulations outlived their time or because technology made them obsolete or because of gridlock and rigidity. There was much variation and disagreement among these different analyses. Yet all the criticisms led to a common conclusion: The regulatory branch of government was inherently flawed, and all too often, it was "private interest," not the public interest, that determined outcomes.

But it was not a conservative Republican who took the first step. In 1974, Senator Edward Kennedy became chairman of a newly created subcommittee on "administrative practice and procedure." For chief counsel, he brought down Stephen Breyer, a Harvard Law School professor, who had worked in the Watergate investigation. At Kennedy's request, Breyer came up with a list of possible investigations for the subcommittee. One of the items, airline regulation, interested Breyer the most. Kennedy checked it off. And that is how deregulation began in the United States.[8]

"Plums" and "Dogs"

Breyer taught antitrust and administrative law at Harvard. He believed in free markets and in ensuring that they worked through competition. Indeed, he could not understand the rationale for regulating markets that were structurally competitive. "Why regulate something," he asked, "if it can be done better by the market?" At the same time, he had become increasingly skeptical about the "science of administration" that had been the goal of James Landis. "During the New Deal," said Breyer, "people were deeply suspicious of the marketplace because of the Depression. People had tremendous confidence in the science of administration, the science of law. Regulation was regarded as a scientific method, which would produce the correct results and hold industry in check by the conscious application of the discipline. It turned out that there was no such science." Breyer was further influenced by the many volumes on regulation produced by the Brookings Institution. "Economics was verifying the suspicion that regulation can't do the job," he said. "People began to think that free markets were not so terrible."

Airline regulation offered a particularly tempting target. The Civil Aeronautics Board (CAB) had been established in 1938 to deal with what was described at the time as "near chaos" and "uneconomic, destructive competition and wasteful duplication of services" in U.S. aviation. The issue then was the rampant instability of the fledgling airline industry. The specific problem was airmail. The contracts let by the post office for airmail provided subsidies for the new business, and companies that were desperate to win those contracts wildly undercut each other in their bids. Losers accused the post office of favoritism. Regulation was introduced to bring some order to what was seen as a public service, both to meet the nation's needs and—at a time when war was on the horizon—to ensure stability in a civilian aviation industry that would be a very important foundation for military power.

What resulted, as the years passed, was a government-run cartel based upon a symbiotic relationship between regulator and regulatee, a system characterized by the allocation of what had become known as "plums" and "dogs." The CAB decided what tickets would cost on all routes, which meant that all airlines charged the same price on the same route. The CAB also decided who could fly the various interstate routes. This was the deal: Airlines would agree to provide unprofitable service along some routes— the dogs—for instance, to smaller cities. In turn, they would be compensated with high-volume, profitable routes—the plums. The CAB conducted lengthy and tedious public hearings, very much in the Brandeisian tradition and without much relation to the actual economics of the business. Then the commissioners would retire to a private room, make their decisions, and hand out the plums and the dogs.

"The CAB was supposed to be protecting the public," said Breyer. "But regulation was leading to higher prices. It spent 95 percent of its time keeping prices from being too low instead of pushing to get them lowered." The Kennedy hearings, in Breyer's mind, unfolded almost like a symphony. They were, he said, "beautiful. Everything emerged in detail just as the score had predicted." The hearings demonstrated how the system prevented competition and thus denied the public the price benefits that would otherwise result.

Yet it was one thing to so demonstrate the flaws of the system; it was quite another to change it in the face of the entrenched opposition by most of the airline industry. In the aftermath of the hearings, President Ford's CAB began to explore how to implement deregulation, but the Ford administration lasted only two and a half years. The Carter administration picked up the theme. The attack on regulation was thereafter led by an economist who was not at all part of the Chicago School. Indeed, he was a liberal Democrat in everything but, as it turned out, economic theory.

"Marginal Costs with Wings"

Something of a prodigy, Alfred Kahn graduated from New York University summa cum laude at age eighteen and then went on to Yale for his Ph.D. in economics, which he obtained at age twenty-four. Endowed with a quick mind and a passion for Gilbert and Sullivan operettas, he enjoyed playing with words, sometimes quite slyly. A professor of economics at Cornell University, he published his masterwork *The Economics of Regulation* at the right time, in 1970. It has been described as the "most influential work ever written on the subject."

The problem with so much regulation, said Kahn, was that it did not reflect the realities of the marketplace, and prevented price from doing its essential job. He explained, "The only economic function of price is to influence behavior—to elicit supply and to regulate demand." But much regulation seemed to do just the opposite—it sent signals quite at variance with the realities of supply and demand. Regulators often did not seem to understand the economics of the industries they were regulating—or the economic consequences of their own decisions. The guiding star of regulation Kahn said, should be marginal cost pricing—that is, prices should be determined by the cost of providing one additional unit of whatever the good or service.

Kahn's book appeared just at the time when the traditional regulatory

343

system was showing signs of severe malfunction, particularly in the energy and electric power sectors. His first opportunity to begin reforming regulation came when he was selected to head the New York State Public Service Commission, where he pushed through a complete redesign of electric power rates, keyed to marginal costs. Kahn developed a reputation as a regulatory reformer. In 1977, President Carter plucked him out of Albany and made him chairman of the Civil Aeronautics Board. At the time Kahn became chairman, a daunting six hundred separate route applications were waiting adjudication. He knew what he wanted to do: introduce competition and let the market take over the economic decisions now being made by the five CAB commissioners. To the swift, or at least the "on-time"—the spoils. To those who got it wrong—losses or, the ultimate sanction, bankruptcy. In the process, Kahn intended to eliminate the long and laborious hearings that owed more to what he called "Perry Masonisms," referring to the famous fictional litigator, than to sound economic analysis.

Kahn had little patience with the hearing process. "Due process in the fashioning of economic policy," he protested, "is not the same as due process in a criminal trial." But one would not know that from the way the CAB operated. He was amazed by the kind of questions the CAB was forced to consider: "May an air taxi acquire a fifty-seat plane? May a supplemental carrier carry horses from Florida to somewhere in the Northeast? May a carrier introduce a special fare for skiers that refunds the cost of their ticket if there is no snow?" And one of the most momentous questions of all: "May the employees of two financially affiliated airlines wear similar-looking uniforms?" All this—and much more—was being decided by government regulators. "Is there any wonder," said Kahn, "that I ask myself every day: Is this action necessary? Is this what my mother raised me to do?"

His major assault on the system was to allow flexibility in pricing, which meant discount fares. By the summer of 1978, over half of coach-class miles were being flown on "peanut," supersaver, and other discount fares. Kahn personally fielded many irate complaints. When Senator Barry Goldwater, the 1964 Republican presidential candidate and author of the best-selling *Conscience of a Conservative,* wrote him to complain about unpleasant conditions aboard now-packed flights, Kahn replied that this was the inevitable consequence of breaking up a "cartel-like regime." He added, "When you have further doubts about the efficiency of a free market system, please do not hesitate to convey them to me. I also warmly recommend some earlier speeches and writings of one Senator Barry Goldwater." When a friend wrote him about how unpleasant it had been to sit next to a hippie on a flight, Kahn replied, "Since I have not received any complaints from the hippie, I assume the distaste was not reciprocated."

Kahn's biggest battles were with the airlines and groups that had grown up with regulation and did not want it changed. In one hearing, former astronaut Frank Borman, president of Eastern Airlines, was seeking to clarify the advantages of different types of aircraft. "I really don't know one plane from another," Kahn shot back. "To me they are all marginal costs with wings." In October 1978, airline deregulation became law: The plums and dogs were gone. Airlines were free to set fares competitively. They could decide whether to enter or exit markets and routes. And entry was now open to new companies. The CAB itself went out of business in 1985. Safety remained the province of the Federal Aviation Administration.

This was deregulation—the first major rolling back of the New Deal system. And how did it work out? It is estimated that on average, air travelers in 1996 paid 26 percent less for trips than they would have if regulation had stayed in place—although business travelers are clearly disadvantaged compared to leisure travelers. Some of the most established carriers have gone bankrupt, although some operated through bankruptcy and came out on the other side. Instead of ten trunk (i.e., major) carriers in the United States, there are now six. In the early years of deregulation smaller cities and towns either lost their air service (especially jets) or were threatened with such loss. Commuter airlines stepped into the breach, replacing one or two jet touchdowns a day with much more frequent small-plane service. One of the unanswered questions is what effect the loss of jet service has had on economic development in smaller cities and towns. But in the larger context, airline deregulation did mark a turning point, a reversal of the regulatory thrust of the preceding forty years and a turn to the market.[9]

Airlines were only the most visible example of economic deregulation. The overall process touched other areas of daily life. Railroads and trucking were also targets. Railroad regulation had been based upon the natural-monopoly argument. As early as the mid-1930s, some New Dealers had pointed out that competition did exist—from trucks, which could also carry freight. But this was disregarded until the 1970s, when it became apparent that the highly irrational regulatory system was destroying not only the economic viability of railroads but even their ability to serve customers. Rate setting did not accord with the economics of efficiently running a railroad.

One of the leaders in the decontrol movement in the 1970s was Edward Jordan, chairman of Conrail, which was created on an emergency basis in the early 1970s as a government-sponsored company to pick up the pieces after the bankruptcy of Penn Central and several other railroads. "Regulation froze managers into a mind-set that did not allow them to run their business," he explained. "Their control over revenue generation was not significant; that was determined by regulators in Washington. This meant that they could not tailor their business to their customers' service needs. The typical railroad executive was either a trainman or a lawyer—who knew how to interact with the commission—rather than a businessman. The people who made the change came from the outside. They were not bound by the regulatory mind-set." These efforts culminated in almost total deregulation by the beginning of the 1980s, and here the consequences were unambiguous. Cost savings from deregulation are estimated at $50 to $70 billion. Railroads started making profits again. Innovation was encouraged. And freight now moves over cost-efficient routes rather than the ludicrously circular routes that were mandated by regulators.

For Whom the Bell Tolls

The biggest regulated company of all was AT&T—the country's largest enterprise, with over 1 million employees—which provided the bulk of telephone services, local and long distance, in the United States. Other companies, like General Telephone and Electric, competed around the edges. AT&T's operation was based on the idea of a natural monopoly; and its regulation, on the preservation of the public good.

AT&T had quickly risen to preeminence in the last part of the nineteenth century on the basis of Alexander Graham Bell's invention of the telephone in 1876, its control of patents and its strategy of horizontal and vertical integration. At its heart was the vision of cheap universal service— in the words of its 1910 Annual Report, "annihilating time or distance by use of electrical transmission." It was helped by Western Union's early decision to get out of the telephone business in order to protect what Western Union thought—mistakenly, as it turned out—would be the much more lucrative business of intercity telegraph. Its growth by acquisition was financed by J. P. Morgan. AT&T was also shaped by a widespread belief at the federal and state level and in the public that competition was duplicative, inefficient, and wasteful, and would deliver inferior service. The phone business should be a monopoly, but a regulated one. At the state level, public-utility commissions did the regulating. At the federal level, regulatory authority was invested in the Interstate Commerce Commission but then shifted by the New Deal's 1934 Communications Act to a new body, the Federal Communications Commission. As Franklin Roosevelt's secretary of commerce put it, telephone service "by its very character" would be "most efficient and satisfactory if conducted as a monopoly."

AT&T provided everything, from the long-distance service to the equipment in the house. And it delivered a very high quality of service. If a subscriber had a problem, the truck would speedily arrive, the problem would be traced and rectified, and there was no squabbling over jurisdiction. "By comparison to any other national network," observed regulatory historian Richard Vietor, "there is no question that this system worked best— measured by penetration, technical quality, or price." AT&T also jealously guarded its monopoly. "Foreign attachments" were not permitted anywhere. Thus the phone company effectively fought off the competitive challenge posed by the Hush-a-Phone, a sort of small cuplike attachment put around the mouthpiece to increase the privacy of the speaker. Using any foreign attachment meant risking the cutoff of one's phone service.

The system was settled and accepted. Only the most adventurous, and perhaps even foolhardy, would dare to challenge AT&T's formidable position—and expend the time and effort so doing. And it took such a character, William McGowan, a consultant-turned-entrepreneur, who started his attack from the fringes in the late 1960s and pursued it resolutely thereafter. McGowan had grasped a golden opportunity when the founders of a firm called Microwave Communications, Inc. (later just MCI) came to him for advice about securing finance for their venture to connect trucks on the St. Louis–Chicago run by microwave signal. Instead of giving them advice, he bought control of the firm.

McGowan embarked on a crusade to undermine AT&T's monopoly. The first step was to win approval from the FCC for its long-distance private-line service. After six years of interminable hearings, filings, appeals, and rehearings—during which it almost went under—MCI won approval from the FCC to establish its service. The vote among the commissioners was a close four to three. One of those who voted yes explained that he was looking "for ways to add a little salt and pepper of competition to the rather tasteless stew of regulatory protection that this Commission and Bell have cooked up." McGowan continued his campaign against AT&T in the courts. At times, it seemed that pursuing lawsuits was the company's only vocation —as the in-house joke went, the company was "a law firm with an antenna on the roof." But McGowan's perseverance would pay off.

McGowan may have done more than anybody else to upset the long-standing regulatory system. But it was technological change that really undermined AT&T's monopoly and the regulatory system that went with it. The problem was no longer a little cup like the Hush-a-Phone. It was the computer age. The development of computing technology and the tremendous growth in data transmission eroded the traditional concept of long distance, creating new demands by customers and new incentives for competition. Private networks were developing rapidly to meet the demands of large users and data flow. There was no longer any clear difference between switching equipment and data processing. Technological progress was generating a growing pressure on the AT&T monopoly. More and more people were doubting the validity of the existing system, which in any event was eroding. Moreover, it had become very clear that long-distance rates subsidized local rates; that recognition provided an incentive for large corporate users to seek ways around the monopoly in order to get cheaper rates for their long-distance and data services.

AT&T sought to resist the pressure for change. "What do we believe?" the chairman of AT&T rhetorically asked a convention of state utility regulators. "We believe . . . that the public interest . . . cannot help but be impaired by the duplication . . . that will inevitably result from the further encroachment of competition. . . . There is something right about the common carrier principle. There is something right about regulation. And, given the nature of our industry, there is something right about monopoly—regulated monopoly." The message may have rung with a clear tone since the turn of the century, but it did not ring true anymore. The Justice Department filed an antitrust suit against AT&T in 1974. Federal judge Harold Greene took responsibility for the case. The trial opened in 1981. Judge Greene rejected AT&T's motion for dismissal, commenting that the government had presented evidence that "the Bell System has violated the antitrust laws in a number of ways over a lengthy period of time." Concluding that the company was cornered, management made the decision to accept the breakup of the company. The consequence—the result of almost two years of negotiation between the company and the Department of Justice—was "the biggest, most complex restructuring in the history of business." The company was divided into separate "local" (i.e., regional) companies—the Baby Bells—and a long-distance-only company, the successor AT&T, which now competes in the United States against MCI (soon to be merged), Sprint, and a host of others, and is also competing in markets around the world.

For the United States, the result has been a telecommunications system that is partly regulated and partly deregulated—indeed, a system that has been described as regulated competition. The long-distance business is mostly deregulated; local service, which has been regulated, is now opening to competition. Local and long-distance phone companies, along with regulators and consumer groups, are struggling over the degree to which long-distance rates should continue to subsidize local rates—and if they do not, how to ensure that low-income families can still afford basic phone services. In other words, how to maintain the commitment to universal service? For customers, the results have been falling costs for long-distance service, an explosion in innovation, many more options, and much greater flexibility. It has also meant confusion in figuring out whom to call for repairs, frustration with the operations of no-brand pay phones, and rage at the innumerable dinnertime calls selling long-distance service.

Where the Money Is

The New Deal's regulatory legacy is also being reassessed in the financial sector. "Our approach is not deregulation but sensible regulatory reform," said Eugene Ludwig, who, as comptroller of the currency, oversees a major part of the national banking system. One of the first things that Franklin Roosevelt did when he became president in 1933 was declare a "bank holiday"—temporarily shutting their doors to prevent runs—and ever since the New Deal, the financial sector has been heavily regulated. The range of control is extraordinarily broad—from the Glass-Steagal legislation, which until recently forbade overlap between commercial and investment banks, to the requirement that the federal government approve every new automated teller machine—a process that typically, for each ATM, requires thirty-five steps and takes thirty-seven days. The Office of the Comptroller has been reviewing every single one of its seventy-two regulations. "We want to hold up everything to the light," said Ludwig "and ask: Does it make sense? Add value? How much does it matter? Is the burden worth the benefit? Some of the regulations didn't make sense when they were first put in place."

That things can go wrong was underlined by the severe crisis that hit the savings and loan industry in the late 1980s and early 1990s. That crisis was the result of both partial deregulation and what Paul Volcker called "a failure of regulation and supervision." Restrictions were lifted on the interest rates that these institutions could pay for deposits and on what they could invest those deposits in. This led them, in Volcker's words, into "temptation —they could make bigger mistakes than otherwise." But deposits were guaranteed by the federal government, meaning that the savings and loans could take ever-larger risks with a sense of impunity. Government examiners might well have blown the whistle, but executives of savings and loans, big political contributors, applied intense political pressure to avert exposure of the risks. It was only when massive bankruptcy and default were at hand that the full extent of the scandal became apparent. Taxpayers ended up stuck with the tab for a $300 billion bailout. The crisis also left a renewed sense of sobriety about the complexity of regulation in the financial sector.

"The trick in regulation," Ludwig said, "is to get the right balance. There is pretty clear evidence that some of the financial unraveling of the 1980s occurred because of regulatory mistakes. On the other hand, there are knaves and fools, and you can't rely entirely on the market itself. The financial system does benefit from a certain amount of oversight and supervision. Some participants will go way out on the bell curve toward high risk in pursuit of high rewards. Regulation helps to push back toward the center, and ensures that a high risk/reward ratio for individuals does not lead to contagion or a systemic crisis. The financial system is different from other sectors because of its centrality to the economy. It can be manipulated. You don't get a run on Toys "Я" Us because of rumors about Barbie. You can get a run on a bank. Illegal activities can lead to insolvency. There's more of a stake in keeping the financial sector honest than there is, for instance, in cosmetics."

But the biggest deregulation yet is still very much in the process of unfolding. It is transforming an industry that is the most capital intensive in the world and is bigger than airlines and telecommunications combined— electric power. Nothing else is as emblematic of deregulation. It touches everyone—and everyone's monthly bills.[10]

Electricity: The Collapse of the "Compact"

In 1993, Elizabeth Moler and William Massey went to London to present the results of U.S. natural gas deregulation. At that point Moler was the chair and Massey a commissioner of the Federal Energy Regulatory Commission

(FERC), which regulates interstate commerce in electric power and natural gas. It is the modern version of the Federal Power Commission, established in 1920 and bolstered by the New Deal. In the early 1990s, the FERC had just completed deregulating a substantial part of the natural-gas industry. Moler's attention, and that of her colleagues, was now turning to electric power. While in Britain, Moler and Massey investigated the changes in the British power industry that the Thatcher government had implemented. They were impressed by how the once-monolithic state-owned industry had been turned into a competitive business, with prices constantly changing in response to supply and demand. The British experience emboldened them to speed up change in the U.S. electric power industry. When Moler and Massey returned to Washington, they and their colleagues agreed that the FERC should do something bold, very bold: Open up the electric power industry—and as fast as possible.

The challenge was enormous. The U.S. electric power industry was conservative, slow-moving, and cautious, and it was run by very clear, if rigid, rules of the game. The system, as established by the New Deal in the wake of the collapse of Samuel Insull's empire, operated under what was called the regulatory compact. Utilities were natural monopolies. It made no sense to have two sets of wires running down an alley. The utility was given its monopoly franchise in exchange for a limited rate of return and a very high degree of governmental oversight and regulation. Interstate transactions were supervised by the Federal Power Commission, and later the FERC. Intrastate activities, the greater part of the business, were regulated by the states' public utility commissions, which set the rates that consumers would pay. They did so through a laborious, legalistic, highly ritualized process called rate hearings, in which—Kabuki-like—lawyers, lobbyists, corporate officials, experts, intervenors, environmentalists, consumer activists, and regulators all performed their stylized roles. The rates allowed the utility to earn a regulated profit, which was determined as a return on capital. There was nothing flamboyant about the return, but it was predictable, fixed—and essentially guaranteed. Along with that went an extreme emphasis on reliability of service. No blackouts. No brownouts. The Public Utility Holding Companies Act of 1935 sharply constrained combinations among utilities, particularly across state borders. The thought of a national utility was inconceivable. The utility was at the very center of the local economy and community. As often as not, its CEO headed the local United Way campaign.

Until the 1970s, the system had worked brilliantly, delivering ever-cheaper prices to consumers. In inflation-adjusted terms, electricity prices had dropped from thirty-seven cents per kilowatt-hour in 1934 to about five cents in 1970. What an astonishing boon to consumers—and to the economy. Economies of scale worked. Bigger, newer plants lowered costs. But then the system began to buckle under the high inflation, high investment, and high costs of the 1970s. New plants were now costing much more, not less, than older plants. This was especially true of the new nuclear plants, whose costs spiraled up because of constant design revisions during construction to meet changing safety regulations. Higher oil and gas prices also hit the system. Consumers now found that the prices they paid were going up, and sometimes sharply, not down. They were stunned by "rate shock." The economics of the industry had become wacky. For instance, consumers in northern Illinois paid twice as much for electricity as their neighbors in southern Wisconsin. Many utilities staggered under an enormous debt burden, made much heavier by high interest rates. A number of them teetered on bankruptcy.

By the early 1980s, the regulatory compact was broken. One response was "more government"—more regulation, more directives, more intervention—as state public-utility commissions effectively began to assume control over most basic economic decisions. But there was another, more radical, response—based on the heretical thought that perhaps utilities, at least in many of their functions, were not natural monopolies. Perhaps at least parts of the business could be competitive. The first glimmer of this came in the aftermath of the 1978 Public Utility Regulatory Policies Act (PURPA), which permitted entrepreneurs to build a power plant and sell its power to a local utility. The original purpose was to promote conservation and a cleaner environment, as well as to provide bite-size additions to generation, as opposed to the massive additions of a huge nuclear power plant. But as so often happens with new initiatives, the development of "independent power" had an unintended consequence. It demonstrated that utilities did not have an inherent monopoly over the economical generation of electric power. Other people could design, finance, build, and operate a plant just as cheaply if not more so—and sell the electricity they generated to the utility's grid.

By the late 1980s, the elements were in place to promote competition. Major technological innovation, particularly in new turbines based on jet-engine technology, made possible much more efficient use of natural gas—and smaller, environmentally attractive plants. A host of aggressive entrepreneurs were anxious to break into the traditional utility business in a big way. And the market was there. Big industrial consumers of electricity wanted to reduce their power costs. The way to do that, they believed, was to shop around and buy the cheapest kilowatt-hours. That required competition. The utility industry itself was deeply split between those who favored more competition and those who argued that the traditional structure served the customers best—and warned that competition might jeopardize reliability.

The Bush administration initiated a proposal to reduce regulation on investors who put money into power plants. But it soon came up against a second issue, which proved to be the critical one—access to transmission. That is, would the local utility have to open up its wires to competing generators? In other words, would the wires become a highway or, more properly, a tollway—open to anyone who paid the tariff? The stakes were very high, and the ensuing battle was very bitter. "If any of us had realized the scale of the issue we were taking on," said Philip Sharp, who was chairman of the key House subcommittee, "we would have been more cautious, because it was so politically difficult." But the matter was resolved with the passage of the Energy Policy Act of 1992, which provided, in principle, for transmission access but limited it only to wholesale buyers and sellers, not individual customers. This legislation persuaded all participants in the industry—and those outside, looking to get in—that an era of genuine competition was coming. But how far and how fast? That was up to the FERC and, in particular, to its new chairman, Betsy Moler.

"We're Teachable"

Some years earlier, Moler had worked on Capitol Hill as a young Democratic staff member of the Senate Energy Committee. Like many others, she had gone through the traumatic battle over natural-gas legislation in the late 1970s. That legislation had been laboriously constructed to manage a transition for natural gas from price controls to a freer market. "We tried to provide transition mechanisms that would allow us to inch along the way from a regulated to deregulated market," said Moler. "Democrats do equity. We didn't want consumers to experience price gouging. But once we had deregulated the commodity market, we discovered that there were enough players, and prices eventually went down, not up." She added: "Democrats have, I think, increasingly come to respect the power of markets. We recognize what competition can do. We're teachable."

With the mandate provided by the Energy Policy Act of 1992, Moler and her colleagues at the FERC began to issue experimental rulings, opening up the power industry to competition. Three years of work culminated in the mammoth Order 888, a major step in bringing down the New Deal system and implementing competition. Order 888 permitted a local utility in one part of the country to contract for electric power from a cheap generator in another part of the country. This power is "wheeled" across transmission lines belonging to a number of companies and finally sold through the local utility to the final customer. Those with high-cost power would no longer be able to block their low-cost competitors from getting to market. Various states are now working on plans that would permit retail competition. That means final customers—whether industrial firms or individual homeowners —would be able to buy directly from generating companies, which would compete on the basis of price. The only part of the utility industry that is now clearly regarded as a natural monopoly is the "wires business"— transmission and local distribution: It still does not make sense to have two sets of wires running down an alley.

The economic impact of competition is enormous. Subjecting the power industry to market forces will change the dollar value of every power plant, every transmission system, every asset of the industry. Altogether, these assets make up 10 percent of fixed business investment in the United States —and now they are worth something different than before deregulation. The retreat of government is also forcing utilities to make immense organizational and cultural changes. Companies that formerly focused on the legal and regulatory system now must contend with competitors and think about marketing. Companies will have to decide whether to stay in the generation, transmission, distribution, and service parts of the business, or exit one or more. Many companies will merge to lower their costs. Others, seeking to take advantage of their wires, will seek to become service providers—not only of electricity but also of telephone, video, Internet, and home security. A number will seek new growth in markets outside the United States. Companies not now in the power business will battle their way in. Meanwhile, new companies will spring up to market power across the United States.

Insofar as the electric power industry shifts from the traditional regulated monopoly to a more market-based system, electricity regulators will change their jobs. Their new occupation will be to make sure that the market is competitive—and remains so. "Regulators are referees now," said Moler. "They don't set prices. They call balls and strikes." [11]

Social Regulation: Expanding Its Reach

If the general trend in economic regulation is toward greater reliance on the market, somewhat the opposite is happening in the realm of what is called social-value regulation, which encompasses such areas as environmental, antidiscrimination, and workplace regulation. In these realms, the "fourth branch of government" is having a bigger and bigger say. Every administration since Richard Nixon's, whether Democratic or Republican, has declared that there is too much regulation and that it needs serious pruning. But the trend has been the opposite—a vast expansion in the fourth branch, resulting in what has been described by critics as the "criminalization of just about everything." It is very difficult to gain an overall view of the ever-growing edifice of social-value regulation; only those who are touched by this or that part of the regulatory system know it is there. To confuse matters further, the debates are passionate. Emotions run very high, driven by notions of justice and fairness, of safety and risk, and differing fundamentally on facts and theory. There is also, at least in the view of some, an ideological difference.

Whatever the point of view, risk regulation—involving health, safety, and the environment—suffers from what Stephen Breyer, now a Supreme Court Justice, calls "regulatory gridlock." Risk regulation goes back to the desperate need in nineteenth-century America to contain the most immediate and gravest danger—fire. In densely populated areas such as New York City and Philadelphia, city ordinances prohibited wooden or plaster chimneys, straw or reed roofs, and haystacks. Fire wardens patrolled neighborhoods, inspecting the cleanliness of chimneys; state authorities regulated stores of gunpowder. At the turn of the century, the muckrakers' exposés of deplorable sanitary conditions led to the establishment of food and drug regulation. But it was only in the late 1960s and early 1970s that a new spirit of activism initiated a great growth in regulatory activities, at the federal, state, and local levels. Both EPA—the Environmental Protection Agency—and OSHA— the Occupational Safety and Health Administration—were established during the Nixon administration. Pollution—dirty air in cities, dirty water in the nation's lakes and streams—spawned a host of new requirements. Progress has been enormous. It is now possible to fish and swim in the Hudson River. A new car rolling off the assembly line in Detroit in 1997 produced only 5 percent as much pollution as a car built during the early 1970s. Los Angeles is the city that made smog famous. Yet, despite an increase in population of more than 30 percent in Los Angeles since then, the air is 36 percent cleaner.[12]

Overall, the environment in the United States and other industrial countries is much cleaner than it was two decades ago. This has been achieved by a combination of regulation and activism, along with technological innovation and intellectual redefinition. Yet at the same time, the system of environmental regulation that has evolved is increasingly seen as cumbersome, inflexible, and overly prescriptive. Among other reasons, this happens because the Congress writes extremely detailed statutory instructions. Instead of general guidelines and goals, "command and control" regulation tends to be imposed in very defined ways, which deters innovation and efficiency. Moreover, regulations have a habit of growing topsy-turvy. Governmental micromanagement is endemic, further reducing the potential for technological innovation and creativity. Science is often at the center of dispute, and priorities often result from the unpredictable interplay of press, public, special-interest groups, politicians, and what Breyer calls "pseudoscience," rather than some ranking of risk and urgency. In the words of Breyer, "We have substituted fear of the market with fear of what goes up the chimney."

He points to the challenge of building flexibility into regulation. "It is always a problem to get discretion into the process so that the regulator can apply a reasonable amount of cautious regulation. Because no one trusts anyone else, there is less discretion, more rules, more rigid results. The only way to improve this regulation is to give administrators more discretion. But Congress writes the rules to prevent discretion. If there is too much discretion, there is a risk of abusing it. If you stop discretion, you get rules and rigidity. It's always true. The challenge is to find balance between rules and discretion."

Critics of the current system worry about its rationality and the "last five—or ten—percent problem." Remediating 90 or 95 percent of a pollution problem can be done in an efficient, cost-effective fashion. The last 5 or 10 percent—purity—is an almost unachievable goal, and one that diverts resources from more pressing needs. "The drive for perfectionism has created a very big mess," said Justice Breyer. In his recent book *Breaking the Vicious Circle: Toward Effective Risk Regulation,* he cited a case he presided over when he was a federal judge. The case involved a ten-year battle to force the cleanup of a toxic waste dump in New Hampshire: "The site was mostly cleaned up. All but one of the private parties had settled. The remaining private party litigated the cost of cleaning up the last little bit, a cost of about $9.3 million to remove a small amount of highly diluted PCBs and 'volatile organic compounds' (benzene and gasoline components) by incinerating the dirt. How much extra safety did this $9.3 million buy? The forty-thousand-page record of this ten-year effort indicated (and all parties seemed to agree) that, without the extra expenditure, the waste dump was clean enough for children playing on the site to eat small amounts of dirt for 70 days each year without significant harm. Burning the soil would have made it clean enough for the children to eat small amounts daily for 245 days per year without significant harm. But there were no dirt-eating children playing in the area, for it was a swamp. Nor were dirt-eating children likely to appear there, for future building seemed unlikely. The parties also agreed that at least half of the volatile organic chemicals would likely evaporate by the year 2000. To spend $9.3 million to protect non-existent dirt-eating children is what I mean by the problem of the 'last 10 percent.' "

The entire system struggles with the fundamental issue of how to assess and measure risk. One way is to analyze the balance between the costs of a regulation and the benefits achieved, but the results of such cost-benefit analysis have been mixed. The vexing matter of the cost of lives saved demonstrates the difficulties. The range is so wide as to veer into the meaningless. It is estimated that the ban on flammable pajamas for children came out to less than $1 million per life saved. By contrast, a more recent rule limiting exposure to formaldehyde works out to an estimated $93 billion per life saved.

A new approach is evolving to bring greater flexibility and efficiency to environmental protection. It is the application of economic incentives and market mechanisms to solve problems, which supplants traditional bureaucratic methods. Clearly, this is the frontier for ecology in the United States. "After twenty-five years, we are moving into a new generation of environmentalism," explained Daniel Esty, director of the environmental law program at Yale University and former assistant EPA administrator. "Rather than command-and-control, it will be market-based." This emerges from dissatisfaction with the rigidities of regulatory command-and-control systems and a quest for greater effectiveness—along with an overall greater openness to market solutions in the United States than in the past.

This new approach is most evident in the emergence of "emissions trading" as a way to promote better air quality. Under a system known as tradable rights, a company acquires from the government, either by purchase or as a grant, a permit to emit a certain amount of pollution. It can either emit pollution up to that point or sell all or part of its allotment to other companies and clean up some of its own emissions. One consequence is that the government controls the overall allowable pollution in a certain region, but the market portions it out. As a result, environmental quality is optimized for the entire region rather than on a company-by-company or facility-by-facility basis. Although experiments with such market approaches actually began in the late 1970s, they became successfully institutionalized only with the Clean Air Act Amendment of 1990.

The record so far is very encouraging. Indeed, in the words of Daniel Dudek of the Environmental Defense Fund, the results have been "spectacular" in terms of demonstrating "the power of market forces to produce environmental benefits"—as measured in "superior environmental performance, lower cost and a ramping back of otherwise intrusive relationships between regulators and business." Total emissions have been reduced much more rapidly, and at much lower cost than had been anticipated. "What other environmental program can show such dramatic performance in so short a time?" asked Dudek. This kind of approach—providing incentives and allowing choice—is also encouraging innovation in a way that overwritten, highly directive regulations cannot. Market-based systems have one other very promising characteristic: They have the potential to reduce the adversarial conflict between environmentalists and industry and, instead, provide a framework for collaborating on solutions. Can market-based systems work across borders? That will be tested by the attempts to create an international system to respond to global-climate-change concerns.[13]

The "Rights Explosion"

Social regulation has also been mounting since the 1960s in what has been called the rights explosion. This is particularly evident in the expanding definitions of discrimination, which, it is argued, should be corrected through various requirements, tests, and penalties. In turn, all of these have increased. The most prominent rights initiative is affirmative action, the legacy of the civil rights movement, which now inflames opinion on both sides of a very bitter debate. To proponents, affirmative action is a method of correcting past wrongs, creating opportunities where they have been denied, and confronting the persistence of race and gender discrimination. Opponents argue that by submerging people into special-interest groups, the programs run counter to equality of opportunity, brand beneficiaries as inferior, prevent people from being judged on their merits, and depend upon controversial definitions of racism and sexism. Contention has increased as quotas and other methods devised to correct one fundamental problem—racial inequality—have been extended to a host of other issues and as new values are set against traditional meritocracy. The explosion of rights has bred a proliferation of rules and of agencies to administer them.

356

There are many other examples of the ways in which government is extending its regulation and control over the marketplace. The constraints in the processes of hiring and firing are a notable example. In hiring someone, an employer is proscribed from asking about such things as the age of the applicant, his or her marital or family or even health status, for any one of these might be considered a basis of discrimination. Yet critics maintain that all those are reasonable questions in order to get to know applicants and make a judgment about whether or not to hire them. It is also very risky for an employer to provide anything more than the most banal reference for a former employee. Companies are now advised to restrict references to the "former employee's job title and starting and ending dates of employment." Otherwise, they open themselves to being sued.

The direct impact of social-value regulation and legislation is much accentuated by the peculiar American phenomenon of "adversarial legalism"—lawsuits. This form of litigation has been described by Pietro Nivola, a senior fellow at the Brookings Institution, as not merely a "means of resolving personal disagreements" but also as "institutions of governance or social regulation." He explained: "A civil jury that levies millions in punitive damages against a maladroit business is addressing more than a private matter. Much like an injunctive order from the Consumer Product Safety Commission or the Equal Employment Opportunity Commission, the civil verdict supposedly serves the public purpose of deterring some perceived threat to society." An eighty-two-year-old woman sued McDonald's after she burned herself by spilling hot coffee bought from a drive-through line. The jury found that McDonald's was willfully negligent for serving coffee that was too hot and awarded her $2.9 million to send a message (the judgment was subsequently reduced). Universities have grown accustomed to expect lawsuits charging discrimination by professors who do not get tenure. Even corporate results provide a platform for litigation. A company that may have created hundreds of new jobs is vulnerable when it goes public. For if its share price falls because of a poor quarter, the company may well end up in the defendant's chair.

The drive to encourage litigation has been deliberate. The 1991 Civil Rights Act greatly stiffened penalties, promoted punitive damages, allowed claims for emotional injury, and increased attorneys' fees. All this was in line with the act's explicit purpose, in the words of Philip Howard, "to encourage private citizens to sue" because "the principle of anti-discrimination is as important as the principle that prohibits assaults, batteries and other intentional injuries to people." Thus, Congress envisions each employee as deputized to act as a "private attorney general to vindicate these precious rights."

At least one major objective of the new legislation is being achieved: Employment discrimination litigation is mushrooming. Indeed, the regulation/litigation system is expanding so fast that Federal District Judge Stanley Sporkin has warned that "the federal courts are becoming flooded with employment cases." He added, "We are becoming the personnel czars of virtually every one of this nation's public and private companies." [14]

Going Private, American-style

On March 26, 1987, John Weinberg, the managing partner of the investment bank Goldman, Sachs, signed a check for $1.65 billion to the U.S. government. It was not a tax bill. It was the proceeds of what up until then was the largest initial public offering ever made on the New York Stock Exchange. The United States government had sold off its holdings in Conrail, the railroad that had been created a decade earlier to keep freight service going after two major railroads went bankrupt. The circumstances of the sale were unusual. Traditionally, there has been much less public ownership in the United States than in other countries, so there was not a long list of major assets slated to be sold off. Yet the value of Conrail was very large, and the $1.65 billion helped project privatization into the American political vocabulary.

Well before the Conrail privatization, the Reagan administration had already begun to borrow the newly minted term from Mrs. Thatcher's Britain. With the passage of time, privatization has become part of the lexicon of Democrats as well as Republicans. One of the major methods for reinventing government in Vice-President Al Gore's Reinventing Government Initiative is by privatization—in the vice-president's words, "spinning off functions to the private sector that are better accomplished there." Privatization has come to include not only selling off assets; the government's changed contracting and procurement practices and a shift toward outsourcing in the provision of services also fall under this rubric. The purpose is to bring market forces and market tests to bear—to increase efficiency, to reduce both costs and the drain on public budgets, and to improve the quality and effectiveness of services.

In the aftermath of the cold war and in the context of controlling the budget, aspects of the military system are being subjected to a new economic scrutiny. Base closures and reconversions, the sale of unnecessary facilities, and the downsizing of its R&D institutions all appear to be good moves in this direction. The United States Naval Academy at Annapolis, for instance, did not need its own 856-acre dairy farm. After all, the typhoid epidemic at the academy that prompted the navy to establish a dairy farm broke out a century ago. The Elk Hills naval oil reserve in California was established before World War I, on the eve of the modern oil era, to allay fears of an oil shortage at a time when the United States was converting its navy from coal to oil. Today it hardly serves any national-security interest; it produces volumes equivalent to just 0.36 percent of the nation's total consumption. In 1997, it went on the block and was sold. So is the uranium-enrichment facility. The Department of Defense is also turning to private firms to man-

358

age facilities and provide supporting logistics. Similar cost-cutting initiatives are at work in other departments of government. Also under discussion are the privatization of such agencies as the Federal Aviation Administration, which controls air traffic. But the more a government service involves public safety, as with air traffic control, the more reluctant politicians will be to promote a sale.

Much of the real action is taking place in state capitals, county head-quarters, and city halls all across America. It is there that government owner-ship of productive assets is most concentrated, and where government oversees, guarantees, or itself provides the greatest range of public services. In the American tradition, local authorities are responsible for making sure that public services are provided in sufficient quantity and quality and ac-cording to the general wishes of voters. That applies to public transportation and to infrastructure services like ports and airports; it also applies to certain basic health facilities and, most of all, to the public schools.

In all of these areas, the retreat of government becomes a grassroots issue. It is forcing stakeholders in local communities to rethink long-held beliefs that governments must control services if they are to work. After all, public provision of services was expanded in an earlier age, to make up for the inadequacies of private providers. New York City established its street-cleaning department in 1881 after decades of failure by private con-tractors to clean the streets of horse manure, which was the number-one pollution problem of urbanizing America in the nineteenth century. Services were expanded and civil-service systems were instituted to curtail corruption and cronyism. Yet now, the insulation of local government employment, which was intended to improve its quality, has arguably had the opposite effect. In the words of Ed Rendell, the Democratic mayor of Philadelphia, "It became clear to me that we had an incentiveless work force. Through work rules, and past practices, and the overall collective bargaining, and because of civil service, we had created a system of management where we had taken out every incentive for performance. . . . The most difficult job in Philadelphia . . . was being a middle-level manager and trying to get motiva-tion out of your work force." [15]

If privatization challenges views that go back beyond the New Deal to the Progressive era, local control also gives America some big advantages as it embarks on the privatization process. The rift between supporters and opponents of a particular privatization is rarely ideological or partisan. To be sure, there is still a clash of underlying assumptions—as to whether key services, and the people who deliver them, are to be most successfully motivated by profit or by conceptions of public service and the common good. A more straightforward concept of profitability will drive a privatized bus company, leading it to reduce uneconomic services. Yet is that a good enough reason to curtail night service? Does that not penalize the nurses who work the evening shift in a hospital? And if fewer buses run, won't that bring more cars on the road and cause added pollution, congestion, and traffic delays? The drive to privatize can also devalue the commitment of those who have dedicated themselves to careers in public service. Often, fights over privatization tend to bring into opposition direct stakeholders; they argue over just who will bear the costs of the change and who will stand to benefit most from the new opportunities it sets up. Usually, the groups to become most exercised are public-sector unions, which see—correctly—a loss of jobs for their members, less security, and a more critical evaluation of work practices.

Some privatizations are quite straightforward. Turning garbage collection over to private companies is accepted across the country. San Francisco started doing it in 1932. Water services are another target for privatization. Currently, about 20 percent of drinking water in the country is provided by government-owned but privately managed facilities. The rationale for future privatization is lower costs, augmented by the comparative advantage in technology and skills that a large company will have over a city-operated system. Private companies now operate a number of major airports, including Pittsburgh's. Ports are also candidates for privatization. Indianapolis compels city-owned services to compete for contracts against private-sector groups. To win the contract to maintain the city's vehicles, city workers had to beat bids from three national firms. They won—by significantly reducing their costs, improving productivity, and taking wage and benefit cuts—in exchange for a share of the cost saving. The Port Authority of New York and New Jersey, disappointed with the decayed state of the international-arrivals building at Kennedy Airport, has turned it over to a consortium led by the Amsterdam airport operator.

Some functions are being increasingly privatized without being recognized as such. One might think that police and prisons were "core" functions of government. But policing has, in effect, been steadily privatized; today the number of private security guards is three times that of police. Owing to the rapidly growing needs created by the production of felons in the United States, incarceration is emerging as a business. By the end of 1996, 132 private prisons and jails were in operation, with another 39 under construction. Industry revenues are expected to top $1 billion in 1997. States and cities are exploring various methods to contract out the provision of welfare services; but as "outsourcing" and contracting become more common, there is an increased need for overseeing the process—to ensure that the public interest is being served. Such privatizations also open the door to new versions of government failure—long, drawn-out bureaucratic and political wrangles that are dominated by endless due process, one of the banes of the American political system.[16]

Education and the Welfare Frontier

Some of the hardest changes to think through and implement are in education—ironically, one of the areas where the crisis of the current system is most plain to see. Public education was the foundation of the American experience, the flame under the melting pot, up until the 1970s. In the years since, it has been ravaged by the "explosion of rights," the breakdown of discipline and the spread of violence, and the leveling of standards. Responses to the breakdown have been both diverse and controversial. A number of states now permit the establishment of "charter schools"—new public schools that secede from local school districts and set their own curricula and standards, whether to promote a particular educational philosophy or to adapt to the perceived needs of an ethnic or immigrant community. Results are mixed. Even more controversial are proposals to provide parents with vouchers, which they could use at the educational establishment of their choice. The widespread adoption of vouchers would go a long way toward the de facto privatization of the educational system. What makes these reforms the most difficult of all is that public education is not just a basic service that must merely be made to run efficiently. It is basic to the nation's future yet also tangled up in America's contentious struggle with race, ethnicity, and poverty—most vividly exemplified by the furious battles over forced busing.

Rethinking the role of government in all of these areas means contending with the often-ambiguous results of past programs—and the conflicting ways that different stakeholders, operating in good faith, interpret them. The central question on that frontier today is what to do with the welfare system, which in the American political vocabulary refers to programs geared to aid the poor: medical assistance (Medicaid), monthly payments to offset family expenses under Aid for Dependent Children (AFDC), and public housing. A challenge has arisen from many different voices that the remedies have not always reduced the scope of the problem—and indeed have sometimes increased it. These critiques often have in common only an agreement that the present system has failed its promise. They run from the center—the moderate camps of the major parties, which advocate gradual reform under the banner of "welfare to work"—to more thoroughgoing critiques of the dependency fostered by the system and more sweeping views of solutions based on self-reliance.

The debate has focused on welfare-reform legislation at the federal level. The act finally passed in August 1996 has as its centerpiece the revocation of AFDC, a core component of the classic welfare package. Its replacement, Temporary Assistance to Needy Families (TANF), means more than just a cosmetic change. It limits the duration of support and requires recipients to enroll in job searches and take whatever jobs they can find. That approach is now being tested on such critical matters as the supply of decent jobs. But the most enduring aspect of federal welfare reform may turn out to lie elsewhere. It is in the wholesale devolution of the issue from the federal to the state level. States are to receive block grants to apply to welfare reform in whatever way they choose. The race is on among governors and state legislatures to devise reforms that will become the model for other states to follow.

At the national level, the most urgent question about the welfare role of government may well be its responsibility to the elderly. Within six to ten years—by, say, 2005—the funding base of Social Security is expected to be under enormous pressure, leading to the possibility of a bust. In response, there is discussion about investing part of the Social Security trust fund in the stock market or privatizing it altogether by replacing the trust fund with individually managed retirement accounts. But the problem may run deeper than this, for the trends that cause alarm are not simply financial but, more fundamentally, demographic. The rapid growth of the elderly as a share of population means—with the present pay-as-you-go system—fewer workers supporting more older people.

"As Old as the Country"

The redefinition in the relationship between government and marketplace in the United States is being driven by a very basic trend—growing cynicism and skepticism about government itself. "Distrust of government is part of American political culture and always has been," observed political analyst William Schneider. "This distrust is as old as the country. Then why has government gotten so big? The answer is pragmatism. Whenever there is a crisis, people have looked to the government to solve it." The New Deal and World War II built confidence in government. In a way that is hard to recall now, John Kennedy inspired a generation with idealism about public service. In the mid-1960s, however, cynicism began to emerge as a powerful trend, stoked by the Vietnam War and domestic turbulence. Watergate and the economic travails of the 1970s fueled it further. There was a respite during Ronald Reagan's "morning in America," but cynicism has continued to grow since then. The result is lowered expectations for government and for what it can do.

The extent of the change is dramatized by the journey of the Clinton administration. Bill Clinton came into office in 1993 as a New Democrat, though his administration began with a thirteen-hundred-page national health care plan, introduced industrial policies, and pursued "strategic trade." Within a few years, however, Clinton was proclaiming the end of the era of big government, signing a massive welfare reform bill, and promoting free markets as a fundamental objective of American foreign policy after the end of the cold war. But such changes are relative. When a Republican Congress fervently sought to roll back a vast agenda of aid programs, it found that the public was not about to give up its social safety net or its commitment to education and the environment. Between the failure of the Clinton health care plan and the rejection of the Gingrich revolution, a new middle has emerged in American politics. It is characterized by an end to the growth of government in many spheres, some rolling back, some devolution, a continuing battle over government's expansion in the realm of social values, and a drive to adapt the mechanisms of the market to the activities of government. It also includes a consensus emphasizing what not so long ago seemed the quite old-fashioned, even quaint, virtue of fiscal rectitude.[17]

CHAPTER 13

THE BALANCE OF CONFIDENCE

The World After Reform

EVEN AS LANDSLIDES GO, it was overwhelming—a 179-seat majority in Parliament. The victory of Tony Blair's Labour Party on May 1, 1997, exceeded the one by which Clement Attlee's Labour Party had routed Winston Churchill in 1945, at the very moment of triumph in World War II. Not only was it the biggest victory in the history of the Labour Party, but one would have to go all the way back to 1832 to find an election in which the Conservative Party had been so thoroughly trounced.

The Attlee government had invented the mixed economy and the welfare state. They were Labour's answer to the Great Depression, World War II, and needs of reconstruction. In turn, Britain's "postwar settlement" became the model for the relationship of state and marketplace around the world, one in which the state was to play the guiding role. It was a decisive repudiation of the old order.

Tony Blair's victory also amounted to a repudiation of the past, though not of the Thatcherite revolution. The Conservatives were certainly defeated, decisively so, but this was a rejection of their performance, not their basic ideas. Theirs was a party that over eighteen years had become tired and divided, its credibility and integrity eroded by incessant scandals. Yet in the long run-up to the election, Blair and New Labour had campaigned as vigorously against their own past as they had against the Conservatives. New Labour rejected Old Labour, with its commitment to intervention and the expansive state. And by the time of its victory, New Labour had embraced Thatcherism, although a remake of Thatcherism heavily leavened with "compassion" and "inclusiveness." The return of the Labour Party to power after almost two bleak decades in the wilderness represented not a defeat for Margaret Thatcher but a consolidation of her revolution.

The half-century arc from Attlee to Blair captures the story of the movement from an era in which the state sought to seize and control the commanding heights of the economy to an era in which the ideas of free markets, competition, privatization, and deregulation are capturing the commanding heights of world economic thinking. In the postwar decades, the ideas associated with the Attlee government became the rulebook for governments around the world. Similarly, in the 1990s, the ideas that characterized Margaret Thatcher's policies have influenced a new market focus worldwide. Will the Blair policies point to a third revolution—the accommodation of left-wing parties to the market and to a more open global economy?

The changes in the Labour Party that propelled Blair to victory arose from failure, a series of bitter electoral defeats. As late as 1983, the Labour Party had produced a manifesto—once described as the longest suicide note in history—that still called for all the paraphernalia of economic intervention: massive nationalization and renationalization, government central planning, exchange controls, trade barriers. In the decade after the 1983 defeat, Labour's leadership—under Neil Kinnock and then his successor, John Smith—struggled to modernize the party. But they wanted to do it cautiously, in order to avoid a split. They called their strategy "the long game." As Smith explained it, "I don't believe that you should rush forward and put everything in your shop window for the next Wednesday." But then, in 1994, Smith collapsed of a heart attack and died in a London hospital emergency room. Ironically, only weeks earlier he had campaigned to keep the same emergency room open in the face of budget cuts.

His successor was Anthony Blair, as he had been known when he was an up-and-coming young barrister; but he was known better as Tony Blair after he won a seat in Parliament in 1983, despite the overall Labour debacle. In his first years in Parliament, Blair did not stray much from Labour orthodoxy; he advocated "enormous state guidance and intervention." But then, coming to believe that Labour's traditional prescriptions were out of sync with reality, he started to redefine the political challenges in terms of accommodating to the market. In less than three years, he would implement a remarkable and thoroughgoing remodeling of one of the most venerable parties of the left.

Blair was more open to change than many others in the party because he was not so deeply rooted in its past. His father, in fact, had been chairman of the local Conservative Party association in Durham, and had been a prospective Tory parliamentary candidate when he was felled by a massive stroke. Blair was ten at the time. For three years, his father, who made his living as a barrister and orator, was unable to speak. Blair once recalled that he spent "every spare minute" at Durham hospital, seeing either his father, who was recovering from his stroke, or his sister, who was seriously ill.

At Oxford, unlike the conventional ambitious undergraduates, Blair focused on rock music, not politics. While others were declaiming in the Oxford Union, he was performing as lead singer for a group called the Ugly

Rumours. He also became a committed Christian, which, in turn, led him to an adherence to what he later called "ethical socialism," a socialism much more rooted in Christianity, community, and responsibility than in Marxism, the class struggle, and dependence on the state. When his mother died suddenly just after he left Oxford, a roommate observed that Blair sat up at night in bed, reading the Bible. The romance of traditional socialism did not do very much for him. And on the other side, Thatcher was not quite the enemy to him that she was to other Labour politicians. After all, there was his father. "I understood where my father was coming from because he was totally self-made," Blair once said. "He was keen on the Thatcher Revolution." [1]

"It's Simple"

Blair had no taste for remaining permanently in opposition. By the end of the 1980s, working with Gordon Brown—now the chancellor of the Exchequer—Blair emerged as one of the party's most aggressive modernizers. Asked why Labour had been out of power for a generation, he always replied in the same way: "It's simple. The world changed, and the Labour Party did not." He was determined to change it. He sought to distance the Labour Party from the trade unions ("fairness not favors" was what he offered them), supported reductions in union power (anathema to the left, but essential to capture the trust of the country), and courted the new shareholders created by the Thatcher privatizations. His critique of Old Labour began to sound more and more like Thatcher's. "We're not reliving the 1970s," he said before the election. The Labour Party should not be known, he insisted, as a party that "bungs up your taxes, runs a high-inflation economy, and is hopelessly inefficient . . . and, by the way . . . let the trade unions run the show." The Tories were right in 1979 that "there was too much collective power, too much bureaucracy, too much state intervention, and too many interests created around it. . . . The era of corporatist state intervention is over." In private, Blair would go further, saying that he agreed with what Thatcher had done. Blair's march to the market infuriated the traditional left, which took to calling him Tony Blur.

In the clearest rejection of Old Labour orthodoxy, he forced the party to renounce its ideological backbone, Clause IV of its constitution, drafted in 1918 by Sidney Webb, which called for nationalization in the form of "the common ownership of the means of production, distribution, and exchange." It was a furious battle, which threatened to destroy the party. But Blair would not tolerate any backsliding. When a Labour politician advocated renationalization of electric utilities, Blair brusquely told him to "grow up."

In the period leading up to the 1997 election, Blair made his way to the sacred precincts of capitalism—paying the first-ever visit by a Labour Party leader to Wall Street, and later giving an address to the financial community of the City of London, where he buried the mixed economy. He said that the objective of any government should be to lower, rather than raise, taxes. "The presumption should be that economic activity is best left to the private sector," he said. For the first time in its history, the party issued an electoral manifesto for business.

Once ensconced as prime minister, Blair went farther. Britain, he said, should become a "nation of entrepreneurs." But "modernizing the nation" is proving a much less clear project than modernizing the Labour Party. Yet the basic concepts for what Blair variously called the "radical middle" or "third way" are in place: Traditional Keynesian intervention and management of the economy cannot work. Nor can the economy be sheltered from global competition. Rather, government's role is to make the economy work better—and to promote opportunity and greater equality, along with "inclusiveness." This it is to do through "long-termism"—investment in education and other generators of human capital. The welfare state is to be preserved, but slimmed down and reformed. The individual is to have more rights, but also more responsibilities.

Not long after the election, Blair made clear how far he was committed to redefining politics. He invited none other than Margaret Thatcher to come to 10 Downing Street for tea and a chat, which could only enrage the old left. After all, she was the devil incarnate. That did not really bother Blair. He intended to stay on message.[2]

The New Consensus?

The market focus that had seemed radical and beyond the pale when Margaret Thatcher initiated her revolution has become the new consensus in less than two decades. Governments continue to be entrusted with a fundamental responsibility for welfare; but in the industrial world, the debate is now about how to define that responsibility, how broad or limited it should be, and how to deliver services—in short, how to reform the system.

But how much has really changed? How deeply rooted is this new consensus? Less than a month after Blair's election, the French Socialists, led by Lionel Jospin, sailed back into government, delivering a devastating defeat to the French right. But they did not sound like New Socialists. They presented plans that recalled the ill-fated *relance* policies of the early 1980s. With their agenda largely set by the reality of unemployment—twice the level of that in Britain—they promised to expand public-sector employment, increase labor charges, and slow privatization. Once in power, the government soon took a far more pragmatic stance in its economic policies. But the episode showed just how deep was the challenge to an idea of European unity that seemed founded on economic austerity alone. The difference was made clear when Blair and Jospin met at a socialist congress in Sweden just after their victories. The task of the left, Blair told the delegates, was "marrying together an open, competitive and successful economy with a just, decent and humane society." He served notice that "we modernize or die." Jospin made no secret of his disagreement: "Market forces," he said, "if there is no attempt to control them—will threaten our very idea of civilization." He went on to attack what he called "ultracapitalism."

Indeed, whatever the transformations in the world economy, an underlying mistrust of the market persists. Why? George Shultz pointed to one reason when he said, "Markets are relentless." As competition becomes more intense, there is no respite from its pressures. People turn to government to provide shelter from the constant demands of the market. The move to the market may bring a higher standard of living, better services, and more choice. But it also brings new insecurities—about unemployment, about the durability of jobs and the stress of the workplace, about the loss of protection from the vicissitudes of life, about the environment, about the unraveling of the safety net, about health care and what happens in old age. Workers—both white- and blue-collar—fear, and sometimes find, that employers, in order to please financial analysts, will break the social contract and cut salaries, benefits, and jobs of employees who have given fifteen or twenty irretrievable years of their life to the company. Further, the global nature of the marketplace disrupts traditional values and familiar forms of organization, amplifying the sense of a loss of control and generating a nostalgia for the past and its settled order. While there are gains, there are also losses, all of which are given a special edge by the undercurrent of millennial anxiety. There is an ambivalence and an uneasy balance. It is heard when a senior official in the Clinton administration talks about the battle between "the free marketeer in me and the liberal in me." It is encountered in the conviction in some countries that the process of privatization has meant the movement of government assets into the hands of those who are friends of the government, massively enriching them in the process. Even with an expertly executed privatization program, the results mean a redistribution of wealth, power, and status within a society, all of which can be highly unsettling.

Yet despite the doubts and the discontents, the move to the market is being driven by a shift in the balance of confidence—a declining faith in the competence of government, offset by a renewed appreciation of the workings of the market. One's parents and grandparents, so deeply traumatized by the Great Depression, may have lived with the permanent fear of another slump. In the United States, suspicion and criticism of the market historically focused on the tendency toward collusion—the Progressives' critique—and the risk of market failure—the New Deal's preoccupation. Yet over the half century since World War II, market systems have demonstrated extraordinary vitality, enormously enhancing their credibility. One has to pause to grasp the extent of the shift in outlook. In 1975, the economist Arthur Okun —a chairman of the President's Council of Economic Advisers and, of course, a child of the Great Depression—would say, "The market needs a place, and the market needs to be kept in its place. . . . Given the chance, it would sweep away all other values, and establish a vending-machine society. I could not give it more than two cheers." In the two decades since, real GDP in the United States has almost doubled; and that tone, and the mistrust that underlies it, sounds archaic. The contrast is made all the more stark by examining the 1997 annual report of the Council of Economic Advisers, the main theme of which is the "advantage of markets." Indeed, the Council's focus on what it called the "insufficiently appreciated property of markets" —"their ability to collect and distribute information"—is vintage Hayek. And the report criticized the New Deal for having "crystallized" the belief in "the omniscience and the omnipotence" of the government "into a new kind of liberalism." All this is a very different view of the world.[3]

The Woven World

Today, there is a resumption—a relinking—of a global economy after the disruptions of world wars, revolutions, and depression. As the steam engine and the telegraph shrank the dimensions of the nineteenth-century world, so technology today is once again eroding distance and borders. But this time the effects are much more comprehensive, for they leave virtually no country or community untouched. The pattern is evident in a host of measures. The number of international air passengers rose from 75 million in 1970 to 409 million in 1996. Between 1976 and 1996, the cost of a three-minute phone call from the United States to England dropped in real terms from about eight dollars to as low as thirty-six cents—and the number of transborder calls has increased from 3.2 billion in 1985 to 20.2 billion in 1996. Today, the world shares the same images from film and entertainment; the same news and information bounces down from satellites, instantaneously creating a common vocabulary for events.

Amid all this, the decisive new force is computers: Information technology is creating a woven world of distant encounters and instant connections. Knowledge and information do not have to wait. Within, outside, and across organizations and national boundaries, people are tied together, sharing information and points of view, working in virtual teams, bartering goods and services, swapping bonds and currencies, exchanging chatter and banalities, and passing the time. Information of every kind is available. With the establishment of the U.S. government data Web site in 1997, a ten-year-old could gain access to more and better data than a senior official could have done just five years earlier. Libraries are open for business on the Internet. Researchers share their results in real time. Activists band together to promote their causes. Would-be terrorists surf for weapon designs. All this is increasingly heedless of the nation-state and outside the traditional structure of organizations. If the Internet is the new commanding heights, it is also beyond the reach of the state. While governments can promote the Internet, they cannot control it.

The hallmark of this new globality is the mobile economy. Capital sweeps across countries at electron speed; manufacturing and the generation of services move flexibly among countries and are networked across borders; markets are supplied from a continually shifting set of sources. Ideas, insights, techniques all disperse among countries with increasing ease. Access to technology across national boundaries continues to grow. Borders—fundamental to the exercise of national power—are eroded as markets are integrated. International trade between 1989 and 1997 grew at an annual rate of 5.3 percent—nearly four times faster than global output (1.4 percent). Over the same years, foreign direct investment rose even faster—at a rate of 11.5 percent per year. One indicator of the rapidity of change is the transformation of more and more firms into multinationals that provide the world market with goods and services that are conceived, produced, and assembled in several countries. The criterion of "national origin" has given way to "local content," which in turn is becoming harder and harder to pin down. The spread of fast, reliable information and communications technology pushes companies to draw on people and resources the world over.

As the barriers fall, private capital seeks new markets in what had once been the special preserve of state investment: energy, communications, and infrastructure. And governments, anxious to reduce deficits and shift spending to social needs, increasingly welcome this investment. In another telling reminder of a hundred years ago, private firms are taking on an increasing share of new investment, as well as responsibility for management, in telecommunications, waterworks, power utilities, and road construction worldwide. Most countries today have one or several mobile phone operators. A growing number have private electric power providers. Even the remaining large state monopolies are behaving like private companies—and their managers as businessmen—as they compete for major contracts beyond their own national borders in both developed and developing countries.

The integration of financial markets is particularly significant. Information and communications technology has, of course, provided the architecture for globally connected capital markets, but that is only part of the explanation. The big British privatizations in the mid-1980s were the first true global offerings of equity, and they changed the orientation and widened the ken of investment managers throughout the world. Not long after, European companies began to offer their shares. Increasingly, investors around the globe are using the same approach and criteria to make their decisions, and they are looking at the same pool of companies. The distinctions among national markets have become lost. In not so many years, a few national stock exchanges could well become global exchanges, opening for business not long after the sun rises and not closing until well after dark—all in order to deal in the equity of world-class companies, irrespective of their domicile. In turn, shares of leading firms will be traded on a twenty-four-hour basis.

When Harold Wilson was Britain's prime minister in the 1960s, he would blame the "gnomes of Zurich" for the pound's recurrent weakness, suggesting a cabal of a few hard-faced Swiss bankers cynically betting against the British currency. Conspiracy theories die hard: no less colorful allegations—against the "rogues" and "highwaymen" of the international economy—surfaced with the 1997 currency crisis in Southeast Asia. But, in fact, today thousands and thousands of traders drive a foreign-exchange market that has grown from a daily turnover of $190 billion in 1986 to an estimated $1.3 trillion in 1997. Analysts and brokers and strategists see the same information at the same moment and compete in their response time. Performance—whether it is a company's quarterly earnings or a country's inflation or trade balance data or the outcome of a national election—sets off an immediate chain reaction. While the publics vote only every few years, the markets vote every minute. And it is private capital—the pensions and accumulated retirement savings of the first world—that is being courted and lured by what used to be called the third world. But this financial integration comes with a price. National governments, whether in developed or developing countries, must increasingly heed the market's vote—as harsh as it sometimes can be.[4]

"Open capital markets create tremendous opportunity and benefits," observed U.S. Secretary of the Treasury Robert Rubin. "But they create risks as well. World trade is growing, but trading in currency is growing at a much steeper rate. There is a greater risk of these markets causing instability because they are so large, and so much money is moving around in them. If it all moves in one direction, the size of the flows can be destabilizing, and the impact could be substantial."

The Company in the Mobile Economy

The emergence of the market focus around the world changes the position of companies as well. The prospect is both attractive and threatening—wider opportunities and tougher competition. Boundaries of every sort are coming down. Political, economic, and ideological borders among nations continue to erode, promoting the flow of investment and trade. Regulatory systems and national monopolies that provided protection against competition are being altered. Restrictions on the movement of information and knowledge are disappearing in the face of advances in communications technology and computers (and declining costs thereof) and in the freer flow of ideas. The very walls of the company are being made more permeable by computers, alliances, and outsourcing. Indeed, it is becoming more difficult to ascertain where one company ends and another begins. The financial walls are coming down, too, as operations become more transparent and subject to much more aggressive scrutiny and demands by outside investors. All this adds up to a much wider and more diverse range of opportunity. It also means more bracing competition and more risk, along with the relentless pressure generated by capital markets and by customers who have a broader range of choice.

Thus, companies are being forced to think differently. They have to prepare themselves for a world in which these pressures are only going to become more intense. That means fostering a culture that encourages alertness, responsiveness, and flexibility, and speeding up the cycle time of processes and decisions. In the aftermath of "reengineering" and restructuring, competitive forces now demand a rediscovery of employees and of the knowledge they command. Emphasizing the importance of knowledge, harnessing it, and speedily integrating it across the organization—these become the ways to strengthen the firm in the marketplace. Information technology is driving the process; and as a result, the way that companies are organized is undergoing a massive change. The high-rise pyramids of hierarchical corporate structures are being transformed into the low-rise of the flatter organization—less bureaucracy, more teamwork, and greater dispersion of responsibility, information, and decision making.

How much more will companies change? British Petroleum is one of the more advanced large companies in reshaping its organization to fit the computer age. Yet its chief executive, John Browne, argues that the impact of information technology on business is still in its early stages: "Technological advance is not reversible. Political trends can come and go, but we do not throw away new technology. It is a ratchet of progress. This is a wave of new technology of major proportions, probably more deeply rooted and wide-ranging than the development of electricity or the internal combustion engine and, as a result, there is a real possibility that the process of change is still only gathering momentum."

A distinct aspect of cultural change concerns the concept of "entrepreneur." In the past, the word often carried a negative connotation; it sounded unsavory and made someone seem unreliable. To be identified as an entrepreneurial personality within an organization was to be branded as a threat to the established hierarchy. Today, in a fast-moving and more open economy, companies are finding that they need to encourage and nurture entrepreneurial values and attitudes that emphasize initiative and rapid response. Otherwise, they cannot keep up. They hardly want swashbuckling egomaniacs. But they need creators and builders.

At a time when governments are slimming their responsibilities, companies as much as individuals will find that their responsibilities to the community are expanded. Whether that community is defined as a city, a region, or something larger, the corporation is part of it and benefits from it. Whatever the demands for obeisance at the altar of quarterly or half-yearly performance, companies will find that they have to engage with the community's interests, environmental concerns, and social issues. Otherwise, they will eventually be penalized by the political process.

What Government Does

One of the characteristics of the new global marketplace is the apparent precedence of economics over politics. But that means precedence only over traditional ideological politics. A firm would make a terrible mistake if it worked on the assumption that eroding borders meant the end of national politics, national identity, and economic nationalism. These forces will continue to express an amalgam of aspirations and ambitions. Politics within each country will still be shaped by its history, its culture, and its definition of national objectives—a reality that the firm can ignore only at its peril. This is not the end of the nation-state, and even less the end of government. If money and goods travel more freely now than at any time in living memory, individual life continues to be shaped by rules, customs, incentives, and constraints that are fundamentally national and political—the province of government. Personal access to the woven world still remains restricted to a minority of the world's population. The vast majority still get their signals not from global financial markets, let alone cyberspace, but from the national capital.

This leaves governments with a daunting challenge: to figure ways to reduce their intervention in some areas, and to retool and refocus their intervention in others, while preserving the public trust. It is a challenge of imagination. It requires buying into the idea of fundamental global change and taking on the task of translating that change into policies that accord with national culture, history, and temperament.

What will be the new role of government? After all, there is no market without government to define the rules and the context. The state creates and maintains the parameters within which the market operates. And that is the new direction. The state accepts the discipline of the market; government moves away from being producer, controller, and intervenor, whether through state ownership or heavy-handed regulation. The state as manager is an increasing laggard in the competitive, mobile economy. Instead, government shifts toward becoming a referee, setting the rules of the game to ensure, among other things, competition.

Economic imperatives and political interests will also force a reconsideration of the government's role in dealing with the range of social programs that make up the welfare state. For governments do spend a great deal of money. Among industrial countries, public expenditure rose from 28 percent of GDP in 1960 to 46 percent in 1996—a surge driven, most of all, by rapid growth in subsidies, transfer payments, and social spending. But government's performance in these roles will move more clearly into the spotlight as it withdraws from the commanding heights of industry and planning. For the shift of role entails also a shift of resources and the way they are applied. The public money and human skills freed up through privatization and deregulation will be partly invested, in many countries, in "human infrastructure"—health, education, the environment—with, it is hoped, the creativity and success that can come from a clearer and better-focused role. What this means, then, is that for all the erosion of boundaries and fundamental technological change, governments still matter—and, most of all, political leadership matters. It also means that even if change in the direction of "more market" and "less state" is a pervasive global phenomenon, it does not lead to a single, common result.[5]

The World After Reform

The move to the market is beyond doubt a truly global phenomenon. It draws on a stock of ideas and recent experience shared around the world. The processes of change—particularly privatization, deregulation, and trade liberalization—are largely common ones, refined over time to a professional craft by their political champions and expert practitioners. As countries anchor themselves in a world of open and connected markets, they are to a significant degree transferring control of the commanding heights from the traditional state apparatus to the dispersed intelligence of the market. And the extraordinarily fast flow of information, made possible by the rapid diffusion of accessible technologies, has helped reinforce the sense of common momentum. Yet that feeling should not be overstated. For despite the common features, each country and region is executing its move to the market according to its own political and economic history and perception of the national interest. In the postreform world that is now emerging, each major region faces specific challenges in reconciling the increasingly complex demands of global participation with the realities of its own history, politics, economics, and culture—all the things that make up the experience and living memory of individuals and nations.

Each area, then, will grapple in this world after reform with its own agenda for the new century. As the withdrawal of the state from the commanding heights opens new perspectives and opportunities, it also conditions success on understanding the regional dynamics. Indeed, the growing connection of markets means that these regional agendas will feed back ever more directly into the workings of the world economy. The future of the postreform world, and certainly the future health and credibility of markets, will thus be shaped not only by technology and global forces but also by how different regions come to grips with their particular challenges.

Asia: Old Formulas and New Tensions

Two transitions are unfolding in much of Asia. One is in the political system —away from authoritarian regimes. Greater political participation is being promoted by the growth of the middle class and the requirements of service and software economies. For some countries, the transition is proving to be traumatic and sometimes tumultuous. No longer does a dire security threat from communism put survival at risk and thus elevate national cohesion above all else.

The second transition is the result of "making it." The old winning formula no longer works for many countries. The immediate causes of the 1997 currency crisis in Southeast Asia were overheating, real estate speculation, and weaknesses in banking systems. Underlying these, however, was the apprehension that countries' competitive positions were being eroded as they move from low-wage to higher-wage economies. Is their era of consistent high economic growth over, or will the flexibility and adaptability that have served them so well in the past once again come into play? They certainly cannot compete on the basis of cheap labor, and thus they will have to reform and reshape their economic and financial systems and continue to move up the technology ladder. The forging of a regional economy in Asia provides many of them with a local market of some scale, and intraregional trade and investment may prove a source of new strength.

The dominant economy of the entire region is, of course, still Japan, which continues its struggle to redefine its own economic life. The system that worked so brilliantly for so many years badly malfunctioned in the 1990s. The weaknesses were revealed when the bubble burst, ending the speculative mania of the 1980s. In order to drive down costs and restore the competitive position of its industry, Japan is seeking to dismantle its superstructure of regulation and protection, which has proved too cumbersome to keep up with fast-paced markets. At the same time, it is confronting the demographic reality of a rapidly aging society. Despite what has become chronic gloom over the last several years, Japanese industry is clearly going through a painful restructuring of the kind that American business has already passed through. The ailing financial sector continues to be a major drag on recovery. The "big bang" of financial deregulation is supposed to restore the sector to health. But its impact is also meant to be broader, not only revitalizing Tokyo as a financial center but also bringing new financial discipline to bear to spur Japanese business to become more efficient and competitive.

China: The Market and the Party

The two great laboratories of change are China and Russia. They are testing, respectively, whether economic reform better precedes political reform or vice versa. Markets before elections, or elections before markets? In both cases, the scale of the experiment is enormous. The irony is that whatever the results, the experiment will probably never have to be repeated.

Upward of 200 million people have been lifted out of poverty in China over the last two decades. The world has never seen change of that rapidity on that scale. By some estimates, China is already the second-largest economy in the world; and, if current trends continue, its economy will rival that of the United States in size before the next two decades are out. Yet China has still to lay down the explicit rules of a market system; its economy continues to operate much more by *guanxi*—connections—than by law and contract. With the 15th Party Congress and the enshrinement of "Deng Xiaoping Theory" as the canon of the Communist Party, China has jettisoned much of traditional socialism. Facing growing deficits, China has acted more quickly than expected and is seeking to cut loose most of its state-owned companies to sink or swim in the market economy, with ownership to be spread among the public and overseas investors. There will be a big cost—unemployment on a large scale will inevitably result as these firms restructure and seek to become more efficient. The leadership is betting that the liberated vitality of the economy will generate new jobs quickly enough to prevent a political reaction.

To date, the focus has been on economic change. But another question is inescapable: How does a dynamic, rapidly growing market system continue to coexist with the centralization of one-party rule? What will "socialism with Chinese characteristics" mean in the next century? Undoubtedly, generational shift in the leadership, itself a smoother and more confident process than many had anticipated, will bolster a transition in the political system; younger leaders will more confidently countenance changes that would have alarmed their elders.

How will a political transition come about in a country as big and still as poor as China, and how will authority and cohesion be maintained during that period? Time is offered as one answer—enough time to allow democracy to continue to build up from the local level, enough time to allow incomes to reach the levels that have led to greater political participation in other, albeit much smaller, Asian countries. No matter what the political outcome, China is destined to be the dominating economic and political force in the region in the next century, and of course one of the most important in the global economy.

China's increasing integration into the global economy will also promote change. How Hong Kong works out could be a decisive factor. Fifty years is a long time to maintain "one country, two systems," especially when one of the systems is the most freewheeling of all the Asian tigers and the other is not only vastly larger but also so much poorer. The new relationship between Hong Kong and the rest of the mainland could well accelerate the process of change throughout China. That is the core meaning of the piquant question "Will China change Hong Kong or will Hong Kong change China?"

Russia: How Deep Is Reform?

Russia is entering a new phase in its post-Communist history. With communism, for the time being, turned back at the polls, the nation continues to struggle to build and consolidate the market while at the same rebuilding and modernizing itself. The market economy is developing much faster than many had expected, although it continues to coexist with an old Soviet economy that is rudderless and marooned between central planning and competition, lacking in vitality and ill-equipped to make a transition. A good part of the old economy is still in the hands of a state that is weak and infirm in terms of its ability to carry out the most basic functions of a modern government. Authority continues to decay, facilitating crime and corruption and breeding social despair. Reformers are now taxed with restoring competence to a government that can act as the referee and regulator rather than owner and manager. A functioning market requires such a state. Government has to deliver on such basic things as the payment of pensions and a working social safety net to undergird the vast transition through which the Russian people are passing.

Much progress has been made on developing the institutions required for a market economy. One indicator: A half decade after the collapse of the Soviet Union and the descent into the black hole of economic chaos, Russia is now established as a legitimate emerging market. But much remains to be done. Property rights, the fundament of a market economy, are still weak and obscure; competition, restricted; and much strengthening of laws, processes, and norms is required. Without progress here—and without protection against crime—new and small business, on which renewed economic growth depends, will remain stunted.

The system has yet to display the fairness and equity that are required for legitimacy. The country, as Deputy Prime Minister Boris Nemtsov put it, is poised between "bandit capitalism and democratic people's capitalism." The specter of communism has been supplanted by "the reign of the seven banks." Concentration of wealth greatly reduces the chances for a new social consensus around the values of democracy and the market. The government has to demonstrate that it is not beholden to the newly enriched financial oligarchy. The Russian presidential election in the year 2000 will be the next test of reform in terms of its success, renewed growth, and popular support. That means there is not all that much time to persuade the majority of the population that they are better off from the tumultuous changes that have so unexpectedly transformed their lives.[6]

India: The Hindu Rate of Change?

In India, despite its tradition of democratic politics, the trust in government knowledge was embedded to the point of unquestioned faith. The country was ruled by a "Permit Raj," under which any kind of economic initiative required a stamp and in which endlessly waiting around official offices for a government sign-off was essential to daily business. In 1991, India embarked on its historic change, beginning a process of rolling back government control and ownership and opening up the country to participation in the global economy. By the end of the 1990s, the rolling back of the Permit Raj was accepted across much of the political spectrum. But how to build a new system is an exceedingly daunting challenge in a society in which pluralism sharpens people's expectations of government but also imposes the constant requirement to co-opt, convince, and build coalitions. The Indian stance has been that those costs are worth bearing, almost for moral reasons—and it is likely to stay that way. But the benefits must increase enormously to meet aspirations, spread beyond the growing middle class, and truly erode poverty.

With less dependence on central government knowledge, the vital signs of change come from below. India may be a country obsessed with politics; but today, politics is increasingly local and regional, no longer driven by elephantine national political machines but instead by parties with regional agendas. They are prepared to make coalitions and deals when these favor their regional economic interests, and to break them when they do not. The country has an enormous economic potential, which could well make it one of the key forces in the global economy in the twenty-first century. But there is frustration with the pace of reform, and fear that the complexities of coalition politics will retard it. The challenge is to ensure that what Indian economists used to describe as the "Hindu rate of growth" is not succeeded by an equally slow "Hindu rate of change."

Africa: A Fresh Start

If India succeeds, the lessons will be nowhere more carefully followed than in sub-Saharan Africa, where the problems of poverty and economic marginalization have been compounded by extra factors: the imbalanced legacy of colonialism, followed by decades of neglect—in some cases depredations—by national rulers, all of it on a continent of mostly small countries kept apart by artificial political boundaries inherited from colonial times. These forces have contributed, in different ways, to leaving unsettled in Africa questions of sovereignty and national identity that are considered settled elsewhere, leading to far more civil wars and armed ethnic conflicts than in any other region. In recent years, a series of traumatic and ambiguous changes across central Africa have grabbed the world's attention, from the genocide and revolution in Rwanda to the fall of the dictator Mobutu Sese Seko and the restoration to the country he named Zaire of its original independent name Congo. Civil conflict persists in a number of small countries, as well as some large ones, such as Sudan. Nigeria, which by virtue of size and human and natural resources should have been the region's leader, has aborted several "democratic transitions" and remains controlled by the military.

Yet at the same time, economic transformations have mushroomed in recent years in many parts of the continent. A growing number of Africa's small and medium-size economies are experiencing a significant withdrawal of government from the commanding heights. A few have moved to the forefront in the scope of privatization, if not in its aggregate size and value. They are doing so thanks not so much to international prodding, but to a new political will that draws on a vast sense of popular frustration. Uganda was once notorious for the extreme brutality and irrational behavior of General Idi Amin. It now enjoys political stability and sustained output growth of around 8 percent. Ghana languished in severe economic decay from the collapse of Kwame Nkrumah's system through the early 1980s. In the past decade, it has restructured its economy, restored sustained growth, and freed the political system. Guinea suffered under the tyrannical and arbitrary rule of Sekou Toure; it is now returned to growth, and attempting to redevelop its considerable natural resources. All three of these countries had to hit rock bottom before repudiating the old political and economic order and setting off to a fresh start.

The most important change is in South Africa. The majority government inherited from the apartheid order a relatively industrial and commercial economy, by far the most developed in Africa; and it has renounced its former radicalism (the African National Congress was a Marxist party) in favor of a measured, pragmatic tone and acceptance of market-based organization. South Africa is turning into a regional motor of growth. Its firms are masterminding integration of rail and road transport and electric networks far to the north. It will take this dynamic, and others on a smaller scale in West and East Africa, to spread growth from a few pockets— Uganda, Côte d'Ivoire, and others—to a vast hinterland. But the signs from many countries are that governments realize they overstretched themselves and are now prepared to restore faith in a private commercial tradition that existed long before the colonial period and, against all odds and in the face of determined opposition, has endured ever since.

Latin America: Who Plays?

Reform in Latin America is haunted by the "lost decade" of the 1980s, when the debt crisis stanched economic growth and standards of living fell. It became clear that massive government ownership and control were suppressing economic vitality. The result—because there no longer seemed to be a choice—was a massive retreat of government. But now countries in the region have to modernize the state and see that it works both differently and more efficiently than in the past, and that it delivers the proper mix of services. Underlying all this is the quest for the desperately needed rules of the game that will give clear signals and directions to those operating in their economies. At the same time, they must make sure that the benefits of the market flow—through better health care, better education, better opportunities—to the disenfranchised in a way that is timely enough to ensure credibility. The broad population has to be convinced, from its own daily experience, that the opening—to the world economy, foreign investment, expanded trade, and privatization—can add up to a formula that satisfies their aspirations. If people see it instead as mainly a device to enrich a minority, then there will be strong political pressure to revise or reverse the reforms.

Political reform has accompanied economic reform; almost every government in the region is now democratically elected. Yet the results of recent elections in a number of countries point to dissatisfaction with the distributions of the benefits of reform and a backlash against the job loss that privatization and restructuring entail. While change started in relatively smaller countries, like Chile, Bolivia, and Argentina, the focus is now on the two largest countries of Latin America. Mexico is coping with a radical change in its political system—the weakening of the PRI and the bolstering of opposition parties—even as its economy continues to undergo restructuring. The full testing will come with the presidential election of the year 2000. Finally, all of South America will be affected by the degree to which Brazil moves ahead. It is not only one of the largest economies in the world —with a GDP twice that of Russia or India—but it has tremendous potential. The real plan succeeded in bringing inflation down from 5,000 percent in 1994 to under 10 percent in 1997, providing a much more stable business environment. The likelihood of Fernando Henrique Cardoso's reelection as president in 1998 will help to ensure continuity. The country is moving ahead with large privatizations, which is helping to stimulate a surge of foreign investment. The critical issue now is to implement the reforms that will permit stronger economic growth. But reform faces obstacles that result from the division between federal and state authority and the opposition of deeply entrenched interests.

Europe: The Euro and Its Discontents

The large-scale privatization and deregulation that come with open markets are forcing a dramatic transformation of Europe's traditional mixed economy. The imminence of the euro and the pressures of the single market are accelerating the change. Yet Western Europe is seeking to secure the grand historical project of the European Union amid high unemployment and a troubling rethinking of the welfare state. How far and how fast will countries go in harmonizing their economies? Will Europe remain on the timetable for the single currency; and if it is to do so, how much flexibility will be allowed into the process in order to facilitate it? Greater suppleness will likely be required as the approaching date stimulates discontent in a number of countries, Germany included. Indeed, the more Europe moves toward a single market in all its dimensions, including currency, the more intense will be the debates over cultural identity, national differences, and the role of the nation-state. Indeed, as the euro becomes the coin of the continent, a new risk will emerge. Could some countries, in the event of an economic downturn, be under pressure to detach themselves from the currency?

Persistent high unemployment threatens to undermine the credibility of the whole European venture. While the 1991 Maastricht Treaty and austerity are blamed for the high rate of joblessness, much of the explanation must be the inflexibility of labor markets. Part of that rigidity is defined by history. As Felix Rohatyn, U.S. ambassador to France, put the matter, "It's relatively easy for a laid-off Pontiac worker in Michigan to move to Dallas and go to work for Texas Instruments. The analogous Italian worker going from Milan to Frankfurt has to cross several borders, operate in a new language, and put his kids into a strange school, where the customs and language are German, not Italian. That is what makes labor less mobile in Europe."

But rigidity results even more from one of Europe's proudest accomplishments: the welfare state. It delivers a very high degree of security—much higher than that in the United States—in terms of protection to workers and subsidies to nonworkers. But its high costs discourage not only investment by large companies but also the creation of small business. Political commitment to the welfare state is fundamental to social consensus in Europe. Yet until the rigidities of the welfare state are reduced, Europe will battle to bring down unemployment. And until that unemployment is brought down, Europeans will question whether the market focus—whether its instrument is privatization or deregulation or economic integration—is delivering the goods.[7]

The United States: The Market and Its Limits

The United States has arrived at a new consensus. Instead of government's expansion, the focus is now on its efficiency and on fiscal rectitude. Economic regulation is also being reassessed. It is now thought that the public can be protected through competition and that government's role is no longer to substitute administrative processes for the workings of the market but rather to ensure the framework is in place to guarantee competition. Yet paradoxically, the diminution of economic regulation is offset by increased government intervention in the marketplace through social-value regulation, the explosion of claims to rights and entitlements, and the machinery of litigation. One major innovation, however, is the use of market mechanisms for environmental protection.

In the United States, as elsewhere, the market system will be judged by what it delivers, by fairness criteria, and by the quality and cost of services it provides. Americans are willing to tolerate more insecurity than people in other industrial nations, but there are still limits to how much insecurity they will accept. Elections and opinion polls demonstrate that while the public does not want government to extend its reach, neither does it want this rich country to abandon its American-style safety net.

When it comes to the profit motive, there are limits as well. If it seems, for instance, that faceless managers in health maintenance organizations are, in the name of profits, overruling doctors on treatment and medication, then there can be little doubt but that the public will successfully demand that these organizations be subject to increased scrutiny, regulation, and restriction. If companies, notwithstanding the quarterly requirements of Wall Street, do not participate in the broader needs of their communities and society, either they will find themselves on the defensive or government will reextend its control. And, critically, America's market system will be judged by its ability to include that part of the population now left out.

Critical Tests

However different the issues in different parts of the world, a common question underlines the shift away from state and toward the market: Is this move permanent, or will there be a shift back—a recalibration and readjustment in the boundary between state and marketplace—that expands the role and responsibilities of government once more? This is, of course, the appropriate question with which to conclude this book. Of course, there can be no definitive answer. But what people believe and how they interpret the world—the ideas they accept and those they reject—these will do much to shape the answer in the years ahead. And thus it is possible to provide a framework that will help bring the answer into focus as it evolves.

For some, the embrace of the market is a matter of conviction. For many more, it is a matter of practicality, of finding something that works better than the alternatives. Lee Kuan Yew, the progenitor of modern Singapore, summed up the reality. Asked why the turn to the market, he replied pithily, "Communism collapsed, and the mixed economy failed. What else is there?" Results count. The new market consensus will be evaluated by its consequences.

Five tests, in particular, are likely to be decisive in shaping people's thinking and judgments about the market. The outcome of these tests will over time provide the signposts to the future frontier between state and market.[8]

Delivering the Goods?

What made both socialism and the mixed economy and then discredited both will make or break the commitment to markets. Will market economies deliver on what they promise in terms of measurable economic goods—growth, higher standards of living, better quality services, and jobs? After all, it was the failure of markets and the loss of confidence in their capacity that led to governments' assuming a much more assertive role in economic management.

If, in the industrialized countries, privatization, deregulation, and the opening up of economies to competition are seen as job-destroying rather than job-creating, then free-market policies will surely be subject to continuing attack and constant revision. In developing countries, too, employment —along with the overall rate of economic growth—will be critical. Many of these nations confront an explosive social issue: rapid growth in the number of young people of working age but no jobs for them. Failure to incorporate them into productive work will mean that the economic system, along with the political system, will be under stress and at risk. But for developing countries, the most telling measure of success will be a clear-cut one: the degree to which the move to the market delivers such basics as electricity, clean water, and reliable transportation.

Ensuring Fairness?

The economic tests are eminently measurable; they can be counted in national income tables. The second set of tests cannot be expressed in figures, but it is no less powerful. It goes to the basic values by which people judge the world, the system in which they live, and their own lot. For many, the market system will be evaluated not only by its economic success but by the way in which that success is distributed. How widely shared is the success? Is the system fair and just? Or does it disproportionately benefit the rich and the avaricious at the expense of the hardworking of more moderate circumstances? Does it treat people decently, and does it include the disenfranchised and the disadvantaged? Are there equity, fair play, and opportunity?

Market systems, by their very nature, confront the question of fairness. Because of their dynamics, and indeed the very nature of the incentives on which they depend for motivation, they generate a much greater range of inequality of income than more controlled societies in which egalitarian values are so strong. But notions of fairness and justice run very deep and are powerful motivators in their own right. In Britain, Tony Blair's great accomplishment was to fuse social-democratic values of fairness and inclusiveness with the Thatcherite economic program.

Excessive concentration of wealth will undercut the legitimacy that a market-oriented system requires. Of course, the operative word is the altogether subjective *excessive*. What a market advocate describes as "incentives" is translated into "greed" in the vocabulary of a market critic. Conspicuous consumption and the flaunting of wealth weigh the scale toward "greed" and thus accentuate the criticism of inequality. American society accepts much greater income inequality than others. For this, there are many explanations—from the lack of a social-democratic tradition to the confidence that a rising sea really does lift all boats to the celebration of pluck and initiative in the tradition of Horatio Alger. Yet surely there are limits to what is acceptable even in the United States. At least so warns Peter

Drucker, one of the most influential modern thinkers on capitalism. Drucker, credited with inventing the word *privatization,* now foresees a coming backlash of "bitterness and contempt" against the rich in the United States. "I don't know what form it will take," he said, "but the envy developing [in reaction to] enormous wealth will cause trouble" when the business cycle turns down again.

For many, whatever the country, extreme inequality not only fans discontent but also suggests hidden cabals and secret strings—in short, the abuse of power by those with the wealth. Privatization is particularly sensitive in this regard: Who benefits as state-owned assets are transferred to private owners? Yet privatization is bolstered by another powerful trend. Globally, it will become more accepted owing to a profound change in capital markets—toward diffusion of ownership. The shift to pension funds based upon savings—as opposed to pay-as-you-go government pension systems—means that the preponderant owners of privatized firms will be not a few very rich families or big-time capitalists but rather the aggregated savings of present and future retirees, mobilized through stock markets and direct investment. This provides an expanding legitimacy for privatization that would not have existed a quarter century ago.

Confidence in the fairness of the system depends upon the effectiveness of the legal system and the transparency of the rules by which the economy operates. Corruption is a deadly enemy of such confidence. It corrodes the moral bedrock of trust upon which markets depend. To be sure, the institutional setup in traditional state-controlled economies made them fertile spawning grounds for corruption. After all, it was government officials—not only those at the top but also woefully underpaid civil servants—who called the critical shots. But there is also plenty of opportunity for corruption in economies that are releasing assets and creating new opportunities as they move from state control to market focus.[9]

Upholding National Identity?

For many countries, participation in the new global economy is very much a mixed blessing. It promotes economic growth and brings new technologies and new opportunities. But it also challenges the values and identities of national and regional cultures. It can undermine a traditional and comforting sense of security—whether it is the high degree of job security in Europe or the social rules in Asia, or indeed values about family and cooperation and to what the young ought be exposed. People in a number of countries may not believe that their cultural life should be dominated by the satellite-borne media images from the West that globalize the values of Hollywood and New York. Nor, they argue, should their companies be subjected to what has been called the "Anglo-Saxon cult of shareholder value," which would ruthlessly cut away what are seen in other societies as social obligations and responsibilities. If these assaults are too strong or the reaction too bitter, then countries that have reduced their tariffs and other import barriers may respond with renewed nationalism and new barriers in the form of regulations and restrictions. They will not have to renationalize in order to assert sovereignty and control.

The interconnection of financial markets, while promoting investment flows, also makes national economies vulnerable to major shocks and turbulence that call into question what participation in the global economy actually means. Leaders and publics are stunned to see how 20 or 30 percent of a country's economic value, built up over decades by the hard work and sacrifice of the nation, can be destroyed in a matter of weeks.

Yet this new focus on financial vulnerability also reveals a change—that the danger comes from the capital markets, not from multinational corporations, which were seen as the great threat not so many years ago. Indeed, the perspective on multinationals is quite altered. Instead of being seen as predators, they are now courted as investors, who bring capital, technology, skills, and access to global markets. They are also seen as less threatening for other reasons; it is not only because there are now so many of them—over forty thousand, according to one United Nations count—but also because their home countries are so diverse.

This does not mean, however, that there will not be renewed hostility to foreign control and to foreign ownership of domestic industries, particularly industries that are seen as too close and too central to national identity. Local participation and partnerships can help alleviate such conflict, to everybody's benefit. But there will continue to be a clash of interests and inherent tension between multinational corporations and national values. The conflict arises from their fundamental difference in perspective and constituencies. Government's job, after all, is to respond to national interests and concerns, while the multinational unit is driven by the imperatives of an international perspective.

Securing the Environment?

After more than a quarter century of activism, the environment is firmly ensconced as both a national and an international priority. Economic systems will be judged by how they respond to the wide range of environmental concerns, and they will be compelled to find further improvements and new solutions.

For the industrial world, this means continuing on a track along which it is already well advanced. Compared to where they started at the beginning of the 1970s, the 850 hundred million people of the industrial world have experienced dramatic improvements in their national environments. This has been accomplished through legislation and regulation, innovation and technology, changes in practices and behavior—and by spending a great deal of money. But how to go forward? Will it be through command-and-control and familiar forms of regulation or through innovative market-based systems?

The most pressing environmental issues are those that affect the 4.75 billion people in the rest of the world. A large number of those countries start from low levels of standards. Their environments are under stress because of poverty—for example, in many countries, the rural poor have cut down forests for firewood, creating a host of difficulties, including erosion that cripples agriculture. Countries also suffer from the environmental problems that come from climbing on the growth ladder—wretched urban air from unprotected factories and power plants, proliferating automobiles, and poor-quality fuels. These problems can be ameliorated, but the price tag is high, especially for a country that is struggling to raise its income and has many needs but limited resources. How will investment be mobilized? Who will pay the price? Such choices are not limited to developing countries. One of the lasting legacies of communism is the extensive environmental damage that afflicts the former Soviet Union and Eastern Europe. But neither the economic resources nor the means are readily available to remedy the ills in the former communist world.

Increasingly, however, environmental issues are becoming international. Some are regional matters. The burning of forests in Indonesia creates terrible air pollution hundreds of miles away, in Malaysia, Singapore, and Thailand. Some issues are global, and climate change is the best known. As the climate-change debate demonstrates, the first challenge is to come to some rough agreement on the dimensions of the problem. But that is only the beginning. For a multitude of nations then have to come to a meeting of the minds on solutions. Then they face the difficult job of apportioning responsibilities and costs.

In such matters, the potential for conflict between developed and developing countries is considerable. Calls for concerted action by the industrial countries can appear to developing nations as an effort to constrain their growth opportunities—imposed by countries much richer than themselves. The industrial world, for instance, expresses concern at the absolute amounts of carbon emitted by coal-fired electric generation in China. The Chinese reply by observing that on a per capita basis, they use only 5 percent as much electric power as Americans. How, they ask, can they be denied the opportunity to strive toward a higher standard of living, which, even if achieved, will still be only a fraction of that in the developed countries?

In all this, the private sector will find itself carrying an increasing environmental role. Not only will companies be regulated from a multitude of directions and by multiple authorities; they will also find themselves judged by the nature of their commitment and contribution to improving the environment. Focusing on the environment will become a growing responsibility of senior management.

Coping with Demographics?

Population trends will challenge the performance of market economies. The more familiar population issue is in the developing world. Those countries confront an enormous swelling in the younger age groups and the daunting tasks of generating jobs and increasing per capita income. The surge in population creates a combustible mixture of idleness, poverty, disillusionment, and bitterness that can be a tremendous source of political and economic instability. Over time, growth in incomes will lead to a tapering-off of births. In the meantime, liberalized economies will struggle to generate opportunities for their populace. The effects are not limited within borders. For population growth also drives migration both among these countries and into industrial nations, creating new political and social conflicts.

For the developed world, the key population trend is the growing proportion of the elderly, which will add to the critical need to reform the traditional welfare state. The key period will begin toward the end of the first decade of the twenty-first century, when the baby-boom generation starts to retire, putting enormous strains on the health and pension systems. The pressures will grow more severe as the years pass. "There can be little doubt," said economist David Hale, "that the great economic policy challenge of the twenty-first century will be how to finance everyone's retirement." He added, "The only good analogy to the magnitude of the fiscal challenge posed by the aging of . . . population is war."

On whose shoulders, on which age group, will the costs of retirement and health care fall? How much responsibility will belong to government, and thus to taxpayers, and how much will be the responsibility of individuals and the private sector? One can well imagine political conflict along generational lines over health care and pensions. The votes will be there to expand government's role and the share of the national income going to meet the needs of the elderly, and the working population will find an increasing proportion of its output being taxed away to support the older generation. The challenge for each society will be to sort out what it considers entitlements, to be paid out of public funds, and what it regards simply as marketable services, for which the individual is responsible. In the next century, the population issues for the developing and developed countries will converge as the daunting challenge of the elderly becomes a problem for developing countries as well. By the year 2030, China will have 400 million people over the age of sixty-five, compared to 100 million today.

The Balance of Confidence

How successfully these tests will be met will have much to do with how publics around the world respond to the great shift in the commanding heights that is now unfolding. Will confidence in market systems be reaffirmed, or will it be eroded? And confidence, after all, is the heart of the matter. As it is, the world continues to move toward markets. One of the most dramatic signs is the degree to which people around the world are entrusting their savings and their retirements to the stock market. In the United States, which is clearly at the forefront, mutual fund assets by mid-1997 exceeded assets in bank accounts by 25 percent. Similarly, with privatization and deregulation, governments are turning over what had been their province to the marketplace. Yet there is nothing guaranteed about the results. Volatility and risk are inherent. If confidence is to be well grounded, it requires a realistic assessment of what can go wrong.[10]

Of all the dangers, perhaps the greatest threat to the new consensus, and the confidence that underlies it, would arise from massive disruption of the international financial system. Capital markets are growing far faster than the capacity to regulate them—or indeed even to understand them. The very scope and reach of the integrated global markets create financial risks on an unprecedented scale. These dangers result from the interconnection of currency markets, interest rates, and stock markets, along with the extraordinary growth in the various ancillary markets that hinge on them. In the past, financial panics took weeks or even months to unfold. Now contagion can sweep through the world's markets in hours, endangering the entire edifice. To be sure, the financial markets are diverse and, in many cases, dense and enormously liquid. The danger arises not from the possibility of a shock but rather from the convergence of several shocks at one time that together reverberate through the entire system.

The probability of such convergence may be low. But, as Margaret Thatcher reminds one with Thatcher's Law, the unexpected does happen. There has been no shortage of severe shocks over the last decade. In 1995, Latin America suffered from the "tequila effect" resulting from Mexico's devaluation; two years later, in 1997, Southeast Asia underwent a massive currency crisis that started in a weak and overleveraged banking sector. Both resulted in panic selling and stock market collapses. A political crisis—the prospect in 1996 that Boris Yeltsin might lose the presidential election to a communist rival—sent shock waves through the Russian economy. The Persian Gulf military crisis, which began with Iraq's invasion of Kuwait in 1990, shook the world's stock exchanges. And in Japan, the breakdown in business and consumer confidence after the bubble broke in the early 1990s has been one of the main reasons for the long slump that settled over the country. Some of these came as complete surprises. But each of them occurred more or less in isolation and was offset by strength elsewhere. The danger is not that one or the other type of shock takes place. The threat is of an unlucky conjunction.

Of course, national and international authorities would not be watching from the sidelines should such a compounding occur. They could use all the considerable crisis-management machinery available to them, both formal and informal, all the lessons learned over the century, in order to restore steadiness, organize bailouts, and turn the tide. But the complexity and range of such problems could exceed any previous experience. When it is all over, markets might end up restabilized at much lower levels. In the meantime, trillions of dollars of wealth would have evaporated. Liquidity problems would likely be widespread, and some large financial institutions, much more exposed than they had recognized, could teeter on bankruptcy. The consequence could be a protracted period of poor economic performance, even deflation, inviting a return to protectionism. Recrimination and bitterness would abound. The result: a wholesale retreat from confidence in markets themselves.

Financial markets have transcended national boundaries and traditional regulation. But coordination and communication among governments and international institutions can help identify and manage weaknesses before they give rise to contagions that turn into epidemics. New methods need to be developed to keep pace with the growth of the global capital markets. That means more transparency by governments in terms of their financial positions and more disclosure by companies—in particular, by firms in the critical financial sector. Investors and lenders need to maintain a clear-eyed assessment of perils and keep in mind, even as they think about global markets, the realities of national and regional politics, culture, and history. In short, the market consensus is best bolstered not by enthusiasm but by a measured prudence.

The market also requires something else: legitimacy. But here it faces an ethical conundrum. It is based upon contracts, rules, and choice—in short, on self-restraint—which contrasts mightily with other ways of organizing economic activity. Yet a system that takes the pursuit of self-interest and profit as its guiding light does not necessarily satisfy the yearning in the human soul for belief and some higher meaning beyond materialism. In the Spanish Civil War in the late 1930s, Republican soldiers are said to have died with the word *Stalin* on their lips. Their idealized vision of Soviet communism, however misguided, provided justification for their ultimate sacrifice. Few people would die with the words *free markets* on their lips.

Even without that extreme contrast, the moral appeal of socialism and state intervention is clear and explicit: altruism; concern, sympathy, and solidarity with fellow humans; dignity and social betterment; justice and fairness; hope. The market system cannot offer such direct appeals. Its moral basis is more subtle—and indirect—in terms of what it makes possible rather than what it does.

Yet the essential morality of the market is twofold. The first is in the results that it delivers, in what it makes possible for people—which is based upon the premise that the pursuit of individual interest cumulatively adds up to the overall betterment of society. That was, after all, at the heart of Adam Smith's argument for self-interest. The second lies in the conviction that a system based upon property, contracts, and initiative provides protection against the arbitrary and unchecked power of the state. Those two premises are the bedrock of the market, and it is against them, over time, that the workings of the market will be evaluated. Neither of these premises implies that all values are market values, that human endeavor is to be judged only by what it fetches in the commercial arena. Large realms of activity are to be valued—and motivated—in terms that are distinct from dollars and cents. What is being said is that there are better and worse ways to organize economies to achieve objectives. To choose the market focus is not to embrace a money culture.

Yet if the market is seen to fail on either of those two grounds—results and restraint—if its benefits are regarded as exclusive rather than as inclusive, if it is seen to nurture the abuse of private power and the specter of raw greed, then surely there will be a backlash—a return to greater state intervention, management, and control. The state would again step forward to expand its role as protector of the citizenry against the power of private interests, whether exercised through monopoly, wanton behavior, fraud and deception, or exploitation and direct harm.

In the meanwhile, in a vast drama, the state continues to withdraw from the commanding heights, leaving it more and more to the realm of the market. This represents a great reconnecting—a conjoining of the beginning and the end of the twentieth century. The century opened with markets ascendant and an expanding global economy, buttressed by a spirit of optimism. That economy was fractured by war, depression, nationalism, and ideology. Crisis and disaster, human need and suffering, and a profound sense of justice and dignity—these propelled the expansion of the state's responsibilities. The decades after World War II were years of recovery and then of great growth. Today's possibilities are built on those achievements of yesterday. But now, because of experience and reassessment—and also because of technology—the role of the state is being redefined, and the realm of the market is now expanding. Hard questions result: What services should the state provide? What is its welfare role? And how much less "mixed" will its economy be?

These changes signify the establishment of the first truly global economy, integrated and interconnected, in which work and production are networked around the world, and in which everything from knowledge to commerce is taking electronic form. With all its benefits and all the hopes it sparks, this reassertion of the market will nevertheless encounter a host of new challenges and bracing tests in the twenty-first century. The opportunities it can create for people are enormous; yet there is a clear unease with its demands, its impact, and the reordering that it can impose. Risk will be a very evident part of this new world, as it should be. For it is out of risk that emerge the innovation and the incentives—and the imagination—that carry the world forward.

Many forces are driving the shift from state control to market consensus. Yet fundamentally it rests upon a recasting of beliefs and ideas—away from the traditional faith in the state and toward greater credibility for the market. Perhaps, then, what will really determine whether this change will persist, or whether there will be a swing back, is the quality and character of the confidence that underpins the marketplace. Confidence is more likely to endure if it is tempered by a realistic appraisal of risk and uncertainty, and of the benefits and limits of the market and its values. And where will fall the future frontier between state and market? That answer will be found in the cumulative judgments and experience that will orient beliefs and shape the balance of confidence.

CHRONOLOGY

1776	Adam Smith publishes *The Wealth of Nations*.
	American Revolution begins.
1789	French Revolution begins.
1867	Marx begins to publish *Das Kapital*.
1882	Bismarck establishes pension system in Germany.
1887	Interstate Commerce Commission established in the United States.
1890	Sherman Anti-Trust Act in the United States.
1901	Theodore Roosevelt becomes U.S. president and starts "trust-busting."
1906	Reforming Liberal government in Britain lays basis for "ambulance state."
1911	Chinese Revolution.
1914	Outbreak of First World War ends "golden age" of international commerce.
1917	Russian Revolution begins.
1918	World War I ends.
1919	Treaty of Versailles.
	British Labour Party adopts Clause IV, calling for nationalization.
	Amritsar massacre in India.
	Tiananmen Square demonstration in Beijing launches "May 4" nationalist movement in China.
1921–22	Lenin's "New Economic Policy" permits some private economic activity. He replies to critics with "commanding heights" theory.
	Ludwig von Mises publishes *On Socialism* in Vienna.
1927	Stalin consolidates control in Soviet Union.
1929	U.S. stock market crash signals onset of Great Depression.
	First five-year plan in Soviet Union.
1932	Samuel Insull's electric power empire collapses in the United States.
1933	Franklin Roosevelt becomes U.S. president, launching New Deal.
	Mussolini's Fascist regime creates IRI as state holding company in Italy.
1933–35	Establishment of U.S. Securities and Exchange Commission and Tennessee Valley Authority, and passage of Public Utility Holding Company Act.
1934–35	Mao Zedong leads China's communists on the Long March.
1936	John Maynard Keynes publishes *The General Theory*.

1937	War between Japan and China begins.
1938	Mexico nationalizes its oil industry.
	Civil Aeronautics Board is created to deal with "extreme competition" in U.S. aviation.
1939	World War II starts in Europe with German invasion of Poland.
1941	U.S. enters World War II the day after Pearl Harbor attack.
	Altiero Spinelli, imprisoned by Fascists on island of Ventotene, writes his manifesto for a united Europe.
1942	The Beveridge Report in Britain prescribes welfare state programs.
1944	Friedrich von Hayek publishes *The Road to Serfdom*.
	The World Bank is created at the Bretton Woods conference.
1945	World War II ends with Allied victory.
	Labour Party wins British election. Clement Attlee becomes prime minister. Welfare state launched.
1946	France establishes national planning under Jean Monnet.
	Nehru publishes *The Discovery of India*.
	Keynes dies after negotiating British loan from the United States.
	Milton Friedman is appointed to economics faculty at University of Chicago.
1946–47	Economic crisis in Europe.
1947	U.S. initiates Marshall Plan program to support European reconstruction.
	India gains its independence from Britain with Nehru as prime minister.
	Britain nationalizes its coal industry.
1948	Allies institute currency reform in western Germany; Soviets blockade Berlin, signifying the division of Europe.
	German finance minister Ludwig Erhard eliminates price controls, beginning social market economy and German economic miracle.
1949	Mao Zedong's communist forces are victorious and the People's Republic of China is established. Chiang Kai-shek flees to Taiwan.
	Schuman Plan—devised by Jean Monnet—creates Coal and Steel Community.
1950	North Korea invades South, beginning the Korean War.
1951	India's first five-year plan begins.
1952	Argentina's Eva Perón dies and Juan Perón goes into exile.
1955	The Bandung summit of nonaligned nations is held in Indonesia.
	The "1955 System" in Japan lays basis for rapid postwar growth.
1956	Soviet troops violently repress anti-Communist revolution in Hungary.
	Suez crisis creates discord within Western Alliance.
	Sony acquires rights to the transistor from Westinghouse.
	Institute of Economic Affairs is established in London.
1957	The German Bundesbank is created with obligation to fight inflation.
	Ghana and Malaysia gain their independence from Britain; Kwame Nkrumah—"the Redeemer"—becomes Ghana's prime minister, later president.
	The Treaty of Rome establishes the European Economic Community.
	British prime minister Harold Macmillan tells British people, "You never had it so good."
1958–60	The Great Leap Forward in China.

1960	Friedrich von Hayek publishes *The Constitution of Liberty.*
1961	General Park Chung Hee seizes power in South Korea, launching industrialization.
1962	Milton Friedman publishes *Capitalism and Freedom.*
	U.S. president John F. Kennedy delivers "Old Myths, New Realities" speech at Yale.
1964	The Olympics are held in Tokyo, as Japan goes for "income doubling."
	President Lyndon Johnson launches War on Poverty.
	Medicare bill is signed in United States.
	Tonkin Gulf Resolution authorizes presidential action in Vietnam.
	Thoughts of Chairman Mao—"the Little Red Book"—is published.
1965	Collapse of the Malay-Singapore union two years after its initiation.
	Lee Kuan Yew is to lead independent Singapore.
	Keynes posthumously makes the cover of *Time* magazine.
	The Public Interest journal is established in United States.
1966	Mao unleashes Cultural Revolution in China.
	Deng Xiaoping is sent to solitary confinement.
	Kwame Nkrumah inaugurates the Volta Dam in Ghana; shortly after, he is overthrown.
1968	Richard M. Nixon is elected president of the United States.
	Soviet tanks crush Czechoslovakia's "Prague Spring" and "socialism with a human face."
	Texas Instruments invests in Singapore.
1969	Anti-Chinese riots disrupt Malaysia, leading to new policies.
1970	Alfred Kahn publishes *The Economics of Regulation.*
	The socialist government of Salvador Allende comes to power in Chile and embarks upon a program of massive nationalizations.
1971	President Nixon institutes a New Economic Policy, including wage-and-price controls, and closes U.S. gold window, ending Bretton Woods currency system.
1973	Britain joins European Economic Community.
	Oil shock hits global economy.
	Heavy and Chemical Industries initiative launched in South Korea.
	General Pinochet topples Chile's Allende regime in bloody coup. Subsequently implements "the brick"—free-market reforms.
1974	India becomes a nuclear power.
	British coal miners' strike blacks out the country, forcing election.
	Friedrich von Hayek shares the Nobel Prize for Economics with Swedish Keynesian Gunnar Myrdal.
	Keith Joseph establishes Centre for Policy Studies in London.
	Senator Edward Kennedy convenes hearings on airline deregulation with staff counsel Stephen Breyer.
1975	Margaret Thatcher, defeating Edward Heath, becomes leader of Britain's Conservative Party.
1975–76	Oil companies are nationalized in Saudi Arabia, Kuwait, and Venezuela.
1976	Mao Zedong dies.
	Milton Friedman wins the Nobel Prize for Economics.
1977	Alfred Kahn becomes chairman of Civil Aeronautics Board, implementing airline deregulation.

1978	Polish cardinal Karoł Wojtyla becomes Pope John Paul II.
	Eleventh Party Congress introduces economic reform in China. Deng Xiaoping emerges as paramount leader.
	European Monetary System links the franc to the deutsche mark.
1978–79	Public-sector employees strike during Britain's "winter of discontent."
1979	Margaret Thatcher becomes British prime minister.
	General Park assassinated in coup following the Kwangju massacre in Korea.
	Second oil crisis begins with Iranian revolution.
	President Jimmy Carter diagnoses crisis of confidence in American people in "malaise" speech.
	Carter appoints Paul Volcker head of Federal Reserve to slay inflation.
1980	The Polish Solidarity movement begins in the Gdańsk shipyards.
	Ronald Reagan is elected president of the United States.
1981	François Mitterrand becomes the first Socialist president in the Fifth Republic of France.
	U.S. federal air traffic controllers strike.
	Mahathir Mohamad becomes prime minister of Malaysia.
	Martial law in Poland; Solidarity, outlawed, goes underground.
1981–82	Household responsibility system is introduced, breaking grip of collectivization on Chinese agriculture.
1982	George Stigler wins the Nobel Prize for Economics.
	Helmut Kohl becomes chancellor of Germany.
	The Falklands War begins after Argentina seizes islands; Britain victorious.
	Mexico's fiscal collapse triggers debt crisis and "the lost decade" in Latin America.
1982–85	Three elderly Soviet leaders—Brezhnev, Andropov, and Chernenko—die in quick succession.
1983	Thatcher returned in landslide election victory.
1984	Jacques Delors becomes president of the European Community's Commission.
	Assassination of Indira Gandhi.
	Deng Xiaoping publishes *Building of Socialism with Chinese Characteristics*.
	Privatization of British Telecom begins.
	New Zealand launches radical reform program in response to currency crisis.
1985	Decree 21060 in Bolivia signals the start of shock therapy.
	Mikhail Gorbachev comes to power intent on promoting reform.
	British coal strike ends with Thatcher victory.
1986	The International Finance Corporation persuades U.S. international investors to come up with $50 million for the first emerging-market fund.
1987	The Single European Act, to create single market, approved by EC.
	Novelist Mario Vargas Llosa becomes the leader of reform movement in Peru.

1988	The capitalization of the Tokyo Stock Exchange equals that of New York's.
1989	Roundtable talks in Poland between Solidarity, the Catholic Church, and the Communists.
	Chinese student protest suppressed in Tiananmen Square.
	The Berlin Wall comes down, marking end of Europe's division.
	Carlos Menem wins the presidency of Argentina.
	Communist governments fall in Poland, Czechoslovakia, Hungary, Romania, and Bulgaria.
1990	West and East German currencies are unified. The two Germanys unify.
	Balcerowicz's shock therapy goes into effect in Poland.
	Solidarity leader Lech Wałęsa is elected president of Poland.
	Elections in Chile; democratic government retains free-market reforms.
	Iraq invades Kuwait.
1991	The Soviet Union disintegrates and the fifteen Soviet Republics become independent nations.
	Boris Yeltsin becomes president of independent Russian Federation.
	P. V. Narasimha Rao becomes India's prime minister and initiates economic reforms.
	The Maastricht treaty, providing for single European currency, is signed.
	Alberto Fujimori wins the Peruvian presidential election in a runoff against Mario Vargas Llosa.
1992	Deng Xiaoping takes his *nanxun* to southern China to protect economic reforms.
	Japan enters a deep slump as "bubble economy" bursts.
	Russia's massive privatization program starts.
	Gary Becker wins the Nobel Prize in Economics.
	U.S. deficit reaches $290 billion.
	North American Free Trade Agreement signed among United States, Canada, and Mexico.
1993	New Democrat Bill Clinton becomes U.S. president.
	Korean president Kim Young-Sam launches major anticorruption campaign.
	Argentina's oil company, YPF, sells $3 billion of stock in IPO.
1994	Fernando Henrique Cardoso introduces the real to stabilize Brazilian economy.
	The Republican Party proclaims its Contract with America and wins both houses of the U.S. Congress.
	World Trade Organization is established.
1995	Former Communist Alexsander Kwasniewski defeats Lech Wałęsa for the Polish presidency but promises not to alter economic reforms.
	Newt Gingrich, Republican Speaker of the House, is chosen as *Time* magazine's Man of the Year.
	"Tequila effect" hits Latin American stock markets after Mexican devaluation.
1995–96	U.S. federal government shutdown results from budget impasse.

1996   Bill Clinton proclaims the end of big government.

Russian stock market is world's best-performing emerging market.

A native Taiwanese, Lee Teng-hui, is the first democratically elected president of Taiwan.

Former Korean presidents Roh Tae-Woo and Chun Doo Hwan are convicted of corruption.

1997   Deng Xiaoping dies.

Hong Kong returns to China on basis of "one country, two systems."

New Labourite Tony Blair becomes Britain's prime minister on a platform of Thatcherite economics leavened with compassion.

Lionel Jospin wins prime ministership of France and presents plans that recall the Socialist policies of the early 1980s.

Currency crisis hits Southeast Asian "miracle" economies.

Fifteenth Party Congress in China endorses dismantling of massive state-owned sector and adopts "Deng Xiaoping Theory."

U.S. deficit drops to $22 billion.

NOTES

Introduction: At the Frontier

1. Interview with Brian Fall. V. I. Lenin, "Five Years of the Russian Revolution and the Prospects of the World Revolution: Report to the Fourth Congress of the Communist International, November 13, 1922," in Lenin, *Collected Works,* vol. 33 (Moscow: Progress Publishers, 1966), pp. 418–432; E. H. Carr, *The Bolshevik Revolution,* vol. 3 (London: Macmillan, 1953), pp. 441–451.
2. Interview with Paul Volcker. John Maynard Keynes, *The General Theory of Employment, Interest and Money* (London: Macmillan, 1936), pp. 383–384 ("madmen"). On market failure versus government failure, see Nicholas Stern, "The Economics of Development: A Survey," *Economic Journal,* vol. 99, September 1989, pp. 597–685, especially sec. III; Nicholas Stern, "Public Policy and the Economics of Development," *European Economic Review,* vol. 35, 1991, pp. 241–271. On government spending, see World Bank, *World Development Report 1997* (New York: Oxford University Press, 1997); Clive Crook, ed., "The Future of the State: A Survey of the World Economy," *The Economist,* September 20–26, 1997.
3. Ronald D. Rotunda, "The 'Liberal' Label: Roosevelt's Capture of a Symbol," *Public Policy,* vol. 17, 1968, pp. 377–408, 389 ("Radical-Red"), 408; Alan Brinkley, *The End of Reform: New Deal Liberalism in Recession and War* (New York: Vintage Books, 1996), p. 10 ("plain English"); Charles Singer, E. J. Holmyard, A. R. Hall, and Trevor I. Williams, eds., *A History of Technology* (Oxford: Clarendon Press, 1980), vol. 5, p. 144 (Savannah), vol. 4, pp. 660–661 (telegraph cable).

Chapter 1: Thirty Glorious Years: Europe's Mixed Economy

1. Martin Gilbert, *Winston S. Churchill,* vol. 8, *"Never Despair," 1945–1965* (Boston: Houghton Mifflin Company, 1988), p. 108 ("Scurvy" and "effectively disguised"); Peter Hennessy, *Never Again: Britain 1945–1951* (London: Vintage, 1993), p. 6 ("greatest adventurer"); Kenneth Harris, *Attlee* (London: Weidenfeld & Nicolson, 1995), p. 564 ("Christian ethics"); David Holloway, *Stalin and the Bomb: The Soviet Union and Atomic Energy* (New Haven: Yale University Press, 1994), pp. 116–118.

2. Harris, *Attlee,* pp. 262 ("subdued and terse"), 564 ("agnostic"), 266 ("fixed"), 268 ("bark yourself"); Hennessy, *Never Again,* p. 199 ("bonkers").

3. Daniel Yergin, *Shattered Peace* (New York: Penguin Books, 1990), pp. 304 ("worse than anything"), 304–306; Dennis L. Bark and David R. Gress, *A History of West Germany: From Shadow to Substance, 1945–1963* (Oxford: Basil Blackwell, 1989), p. 193 ("Jacobites"); Charles Maier, "The Two Post War Eras," *American Historical Review,* 1981, p. 327; Mario Einaudi, Maurice Byé, and Ernesto Rossi, *Nationalization in France and Italy* (Ithaca, N.Y.: Cornell University Press, 1995), p. 14 ("we are all planners now").

4. Hennessy, *Never Again,* pp. 70 ("stress"), 75 ("five giants"); Nicholas Timmins, *The Five Giants: A Biography of the Welfare State* (London: HarperCollins, 1995), pp. 34, 25, 12–14; Harris, *Attlee,* p. 257 ("pathetic faith"); Richard Cockett, *Thinking the Unthinkable: Think-tanks and the Economic Counter-Revolution, 1931–1983* (London: Fontana Press, 1995), pp. 14–15 ("Collective Welfare" and "installment of Socialism"); Jim Fyrth, ed., *Labour's High Noon: The Government and the Economy 1945–51* (London: Lawrence & Wishart, 1993); Sidney and Beatrice Webb, *Soviet Communism: A New Civilization?,* 2 vols. (London: Longmans, Green and Co., 1935).

5. Hennessy, *Never Again,* pp. 79 ("common ownership"), 183 ("public corporations"), 198 ("socialist principle"), 202; Jim Tomlinson, *Government and the Enterprise Since 1900: The Changing Problem of Efficiency* (New York: Oxford University Press, 1994), pp. 192–203, 162; Richard Saville, "Commanding Heights: The Nationalisation Programme," in Fyrth, *Labour's High Noon,* pp. 37–60.

6. Hennessy, *Never Again,* pp. 434 ("practically"), 195 ("grace of God"), 450–452; Tomlinson, *Government and the Enterprise,* p. 114; Robert Skidelsky, *Interest and Obsessions* (London: Macmillan, 1993), p. 133 ("full employment standard"); Harris, *Attlee,* p. 254 ("mixed economy").

7. Interview with Christian Stoffaes. Stanley Hoffmann, *In Search of France: The Economy, Society and Political System in the Twentieth Century* (Cambridge, Mass.: Harvard University Press, 1963), p. 6 ("rotten" and "freezing"); Einaudi, Byé, and Rossi, *Nationalization in France and Italy,* pp. 136, 33–34, 73–79 ("levers" and "weapon"); François Duchêne, *Jean Monnet: The First Statesman of Independence* (New York: W. W. Norton & Company, 1994), p. 157 ("privileged classes"); Daniel Yergin, *The Prize: The Epic Quest for Oil, Money and Power* (New York: Simon & Schuster, 1991), pp. 190–191.

8. Richard Barnet, *The Alliance: America, Europe, Japan, Makers of the Postwar World* (New York: Simon & Schuster, 1983), pp. 96–98 ("without lawyers"); Richard Mayne, *The Recovery of Europe, 1945–1973* (New York: Anchor Books, 1973), p. 210 ("my horse"); Duchêne, *Jean Monnet,* pp. 55, 89 ("arsenal").

9. Duchêne, *Jean Monnet,* pp. 145 (de Gaulle and Monnet), 157 ("crystallizing"), 145 *("dirigistes"),* 171, 153; Einaudi, Byé, and Rossi, *Nationalization in France and Italy,* p. 80.

10. Duchêne, *Jean Monnet,* pp. 177, 166 ("balance sheets"), 148 ("odd thing"), 178–179 ("relative consensus"); François Caron, *An Economic History of Modern France* (London: Methuen & Co., 1979), p. 274.

11. Herbert Giersch, Karl-Heinz Paqué, and Holger Schmieding, *The Fading Miracle: Four Decades of Market Economy in Germany* (Cambridge, England: Cam-

bridge University Press, 1992), pp. 12, 37 ("capitalist economic system"); Barnet, *The Alliance,* p. 19; Yergin, *Shattered Peace,* pp. 310 ("close to starving"), 306; Jean Edward Smith, *Lucius D. Clay: An American Life* (New York: Henry Holt and Company, 1990), pp. 453–454.

12. Bark and Gress, *From Shadow to Substance,* pp. 207–208 ("Nazi totalitarianism," "hierarchy," and "no restriction").

13. Bark and Gress, *From Shadow to Substance,* pp. 192 ("truly fortunate"), 202 ("Herr General" and "most fateful"); Smith, *Lucius D. Clay,* pp. 484–485; Mayne, *The Recovery,* pp. 197–200.

14. Bark and Gress, *From Shadow to Substance,* pp. 110 ("American army"), 251 ("planned" and "market"), 244 ("My doctor"); Karl Hardach, *The Political Economy of Germany in the Twentieth Century* (Berkeley: University of California Press, 1980), pp. 155–177.

15. Einaudi, Byé, and Rossi, *Nationalization in France and Italy,* p. 199 ("unplanned").

16. Robert Skidelsky, *Keynes* (Oxford: Oxford University Press, 1996), pp. 46 ("*educated* bourgeoisie"), 10 ("from messing" and "always a bet").

17. Skidelsky, *Keynes,* pp. 119, 81 ("somewhat comprehensive"), 2 ("Keynes supplied"), 117 ("market is stupid"); Keynes, *General Theory,* p. 383 ("gradual encroachment"); William J. Barber, *A History of Economic Thought* (London: Penguin, 1967, reprinted 1979), p. 257 ("intellectual foundations").

18. Raymond Vernon and Deborah Spar, *Beyond Globalism* (New York: Free Press, 1989), p. 45 ("State Department"); Duchêne, *Jean Monnet,* p. 126; Mayne, *The Recovery,* pp. 146–148 ("code"); Raymond Vernon, "America's Foreign Trade Policy and the GATT," *Essays in International Finance,* no. 21, October 1954.

19. Giersch, Paqué, and Schmieding, *The Fading Miracle,* p. 4; Mayne, *The Recovery,* pp. 217–277; Hardach, *The Political Economy of Germany,* p. 162; Peter Pulzer, *German Politics, 1945–1995* (Oxford: Oxford University Press, 1995), p. 63 ("prosperity"); Caron, *An Economic History of Modern France,* p. 190; Alistair Horne, *Harold Macmillan,* vol. 2, *1957–1986* (New York: Viking Penguin, 1989), pp. 64 ("You never"), 149.

CHAPTER 2: THE CURSE OF BIGNESS: AMERICA'S REGULATORY CAPITALISM

1. *New York Times,* July 17, 1938 ("Every home"); Arthur M. Schlesinger, Jr., *Crisis of the Old Order, 1919–1933* (Boston: Houghton Mifflin, 1988), p. 255 ("Why am I not"); Forrest McDonald, *Insull* (Chicago: University of Chicago Press, 1962), p. 314 ("the Insulls").

2. Thomas McCraw, *Prophets of Regulation* (Cambridge, Mass.: Belknap Press, 1984), pp. 67, 62; Ida Tarbell, *All in the Day's Work: An Autobiography* (New York: Macmillan Company, 1939), pp. 241–242 ("vile"); Adam Smith, *Inquiry into the Nature and Causes of the Wealth of Nations* (Oxford: Clarendon Press, 1869), p. 148 ("same trade"); Kathleen Brady, *Ida Tarbell: Portrait of a Muckraker* (New York: Seaview/Putnam, 1984), pp. 120–123 ("red hot"); George E. Mowry, *Era of Theodore Roosevelt, 1900–1912* (New York: Harper & Brothers, 1958), pp. 131–132 ("levees").

3. McCraw, *Prophets,* pp. 82 ("people's lawyer" and "curse"), 83 ("in mind" and "The Profs"), 110 ("regulated monopoly" and "regulated competition"), 95 ("Captains"), 112 ("In my opinion").

4. William Leuchtenburg, *The Perils of Prosperity* (Chicago: University of Chicago Press, 1993), pp. 89 ("not heroism"), 190 ("propaganda"), 201 ("big business" and Calvin Coolidge); Justin Kaplan, *Lincoln Steffens, A Biography* (New York: Simon & Schuster, 1974), p. 250 ("I have seen the future").

5. Schlesinger, *Crisis,* pp. 2 ("very solemn"), 116, 152–154; Arthur M. Schlesinger, Jr., *The Coming of the New Deal* (Boston: Houghton Mifflin, 1988), pp. 468, 98 ("laissez-faire" and "Herbert Hoover"); McCraw, *Prophets,* p. 173 ("Not Dick Whitney" and "trustees").

6. McCraw, *Prophets,* p. 178 ("brewery horse" and "What husband?"); James M. Landis, *The Administrative Process* (New Haven: Yale University Press, 1938), pp. 1 ("simple tripartite"), 23 ("52 weeks"), 24 ("expanding interest"); Arthur M. Schlesinger, Jr., *The Politics of Upheaval* (Boston: Houghton Mifflin, 1988), p. 312 ("concentrated" and "private socialism").

7. Robert Skidelsky, *John Maynard Keynes,* vol. 2, *The Economist as Saviour, 1920–1937* (London: Macmillan, 1992), pp. 506 ("grand talk" and "not clever"), 89; Schlesinger, *Crisis,* p. 136 ("Too good"); Paul Samuelson, "In the Beginning," p. 33, and James Tobin, "A Revolution Remembered," pp. 38–39, both in "Keynesian Economics and Harvard," *Challenge,* July–August 1988 ("statist features" and "Hansen").

8. Alan Brinkley, *The End of Reform: New Deal Liberalism in Recession and War* (New York: Vintage Books, 1996), pp. 147 ("jarring reversal"), 176 ("In 1945").

9. Brinkley, *The End of Reform,* pp. 261 ("remunerative"), 263 (American Beveridge Plan and "to foster and promote"); Otis Graham, Jr., *Toward a Planned Society* (New York: Oxford University Press, 1976), p. 94 ("Saint Peter").

10. McCraw, *Prophets of Regulation,* pp. 217–219 ("jaunty," "hallmark," and "breakdown").

11. Herbert Stein, *Presidential Economics: The Making of Economic Policy from Roosevelt to Reagan and Beyond* (New York: Touchstone, 1985), pp. 393, 135–136 ("financial types" and "I am a Keynesian"), 162, 146 ("power, status"), 162 (Connally); Richard Nixon, *RN: The Memoirs of Richard Nixon* (New York: Grosset & Dunlap, 1978), pp. 517–518 ("burn up"); John F. Kennedy, "The Myth and Reality in our National Economy," *Vital Speeches* July 15, 1962, pp. 378–381 ("Harvard education").

12. Stein, *Presidential Economics,* pp. 157, 186, 190 ("more new regulation"); H. R. Haldeman, *The Haldeman Diaries: Inside the Nixon White House* (New York: G. P. Putnam's Sons, 1994), p. 346 ("mystic moods"), 308 ("jawboning"); Nixon, *RN,* pp. 519 *("Pravda"),* 520 ("evils"), 521 (Shultz); George P. Shultz and Kenneth W. Dam, *Economic Policy Beyond the Headlines* (New York: W. W. Norton, 1977).

13. Daniel Yergin, *The Prize: The Epic Quest for Oil, Money, and Power* (New York: Simon & Schuster, 1991), p. 695 ("worst"); Stein, *Presidential Economics,* pp. 221 ("two decades"), 224 ("fanciful ideology"). On economic policy in the crisis, see Shultz and Dam, *Economic Policy Behind the Headlines.*

CHAPTER 3: TRYST WITH DESTINY: THE RISE OF THE THIRD WORLD

1. M. J. Akbar, *Nehru: The Making of India* (New York: Viking Penguin, 1988), p. 426 ("tryst"). A recent biography of Nehru is Stanley Wolpert, *Nehru: A Tryst with Destiny* (New York: Oxford University Press, 1996).

2. Akbar, *Nehru,* pp. 73 ("gambler"), 129 ("Indian sahib"), 130 ("shame and sorrow"), 122 ("Greatness").

3. Akbar, *Nehru,* pp. 132 ("Russian system"), 468 ("embody truth"), 465 ("chains of imperialism"); Jawaharlal Nehru, *Discovery of India* (New Delhi: Oxford University Press, 1989; originally Calcutta, Signet Press, 1946), pp. 397 ("appalling poverty"), 406 ("tractors"), 410 ("plus electrification" and "heavy engineering"), 29 ("Soviet Revolution").

4. Nehru, *Discovery,* p. 501 ("planned society"); Sukhamoy Chakravarty, "P. C. Mahalanobis: A Personal Tribute," in Sukhamoy Chakravarty, *Selected Economic Writings* (New Delhi: Oxford University Press, 1993), p. 523 ("qualitative reasoning"). On planning in India, see A. H. Hanson, *The Process of Planning: A Study of India's Five-Year Plans* (London: Oxford University Press, 1966); Sukhamoy Chakravarty, *Development Planning: The Indian Experience* (Oxford: Clarendon Press, 1987).

5. Gerald M. Meier, "The Formative Period," in Meier and Dudley Seers, eds., *Pioneers in Development* (New York: Oxford University Press, 1984), p. 3 ("opulence"); Albert O. Hirschman, "A Dissenter's Confession: 'The Strategy of Economic Development' Revisited," in Meier and Seers, *Pioneers,* p. 111 ("Agenda for a Better World"); Walt Whitman Rostow, "Development: The Political Economy of the Marshallian Long Period," in Meier and Seers, *Pioneers,* pp. 240–245, 277 ("P. C. Mahalanobis"). On Keynes, see Edward Sagendorph Mason and Robert Asher, *The World Bank Since Bretton Woods* (Washington, D.C.: Brookings Institution, 1973), p. 2; Albert O. Hirschman, ed., *Essays in Trespassing* (New York: Cambridge University Press, 1981), pp. 20–23 ("not as narrow" and "backwardness").

6. Paul N. Rosenstein-Rodan, "*Natura Facit Saltum:* Analysis of the Disequilibrium," in Meier and Seers, *Pioneers,* pp. 207, 221 ("status quo" and "real moral crisis"); Jan Tinbergen, "Development Cooperation as a Learning Process," in Meier and Seers, *Pioneers,* pp. 317–318 ("poverty prevailing"); Sir W. Arthur Lewis, "Development Economics in the 1950s," in Meier and Seers, *Pioneers,* p. 130 ("My mother"); Jagdish N. Bhagwati, "Comments," in Meier and Seers, *Pioneers,* p. 201 ("together sail"); P. T. Bauer, "Remembrance of Studies Past: Retracing First Steps," Meier and Seers, *Pioneers,* pp. 27–43; Hirschman, *Essays,* p. 10 ("conviction").

7. Mason and Asher, *World Bank,* pp. 698 ("pattern and flow"), 201 ("essential precondition" and "emergency"), 692 (TVA as model).

8. Mason and Asher, *World Bank,* p. 473; Tinbergen in Meier and Seers, *Pioneers,* p. 326 ("quality of its management" and "stumbling block").

9. Alistair Horne, *Harold Macmillan,* vol. 2, *1957–1986* (New York: Viking Penguin, 1989), p. 195 ("wind of change"); Tony Killick, *Development Economics in Action: A Study of Economic Policies in Ghana* (London: Heinemann Educational Books, 1978), p. 34 ("If we get self-government"); Kwame Nkrumah, *The Autobiography of Kwame Nkrumah* (London: Thomas Nelson and Sons, 1961), p. x ("Capitalism is too complicated"); Crawford Young, *Ideology and Development in Africa* (New Haven: Yale University Press, 1982), p. 1 (Nkrumah's "political kingdom").

10. James Moxon, *Volta: Man's Greatest Lake* (London: Andre Deutsch, 1984), p. 115 ("Roumanian bonds"); *New York Times,* February 25, 1966, p. 1 ("myth"); Horne, *Macmillan,* vol. 2, pp. 397–399 ("greatest socialist mon-

arch" and "risked my Queen"); Killick, *Development Economics in Action,* p. 45 ("establish factories").

11. Arthur Lewis, "Development Economics in the 1950s," in Meier and Seers, *Pioneers,* p. 128 ("ministerial speeches").

CHAPTER 4: THE MAD MONK: BRITAIN'S MARKET REVOLUTION

1. Interview with David Young. Morrison Halcrow, *Keith Joseph: A Single Mind* (London: Macmillan, 1989), pp. 149 ("madman"), 152 *("believe").*

2. Margaret Thatcher, *The Downing Street Years* (New York: HarperCollins, 1993), pp. 251 ("without Keith"), 405 ("torpid socialism"); Margaret Thatcher, *The Path to Power* (New York: HarperCollins, 1995), p. 26 ("political friend"); Lord Blake, quoted in Richard Cockett, *Thinking the Unthinkable: Think-tanks and the Economic Counter-Revolution, 1931–1983* (London: Fontana Press, 1995), p. 217.

3. Halcrow, *Keith Joseph,* pp. 14 ("increasing supply"), 132 ("unjustified fear"), 22, 26 ("any consolation"), 23 ("live interview" and "Minister of Thought").

4. Nicholas Timmins, *The Five Giants: A Biography of the Welfare State* (London: HarperCollins, 1995), p. 264 ("jingling"); Peter Hennessy, *Whitehall* (London: Fontana Press, 1990), p. 324 (vicar of Trumpington).

5. Halcrow, *Keith Joseph,* pp. 56 ("I had thought"), 67 ("our ruddy neighbors"); Cockett, *Thinking the Unthinkable,* pp. 236 (Heath), 142, 133–135 ("anti-Fabian"), 161 ("radical reaction"), 160, 139 ("trench warfare"), 146, 154–155 (Alan Walters), 173 ("bashing"), 145, 158 (Milton Friedman), 236–237 ("My aim" and "chemistry set").

6. Cockett, *Thinking the Unthinkable,* pp. 241, 237–238 (Alfred Sherman, *market economy* and "compassionate"); Thatcher, *The Downing Street Years,* p. 253 ("contradictions" and "thirty years").

7. Thatcher, *The Path to Power,* pp. 266–267 ("I am sorry" and "If you must"); Hugo Young, *One of Us: A Biography of Margaret Thatcher* (London: Pan Books, 1993), pp. 94 ("unacceptable face"), 97 ("filly"), 269 ("destroyed Keith"); Halcrow, *Keith Joseph,* pp. 93 ("instinct"), 82 ("battle of ideas").

8. Cockett, *Thinking the Unthinkable,* pp. 241–243 ("mealy-mouthed" and "reverse the trend"), 248 ("over-governed"); Thatcher, *The Downing Street Years,* p. 255 ("generation's"); Young, *One of Us,* p. 103; Robert Skidelsky, *Thatcherism* (London: Chatto & Windus, 1988), p. 14.

9. Halcrow, *Keith Joseph,* pp. 104 ("It was lovely"), 72 ("We were haunted"), 100 ("indispensable base"), 104 ("moral case"), 112 ("more millionaires"), 105 ("free-for-all"); Cockett, *Thinking the Unthinkable,* p. 278 ("ambitious tutor").

10. Halcrow, *Keith Joseph,* pp. 87 ("re-somethinging"), 127 ("He crouches"); Cockett, *Thinking the Unthinkable,* pp. 245 ("practical people"); Bernard Donoghue, *Prime Minister: The Conduct of Policy Under Harold Wilson and James Callaghan* (London: Jonathan Cape, 1987), p. 190 ("sea-change"); Richard Coopley and Nicholas Woodward, *Britain in the 1970s: The Troubled Economy* (London: University College London, 1996), pp. 74–77 ("For too long"); James Callaghan, *Time and Chance* (London: Collins, 1987); Denis Healey, *The Time of My Life* (London: Penguin, 1989), Chapter 20; Tony Benn, *Against the Tide: Diaries, 1973–76* (London: Hutchinson, 1989), Chapter 5.

11. Interview with John Wakeham. Cockett, *Thinking the Unthinkable,* p. 265 ("the

first hurdle"); Young, *One of Us,* pp. ix ("synonymous"), 4 ("I owe" and "integrity"), 5 ("homilies"), 21 ("age of 19"), 30 ("political career"); Thatcher, *The Downing Street Years,* p. 37 ("a starter").

12. Thatcher, *The Downing Street Years,* pp. 66 ("plastics"), 116 ("prevailing orthodoxy"), 163 ("his daughter"); Young, *One of Us,* pp. 37 ("Should a woman arise"), 19 ("natural path" and "New Deal Conservative"); Cockett, *Thinking the Unthinkable,* p. 174 ("This is what we believe"), 176 ("She's so beautiful"), 173 ("foundation work"); Alistair Horne, *Harold Macmillan,* vol. 1, *1894–1956* (New York: Viking Penguin, 1989), pp. 106–109; Alistair Horne, *Harold Macmillan,* vol. 2, *1957–1986* (New York: Viking Penguin, 1989), p. 70 ("Keynes always said to me").

13. Young, *One of Us,* pp. 147 ("not expect the state"), 207 ("The two great problems"); Thatcher, *The Path to Power,* pp. 26 ("Nanny State" and "philosophy in action"), 149 ("six strong men"); Halcrow, *Keith Joseph,* pp. 136–138 ("Talking to you"); Christopher Beauman, "The Turnaround: The British Steel Corporation from the Mid-1970s to the Mid-1980s—And Beyond," Centre for Economic Performance, London School of Economics, April 23, 1996.

14. Halcrow, *Keith Joseph,* pp. 136–137; Young, *One of Us,* pp. 157 ("We're all Keynesians"), 200–202 ("à la Professor Hayek"), 217 ("364 academic economists"), 240–242 ("rebel head"), 221 ("That Woman"); Thatcher, *The Path to Power,* pp. 122 ("The lady's not for turning"), 151 ("his housemaid"), 130.

15. Interview with Margaret Thatcher. Thatcher, *The Path to Power,* p. 234 ("a nation in retreat"); Thatcher, *The Downing Street Years,* p. 304 ("New Jerusalem").

16. Interviews with Margaret Thatcher, John Wakeham, David Young, and Christopher Beauman. For birth of privatization, letter from David Howell, October 22, 1996. Young, *One of Us,* pp. 358–359; Nigel Lawson, *The View from No. 11: Memoirs of a Tory Radical* (London: Corgi Books, 1993), pp. 203 ("zebra"), 202 ("no unique hot line," "bottomless public purse" and "What public ownership does"), 213 ("chain of shops" and "what a storm"), 198 ("from Siberia to Patagonia"); John Vickers and George Yarrow, *Privatization: An Economic Analysis* (Cambridge, Mass.: MIT Press, 1993), p. 127 ("be-all and end-all"). On the coal strike, see Jonathan Winterton, *Coal, Crisis and Conflict: The 1984–85 Miners' Strike in Yorkshire* (New York: Manchester University Press, 1989).

17. Interview with David Young. Lawson, *The View from No. 11,* pp. 198 ("dossier"), 217 ("too cheap"), 226, 222 ("East European style"), 219 (" 'golden share' "); Beauman, "The Turnaround," LSE, April 23, 1996.

18. Interviews with David Young and Christopher Beauman. On the regulation of privatized utilities, see M. E. Beesley, ed., *Utility Regulation: Challenge and Response* (London: Institute of Economic Affairs, 1995) and Matthew Bishop, John Kay, and Colin Mayer, eds., *The Regulatory Challenge* (New York: Oxford University Press, 1995).

19. Interviews with Margaret Thatcher and David Young. Young, *One of Us,* pp. 518 ("a bit of an institution"), 427, 574 ("Remember, George"), 587 ("it's all over"), 605; Geoffrey Howe, *Conflict of Loyalty* (London: Pan Books, 1995), pp. 637–652 (resignation), p. 691 ("great prime minister").

20. Interview with Margaret Thatcher.

1. Elizabeth Pond, *Beyond the Wall: Germany's Road to Unification* (Washington, D.C.: Brookings Institution, 1993), pp. 132–133 ("hit" and "small mistake"); Charles Maier, *Dissolution: The Crisis of Communism and the End of East Germany* (Princeton, N.J.: Princeton University Press, 1997), p. 163 ("kaput").

2. Interviews with Valéry Giscard d'Estaing, Jesús Silva Herzog, and Paul Volcker. Paul Volcker and Toyoo Gyohten, *Changing Fortunes: The World's Money and the Threat to American Leadership* (New York: Times Books, 1992), pp. 194–202 ("Third World"); *World Debt Tables, 1992–1993,* p. 46 ("problem in history"); Daniel Yergin, *The Prize: The Epic Quest for Oil, Money, and Power* (New York: Simon & Schuster, 1991), p. 667 ("borrower of the year").

3. Interviews with Franco Bernabè and Vijay Kelkar.

4. Interviews with G. V. Ramakrishna and Gary Becker. R. H. S. Crossman, *The God That Failed* (New York: Harper, 1949).

5. Interviews with Gary Becker and Dani Kauffmann. On New Zealand, see M. A. Smith, "Deregulation, Privatization, and Economic Reform in New Zealand," *Fletcher Challenge Energy,* September 25, 1997; Graham C. Scott, *Government Reform in New Zealand* (Washington, D.C.: IMF, 1996).

6. F. A. Hayek, *Hayek on Hayek: An Autobiographical Dialogue* (Chicago: University of Chicago Press, 1994), p. 48 ("eleven different languages"); Jeremy Shearmur, *Hayek and After: Hayekian Liberalism as a Research Program* (London: Routledge, 1996), pp. 26–34; Peter Klein, ed., *The Fortunes of Liberalism: The Collected Works of F. A. Hayek* (London: Routledge, 1992), vol. 4, pp. 136–139 ("civilization," "*Socialism* shocked," and "wrong direction"), 170; F. A. Hayek, *The Constitution of Liberty* (London: Routledge, 1993), p. 280; Robert Skidelsky, *John Maynard Keynes: The Economist as Saviour,* vol. 2, *1920–1937* (London: Macmillan, 1992), pp. 457–459 ("mistake" and "what rubbish"); W. W. Bartley and Stephen Kresge, *F. A. Hayek: The Trend of Economic Thinking* (London: Routledge, 1991), p. 40 ("too glad").

7. Interview with Gary Becker. F. A. Hayek, "The Use of Knowledge in Society," in Hayek, *Individualism and Economic Order* (Chicago: University of Chicago Press, 1980), p. 87 ("a marvel"); Richard Cockett, *Thinking the Unthinkable: Think-tanks and the Economic Counter-Revolution* (London: Fontana Press, 1995), pp. 89–90 ("a grand book" and "Don Quixote"), 96 ("ten or twenty years"), 105 ("contemporary observer"); Hayek, *The Constitution of Liberty;* Robert Skidelsky, *The World After Communism: A Polemic for Our Times* (London: Macmillan, 1995), pp. 78–83; *Hayek on Hayek,* p. 103 (popularity of *Road to Serfdom*).

8. Interviews with Milton Friedman, Gary Becker, and George Shultz. Melvin Reder, "Chicago Economics: Permanence and Change," *Journal of Economic Literature,* March 1982, pp. 1–38; Milton Friedman, untitled essay, in William Briet and Roger W. Spencer, eds., *Lives of the Laureates: Thirteen Nobel Economists* (Cambridge, Mass.: MIT Press, 1995), pp. 84–85 ("1932" and "actuary"); Milton Friedman and George Stigler, "Roofs or Ceilings? The Current Housing Problem," in *Popular Essays on Current Problems,* vol. 1, no. 2, September 1946; see also George J. Stigler, *Memoirs of an Unregulated Economist* (New York: Basic Books, 1988), especially Chapter 10. A thorough compendium of Chicago School perspectives is Warren J. Samuels, ed., *The*

Chicago School of Political Economy (New Brunswick, N.J.: Transaction Publishers, 1993; originally Michigan State University, 1976).

9. Interviews with Milton Friedman, Gary Becker, and Rudolph Penner. Milton Friedman, "Receiving the Nobel Prize for Economics, 1976" (speech given January 29, 1977, Income Distribution Conference, Hoover Institution), p. 5 ("John F. Kennedy"); Milton Friedman, *Capitalism and Freedom* (Chicago: University of Chicago Press, 1982 edition, orig. pub. 1962), pp. vi–vii ("beleaguered" and "broader public"), 128 ("monopoly"); Gary Becker, *Human Capital and the Personal Distribution of Income* (Ann Arbor, Mich.: Institute of Public Administration, 1967), p. 81; Paul Krugman, *Peddling Prosperity: Economic Sense and Nonsense in the Age of Diminished Expectations* (New York: W. W. Norton and Company, 1994), p. 34 ("world's best known economist").

10. Interviews with Jeffrey Sachs and Lawrence Summers. World Bank, *World Development Report, 1991* (New York: Oxford University Press, 1991).

11. Interviews with Thomas Hansberger, Antoine M. van Agtmael, Vijay Kelkar, Valéry Giscard d'Estaing. Antoine M. Van Agtmael, *Emerging Securities Markets: Investment Banking Opportunities in the Developing World* (London: Euromoney Publications, 1984); International Finance Corporation, *Emerging Stock Markets Factbook, 1997* (Washington, D.C.: IFC, 1997).

CHAPTER 6: BEYOND THE MIRACLE: ASIA'S EMERGENCE

1. Interviews with Mahathir Mohamad and Anwar Ibrahim. World Bank, *The East Asian Miracle* (New York: Oxford University Press, 1994); José Campos, *The Key to the Asian Miracle: Making Shared Growth Credible* (Washington, D.C.: Brookings Institution, 1996).

2. Yutaka Kosai, *The Era of High-Speed Growth: Notes on the Postwar Japanese Economy,* translated by Jacqueline Kaminski (Tokyo: University of Tokyo Press, 1986), pp. 27, 17 ("Come, Come"), 77 ("feather!"), 130 ("Isn't it all"), 153 ("19 postwar years"), 76 ("three C's").

3. Kosai, *The Era of High-Speed Growth,* p. 80; Yukio Noguchi, "The 1940 System," July 7, 1996, manuscript; Ezra F. Vogel, *The Four Little Dragons: The Spread of Industrialization in East Asia* (Cambridge, Mass.: Harvard University Press, 1991), pp. 51–52 ("natural component" and "promotion"), 52; Hugh Patrick, "Crumbling or Transforming? Japan's Economic Success and its Postwar Economic Institutions," Working Paper 98, Columbia Business School, September 1995; Steven Vogel, *Freer Markets, More Rules: Regulatory Reform in Advanced Industrial Countries* (Ithaca, N.Y.: Cornell University Press, 1996), p. 52 ("supply and demand adjustment"); World Bank, *The East Asian Miracle,* p. 101. For differing views of MITI's role, see Chalmers Johnson, *Japan: Who Governs? The Rise of the Developmental State* (New York: W. W. Norton, 1995); Raymond Vernon, *Two Hungry Giants: The United States and Japan in the Quest for Oil and Ores* (Cambridge, Mass.: Harvard University Press, 1983).

4. Interview with Masahisa Naitoh. On Japan's "bubble," see Christopher Wood, *The Bubble Economy: The Japanese Economic Collapse* (Tokyo: Tuttle Books, 1992); a description of Japan's economic model by an influential civil servant is Eisuke Sakakibara, *Beyond Capitalism: The Japanese Model of Market Economics* (Lanham, Md.: University Press of America, 1993).

5. Interview with Dwight Perkins. *Far Eastern Economic Review,* October 20, 1983, pp. 16–19, November 2, 1995, p. 48; Vogel, *Four Little Dragons,* pp. 44, 47–49, 61, 53; World Bank, *East Asian Miracle,* p. 309, 129; Joseph J. Stern, Ji-hong Kim, Dwight Perkins, and Jung-ho Yoo, *Industrialization and the State: The Korean Heavy and Chemical Industry Drive* (Cambridge, Mass.: Harvard University Press, 1995), pp. 24, 20.

6. World Bank, *East Asian Miracle,* pp. 97, 131; *Far Eastern Economic Review,* November 30, 1995, p. 66; Vogel, *Four Little Dragons,* pp. 9, 65 ("unrivaled" and "No nation"); Stern et al., *Industrialization and the State,* p. 33; *Financial Times,* October 17, 1983 ("dour soldier" and "explained economics"); *Financial Times,* July 12, 1984 ("biggest loss" and "legendary"); *Economist,* September 14, 1996, p. 63; Alice Amsden, *Asia's Next Giant: South Korea and Late Industrialization* (New York: Oxford University Press, 1989).

7. Hollington K. Tong, *Chiang Kai-shek* (Taipei: China Publishing Company, 1953), p. 477; Robert Wade, *Governing the Market: Economic Theory and the Role of Government in East Asian Industrialization* (Princeton: Princeton University Press, 1990), p. 246 ("fierce" and "myth"); K. T. Li, *Economic Transformation of Taiwan, ROC* (London: Shepheard-Walwyn, 1988), pp. 109, 227; Alan P. L. Liu, *The Phoenix and the Lame Lion: Modernization in Taiwan and Mainland China 1950–1980* (Stanford: Hoover Institution Press, 1987), pp. 24–25 ("Confucian capitalism"), 30, 48; Vogel, *Four Little Dragons,* pp. 21–31; K. T. Li, *The Evolution of Policy Behind Taiwan's Development Success* (Singapore: World Scientific Publishing, 1995), pp. 7 ("depoliticization"), 215, 240; World Bank, *East Asian Miracle,* p. 131 ("Gradual").

8. Wade, *Governing the Market,* pp. 207–208, 217; Vogel, *Four Little Dragons,* pp. 27 ("Confucian advisors"), 38 ("brain bank"); Liu, *The Phoenix and the Lame Lion,* pp. 52 ("father"), 60 ("An engineer"), 52–56 ("Made in Taiwan"), 61 ("modernization"), 58 ("textbook"); Li, *The Evolution of Policy,* pp. 95–96, 227, 102 ("arbitrary" and "openness"), 217 ("glorification"), 259 ("Chinese cultural tradition"); World Bank, *The East Asian Miracle,* p. 133; Glen Rifkind, "Nation of Notebooks," *Fast Company,* July 1997, pp. 153–154.

9. Interviews with Goh Keng Swee and Yeo Chow Tong. National Day Rally, August 20, 1989 ("passion"); Linda Low, "Privatization Options and Issues in Singapore," in Dennis J. Gayle and Jonathan N. Goodrich, eds., *Privatization and Deregulation in Global Perspective* (New York: Quorum Books, 1990), p. 291 ("cooked up"); Vogel, *Four Little Dragons,* pp. 77 ("administrative state"), 79 ("socialistic characteristics").

10. Interviews with Mahathir Mohamad and Anwar Ibrahim. Mahathir Mohamad, "Toward an Asian Renaissance," speech, January 11, 1996 ("Not bad"); James Fallows, *Looking at the Sun: The Rise of the New East Asian Economic and Political System* (New York: Pantheon, 1994), pp. 304, 250 ("spirit"), 310 ("arrogant"); *Far Eastern Economic Review,* December 21, 1995, p. 27 ("Malay education"); Mahathir Mohamad, speech, Asia Society, September 25, 1996 ("rice farmers," "touching," and "The private sector"); also Mahathir Mohamad, *The Malay Dilemma* (Singapore: Times Books, 1970); Mahathir Mohamad, speech at World Bank Meeting, Hong Kong, September 20, 1997.

11. Interview with Anand Panyarachun. Ali Wardhana, "Structural Adjustment in

Indonesia: Export and the 'High-Cost' Economy," speech, January 25, 1995 ("Bureaucrats").

12. Interview with Anand Panyarachun. James Rohwer, *Asia Rising: Why America Will Prosper as Asia's Economies Boom* (New York: Simon & Schuster, 1995), Chapter 11; United Nations, *World Economic and Social Survey 1995,* pp. 171–178; *New York Times,* July 29, 1997; Business in Asia survey, *The Economist,* March 9, 1996; *The Economist,* July 18, 1992; Sterling Seagrave, *Lords of the Rim: The Invisible Empire of the Overseas Chinese* (New York: G. P. Putnam's Sons, 1995).

CHAPTER 7: THE COLOR OF THE CAT: CHINA'S TRANSFORMATION

1. David S. G. Goodman, *Deng Xiaoping and the Chinese Revolution: A Political Biography* (London: Routledge, 1994), pp. 18 ("elder brother"), 27–28, 46, 43 ("Some comrades say"). Other biographies are Richard Evans, *Deng Xiaoping and the Making of Modern China* (London: Penguin, 1993), and Deng Maomao, *Deng Xiaoping: My Father* (New York: Basic Books, 1995).

2. Goodman, *Deng Xiaoping,* pp. 3 ("cat"), 76 ("dead parent"), 4; Nikita Khrushchev, *Khrushchev Remembers,* vol. 1 (Harmondsworth, England: Penguin, 1977), p. 301 ("little man"); David S. G. Goodman and Gerald Segal, *China Without Deng* (Sydney: HarperCollins, 1995), p. 28; Richard Baum, *Burying Mao: Chinese Politics in the Age of Deng Xiaoping* (Princeton: Princeton University Press, 1994), pp. 51–55 ("I'm at ease"); Joseph Fewsmith, *Dilemmas of Reform in China: Political Conflict and Economic Debate* (Armonk: M. E. Sharp, Inc., 1994), p. 11 ("whateverist").

3. Fewsmith, *Dilemmas of Reform in China,* pp. 23 ("cry out"), 28 ("grief"); Dwight Perkins, "Completing China's Move to the Market," *Journal of Economic Perspectives,* vol. 8, no. 2, Spring 1994, pp. 26, 27 ("clear winner").

4. Fewsmith, *Dilemmas of Reform in China,* pp. 78–79 ("feeling the stones" and "fast ox"), 56, 76, 67 ("invisible hand" and "consumers").

5. Fewsmith, *Dilemmas of Reform in China,* pp. 89 ("rashness"), 92, 108 ("foreign capitalists"), 89 ("pollution" and "primary"), 63, 114 (Chen on the birdcage), 104 ("did not pay attention"), 108 ("stability and unity"), 102 ("Without such a Party"), 37 (report on Japanese standard of living), 110 ("chessboard").

6. Fewsmith, *Dilemmas of Reform in China,* pp. 135 ("our comrades"), 124 ("asked-to-help"), 211 ("contract"), 164, 188 (Wu Jinglian), 194 ("building").

7. Kenneth Lieberthal, *Governing China: From Revolution Through Reform* (New York: W. W. Norton, 1995), p. 244 ("technological revolution"); Goodman and Segal, *China Without Deng,* p. 25 ("cycle of development"); Fewsmith, *Dilemmas of Reform in China,* pp. 123, 214–215 ("China should seize"); Alvin Toffler, *The Third Wave* (New York: Morrow, 1980).

8. Fewsmith, *Dilemmas of Reform in China,* pp. 196 ("moon . . . is fuller"), 204 ("brighter . . . sun"), 231 ("Mao Zedong craze"), 220 ("Honest people"), 225 ("stormy weather").

9. Goodman, *Deng Xiaoping,* pp. 109 ("Concessions in Poland"), 110; Baum, *Burying Mao,* pp. 337 ("proper ratio"), 340; *Beijing Review,* June 11–17, 1990, p. 19 ("studying philosophy"); *Far Eastern Economic Review,* May 10, 1990, pp. 8–9.

10. Roderick MacFarquhar, "Deng's Last Campaign," *The New York Review of Books,* December 17, 1992, p. 22 ("confidence"); Baum, *Burying Mao,* pp. 342 ("surnamed capitalism" and "stepping stones"), 344 ("watch out"), 353 ("special Leftist zones").

11. Interview with Dwight Perkins. Yun-Wing Sung, Pak-Wai Liu, Yue-Chim Richard Wong, and Pui-King Lau, *The Fifth Dragon: The Emergence of the Pearl River Delta* (Singapore: Addison Wesley, 1995), pp. 23, 136; *Financial Times,* June 11, 1997, p. 4 (labor forces and "too tired"); Perkins, "Completing China's Move," pp. 24, 41, 43, 37; James Rohwer, *Asia Rising: Why America Will Prosper as Asia's Economies Boom* (New York: Simon & Schuster, 1995), pp. 103, 135.

12. Sung et al., *Fifth Dragon,* pp. 6 ("crown jewel"), 8, 13.

13. Baum, *Burying Mao,* p. 390; Jiang Zemin, Oration at Comrade Deng Xiaoping's Memorial Meeting, February 25, 1997. On the Chinese bean curd shop: *The Shanghai Ximin Evening News,* cited in *Los Angeles Times,* October 19, 1992; World Bank, *China 2020: Development Challenges in the New Century* (Washington, D.C.: World Bank, 1997), pp. 1–4, 84–85; Jiang Zemin, "Report to the 15th Party Congress," Beijing, September 12, 1997; *Financial Times,* September 22, 1997 (Zhu Rongji); *Wall Street Journal,* September 18, 1997, p. 10.

CHAPTER 8: AFTER THE PERMIT RAJ: INDIA'S AWAKENING

1. Interviews with P. Chidambaram and Jairam Ramesh. *India Today,* July 31, 1991, p. 10 ("Sudden work").

2. Jagdish Bhagwati, *India in Transition: Freeing the Economy* (New York: Oxford University Press, 1995), pp. 54 ("not entirely wrong"), 51, 11, 14; Vijay Joshi and I. M. D. Little, *India's Economic Reform, 1991–2001* (New York: Oxford University Press, 1996).

3. Vijay L. Kelkar and V. V. Bhanoji Rao, *India: Development Policy Imperatives* (New Delhi: Tata McGraw-Hill Publishing Company, 1996), pp. 165, 200, 193 ("rewards"); Bhagwati, *India in Transition,* pp. 18, 53 ("corruption"), 63 ("up the Marxist mountain"); Steven R. Weisman, "India Budget Recalls Reagan Plan for Stimulus," *New York Times,* March 25, 1985.

4. *Far Eastern Economic Review,* August 8, 1991, p. 48.

5. Bhagwati, *India in Transition,* p. 79 ("honest work"); Weisman, "India Budget," *New York Times,* March 25, 1985 ("common man").

6. *India Today,* July 15, 1991, p. 10 ("old wine").

7. James Manor, "The Political Sustainability of Economic Liberalization in India," in Robert Cassen and Vijay Joshi, eds., *India: The Future of Economic Reform* (New Delhi: Oxford University Press, 1995), pp. 346 ("trickle down economics"), 351 ("a railway platform"); *Financial Times,* September 2, 1991, p. 30 ("no head").

8. Interviews with P. Chidambaram and Vijay Kelkar.

9. Interviews with Jairam Ramesh and G. V. Ramakrishna. Kelkar and Rao, *India,* p. 40 ("way of socialism"); *Business India,* July 8–12, 1992, p. 49; Bhagwati, *India in Transition,* pp. 58–59.

10. Manmohan Singh, budget speech, July 24, 1991, paragraphs 4, 5; *Business World,* March 6–9, 1996, pp. 32 ("position was bad"), 33 ("For 20 or 30 years"), 40 ("technocrats?"), 33 ("cobwebs"); *Business India,* July 8–12, 1991,

p. 49 ("functionless capitalism"); *India Today,* July 31, 1991, pp. 12, 13 ("old methods").

11. Singh, budget speech, July 24, 1991, paragraphs 2, 7, 50, 126; *Business World,* March 6–9, 1996, pp. 38–39 ("We're in the business" and "trade and not aid").

12. Kelkar and Rao, *India,* p. 19 ("vastly different role"); James Manor, "How Steady? India's New Course: Economic Liberalization and Energy Investment" (Cambridge, Mass.: CERA Private Report, November 1995).

13. Interviews with P. Chidambaram, Vijay Kelkar, and Kenneth Lay. Larry Ellison, speech at CERA Executive Conference, Houston, February 10–13, 1997; Manor, "Political Sustainability," in Cassen and Joshi, *India;* Singh, budget speech ("No power" and "The emergence").

CHAPTER 9: PLAYING BY THE RULES: THE NEW GAME IN LATIN AMERICA

1. Interviews with Gonzalo Sánchez de Lozada and Jeffrey Sachs. Robert Skidelsky, *The World After Communism* (New York: Penguin Press, 1996), pp. 139–140.

2. Raúl Prebisch, "Five Stages of My Thinking," in Gerald M. Meier and Dudley Seers, eds., *Pioneers in Development* (New York: Oxford University Press, 1984), pp. 175 ("neoclassical theories" and "great crisis"), 179; Gert Rosenthal, "Development Thinking and Policies in Latin America and the Caribbean: The Way Ahead," paper prepared for Development Thinking and Practice Conference, September 3–5, 1996, Washington, D.C., p. 5. On the national-security rationale, see John Wirth, ed., *Latin American Oil Companies and the Politics of Energy* (Lincoln: University of Nebraska Press, 1985).

3. Sebastian Edwards, *Crisis and Reform in Latin America: From Despair to Hope* (New York: Oxford University Press, 1995), p. 17.

4. Interview with Enrique Iglesias. Edwards, *Crisis and Reform in Latin America,* pp. 70, 49, 48 ("outward oriented"); John Williamson, "The Washington Consensus Revisited," paper prepared for Development Thinking and Practice Conference, September 3–5, 1996, Washington, D.C., pp. 2 (Washington Consensus and "diplomatic label"), 3 (distorting markets); Frances Stewart, "John Williamson and the Washington Consensus," paper for Development Thinking and Practice Conference, September 3–5, 1996, Washington, D.C., p. 1 ("shadowy master"); David Hojman, "The Political Economy of Recent Conversions to Market Economics in Latin America," *Journal of Latin American Studies,* vol. 26, pp. 191–219.

5. Interviews with Domingo Cavallo and Benjamin Friedman. Matt Moffett, "Key Finance Ministers in Latin America Are Old Harvard and MIT Pals," *Wall Street Journal,* August 1, 1994; "Latin America Within the World Economy" (Foxley interview), *Challenge,* January–February 1993, pp. 18–23 ("persuade antagonists").

6. Arnold C. Harberger, "Secrets of Success: A Handful of Heroes (Political Economy of Policy Reform: Is There a Second Best?)," *American Economic Review,* May 1993, pp. 343–351; Pamela Constable and Arturo Valenzuela, *A Nation of Enemies: Chile Under Pinochet* (New York: W. W. Norton, 1991), pp. 167 ("kind of therapy"), 169 ("trying to explain"), 173 ("pot by the handle"); Juan Gabriel Valdez, *Pinochet's Economists: The Chicago School in Chile* (New York: Cambridge University Press, 1995).

7. Interviews with Alejandro Jadresic and Dani Kauffmann. Juan Gabriel Valdez, *Pinochet's Economists,* p. 263 ("road to socialism"); Jorge I. Dominguez, *Technopols: Freeing Politics and Markets in Latin America in the 1990s* (University Park, Pa.: Pennsylvania State University Press, 1997), pp. 232 ("the competent state"), 258 ("progressive"); *Wall Street Journal,* August 1, 1994 (winners).

8. William C. Smith, *Authoritarianism and the Crisis of the Argentine Political Economy* (Palo Alto, Calif.: Stanford University Press, 1991), pp. 257–258, 267; Dominguez, *Technopols,* p. 255; *The Economist,* November 26, 1994 ("nightmare" and "movie").

9. Interviews with Domingo Cavallo and Carlos Bastos. Dominguez, *Technopols,* pp. 54–56 ("It is in the provinces" and "socialism without plans"), 67.

10. Interviews with Domingo Cavallo and Carlos Bastos. Edwards, *Crisis and Reform in Latin America,* p. 196; José Estenssoro, "The New Competitive Frontiers: Argentina," in William Durbin and Penny Janeway, eds., *Transforming Latin America's Energy Future: Cambridge Energy Forum* (Cambridge, Mass.: CERA, December 1995), pp. 7–24.

11. Mario Vargas Llosa, *A Fish in the Water* (London: Faber & Faber, 1994), pp. 31 ("barbarism"), 34 ("Totalitarian Peru"), 214, 224; Edwards, *Crisis and Reform in Latin America,* p. 33; Kenneth M. Roberts, "Neoliberalism and the Transformation of Populism in Latin America: The Peruvian Case," *World Politics,* vol. 48, October 1995, p. 93; Mario Vargas Llosa, "In Defense of the Black Market," *New York Times Sunday Magazine,* February 22, 1987, p. 46 ("register the workshop"); Gustavo Gorriti, "The Fox and the Hedgehog," *New Republic,* February 12, 1990, pp. 20–25.

12. Gorriti, "Fox," *New Republic,* February 12, 1990, p. 25 ("cut-rate" and "modern man"); Vargas Llosa, *A Fish in the Water,* pp. 216 ("lack of economic knowledge"), 41 ("I see it"), 261 ("economic freedom"), 264 ("a semicolonial factory"); Alvaro Vargas Llosa, "The Press Officer," *Granta,* vol. 36, Summer 1991, p. 80 ("loneliness").

13. Interview with Alberto Fujimori. Roberts, "Neoliberalism," pp. 107, 82–116 (tiger and puma).

14. Interviews with Carlos Salinas, Jesús Silva Herzog, and Pedro Aspe. William Orme, "Fire in the Pan," *New Republic,* May 6, 1985, pp. 20–21; Banco de México, *The Mexican Economy,* pp. 6–7; *The Economist,* December 14, 1991, p. 19, cited in Dominguez, *Technopols,* p. 98 ("economically literate").

15. Dominguez, *Technopols,* pp. 145 ("radical tradition"), 171 ("regulated free market"), 166–167 ("In the whole world"), 175 ("smaller the state"); *Wall Street Journal,* August 1, 1994; James P. Hoge, Jr., "Fulfilling Brazil's Promise: A Conversation with President Cardoso," *Foreign Affairs,* August 1995, p. 64 ("rule of law" and "Reforms are needed").

16. Moises Naim, *Latin America's Journey to the Market: From Macroeconomic Shocks to Institutional Therapy* (San Francisco: ICS Press, 1995), pp. 17–26, 2 ("The discovery"); Moises Naim, "Latin America—The Morning After," *Foreign Affairs* July–August 1995, pp. 45–62; Shahid Javed Burki and Sebastian Edwards, *Dismantling the Populist State: The Unfinished Revolution in Latin America and The Caribbean* (Washington, D.C.: World Bank, 1997).

1. Timothy Garton Ash, *The Polish Revolution: Solidarity* (London: Granta Books, 1991), p. 34 ("self-defense").
2. Interview with Jeffrey Sachs. Jeffrey Sachs, *Poland's Jump to the Market Economy* (Cambridge, Mass.: MIT Press, 1993), p. 44.
3. Sachs, *Poland's Jump,* p. 44 (searching for his Ludwig Erhard); Leszek Balcerowicz, *Socialism, Capitalism, Transformation* (Budapest: Central European Press, 1995), pp. 341–342 ("change their attitudes").
4. Balcerowicz, *Socialism,* pp. 366 (*shock therapy* and *market revolution*), 344, 354; Sachs, *Poland's Jump,* pp. 64–65.
5. Balcerowicz, *Socialism,* pp. 356 ("old habits"), 362 ("just market"), 349, 343 ("chaos"), 182 ("key part"); Sachs, *Poland's Jump,* pp. 63–65; European Bank for Reconstruction and Development, *Transition Report 1996* (London: EBRD, 1996), pp. 17, 112, 165–167.
6. Otto Ulč, "Czechoslovakia's Velvet Divorce," *East European Quarterly,* vol. 30, Fall 1996, pp. 331–352; *Wall Street Journal,* May 30, 1996 ("choice"); European Bank, *Transition Report,* pp. 146–148; Václav Klaus, *Renaissance: The Rebirth of Liberty in the Heart of Europe* (Washington, D.C.: Cato Institute, 1997), pp. 28, 151–153.
7. Interview with Yegor Gaidar. Daniel Yergin and Thane Gustafson, *Russia 2010 —And What It Means for the World* (New York: Vintage, 1995), Chapter 4; Yegor Gaidar and Karl-Otto Pöhl, *Russian Reform: International Money* (Cambridge, Mass.: MIT Press, 1995), pp. 48, 7 ("For twenty years"); Maxim Boycko, Andrei Shleifer, and Robert Vishny, *Privatizing Russia* (Cambridge, Mass.: MIT Press, 1995), p. 119. The classic work on the failure of innovation is Joseph Berliner, *The Innovation Decision in Soviet Industry* (Cambridge, Mass.: MIT Press, 1976), and the classic work on the development of the Soviet oil and gas industry is Thane Gustafson, *Crisis amid Plenty: The Politics of Soviet Energy under Brezhnev and Gorbachev* (Princeton: Princeton University Press, 1989).
8. Anders Åslund, *How Russia Became a Market Economy* (Washington, D.C.: Brookings Institution, 1995), pp. 28–30, 42–46; Boris Yeltsin, "We Are Taking Over" (interview, *Newsweek,* January 6, 1992), pp. 11–12 ("hedgehog"). Gorbachev's characterization of himself as a child of the secret speech is in Angela Stent, *Russia and Germany Reborn: Unification, the Collapse of the Soviet Union, and the Future of Europe* (Princeton: Princeton University Press, forthcoming). On the devastating impact of the unearthing of Soviet history, see David Remnick, *Lenin's Tomb: The Last Days of the Soviet Union* (New York: Random House, 1993).
9. Interviews with Yegor Gaidar and Andrei Konoplyanik. Boris Pankin, *The Last Hundred Days of the Soviet Union* (London: I. B. Tauris, 1996), p. 25; János Kornai summed up three decades of work dissecting communist economics in Kornai, *The Socialist System: The Political Economy of Communism* (Princeton: Princeton University Press, 1992).
10. Interview with Grigorii Yavlinsky. Balcerowicz, *Socialism,* p. 365 ("Polish path"); Åslund, *How Russia Became a Market Economy,* p. 71 (military-industrial complex); Boris Yeltsin, *The Struggle for Russia* (New York: Times Books, 1994), pp. 125–126 ("get going!").

11. Interview with Yegor Gaidar. Åslund, *How Russia Became a Market Economy,* pp. 64–69 ("small steps" and "political freedom").
12. Interview with Yegor Gaidar. Åslund, *How Russia Became a Market Economy,* pp. 85, 94 ("pink shorts").
13. Interview with Sergei Vassilyev. Åslund, *How Russia Became a Market Economy,* pp. 69, 228 ("For impermissibly long"), 240 ("broad stratum"); Thane Gustafson, *Capitalism Russian Style* (Cambridge, Mass.: Cambridge University Press, forthcoming).
14. Boycko, *Privatising Russia,* pp. 8–14 ("by the power"), 71; Åslund, *How Russia Became a Market Economy,* p. 247.
15. Åslund, *How Russia Became a Market Economy,* p. 235 ("millionaires"); Gustafson, *Capitalism Russian Style* ("carrots or cabbages"); Boycko, *Privatizing Russia,* pp. 63 ("our ideology"), 108.
16. Joseph A. Blasi, Maya Kroumova, and Douglas Kruse, *Kremlin Capitalism: Privatizing the Russian Economy* (Ithaca, N.Y.: Cornell University Press, 1997), pp. 2, 26, 167, 178; *Financial Times,* September 17, 1997; Alessandra Stanley, "The Power Broker," *New York Times Sunday Magazine,* August 31, 1997.
17. Interviews with Yegor Gaidar and Sergei Vassilyev. Peter Boone and Boris Federov, "The Ups and Downs of Russian Economic Reforms," in Wing Thye Woo, Stephen Parker, and Jeffrey Sachs, eds., *Economies in Transition: Comparing Asia and East Europe* (Cambridge, Mass.: MIT Press, 1997), pp. 186–188. Nemtsov in *Financial Times,* March 18, 1997. On crime, see Stephen Handelman, *Comrade Criminal: The Theft of the Second Russian Revolution* (London: Michael Joseph, 1994). On a possible Russian economic miracle, see Yergin and Gustafson, *Russia 2010,* Chapter 12; Cambridge Energy Research Associates, *Former Soviet Union Watch* (Cambridge, Mass.: CERA, 1996, 1997); *Financial Times,* September 20, 1997; *Washington Post,* September 25, 1997; Lilia Shevtsova, *Yeltsin's Russia: Challenges and Constraints* (Moscow: Carnegie Center, 1997); *Financial Times,* May 29, 1997, p. 21 (Nemtsov and Yeltsin).
18. Interview with Vladimir Dovgan. Gustafson, *Capitalism Russian Style.*

CHAPTER 11:
THE PREDICAMENT: EUROPE'S SEARCH FOR A NEW SOCIAL CONTRACT

1. Altiero Spinelli and Ernesto Rossi, *Il Manifesto de Ventotene* (Naples: Guida Editori, 1982); Juliet Lodge, ed., *European Union: The European Community in Search of a Future* (London: Macmillan, 1986), pp. 174–185; European Community, *Battling for the Union: Altiero Spinelli 1979–1986* (Luxembourg: European Community Press, 1988), pp. 47–58 ("Hemingway").
2. Vivien A. Schmidt, *From State to Market? The Transformation of French Business and Government* (New York: Cambridge University Press, 1996), Chapter 4; *Le Monde,* June 25, 1981; Andrea Boltho, "Has France Converged on Germany? Policies and Institutions Since 1958," in Suzanne Berger and Ronald Dore, eds., *National Diversity and Global Capitalism* (Ithaca, N.Y.: Cornell University Press, 1991); Marie-Paule Virard, *Comment Mitterrand a découvert l'économie* (Paris: Albin Michel, 1993), p. 24.
3. Charles Grant, *Delors: Inside the House That Jacques Built* (London: Nicholas

Brealey, 1994), pp. 12 ("most successful"), 8, 11 ("good workhorse"), 13 ("never been fascinated"), 15 ("How do you manage it?").

4. Gabriel Milesi, *Delors: L'homme qui dit non* (Paris Edition 1, 1995), pp. 214 ("Jacobins"), 219 ("There is no option" and "Mrs. Thatcher's policies"); Grant, *Delors,* p. 47 ("locomotive"); Schmidt, *From State to Market?,* p. 122 ("cash-flow").

5. Milesi, *Delors,* p. 248 ("Helping Creusot-Loire").

6. Schmidt, *From State to Market?,* p. 111 ("efface itself"); Grant, *Delors,* pp. 56 ("smells"), 54 ("grand vizier"), 59 ("French social democracy and presidential majority").

7. Spinelli and Rossi, *Il Manifesto de Ventotene,* p. 188 ("European unification"); Grant, *Delors,* p. 66 ("money back").

8. European Community, *Battling for the Union,* pp. 47–58 ("ridiculous mouse"); Grant, *Delors,* pp. 74–75, 88; Berger and Dore, *National Diversity,* p. 231; *Financial Times,* October 24, 1997 (milk chocolate).

9. Interview with Margaret Thatcher. Geoffrey Howe, *Conflict of Loyalty* (London: Macmillan, 1994), p. 537 ("European superstate"); Thatcher, *Downing Street Years,* p. 558 ("new breed").

10. David Marsh, *Germany and Europe: The Crisis of Unity* (London: Heinemann, 1994), p. 10.

11. Interview with Karl-Otto Pöhl. Marsh, *Germany and Europe,* pp. 70–77 ("deutschmark"); Horst Tetschik, *329 Tage: Innenansichten der Einigung* (Berlin: Seidler Verlag, 1991), pp. 129–133. See Stent, *Germany and Russia Reborn;* Maier, *Disillusion;* Helmut Kohl, *Ich Wollte Deutschlands Einheit* (Berlin: Propyalaen Verlag, 1996), pp. 259–265.

12. Marsh, *Germany and Europe,* p. 61 ("heart transplants").

13. Interview with Karl-Otto Pöhl. Rudi Dornbusch, "Euro Fortress," *Foreign Affairs,* September–October 1996, pp. 116–124.

14. Interviews with Valéry Giscard d'Estaing, Jens Stoltenberg, Christian Stoffaes, and Alberto Clô.

15. Interviews with Valéry Giscard d'Estaing, Oscar Fanjul, Helmut Schmidt, Herbert Detharding, Jens Stoltenberg, Karl-Otto Pöhl, and Peter Sutherland. Peter Sutherland, speech to Confederation of British Industry Conference, November 12, 1996; International Monetary Fund, *World Economic Outlook: EMU and the World Economy,* part I (Washington, D.C.: IMF, October 1997), pp. 60–61; *International Herald Tribune,* September 16, 1997; Barry Bosworth and Gary Burtless, "Budget Crunch Population Aging in Rich Countries," *The Brookings Review,* Summer 1997, pp. 10–15.

16. Interview with Helmut Schmidt.

CHAPTER 12: THE DELAYED REVOLUTION: AMERICA'S NEW BALANCE

1. *Dayton Daily News,* December 28, 1995, p. 7; *Arkansas Democrat-Gazette,* November 17, 1995, p. 1; *Sun-Sentinel,* December 29, 1995, p. 1 (BUDGET IMPASSE and "politics with people's lives"); *Seattle Times,* December 29, 1995, p. 1; *New York Times,* December 29, 1995, p. 1; *Bergen* (N.J.) *Record,* December 29, 1995, p. 1.

2. Elizabeth Drew, *Showdown: The Struggle Between the Gingrich Congress and the Clinton White House* (New York: Touchstone, 1997), pp. 305–381; Dick

Morris, *Behind the Oval Office: Winning the Presidency in the 1990s* (New York: Random House, 1997), pp. 183–184; George Hagar, "Reconciliation: A Battered GOP Calls Workers Back to Work," *Congressional Quarterly Weekly Review,* January 6, 1996, pp. 53–56.

3. Lou Cannon, *Reagan* (New York: G. P. Putnam's Sons, 1982), pp. 262–268 ("super executive").
4. Interviews with Irving Kristol, William Kristol, and George Shultz (underestimated); Christopher DeMuth and William Kristol, eds., *The Neo-Conservative Imagination: Essays in Honor of Irving Kristol* (Washington, D.C.: American Enterprise Institute Press, 1995), pp. 166 ("mugged by reality"), 180 ("The truth" and "leverage of ideas"), 60 ("besmirched" and "fight to rehabilitate"); *Bangor* (Maine) *Daily News,* March 28, 1996 (McGovern as innkeeper); Irving Kristol, *Neo-Conservativism: The Autobiography of an Idea* (New York: Free Press, 1995), pp. 12–13, 379, 18, 32 ("Though none" and "political landscape").
5. Interview with Paul Volcker. Paul Volcker and Toyoo Gyohten, *Changing Fortunes: The World's Money and the Threat to American Leadership* (New York: Basic Books, 1992), p. 170 ("euphoria" and "inflationary dragon"); Elisabeth Bumiller, "Two for the Money," *Washington Post,* August 7, 1979, p. B3 ("I'm boring"); William R. Neikirk, *Volcker, Portrait of the Money Man* (New York: Congdon & Weed, 1987), pp. xx, 28, 78–79.
6. Interviews with George Shultz and Paul Volcker. Volcker and Gyohten, *Changing Fortunes,* p. 166 ("bet on inflation"); Neikirk, *Volcker,* pp. 137–138, 219 ("compliment"); William Greider, *Secrets of the Temple: How the Federal Reserve Runs the Country* (New York: Simon & Schuster, 1987).
7. Interviews with Robert Rubin, Lawrence Summers, Benjamin Friedman, Michael Levy, and others. Herbert Stein, *Presidential Economics: The Making of Economic Policy from Roosevelt to Reagan and Beyond* (New York: Touchstone, 1985), pp. 263–307 ("punk" supply-side); Congressional Budget Office, "The Economic and Budget Outlook: Fiscal Years 1998–2005," January 1997, p. 105; David A. Stockman, *The Triumph of Politics: How the Reagan Revolution Failed* (New York: Harper & Row, 1986), p. 14 ("radical ideologue"); Elizabeth Drew, *On the Edge: The Clinton Presidency* (New York: Touchstone, 1995); *Newsweek,* June 23, 1997, p. 16 (Robert Rubin); Martin Feldstein, ed., *American Economic Policy in the 1980s* (Chicago: University of Chicago Press, 1994); William A. Niskanen, *Reaganomics: An Insider's Account of the Policies and the People* (New York: Oxford University Press, 1988); Council of Economic Advisers, *Economic Report of the President* (Washington, D.C.: U.S. Government Printing Office, 1997); Richard Darman, *Who's in Control? Polar Politics and the Sensible Center* (New York: Simon & Schuster, 1996), pp. 113 ("tax increase"), 73 ("prior history"). On "declinism," see Joseph Nye, Jr., *Bound to Lead: The Changing Nature of American Power* (New York: Basic Books, 1990).
8. Interviews with Stephen Breyer, Dick Cheney, and Rudolph Penner. William Breit and Roger W. Spencer, eds., *Lives of the Laureates: Seven Nobel Economists* (Cambridge, Mass.: MIT Press, 1986), p. 107 ("My findings" and "widows and orphans"); George J. Stigler, *Memoirs of an Unregulated Economist* (New York: Basic Books, 1988); Harry M. Trebing, "The Chicago School Versus Public Utility Regulation," in Warren J. Samuels, ed., *The Chicago*

School of Political Economy (New Brunswick, N.J.: Transaction Publisher, 1993), pp. 311–340; The Brookings Institution series on regulation was greatly influential. On public choice theory, see James Buchanan and Gordon Tullock, *The Calculus of Consent* (Ann Arbor: University of Michigan Press, 1962); Richard H. K. Vietor, *Contrived Competition: Regulation and Deregulation in America* (Cambridge, Mass.: Harvard University Press, 1996). On Kahn, see Thomas McCraw, *Prophets of Regulation* (Cambridge, Mass.: Harvard University Press, 1984), Chapter 7.

9. Interview with Stephen Breyer. Robert Burkhardt, *CAB—The Civil Aeronautics Board* (Dulles International Airport, Va.: Green Hills Publishing Company, 1974), p. 12 ("near chaos").

10. Interviews with Edward Jordan and Eugene Ludwig. *Business Week,* June 22, 1992, p. 146; *New York Times,* June 9, 1992, p. 1 ("antenna"); Alfred Kahn, *Economics of Regulation* (New York: Wiley, 1970); Vietor, *Contrived Competition,* pp. 168–172 ("annihilating"), 176 ("monopoly"), 197 ("tasteless stew"), 206–207 ("common carrier"), 211 ("history of business"), 231–233 ("technical quality"). Steven A. Morrison and Clifford Winston, "The Fare Skies: Air Transportation and Middle America," *Brookings Review,* Fall 1997, pp. 42–45.

11. Interviews with Elizabeth Moler and Philip Sharp. Cambridge Energy Research Associates, *Electric Power Trends 1996–97,* p. 8; Bruce Humphrey, *Notes on Deregulation* (Cambridge, Mass.: Cambridge Energy Research Associates, 1997); Larry Makovich, *Cost Versus Value: Private Report* (Cambridge, Mass.: Cambridge Energy Research Associates, 1997); Gary Simon et al., *North American Power Watch* (Cambridge, Mass.: Cambridge Energy Research Associates, various editions).

12. Pietro Nivola, *Comparative Disadvantages? Social Regulations and the Global Economy* (Washington, D.C.: Brookings Institution Press, 1997), p. 10 ("criminalization"); Stephen Breyer, *Breaking the Vicious Circle: Toward Effective Risk Regulation* (Cambridge, Mass.: Harvard University Press, 1993), p. 51 ("regulatory gridlock"); William J. Novak, *The People's Welfare: Law and Regulation in Nineteenth-Century America* (Chapel Hill: University of North Carolina Press, 1996), pp. 56–57.

13. Interviews with Stephen Breyer and Daniel Esty. Breyer, *Breaking the Vicious Circle,* pp. 39–40, 12 ("The site"); Nivola, *Comparative Disadvantages?,* p. 20; Daniel J. Dudek, "Emissions Trading: Practical Lessons from Experience," testimony before the Joint Economic Committee, U.S. Congress, July 9, 1997, pp. 3–4 (success of emissions trading); American Enterprise Institute, "How Economics Can Inform the Global-Climate Change Debate," conference summary, March 1997; Congressional Research Service, "Market-based Environmental Management: Issues and Implementation," March 1994, Washington, D.C.

14. Lincoln Caplan, *Up Against the Law: Affirmative Action and the Supreme Court* (New York: Twentieth Century Fund Press, 1997); Littler, Mendelson, Fastiff, Tichy, and Mathiason, *The 1996 National Employer,* 1996, p. 153 ("former employee's"); Nivola, *Comparative Disadvantages?,* p. 11 ("personal disagreements" and "levies millions"); Philip Howard, *The Death of Common Sense: How Law Is Suffocating America* (New York: Warner Books, 1996), p. 142 ("sue" and "precious rights"); *Washington Post,* May 12, 1997, pp. A1, A10 (Stanley Sporkin).

417

15. Al Gore, *Common Sense Government: Works Better and Costs Less* (New York: Random House, 1995), p. 117 ("spinning off"); Moshe Adler, "In City Services, Privatize and Beware," *New York Times,* April 7, 1996; Reason Foundation, *Privatization 1996,* p. 15 (Ed Rendell); *New York Times,* February 12, 1989 (Conrail).
16. *Wall Street Journal,* May 13, 1997; Reason Foundation, *Privatization 1996,* pp. 7, 8; *Atlanta Journal and Constitution,* August 2, 1996, p. 14A; *Economist,* April 19, 1997 (private police); *Security Management,* November 1994; *General Accounting Office Report,* January 1994; information from Douglas MacDonald (private prisons).
17. Interviews with William Schneider and Rudolph Penner.

CHAPTER 13: THE BALANCE OF CONFIDENCE: THE WORLD AFTER REFORM

1. Jon Sopel, *Tony Blair: The Modernizer* (London: Bantam Books, 1995), pp. 54, 150 ("long game"), 63 ("enormous state guidance"), 13 ("every spare minute"), 35 ("ethical socialism"), 39, 10 ("totally self-made").
2. *New Statesman,* Special Edition, May 1997, p. 42 ("It's simple" and "bungs up"), p. 64 ("presumption"); Sopel, *Tony Blair,* pp. 208 ("too much bureaucracy"), 285 ("common ownership" and "grow up"), 246.
3. *New York Times,* June 7, 1997 (Blair and Jospin); Arthur M. Okun, *Equality and Efficiency: The Big Tradeoff* (Washington, D.C.: Brookings Institution, 1975), p. 119 ("more than two cheers"); Council of Economic Advisers, *Economic Report of the President* (Washington, D.C.: U.S. Government Printing Office, 1997).
4. Interviews with Robert Rubin and Eric Dobkin. On foreign exchange, see McCarthy, Crisanti, and Maffei (MCM).
5. Interview with John Browne. On BP's transformation, see Steven E. Prokesch, "Unleashing the Power of Learning," *Harvard Business Review,* September–October 1997; Vito Tanzi and Ludger Schuknecht, "The Growth of Government and the Reform of the State in Industrial Countries," IMF Working Paper W/95/130, December 1995; Clive Crook, ed., "The Future of the State: A Survey of the World Economy," *The Economist,* September 20–26, 1997.
6. *Financial Times,* September 26, 1997, p. 13 (Nemtsov).
7. Interview with Felix Rohatyn.
8. Lee Kuan Yew, discussion, International Institute for Strategic Studies meeting, Singapore, September 12, 1997.
9. *Forbes,* March 10, 1997, p. 124 (Drucker).
10. David Hale, "How the Rise of Pension Funds Will Change the Global Economy in the 21st Century," manuscript; Eugene Ludwig, speech to American Bankers Association, October 5, 1997 (mutual funds).

INTERVIEWS

Many people generously made themselves available for interviews, which were essential to the writing of this book. We would like to express our great appreciation to all of them for their graciousness and consideration. None of them is responsible for the interpretations and judgments in this book.

Anand Panyarachun
Anwar Ibrahim
Pedro Aspe
Carlos Bastos
Gary Becker
Franco Bernabè
Carlos Bernardez
Albert Bressand
Stephen Breyer
John Browne
Domingo Cavallo
Richard Cheney
P. Chidambaram
Alberto Clô
Herbert Detharding
Eric Dobkin
Vladimir Dovgan
Caspar Einem
Daniel Esty
Sir Brian Fall
Oscar Fanjul
Benjamin Friedman
Milton Friedman
Alberto Fujimori
Yegor Gaidar
Valéry Giscard d'Estaing
Luis Giusti

Goh Keng Swee
Gong Wee Lik
Thane Gustafson
Thomas Hansberger
Yukon Huang
Enrique Iglesias
Alejandro Jadresic
Edward Jordan
Dani Kauffmann
Vijay Kelkar
Christine Keung
Kim Il Sup
Irving Kristol
William Kristol
Kenneth Lay
Hoesung Lee
Michael Levy
Linda Low
Eugene Ludwig
Claude Mandil
Edward McCracken
Mahathir Mohamad
Dominique Moisi
Elizabeth Moler
Masahisa Naitoh
Pietro Nivola
R. K. Pachauri

Rudolph Penner
Dwight Perkins
Karl-Otto Pöhl
Roger Porter
G. V. Ramakrishna
Jairam Ramesh
Bhanoji Rao
Felix Rohatyn
Robert Rubin
Jeffrey Sachs
Gonzalo Sánchez de Losada
James Schlesinger
Helmut Schmidt
William Schneider
Philip Sharp
George Shultz
Jesús Silva Herzog

Helga Steeg
Joseph Stiglitz
Christian Stoffaës
Jens Stoltenberg
Lawrence Summers
Peter Sutherland
Margaret Thatcher
Felipe Thorndike
Antoine van Agtmael
Sergei Vasiliev
Paul Volcker
John Wakeham
John Wing
Wong Wee Kim
Grigorii Yavlinsky
Yeo Cheow Tong
David Young

SELECTED BIBLIOGRAPHY

Aharoni, Yari. *The Evolution and Management of State Owned Enterprises.* Cambridge, Mass.: Ballinger Publishing Company, 1986.

Akbar, M. J. *Nehru: The Making of India.* London: Viking Penguin Group, 1988.

Allen, Frederick Lewis. *Only Yesterday: An Informal History of the Nineteen-Twenties.* New York: Blue Ribbon Books, 1931.

Ambrose, Stephen E. *Nixon.* 3 vols. New York: Simon & Schuster, 1987–91.

Amsden, Alice H. *Asia's Next Giant: South Korea and Late Industrialization.* New York: Oxford University Press, 1989.

Anderson, Martin. *Welfare: The Political Economy of Welfare Reform in the United States.* Stanford: Hoover Institution Press, 1979.

Ash, Timothy Garton. *The Polish Revolution.* London: Granta Books, 1991.

Åslund, Anders. *Gorbachev's Struggle for Economic Reform.* Ithaca, N.Y.: Cornell University Press, 1991.

———. *How Russia Became a Market Economy.* Washington, D.C.: Brookings Institution, 1995.

Balcerowicz, Leszek. *Socialism, Capitalism, Transformation.* London: Central European University Press, 1995.

Balze, Felipe A. M. de la. *Remaking the Argentine Economy.* New York: Council on Foreign Relations Press, 1995.

Barber, William J. *A History of Economic Thought.* London: Penguin, 1967, reprinted 1979.

Bark, Dennis L., and David R. Gress. *A History of West Germany: From Shadow to Substance, 1945–1963.* Vol. 1. Oxford: Basil Blackwell Ltd., 1989.

Barnet, Richard. *The Alliance: America, Europe, Japan, Makers of the Postwar World.* New York: Simon & Schuster, 1983.

Barro, Robert J. *Getting It Right: Markets and Choices in a Free Society.* Cambridge, Mass.: MIT Press, 1996.

Bartley, W. W., III, ed. *The Collected Works of Friedrich August Hayek,* vol. 1, *The Fatal Conceit: The Errors of Socialism.* London: Routledge, 1988.

Bastos, Carlos Manuel, and Manuel Angel Abdala. *Reform of the Electric Power Sector in Argentina.* Trans. Inès Drannly and Suzzane Maia. Buenos Aires, 1996.

Bauer, P. T. *Dissent on Development.* Cambridge, Mass.: Harvard University Press, 1979.

———. *West African Trade: A Study of Competition, Oligopoly and Monopoly in a Changing Economy.* Cambridge, England: Cambridge University Press, 1954.

Baum, Richard. *Burying Mao: Chinese Politics in the Age of Deng Xiaoping.* Princeton: Princeton University Press, 1996.

Beauman, Christopher. "The Turnaround: British Steel Corporation from the Mid-1970s to the Mid-1980s—And Beyond." Centre for Economic Performance, London School of Economics, April 23, 1996.

Becker, Gary S. *Human Capital and the Personal Distribution of Income.* Ann Arbor, Mich.: Institute of Public Administration, 1967.

——— and Guity Nashat Becker. *The Economics of Life: From Baseball to Affirmative Action to Immigration, How Real-World Issues Affect Our Everyday Life.* New York: McGraw-Hill, 1997.

Beckner, Stephen K. *Back from the Brink: The Greenspan Years.* New York: John Wiley & Sons, Inc., 1996.

Beesley, E. M., ed. *Utility Regulation: Challenge and Response.* London: Institute of Economic Affairs, 1995.

Bell, Daniel. *The Cultural Contradictions of Capitalism.* New York: Basic Books, 1976.

Benn, Tony. *Against the Tide: Diaries 1973–76.* London: Hutchinson, 1989.

Berger, Suzanne, and Ronald Dore, eds. *National Diversity and Global Capitalism.* Ithaca, N.Y.: Cornell University Press, 1991.

Berliner, Joseph S. *The Innovation Decision in Soviet Industry.* Cambridge, Mass.: MIT Press, 1976.

Bernstein, Richard, and Ross H. Munro. *The Coming Conflict with China.* New York: Alfred A. Knopf, 1997.

Bhagwati, Jagdish. *India in Transition: Freeing the Economy.* Oxford: Oxford University Press, 1995.

Bishop, Matthew, John Kay, and Colin Mayer, eds. *The Regulatory Challenge.* Oxford: Oxford University Press, 1995.

Blasi, Joseph A., Maya Kroumova, and Douglas Kruse. *Kremlin Capitalism: Privatizing the Russian Economy.* Ithaca, N.Y.: Cornell University Press, 1997.

Booth, Anne, ed. *The Oil Boom and After: Indonesian Economic Policy and Performance in the Soeharto Era.* Shah Alam, Malaysia: Oxford University Press, 1995.

Bosworth, Barry P., Rudiger Dornbusch, and Raúl Labán, eds. *The Chilean Economy: Policy Lessons and Challenges.* Washington, D.C.: Brookings Institution, 1994.

Boycko, Maxim, Andrei Shleifer, and Robert Vishny. *Privatizing Russia.* Cambridge, Mass.: MIT Press, 1995.

Brady, Kathleen. *Ida Tarbell: Portrait of a Muckraker.* New York: Seaview/Putnam, 1984.

Breit, William, and Roger W. Spencer, eds. *Lives of the Laureates: Seven Nobel Economists.* Cambridge, Mass.: MIT Press, 1986.

Bresnan, John. *Managing Indonesia: The Modern Political Economy.* New York: Columbia University Press, 1993.

Breyer, Stephen. *Breaking the Vicious Circle: Toward Effective Risk Regulation.* Cambridge, Mass.: Harvard University Press, 1994.

———. *Regulation and Its Reform.* Cambridge: Harvard University Press, 1982.

Brinkley, Alan. *The End of Reform: New Deal Liberalism in Recession and War.* New York: Vintage Books, 1995.

Brittan, Samuel. *Capitalism with a Human Face.* London: Fontana Press, 1995.

Bryan, Lowell, and Diana Farrell. *Market Unbound: Unleashing Global Capitalism.* New York: John Wiley & Sons, 1996.

Burkhardt, Robert. *CAB—The Civil Aeronautics Board.* Dulles International Airport: Green Hills Publishing Company, 1974.

Burki, Shahid Javed, and Sebastian Edwards. *Dismantling the Populist State: The Unfinished Revolution in Latin America and the Caribbean.* Washington, D.C.: The World Bank, 1996.

Cairncross, Alec. *Years of Recovery: British Economic Policy, 1945–1951.* London: Methuen, 1985.

Caldwell, Bruce, ed. *The Collected Works of F. A. Hayek,* vol. 9, *Contra Keynes and Cambridge, Essays, Correspondence.* London: Routledge, 1995.

Cambridge Energy Research Associates. *Former Soviet Union Watch.* Various editions.

Campos, Jose Edgardo, and Hilton L. Root. *The Key to the Asian Miracle: Making Shared Growth Credible.* Washington, D.C.: Brookings Institution, 1996.

Cannon, Lou. *Reagan.* New York: G. P. Putnam's Sons, 1982.

———. *President Reagan: The Role of a Lifetime.* New York: Simon & Schuster, 1991.

Caplan, Lincoln. *Up Against the Law: Affirmative Action and the Supreme Court.* New York: Twentieth Century Fund Press, 1997.

Cardoso, Fernando Henrique, and Enzo Faletto. *Dependency and Development in Latin America.* Berkeley: University of California Press, 1979.

Caron, François. *An Economic History of Modern France.* Trans. Barbara Bray. New York: Columbia University Press, 1979.

Carr, Edward Hallett. *The Bolshevik Revolution, 1917–1923.* 3 vols. London: Macmillan, 1950–53.

Cassen, Robert, and Vijay Joshi, eds. *India: The Future of Economic Reform.* New Delhi: Oxford University Press, 1995.

Chakravarty, Sukhamoy. *Selected Economic Writings.* New Delhi: Oxford University Press, 1993.

———. *Development Planning: The Indian Experience.* Oxford: Clarendon Press, 1987.

Chertow, Martin R., and Daniel Esty. *Thinking Ecologically: The Next Generation on Environmental Policy.* New Haven: Yale University Press, 1997.

Clawson, Marion. *New Deal Planning: The National Resources Planning Board.* Baltimore: Johns Hopkins University Press, 1981.

Cockett, Richard. *Thinking the Unthinkable: Think-tanks and the Economic Counter-Revolution, 1931–1983.* London: Fontana Press, 1995.

Colclough, Christopher, and James Manor, eds. *States or Markets? Neo-liberalism and the Development Policy Debate.* Oxford: Oxford University Press, 1995.

Conaghan, Catherine M., James M. Malloy, and Luis A. Abugattas. "Business and the 'Boys': The Politics of Neoliberalism in the Central Andes." *Latin American Research Review* #32 (Spring 1990): 3–30.

Congressional Budget Office. *The Economic and Budget Outlook: Fiscal Years 1998–2007.* Washington, D.C.: Congressional Budget Office, 1997.

Congressional Research Service. "Market-based Environmental Management: Issues and Implementation." Washington, D.C.: Congressional Research Service, 1994.

Constable, Pamela, and Arturo Valenzuela. *A Nation of Enemies: Chile Under Pinochet.* New York: W. W. Norton & Company, 1991.

Coopey, Richard, and Nicholas Woodward, eds. *Britain in the 1970s: The Troubled Economy.* London: University College London Press, 1996.

Council of Economic Advisers. *Economic Report of the President.* Washington, D.C.: U.S. Government Printing Office, 1997.

Crook, Clive, ed. "The Future of the State: A Survey of the World Economy." *The Economist* (September 20–26, 1997).

Crossman, R. H. S., ed., *The God That Failed.* New York: Harper, 1949.

Dahrendorf, Ralf. *A History of the London School of Economics and Political Science: 1895–1995.* Oxford: Oxford University Press, 1995.

Dam, Kenneth W. *The GATT: Law and International Economic Organization.* Chicago: University of Chicago Press, 1970.

———. *The Rules of the Game: Reform and Evolution in the International Monetary System.* Chicago: University of Chicago Press, 1982.

Darman, Richard. *Who's In Control? Polar Politics and the Sensible Center.* New York: Simon & Schuster, 1996.

Delors, Jacques. *Our Europe: The Community and National Development.* Trans. Brian Pearce. London: Verso, 1992.

———. *L'Unité d'un homme: Entretiens avec Dominique Wolton.* Paris: Éditions Odile Jacob, 1994.

DeMuth, Christopher, and William Kristol, eds. *The Neoconservative Imagination.* Washington, D.C.: AEI Press, 1995.

Deng Mao-mao. *Deng Xiaoping: My Father.* New York: Basic Books, 1995.

Dominguez, Jorge I., ed. *Technopols: Freeing Politics and Markets in Latin America in the 1990s.* University Park: Pennsylvania State University Press, 1997.

Donaldson, David J. *Privatization: Principles and Practice.* Lessons of Experience Series from the International Finance Corporation. Washington, D.C.: World Bank, 1995.

Donoghue, Bernard. *Prime Minister: The Conduct of Policy Under Harold Wilson and James Callaghan.* London: Jonathan Cape, 1987.

Dornbusch, Rudiger, and F. Leslie C. H. Helmers, eds. *The Open Economy: Tools for Policymakers in Developing Countries.* New York: Oxford University Press for the World Bank, 1988.

Drew, Elizabeth. *On the Edge: The Clinton Presidency.* New York: Simon & Schuster, 1994.

——— *Showdown: The Struggle Between the Gingrich Congress and the Clinton White House.* New York: Touchstone, 1997.

Duchêne, François. *Jean Monnet: The First Statesman of Interdependence.* New York: W. W. Norton & Company, 1994.

Durbin, Elizabeth. *New Jerusalems: The Labour Party and the Economics of Democratic Socialism.* London: Routledge, 1985.

Edwards, Sebastian. *Crisis and Reform in Latin America: From Despair to Hope.* Oxford: Oxford University Press for the World Bank, 1995.

Einaudi, Mario, Maurice Byé, and Ernesto Rossi. *Nationalization in France and Italy.* Ithaca, N.Y.: Cornell University Press, 1955.

Ekiert, Grzegorz. *The State Against Society: Political Crises and Their Aftermath in East Central Europe.* Princeton: Princeton University Press, 1996.

Enright, Michael J., Edith E. Scott, and David Dodwell. *The Hong Kong Advantage.* Hong Kong: Oxford University Press, 1997.

European Bank for Reconstruction and Development. *Transition Report.* London: EBRD, annual.

European Community. *Battling for the Union: Altiero Spinelli 1979–1986.* Luxembourg: European Community Press, 1988.

Evans, Richard. *Deng Xiaoping and the Making of Modern China.* London: Penguin Books, 1993.

Fairbank, John King. *China: A New History.* Cambridge, Mass.: Belknap Press of Harvard University Press, 1992.

Fallows, James. *Looking at the Sun: The Rise of the New East Asian Economic and Political System.* New York: Pantheon, 1994.

Febrero, Ramon, and Pedro S. Schwartz, eds. *The Essence of Becker.* Stanford: Hoover Institution Press, 1995.

Feldstein, Martin, ed. *American Economic Policy in the 1980s.* Chicago: University of Chicago Press, 1994.

Ferdinand, Peter, ed. *Take-off for Taiwan?* London: Royal Institute of International Affairs, 1996.

Fewsmith, Joseph. *Dilemmas of Reform in China: Political Conflict and Economic Debate.* Armonk: M. E. Sharpe, 1994.

Foss, Nicolai Juul. *The Austrian School and Modern Economics: Essays in Reassessment.* Copenhagen: Handelshøjskolens Forlag, 1994.

Foster, Christopher D. *Privatization, Public Ownership and the Regulation of Natural Monopoly.* Oxford: Blackwell, 1992.

Foxley, Alejandro. *Latin American Experiments in Neo-Conservative Economics.* Berkeley: University of California Press, 1983.

Francis, John. *The Politics of Regulation: A Comparative Perspective.* Oxford: Blackwell, 1993.

Friedman, Benjamin M. *Day of Reckoning: The Consequences of American Economic Policy.* New York: Vintage Books, 1989.

Friedman, Milton. *Capitalism and Freedom.* Chicago: University of Chicago Press, 1982.

———. *Free to Choose.* New York: Harcourt Brace Jovanovich, 1980.

———. "The Nobel Prize in Economics, 1976: A Talk by Milton Friedman." Speech delivered at the Income Distribution Conference sponsored by the Hoover Institution at Stanford University, January 29, 1977.

——— and George Stigler. "Roofs or Ceilings? The Current Housing Problem." *Popular Essays on Current Problems,* vol. 1, no. 2 (September 1946).

Frydman, Roman, Andrzej Rapaczynski, and John S. Earle, eds. *The Privatization Process in Central Europe.* Budapest: Central European University Press, 1993.

Fukuyama, Francis. *The End of History and the Last Man.* New York: Free Press, 1992.

Fyrth, Jim, ed. *Labour's High Noon: The Government and the Economy 1945–51.* London: Lawrence & Wishart, 1993.

Gaidar, Yegor, and Karl Otto Pöhl. *Russian Reform/International Money.* Cambridge, Mass.: MIT Press, 1995.

Galbraith, John Kenneth. *The Affluent Society.* London: H. Hamilton, 1958.

———. *The Great Crash 1929.* Boston: Houghton Mifflin, 1954.

425

———. *The World Economy Since the Wars: A Personal View.* London: Mandarin, 1995.

Giddens, Anthony. *Beyond Left and Right: The Future of Radical Politics.* Cambridge, Mass.: Polity Press, 1994.

Giersch, Herbert, Karl-Heinz Paqué, and Holger Schmieding. *The Fading Miracle: Four Decades of Market Economy in Germany.* Cambridge, England: Cambridge University Press, 1992.

Gilbert, Martin. *Winston S. Churchill,* vol. 8, *Never Despair 1945–1965.* Boston: Houghton Mifflin, 1988.

Goodman, David S. G. *Deng Xiaoping and the Chinese Revolution.* London: Routledge, 1994.

——— and Gerald Segal, eds. *China Deconstructs.* London: Routledge, 1994.

———. *China Without Deng.* Sydney: Editions Tom Thompson, 1995.

Gorbachev, Mikhail. *Memoirs.* New York: Doubleday, 1995.

Gore, Al. *Common Sense: Works Better and Costs Less.* New York: Random House, 1995.

———. *Earth in the Balance: Ecology and the Human Spirit.* Boston: Houghton Mifflin, 1992.

Graham, Otis, Jr. *Toward a Planned Society.* New York: Oxford University Press, 1976.

Grant, Charles. *Delors: Inside the House That Jacques Built.* London: Nicholas Brealey, 1994.

Gray, John. *The Moral Foundations of Market Institutions.* London: The IEA Health and Welfare Unit, 1992.

Greenleaf, W. H. *The British Political Tradition.* 2 vols. London: Methuen & Co., 1983.

Greider, William. *One World, Ready or Not: The Manic Logic of Global Capitalism.* New York: Simon & Schuster, 1998.

———. *Secrets of the Temple: How the Federal Reserve Runs the Country.* New York: Simon & Schuster, 1987.

Gustafson, Thane. *Crisis amid Plenty: The Politics of Soviet Energy Under Brezhnev and Gorbachev.* Princeton: Princeton University Press, 1989.

———. *Capitalism Russian Style.* Cambridge, England: Cambridge University Press, forthcoming.

Haggard, Stephan. *Pathways from the Periphery: The Politics of Growth in the Newly Industrializing Countries.* Ithaca, N.Y.: Cornell University Press, 1990.

———. *Developing Nations and the Politics of Global Integration.* Washington, D.C.: Brookings Institution, 1995.

Halberstam, David. *The Reckoning.* New York: Avon Books, 1987.

Halcrow, Morrison. *Keith Joseph: A Single Mind.* London: Macmillan Press, 1989.

Haldeman, H. R. *The Haldeman Diaries: Inside the Nixon White House.* New York: G. P. Putnam's Sons, 1994.

Hale, David. "How the Rise of Pension Funds Will Change the Global Economy in the 21st Century."

Hall, Peter. *Governing the Economy: The Politics of State Intervention in Britain and France.* New York: Oxford University Press, 1986.

Handelman, Stephen. *Comrade Criminal: The Theft of the Second Russian Revolution.* London: Michael Joseph, 1994.

Hanson, Albert H. *The Process of Planning: A Study of India's Five-Year Plans.* London: Oxford University Press, 1966.

Harberger, Arnold C. "Secrets of Success: A Handful of Heroes (Political Economy of Policy Reform: Is There a Second Best?)." *American Economic Review* (May 1993): 343–351.

Hardach, Karl. *The Political Economy of Germany in the Twentieth Century.* Berkeley: University of California Press, 1980.

Harris, Kenneth. *Attlee.* London: Weidenfeld & Nicolson, 1982.

Hayek, F. A. *The Constitution of Liberty.* Chicago: University of Chicago Press, 1960.

———. *Hayek on Hayek: An Autobiographical Dialogue.* Chicago: University of Chicago Press, 1994.

———. *Individualism and Economic Order.* Chicago: University of Chicago Press, 1980.

———. *The Road to Serfdom.* Chicago: University of Chicago Press, 1994.

Healey, Denis. *The Time of My Life.* London: Penguin, 1990.

Heilbroner, Robert. *21st Century Capitalism.* New York: W. W. Norton & Company, 1994.

———. *The Worldly Philosophers.* London: Penguin, 1983.

Hennessy, Peter. *Never Again.* London: Vintage Books, 1993.

———. *Whitehall.* London: Fontana Press, 1990.

Herring, Richard J., and Robert E. Litan. *Financial Regulation in the Global Economy.* Washington, D.C.: Brookings Institution, 1995.

Hirschman, Albert O., ed. *Essays in Trespassing: Economics to Politics and Beyond.* Cambridge, England: Cambridge University Press, 1981.

Hoffmann, Stanley. *In Search of France: The Economy, Society and Political System in the Twentieth Century.* Cambridge, Mass.: Harvard University Press, 1963.

Hoge, James F., Jr. "Fulfilling Brazil's Promise: A Conversation with President Cardoso." *Foreign Affairs* (July–August 1995): 62–75.

Hojman, David. "The Political Economy of Recent Conversions to Market Economies in Latin America." *Journal of Latin American Studies* 26 (February 1994): 191–219.

Holden, Paul, and Sarath Rajapatirana. *Unshackling the Private Sector: A Latin American Story.* Washington, D.C.: World Bank, 1995.

Holloway, David. *Stalin and the Bomb: The Soviet Union and Atomic Energy.* New Haven: Yale University Press, 1994.

Horne, Alistair. *Harold Macmillan.* 2 vols. New York: Viking Penguin, 1989.

Hough, Jerry F., Evelyn Davidheiser, and Susan Goodrich Lehmann. *The 1996 Russian Presidential Election.* Brookings Occasional Papers. Washington, D.C.: Brookings Institution Press, 1996.

Howard, Philip K. *The Death of Common Sense: How Law Is Suffocating America.* New York: Warner Books, 1994.

Howe, Geoffrey. *Conflict of Loyalty.* London: Pan Books, 1995.

Huff, W. G. *The Economic Growth of Singapore: Trade and Development in the Twentieth Century.* Cambridge, England: Cambridge University Press, 1997.

Huntington, Samuel P. *The Clash of Civilizations and the Remaking of World Order.* New York: Simon & Schuster, 1996.

Interamerican Development Bank. Papers presented at Development Thinking and Practice Conference, Washington, D.C., September 3–5, 1996.

International Finance Corporation. *Emerging Stock Markets Factbook, 1997.* Washington, D.C.: IFC, 1997.

International Monetary Fund. *World Economic Outlook: EMU and the World Economy.* Washington, D.C.: IMF, 1997.

Irwin, Douglas A. *Against the Tide: An Intellectual History of Free Trade.* Princeton: Princeton University Press, 1996.

Jadresic, Alejandro. "Reforms in Latin American Energy Markets." Presented at the 15th Annual CERA Executive Conference on "Global Energy Strategies: Looking over the Horizon," February 13–14, 1996, Houston, Texas.

Jayarajah, Carl, and William Branson. *Structural and Sectoral Adjustment: World Bank Experience,* 1980–1992. Washington, D.C.: World Bank, 1995.

Jenkins, Simon. *Accountable to None: The Tory Nationalization of Britain.* London: Penguin Books, 1996.

Johnson, Chalmers. *Japan: Who Governs? The Rise of the Developmental State.* New York: W. W. Norton & Company, 1995.

Johnson, Christopher. *The Economy Under Mrs. Thatcher, 1979–1990.* London: Penguin Books, 1991.

Joshi, Vijay, and I. M. D. Little. *India's Economic Reform 1991–2001.* New York: Oxford University Press, 1996.

Kahn, Alfred. *Economics of Regulation: Principles and Institutions.* New York: Wiley, 1970.

Kanter, Rosabeth Moss. *World Class: Thriving Locally in the Global Economy.* New York: Simon & Schuster, 1995.

————. *When Giants Learn to Dance: Mastering the Challenge of Strategy, Management, and Careers in the 1990s.* New York: Simon & Schuster, 1989.

Kaplan, Justin. *Lincoln Steffens: A Biography.* New York: Simon & Schuster, 1974.

Kapstein, Ethan B. *Governing the Global Economy: International Finance and the State.* Cambridge, Mass.: Harvard University Press, 1996.

Kelkar, Vijay L., and V. V. Bhanoji Rao. *India Development Policy Imperatives.* New Delhi: Tata McGraw-Hill, 1996.

Kenwood, A. G., and A. L. Lougheed. *The Growth of the International Economy, 1820–1960.* London: George Allen & Unwin, 1975.

Keynes, John Maynard. *The General Theory of Employment, Interest and Money.* London: Macmillan, 1936.

Khatkhate, Deena. "Intellectual Origins of Indian Economic Reform." *World Development* 22(7) (1994): 1097–1102.

Khrushchev, Nikita. *Khrushchev Remembers.* 2 vols. Trans. Jerrold L. Schecter. Harmondsworth: Penguin, 1977.

Kikeri, Sunita, John Nellis, and Mary Shirley. *Privatization: The Lessons of Experience.* Washington, D.C.: World Bank, 1994.

Killick, Tony. *Development Economics in Action: A Study of Economic Policies in Ghana.* London: Heinemann, 1978.

Kindleberger, Charles P. *Europe's Postwar Growth: The Role of Labor Supply.* Cambridge, Mass.: Harvard University Press, 1967.

————. *World Economic Primacy: 1500–1990.* New York: Oxford University Press, 1996.

————. *The World in Depression: 1929–39.* London: Allen Lane Penguin, 1973.

Klaus, Václav. *Renaissance: The Rebirth of Liberty in the Heart of Europe.* Washington, D.C.: Cato Institute, 1997.

Klein, Peter, ed. *The Fortunes of Liberalism: The Collected Works of F. A. Hayek.* London: Routledge, 1992.

Kohnstamm, Max. *The European Community and Its Role in the World.* Columbia: University of Missouri Press, 1964.

Kornai, János. *The Socialist System: The Political Economy of Communism.* Princeton: Princeton University Press, 1992.

Kosai, Yutaka. *The Era of High-Speed Growth: Notes on the Postwar Japanese Economy.* Trans. Jacqueline Kaminski. Tokyo: University of Tokyo Press, 1986.

Kotlikoff, Laurence J., and Jeffrey Sachs. "Privatizing Social Security." *The Brookings Review* 15(3) (Summer 1997): 16–24.

Krauze, Enrique. *Mexico: Biography of Power. A History of Modern Mexico, 1810–1996.* Trans. Hank Heifetz. New York: HarperCollins, 1997.

Kresge, Stephen, and Leif Wenar, eds. *Hayek on Hayek: An Autobiographical Dialogue.* London: Routledge, 1994.

Kristol, Irving. *Neoconservativism: The Autobiography of an Idea.* New York: Free Press, 1995.

Krugman, Paul. *The Age of Diminished Expectations: U.S. Economic Policy in the 1990s.* Cambridge, Mass.: MIT Press, 1995.

———. *Peddling Prosperity: Economic Sense and Nonsense in the Age of Diminished Expectations.* New York: W. W. Norton & Company, 1994.

———. *Pop Internationalism.* Cambridge, Mass.: MIT Press, 1997.

———. *Geography and Trade.* Cambridge, Mass.: MIT Press, 1993.

Kurtzman, Joel. *The Death of Money: How the Electronic Economy Has Destabilized the World's Markets and Created Financial Chaos.* New York: Simon & Schuster, 1993.

Kuttner, Robert. *Everything for Sale: The Virtues and Limits of Markets.* New York: Alfred A. Knopf, 1997.

Lam, Willy Wo-Lap. *China After Deng Xiaoping: The Power Struggle in Beijing Since Tiananmen.* Singapore: John Wiley & Sons, 1995.

Landis, James. *The Administrative Process.* New Haven: Yale University Press, 1938.

Lawrence, Robert Z. *Single World, Divided Nations: International Trade and OECD Labor Markets.* Paris: Organization for Economic Cooperation and Development, 1996.

Lawson, Nigel. *The View from No. 11: Memoirs of a Tory Radical.* London: Corgi Books, 1993.

Lazear, Edward P., ed. *Economic Transition in Eastern Europe and Russia: Realities of Reform.* Stanford: Hoover Institution Press, 1995.

Lear, John, and Joseph Collins. "Working in Chile's Free Market." *Latin American Perspectives* 84 (Winter 1995): 10–29.

Lee, Chae-jin. *Zhou Enlai: The Early Years.* Stanford: Stanford University Press, 1994.

Lee, Susan. *Hands Off: Why the Government Is a Menace to Economic Health.* New York: Simon & Schuster, 1995.

Leibfried, Stephan, and Paul Pierson, eds. *European Social Policy: Between Fragmentation and Integration.* Washington, D.C.: Brookings Institution Press, 1995.

Lenin, V. I. *Collected Works,* vols. 32, 33. Moscow: Progress Publishers, 1965.

Leuchtenberg, William E. *The Perils of Prosperity: 1914–32.* Chicago: University of Chicago Press, 1993.

————. *The FDR Years: On Roosevelt and His Legacy.* New York: Columbia University Press, 1995.

Li, Kwoh-ting. *Economic Transformation of Taiwan, ROC.* London: Shepheard Publishers, 1988.

————. *The Evolution of Policy Behind Taiwan's Development Success.* New Haven: Yale University Press, 1988.

Lieberthal, Kenneth. *Governing China: From Revolution Through Reform.* New York: W. W. Norton & Company, 1995.

Liu, Alan P. L. *The Phoenix and the Lame Lion: Modernization in Taiwan and Mainland China 1950–1980.* Stanford: Hoover Institution Press, 1987.

Lodge, Juliet, ed. *European Union: The European Community in Search of a Future.* London: Macmillan, 1986.

MacFarquhar, Roderick. "Deng's Last Campaign." *New York Review of Books,* December 17, 1992.

Macintyre, Andrew. *Business and Politics in Indonesia.* Kensington, Australia: Allen & Unwin, 1991.

Macmillan, Harold. *Tides of Fortune: 1945–1955.* New York: Harper & Row, 1969.

Mahathir, Mohamad. *Malaysia: The Way Forward: Vision 2020.* Working paper presented at the inaugural meeting of the Malaysian Business Council, February 28, 1991.

————. *The Malay Dilemma.* Singapore: Times Books, 1970.

Maier, Charles. *Dissolution: The Crisis of Communism and the End of East Germany.* Princeton: Princeton University Press, 1997.

Marsh, David. *Germany and Europe: The Crisis of Unity.* London: Heinemann, 1994.

Mason, Edward Sagendorph, and Robert Asher. *The World Bank Since Bretton Woods.* Washington, D.C.: Brookings Institution Press, 1973.

Mayer, Martin. *The Bankers: The Next Generation.* New York: Truman Talley Books, 1997.

Mayne, Richard. *The Recovery of Europe: 1945–1973.* Garden City, N.Y.: Anchor Books, 1973.

McCraw, Thomas K. *Prophets of Regulation.* Cambridge, Mass.: Belknap Press of Harvard University Press, 1984.

McDonald, Forrest. *Insull.* Chicago: University of Chicago Press, 1962.

Meier, Gerald M., and Dudley Seers, eds. *Pioneers in Development.* New York: Oxford University Press, 1984.

Menem, Carlos, and Roberto Dromi. *Reforma del Estado y Transformación Nacional.* Buenos Aires: Ciencias de la Administración S.R.L., 1990.

Milesi, Gabriel. *Jacques Delors: L'homme qui dit non.* Paris: Edition 1, 1995.

Milward, Alan S. *The German Economy at War.* London: Athlone Press, 1965.

————. *The Reconstruction of Western Europe 1945–51.* London: Methuen & Co., 1984.

Morishima, Michio. *Why Has Japan "Succeeded"? Western Technology and the Japanese Ethos.* Cambridge, England: Cambridge University Press, 1982.

Morris, Dick. *Behind the Oval Office.* New York: Random House, 1997.

Morrison, Steven A., and Clifford Winston. *The Evolution of the Airline Industry.* Washington, D.C.: Brookings Institution, 1995.

Mosley, Paul, Jane Harrigan, and John Toye. *Aid and Power: The World Bank & Policy-Based Lending,* vols. 1 and 2. London: Routledge, 1991.

Mowry, George E. *The Era of Theodore Roosevelt: 1900–1912.* New York: Harper & Brothers, 1958.

Moxon, James. *Volta: Man's Greatest Lake.* London: Andre Deutsch, 1984.

Moynihan, Daniel Patrick. *Miles to Go: A Personal History of Social Policy.* Cambridge, Mass.: Harvard University Press, 1996.

Muller, Jerry Z. *Adam Smith in His Time and Ours.* Princeton: Princeton University Press, 1993.

Naim, Moises. "Latin America: Post-Adjustment Blues." *Foreign Policy* 92 (Fall 1993): 133–150.

———. *Latin America's Journey to the Market: From Macroeconomic Shocks to Institutional Therapy.* San Francisco: ICS Press, 1995.

Nehru, Jawaharlal. *The Discovery of India.* New Delhi: Oxford University Press, 1989. Originally published in 1946.

Neikirk, William R. *Volcker: Portrait of the Money Man.* New York: Congdon & Weed, 1987.

Niskanen, William A. *Reaganomics: An Insider's Account of the Policies and the People.* New York: Oxford University Press, 1988.

Nivola, Pietro S., ed. *Comparative Disadvantages? Social Regulations and the Global Economy.* Washington, D.C.: Brookings Institution, 1997.

Nixon, Richard. *RN: The Memoirs of Richard Nixon.* New York: Grosset & Dunlap, 1978.

Nkrumah, Kwame. *The Autobiography of Kwame Nkrumah.* London: Thomas Nelson and Sons, 1961.

Noguchi, Yukio. "The 1940s System." Manuscript.

Novak, William J. *The People's Welfare: Law & Regulation in Nineteenth Century America.* Chapel Hill: University of North Carolina, 1997.

Nove, Alec. *An Economic History of the U.S.S.R.* London: Penguin Books, 1969.

Nye, Joseph, Jr. *Bound to Lead: The Changing Nature of American Power.* New York: Basic Books, 1990.

Ohmae, Kenichi. *The End of the Nation State: The Rise of Regional Economies.* London: HarperCollins, 1995.

———. *The Borderless World: Power and Strategy in the Interlinked Economy.* New York: HarperBusiness, 1990.

Okun, Arthur M. *Equality and Efficiency: The Big Tradeoff.* Washington, D.C.: Brookings Institution, 1975.

Oliver, Robert W. *George Woods and the World Bank.* Boulder, Colo.: Lynne Rienner Publishers, 1995.

Ostry, Sylvia. *The Post-Cold War Trading System: Who's on First?* Chicago: University of Chicago Press, 1997.

Overholt, William H. *The Rise of China: How Economic Reform Is Creating a New Superpower.* New York: W. W. Norton & Company, 1993.

Patrick, Hugh. "Crumbling or Transforming? Japan's Economic Success and Its Postwar Economic Institutions." Working Paper 98, Columbia Business School, September 1995.

Perkins, Dwight. "Completing China's Move to the Market." *Journal of Economic Perspectives* 8 (Spring 1994): 23–46.

Pond, Elizabeth. *Beyond the Wall: Germany's Road to Unification.* Washington, D.C.: Brookings Institution, 1993.

Pulzer, Peter. *German Politics, 1945–1995.* Oxford: Oxford University Press, 1995.

Ramamurti, Ravi, and Raymond Vernon, eds. *Privatization and Control of State-owned Enterprises.* Washington, D.C.: World Bank, 1995.

Ramanadham, V. V. *Privatization and After: Monitoring and Regulation.* London: Routledge, 1994.

————, ed. *Privatization and Equity.* London: Routledge, 1995.

Reason Foundation. *Privatization.* Annual, 1996.

Reder, Melvin. "Chicago Economics: Permanence and Change." *Journal of Economic Literature* (March 1982).

Reich, Robert. *Locked in the Cabinet.* New York: Alfred A. Knopf, 1997.

Remnick, David. *Lenin's Tomb: The Last Days of the Soviet Union.* New York: Random House, 1993.

Roberts, Jane, David Elliott, and Trevor Houghton. *Privatising Electricity: The Politics of Power.* London: Bellhaven Press, 1991.

Roberts, Kenneth M. "Neoliberalism and the Transformation of Populism in Latin America: The Peruvian Case." *World Politics* 48 (October 1995).

Rohwer, Jim. *Asia Rising: Why America Will Prosper as Asia's Economies Boom.* New York: Simon & Schuster, 1995.

Roll, Eric. *A History of Economic Thought.* London: Faber and Faber, 1992.

Rosenberg, Nathan. *The Emergence of Economic Ideas: Essays in the History of Economics.* Aldershot, Hants, England: Edward Elgar, 1994.

Rotunda, Ronald D. "The 'Liberal' Label: Roosevelt's Capture of a Symbol." *Public Policy* 17 (1968): 377–408.

Sachs, Jeffrey. *Poland's Jump to the Market Economy.* Cambridge, Mass.: MIT Press, 1994.

Sakakibara, Eisuke. *Beyond Capitalism: The Japanese Model of Market Economics.* Lanham, Md.: University Press of America, 1993.

Salmon, Keith. *The Modern Spanish Economy: Transformation & Integration into Europe.* London: Pinter, 1995.

Samuels, Warren J., ed. *The Chicago School of Political Economy.* New Brunswick, N.J.: Transaction Publishers, 1993.

Schlesinger, Arthur M., Jr. *The Age of Roosevelt.* 3 vols. Boston: Houghton Mifflin Company, 1988.

————. *A Thousand Days: John F. Kennedy in the White House.* Greenwich, Conn.: Fawcett, 1965.

Schmidt, Vivien A. *From State to Market? The Transformation of French Business and Government.* New York: Cambridge University Press, 1996.

Schubert, Aurel. *The Credit-Anstalt Crisis of 1931.* Cambridge, England: Cambridge University Press, 1991.

Schumpeter, Joseph A. *Capitalism, Socialism, and Democracy.* London: Routledge, 1994.

Seagrave, Sterling. *Lords of the Rim: Invisible Empire of the Overseas Chinese.* New York: G. P. Putnam's Sons, 1995.

Shearmur, Jeremy. *Hayek and After: Hayekian Liberalism as a Research Programme.* London: Routledge, 1996.

Shevtsova, Lilia. *Yeltsin's Russia: Challenges and Constraints.* Moscow: Carnegie Center, 1997.

Shirley, Mary, and John Nellis. *Public Enterprise Reform: The Lessons of Experience.* Washington, D.C.: World Bank, 1991.

Shultz, George P. *Turmoil and Triumph: My Years as Secretary of State.* New York: Maxwell Macmillan International, 1993.

———— and Kenneth W. Dam. *Economic Policy Behind the Headlines.* New York: W. W. Norton, 1977.

Singer, Charles, E. J. Holmyard, A. R. Hall, and Trevor I. Williams, eds. *A History of Technology.* 8 vols. Oxford: Clarendon Press, 1980.

Singh, Manmohan. *India's Export Trends and the Prospects for Self-Sustained Growth.* Oxford: Clarendon Press, 1964.

Skidelsky, Robert. *Beyond the Welfare State.* London: Social Market Foundation, 1997.

————. *Interests and Obsessions: Historical Essays.* London: Macmillan, 1994.

————. *John Maynard Keynes.* 3 vols. London: Macmillan, 1983–1994.

————. *Keynes.* Oxford: Oxford University Press, 1996.

————, ed. *Thatcherism.* London: Chatto & Windus, 1988.

————. *The World After Communism.* London: Macmillan, 1995.

Skidmore, Thomas E., and Peter H. Smith. *Modern Latin America.* New York: Oxford University Press, 1992.

Smith, Adam. *The Wealth of Nations.* New York: Modern Library, 1994.

Smith, William C. *Authoritarianism and the Crisis of the Argentine Political Economy.* Palo Alto: Stanford University Press, 1991.

Solovyov, Vladimir, and Elena Klepikova. *Boris Yeltsin: A Political Biography.* Trans. David Gurevich. New York: G. P. Putnam's Sons, 1992.

Sopel, Jon. *Tony Blair: The Moderniser.* London: Bantam Books, 1995.

Soros, George. "The Capitalist Threat." *The Atlantic Monthly* (February 1997).

Spence, Jonathan D., and Annping Chin. *The Chinese Century: A Photographic History of the Last Hundred Years.* New York: Random House, 1996.

Spinelli, Altiero, and Ernesto Rossi. *Il Manifesto di Ventotene.* Naples: Guida Editori, 1982.

Stein, Herbert. *Presidential Economics: The Making of Economic Policy from Roosevelt to Reagan and Beyond.* New York: Touchstone, 1985.

Stent, Angela. *Russia and Germany Reborn: Unification, the Collapse of the Soviet Union and the Future of Europe.* Princeton: Princeton University Press, forthcoming.

Stern, Joseph J., Ji-hong Kim, Dwight H. Perkins, and Jung-ho Yoo. *Industrialization and the State: The Korean Heavy and Chemical Industry Drive.* Cambridge, Mass.: Harvard Institute for International Development, 1995.

Stigler, George J. *Memoirs of an Unregulated Economist.* New York: Basic Books, 1988.

Stiglitz, Joseph E. *Whither Socialism?* Cambridge, Mass.: MIT Press, 1995.

Stockman, David A. *The Triumph of Politics: How the Reagan Revolution Failed.* New York: Harper & Row, 1986.

Sung, Yun-Wing, Pak-Wai Liu, Yue-Chim Richard Wong, and Pui-King Lau. *The Fifth Dragon: The Emergence of the Pearl River Delta.* Singapore: Addison Wesley Publishing Company, 1995.

Tanzi, Vito, and Ludger Schuknecht, "The Growth of Government and the Reform of the State in Industrial Countries," IMF Working Paper W/95/136, December 1995.

Tarbell, Ida M. *All in the Day's Work: An Autobiography.* New York: Macmillan, 1939.

433

Temin, Peter, with Louis Galambos. *The Fall of the Bell System: A Study in Prices and Politics*. New York: Cambridge University Press, 1987.

Thatcher, Margaret. *The Downing Street Years*. New York: HarperCollins, 1993.

————. *The Path to Power*. New York: HarperCollins, 1995.

Thurow, Lester C. *The Future of Capitalism: How Today's Economic Forces Shape Tomorrow's World*. New York: William Morrow and Company, 1996.

Timmins, Nicholas. *The Five Giants: A Biography of the Welfare State*. London: HarperCollins, 1995.

Toffler, Alvin. *The Third Wave*. New York: Morrow, 1980.

Tomlinson, Jim. *Government and the Enterprise Since 1900: The Changing Problem of Efficiency*. New York: Oxford University Press, 1994.

Tong, Hollington K. *Chiang Kai-shek*. Taipei: China Publishing Company, 1953.

Tsang, Steve. *Hong Kong: An Appointment with China*. London: I. B. Tauris, 1997.

Tsuru, Shigeto. *Japan's Capitalism: Creative Defeat and Beyond*. Cambridge, England: Cambridge University Press, 1996.

Ulč, Otto. "Czechoslovakia's Velvet Divorce." *East European Quarterly* 30 (Fall 1996): 331–352.

Valdez, Juan Gabriel. *Pinochet's Economists: The Chicago School in Chile*. New York: Cambridge University Press, 1995.

van Agtmael, Antoine M. *Emerging Securities Markets: Investment Banking Opportunities in the Developing World*. London: Euromoney Publications, 1984.

Vargas Llosa, Alvaro. "The Press Officer." *Granta* 36 (Summer 1991).

Vargas Llosa, Mario. *A Fish in the Water: A Memoir*. Trans. Helen Lane. London: Faber and Faber, 1994.

————. *Vargas Llosa for President*. New York: Granta Publications, 1991.

Vernon, Raymond. *America's Foreign Trade and the GATT*. Princeton: Princeton University Department of Economics and Sociology, 1954.

————. *Privatization and Control of State Owned Enterprises*. Washington, D.C.: World Bank, 1991.

————. *The Promise of Privatization: A Challenge for U.S. Policy*. New York: Council on Foreign Relations, 1988.

————. *Storm over the Multinationals: The Real Issues*. Cambridge, Mass.: Harvard University Press, 1977.

————. *Two Hungry Giants: The United States and Japan in the Quest for Oil and Ores*. Cambridge, Mass.: Harvard University Press, 1983.

———— and Debora Spar. *Beyond Globalism: Remaking American Foreign Economic Policy*. New York: The Free Press, 1989.

Vickers, John, and George Yarrow. *Privatization: An Economic Analysis*. Cambridge, Mass.: MIT Press, 1993.

Vietor, Richard H. K. *Contrived Competition: Regulation and Deregulation in America*. Cambridge, Mass.: Harvard University Press, 1996.

Virard, Marie-Paule. *Comment Mitterrand a découvert l'économie*. Paris: Albin Michel, 1993.

Vogel, Ezra F. *The Four Little Dragons: The Spread of Industrialization in East Asia*. Cambridge, Mass.: Harvard University Press, 1991.

Vogel, Stephen. *Freer Markets, More Rules: Regulatory Reform in Advanced Industrial Countries*. Ithaca, N.Y.: Cornell University Press, 1996.

Volcker, Paul, and Toyoo Gyohten. *Changing Fortunes: The World's Money and the Threat to American Leadership*. New York: Times Books, 1992.

Wade, Robert. *Governing the Market: Economic Theory and the Role of Government in East Asian Industrialization.* Princeton: Princeton University Press, 1990.

Webb, Sidney. *The History of Trade Unionism.* New York: AMS Press, 1975.

────── and Beatrice Webb. *Soviet Communism: A New Civilization?* London: Longmans, Green and Co., 1935.

──────. *The Truth About Soviet Russia.* London: Longmans, Green and Co., 1942.

Weber, Max. *The Protestant Ethic and the Spirit of Capitalism.* London: Unwin Hyman, 1989.

Winiecki, Jan. *Five Years After June: The Polish Transformation, 1989–1994.* Trans. Robert Clarke. London: Centre for Research into Communist Economies, 1996.

Winterton, Jonathan. *Coal, Crisis and Conflict: The 1984–85 Miners' Strike in Yorkshire.* New York: Manchester University Press, 1989.

Wirth, John D., ed. *Latin American Oil Companies and the Politics of Energy.* Lincoln: University of Nebraska Press, 1985.

Wolpert, Stanley. *Nehru: A Tryst with Destiny.* New York: Oxford University Press, 1996.

Woo, Wing Thye, Stephen Parker, and Jeffrey Sachs, eds. *Economies in Transition: Comparing Asia and East Europe.* Cambridge, Mass.: MIT Press, 1997.

Wood, Christopher. *The Bubble Economy: The Japanese Economic Collapse.* Tokyo: Charles E. Tuttle Company, 1993.

World Bank. *Adjustment in Africa: Reforms, Results, and the Road Ahead.* New York: Oxford University Press, 1994.

──────. *Bureaucrats in Business: The Economics and Politics of Government Ownership.* New York: Oxford University Press, 1995.

──────. *China 2020: Development Challenges in the New Century.* Washington, D.C.: World Bank, 1997.

──────. *The East Asian Miracle: Economic Growth and Public Policy.* New York: Oxford University Press, 1993.

──────. *Global Economic Prospects and the Developing Countries.* Washington, D.C.: World Bank, 1997.

──────. *Private Capital Flows to Developing Countries: The Road to Financial Integration.* New York: Oxford University Press, 1997.

──────. *World Debt Tables.* New York: Oxford University Press, annual to 1998.

──────. *World Development Report.* New York: Oxford University Press, annual.

Wright, Vincent, ed. *Privatization in Western Europe: Pressures, Problems, and Paradoxes.* London: Pinter Publishers, 1994.

Yeltsin, Boris. *The Struggle for Russia.* New York: Random House, 1994.

Yergin, Daniel. *The Prize: The Epic Quest for Oil, Money and Power.* New York: Simon & Schuster, 1991.

──────. *Shattered Peace: The Origins of the Cold War.* New York: Houghton Mifflin, 1977.

────── and Thane Gustafson. *Russia 2010 and What It Means for the World.* New York: Vintage Books, 1995.

Young, Hugo. *One of Us.* London: Pan Books, 1993.

Youngson, A. J. *The British Economy: 1920–1957.* Cambridge, Mass.: Harvard University Press, 1960.

ACKNOWLEDGMENTS

In the course of its research and writing, this book turned into a much larger inquiry than we had initially anticipated. We found ourselves writing about the twenty-first century and, from a particular perspective, about the history of the last half of the twentieth century. In so doing, we acquired debts to many people, which we wish to acknowledge.

Three people had special impact on this book. And to them we are especially grateful.

Sue Lena Thompson, who is director of special projects at CERA, guided this as a very special project. This book benefited enormously from the intelligence, dedication, grasp, and conviction that she brought to bear on every dimension of this project. She had a vision of what this book could be before we did, and she contributed a particular insight into the interaction of ideas and people.

Siddhartha Mitter is a young scholar of uncommon ability. He temporarily put aside his own work on the new Africa to apply his talent and analytic capabilities to our task. His intellectual rigor was invaluable, as was his unique feel for the interplay of politics and economics and the dynamics of change. Both Sue Lena and Siddhartha balanced their focus on the challenge with humor, spirit, and much-needed flexibility, and they never wavered in their extraordinary commitment.

Our editor at Simon & Schuster, Frederic Hills, saw the possibilities and challenged us to stretch the book. He conceptualized the themes and joined us in the thinking and design. He was always demanding, usually relentlessly so; he was also supportive, stood by us throughout, and went several extra miles, more miles perhaps than he even expected. His commitment was absolute. He is an editor that any author is lucky to have.

We are also deeply grateful to the others who were integral to the team: Bridgett Neely kept this far-flung project organized and coordinated the effort. She also made an important contribution to the research and resolutely carried the spirit. Meghan Oates was a superb researcher, integral to our ability to tell this story. She responded to the most impossible assignments with unfailing perseverance and creativity. Peter Spiegler brought an incisive mind and a scholarly thoroughness and contributed a deft understanding of history and economics. Johanna Klein was also an intrepid researcher and insightful analyst. Susan Nardone supported us throughout this venture with patience and consideration, coordinating interviews and other aspects of this project balanced against the barrage of other demands. In production, Teresa Chang helped us with great skill in the face of many pressures, and Mike Kelly and Gig Moineau also kindly assisted us. In Paris, Dagmar Wulf was gracious and thoughtful in her organizational work, and Arnette de Mille also capably supported the interviewing process.

The picture section, which started with 1,200 photos, was created—with much determination in the making—by Sue Lena Thompson and Bridgett Neely with the help of Siddhartha Mitter.

We certainly are most appreciative to those we interviewed, who took the time to share their thinking and experience. They are listed in the interview section. But we wish to express our special gratitude to Baroness Thatcher. And we particularly want to thank Lord Wakeham.

We want to convey our gratitude to our colleague and partner James Rosenfield, who saw the story, encouraged us to take it on, helped create the space to make it possible, and brought his own intellectual strengths to the structure and substance.

We owe a special thank-you to two mentors, in whose professional lives issues of state and marketplace have been central. It is impossible to write about these issues without acknowledging the profound intellectual impact that Professor Raymond Vernon has had on them over the half century. Edward Jordan was at the center of these issues at a critical time. Both were always available to us as advisers as we negotiated our way through this book.

We are most grateful to Amanda Urban and Jim Wiatt at ICM for their commitment, encouragement, and support.

Angela Stent read this manuscript through many incarnations and advised us at every stage. We benefited greatly from her incisive comments and her command of twentieth-century history.

We are deeply appreciative to those who commented substantially on the manuscript: Christopher Beauman, John Browne, Valéry Giscard d'Estaing, Ian Hargreaves, Rudolph Penner, Nicholas X. Rizopoulos, Augusta Stanislaw, and Steven R. Weisman gave us in-depth and insightful readings from which we greatly benefited. They also gave generously of their time. We thank them.

For their informed and thoughtful comments on chapters we thank: Anders Aslund, Carlos Bastos, Roger Beach, William Bonse-Geuking, Jinyong Cai, Jonathan Davidson, Vera de Ladoucette, Herbert Detharding, Benjamin Friedman, Yukon Huang, John Imle, Alejandro Jadresic, Yoriko Kawaguchi, Vijay Kelkar, Constantine Krontiras, Francois LaGrange, James Manor, Masahisa Naitoh, Tadahiko Ohashi, Rene Ortiz, R. K. Pachauri, Martin Peretz, Dwight Perkins, Jairam Ramesh, Henry Rosovsky, Neal

Schmale, William Schneider, Gerald Segal, Marcella Serrato, Lilia Shevtsova, Manmohan Singh, Ronald Stent, Felipe Thorndike, Ezra Vogel, Steven Vogel, and John Walmsley.

We are appreciative to the following people for their dialogue and advice on these issues: John Andrews, Nicola Beauman, David Bell, Kenneth Cheng, Clive Crook, Raj Desai, Everett Erlich, Jean-Michel Fauve, Stuart Gerson, the late Pamela Harriman, Paul Krugman, Kenneth Lay, Michael Levy, Paul London, Rebecca Mark, Dana Marshall, Jane Prokop, Dennis Riley, John Starrels, Edward Steinfeld, Richard Stern, William Sword, and John Wing.

We thank the following people for help on specific substantive issues: Daniel Bell, Sidney Blumenthal, Donald Carr, Philippe de Ladoucette, Ruth Fleischer, Susan Friedman, Svetlana Gromova, Barbara Grufferman, David Hale, David Howell, Vidar Jorgensen, Barbara Kafka, Beate Lindemann, Claire Liuksila, Shelley Longmuir, Douglas MacDonald, Hashim Makaruddin, Leonardo Maugeri, Thomas Mayer, Cyril Murphy, Hugh Patrick, Pedro Sanchez, John Schmitz, Adam Shub, Peter Susser, Gloria Valentine, Gina Weiner, Clifton Winston, Mark Wolf, Mark Worthington, and Joanne Young.

We greatly benefited from the criticism, advice, help, and support of our colleagues at Cambridge Energy Research Associates. We are grateful to colleagues who contributed to this project: Steve Aldrich, Simon Blakey, I. C. Bupp, James Clad, William Durbin, Dennis Eklof, Thane Gustafson, Ann-Louise Hittle, Peter Hughes, Bruce Humphrey, Kevin Lindemer, Huaibin Lu, Daniel Lucking, Elizabeth McCrary, Philippe Michelon, James Placke, Tom Robinson, Sondra Scott, Gary Simon, and Julian West. Other colleagues who helped us at CERA include: Alice Barsoomian, Jennifer Battersby, Barbara Blodgett, Peter Bogin, Sara Burr, Diana Frame, William Hamilton, John Hoffmann, Kelly Knight, Susan Krouscup, Susan Leland, Micheline Manoncourt, Susan Ruth, Helen Sisley, and Tanya Ustyantseva.

The role of state and marketplace has been a central theme of CERA over the last decade, and thus we really owe our thank-you to the entire staff, who supported us both intellectually and in their work.

At the Kennedy School of Government at Harvard University, our deep appreciation to Roger Porter, director of the Center for Business and Government, and Joseph Nye, dean.

At Global Decision Group, we want to express our appreciation to Alberto Cribiore, Gordon McMahon, and David Nixon, and to Peter Derow, whose reading was most helpful. We want to thank David Leuschen, Eric Dobkin, Richard Hayden, Peter Wheeler, Varkki Chacko, and their colleagues for their continuing dialogue. And we thank Leslie Dach, Michael Connelly, and their colleagues.

The people at Simon & Schuster have treated the authors as well as any authors deserve. Burton Beals, a wonderful and considerate editor, brought a thoughtfulness and commitment that made a real difference. Hilary Black was committed to the project and played a key role. We greatly valued her gracious temperament. Veronica Windholz was a superb and understanding copy editor. We are especially grateful to Leslie Ellen, who oversaw the effort and went out of her way to make the daunting possible. Her high standards were matched by her ability to do the impossible. Lynn Anderson was our eagle-eyed and vigilant proofreader. We are also very appreciative to John Wahler, the head of production, who made sure that the schedule was met against all odds; and we are most grateful to Victoria Meyer, John Mooney, Kate Larkin, and Karen Weitzman. The support of Carolyn Reidy, David Rosenthal, and Annik LaFarge was essential and is much appreciated.

At Simon & Schuster in London we want to express our appreciation to Nick Webb, who was committed to the book from early on, and also to Catherine Schofield.

The creation of the photo section was in itself a year-long task, and our thanks to the following people and archives: Archive Photos, Larry Schwartz; Corbis-Bettmann, Talya Schaeffer; Hulton-Getty, Henry Wilks; Tony Stone Images, Kathy Carcia; and SYGMA, Anne Manning.

We conclude by thanking our families—Angela Stent, and Rebecca and Alexander Yergin; and Augusta, Louis, Katrina, and Henry Stanislaw. Their understanding and forbearance were tested repeatedly and their support, encouragement, and engagement were more than essential. We surely cannot thank them enough.

INDEX

441

442

high-speed growth of, 207–8, 211–12
Hong Kong and, 208–9, 210, 211, 376
household responsibility system in, 196–97, 201
industrial reform in, 197–200
Japanese invasion of, 193–94
Japan's economic success and, 200
Long March and, 193
market economy debate in, 200–201
May 4 Movement and, 193
"one country, two systems" concept and, 210–11, 212, 376
overseas Chinese (*guanxi*) and, 207, 376
"people-owned" companies (*ming ying*) in, 212–13
postreform era in, 375–76
privatization in, 212–13, 376
property rights in, 201–2
Revolution of 1911 in, 192, 196, 208
Special Economic Zones (SEZs) of, 202, 204–5, 207, 209–10
state-owned companies of, 201, 206, 212
Taiwan's relationship with, 178–79
Yugoslav model and, 198, 199
Christian Democrat party, German, 33, 37, 312
Christian Socialist party, German, 37
Chubais, Anatolii, 284–85, 291
Chun Doo Hwan, 167, 171, 173
Churchill, Winston, 19–20, 25, 27, 40, 44, 103, 111, 119, 364
Attlee contrasted with, 20
Civil Aeronautics Board (CAB), 55, 58, 342–345
Civil Rights Act (1991), 357
Clark, Colin, 98
Clay, Lucius, 33
Erhard's meeting with, 36
Clayton, Will, 31
Clean Air Act Amendment (1990), 356
Clean Hands investigation (Italy), 134
Clinton, Bill, 325, 326–27, 328, 337, 362, 363
"triangulation" by, 338
Clinton administration, 362, 368
Clô, Alberto, 318
Coca-Cola, 90
Cocoa Marketing Board, 86
Colbertism, 298
cold war, 26, 29, 75, 79, 174, 297, 310, 358
end of, 125–26
nonaligned movement and, 89
Cologne, Archbishop of, 33
Colombia, 77
Colorni, Eugenio, 297
Colosio, Luis Donaldo, 256
Comintern, 193, 198
"commanding heights," origin of term, 11–12
Commentary, 331, 332
Commissariat Général du Plan, 32, 301

Committee on Social Thought (University of Chicago), 144
Common Market, *see* European Community; European Economic Community; European Union
Communication Act (1934), 346
communism, 15, 17, 23, 29, 71, 75, 158, 328, 330, 386, 389
central planning and, 11–12
collapse of, 9, 12, 14, 125–26, 137–38, 187, 203–4, 221, 262–63, 266–67, 310–11
Communist International, 12
Communist Party, Chinese, 193, 194, 195, 196, 200, 203, 205, 211, 212, 376
Communist Party, East German, 125–26
Communist Party, French, 300, 305
Communist Party (Marxist), Indian, 228
Communist Party, Italian, 296, 300
Communist Party, Polish, 264, 265, 266
Communist Party, Soviet, 211, 272, 278, 284
Khrushchev's secret speech, 274, 277
Communist Party, Spanish, 300
Compagnie Française des Pétroles, 28
computers, *see* technology
Confucianism, 175
Congo, 91, 378
Congress, Argentine, 243
Congress, Brazilian, 258
Congress, Peruvian, 251
Congress, U.S., 44, 61, 331, 335, 337–38, 354, 357, 362–63
government shutdown and, 325–26
Congressional Budget Office, U.S., 327, 338
Congress Party, Indian, 12, 68, 69, 70, 71, 72, 74, 82, 214, 215, 217, 218, 219, 220, 221, 222, 223, 224, 225
National Planning Committee of, 72
Connally, John, 61–62
Conrail, 345
privatization of, 358
Conscience of a Conservative (Goldwater), 344
conservatism, 15
Conservative Party, British, 20, 92, 93, 94, 98, 105, 107–8, 122, 124, 364, 365
1980 conference of, 110
"wets vs. drys" debate and, 108–9
Constituent Assembly, Indian, 67
Constitution of Liberty, The (Hayek), 107, 144
Consumer Product Safety Commission, 357
contract responsibility system, 201
Contract with America, 326, 327, 337
Convention People's Party (CPP), Gold Coast, 84
Convertibility Law, Argentine, 244
Coolidge, Calvin, 51, 132
Cost of Living Council, 63
Côte d'Ivoire, 379
Council of Economic Advisers, 330, 368–69

444

India, 12, 17, 79, 88, 90, 183, 191, 214–29
  collapse of communism and, 221–22
  decision for reform in, 223–25
  democracy in, 214–15
  development economics and, 76–77
  disinvestment (privatization) program of,
    226–27
  East Asia compared with, 222
  Fabian influence on, 216, 222
  foreign investment in, 225–26, 228
  Gandhi regime of, 217–19
  Gulf crisis and, 220
  independence of, 67–68
  middle class of, 227
  mixed economy of, 71–73
  as model for decolonialization, 82, 84
  nationalization in, 73, 90
  Nehru-Gandhi economic programs and, 71–
    72
  1990–91 economic crisis in, 216, 219–20,
    228–29
  nonresident Indians (NRIs) and, 223, 227
  onset of reform in, 218–19, 221
  Permit Raj of, see Permit Raj
  postreform era in, 377–78
  religious and ethnic strife in, 68–69, 215,
    218, 226, 228
  Soviet model and, 215, 217, 221–22
  state-owned companies in, 216–17, 218,
    226–27
Indonesia, 89, 139, 182, 186, 188, 189, 386
Industrial Policy Bureau, MITI, 165
Industry Department, British, 116
inflation, 92, 95, 96, 101, 104, 107, 108, 110,
    202, 211, 235, 257–58, 267, 289, 300,
    311, 316, 319
  mixed economy and, 128–29
  of 1970s, 332–35
  oil crises and, 128–29
  regulation and, 64–65, 341
  supply-side economics and, 330
information technology, 14, 154–55
Institute of Economic Affairs (IEA), 97–98,
    104, 107–8, 124
Institute of System Analysis, 275
Institutional Revolutionary Party (PRI),
    Mexican, 252–53, 254, 255, 257, 380
Instituto de Estudios Económicos Sobre la
    Realidad Argentina y Latinoamericana
    (IEERAL), 242, 243
Insull, Samuel, 46–47, 350
"Intellectuals and Socialism, The" (Hayek), 145
Inter-American Development Bank, 236
interest rates, 334–35
Interior Ministry, East German, 125
International Bank for Reconstruction and
    Development, see World Bank
International Finance Corporation (IFC), 80,
    152–53

International Monetary Fund, 42, 44, 104, 223,
    302
  Asian currency crisis and, 190
  debt crisis and, 132–33
  Latin America and, 233, 235, 237
International Trade Organization (ITO), 44
Internet, 156, 293, 353, 369–70
Interstate Commerce Commission (ICC), 48,
    55, 340, 346
Iran, 65
  hostage crisis of, 334
Iraq, 388
Ireland, 306
Israel, 89
Istituto per la Ricostruzione Industriale (IRI),
    38, 39, 318
Italy, 297, 305–6, 323
  "Clean Hands" investigation in, 134
  postwar era in, 38–39
  privatization in, 133–34, 136–37, 318
Izmailovo market, Moscow, 9–10

Jadresic, Alejandro, 240
Jamaica, 88
Janata Party, Indian, 90
Japan, 19, 51, 79, 139, 151, 158, 159–67, 172,
    189, 222, 279, 293, 306, 323, 339, 375,
    388
  Big Bang liberalization in, 166–67
  China invaded by, 193–94
  deregulation in, 164–67
  government-business collaboration in, 161–
    163
  "iron triangle" of, 161–64
  MITI's role in, 162–65, 167
  1955 system of, 161–62, 165, 167
  postwar era and, 159–61
  structural reform in, 166–67
  U.S. occupation of, 159, 160–61
Jaurès, Jean, 299
Jay, Peter, 104
Jiang Zemin, 212–13
John Paul I, Pope, 264
John Paul II, Pope, 264, 269
  assassination attempt on, 265
Johnson, Hugh, 52
Johnson, Lyndon Baines, 59
Johnson administration, 333, 341
Jordan, Edward, 345
Joseph, Keith, 15, 93, 97, 107, 109, 110–11,
    112, 114, 116, 119, 123
  anti-Keynesianism campaign of, 101–4, 108
  background of, 94–95
  leadership battle and, 100–101
  Thatcher and, 98–99
Joseph, Samuel, 94
Jospin, Lionel, 367–68
J. P. Morgan, 346
Justice Department, U.S., 348

448

Kahn, Alfred, 343–45
Kaiser Aluminum, 86
Kapital, Das (Marx), 137, 205
Kaunda, Kenneth, 84, 90
Keidanren (Federation of Employers), 165
Kelkar, Vijay, 135–36, 154, 221, 228
Kelvin, William, 73
Kennedy, Edward M., 341–42, 343
Kennedy, John F., 58–59, 60, 61, 87, 148, 262, 272, 362
Kennedy, Joseph P., 52, 58
Kennedy administration, 58–59, 333
Kenya, 84
Kenyatta, Jomo, 84
Keynes, John Maynard, 14–15, 55–56, 60, 76, 79, 98, 101, 107, 149, 177, 241
  background of, 39–40
  Hayek's criticism of, 142–43
  Road to Serfdom criticized by, 143–44
  writings of, 40–41
Keynesianism, 96, 127, 129, 234, 299, 312
  British economy and, 97–98
  capitalism and, 41, 42
  government's role and, 128
  Hayek's criticism of, 142–43
  mixed economy and, 39–42
  poverty and, 76–77
  regulation and, 55, 59–60, 65
  Thatcherism's rejection of, 101–2, 112
KGB, 138, 278
Khrushchev, Nikita, 194, 262, 274, 277
Kim Il Sung, 168
Kim Jae-Ik, 167, 171
Kim Young-Sam, 173
Kinnock, Neil, 365
Kirkpatrick, Jeane, 331
Klaus, Václav, 270
Knight, Frank, 145
Kohl, Helmut, 126, 305, 310, 312–14
Konoplyanik, Andrey, 275–76
Korea, Democratic People's Republic of (North), 167–68, 169, 246
Korea, Republic of (South), 139, 167–73, 174, 189, 206, 222, 267
  chaebols of, 169, 170–71, 172, 173
  corruption in, 172–73
  heavy industries initiative of, 169–70, 171
  Japanese model and, 168–69
  liberalization policy of, 171–72
  North Korean threat and, 167–68, 169
  reunification issue and, 172
  U.S. troops in, 169–70
Korea Fund, 152
Korean Central Intelligence Agency (KCIA), 171
Korean War, 44, 159, 168, 279
Kornai, János, 199, 277
Krenz, Egon, 125
Kristol, Irving, 330, 331–32

Krugman, Paul, 148
Kuomintang, 178
Kuwait, 89–90, 122, 220, 388
Kwasniewski, Alexsander, 269

labor, 13, 95–96, 109, 335
Labor Party, Norway, 318
labor unions, *see* trade unions
Labour Party, British, 12, 20, 21, 27, 33, 71, 81, 96, 106, 108, 112, 115, 117, 140, 181
  Blair's modernization of, 364–68
  nationalization policy of, 25–26
  postwar government of, 22–25
  strike of 1978–1979 and, 104–5
Lambsdorff, Otto von, 314
Landis, James, 53–55, 58–59, 340, 342
Lange, Oskar, 145, 201
Latin America, 10, 13, 17, 75, 76, 78, 79, 91, 130, 150, 230–61, 266, 267
  collapse of communism and, 236–37
  dependency (*dependencia*) theory and, 233–235, 237, 243, 258, 259
  ECLA and, 236, 237
  IMF and, 233, 235, 237
  ISI and, 234
  "lost decade" of, 235, 379
  postreform era in, 379–80
  privatization in, 259–60, 380
  role of state in, 234, 235–36, 259–61
  Soviet model and, 234, 235, 236–37
  technopols of, 237–38, 260
  traditional governments of, 233
  Washington Consensus and, 236
  see also specific countries
Lawson, Nigel, 115, 117, 122
  "golden share" concept of, 118
Lay, Kenneth, 226
League of Nations, 30
Lee Kuan Yew, 157, 179, 180–81, 220
Lee Teng-hui, 178
Lenin, V. I., 9, 12, 25, 61, 71, 271, 278
Lewis, Arthur, 77, 91, 177
Li, K. T., 177–78, 179
Liberal Democratic Party, Japanese (LDP), 162, 164, 166
liberalism, 10, 16, 24, 97, 107, 142
  Hayek's criticism of, 99
  neoconservatives vs., 330–31
  U.S. vs global meaning of, 15
Libertad movement, Peru, 247, 248, 250
Libya, 113
Lilienthal, David, 80
Lincoln University, 83–84
Lipton, David, 266
Li Yining, 201
Lloyd George, David, 22–23
Locke, John, 15
London School of Economics (LSE), 24, 77, 97, 142, 180

449

450

451

oil crises (*cont.*)
  Siberian reserves and, 273
  third world and, 89–90
  U.S. economy and, 63–65, 341
Okun, Arthur, 368–69
Old Man and the Sea, The (Hemingway), 297
"one country, two systems" concept (China), 210–11, 212, 376
Opium Wars, 208
Oracle Corporation, 227
Order 888, 352
Ordoliberals, 34–35, 144, 312
Organization for Economic Cooperation and Development (OECD), 164, 172, 222
Other People's Money and How the Bankers Use it (Brandeis), 50, 52
Otro Sendero, El (*The Other Path*) (de Soto), 247
overseas Chinese, 176, 207, 376
Owen, Robert, 27

Paine, Tom, 117
Pakistan, 68, 217, 220
PAN (National Action Party), Mexican, 255
Panyarachun, Anand, 187, 188
"parastatals," *see* state-owned companies
Park Chung Hee, 168, 169, 170–71
Parliament, British, 95, 102, 106, 107, 109, 119, 364, 365
Parliament, European, 307
Parliament, Indian, 72, 224
Parliament, Polish, 265–66
Parliament, Russian, 291, 292
Party of the Democratic Revolution (PRD), Mexican, 254–55
Penn Central railroad, 345
perestroika (restructuring), 274
Pérez de Cuéllar, Javier, 251
Perkins, Dwight, 169, 197, 207
Permit Raj, 17, 73–75, 216–17, 218, 221, 222, 225, 226, 377–78
Perón, Evita, 240
Perón, Isabel, 241
Perón, Juan, 240, 242
Perot, Ross, 337
Persian Gulf crisis, 220, 388
personalism, 301
Peru, 246–52
  Fujimori regime in, 249–52
  Libertad movement in, 247, 248, 250
  nationalization in, 246, 247, 248
  1990 election in, 248–49
  Shining Path insurrection in, 246–47, 248, 251–52
peso, Argentine, 244
peso, Mexican, 256
"petrodollars," 131
Petronas, 156–57

Philippines, 91, 139, 187–88, 189
Pilgrim's Progress (Bunyan), 48
Pinochet Ugarte, Augusto, 238, 239
planification, 29
Planning Commission, Indian, 72
Podhoretz, Norman, 331, 332
Pöhl, Karl-Otto, 311–16, 322
Poland, 145, 199, 203, 217, 263–69, 271, 273, 275, 278, 280, 285, 310
  debt burden of, 264–65, 267
  Gorbachev phone call and, 266, 277
  Jean Paul II and, 264–65
  market revolution in, 267–69
  1995 election in, 269
  privatization in, 269
  Solidarity movement in, 263–65, 266, 267, 268, 269
  Soviet Union and, 265–66
Popper, Karl, 249
Port Authority of New York and New Jersey, 360
Portugal, 82, 307–8
postreform era, 364–91
  in Africa, 378–79
  in Asia, 375
  in China, 375–76
  climate-change debate and, 386
  computer technology and, 369–72
  critical tests of, 382–84
  and decline of faith in government, 368
  delivering the goods in, 382–83
  entrepreneur concept and, 372
  environmentalism in, 385–86
  in Europe, 380–81
  fairness and, 383–84
  financial vulnerability in, 388–89
  global economy and, 369–71
  income inequality and, 383–84
  in India, 377–78
  information technology and, 370–72
  in Latin America, 379–80
  and mistrust of market, 368–69
  mobile economy and, 369–71
  national borders and, 370–71, 373
  national identity and, 384–85
  population issue and, 387
  role of company and, 371–73
  role of government in, 373–74
  in Russia, 375, 377
  in U.S., 381–82
  see also market system
Potsdam Conference (1945), 19–20
pound, British, 371
Pravda, 62
PRD (Party of the Democratic Revolution), Mexican, 254–55
Prebisch, Raúl, 234, 236, 258
PRI (Institutional Revolutionary Party), Mexican, 252–53, 254, 255, 257, 280

452

Prices and Incomes Act, British, 96
Principles of Economics, The (Barre), 242
privatization, 13, 279, 298, 374, 387
  in Africa, 379
  anxiety and, 368
  in Argentina, 244–45
  in Bolivia, 261
  of Bolshevik Biscuit Factory, 286
  in Brazil, 258–59, 380
  of British Telecom, 119–20
  as "capitalization," 261
  in China, 212–13, 376
  of Conrail, 358
  consequences of, 123
  Defense Department and, 358–59
  of education, 361
  of ENI, 133–34, 136–37
  European unification and, 317–19, 380
  golden share idea and, 118
  in Great Britain, 114–20, 370
  in India, 226–27
  in Italy, 133–34, 136–37, 318
  in Latin America, 259–60, 380
  local control and, 359–60
  in Malaysia, 185
  in Mexico, 255
  nationalization and, 114–19
  in New Zealand, 140
  in Poland, 269
  public service sector and, 360
  regulation and, 120–21
  reinventing government and, 358
  restructuring and, 117–18
  in reunified Germany, 318–19
  in Russian Federation, 281, 283–88
  in Soviet Union, 279
  "spontaneous," 267
  technology and, 318
  Thatcherism and, 114–20
  unemployment and, 120
  in U.S., 120–21, 328, 358–60
  voucher system of, 271, 285–86
  welfare reform and, 361–62
Profiles in Courage (Kennedy), 58
progressivism, 15*n*
"public choice" theory, 149, 330
Public Interest, 331, 332
Public Utilities Regulatory Policies Act
  (PURPA) (1978), 351
Public Utility Holding Company Act (1935),
  53–54, 350
Punch, 70

Qaddafi, Muammar, 113

Radio Liberty, 154
Raffles, Thomas Stamford, 180
Ramesh, Jairam, 222
Ramos, Fidel, 187–88

Rao, P. V. Narasimha, *see* Narasimha Rao,
  P. V.
"rational expectations," 148
Reader's Digest, 143
Reagan, Ronald, 15, 148, 299, 329, 334, 362
  air controller's strike and, 335
  economic policies of, 335–36
Reagan administration, 332, 335–36
Real Plan, 258
recolonialization, 73
Red Guards, 195
regulation, 158, 161, 319, 328
  Carter and, 64–65, 340
  decline of, 339–40
  Eisenhower administration and, 58
  environmental, 353–56
  flexibility and discretion as problem of,
    354–55
  gold standard and, 62
  Great Depression and, 51–52, 55
  inflation and, 64–65, 341
  Kennedy administration and, 58–59
  Keynesianism and, 55, 59–60, 65
  Landis and, 53–55, 58–59, 340
  litigation and, 357–58, 381
  muckrakers and, 48–49
  New Deal approach to, 48, 51–55, 57, 58,
    66, 339, 340
  Nixon's New Economic Policy and, 60–64
  postwar era and, 57–58
  social, 353–58, 381
  tradeable rights system of, 355–56
  trusts issue and, 48–49
  wage and price controls and, 60–64, 341
  World War II and, 56–57
  see also deregulation
regulatory capture, theory of, 340
Reinventing Government Initiative, 358
Renault, 29, 317
Rendell, Ed, 359
rent control, 147
Republican Party, U.S., 12, 331–32, 358, 362
  government shutdown and, 325–28
  1992 election and, 337–38
Reuters, 156
Revolution of 1911, Chinese, 192, 196, 208
Reynolds, 86
Rhee, Syngman, 168
Road to Serfdom, The (Hayek), 99, 109
  Keynes's criticism of, 143–44
Robbins, Lionel, 142
Roberts, Alfred, 105–6
Rockefeller, John D., 50
Rohatyn, Felix, 381
Roh Tae-Woo, 173
Romania, 266–67, 310
Rome, Treaty of, 305–6, 307
"Roofs or Ceilings? The Current Housing
  Problem" (Friedman and Stigler), 147

454

central planning in, 11–12
collapse of, 10, 14, 16, 137–38, 221, 262–263, 279–80, 317
command economy of, 271–73
Czechoslovakia and, 270
ethnic nationalism in, 279
Gorbachev's reforms and, 273–75
Hungarian Revolution crushed by, 43
India's economy and, 215, 217, 221–22
industrial sector of, 274–75
Japanese model and, 279
market economy transition of, 275–79
military-industrial complex of, 272–73, 274
Nkrumah's visit to, 87
Polish model and, 278
as postwar economic model, 22, 23
Sputnik launched by, 44–45, 262, 282
third world and, 75
Yavlinsky plan and, 278–79
see also Russia, Russian Federation
Soviet Union, former, 13, 150, 386
Spain, 307–8
Spanish Civil War, 389
Special Economic Zones (SEZs), 202, 204–5, 207, 209–10
Spinelli, Altiero, 296–98, 305, 306, 308, 324
Sporkin, Stanley, 357–58
Sprint, 348
Sputnik, 44–45, 262, 282
Sri Lanka, 219
stagflation, 129, 131, 149
Stalin, Joseph, 19–20, 193, 271, 272, 274, 277, 278, 296,
Stalinism, 12, 274
Standard Oil, 50
"Star Wars" program, 335
Stasi, 313
State Committee on the Management of State Property (GKI), 284, 285
State Department, U.S., 44, 161
state-owned companies, 88, 90, 114, 116, 117, 285
Chinese, 201, 206, 212
contribution of, 25, 80–82, 128
corruption and, 135–36
development economics and, 80–82
Giscard on, 317–18
human capital and, 82
Indian, 216–17, 218, 226–27
shortcomings of, 134–37
third world and, 80–82
"statism," 97, 99, 330
Steffens, Lincoln, 50–51
Stein, Herbert, 61, 64, 65, 335
Stigler, George, 147, 340, 341
Stimson, Henry L., 21
Stockman, David, 336
stock market, Russian, 292
stock market crash (1929), 47, 51

Stoltenberg, Jens, 318, 322
Sudan, 378
Suez Crisis, 43
Suharto, T.N.J., 186
Sukarno, Achmed, 89
Summers, Lawrence, 150–51, 237, 339
"supply-and-demand adjustment" (*jukyu chosei*), 162
supply-side economics, 330, 335–36, 339
Supreme Court, U.S., 50
Sutherland, Peter, 322
Sweden, 323
Switzerland, 297
Syria, 89

Taiwan, 139, 173–79, 182, 189, 206, 208, 210, 249, 267
China's relationship with, 178–79
export policy of, 175–76
Japanese economic model and, 177–78
overseas Chinese (*guanxi*) and, 176
postwar era and, 173–75
supertechnocrats of, 176–78, 179
U.S. aid to, 175–76
Tanzania, 84, 222
Tata family, 73, 226
Taylor, A.J.P., 22
Teapot Dome scandal, 50
technology, 13, 74, 153, 161, 170, 217, 273, 318
deregulation of AT&T and, 347
information, 14, 154–55
market system and, 390
19th century, 16
in postreform era, 369–72
technopols, 237–38, 260
telecommunications, 154–55
Templeton, John, 151, 152–53
Templeton Investment, 151
Temporary Assistance to Needy Families (TANF), 361–62
Tennessee Valley Authority (TVA), 48, 54
as model for World Bank, 80
"tequila effect," 256, 388
Texas Instruments, 182
Thailand, 139, 152, 182, 190, 386
growth of, 186–87
regional market and, 188–89
Thatcher, Denis, 106
Thatcher, Margaret, 15, 93, 94, 97, 107, 111, 143, 173, 185, 220, 222, 232, 249, 261, 299, 306, 309, 364, 365, 366, 367
assessment of, 123, 124
background of, 105–7
Centre for Policy Studies and, 98–99
conservative philosophy of, 108–9
Falklands War and, 111–12, 113, 241
Hayek and, 107–8
Joseph and, 98–99

PHOTO CREDITS

ABOUT THE AUTHORS

A writer of international renown, **Daniel Yergin** is the author of *The Prize: The Epic Quest for Oil, Money, and Power,* the global best-seller and winner of the Pulitzer Prize and the Eccles Prize that was made into an eight-part PBS series. He is also the author of *Shattered Peace,* the classic account of the Cold War, and coauthor of the best-seller *Energy Future* and *Russia 2010 and What It Means for the World.* Yergin is president of Cambridge Energy Research Associates, a leading analytic firm in the energy industries, and vice-chairman of Global Decision Group, which provides economic and risk analysis on major global markets. He is a Fellow of the Center for Business and Government at Harvard's Kennedy School. He received a B.A. from Yale University and a Ph.D. from Cambridge University, where he was a Marshall Scholar. He lives in Cambridge, Massachusetts, and in Washington, D.C.

A leading adviser on international markets and politics, **Joseph Stanislaw** is managing director of Cambridge Energy Research Associates, head of global research, and director of its European office in Paris. Dr. Stanislaw travels extensively worldwide, advising companies and countries on strategies to deal with the risks and opportunities in the newly evolving marketplace. He holds a B.A. from Harvard University and a Ph.D. from Edinburgh University and was formerly a professor at Cambridge University. He was senior economist at the OECD International Energy Agency in Paris and currently serves on the board of the Global Decision Group and of the American University in Paris. He lives in Paris, France.